Communications Systems
Engineers' choices

*Dedicated to the Installation and Service Engineers,
the unsung heroes of the telecommunications industry.*

Communications
Systems
Engineers' choices

Third edition

Geoff Lewis
BA, MSc, MIEEE, MRTS, MIEIE

OXFORD AUCKLAND BOSTON JOHANNESBURG MELBOURNE NEW DELHI

Butterworth-Heinemann
Linacre House, Jordan Hill, Oxford OX2 8DP
225 Wildwood Avenue, Woburn, MA 01801-2041
A division of Reed Educational and Professional Publishing Ltd

R̵ A member of the Reed Elsevier plc group

First edition published as *Communication Services via Satellite*
  by BSP Professional Books Ltd 1988
Second edition published 1992
Reprinted 1995
Third edition 1999

British Library Cataloguing in Publication Data
A catalogue record for this book is available from the British Library

Library of Congress Cataloguing in Publication Data
A catalogue record for this book is available from the Library of Congress

ISBN 0 240 51494 7

Composition by Genesis Typesetting, Rochester, Kent
Printed and bound in Great Britain by
Biddles Ltd, Guildford and King's Lynn

Contents

Preface

The rapid convergence that is occurring within the general concept of the telecommunication and associated industries means that choices have to be made. Is the convergence or synergic approach the best way forward? Computer system users have already experienced the problems associated with being locked in to one supplier of services. Not only does all this affect the engineering fraternity who have to select and provide the best means of achieving some end, but it also affects the service or programme provider, not forgetting the final arbiter in all this – the end user. For example, the multimedia business is now a confirmed technology – but how can it all be used to the maximum advantage of the populace? Again, choices are necessary. Many promises have been made about the delivery of more than 200 television channels directly into each home. Will this mean that more time will be spent on viewing, or will the end user become more selective? Certainly past experience suggests that providing more programmes does not increase the time spent on watching television. How then are the extra channels to be used? What services can be economically provided to finance the developments? Education, entertainment, the Internet or what? Again, choices are necessary and some have already been made, but what will survive in this jungle called telecommunications? Newly developed engineer-driven systems in the past have not had a particularly good track record of success. Similarly, many financially driven systems have also had their calamities. Choices and cooperation for the long-term development are therefore needed as never before.

Is instant communication even desirable, is it a feature for good or evil? Instant information often drives an instantaneous response, leading to ill-thought-out decisions with unfortunate consequences. Examples can be seen almost every day in the business, financial and stock markets. Again, communication choices, but for the benefit of whom? The long-term views of the engineering researcher are often circumvented by the needs of the financial masters, creating the short-termism concept that bedevils much of today's industrial development.

Acknowledgements

During the research and writing period for this book, I became aware of the following thoughts about the engineering fraternity. Engineers in modern society do not often receive their rightful recognition for their contributions to everyday life. Without design engineers there are no telecommunications systems; without installation and service engineers there is no maintenance of these systems; hence ultimately there are no systems. Such a situation is not the fault of the enthusiastic engineers that I corresponded with and met during the gestation period. All provided me with much encouragement, provided many useful ideas and gave valuable guidance. To all of those who read this work, I offer my grateful thanks in appreciation of their help. Such is the enthusiasm found among the practitioners of telecommunications that the task of writing this book was made very much easier and most stimulating.

While I have acknowledged all sources of help in the References, I feel that I must express my particular thanks to the following organizations and companies and their personnel:

Arrowe Technical Services, Merseyside, UK: D.J. Stephenson.
BICC Research and Engineering, London, UK: R. Grigsby, J.S. Buck.
DRA Farnborough, UK: Technical Manager Navigation, J.I.R. Owen.
Eutelsat, Paris, France: P. Binet, G. De La Villetanet.
European Space Agency, Toulouse, France: O. Ferrand.
European Space Agency (Meteosat Operations), Paris, France: C Honvault.
European Space Operations Centre, Darmstadt, West Germany: A. Robson.
European Space Research and Technology Centre, Noordwijk, Holland:
    N. Longdon.
Feedback Instruments Ltd, Crowborough, UK: M.L. Christieson.
INMARSAT, London, UK: Häkan Olsson.
Magellan Systems Corp., San Dimas, California, USA: Jim White.
Marconi International Marine Ltd, Chelmsford, UK: C. Riches.
Meteorological Office, Bracknell, UK: D.R. Maine, J. Turner.
Multipoint Communications Ltd, Witham, UK: J.K. Player.
Pascall Electronics Ltd, Ryde, Isle of Wight, UK: Stuart Chiplin,
    Mervyn Fretter.

Plessey Semiconductors Ltd, Swindon, UK: J. Salter.
Polytechnic Electronics Ltd, Daventry, UK: M. Warman, E.L. York.
Rohde & Schwarz GmbH & Co, München, Germany: Dr Waibel.
Royal National Institute for the Blind, London, UK: John Gill.
Scientific Atlanta Inc., Atlanta, USA: P.C. Bohana, K. Lucas.
Slater Electronic Services, Salisbury, UK: Jim Slater.
Swift Television Publications, Cricklade, Wilts, UK: John Breeds.
Texas Instruments Ltd, Northampton, UK: Colin Hinson, Colin Davies.
Trimble Navigation Ltd, Sunnyvale, California, USA: Tricia Tan.
University of Hertfordshire, Hatfield, UK: Hatfield Campus, Dr Helen Petrie.
University of Kent at Canterbury, UK: Dr R. Collier, Dr G. McDonald,
    Dr E.A. Parker.
Video Systems (SVT) Ltd, Maldon, UK: G. Steele.
Wegener Communications Inc., Atlanta, USA: N.L. Mountain.

Chapter 1
Basic communications concepts

1.1 CHOICES AND COMPROMISE

For many years the development of new communications services, be they the broadcasting of television or sound by radio frequency carriers, or telephony via wires, have involved the use of analogue concepts. The chief reason for this is that this form of transmission is based on a mature technology that can be readily mathematically modelled in a way which is well understood. Up to well into the 1970s such communications were regularly carried out via terrestrial, cable or satellite methods. At about this time, the concept of digital teletext was added to television services, showing that digital and analogue formats could well be carried via the same medium without mutual interference. Even by the mid-1980s digital communications were chiefly found in the domain of the computer which at this time was becoming more involved with local area networking to increase the sphere of influence. Thus digital communications were beginning to converge with telephony concepts and since television and sound broadcast services had long been carried over limited cable distribution systems, the basis for the complete integration of the home or personal computer (PC) with all forms of corporate and entertainment services became established. By the turn of the century, it will be common practice to view television via the home PC or gain access to the Internet via the home TV receiver. Thus work and leisure time will also converge even further with these multimedia services.

When developing new broadcasting or corporate data services, the design engineer is presented with a number of choices for the carrier medium: terrestrial radio, cable systems or satellite delivery. In addition, the electromagnetic frequency spectrum is a saturable commodity. Each of these options presents its own particular advantages or problems. The first consideration must be the needs of the user or audience base area, with consideration for the terrain between transmitters and receivers being important. As we approach the end of the twentieth century, the analogue or digital dichotomy would appear to be virtually dead, to some extent because of the fact that analogue signals have noise-like characteristics and therefore in general require to be transmitted at higher power levels. So why has the digital concept quite suddenly taken precedence? When building equipment for any new service, the scale of production and end-user costs becomes paramount. For analogue systems, most of the component parts are specific to a particular service or system and are thus produced in relatively smaller quantities. For digital systems the piece parts are common to many different systems and are therefore manufactured in very large quantities with the attendant lower costs due to the scale of production. Hence any new digital service should ultimately be more economic than an equivalent analogue service. Furthermore, it is possible to multiplex several digital signals on to the same radio frequency carrier, thus reducing the pressures on the already well-loaded electromagnetic frequency spectrum.

Technically all systems are either power or bandwidth limited with the former being particularly important with satellite systems. The bandwidth required is related to the amount of information that has to be transmitted per unit time and this influences the lowest level of carrier frequency employed. Higher carrier frequencies also demand higher levels of electronic technology. Although digital systems can overcome many of the problems associated with analogue transmissions, they are generally less well understood and even their mathematical modelling is more complex.

Although a fairly mature technology, cable distribution systems also provide many choices and compromises. Perhaps the most important is having to bury the cables underground to avoid the environmental impact. Then there is the choice of copper cables or optical fibres. Here the problems of attenuation have to be considered, together with the basic cost. Although copper is an expensive ore to mine and refine, the production of wire is relatively cheaper than optical fibre even though it is basically made from the second most common element on earth – silica (sand). By comparison, the attenuation of optical fibre is considerably less than that of copper cable and so needs fewer relay amplifiers along the path to make good the signal losses. In addition, cable distribution probably provides the least noisy environment available. The new broadband cable networks employ optical fibre for the major sections of the network and only use copper cable as the final drop to a subscriber's premises. Used in this way, the bandwidth and signal handling capacity of such a network are considerably improved.

For terrestrial broadcast purposes, the choices virtually all involve noise and mutual interference with other services. All the frequency bands from very low (about 16 kHz) up to very high (around 30 GHz) are currently well loaded with both analogue and digital signalling, for both entertainment and corporate communications. To operate new services within these constraints involves extensive band-planning to minimize the interference problems. The choices here now involve the bandwidth needed to accommodate the transmission signal and the level of power output required to cover the service area without creating unacceptable interference to other users. As operations are driven above about 300 Mhz, geographical and meteorological conditions need to be considered. High-rise building, hills and mountains create blind spots and weather conditions can give rise to interference effects between transmissions from different stations. Even the variation of tree leaf growth between summer and winter can have its effect. Thus for earth-bound systems, a rain fade margin of as much as 30 dB may need to be built into the transmission power budget.

Satellite radio communications systems are an extension of the relay systems that were developed for terrestrial communications, but with the difference that the receiver/transmitter, known in this case as the *transponder*, is now located in space. In spite of the high costs involved, the flexibility and advantages gained allow satellites to make a valuable contribution to worldwide communications. All the propagation parameters are well defined, well understood and capable of being accurately modelled mathematically. A single satellite can provide communications coverage for almost one-third of the earth's surface, using much less radio frequency power than would be required for an equivalent terrestrial system. Even though the signal attenuation due to the long path lengths involved is high, it is fairly constant. A *signal fade margin* allowance of only about 3–5 dBs needs to be made to account for the variability due to local atmosphere and weather conditions. To some extent, the high costs associated with high-altitude satellites are due to the lack of service access, thus on-board equipment redundancy and back-up satellites have to be be provided to ensure continuity of service. By comparison, low-altitude satellites can be serviced from an earth-launched space shuttle vehicle and these are set to become much more predominant in the near future. The high level of reliability of current technology is such that the operational lifetime of a satellite is now in the order of fifteen years. When compared with terrestrial microwave relays and undersea cables, and taking into consideration the fact that in some areas of the world satellites are the only possible way of providing radio communications, the system becomes very cost-effective.

1.2   SATELLITE ORBITS IN USE

Communications satellites occupy either an *equatorial*, an *elliptical* or a *polar* orbit, as depicted in Figure 1.1(a). *Geosynchronous* satellites are those whose period of rotation is synchronized to that of the earth or some multiple of it. The *geostationary* (GEOs) orbit is a unique geosynchronous one, located over the equator. The satellite in geostationary orbit has a height and velocity such that it appears stationary to earth-bound observation. In this context, it is the earth's period of rotation relative to the fixed stars in space (the *sidereal* time) that is important. This is slightly less than the *solar* period and is approximately 23 hours, 56 minutes, 4.1 seconds (23.9345 hrs). The height above the earth's surface of 35 765 km and velocity of 3.073 km/sec (see Appendix A1.1) required for the geostationary orbit was first calculated by the engineer and science fiction writer, Arthur C. Clarke (1), and presented in an article published in the October 1945 issue of *Wireless World*. This effectively set out the ground rules for satellite communications, so that the geostationary orbit is now named after

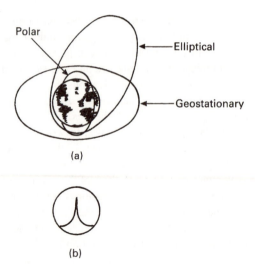

(a)

(b)

Figure·1.1 (a) Orbits used for satellite communication. (b) Track of elliptical orbit over service area.

Clarke in recognition of this work. The 'Clarke Orbit' is used to provide worldwide *point-to-point* (narrowcasting) and *point-to-multi-point* (broadcasting) services.

The elliptical orbiting satellites (or high earth orbiters (HEOs)) operate with the earth's centre as one of the two focus points of an ellipse, which is inclined at a suitable angle to the polar axis. Such an orbit has the advantage that the launch is achieved for a lower expenditure of energy. A typical satellite has an *apogee* (highest point) of about 35 600 km and a *perigee* (lowest point) of about 3960 km above the earth's surface, and a period of slightly less than twelve hours (see Appendix A1.2). Around the apogee, the satellite appears *pseudo-stationary*, remaining within a beamwidth of less than ±15° for more than eight hours over the service area. Three satellites in such an orbit can therefore provide twenty-four-hour service. These orbits, sometimes described as *super-synchronous*, are also known as *Molniya* orbits after the Russian communication satellites that used them. The track of such a satellite over its service area is shown in Figure 1.1(b). With the crowding of the Clarke orbit that occurred as the use of satellites increased, the elliptical and polar orbits are set to become increasingly important for future communications.

The low polar orbits (LEOs), with a typical height that ranges from about 700 to 1600 km and a period of around 100 minutes, have proved invaluable to navigation and weather forecasting. These satellites traverse the north and south poles, covering the earth's surface in a series of strips, to scan weather conditions around the world. Radio beacons are also carried for navigational purposes. Personal mobile satellite communications can be established in the frequency band 1–2 GHz. Here the low level of propagation attenuation allows the use of small and simple antennas. By combining this technique with a number of *low earth orbiters* (LEOs) equipped for inter-satellite communications and using modern integrated circuit technology, the concept of a worldwide *personal communication network* (PCN) becomes a reality. A further sub-group of LEOs are described as medium earth orbiters (MEOs) and are generally located at heights ranging from about 6000 to 19 000 km.

1.3 SATELLITE CHOICES – GEOs OR LEOs

Geostationary satellites, once launched into their operational orbit, appear stationary to earth-bound observation and therefore require no special tracking antenna system to receive their signals. However, if left to their own devices, these satellites would drift into a daily north–south figure-of-eight track under gravitational influences. GEOs therefore need to carry enough station-keeping fuel to maintain their special orbit. At the end-of-life period, these satellites can be given over to telecommunications services that must employ tracking antenna systems and so make further short-term use of what otherwise would become a dead bird. Operated in this way, the lifetime of GEOs can probably be extended to 18–20 years. Offset against this is the signal attenuation of the long path length that has to be countered by on-board power delivered from solar panels. Another feature that may be disconcerting is the propagation time delay of about 250 ms for the total loop path length. The rain fade and other propagation anomalies which are relatively small are easily countered. A particularly troublesome problem arises when the satellite, earth and sun are in alignment. When the earth casts its shadow over the satellite, the electrical output from the solar panels falls to zero and the on-board systems then have to rely on back-up batteries and operate on reduced power. As the sun passes behind the satellite, a signal outage occurs and the radio frequency (RF) signal received by the ground antenna becomes swamped with solar radiation. This eclipse period typically falls twice a year between the end of February and the middle of March and during August and September. The effect lasts for a period of about ten minutes over five consecutive days. The eclipse by the moon is relatively rare and may last for up to fifty-one minutes; the next event is due during 1999. The location of GEOs is defined in one of two ways; either in degrees east or west of the Greenwich meridian, between 0° and 180°, or as a purely easterly value (30° W = 330° E) (2). Once on-station, the GEOs are virtually non-servicable apart from the option of switching between failed equipment and on-board redundant components, usually under control from the ground station.

Since LEOs operate at very much lower altitudes, the path length is shorter and the signal attenuation is lower. The on-board power requirement is thus much lower. These birds track across the earth surface much faster with the result that signal outage due to the eclipse effect produces only short bursts of noise. The propagation delay is very short and together with the low power requirement, these satellites are particularly useful for hand-held system operations such as mobile phones, portable navigation devices and computers (laptops). LEOs may be launched and serviced from earth-launched space vehicles. This may make these birds particularly attractive for the operators of corporate communications networks using store-and-forward message transfers and inter-satellite wireless links. Both GEOs and LEOs have similar life expectancies but the latter are cheaper to build and maintain in service and are thus likely to be the mainstay of communications well into the next century.

GEOs are most commonly launched via large three-stage rocket systems and the process is carried out over several days (3). All such launches are initiated from as close to the equator as possible to maximize the slingshot effect of the earth's rotation. The first stage of launch places the satellite in an inclined orbit at an altitude of about 250 km. At the appropriate moment, a rocket is fired to drive the bird into a highly elliptical orbit with an apogee of about 36 000 km. At the next firing, the satellite is driven into an orbit close to its final geostationary one, but with a perigee of about 15 000 km. This is followed by a further firing which brings the satellite close to its equatorial geostationary orbit. Finally, the satellite has to be driven into its allocated positional slot. If the bird's forward velocity is reduced, it will fall into a lower orbit with a smaller circumference and then move forwards easterly. Increasing the velocity will have the opposite effect and drive the satellite westwards.

1.4 FREQUENCY RANGES IN USE

Theoretically all radio frequency signals above dc will radiate electromagnetic energy and thus propagate through space. However, for those frequencies below about 16 kHz the radiation is insignificant. This figure should not be confused with the higher limit of the audibility of sound waves by the human ear. Radio and sound waves propagate via completely different phenomena. Typically then, the part of the electromagnetic spectrum that is suitable for radio communications lies in the range 16 kHz to 300 GHz, although current applications above about 30 GHz are very limited. The ranges and nomenclature of the various sub-bands in use are shown in Table 1.1. The frequency ranges used for microwave

Table 1.1

Frequency	Name	Wavelength
Up to 30 kHz	Very low frequency (VLF)	> 10 km
30 kHz to 300 kHz	Low frequency (LF)	10 km to 1 km
300 kHz to 3 MHz	Medium frequencies (MF)	1 km to 100 m
3 MHz to 30 MHz	High frequencies (HF)	100 m to 10 m
30 MHz to 300 MHz	Very high frequencies (VHF)	10 m to 1 m
300 MHz to 3 GHz	Ultra high frequencies (UHF)	1 m to 10 cm
3 GHz to 30 GHZ	Super high frequencies (SHF)	10 cm to 1 cm
30 GHz to 300 GHz	Extra high frequencies (EHF)	1 cm to 1 mm

communications are commonly known by the American Radar Engineering Standard and since these differ slightly from the European classifications (see Appendix A1.3) some confusion can occur.

Radio propagation is such that frequencies below about 500 kHz are trapped between the lower ionosphere and the surface of the earth and therefore propagate chiefly as surface waves. Frequencies in the range of about 3–30 MHz propagate mostly by reflection and refraction between the earth and the ionosphere as a sky wave. Above about 30–40 MHz the wave energy escapes into space so that radiation then is via space waves. These critical frequencies vary during the eleven-year sunspot cycle and with atmospheric conditions, but the space waves seldom exist below 30 MHz. For this reason, only frequencies above about 100 MHz are reliable enough to be used for space communications.

The general allocation of parts of the frequency spectrum for various operations are made through the offices of the International Telecommunications Union (ITU) via World Administrative Radio Conferences (WARC). The actual frequency allocations are confirmed by the International Frequency Registration Board (IFRB), one of the bodies associated with the ITU. Because of the way in which cable network signals propagate, these systems are not constrained in the same way. Table 1.2 gives an indication of the way in which just a few of the satellite applications are handled.

Table 1.2 indicates generally how the microwave part of the frequency spectrum has been allocated for the most popular satellite services. Table 1.3 further indicates the way in which C and K band frequencies are allocated for system up- and down-link applications. In general, the up-link service is provided in the higher-frequency sub-band and the corresponding down-link on a lower

Table 1.2

Approximate frequency (Ghz)	Application
0.137	Weather satellite
0.145	Amateur
0.400	Satellite navigation
0.435	Amateur
0.714	Television – China
0.70–0.79	Television – Russia
0.860	Television – India
1.269	Amateur
1.5–1.6	Mobile – INMARSAT
1.7	Weather satellite
2.5–2.6	Television – Arabsat
3.7–7.75	C band television and communications
10.7–12.75	Ku band communications and television
40.5–42.5	Experimental – future expansion
84–86	Experimental – future expansion

Table 1.3

Band	Up-link (GHz)	Down-link (GHz)
C	5.8–8.4	3.7–7.75
Ku	12.75–14.5	10.7–12.75
K	27.5–31.0	17.7–21.2

one. There are economic and technical advantages in using this arrangement (4). It will be shown in Chapter 3 that the gain of an antenna is proportional to the operating frequency and inversely proportional to its beamwidth. If the high band were used for the down-link, any given antenna would have a narrower beamwidth, increasing the problems of maintaining antenna alignment as the satellite drifts around in space about its mean position. Compensation for this would require a servo-controlled steering system to be added to each receiver site. By using the high band for the up-link, the extra gain achieved can be usefully employed to make up for the extra path length attenuation which increases with frequency. With this arrangement, the overall system SNR can be better managed. The large dish ground-transmitting station would in any case require a servo-controlled tracking system, so that there is no addition to this side of the cost budget.

1.5   MAXIMIZING THE AVAILABILITY OF THE FREQUENCY SPECTRUM

The original methods used to regulate the exploitation of the frequency spectrum for terrestrial systems provided unfair advantage to those nations first in the field of radio communications. The result, in some cases, of almost haphazard development can be heard in nearly all the wavebands used for terrestrial radio services (5). In certain parts of the spectrum, the level of mutual interference produced by transmitters has become intolerable. When a frequency is occupied by one transmitter, it is of little use to any other within the same coverage area, so that in a restricted sense, the frequency spectrum is a non-renewable resource. From around 1977, a series of World Administrative Radio Conferences were convened in order to manage the spectrum for space communications and minimize the effects on terrestrial systems, and to ensure a more equitable distribution of this very important resource. The problem of avoiding interference in space-based communications systems has a significant effect on the way in which geostationary satellites are managed. In these cases, mutual interference can be minimized by controlled allocation of orbit position, the use of frequency division, time division and code division multiple access techniques, and the use of various forms of signal polarization (6).

The number of satellites that the Clarke Orbit will support depends upon the antenna pointing accuracy that can be achieved and maintained. Satellite operational lifetime is to a large extent dependent upon the amount of fuel it can carry for station keeping. The accuracy required is within an arc of ± 0.1°. A simple calculation shows that such a satellite can wander about its mean position within a diameter of about 62.4 km. Taking these points into consideration, it is unlikely that GEO satellite spacings closer than about 2° can be accepted if the level of interference to ground-based receivers is not to become intolerable. In spite of this restriction, it has been shown by the Société Européenne des Satellites (SES), which operates the ASTRA system, that up to eight satellites can be controlled within this 62.4 km space to provide at least 120 transponders each capable of transmitting television and radio programmes, plus some digital services.

Frequency division multiple access (FDMA) is the very common method that was employed for terrestrial and cable distribution systems long before satellite broadcasting became feasible (7), where each transmitting station is allocated different carrier frequencies, as indicated in Figure 1.2(a). Many stations may use the same transponder amplifiers simultaneously within the limit of the total

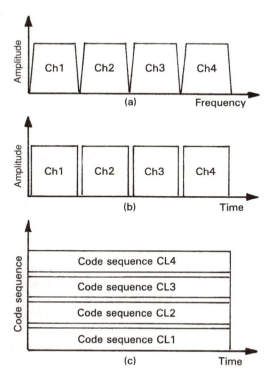

Figure 1.2 (a) Frequency division multiplex. (b) Time division multiplex. (c) Code division multiplex.

channel bandwidth. Capacity allocation is simple and the system requires no complex timing or synchronism. The required baseband signal is easily recovered using relatively simple and inexpensive receivers. The system can easily be computer modelled to minimize the risk of adjacent and co-channel interference from adjacent satellites even before these have been launched. The major disadvantage lies in the non-linearity of the transponder's travelling wave tube (TWT) high-power amplifier. Because several carriers are present simultaneously, intermodulation (IM) can arise. This is normally countered by *backing-off* the TWT power output, thus reducing the signal level received by the ground station.

Time division multiple access (TDMA) allows each earth station to be assigned a time-slot for transmission using the entire transponder resources as illustrated in Figure 1.2(b). Each ground station transmitter uses the same carrier frequency within a particular transponder and transmits in bursts (8). As each burst must carry a destination address, the flexibility of interconnection is improved. Since only one carrier is present at any one time, the transponder's TWT can be operated near to saturation, for greater power output. There is no intermodulation or adjacent channel interference from the same satellite. This leads to an improved signal-to-noise ratio (SNR) at the ground receiver and hence improved service quality. The cost of these improvements is the extra complexity of the equipment but since the concept is compatible with digital processing developments, this overhead is minimal. A ground control station is necessary to maintain control and synchronize the system network. The throughput of data is better than FDMA by a factor of about two because this system makes better use of the gaps in normal transmissions.

Code division multiple access (CDMA) is a method well suited to digital transmission. All users operate at the same carrier frequency simultaneously and use the whole channel bandwidth. A unique digital *key* is added to each digital transmission sequence and the intended receiving station is equipped with the same key. (See Figure 1.2(c).) By using *correlation detection*, the receiver extracts the wanted signal from the noise of all the other transmitters. As the number of simultaneous users increases, the system performance degrades gracefully, unlike normal digital systems whose performance *crashes* when overloaded. When the system is under-used, there is an automatic improvement in the signal error margin.

Signal polarization variation can permit *frequency reuse* to extend the occupancy of a waveband and, provided that the services are separated by sufficient distance, there will be minimum mutual interference. 'x' and 'y' linear and left- and right-hand circular polarization can be used in the same way as vertical, horizontal and circular polarizations have been used for terrestrial systems.

By using all these concepts, an equitable share of the frequency spectrum can be made available to all who need to use it, even well into the next century. In addition, there should be much less mutual interference between users than has been the case with earth-bound communication systems in the past.

1.6 SYSTEM CONSTRAINTS IMPOSED BY TRANSPONDER CHARACTERISTICS

Apart from producing a change of carrier frequency, the satellite's transponders should be *transparent* to the ground station receivers. In such applications as inter-satellite links, *on-board* demodulation, noise reduction/error correction and remodulation can be usefully employed to improve the ground station's received signal quality. However, this makes further demands on the power available, which has to be shared between all the transponders covering the operating bandwidth and services. Thus the satellite transponders are both power and bandwidth limited. The down-link antenna beams are specifically shaped to cover the required service area. Global coverage requires a beamwidth of about 17.5° to cover a little over one-third of the earth's surface. Relative aerial gains can be expressed in terms of beamwidth. The square of the beamwidth is approximately proportional to the antenna aperture. A typical *spot beam* might have a width of about 4°. Thus the relative gains would be $(17.5/4)^2 = 19$ or 13 dB. Therefore, for the same signal level at the ground receiver, the global beam makes a much greater demand on the available power and limits the services available through the satellite. Higher effective radiated down-link power leads to smaller and lower-cost receiver antennas.

The transponder high-power stages commonly use *travelling wave tube* (TWT) or modular solid state amplifiers. The former have the advantage of relatively low weight and high power efficiency while the latter, which are assembled from a number of low-power stages in parallel, have the advantage that if one unit fails, the loss of signal power output is relatively small. Figure 1.3 shows the shape of the amplitude and phase response of a typical TWT. When

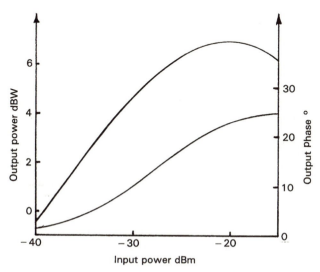

Figure 1.3 Characteristics of a typical travelling wave tube amplifier.

operated near to saturation, the non-linearity and *group delay* (rate of change of the phase response) will seriously distort amplitude-modulated signals, and cause intermodulation when several carriers are present simultaneously. Such operation requires the TWT operating conditions to be backed-off, reducing the effective output power. Using frequency modulation, however, both types of amplifier can be operated nearer to saturation for better efficiency.

1.7   CHARACTERISTICS OF MODULATION SYSTEMS

Before making a choice between the two basic systems of amplitude modulation or frequency modulation (AM and FM), two special cases need to be considered: those of analogue and digital baseband signals. The analogue signals will include voice telephony, audio and television (narrow and wideband). Digital signals may be derived from sources other than computer-compatible systems. The case of digital signals derived from analogue ones also needs to be considered.

Taking analogue signals first, although from a frequency spectrum conservation viewpoint AM or single side band suppressed carrier (SSBSC) methods are more acceptable, they are not commonly used for satellite communications. A noise signal is strictly a random variation of amplitude, thus any receiver designed for AM will be responsive to noise. In addition, the amplitude-varying nature of the AM signals requires that processing amplifiers should have linear characteristics, otherwise distortion will arise. This feature of the signal also imposes a varying demand on the power supply which must be capable of meeting the demand of peak modulation. In turn, this poses a serious problem for the satellite power supply and its output power amplifiers.

By comparison, FM is a constant power method due to the constant amplitude nature of the signal. Thus there is no power supply problem and the high-power amplifiers can operate in Class C for maximum power efficiency. Also in the AM case, at least 50 percent of the available power is used to provide the carrier component which contains no information. In the FM case, all the transmitted power components carry information, so that for the same total power output FM produces a 3 dB more useful signal to a receiver.

It is demonstrated in Appendix A1.4 that the FM system of modulation has an SNR (S/N ratio) advantage over AM of $3M^2$, where M is the deviation ratio. In the case where $M = 5$, which is typical for wideband FM, the improvement is of the order of 19 dB. It is also shown here that noise is least troublesome at the lower baseband frequencies. This is due to differentiating action of the FM demodulator that reduces the noise power spectral density at the lower end. If a low-pass filter is added to follow the demodulator, this will cut the high-frequency noise component. The attenuation of the high-frequency baseband components can be compensated by boosting these in the transmitter in a complementary manner before modulation. The use of this *pre-emphasis* and *de-emphasis* (see Figure 1.4), which is not really available to AM systems, can give rise to an average improvement of about 6 dB in the overall SNR (see Appendix A1.5).

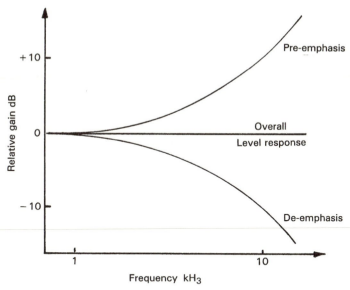

Figure 1.4 Pre-emphasis/de-emphasis characteristics.

The FM receiver has another unique property, that of a *capture effect*. This is the ability of the receiver to lock on to the modulation of the stronger of two signals on the same or nearby frequency. Typically, a receiver can reject such signals that are only about 1 dB less than the wanted signal. Thus FM gives a superior rejection ratio for adjacent and co-channel interfering signals.

FM analogue signal processing can be further improved by the use of *companding* where the dynamic range of the baseband signal is compressed before transmission and expanded in a complementary manner at the receiver. Not only does this improve the SNR by perhaps as much as 9 dB, it also reduces the deviation ratio which reduces the modulated signal bandwidth and increases the satellite channel capacity.

Unlike AM detectors, FM demodulators can enhance the SNR. The quality of the modulated signal is usually referred to by its *carrier-to-noise ratio* (CNR), and after demodulation by its SNR. Ignoring any small signal degradation, the AM detector's SNR at the output will be equal to its CNR. Within certain limitations depending on the deviation ratio, an FM demodulator can give a 15 dB improvement over AM (7), provided that the CNR is above the 14 dB threshold. These features are displayed in Figure 1.5. Recent circuit developments have produced FM demodulators with the threshold extended down to 3 dB, giving a further 11 dB improvement in the signal levels of FM. Figure 1.6 shows descriptively how the FM demodulator achieves the improvement derived in Appendix A1.4. The information signal bandwidth is halved and compressed back into its original baseband value, whereas the noise bandwidth is only halved. The important feature of any signal processing must be to maximize the

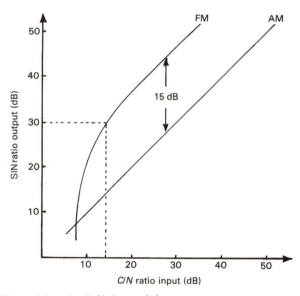

Figure 1.5 FM demodulator threshold characteristics.

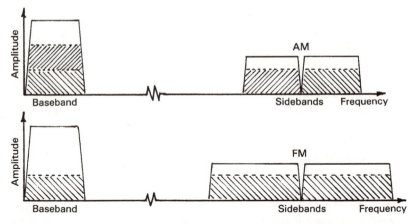

Figure 1.6 Comparison of the effects of sideband noise between AM and FM.

SNR to obtain a high-quality analogue signal or a low error rate in a digital signal. This should be achieved while trying to transmit the maximum information within the available bandwidth, thus conserving the frequency spectrum. Carson's rule gives the approximate bandwidth B Hz for an FM signal as:

$$2(f_d + f_m) = 2(m + 1)fm \tag{1.1}$$

where f_d is the frequency deviation in Hz, f_m is the modulating frequency in Hz, and $m = f_d/f_m$ the modulation index. This rule is illustrated in Figure 1.7.

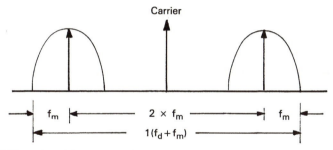

Figure 1.7 Illustration of Carson's rule for FM bandwidth.

Shannon's rule for channel capacity using binary signalling is given by:

$$C = B \log_2(1 + SNR) \text{ bits per second} \tag{1.2}$$

where C is the channel capacity, B is the bandwidth in Hz, and SNR is the signal-to-noise ratio. Shannon suggests that the capacity of a communications channel can be increased by increasing the bandwidth or the SNR. Thus for an acceptable channel capacity, bandwidth can be traded for SNR and vice versa. This is effectively what happens in the analogue FM case. Many coding and modulation combinations used for satellite communications operate within this trade-off.

It has thus been demonstrated that, under favourable conditions, FM can show a very significant SNR improvement if the bandwidth is available, as is the case in many satellite communications links.

1.8 COMPANDING

Companding is the name given to the signal process that *compresses* the dynamic range of a signal before transmission and expands it in a complementary manner in the receiver. This is achieved by using amplitude-dependent (non-linear) amplifiers with characteristics such as those of Figure 1.8(a). The compressing amplifier in this example has a characteristic slope of 0.5. The receiver expanding amplifier therefore has a slope of 2, to give an overall unity response. Figure 1.8(b) shows how the process functions.

Signals above the level 0 dBm (1 mW) are assumed to be either nonexistent or unaffected by companding. During the compression stage, the dynamic range is halved by increasing the relative amplitudes of the lower-level signals, which in turn reduces the FM deviation necessary.

Assume that there is −30 dBm (1 μW) of noise present in the transmission media. This would have swamped the original low-level signal components, but now is only comparable with them. The expansion process at the receiver effectively depresses the low-level signal components (and the noise) to restore the dynamic range to its original value and improve the SNR at the same time.

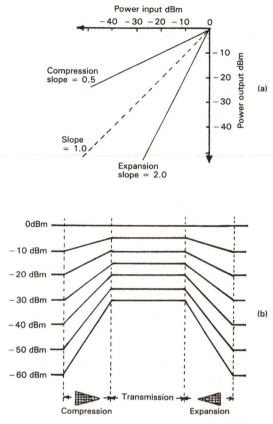

Figure 1.8 Companding. (**a**) Characteristics of compression/expansion circuits. (**b**) Overall system characteristics.

1.9 ENERGY DISPERSAL

The demands on the radio frequency spectrum are such that every possible technique must be used to minimize the interference between communication networks. Worst-case conditions are usually caused by unmodulated carriers. The effects are reduced if the signal energy is spread evenly throughout the bandwidth in use (2). Figure 1.9 represents part of the frequency spectrum associated with the luminance component of a TV video signal, with the energy being concentrated into small regions. Because the luminance signal rests at various dc levels for about 14 percent of the time (blanking levels), short bursts of single frequencies are produced when using FM. The burst repetition frequency is harmonically related to the line time base frequency. During these burst of effectively unmodulated carriers, interference can be caused to other services. The problem is particularly significant in the C band, where up- and down-link TV signals can cause interference with terrestrial microwave links.

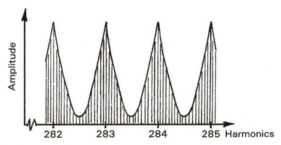

Figure 1.9 TV luminance signal spectra.

The technique of *energy dispersal* simply adds a triangular waveform to the video signal so that the FM carrier is continually varied. This spreads the spectral energy more evenly by reducing the peak amplitudes. The frequency of this waveform is usually related to the frame timebase frequency (25 or 30 Hz). It has been shown experimentally (4) that its amplitude should be such as to produce a peak-to-peak deviation of 600 KHz.

In at least one TV service (Russian Gorizont), a dispersion frequency of 2 Hz is used, a frequency easily removed at the receiver by a good automatic frequency control (AFC) system. For higher frequencies, a video clamp circuit is necessary.

1.10 DIGITAL MODULATION SYSTEMS

As with analogue transmission, the main criterion for digital communications is still the accuracy of the received information. Therefore the aim must again be to maximize the SNR-to-bandwidth trade-off. It is shown (7) that any signalling pulse has an inverse *pulse width* to *pulse bandwidth* relationship. If the processing circuit bandwidth is less than the pulse bandwidth, distortion occurs and this leads to bit errors. To ease this problem, the data stream is usually prefiltered before modulation to produce a shape similar to (sin x)/x or related cosine pulses.

Whereas the CNR or SNR was a valuable indicator of analogue signal quality, the ratio of energy per bit (E_b), per watt of noise power, per unit bandwidth (N_0) is often used for digital systems. (This ratio is dimensionless – joules = watts/ sec.) The two ratios are related by

$$E_b/N_0 = CNR \times B/R$$

where $N_0 = N/B$, CNR is the carrier-to-noise ratio in bandwidth B and R is the serial bit rate. The *bit error rate* (BER) is the ratio of the number of bits received in error to the total number of bits transmitted per second. It is often typically expressed as BER = e $\times$ 10^{-3} per sec.

The most significant, and fairly predictable, problem is that of *white noise*, so called because its power spectral density (PSD) per unit bandwidth is constant. Statistically, such noise has a *Gaussian* or *normal* distribution, as shown in Appendix A1.6.

There are many ways of representing a binary message sequence with a series of pulses. The method chosen is always a compromise and two possible ways are shown in Figure 1.10. The *non-return-to-zero* (NRZ) sequence minimizes the energy per pulse and reduces the bandwidth needed. The *bipolar* sequence has a spectrum with a zero dc component, a feature that is very useful if the signal is to be passed through ac circuits.

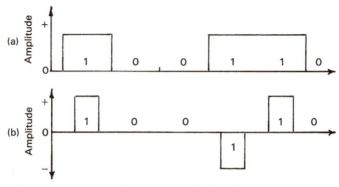

Figure 1.10 (a) Non-return-to-zero pulse train. (b) Equivalent bipolar sequence.

The three principal methods used to carry digital signals over radio frequency (RF) communication links are derived from the analogue concepts of amplitude, frequency and phase modulation.

On-off keying (OOK)

This is a limiting case of amplitude shift keying (ASK), where the carrier level is varied in discrete steps. In this case there are only two levels: on and off, 1 and 0. The RF pulse stream and frequency spectrum of such a signal are depicted in Figures 1.11(a) and (b) respectively. It will be seen that the spectrum bandwidth is twice the baseband signalling frequency. It is explained in Appendixes A1.6 and A1.7 that the probability of error (P_e) in a digital signal, in the presence of Gaussian noise, depends on the complementary error function (erfc) and a kind of SNR. Assuming that the signal has a peak amplitude of A volts, that zeros and ones occur with equal probability and that the total noise power is N watts, then the error probability can be deduced from the SNR:

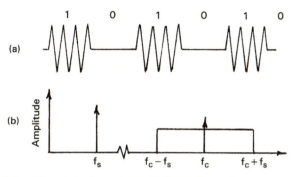

Figure 1.11 (a) On-off keyed signal waveform. (b) Frequency spectra.

$$\text{RMS signal amplitude} = (A/2)/\sqrt{2}$$

$$\text{RMS noise amplitude} = \sqrt{N}$$

$$\text{SNR} = A/(2\sqrt{(2N)})$$

$$P_e(\text{OOK}) = \tfrac{1}{2}\,\text{erfc}(A/(2\sqrt{(2N)}))$$

A similar expression based on the energy per bit ratio is:

$$P_e(\text{OOK}) = \tfrac{1}{2}\,\text{erfc}\sqrt{(E_b/4N_o)}$$

Frequency shift keying (FSK)

This method involves switching the RF carrier frequency between two discrete values, each representing logic 0 or logic 1. Figure 1.12 shows the modulated wave at (a) and the frequency spectrum at (b). The upper and lower frequencies each have a spread of energy due to the baseband signalling frequency, so that it

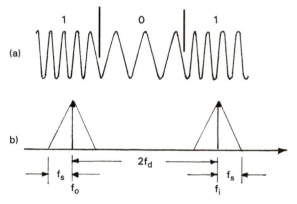

Figure 1.12 (a) Frequency shift keyed signal waveform. (b) The frequency spectrum.

is apparent that FSK obeys Carson's rule (bandwidth = $2(f_d + f_s)$). Again, the probability of error can be deduced using similar assumptions as above. The RF signal is present at all times so that its RMS voltage is $A/\sqrt{2}$.

There are now two noise channels, one for each frequency, so that the noise bandwidth is doubled. The RMS noise voltage is thus $\sqrt{(2N)}$.

$$\text{SNR} = (A/\sqrt{2})/\sqrt{(2N)}$$

$$P_e(\text{FSK}) = \tfrac{1}{2}\,\text{erfc}\;A/(2\sqrt{N})$$

Alternatively:

$$P_e(\text{FSK}) = \tfrac{1}{2}\,\text{erfc}\;\sqrt{E_b/(2N_o)}$$

Phase shift keying (PSK)

This is essentially a single frequency method where the data stream causes the carrier phase to change. Figures 1.13(a) and (b) show the modulated waveshape and the phasor diagram. The signal is again present at all times, so there is only one signal channel and one noise channel. The SNR is, therefore,

$$(A/\sqrt{2})/\sqrt{N}$$

giving a probability of error

$$P_e = \tfrac{1}{2}\,\text{erfc}\;A/\sqrt{(2N)}$$

or alternatively

$$P_e = \tfrac{1}{2}\,\text{erfc}\sqrt{(E_b/N_o)}$$

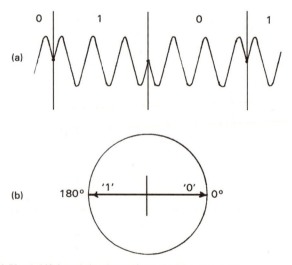

Figure 1.13 (a) Phase shift keyed signal waveform. (b) The phasor diagram.

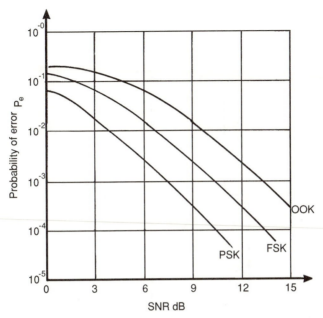

Figure 1.14 Probability of data errors vs. SNR for binary transmissions.

By comparison of these three terms for the probability of error, it can be seen that for the same value of P_e, PSK has a 3 dB advantage over FSK, which in turn has a 3 dB advantage over OOK. PSK also has the advantages of the narrowest bandwidth and the capability of expansion to carry even more data without an increase in bandwidth. These features are clearly shown in Figure 1.14. (See also Appendix A1.7.)

Gaussian minimum shift keying (GMSK)

This hybrid form of modulation can be represented by a vector of constant amplitude that rotates with the signal information and is a continuous phase type of FSK. If the phase change $\delta\phi$ that occurs over the bit period is expressed as a multiple h of π, h is referred to as the modulation index. If h = 0.5, the phase shift over 1 bit period is $0.5 \times \pi = 90°$, and the corresponding frequency deviation $\delta f = 1/(4.T_{bit}) = f_{bit}/4$.

Thus the vector turns through 90° during the bit period for an arbitrary bit, say clockwise for a 1 and anticlockwise for a 0. If a series of 1s or 0s is encountered, the vector continues to rotate in the same direction for the total period as indicated by Figure 1.15.

Before modulation, the baseband signal is passed through a filter to restrict the bandwidth and by using a filter with a Gaussian response, the modulation

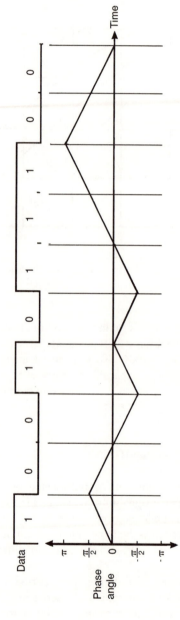

Figure 1.15 Principle of GMSK modulation.

becomes known as GMSK. The filter bandwidth B is normalized to the bit frequency and the 3 dB range of frequencies.

Thus if $B.T_{bit} = \infty$, the system is using straight MSK. Typically for the GSM system, $B.T_{bit} = 0.3$ and with a bit frequency of 270 kbit/s, the bandwidth $B = 270 \times 0.3 = 81$ kHz.

REFERENCES

(1) Clarke, Arthur C. 'Extra-Terrestrial Relays'. *Wireless World*, Oct. 1945.
(2) Slater, J.N. and Trinogga, L.A. (1986) *Satellite Broadcasting Systems*. Chichester: Ellis Horwood Ltd.
(3) Rainger, P., Gregory, D., Harvey, R. and Jennings, A. (1985) *Satellite Broadcasting*. London: John Wiley & Sons.
(4) Griffiths, D.C. (1982) *IBA Technical Review No. 18*. Independent Broadcasting Authority.
(5) Withers, D. 'Equitable Access to Satellite Communication' (review of WARC '85). *Electronics and Wireless World*, Dec. 1985.
(6) Ackroyd, B. (1990) *World Satellite Communications and Earth Station Design*. Oxford: BSP Professional Books.
(7) Schwartz, M. (1970) *Information Transmission, Modulation and Noise*, 2nd edn (International student edition). London: McGraw-Hill Kogakusha.
(8) Mazda, F. (1993) *Telecommunications Engineers Reference Book*, Oxford: Butterworth-Heinemann.

Chapter 2
Noise and interference

2.1 NOISE SOURCES

Noise in the communications sense is any spurious signal that tends to corrupt a wanted one. It is thus a destroyer of information and can be the ultimate limiting factor in a communications link. Noise may be *natural* or *artificial* (man-made) in origin. The former, which includes electromagnetic radiation from such as solar, galactic or thermal sources, is often described collectively as *sky noise*. It usually enters a communications system via a receiving antenna. Artificial noise is largely created by arcing contacts from sources such as vehicle ignition systems, commutator-type motors and generators, etc. It can include radiation from electrical supply systems, or even be carried by the mains wiring (mains-borne).

The effects of noise cannot be eliminated entirely, but by careful design and construction can be reduced to very acceptable levels.

Noise appears as random variation of signal voltages or currents, unrelated in phase or frequency. Such signals have a large peak-to-RMS ratio (*crest factor*) typically in the order of more than 4:1, so the annoyance factor is related to the noise power, or its mean square voltage or current.

A further type of noise that is usually described as interference is produced by other RF carriers present. In this case the noise tends to be periodic and regular in form.

Nevertheless, it creates a major problem. Even a transmitter itself generates noise. Its non-linearities cause distortion which in turn produce unwanted radiation of harmonics. It also generates and radiates some thermal noise, so that even close to the transmitter there is an SNR that is less than ideal.

2.2 SYSTEM NOISE FACTOR

Thermal noise, like white noise (described in Chapter 1), has a statistically normal distribution. The annoyance factor of such noise is quantified (1) by the equation:

$$(\overline{v_n^2}) = 4kTBR \tag{2.1}$$

where: $(\overline{v_n^2})$ is the mean square noise voltage,
        k is Boltzman's constant, 1.38×10^{-23} J/K,
        T is the absolute temperature K,
        B is the system bandwidth Hz, and
        R is the source resistance.

When a noise source is connected to a receiver, the worst-case SNR exists under maximum transfer of power conditions; that is, when the source and input resistances are equal. From Figure 2.1, it can be seen that the maximum thermal noise power P_n, developed in the input load resistance, is given by:

$$(\overline{v_n}/2)^2/R = (\overline{v_n^2}/4R)$$

$$= 4kTBR/4R$$

$$= kTB \text{ watts or } kT \text{ watts/Hz} \tag{2.2}$$

Thus the maximum available noise power is proportional to both temperature and bandwidth.

A receiver itself generates thermal noise power distributed throughout its stages. The measure of the input SNR degradation so produced is described by the system *noise figure or factor* F, which is variously defined as:

(1) $\dfrac{\text{SNR at system input}}{\text{SNR at system output}}$

(2) $\dfrac{\text{SNR of an ideal system}}{\text{SNR of a practical system}}$

(3) $\dfrac{\text{Total noise power at output}}{\text{Noise power at output due to input alone}}$

F may be quoted as a simple ratio or in decibels.

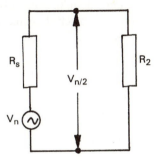

Figure 2.1 Maximum available noise power conditions.

It is shown in Appendix A2.1 that the overall receiver noise factor F_0 is given by:

$$F_0 = F_1 + (F_2 - 1)/G_1 + (F_3 - 1)/G_1 G_2 \tag{2.3}$$

where F_1, G_1, etc. are the individual noise factors and power gains of successive stages of the receiver.

Equation 2.3 shows the importance of low-noise design for the system first stage, as this contributes most to the total degradation. The noise contributions of successive stages are smaller because these pass through fewer stages of amplification.

It should be pointed out here that an attenuator or other device that produces a signal level reduction has a noise factor numerically equal to its loss ratio L. Such a device should not therefore be used in the first stage if it can possibly be avoided. The second term of equation 2.3 then becomes:

$$(F_2 - 1)(1/L)$$

so that the second stage makes a large contribution to the overall noise performance.

2.3 EQUIVALENT NOISE TEMPERATURE

It has been shown that the thermal noise power P_n, available from a resistor over a bandwidth of B Hz, is kTB watts, where T is the absolute temperature of the resistor. Equation 2.2 can be rearranged to give $T_e = P_n/kB$, where T_e is the effective temperature of the resistor that gives the same noise power. This concept can be extended to other noisy sources not necessarily associated with a physical temperature. For example, an antenna collects noise as random electromagnetic radiation and this may be associated with an *equivalent noise temperature*. If a noise power P_n watts is received by the antenna over a bandwidth of B Hz, then the antenna has an equivalent noise temperature, $T_a = P_n/kB$. Of course, T_a will depend very much upon the direction in which the antenna is pointed, thus showing that even the sky has an equivalent noise temperature. This is illustrated in Figure 2.2.

Figure 2.3 shows how the third definition of noise factor is derived. The receiver is connected to a correctly matched source and assumed to be ideal (noise free). An auxiliary noise input T_r accounts for the equivalent noise temperature of the receiver.

$$F = \frac{\text{Total noise power at output}}{\text{Noise power at output due to input alone}}$$

$$= (GkT_s B + GkT_r B)/GkT_s B$$

$$= (T_s + T_r)/T_s = 1 + T_r/T_s$$

or $\quad F - 1 = T_r/T_s.$

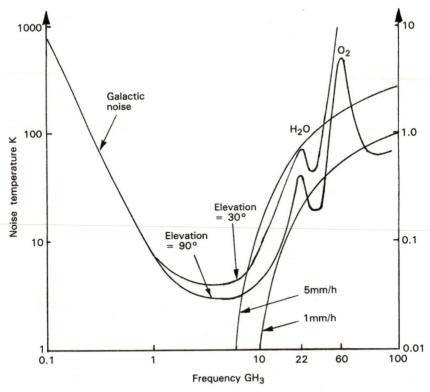

Figure 2.2 Variation of sky noise and atmospheric attenuation with frequency.

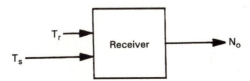

Figure 2.3 Receiver noise factor.

By making this substitution in equation 2.3, an alternative expression for F_0 can be derived.

$$F_0 = 1 + T_1/T_5G_1 + T_2/T_sG_1G_2, \text{ etc.} \tag{2.4}$$

The excess noise ratio (ENR) is often expressed as:

$$10 \log(T_e - 290)/290 \tag{2.5}$$

where T_e is the effective noise temperature of a source and 290k is considered as the reference temperature. The noise spectral density (N_0), is then quoted as the noise power in each Hz of bandwidth (dBm/Hz), hence the total noise power is equal to N_0 times the bandwidth, or in decibels as $10 \log N_0 + 10 \log B$, where B is the bandwidth.

2.4   COMPARISON OF NOISE FACTOR AND TEMPERATURE

When evaluating the performance of systems with low noise factors (less than about 5 dB), the scale for comparison becomes rather cramped. The graph of Figure 2.4, which is a plot of equation 2.4 using a standardized source temperature of 290k, illustrates how an improvement in F of 1 dB is equivalent to an improvement of noise temperature of about 130k, thus showing the scale expansion that is available using the equivalent noise temperature concept.

2.5   ATMOSPHERIC EFFECTS

The atmosphere works in two ways to degrade the SNR: by increasing the attenuation to lower the signal level, and by increasing the noise component. Figure 2.2 shows how both sky noise and rain effects are frequency dependent. Galactic noise falls significantly as frequency rises up to about 1 GHz. The noise level then remains fairly constant, depending upon the angle of elevation of the

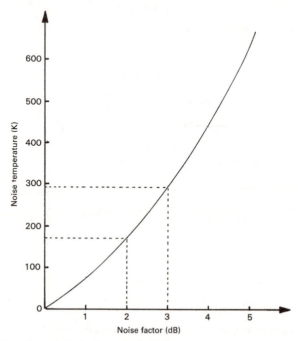

Figure 2.4 Noise temperature/noise factor relationship.

antenna, at about 4k up to 12 GHz. This background noise is considered to be due to *black body* radiation of the expanding universe (the 'big bang' theory). The graph shows quite clearly why this range of frequencies is popular for satellite communications operations.

Both water (H_2O) and oxygen (O_2) molecules are capable of absorbing energy from electromagnetic radiation and then reradiating some of this as noise (scattering). This effect accounts for the two peaks in the curve at about 22 and 60 GHz.

Raindrops vary in size from a few microns to several millimetres in diameter, so storms can produce variation in absorption and scattering to degrade the SNR. The effects of rain are also depicted in Figure 2.2, light drizzle being rated at 1 mm/hr and moderate rain at 5 mm/hr. Except for the case of heavy rain, this form of attenuation is most noticeable above about 6–8 GHz and generally a 3 dB allowance needs to be made for this. However, if the transmitting and receiving stations are close to each other, as may be the case for television distribution, both the up-and down-links can be simultaneously affected. In this case the rain fade margin will need to be doubled.

As the rain attenuation depends on the propagation path length through the storm, the effect increases as the angle of elevation of the antenna decreases. Assuming a storm depth of, say, 5 km and an elevation angle of 25°, the storm path length becomes 5/sin 25° = 11.83 km. Thus at the higher-latitude receiving stations, a greater margin must be allowed for. If the rain is frozen as hail or snow, the attenuation falls to a relatively low level, perhaps 1 percent of that for liquid water (2). However, a special case exists. When the particles contain about 20 percent of liquid water, the attenuation can be about double that when the particles are completely melted.

The frequency ranges of approximately 18–20 GHz and 27.5–31 GHz (Ka band) can provide a further useful *window* for satellite communications (3). However, because of the rain effect, a fade margin in the order of 17 dB will need to be made (4).

2.6 INTERFERENCE WITH ANALOGUE SIGNALS

The major requirements of any receiver can be summarized as:

(1) To select the wanted frequency and reject all the unwanted signals that are present in any waveband.
(2) To recover the information from the modulated signal.
(3) To reproduce the information in a suitable manner.
(4) To carry out these functions without adding too much noise to the wanted signal.

The need to ensure that the SNR remains as high as possible rests not only with the system designer but also, ultimately, with the service engineer. It is therefore important to analyse the sources of interference to the systems.

Since the receivers in use for satellite reception are almost entirely double or triple conversion superhets, interference problems tend to be more complex than those found in the usual terrestrial equipment. Four basic forms of interference are due to *adjacent* and *co-channel, image* or *second channel* and *intermediate frequency* (IF) breakthrough. Co-channel interference results from unusual propagation conditions and/or frequency reuse. Adjacent channel interference implies a lack of intermediate frequency (IF) selectivity within the receiver or discrimination at the antenna. Both are to some extent features of system design and band-planning, but when the problem arises in service, careful attention to the installation can often minimize the effects. Co-channel interference creates *whistles* on audio channels and *patterning* on television displays. In the latter case, high levels of interference can also give rise to *line tearing* because of the interfering synchronizing (sync) pulses.

Adjacent channel interference is most likely to be apparent as sideband interference, as shown in Figure 2.5(a), the higher baseband frequency components from each channel causing mutual interference.

Image or second channel interference is an unwanted feature of the superhet receiver concept. The wanted IF is the difference between the local oscillator and wanted carrier frequencies. Unfortunately, there are two carrier frequencies that give this result. These are shown in Figure 2.5(b), where the first and second channels can be seen to be separated by twice the IF. Receivers of the double or triple conversion types thus make the problem of image channel rejection more complex.

Chosing a high-value IF at the design stage allows the RF stages ahead of the mixer to give good image channel rejection. However, this restricts the adjacent

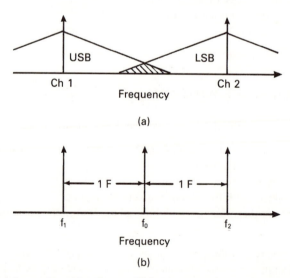

Figure 2.5 (a) Adjacent channel interference. (b) Image or second channel interference.

channel rejection properties of the IF stages, thus clearly indicating some of the design compromises that have to be made.

The superhet receiver can also suffer *IF breakthrough*. A strong signal present at the IF might break through into the IF stages where it will produce an effect similar to co-channel interference. For double or triple conversion receivers, this problem requires the use of efficient screening and filtering. From this can be seen the importance of choosing IFs from little-used parts of the frequency spectrum – another feature that calls for international agreement.

The ability of a receiver to reject these forms of interference is reflected in its *interference rejection ratios*. These are expressed in decibels as:

$$20 \log \frac{\text{(Wanted signal input voltage)}}{\text{(Interfering signal input voltage)}} \quad \text{(each producing the same output level)}$$

or:

$$10 \log \frac{\text{(Wanted signal output power)}}{\text{(Interfering signal output power)}} \quad \text{(each for the same input level)}$$

WARC '77 adopted a figure of merit for direct broadcasting by satellite (DBS or direct to home) television services that is valid for analogue systems. This was based on the *carrier-to-interference ratio* (C/I ratio or CIR) that produces just *perceptible* interference to the picture and is used to define the *service area* of a given channel. The *protection ratio* is quoted in decibels and, to a certain extent, is a subjective value (5). Protection levels of 31 dB for co-channel interference (CCI) and 15 dB for adjacent channel interference (ACI) were set as minimum requirements. In a practical situation, the *protection margin* is the value by which the actual C/I ratio exceeds these values. WARC '77 also proposed an *equivalent protection margin*, based on the summation of upper and lower adjacent channels and co-channel interferences, and the difference between this and the protection margin. Unless this value is positive, the level of interference will be greater than 'just imperceptible'.

It is common receiver practice to use a *low-noise block converter* (LNB) for the first stages. This wideband stage converts blocks of channels down to the first IF. Since there are several carriers present simultaneously, any non-linearity in the LNB will produce *intermodulation interference*. Some possible products of intermodulation are represented in Figure 2.6.

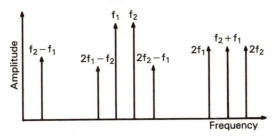

Figure 2.6 Products of intermodulation.

2.7 SIGNAL-TO-NOISE RATIOS

The signal + noise to noise ratio is often used to describe the receiver sensitivity characteristic. This refers to the minimum input signal voltage required to produce a given output signal-to-noise ratio above the noise level for a specified degree of selectivity.

The SINAD ratio takes into consideration the noise contribution produced by the distortion due to non-linear signal processing. It therefore relates to the signal + noise + distortion to noise + distortion ratio that results from processing a modulated carrier.

Table 2.1 gives a few of the decibel ratios that are used in communications engineering for special applications.

Table 2.1 Special dB ratios

dBc	decibels relative to the carrier level
dBi	decibels relative to an isotropic radiator
dBk	decibels relative to degrees Kelvin
dBm	decibels relative to the 1 mW level
dBm0	decibels relative to 1 mW which is also the zero reference level
dBv	decibels relative to 1 volt
dBW	decibels relative to 1 watt
dBpW	decibels relative to 1 picaWatt
dBμV	decibels relative to 1 microvolt
dBμW	decibels relative to 1 microwatt

2.8 INTERFERENCE WITH DIGITAL CHANNELS

Noise and interference create similar problems for digital signals, distorting pulse shapes so that the pulses of adjacent symbols overlap, giving rise to *inter-symbol interference* (ISI) and creating bit errors at the detector stages. Digital processing by *slicing* and/or *sampling* can actually improve the SNR ratio, as shown by Figure 2.7, but the price paid for this advantage is loss of accuracy of decoding under high noise conditions. The accuracy can be recovered by adding redundant bits to the message signal in the form of *error detection/correction codes*. However, this reduces the signalling rate by a factor:

$$\frac{\text{Number of message bits}}{\text{Number of message bits} + \text{Number of redundancy bits}}$$

The performance of analogue and digital signals under noisy conditions is compared in Figure 2.7(c). As the input SNR ratio decreases, the output quality for the analogue system degrades gracefully, but the digital system is relatively

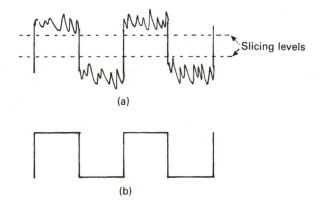

(a)

(b)

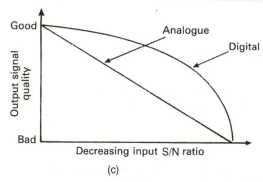

(c)

Figure 2.7 Comparison of analogue and digital signals. **(a)** Digital signals in noisy environment. **(b)** Regenerated digital signal. **(c)** Comparison of signal behaviour in the presence of noise.

unaffected until it suddenly *crashes*. Up to the point where the noise level becomes comparable with the wanted signal level, the action of slicing regenerates an accurate version of the original. As the noise level increases further, bit errors are created and these are generally correctable by the forward error control (FEC) method employed. Eventually, even FEC fails to correct the errors and then the system crashes (6).

2.9 ELECTROMAGNETIC COMPATIBILITY

Electromagnetic compatibility is defined as the ability of a device or system to function satisfactorily in its electromagnetic environment without introducing intolerable interference to any other system. At the same time, its own performance should not be impaired by inteference from other sources.

Noise and interference can enter or escape from equipment in several ways, but chiefly by direct radiation or conduction. The former is controlled by using adequate screening and the latter by suitable filtering to all inputs and outputs. The measurement of radiation and induced susceptibility is measured in a Faraday cage which is itself free from extraneous interference sources. By measuring the radiation from the unit under test over a suitable frequency range, the efficiency of the shielding can be established. Furthermore, the unit should be exposed to radiation to study its behaviour under induced noise conditions. Power filters should be entirely inductive and capacitive so that they do not dissipate any interference energy. The insertion loss performance is then achieved by reflecting unwanted energy back to its source. Generally, these have either low-pass or bandpass characteristics so that they do not attenuate the wanted signals but at the same time provide a high rejection to the interfering noise components.

2.10   NOISE CANCELLATION

This is a new developing technology that owes its origins to the echo-cancelling concept that has for some time been employed in speech telephony circuits. This technique involves filtering off the unwanted signal component, amplifying and phase inverting it, before adding it back to the original signal to cancel out the unwanted effect.

There are two cases to consider which are described as *reference* or *blind*. In the former case a sample of the noise without the signal is available. Hence observation of the noise and signal separately allows an anti-phase noise component to be generated which when added to the wanted signal provides very good noise cancellation.

Blind processing is much more difficult as only one access to the signal and noise is available. In this case, the signal has to be inferred from the different characteristics of the signal and noise. A prime example of this situation relates to the use of in-car mobile telephones which can be expressed as:

Car noise + acoustic characteristics of the car body + speech
    = Impaired intelligibility

Hand-held cellular phones operated within city streets also face similar problems. During signal processing, the filtering action must extract the component with noise-like characteristics; an operation that is easier to perform when the wanted signals are in digital form. The recovered noise component is then processed through adaptive gain and phase shift circuits before being added anti-phase to the original time-shifted wanted signal component. By using complex digital signal processing (DSP) integrated circuits (ICs), the effects of noise can be considerably reduced.

REFERENCES

(1) Connor, F.R. (1976) *Introductory Topics in Electronics and Telecommunication: Noise.* London: Edward Arnold Ltd.
(2) Wise, F. (1979) 'Fundamentals of Satellite Broadcasting'. *IBA Technical Review 11*, March.
(3) Rose, J., Principal Consultant, Communications Systems Ltd, London. Private communication to author.
(4) Mazda F. (1993) *Telecommunications Engineers' Reference Book.* Oxford: Butterworth-Heinemann.
(5) Hopkins, D.K.W. Interference Protection Ratios for C-MAC Vision. *IBA Technical Report No. 126/83.*
(6) Lewis, G.E. (1997) *Communications Technology Handbook.* Oxford: Butterworth-Heinemann.

Chapter 3

Electromagnetic waves, propagation and antennas

3.1 ENERGY IN FREE SPACE

Electromagnetic waves consist of energy in the form of *electric* (E) and *electromagnetic* (H) fields that are interdependent. The waves propagate through space due to an energy source, with the two fields acting at right angles to each other and mutually at right angles to the direction of propagation. Such waves occupy three-dimensional space and are said to be *orthogonal*. The ratio E/H is referred to as the *characteristic impedance* of free space and is equal to 120π ohms or about $377\,\Omega$. A very readable explanation of the way in which electromagnetic waves are forced to propagate is given in reference (1).

By convention, the *plane of polarization* of these waves is associated with the E field. Vertical and horizontal polarizations are used extensively in terrestrial communication frequency reuse systems. Here the E field is either vertical or horizontal in respect of the earth's surface.

3.2 POLARIZATION AND THE TWO COMPONENTS OF THE E FIELD

Figure 3.1 shows the *Poincaré sphere*, a type of spherical quadrant, with centre O and the edges representing the three axes x, y and z. Consider O as the source of energy, generating an electric field, propagating in the arbitrary direction OP. At the surface of the sphere, the wavefront is perpendicular to the direction OP. Due to the angles θ and ϕ there will be components of the electric field in both horizontal (E_x) and vertical (E_y) directions, the total field E being given by $(E_x^2 + E_y^2)^{1/2}$. These two components, shown as being sinusoidal in Figure 3.2, can be represented by:

$$E_x = E_1 \sin(\omega t) \text{ and}$$

$$E_y = E_2 \sin(\omega t + \delta)$$

where E_1 = amplitude of wave polarized in the x direction, E_2 = amplitude of wave polarized in the y direction, and δ = time-phase angle by which E_y leads E_x. In Figure 3.2(b), δ is shown as $-90°$.

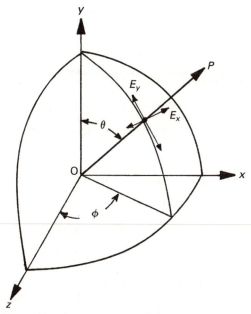

Figure 3.1 The Poincaré sphere and electric field vectors.

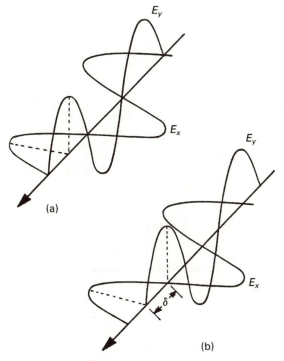

Figure 3.2 (a) Linear polarization. (b) Circular polarization.

The polarization of the wave depends on the relative magnitudes of E_1, E_2 and δ as tabulated below.

$\underline{\delta = 0}$

$E_1 = 0$, linear polarization in the y direction

$E_2 = 0$, linear polarization in the x direction (Figure 3.3(a))

$E_1 = E_2$, linear polarized at 45° in the x, y direction.

$\underline{\delta = \pm 90°}$

$E_1 \neq E_2$, elliptical polarized (Figure 3.3(b))

$E_1 = E_2$, circular polarized (Figure 3.3(c))

δ *positive*, left-hand circular (LHC) or elliptical polarized

δ *negative*, right-hand circular (RHC) or elliptical polarized

It should be noted here that the convention for the direction of circular or elliptical polarization as adopted by the Institute of Electrical and Electronic Engineers (IEEE) is such that left-hand circular polarization is defined as the wavefront rotating clockwise approaching the receiver. This is the opposite of that taken from classical optics.

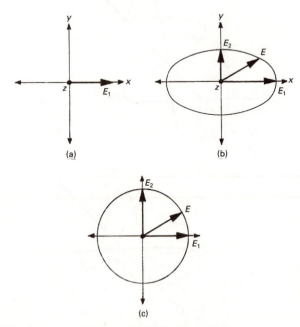

Figure 3.3 Polarization vectors: **(a)** linear; **(b)** elliptical; **(c)** circular.

3.3 PRIMARY PROPERTIES OF ANTENNAS

The terminology aerial and antenna are alternatives for the same device. However, the former is often applied to operational frequencies below about 1 GHz. Virtually any metallic structure can behave as a radiator or receptor, either intentionally or otherwise. An antenna is essentially a transducer designed to obtain maximum transfer of energy from a transmitter into a communications medium or, alternatively, from the medium into a receiver. Because of the reciprocal properties of these devices, their characteristics can be measured or analysed in either the transmit or receive modes, as convenient, with the qualifications that the medium must be both linear and isotropic. Of the many types of antenna available, those based on the parabolic reflector are most commonly used for satellite communication purposes, while those based on the dipole structure with lengths that are either multiples or sub-multiples of a wavelength are used at lower frequencies. However, the reflector type often incorporates a monopole or dipole structure in its feed system. The most important primary properties of antennas are: power gain, directivity, efficiency and equivalent noise temperature, for which there are various definitions.

Power gain is formally defined as:

$$G(\theta, \phi) = \frac{4\pi(\text{Power radiated per unit solid angle in direction } \theta, \phi)}{\text{Total power accepted by antenna from source}} \quad (3.1)$$

or alternatively by:

$$\frac{\text{Power radiated by practical antenna in preferred direction}}{\text{Power radiated in same direction from an isotropic antenna}} \quad (3.2)$$

with both antennas being supplied with the same power levels.

An isotropic antenna is a hypothetical device that radiates energy equally well in all directions. Such a device cannot be achieved in practice, but is a valuable theoretical reference resource with which to compare the properties of practical antennas.

Dipole-based aerials

If a power of P watts is applied to an isotropic radiator, then the electric field strength at a distance d metres is given by $E = \sqrt{(30P)}/d = (5.48\sqrt{P})/d$ V/m. If the isotropic device is replaced by a half-wave dipole ($\lambda/2$) then the electric field strength in the preferred direction rises to $E = (7.014\sqrt{P})/d$ V/m. Thus the $\lambda/2$ dipole has a relative gain of $7.014/5.48 = 1.279$ or 2.14 dBi.

The dipole has many of the properties of a resonant circuit, particularly when cut to multiples of half-wave lengths. In practice, due to capacitive end-effects the optimum length is approximately 0.46λ which produces a centre impedance of about 73 Ω. Figure 3.4(a) shows the voltage and current distribution along a

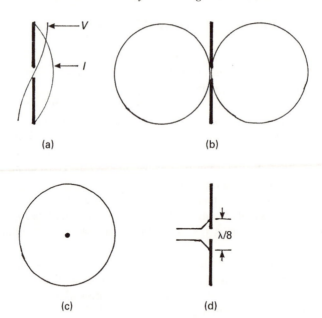

Figure 3.4 **(a)** Voltage/current distribution along $\lambda/2$ dipole. **(b) and (c)** Direction of radiation from a dipole. **(d)** Delta-match feeder.

dipole when energized under resonant conditions. This clearly shows how the low impedance is derived. Figures 3.4(b) and (c) show the broadside and plan radiation patterns respectively. When it is more convenient to feed the dipole via $600\,\Omega$ balanced twin cable, the delta-match concept shown in Figure 3.4(d) can be employed. The gain can be increased by the addition of so-called parasitic elements in front and/or behind the dipole as indicated in Figure 3.5(a). These are respectively referred to as reflectors and directors and for maximum effect are cut slightly longer and shorter than $\lambda/2$ as indicated. Typically the reflector is cut to $\lambda/2$, with the dipole and director to 0.46λ and 0.43λ respectively, while the spacing varies between about 0.15λ and 0.3λ. This type of structure may be extended to as many as eighteen elements before becoming unwieldy. Typical approximate gains for these Yagi-Uda arrays relative to a standard dipole are as follows: five or six elements – 10 dB, nine or ten elements – 13 dB, eighteen elements – 16 dB. Thus doubling the number of parasitic elements increases the gain by about 3 dB. Apart from increasing the gain, the addition of extra elements has the effect of reducing the feed point impedance and the aerial bandwidth. However, these disadvantages can be countered by folding the dipole as shown in Figure 3.5(b). A single fold increases the impedance by a factor of 4, while a double fold increases it by 4^2 or 16. These values can be modified by changing the length to diameter ratio as indicated in the last two diagrams. While folding the dipole has no effect on the gain, it increases both the feed point impedance and the bandwidth.

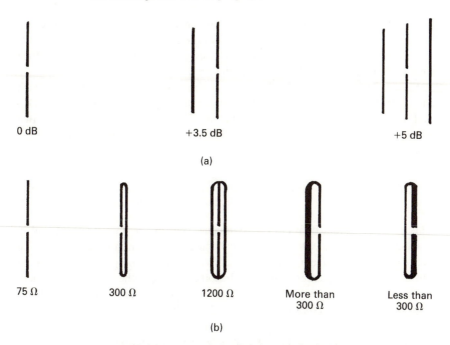

0 dB   +3.5 dB   +5 dB

(a)

75 Ω   300 Ω   1200 Ω   More than 300 Ω   Less than 300 Ω

(b)

Figure 3.5 (a) Relative gain of dipole-based aerials. (b) Relative impedances of dipole structures.

The universal antenna constant which applies specifically to reflector type antennas:

$$G/A_e = 4\pi/\lambda^2 \tag{3.3}$$

is derived in Appendix A3.1,

where: G = power gain
         A_e = effective antenna area
         λ = operational wavelength

Also $A_e = A\eta$,

where: A = physical area of antenna
         η = coefficient of efficiency

It therefore follows that:

$$G = 4\pi A_e/\lambda^2 = \eta\pi^2 d^2 f^2/c^2 \tag{3.4}$$

where: d = diameter of antenna
         f = operational frequency
         c = velocity of electromagnetic propagation

thus showing that gain is dependent upon dish diameter and operating frequency. Doubling either theoretically increases the gain by a factor of 4 or 6 dB.

Directivity is the ability of an antenna to concentrate the radiated energy in a preferred direction in the transmit mode, or to reject signals that are received off-axis to the normal or *antenna boresight*. This gives rise to an amplifying effect on signals being received from the preferred direction.

Figure 3.6(a) shows this directivity as a polar response diagram which indicates the difference between the forward and backward gains (G_F and G_B) and defines the aerial beamwidth as the angle subtended (α) between the two −3 dB points.

The directivity is given by:

$$D(\theta, \phi) = \frac{4\pi(\text{Power radiated per unit solid angle in direction } \theta, \phi)}{\text{Total power radiated by antenna}} \quad (3.5)$$

This property should be rotational symmetric, but this is not often achieved in practice. The directivity for one practical antenna is shown in Figure 3.6(b). The peaks and nulls are due to the phasor addition of signal components incident on different parts of the antenna surface. In some directions these components add, while in others phase cancellations occur, depending on the angles θ and ϕ of Figure 3.1. The side lobes are produced chiefly by:

● reflector surface irregularities that give rise to scattering
● absorption losses at the reflector surface
● diffraction effects at the reflector edges
● the feedhorn *sees* a greater space than that occupied by the focal point thus producing an off-axis response.

These result in the antenna generating spurious emission or reception in unwanted directions, thus giving rise to interfering effects. To minimize this, the Consultative Committee for International Radio (CCIR and now the ITU-RS) and the Federal Communication Commission (FCC of the USA) have adopted standards for geostationary satellite communications that ensure that the amplitude of side lobes will generally be below the level 29−25 log θ dBi (θ = the angle off-boresight), as shown in Figure 3.6(b).

These authorities have adopted slightly different standards to cater for satellite spacing at 2° and for varying European and American operational conditions.

CCIR	FCC
29−25 log θ dBi for $\theta < 20°$	29−25 log θ dBi for $\theta < 7°$
32−25 log θ dBi for $20° < \theta < 48°$	8 dBi for $7° < \theta < 9.2°$
< 10 dBi for $\theta > 48°$	32−25 log θ dBi for $9.2° < \theta < 48°$
	10 dBi for $\theta > 48°$

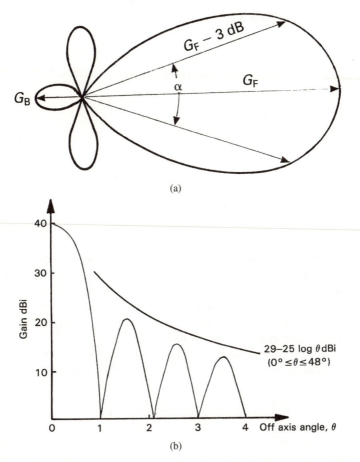

(a)

(b)

Figure 3.6 (a) Directivity and gain of a Yagi array. (b) Directivity patterns of main and side lobes for a reflector antenna.

It is shown in reference (2) that the graphical form of Figure 3.6(b) can be represented by the equation:

$$E_0 = 2\lambda J_1((\pi d/\lambda)\sin\phi)/(\pi d\sin\phi), \tag{3.6}$$

where for $\theta = 90°$:

J_1 = Bessel function of first order
d = antenna diameter
λ = operational wavelength
ϕ = angle with respect to boresight

Bessel functions, which were derived by F.W. Bessel (1784–1846) to solve Kepler's problem relating to the gravitational effects between three bodies in space, are similar in form to sinusoids of diminishing amplitude. These functions

Table 3.1

x	$J_1(x)$	
1	0.4401	
2	0.5767	
3	0.3391	
4	−0.0660	zero crossing
5	−0.3276	
6	−0.2767	
7	−0.0047	
8	0.2346	zero crossing
9	0.2453	
10	0.0435	
11	−0.1768	zero crossing

are particularly flexible and have many uses in communications theory. They are usually presented in table or graphical form and Table 3.1 is a short extract from one such table that indicates the zero crossing points. Figure 3.7 shows a graphical plot of the Bessel function of the first kind that, in terms of frequency modulation, indicates the amplitude variation of the carrier and first three sideband pairs with change of modulation index.

By using linear interpolation to obtain approximation, the first three zero crossings occur at 3.84, 7.02 and 10.2. Thus the values that make $E_0 = 0$ occur when:

$$J_1((\pi d/\lambda) \sin\phi) = J_1(3.84), J_1(7.02), J_1(10.2), \text{ etc.}$$

when:

$$(\pi d/\lambda) \sin \phi = 3.84, 7.02, 10.2, \text{ etc.}$$

so that $\sin \phi = 1.22(\lambda/d), 2.25(\lambda/d), 3.25(\lambda/d)$, etc.

Now since $\phi < 0.1$ rd, $\sin \phi = \phi$ (approx), so that:

$$\phi(\text{rd}) = 1.22(\lambda/d), 2.25(\lambda/d), 3.25(\lambda/d) \ldots \text{ and}$$

$$\phi(°) = 70(\lambda/d), 129(\lambda/d), 186(\lambda/d) \tag{3.7}$$

It is also shown in Appendix A3.2 that the half-power (−3 dB) beamwidth is given by $57.3(\lambda/d)$.

The literature quotes two versions for the *efficiency* parameter. The one applying particularly to the transmit mode is the *radiation efficiency* (η):

$$\eta = \frac{\text{Total power radiated by antenna}}{\text{Total power accepted by antenna from source}}$$

$$= G(\theta, \phi)/D(\theta, \phi) \tag{3.8}$$

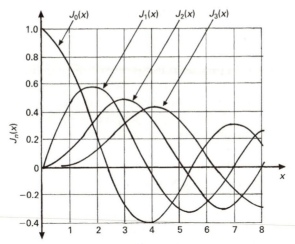

Figure 3.7 Graphical plot of Bessel function of the first kind.

The alternative ratio that is usually applied to the receive mode is known as the *aperture efficiency* (η):

$$\eta = \frac{\text{Effective area of antenna}}{\text{Physical area of antenna}}$$

Typical practical values for both ratios lie in the range 50–75%. The antenna equivalent noise temperature is most important in the receive mode and is related to the antenna radiation resistance, which is not a physical value but more an equivalent one. If a transmitter is loaded with a resistor of $R\,\Omega$ and it dissipates the same amount of heat energy as an antenna radiates in the form of electromagnetic energy, then the antenna radiation resistance is $R\,\Omega$.

This noise component is generally relatively small. A typical antenna noise temperature might lie in the range 50–100k. However, the overall noise temperature depends upon the direction in which the antenna is *looking*, as shown in Figure 3.8. In addition, the noise temperature can be exaggerated by a side lobe that *looks* along a noisy earth.

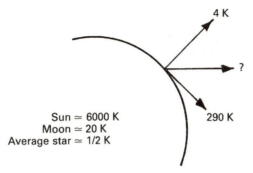

Figure 3.8 Noise temperature 'seen' by an antenna.

3.4   SECONDARY ANTENNA PROPERTIES

The G/T ratio

This is one of the system parameters that is very much controlled by the antenna. The factors that affect this gain/temperature (G/T) ratio are the antenna gain (G_a), its equivalent noise contribution (T_a), and the system equivalent noise temperature (T_s). Since G_a is a function of operating frequency and T_a depends on the angle of elevation of the antenna, both should be stated in a system specification. The importance of this *figure of merit* lies in the choice that it presents to the system designer. A particular G/T ratio can be achieved with a large, high-gain antenna, or a smaller antenna combined with a lower noise specification system.

A receiving system has a sensitivity threshold specification, effectively related to the overall gain. This represents the lowest input signal level that will produce just acceptable quality of output or bit error rate.

The ratio is usually expressed in decibels per degree Kelvin and the following equation is commonly used:

$$G/T = 10 \log[\alpha\beta G_a/(\alpha T_a + (1 - \alpha)290 + T_s)] \, dB/K \qquad (3.9)$$

where α represents the coupling losses between the antenna and the system, and β represents the pointing and polarization losses.

Both coefficients are typically of the order of 0.5 dB. The coupling losses are caused by the small impedance mismatch that occurs between the antenna and block converter. These are usually shown in the system specification under *voltage standing wave ratio* (VSWR) for the antenna output and block converter input. The total standing wave ratio is then the product of the two values. It is shown (3) that α can be calculated from the equation:

$$\alpha = \frac{4}{(2 + VSWR + (1/VSWR))}$$

The following figures are extracted from typical systems designed for Ku band television reception and are presented here to show the relationship between the specification and the G/T ratio.

Antenna gain	48 dB
Pointing and coupling losses	1 dB
Antenna noise temperature	60 K
System noise factor	2.7 dB
Total noise temperature	310 K
Total noise temperature (dBK)	24.9 dBK
G/T ratio	22.1 dB/K

It will be recalled from Chapter 2 that the effective equivalent noise temperature (T_e) referred to the system input is given by:

$$T_e = T_a + T_s/G_a$$

and the overall noise factor by:

$$F_0 = F_a + (F_s - 1)/G_a$$

where
$$F_a = 1 + T_a/290$$

$$\text{Noise factor } 2.7\,\text{dB} = 1.86 = F_s = 1 + T_s/290$$

$$F_s = 1 + T_s/290 = 1.86$$

$$T_s = 250\,\text{K}$$

$$\text{Total noise temperature} = 250 + 60 = 310\text{K},$$

$$\text{or in dBk} = 10\,\log\,310 = 24.9\,\text{dBK}$$

$$\text{System G/T ratio} = 48 - 1 - 24.9 = 22.1\,\text{dB/K}$$

(To convert K into dB, the formula dB = 10 log (K/290 + 1) can be used.)

The parabolic reflector

The mathematical equation for a parabola is:

$$y^2 = 4ax \tag{3.10}$$

Such a shaped curve, shown in Figure 3.9, has some special properties. Any ray emanating from point 'a' will reflect off the curve along a path parallel to the x axis. If the curve is rotated around the x axis, the *surface* so produced is a

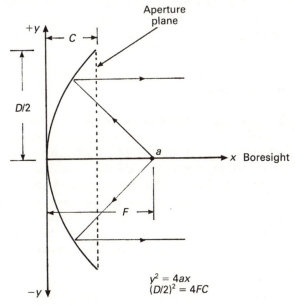

Figure 3.9 The parabolic reflector.

parabolic dish. If this surface is used as a transmitting device, energy emanating from 'a' will be reflected to form a beam parallel to the x axis. Conversely, energy received along a complementary path will be concentrated at 'a', the *focal point.*

Another property of the surface is that the total distance, by any path, from the focal point to the *aperture plane* by reflection is constant. Thus as a transmitting device, any energy leaving 'a' will theoretically pass through the aperture plane completely in phase. It is these properties that are responsible for the forward gain of the device.

For a practical dish of diameter D, centre depth C and focal length F, equation 3.11 can be rewritten as:

$$(D/2)^2 = 4FC$$

$$D^2 = 16FC$$

$$C = D^2/16F$$

$$C = D/(16(F/D)) \qquad (3.11)$$

showing that the depth of dish depends on the diameter and the F/D ratio. The dish shape can be completely described from a knowledge of this ratio and either F or D. With the F/D ratio = 0.25 the focal point lies on the aperture plane. For F/D less than this the focal point lies within the dish volume. While this gives a good side-lobe response, the forward gain is lower because the feedhorn fails to *see* the whole surface. For F/D greater than 0.25, *spill-over* can occur and the side-lobe response degrades. In general, a high F/D ratio produces a flatter dish and optimizes the forward gain, while a lower value gives a better degree of side-lobe suppression. For a typical compromise, values between 0.35 and 0.45 are commonly used for prime focus dishes and between 0.6 and 0.7 for the offset focus versions.

Accuracy of parabolic profile

The overall efficiency of the reflector depends on the aperture efficiency, phase errors at the aperture plane, *spill-over*, and *blocking losses*. The latter two points will be dealt with in the next sections. The aperture efficiency has been shown as the ratio of effective and physical areas, where the effective area is related to the area of the aperture plane. The efficiency will be greatest when the transmitted energy evenly illuminates the whole surface. It is shown in the literature (4) that because of the small space attentuation between the focal point and the dish surface, the illumination will tend to diminish towards the edge. This depends on the F/D ratio, and the edge illumination relative to that at the centre is given by:

$$\{1+(D/4F)^2\}^{-2} \qquad (3.12)$$

Substituting typical values for F/D in this equation shows that the edge illumination improves with an increase in F/D.

Phase errors are largely affected by surface inaccuracies, and so are wavelength dependent. As a general rule of thumb, the peak discrepancies should not exceed ±λ/8 from the true shape. The problem thus becomes exaggerated as operating frequency rises. Often the surface errors for a dish are quoted in RMS values and these can be misleadingly small when compared with peak values. The surface shape may well become distorted by changes of ambient temperature. Therefore for the higher operating frequencies (Ku band and above), even though perforated dishes may be used to reduce wind loading, rigid construction is very important. For the lower frequencies (C band), wire mesh surfaces for reduced windage are sometimes used. Here a useful rule of thumb suggests that the holes should not be greater than about λ/10. These features are often responsible for the poor results that are sometimes obtained when upgrading a system from C to Ku band.

Spill-over

The most effective way to utilize the surface of a reflector antenna is to ensure that the energy radiated from the feed is distributed across its area. With simple feeds, any attempt to achieve this state will result in radiating a significant amount of energy into the angular regions exceeding the angle 2θ of Figure 3.10(a). The resulting *spill-over* of energy represents a signal loss to the forward radiation, as well as radiating possible interference in an unwanted direction. The *spill-over efficiency* can be defined as the percentage of the total energy radiated that actually falls on the reflector. In the receive mode, spill-over will make the antenna responsive to interference from behind the antenna.

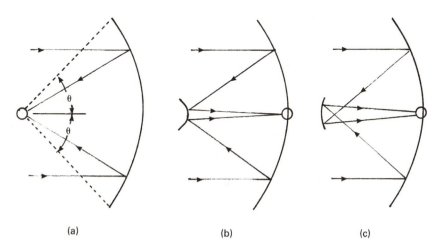

(a)   (b)   (c)

Key: ◯ = Electronics unit

Figure 3.10 Three methods of feeding the parabolic antenna: **(a)** prime focus; **(b)** Cassegrain sub-reflector; **(c)** Gregorian sub-reflector.

It is shown in reference (5) that the most effective way of using the source energy is to arrange for an *illumination taper* with the energy level at an angle of 2θ to be approximately $-10\,\text{dB}$ relative to that at the reflector centre. It is also shown that this can be achieved using a tapered feedhorn, either rectangular or circular, similar to that shown in Figure 3.11(a). Since the angle 2θ is dependent upon the dish F/D ratio, there is an optimum relationship between these parameters and the feedhorn taper, the design of which has to take into consideration the fact that the radiation amplitudes in the E and H planes might not be symmetric. It is conjectured that this is due to E field fringing which results in the two components of the wavefront *seeing* different values of free space impedance. In the receive mode, this produces different focal points or phase centres for each of the E and H components.

Scalar feedhorns of the type shown in Figure 3.11(b) are commonly used for reception purposes. These have three to seven concentric rings, which behave as

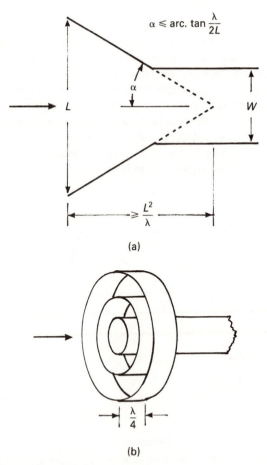

(a)

(b)

Figure 3.11 Feedhorns: **(a)** tapered; **(b)** scalar.

quarter-wave chokc slots, to correct the E field fringing problem. Such horns are insensitive to polarization, have good beamwidth and bandwidth, very low VSWR and good side-lobe discrimination.

Feedhorns are designed to match the impedance of free space to that of the waveguide structure, and for this reason, the position of the scalar rings is often adjustable. These should be slid along the tube and locked into the position that give maximum response. If a weak signal is used for this purpose, it avoids the receiver AGC system masking the adjustment effect. Such feed adapters can add an extra gain to the antenna system of about 1–2 dB. In general, for reception purposes, the tapered feedhorn is often used with offset fed systems, while the scalar device is used with prime focus feeds.

Blocking losses

There are two basic methods of illuminating the reflector antenna: either from the focal point using the *prime focus* method depicted in Figure 3.10(a), or by using a sub-reflector as in Figures 3.10(b) and (c). The latter diagrams show two alternative sub-reflectors: the convex hyperbolic shape of the *Cassegrain* feed, and the concave elliptical shape of the *Gregorian* feed. All three methods have certain advantages, but in general the sub-reflector methods yield an overall antenna gain of about 75–80 percent compared to about 55 percent for the prime focus feed system. The accuracy of the sub-reflector surface is most important, otherwise spill-over will be increased.

The prime focus system is the easiest to set up, but with the electronics unit positioned near to the focal point, heat from the sun's rays can produce a problem. Using sub-reflectors places the electronics unit at the back of the dish and in a more convenient position for servicing. Using either method results in physical components being mounted near to the focus. These and their support structure then throw a shadow on the dish surface that reduces the effective area by *blocking*, as shown in Figure 3.12(a). The structure in front of the dish causes scattering of the electromagnetic energy, which leads to a loss of gain and degradation of side-lobe and cross-polar discrimination.

The blocking effect can be completely eliminated by using an *offset* feed, as shown in Figure 3.12(b). The main reflector is a section of a larger paraboloid, which can be illuminated by either of the three methods described above. It should be noted that the offset feed produces a boresight that is approximately 28° off-centre in the elevation plane (6). This is shown in Figure 3.12(b), together with a representation of the effective area of the reflector surface. In the transmit mode, the offset feed antenna introduces a small cross-polar component, which can be corrected by using a suitably shaped sub-reflector. The focal point for either the Cassegrain or Gregorian sub-reflector should coincide with the focal point of the main reflector. The removal of the blocking effect gives increased gain, better side-lobe and cross-polar discrimination and a good VSWR.

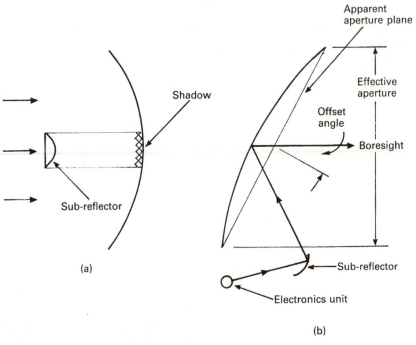

Figure 3.12 (a) Blocking losses. (b) Offset feed antennas.

Antenna pointing losses

The sun and moon, in particular, exert gravitational forces on a geostationary satellite that cause it to drift in a north/south-oriented figure-of-eight path during each sidereal day. By comparison, the drift in the east/west direction is small, but the satellite has to carry fuel for *station keeping* to constrain this drift within acceptable bounds. The larger ground stations with high-gain, narrow-beamwidth antennas need to use servo-controlled tracking systems to maintain a good SNR. But when using small fixed receiving antennas, there will be a small daily change in signal level.

It has been shown that the approximate beamwidth (−3 dB) is given by 57.3λ/D. Using a 1.8 m antenna at 10 GHz gives a beamwidth of about 1°, so a pointing error of 0.5° will give rise to a loss in signal level of about 1 dB. Such a calculation also shows the importance of a rigid mounting construction even for a small dish, particularly in windy environments.

Tracking systems for satellite operation

The master ground station has to maintain the satellite's location throughout its operational lifetime and to this end it is equipped with a highly accurate tracking system. Any drift in the satellite position demands an early correction command if services to customers are not to be lost. A constant amplitude down-link beacon signal is transmitted within the satellite's housekeeping multiplex of signals. As the bird drifts away from its nominal position, the strength of the beacon signal received by ground control will decrease, indicating that some correction is necessary. The control technique is based on a step-tracking process that operates identically but alternately in the azimuth and elevation planes. If the beacon signal level falls below some selected threshold, then the antenna is realigned to recover the original maxima. The satellite's position is now compared with its nominal location and it is then instructed to move. As this occurs, the antenna continues to track the moving satellite until both are again in correct alignment. By studying the behaviour pattern over several days, it becomes possible, under computer control, to predict the bird's movements. In fact it has been found possible to quickly relocate a satellite several days after a ground station power failure. As an example of the degree of accuracy of this mode of control, SES (Societé Européene des Satellites) are able to control up to eight ASTRA satellites within ±0.1° of the nominal location at 19.2° East without collisions or radio frequency shadowing.

The level of the beacon signal can also be used by portable ground stations such as those used for satellite news gathering (SNG) to allow the operators to align their antenna system on the allocated satellite before starting transmissions.

For SNG operation, transportability is an essential feature and to this end a number of interesting reflector systems have been developed. Among these are the elliptical devices, such as that provided by Advent (UK) Ltd for use with the Newshawk SNG system. The main reflector has a width-to-height ratio of 2:1 and uses a Gregorian-type sub-reflector with an offset feed for both the receive and transmit modes. The whole construction makes for high efficiency, portability and flexible operation. The width gives high gain and narrow beamwidth in the azimuth plane, to discriminate between adjacent satellites. The reduced height gives a wider beamwidth in the elevation plane to minimize the pointing loss effect due to satellite drift.

The main reflector, sub-reflector and waveguide feedhorn are closely matched and the surface shapes and illumination taper have been produced by an iterative computer-controlled process known as *diffraction profile synthesis*. As a result, the surfaces are complex and not describable by any simple mathematical function. The design technique has produced an antenna with very good side-lobe rejection and cross-polar discrimination, with low noise temperature and high efficiency.

Towards the end of a satellite's lifetime, dictated by the supply of station-keeping fuel, it is common to allow the bird to drift into an inclined orbit so that it can still be used by ground stations equipped with tracking aerial systems.

3.5   CHOICE OF ANTENNA TYPE

The performance of a wide range of aerials can be compared with a number of standard devices. For low and medium frequencies (LF and MF) that have corresponding long wavelengths, the standard is based on a vertical radiator or mast that has a height of less then 0.1λ which acts as a monopole. When this is compared with the radiation from a 0.55λ mast, it is found that the latter has a gain of about 2 dB. For high and microwave frequencies (HF and µw) the standard is based on the isotropic radiator or a standard dipole which has a gain of 2.15 dBi.

Satellite communications provide applications for a very wide range of frequencies, extending from about 135 MHz upwards. It has been shown (equation 3.4) that the gain of a parabolic reflector antenna is proportional to its diameter and the operating frequency. Therefore below some frequency its gain must fall below an acceptable level. It is shown (5) that this is likely to be around a diameter of 0.1λ, below which it might be practicable to change to an alternative type. The Yagi array has been extensively used for terrestrial systems up to about 1 GHz for linear polarized signals, but for circular polarization its use invokes a 3 dB penalty. Typical maximum gain for a Yagi is around 18 dB. Stacking two similar arrays in parallel yields only a further theoretical gain of 3 dB. Therefore at this stage the Yagi becomes unwieldy, particularly if it is to be steerable. Helical antennas have a useful gain up to about 20 dB for circular polarization with good directivity. A small commercially available antenna is available for operation in the 1.50–1.55 GHz band. This has a figure of merit (G/T) of 23 dB/K down to 5° of elevation. However, as with the Yagi, any further increase in gain tends to be mechanically inconvenient.

There are applications where the antenna gain is of secondary importance to a wide beamwidth. Services using the polar orbiting satellites often need a beamwidth in the order of 180°. The *resonant quadrifilar helix antenna* can meet such a need.

3.6   HELICAL ANTENNAS

The helical beam antenna depicted in Figure 3.13 is particularly suitable at frequencies below about 500 MHz. The polarization is circular along the helix axis and dependent upon the winding direction. A helix for left-hand circular (LHC) polarization is shown in Figure 3.13(a). The dimensions that are important to the characteristics are shown in Figure 3.13(b). The antenna radiation resistance is low and suitable for use with coaxial cable feeders.

When the circumference of the antenna is approximately one wavelength (λ), the radiation pattern is almost entirely in front of the ground plane. The directivity is empirically given (7) by:

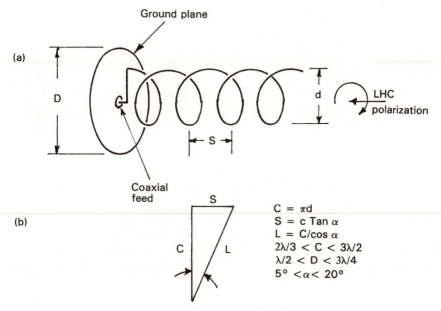

Figure 3.13 The helical beam antenna and its important dimensions.

$$D = 15n(S/\lambda)(C/\lambda)^2 \qquad (3.13)$$

where: $C = \pi d$ the circumference
d = diameter
$S = C \tan \alpha$
α = helix angle
n = number of turns
λ = operational wavelength

For the commonly used values of $\alpha = 12°$, $C = \lambda$, the forward gain for n between 3 and 25 turns is given approximately by:

$$GdB = 7 + 2\sqrt{n} \qquad (3.14)$$

Additionally, the antenna has a wide bandwidth and very good VSWR. Due to the helical construction, it is physically short in terms of wavelengths.

The helix antenna has been further developed for use at L band. Two small helices each of seven turns, are mounted in parallel above a ground plane, with a dielectric strap across the top to increase mechanical stability. This in turn also helps to maximize the overall gain across the bandwidth to achieve a value of 13 dBi extending from 1.5 to 1.6 GHz. The cross-circular polar rejection is in the order of −20 dB. The ground plane measures 11 × 30 cm, and the structure has a height including radome of 12.5 cm.

Resonant quadrifilar helix antennas

Circular polarized antennas with a beamwidth approaching 180° find applications as receiving devices for the navigation and weather services provided from polar-orbiting satellites. Due to such a beamwidth, the receiver remains within a good SNR area for the duration of the satellite pass. Most antennas that meet this requirement for VHF and low UHF are mechanically cumbersome. However, the resonant quadrifilar helix antenna not only has a wide beamwidth but also a useful gain and small size (8).

There is a family of these devices, whose construction is typified by Figure 3.14. The helix shown is wound for RHC polarization (reversing the helix reverses the polarization). The helices consist of thin brass tapes wound on to a dielectric material cylinder, with the lower ends short circuited and the upper ends connected in parallel pairs as shown. The total length of each helix is a multiple of two or more quarter-wavelengths. That shown has two loops, each of one wavelength total length. The antenna forms a balanced circuit with a radiation resistance of 25 Ω. It is usual to feed these antennas via a sheathed

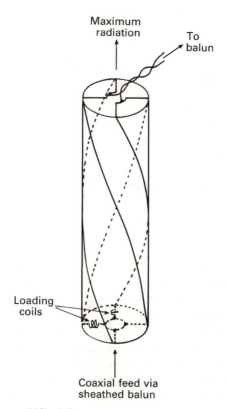

Figure 3.14 A half-turn quadrifilar helix antenna.

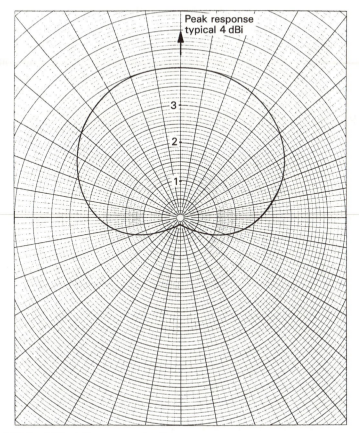

Figure 3.15 Quadrifilar helix antenna polar diagram.

balanced-to-unbalanced (balun) transformer through the aperture at the short-circuit end and using coaxial cable. The antennas with three or more quarter-wavelength helices have a higher gain, but the half-wavelength version has a better front-to-back ratio.

In order to obtain the correct polar diagram with maximum response along the helix axis as shown in Figure 3.15, it is necessary to feed the two loops in phase quadrature (90°). This can be achieved either by using a 3 dB directional coupler and feeding each loop from separate outputs, or by making one loop resonant at a higher frequency than the other but equally spaced across the operating frequency. By careful control of the reactive components, the current in one loop then leads the applied voltage by 45° while the current in the second lags by 45°. The operational bandwidth depends on maintaining this phasing relationship.

Feedback Instruments Ltd UK have produced such an antenna for their Weather Satellite Receiving System, where the two loops are identical except that one contains a pair of loading coils. The two loops are connected in parallel through a balun to give a feed impedance of 25 Ω. Their design includes a built-in high-gain pre-amplifier and a five-section low-pass filter, which avoids the need to match the 25 Ω to a 50 Ω coaxial cable, thus removing one source of signal loss. The amplifier power is provided over the feeder cable. The complete antenna is coated with glass fibre to give protection from the elements.

3.7   REFLECTION, REFRACTION, DEPOLARIZATION AND FEEDS

The behaviour of light waves incident upon a boundary layer between two media is described by two laws:

(1)   The incident ray, reflected ray and the normal to the separation surface between the two media lie in the same plane at the point of incidence.
(2)   Snell's law, which states that the ratio of the sines of the incidence and refraction angles is constant for a given pair of media. When one of the media is a vacuum (air is also a close approximation), this ratio gives the *refractive index* n for the second medium. The refractive index is also the ratio of the velocity of light in free space to its velocity in the medium.

Using Figure 3.16(a), Snell's law can be expressed as:

$$\sin \theta_3 / \sin \theta_1 = n_1/n_2 = \text{constant} \tag{3.15}$$

where: θ_1 = angle of incidence
$\theta_2 = \theta_1$ = angle of reflection
θ_3 = angle of refraction
n_1, n_2 = optical refractive indices for the two media

It will be recalled from electromagnetic wave theory that the velocity of light c in free space is given by:

$$c = 1/\sqrt{(\mu_0 \varepsilon_0)}$$

where μ_0 and ε_0 are the absolute values of permeability and permittivity for free space respectively.

The behaviour of electromagnetic waves (which, like light waves, are part of the same electromagnetic radiation spectrum) incident upon a surface is a fundamental feature of several antenna types.

For electromagnetic waves, equation 3.15 can be rewritten as:

$$\sin \theta_3 / \sin \theta_1 = \sqrt{(\mu_1 \varepsilon_1 / \mu_2 \varepsilon_2)} \tag{3.16}$$

where μ_1, μ_2, ε_1 and ε_2 are the relative permeabilities and permittivities of the two media respectively. If one of the media is air and the other a dielectric material, μ is approximately equal to μ_0 so that equation 3.16 simplifies to:

$$\sin \theta_3 / \sin \theta_1 = \sqrt{(\varepsilon_0 / \varepsilon_2)} \tag{3.17}$$

Since $\varepsilon_2 < \varepsilon_0$, the velocity of propagation and the wavelength in the dielectric will be less than in air. From equations 3.15 and 3.17, it can be shown that the proportional reduction of velocity and wavelength is dependent upon $\sqrt{\varepsilon_r}$, where ε_r is the relative permeability of the second medium.

If a wave is incident upon a perfect conducting surface, the angle of reflection will be equal to the angle of incidence but the wave polarization will have been changed. If the incident wave is right-hand circular polarized (RHCP), the reflected wave will be left-hand circular polarized (LHCP) and vice versa, as shown in Figure 3.16(b).

Figure 3.16(c) shows the wave incident upon a dielectric material, with the H field perpendicular to the boundary layer. A critical angle (Brewster angle) can be found, where the wave is totally transmitted into medium 2. If the incident

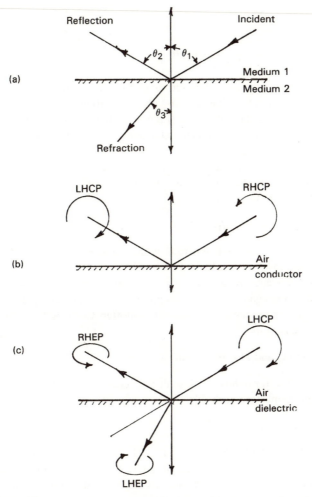

Figure 3.16 (a) Reflection and refraction. (b) Reflection from a conductor surface. (c) Refraction in a dielectric material.

wave were circular polarized (CP) or elliptically polarized (EP), the transmitted wave would be elliptically or linearly polarized respectively.

All four states of polarization are used for different satellite services, the state chosen for a particular application depending upon some particular attribute of that state. For instance, *Faraday rotation* within the ionosphere, the change of satellite attitude or the misalignment of an antenna feed can each give rise to a change of plane of polarization, with the attendant loss of received signal. Therefore circular polarization, which is not affected in this way, would be used. Both opposite linear and circular polarizations give rise to similar degrees of isolation under frequency reuse conditions. A linear feed will receive both RHCP and LHCP equally well, but will only respond to one component in the wavefront, resulting in a 3 dB loss of possible signal level.

Dielectric depolarizer for CP feeds

The dielectric depolarizer can be used to modify circular polarized waves so that they may be received by a linear feed without significant loss of signal. This can be done by reducing the value of δ (Figure 3.2(b)) to zero. To understand how this can be achieved, some fundamental features of wave motion are now re-examined.

The phase velocity, v_p of a wave $= \lambda/T = \lambda.f$, where λ, T and f have their usual meanings. If the phase velocity per unit length is β, then over a wavelength λ the phase shift is 2π radians, so that:

$$\beta = 2\pi/\lambda \text{ or } \lambda = 2\pi/\beta$$

Now $v_p = \lambda.f = 2\pi f/\beta = \omega/\beta$ where ω is the angular velocity in rd/sec.

Consider the case of a thin slab of dielectric as shown in Figure 3.17(a), which is placed in a waveguide through which a wavefront is flowing. The component E_y will still propagate largely through air, while the component E_x must propagate through the dielectric, but with a shorter wavelength, so that its phase shift is represented by:

$$\beta_y = 2\pi/\lambda_y \text{ and also } \beta_x = 2\pi/\lambda_x$$

For the dielectric to produce a phase difference of $\pi/2$ rd (90°) between E_x and E_y, its length L must be such that:

$$\beta_y L - \beta_x L = \pi/2 \tag{3.18}$$

Then the slab effectively converts circular into linear polarization. The slab must be mounted in the waveguide/feedhorn at an angle of $\pm 45°$ to the feed probe as shown by Figure 3.17(b). In a practical feed system, it is possible to arrange for the depolarizer to be rotated through 90° to change from RHCP to LHCP, and vice versa.

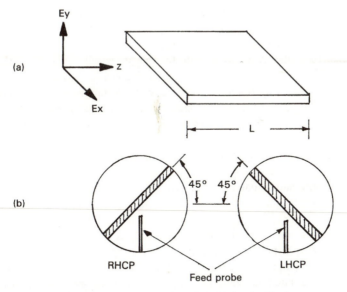

Figure 3.17 (a) The dielectric depolarizer. (b) View of depolarizer looking into a waveguide/feedhorn.

Feeds for linear polarization

To receive signals of both x and y linear polarizations usually requires the use of two low-noise block converters (LNBs). These may be mounted in series along a circular waveguide as shown in Figures 3.18(a) and (b). Each LNB has its own feed probe and the two are at right angles to each other. Rotating the assembly

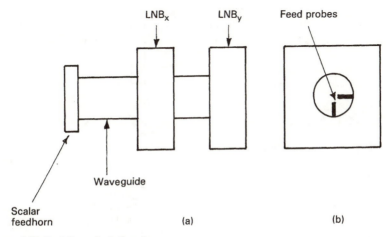

Figure 3.18 Dual linear feeds in series.

to maximize the signal level for one polarization automatically assures maximum signal at the output of the alternate LNB, selection of the necessary LNB being achieved by switching dc power supplies.

Alternatively, the two LNBs can be fed in parallel via an *orthomode-transducer* (OMT) in the manner indicated in Figures 3.19(a) and (b). The OMT consists of a circular section of waveguide with a rectangular branch section. By rotating the OMT, the linear polarized E_y field will couple with the narrow dimension of the rectangular waveguide to transfer its signal to LNB_y, leaving the E_x component to continue straight through to LNB_x. The rectangular opening thus behaves as a low impedance to one component and a very high impedance to the other.

A further alternative that avoids the use of a second LNB involves rotating the feed probe within the waveguide by 90° using an electromechanical polarizer driven by a stepper or servo motor. While this gives a good cross-polar response, the mechanical parts tend to wear, or seize up due to weather conditions. A variation on this principle involves an LNB equipped with a pair of monopole pick-ups each feeding separate RF amplifiers which can be selected for either vertical or horizontal polarization by switching on the appropriate amplifier. (For

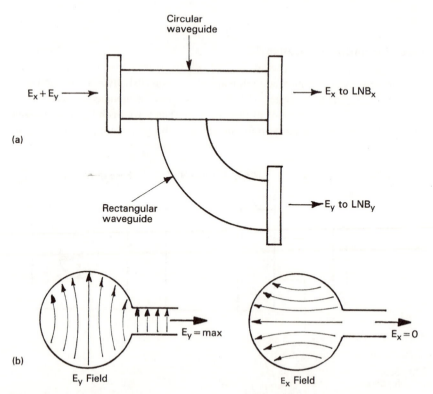

Figure 3.19 (a) The orthomode transducer. (b) Coupling of E field into rectangular section.

control of such schemes, see Chapter 8.) For reception from two co-located satellites it is possible to mount two LNBs in parallel at the common focus point, with the selection being achieved by switching the dc power supply to the wanted device over its own coaxial cable feed. Both LNBs may then be capable of responding to either vertical or horizontal polarized signals.

Faraday rotation and dual feeds

An electromagnetic wave is influenced by the earth's magnetic field as it propagates through the ionosphere, in such a way that causes a rotation of the plane of polarization of a linear polarized wave. This is known as *Faraday rotation*, the degree of rotation depending on the ionospheric path length and the intensity of the magnetic field. This phenomenon forms the basis of operation of several microwave devices.

Faraday rotation is increased if the wave is constrained within a waveguide, with a dc magnetic field applied externally. The effect can be further enhanced if a relatively small piece of ferrite is judiciously placed in the waveguide. Ferrite has the highly desirable magnetic properties of high permeability and high internal molecular resistance with very low loss, even when used at microwave frequencies.

By a suitable choice of ferrite dimensions and strength of magnetic field, the plane of polarization can be rotated through 90° over a fairly short distance. Alternatively, the external magnetic field can be switched, to provide ±45° of rotation with about ±40 mA of current. The degree of loss with such a dual polarity feed is typically less than 0.2 dB. A cross-polar attenuation of better than 20 dB is typically achieved with such a device, and a *fine* or *skew* adjustment is often provided to maximize the performance.

3.8 FREQUENCY-SELECTIVE SURFACES AND PLANAR ANTENNAS

In certain applications, it may be necessary to operate on two different frequencies simultaneously. This could, of course, be achieved with two antenna systems. However, if a sub-reflector is constructed from dichroic material, which is transparent at the prime focus feed frequency and highly reflective at the frequency provided from a Cassegrain/Gregorian feed mounted in the conventional position, the cost of an antenna system can be saved. *Frequency-selective surfaces* have such properties.

These are arrays of metallic elements printed over the surface of a suitably shaped dielectric substrate, using normal printed circuit techniques. The surfaces behave as high-pass filters, transparent to the prime focus feed while being highly reflective to the lower frequencies. The elements have a self-resonant frequency that depends upon their dimensions and is responsible for these

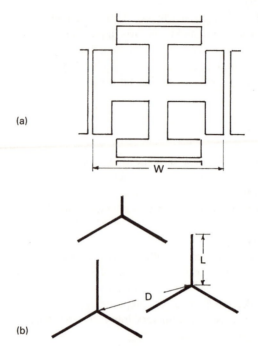

Figure 3.20 Frequency-selective surface patterns: **(a)** Jerusalem cross; **(b)** tripole.

characteristics. Much work has been reported (9) using arrays of elements of various shapes, ranging from the *Jerusalem cross* of Figure 3.20(a), through concentric rings and squares, to the *tripoles* shown in Figure 3.20(b). Very low losses, ranging from 0.1 to 0.5 dB, have been reported for both transmissive and reflective modes, with good cross-polar performance for linear polarized signals.

In the reflective mode, the elemental microwave patches of the frequency-selective surface radiate as antennas that have been fed from the incident energy of the electromagnetic waves. If the patches on such a surface are coupled together and fed from a source such as a transmitter, then the surface will radiate energy in a similar way.

Figure 3.21 shows how using a frequency-selective surface that is reflective to one band of frequencies and transparent to another range can allow one antenna to perform the functions of two. In this case the system is capable of transmitting on both the X and Ka bands and receiving on the S and Ku bands (see Appendix A1.3).

Although radiation emanates from the satellite antenna as a spherical wave, when received at the earth station it has become a very close approximation to a plane wave. Under such conditions, any flat panel carrying an array of resonant circuits will collect radiated energy that lies within some particular bandwidth. The *printed planar antenna* is an array of microstrip radiating elements fed by

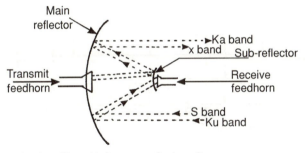

Figure 3.21 Four-band working with frequency-selective reflectors.

microstrip transmission lines, the construction being similar to double-sided printed circuit boards. The patterns for the elements and feed lines are formed by etching away copper cladding from one side of the substrate, leaving the other side to act as a ground plane. The substrate used has varied from high-grade glass fibre to polythene, but needs to be chosen for low loss with adequate mechanical stiffness.

Over the development period, many different patch shapes have been studied, showing that both linear and circular polarizations can be radiated or received. Gains in excess of 35 dBi and operating frequencies beyond 85 GHz have been reported (10, 11), showing that the concept is a valuable alternative antenna for mobile satellite communications. Because of their flat nature, they adapt well to use with ground vehicles or aircraft. In these cases, the vehicle's metallic skin can act as the ground plane, giving rise to the term *conformal antennas*.

The chief advantages of planar arrays lies in the thin profile. This makes them less obtrusive and adaptable as conformal antennas, with acceptable side-lobe rejection. Further, if these units are fed from a corner, then it becomes very easy to connect four in parallel to improve the overall performance.

Of the many different configurations that have been used, the patterns shown in Figure 3.22 are popular. The antennas are either made as a complete panel (Figure 3.22(a) or in sections that can be coupled together to form a large array (Figure 3.22(b)).

It should be pointed out that when a radome is fitted, this results in a detuning effect. For a single patch antenna designed to work at 1.5 GHz, the fitting of this protective cover will lower the working frequency by about 5 MHz.

In terms of directivity, if the panel is fed from the centre then the major part of the radiation will be normal to the ground plane. However, the antenna of Figure 3.22(a) can be fed from any of the four corners, and this gives rise to four different off-centre beams (11). An alternative way of making the array *squint* is to insert ferrite phase shifters in the feeds between panel sections. By carefully controlling the reactive components, the beam can then be directed in a preferred direction. Multiple patches may either be edge or aperture coupled but the former can become difficult and costly for very large arrays. In addition, such arrays usually have a relatively narrow bandwidth, typically in the order of 2 percent of

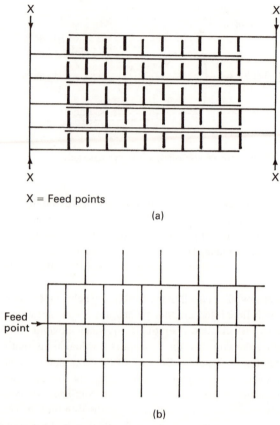

X = Feed points

(a)

Feed point →

(b)

Figure 3.22 Microwave planar antenna arrays: (a) end sections of square array with steerable directivity; (b) single section of multiple array.

centre frequency. Aperture coupling allows for a sandwich type of construction where a thicker layer of plastic foam can be used to separate the patch, coupling and ground plane panels. This then provides for a bandwidth of around 10 percent which is necessary for video and multimedia applications. Such a structure can achieve a bandwidth of 1 GHz in the Ku band with a forward gain of 25 dB and side lobes at least 10 dB down on the main response, together with a beamwidth of 20° (12).

For receiving circular polarized waves, a dielectric depolarizer can be placed in front of the array, with the dielectric slats at 45° to the elements (see Figure 3.23). This functions in the manner of the depolarizer previously described and gives rise to a 3 dB signal penalty.

Diamond-shaped (squarial) devices have been used for the DBS service provided from a high-power satellite (approximately 60 dBW). This 40 or 50 cm sided unit provides enough gain to produce excellent picture quality even when

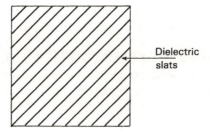

Figure 3.23 Depolarizer for planar antenna array.

working with a CNR as low as 11 dB. The basic structure is designed around either 144 or 256 resonant cavities separated by 0.9λ, each with separate probes. These are arranged to feed an embedded low-noise block converter (LNB) via a combining network, which introduced some attenuation that can be countered by using a dielectric material with very low loss (12).

3.9 FRESNEL ZONE PLATE ANTENNAS (13)

This antenna is based on the Fresnel principle of a series of concentric rings, alternately transparent and opaque and deposited on a transparent surface. This has the ability to focus electromagnetic waves on to a point behind the surface. The alternate zones are formed by screen printing on to a clear plastic layer or flat glass sheet using reflective or absorbing inks. Silver or graphite loaded ink is used for the plastic surface and metallic oxides can be used on glass. This last form leaves the structure completely transparent to visible light. If the dielectric

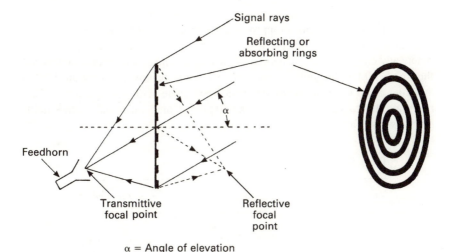

α = Angle of elevation

Figure 3.24 The elliptical zone plate.

layer is backed by a metallic surface acting as a reflecting ground plane, the focal point switches to being a mirror image of the transmissive version. This has the effect of increasing the gain of the reflector by almost 3 dB. The principle of both modes is shown in Figure 3.24. Furthermore, if the rings are made elliptical, the focal point shifts so that electromagnetic waves approaching from a suitable angle *see* concentric circles. The secant of this angle is proportional to the ratio

semi-major axis

semi-minor axis

of the ellipsoid. This feature is therefore used to give the reflector surface a *squint*. Figure 3.25 shows the relationship between the wavelength-dependent dimensions.

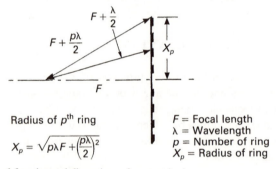

Radius of pth ring

$$X_p = \sqrt{p\lambda F + \left(\frac{p\lambda}{2}\right)^2}$$

F = Focal length
λ = Wavelength
p = Number of ring
X_p = Radius of ring

Figure 3.25 Signal focusing and dimensions of concentric rings.

The gain of the reflector is approximately proportional to the number of rings and the beamwidth is inversely proportional to the area. The bandwidth is practically equal to $2\omega_0/N$ where ω_0 represents the mid-band frequency and N is the number of rings. For a typical reflector, the bandwidth is about $15\%\omega_0$. Working at 11 GHz, a 90 cm diameter zone plate will give good television reception from a signal source of about 50 dBW. Comparative gain values in dBi are shown in Table 3.2.

Table 3.2

Number of zones	Theoretical gain	Practical gain
1	6.0	4.5
2	11.8	9.0
3	15.2	11.5

3.10 SIGNAL STRENGTH CONTOUR MAPS OR FOOTPRINTS

The contour lines of the satellite's transponder footprint, as depicted by Figure 3.26 (14), represent the level of signal receivable by a ground station. Unlike the maps used for terrestrial transmission systems, which are usually scaled in volts/metre (dBV) or microvolts/metre (dBμ), the satellite's contours are generally scaled either in terms of power flux density (PFD) or effective isotropically radiated power (EIRP). PFD represents the signal level received on earth per square metre of surface (W/m^2) or decibels relative to 1 W/m^2 (dBW/m^2). As an example, if an antenna of effective area of 1 m^2 is exposed to a PFD of -120 dBW/m^2, it will collect -120 dBW of power.

$$-120 \, \text{dBW} = 10^{-12}\text{W} = 1 \, \text{pW}$$

Since power is given by V^2/R and R in this case is the free space impedance of 120π ohms, V = 19.42 μV or 25.76 dBμ.

EIRP is related to the transmission polar diagram, and is the product of the signal power fed to the antenna and the transmitting antenna gain in a preferred direction. If the power transmitted from an isotropic source is P_t watts, the PFD at the surface of a sphere will be $P_t/4\pi r^2$ W/m^2, where r is the spherical radius.

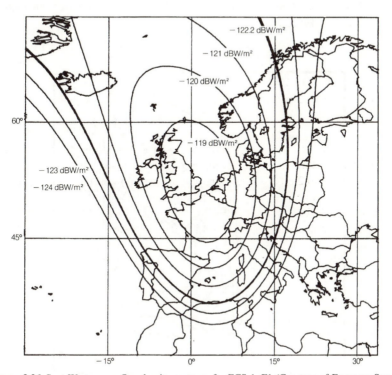

Figure 3.26 Spot West power flux density contours for ECS-1, F1 (Courtesy of European Space Agency (ESA)).

If the isotropic source is now replaced with an antenna of gain G_t, then assuming the same power input, the PFD at the surface will be $G_tP_t/4\pi r^2$ W/m^2 in some direction. If this energy is incident upon a receiving antenna with an effective area of A_e m^2, the total received power P_r will be:

$$G_tP_tA_e/4\pi r^2 \text{ watts} \tag{3.19}$$

From equation 3.3, $A_e = G_r\lambda^2/4\pi$, where G_r is the gain of the receiving antenna, and making a substitution in equation 3.19, this gives:

$$P_r = G_tP_tG_r\lambda^2/(4\pi r)^2 \text{ watts}$$

$$= G_tP_tG_r(\lambda/4\pi r)^2 \text{ watts and}$$

$$P_r/G_r = P_tG_t(\lambda/4\pi r)^2 \text{ watts} \tag{3.20}$$

Now $P_r/G_r = $ PFD, $P_t/G_t = $ EIRP, and the term $(\lambda/4\pi r)^2$ is usually referred to as the *free space attenuation*. Figure 3.27 thus indicates the equivalence between these two methods of scaling the footprint contours which can be summarized as:

$$\text{PFD dBW} = \text{EIRP dB} - \text{free space attenuation dB} \tag{3.21}$$

For a geostationary satellite receiving station for 12 GHz, the minimum value of r is 35 775 km. Therefore at this frequency the minimum free space attenuation is approximately 195.1 dB.

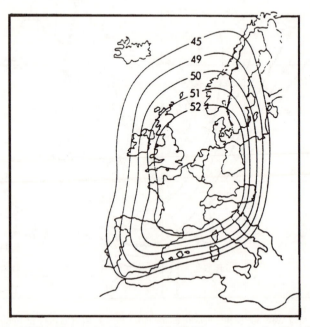

Figure 3.27 An ASTRA 1B footprint (Courtesy of Société Européene des Satellites (SES)).

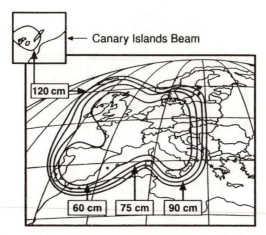

Figure 3.28 An ASTRA 1F footprint (Courtesy of Société Européene des Satellites (SES)).

Figure 3.28 shows a further method that can be used to describe the signal coverage area. In this case all the parameters are considered as constants so that the footprint can be defined in terms of the minimum reflector diameter needed to provide a signal such the received images will be of a quality better than CCIR Grade 4 for 99.9 percent of an average year for digital transmissions. An approximate relationship between PFD and antenna diameter is given in Table 3.3. In order to obtain a fair comparison between the values, ASTRA 1B provides an output of 60 W per transponder against the 82 W provided by ASTRA 1F (a little more than a 4 dBW increase).

Table 3.3

Diameter	PFD
60 cm	51 dBW
75 cm	49 dBW
90 cm	47 dBW
120 cm	45 dBW

3.11 ANTENNA POINTING AND MOUNTING

In addition to the adjustment for focus, the ground station antenna needs to be mounted with two degrees of freedom of movement. This allows the correct angles of *elevation* (El) to the tangent plane on which the antenna is assumed to be located, and *azimuth* (Az) or bearing. These two angles are shown as α and ϕ in Figure 3.29, and are dependent upon the latitude and longitude differences

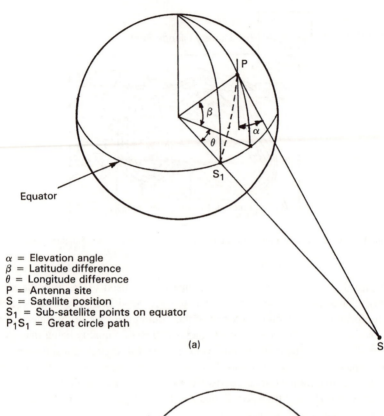

α = Elevation angle
β = Latitude difference
θ = Longitude difference
P = Antenna site
S = Satellite position
S_1 = Sub-satellite points on equator
P_1S_1 = Great circle path

(a)

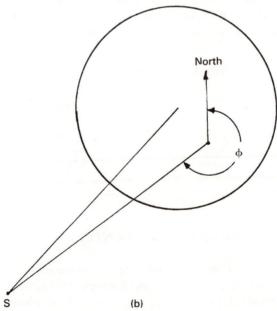

(b)

Figure 3.29 (a) and (b) The pointing angles (look angles).

between the satellite's orbital location and the earth station's position, shown as S and P respectively in Figure 3.29(a). Point S_1 is the sub-satellite point on the equator and the line P, S_1 is a 'Great circle' path. The angle of elevation α is the angle between the line-of-sight path to the satellite P, S and the tangent plane at P along the line P, S_1. The azimuth angle ϕ in Figure 3.29(b) is the angle between P, S and the true north (relative to the fixed stars).

The angle of elevation can be obtained (15) from:

$$\alpha = \text{arc.tan}((\cos \gamma - 0.151\ 269)/\sin \gamma \tag{3.22}$$

where:

$$\gamma = \text{arc.cos}(\cos \beta \times \cos \theta) \tag{3.23}$$

For latitudes above 81°, this value of γ is negative because the satellite is below the horizon.

The angle of azimuth is given by:

$$\phi = \text{arc.tan}(\tan \theta/\sin \beta) \tag{3.24}$$

(adding 180° if the satellite is west of the Greenwich meridian).

The path length d needed to calculate the free space attenuation can be found from:

$$d\,km = 35\,765\sqrt{(1 + 0.41999(1 - \cos \gamma))} \tag{3.25}$$

The mathematical proof of these equations can be found in reference (16). A pocket calculator approach is provided in Appendix A3.3.

As an alternative, the antenna can be provided with a *polar mount*, the principle of which is sketched in Figure 3.30(a). In this case, it is theoretically only necessary to calculate the elevation angle α and adjust this by positioning the king post at an angle of $(90° - \alpha)$ with the antenna pointing due south. Swinging the antenna around the king-post bearings then allows the antenna to sweep out an equatorial arc. In practice, an additional fine adjustment is provided (declination adjustment) to account for the system vagaries. The proof and method for the calculation of α in the polar mount case is given in Appendix A3.4/5, where it is shown that a good approximation for α can be obtained from:

$$\alpha = 90° - 1.15385 \text{ (station latitude°)} \tag{3.26}$$

Since the antenna beamwidths are small, and the dish provides a significant wind surface, the nature of the mount must take this into account. Wind vibrations of about 0.5° or so can cause a fluctuation in received SNR. Thus the relative merits of the two mounting methods tend to depend on antenna size. For a larger antenna, the Az/El method using an A frame approach is more stable. For antennas with a diameter of less than about 2 m, the polar mount is useful. This has a significant advantage if reception from more than one satellite is intended, as it only requires one servo drive system to track all equatorial orbits.

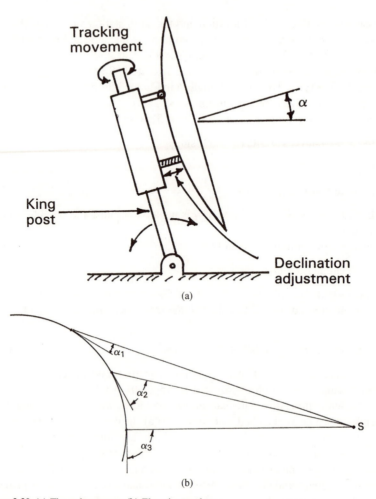

Figure 3.30 (a) The polar mount. **(b)** Elevation angles.

In those conditions where a greater pointing accuracy is needed, the *step-track* servo control technique may be used. To offset the problems of system backlash and propagation variation, a threshold level is set so that such a system is inoperative unless the signal level falls below some predetermined value.

3.12 SYSTEM DESIGN AIDS

With the introduction of computing power, the task of communication system design has become much simpler. It is now only necessary to input the important parameters and then run a program to obtain all the design data in an iterative manner. Calculations for link power budgets, aerial design and configuration, propagation path vagaries of noise and interference, may all be performed even before any hardware has been commissioned. This generally allows a new system to be economically configured from custom built and designed components. Two particular examples have been tested and proved to produce first-rate results, even showing up problems that might eventually arise during development.

Propagation Wizard (Courtesy of Dr Haus Waibel, Rohde & Schwarz, Munchen, Germany)

This suite of programs is available for both desk and laptop personal computers (PC) and is therefore readily portable. It runs under Windows 3.1 or higher and is complete with Menu bar, Command buttons and Short-cut keys, is well documented and easy to use. It provides a valuable tool for the development of high-frequency (HF) radio systems for both analogue and digital modulation systems.

The processing algorithm uses the prediction of the Maximum Usable Frequency (MUF) to calculate the field strength at a distant receiver site, taking into consideration the location, seasonal variations, atmospheric and man-made noise, using CCIR recommendations. (The Optimum Working Frequency – OWF – is typically 10 percent lower than the MUF.) The program calaculates the signal-to-noise ratios (SNR) in a given bandwidth, for a particular receiver noise factor and antenna gain. Data that is taken into consideration includes the year, month, sunspot number and ground characteristics. It then calculates and compares the necessary SNR margins for a given bandwidth and modulation scheme. The calculations include an iterative process to determine the availability of the proposed link in hours per day. In the light of these calculations, the user can then input further data to modify the proposed system.

Finally, the program outputs the data in a graphical manner so that the designer can have a clear overall view of the proposal's chances of meeting the design specification.

Because the time-of-day is based on UTC, there is provision for conversion to local solar time. The details of transmitter and receiver sites and their data can be stored as a database for future use.

Satmaster Pro (Courtesy of D.J. Stephenson IEng, FIEIE, Arrowe Technical Services, Merseyside, UK)

This relatively low-cost suite of programs provides a professional approach to the calculations needed for satellite TV system design. Again, this system runs under Windows 3.1 or higher, requires a relatively low level of PC capability and can operate on a laptop PC for portability. The program calculates all the look angles for geostationary satellite reception, including parameters for polar mount antenna systems. The program is comprehensive, easy to use and well documented. It calculates the link power budgets, bandwidth, SNR margins, antenna sizing and pointing, and antenna side-lobe patterns that might create interference from neighbouring satellites, together with tropospheric effects and solar outages.

Hardcopy printouts provide a permanent reference of all the calculated data, together with predicted footprint diagrams. In addition, there are a number of look-up tables that are of direct use to the designer. These include conversion between noise figure and noise temperature, world time zone, world TV standards listings and many more.

REFERENCES

(1) 'Cathode Ray'. *Wireless World*, Oct. (1975). Radio Waves – What makes them go. Pages 469–72.
(2) Slater, J.N. and Trinogga, L.A. (1985) *Satellite Broadcasting Systems: Planning and Design*. Chichester: Ellis Horwood Ltd.
(3) Rijssemus, M., Tratec Bv, Veenendaal, Holland. Private communication to author.
(4) Rudge, A.W. *et al.* (1982) *Handbook of Antenna Design*, Vol. 1. London: Peter Peregrinus Ltd.
(5) Christieson, M.L. (1982) 'Parabolic Antenna Design'. *Wireless World*, Oct.
(6) Butcher, M.E., British Telecom Research Laboratories, Martlesham Heath, UK. Private communication to author.
(7) Kraus, J.D. (1984) *Electromagnetics*, 3rd edn. New York: McGraw-Hill Book Co.
(8) Christieson, M.L., Feedback Instruments Ltd, Crowborough, UK. Private communication to author.
(9) Parker, E.A. and Langley, R.J., Antenna Group, University of Kent at Canterbury, UK. Private communication to author.
(10) Lafferty, A. and Stott, J.H., BBC UK Engineering Information Department Private communication to author.
(11) Mullard Ltd UK (1982) *Mullard Technical Publication M81-0147*.
(12) *Microwave Journal* (Euro-Global Edn), Vol. 40, No. 5. May 1997. Special reports and Technical features.
(13) Wright, W., Mawzones Ltd, Baldock, UK. Private communication to author.
(14) European Space Agency (1983). ECS Data Book *Esa BR-08*.
(15) Wise, F. (1979) 'Fundamentals of Satellite Broadcasting'. *IBA (UK) Technical Review No. 11*.
(16) Rainger, P. *et al.* (1985) *Satellite Broadcasting*. London: John Wiley & Sons.

Chapter 4

Microwave circuit elements

4.1 TRANSMISSION LINES

When electromagnetic energy flows along a transmission line, the voltage and current distribution along the line depend on the nature of the load at the far end. If the load impedance correctly matches the characteristic impedance of the line, then all the energy travelling on the line will be absorbed by the load. Under mismatch conditions, the load can only absorb an amount of power that is dictated by Ohm's law, any surplus energy being reflected back along the line towards the generator. The forward and reflected waves combine to form *standing waves* all along the line that are indicative of the degree of mismatch. Figure 4.1(a) shows the voltage and current distribution near to the load for two extreme cases of mismatch, where the load is either an open or a short circuit. In either case, there will be no power absorbed in the load, because either the current or the voltage is zero. Hence there will be a total reflection of energy.

The standing wave pattern depends on the wavelength/frequency of the transmitted signal and is repetitive every half-wavelength, as shown by Figure 4.1(a). The impedance (V/I ratio) seen by the signal thus varies all along the line, being purely resistive of very high or very low value at the λ/4 points and either capacitive or inductive reactive in between. An open circuit at the end behaves as a very low resistance just λ/4 away, while the short-circuit case behaves in the opposite way.

This impedance transformation property allows transmission lines to be supported on metallic λ/4 stubs, as shown by Figure 4.1(b), without affecting the signal power flow in any way. If the signal frequency is reduced, the stub becomes less than λ/4 long at the new frequency and so behaves as an inductive reactance to give rise to low-frequency losses. In a similar way, an increase of frequency causes the stub to develop capacitive reactance to limit the high frequencies.

If an infinity of λ/4 stubs are connected in parallel all along the lines, a rectangular box shape develops which will continue to carry energy. Such a structure is described as a *waveguide*.

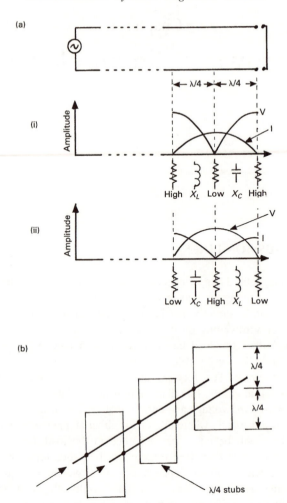

Figure 4.1 (a) Standing waves on (i) open circuit line, (ii) short circuit line. (b) Transmission line supported by λ/4 stubs.

4.2   WAVEGUIDES

At frequencies above about 1 GHz or so, the losses in coaxial cable transmission lines become unacceptable and waveguides are commonly used. Although the latter are physically larger, mechanically stiffer and more expensive than cables, these disadvantages are outweighed by the very low losses at microwave frequencies. The electromagnetic energy propagates through the guide by reflections off the side walls. The common mode for rectangular waveguide propagation is referred to as the *transverse electric* (TE) mode with the E field acting across the guide and with the H field creating magnetic loops along the guide in the direction of propagation. The dominant or first-order mode is usually described as the TE_{01} mode. For the transverse magnetic (TM) mode, which is less common, the field conditions are the exact opposite.

Figure 4.2(a) shows this behaviour for a range of frequencies, with the lower frequencies being reflected off the walls at the sharpest angles. The guide behaves as a high-pass filter (HPF), because at some low frequency a critical wavelength occurs (*cut-off wavelength* λ_c) where the energy is simply reflected back and forth across the guide so that propagation ceases. For the *dominant* or fundamental mode of propagation, the cut-off wavelength is proportional to the transverse dimension 'a' in Figure 4.2(b), λ_c being equal to 2a. The narrow dimension 'b' is not so critical and is usually equal to a/2. However, the 'b' dimension does affect the impedance, attenuation and power handling capability of the guide.

The velocity of propagation within waveguides is similar to that in coaxial cables. In the latter case, the wave travel is slowed by the charging and discharging of the cable self-capacitance by a current flowing against its self-inductance. In the waveguide, the energy has to travel via the rather longer reflective path.

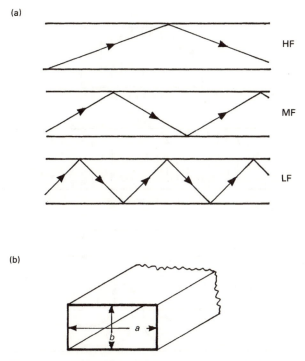

(a)

HF

MF

LF

(b)

Figure 4.2 **(a)** Waveguide reflective paths for a range of frequencies. **(b)** Dimensions of rectangular waveguide.

For sinusoidal signals, the dominant mode of propagation gives the longest value of critical wavelength and so determines the lower cut-off frequency. Figure 4.3 shows the distribution of the E and H field force lines. The E field lines terminate on the side walls and the H field lines create the current loops that generate the propagation through the guide. The lengths of the E field force lines in Figures 4.3(a) and (b) represent the sinusoidal variation of field intensity.

Higher-order modes can propagate as indicated by Figure 4.4. In fact, the larger the waveguide (in terms of wavelengths), the greater the number of modes that can propagate. However, the presence of very many modes all travelling at different velocities and following different reflective paths is clearly undesirable. It is therefore usual to choose the waveguide dimension large enough to support only the dominant mode. This restricts the use of given rectangular waveguide to a relatively narrow range of frequencies.

Similar modes of propagation occur in circular waveguides, but because of the narrow range between the cut-off frequency of the dominant mode and the next higher mode, the bandwidth is somewhat restricted. Also, because of the circular cross-section the guide cannot prevent the rotation of the plane of polarization. Although these are more flexible for installation purposes, they are commonly restricted to acting as couplings to rotating waveguide applications. Many of the

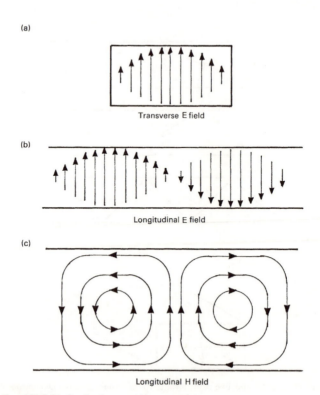

(a)

Transverse E field

(b)

Longitudinal E field

(c)

Longitudinal H field

Figure 4.3 E and H fields for dominant mode propagation.

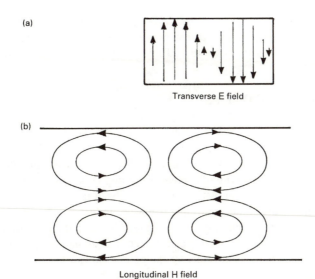

(a)

Transverse E field

(b)

Longitudinal H field

Figure 4.4 Second-order mode of propagation.

circular waveguide problems can be resolved by using elliptical guides. Higher-order modes may propagate but these can create intermodulation and distortion which needs to be resolved by using mode filters at the terminations. Unlike rectangular waveguides, over-moded elliptical guides can be fabricated, bent, and laid in one length. Typical attenuation per 100 m length for elliptical guides varies for a range of frequencies from about 14 dB at 14 GHz, to 28 dB at 28 GHz. These figures might be reduced to 7 and 14 dB respectively when using mode filters.

Table 4.1 shows the approximate internal dimensions for the popular rectangular waveguides in both inches and millimetres, together with the

Table 4.1

Type number	Internal dimensions (a, b, in (mm))	Frequency range (Dominant mode GHz)
WG6	6.5, 3.25 (16.5, 8.25)	1.12–1.7
WG8	4.3, 2.15 (10.9, 5.46)	1.7–2.6
WG10	2.84, 1.34 (7.2, 3.4)	2.6–3.95
WG12	1.87, 0.87 (4.75, 2.22)	3.95–5.85
WG14	1.37, 0.62 (3.49, 1.58)	5.85–8.2
WG16	0.9, 0.4 (2.29, 1.02)	8.2–12.4
WG18	0.62, 0.31 (1.58, 0.79)	12.4–18
WG20	0.42, 0.17 (1.07, 0.43)	18–26.5
WG22	0.28, 0.14 (0.71, 0.36)	26.5–40

operating frequency ranges. The *breakdown power rating* for these waveguides is approximately proportional to the cross-sectional area, ranging from about 50 mW for WG6 linearly down to 100 μW for WG22.

4.3   RESONANT CAVITIES

At lower frequencies, a parallel combination of inductance (L) and capacitance (C) provides a resonant circuit across which maximum voltage will be developed at some frequency. Progressive reduction of both L and C will cause the resonant frequency to increase. Figure 4.5 shows a limiting condition where C has been reduced to a pair of parallel plates, while L has been reduced by connecting the plates together with parallel straps that behave as inductors. The ultimate limit is reached where the two plates are connected together with the four sides of a box. This structure is a *resonant cavity*, and if energized at an appropriate frequency will develop maximum voltage across the points shown.

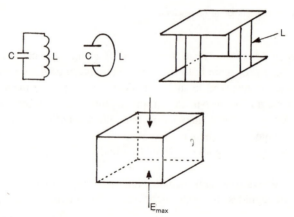

Figure 4.5 Development of resonant cavity.

Figure 4.6(a) shows that this structure has a resonant wavelength dictated by the length of its diagonal, the electromagnetic field reflecting off the sides as indicated. Figure 4.6(b) shows how the fields oscillate at quarter-period intervals when the cavity is energized, the total energy being transferred between the electric and magnetic fields in an oscillatory manner.

The Q factor, which is very high, is typically about 15 000 (unloaded) and is given by:

$$Q = 2\pi \text{ (Total energy stored in cavity/Energy lost in 1 cycle}$$
$$\text{due to resistivity of walls)} \qquad (4.1)$$

from which it can easily be deduced that Q is proportional to the ratio of cavity volume to interior surface area.

(a)

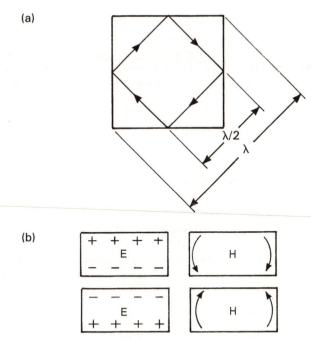

(b)

Figure 4.6 Oscillators in resonant cavities: (a) resonant wavelength; (b) oscillating E and H fields.

4.4 COUPLING TO CAVITIES AND WAVEGUIDES

Of the various ways in which signals may be coupled into cavities and waveguides, those shown in Figure 4.7 are common. The probe in Figure 4.7(a) acts as a dipole aerial generating or responding to the E field. The current loop either generates or responds to the H field. Figure 4.7(b) shows how a resonant cavity can be coupled to a waveguide via a hole or *iris*, coupling being achieved

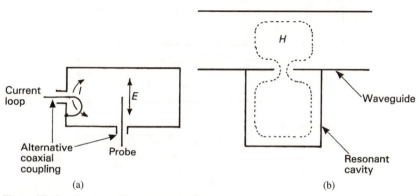

Figure 4.7 Coupling to cavities and waveguides.

through the H field. Cavities of different resonant wavelengths may be coupled to a waveguide in this way, to form a filter circuit. Cavities can be retuned by introducing a metallic screw or dielectric rod into the cavity, from the centre of either of the large area sides. In each case, either the inductance or the capacitance of the cavity is increased, to lower the resonant frequency.

4.5   CIRCULATORS AND ISOLATORS

Two ferrite devices that are used extensively in microwave circuits are circulators and isolators. The most commonly used circulator, shown schematically in Figure 4.8(a), has three ports each spaced by 120°. When each port is correctly terminated, a signal input at one port appears as an output at the next, the third port being isolated from the signal. The behaviour at each port changes in a cyclic manner as indicated in Table 4.2.

Such a device is very suitable for separating incident and reflected signals. The insertion loss in the transmissive direction is typically less than 0.5 dB,

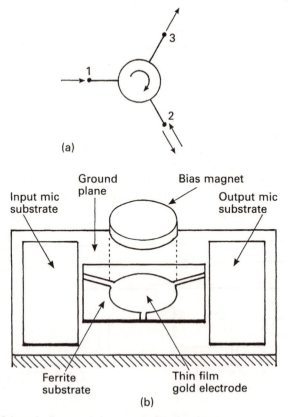

(a)

(b)

Figure 4.8 (a) Schematic diagram of circulator. (b) Circulator construction.

Table 4.2

	Ports	
Input	*Output*	*Isolated*
1	2	3
2	3	1
3	1	2

while the attenuation at the isolated port is better than 20 dB. As an example, port 1 might be driven from a transmitter, while port 2 provides the antenna feed. In the receive mode, port 2 becomes the input and the circulator passes this signal to port 3, providing an isolation between transmitter and receiver of better than 20 dB. For this high-power application, the circulator would be positioned within the waveguide feed to the antenna. The basic construction of a low-power device is shown in Figure 4.8(b). A small, thin slab of ferrite acts as a substrate for a thin film of deposited gold electrode. A permanently magnetized bias magnet sits on top of the electrode structure, to generate Faraday rotation within. Inputs and outputs are provided by *microwave integrated circuits* (MIC).

The behaviour of the device depends upon the combined effects of the magnetic fields due to the input signal power and that provided by the bias magnet.

Figure 4.9(a) shows the lines of the electric and magnetic fields within the substrate when the bias magnet is not in place. Ports 2 and 3 are at the same potential and are effectively isolated from port 1. By applying a correctly chosen

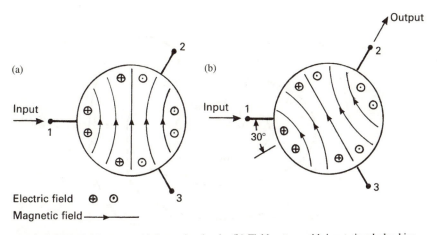

Figure 4.9 (a) Field pattern with input signal only. (b) Field pattern with input signal plus bias.

bias level from the permanent magnet, the field components can be rotated by 30°. Port 3 is now at a null in the electric field, while ports 1 and 2 are at equal but opposite potentials. Conduction can occur between ports 1 and 2 but port 3 will be isolated from the signal. By reversing the bias field, the signal circulation would be reversed.

An isolator is a two-port device that functions in a similar way, with similar levels of insertion loss and attenuation. In fact, a circulator can behave as an isolator if the third port is terminated in a resistance equal to its characteristic impedance. Used in this way, the reflected energy is absorbed in the resistive load. Such a device is ideal to use in the coupling path between an RF oscillator and its load, to prevent frequency pulling.

4.6   DIELECTRIC RESONATORS

These ceramic devices, made as small discs of sintered *barium titanate*, are used at microwave frequencies in the same way as quartz crystals are used at lower frequencies to control the frequency of an oscillator directly and without frequency multiplication. They are much smaller than resonant cavities and have a similar degree of stability. Dielectric resonators are placed in the oscillator feedback path, with coupling being achieved via the magnetic field as shown by Figure 4.10. Dielectric resonator oscillators (DRO) suffer less frequency pulling than an unstabilized oscillator, a characteristic that can be further improved by the use of an isolator. DROs can be tuned over a range of about 1 percent (100 MHz in 10 GHz) by perturbing the resonator's magnetic field by varying an air gap between the disc and the circuit's metallic enclosure.

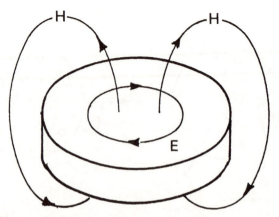

Figure 4.10 Field patterns in dielectric resonators.

4.7   MICROWAVE CIRCUIT SUBSTRATES AND TRANSMISSION LINES

The printed circuit board concept used for lower frequencies is retained for microwave applications. But the behaviour is now more closely related to transmission lines. Planar construction is used because it is compatible with solid state and surface mounted components and provides low loss and stable circuits, which are very reproducible and hence cost-effective.

The dielectric substrates used include such proprietary materials as Rexolite, Cuflon and RT Duroid, PTFE, Alumina and Sapphire. The relative permittivities (ε_r) range from around 2.2 to 11.5. The factors that affect the choice of a particular substrate include operating frequency, thermal conductivity, mechanical stiffness, cost, fabrication tolerances and reproducibility, with surface finish being important for conductor adhesion. For applications above about 5 GHz, alumina is very popular.

The microwave energy propagates in the dielectric substrate and the surrounding air, rather than through the conductors, which simply behave as waveguides. The combined structure then has an *effective relative permittivity* (ε_{reff}) somewhere between that for air and the substrate ($1 < \varepsilon_{reff} < \varepsilon_r$). It is shown in the literature (1) that:

$$\varepsilon_{reff} = (\lambda_o/\lambda_g)^2 \tag{4.2}$$

where λ_0 = wavelength in free space, and λ_g = wavelength in guiding structure.

Low dielectric constant substrates have the advantage of producing longer circuit elements, which eases the reproduction of dimensional tolerances.

With rising frequency, the propagation tends to concentrate more in the substrate and less in the air, so that λ_g tends to increase with frequency.

Transmission line structures

Microstrip
As with most of the structures used at microwave frequencies, the substrate is used to support the metallic conductor patterns. These are commonly gold on a thin film of chromium for better adhesion, and copper. Figure 4.11(a) shows the typical construction of microstrip together with the important dimensions. Figure 4.11(b) indicates how the electric field is set up between the conductor pattern and the ground plane.

The design details for microstrip circuits are quite complex and are best managed using computer aided design (CAD). Design tables are provided in reference (2) and a suitable design program (STRIP) is given in reference (3). In essence, the characteristic impedance of each conductor strip is dependent upon the frequency, the width (w) of the strip, and the height (h) and relative permittivity ε_r of the substrate. Each conductor element must be capable of

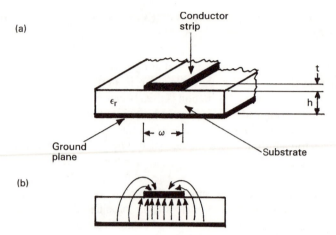

Figure 4.11 Microstrip waveguide construction and **(a)** important dimensions; **(b)** E field.

supporting any dc supply current and dissipating the resulting heat. With suitable components and substrate, microstrip can operate satisfactorily up to about 55 (GHz).

Inverted microstrip
In this version, depicted in Figure 4.12, the substrate simply supports the guiding conductors in air, so that the effective relative permittivity for this structure is practically that of air ($\varepsilon_{reff} = 1$). Thus λ_g is relatively longer than for microstrip, which allows for operation at even higher frequencies.

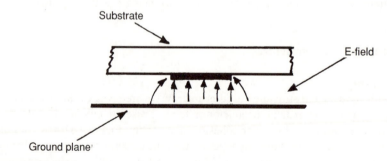

Figure 4.12 Inverted microstrip.

Fin-line or E-plane
This less common structure is illustrated in Figure 4.13. It consists of a thin dielectric substrate, typically of glass-fibre-reinforced PTFE, metallized with copper and bridging the broad walls of a section of rectangular waveguide of suitable dimensions. The conductor patterns which form the various circuit

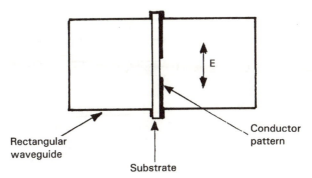

Figure 4.13 Fin-line or E-plane structure.

elements are defined on one or both sides of the substrate. The losses with fin-line are significantly less than with microstrip and this allows operations up to and even beyond 100 GHz (4).

4.8 SOME MICROWAVE CIRCUIT ELEMENTS (5, 6)

Because of the very short wavelengths involved and the transmission-line-like behaviour of microstrip circuits, many different circuit elements can be fabricated directly on to the substrate. Lumped inductors and capacitors can be provided from open circuit conductor strips. At 10 GHz, λ_0, the free space wavelength, is 30 mm. If a microstrip circuit has an effective relative permittivity of 4, then λ_g the wavelength on the structure, is 15 mm. Thus $\lambda_g/4$ is only 3.75 mm.

Impedance transformers

A capacitive element can be produced by using an open circuit strip of conductor of length 1, such that $0 < 1 < \lambda_g/4$, while, an inductive element is produced if $\lambda_g/4 < 1 < \lambda_g/2$. When $1 = \lambda_g/4$, the strip ends both appear resistive, one end of very low value and the other end very high. This impedance transformation allows a quarter-wavelength strip to be used as a matching device. In Figure 4.14(a), a quarter-wavelength strip of impedance Z_2 is used to provide this match where:

$$Z_2 = \sqrt{(Z_1 Z_3)} \tag{4.3}$$

Z_2 is thus the geometric mean between Z_1 and Z_3. Alternatively, a tapered section of line as shown in Figure 4.14(b) may be used to affect the impedance match.

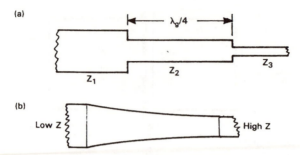

Figure 4.14 Matching transformer elements.

Filters

The high-impedance strip of length $L < \lambda_g/4$, connected between two low-impedance sections as shown in Figure 4.15(a), behaves predominantly as an inductor. The two low-impedance sections have significant shunt capacitance, so that the combination acts as a low-pass filter (LPF). In Figure 4.15(b), again $L < \lambda_g/4$, but this low-impedance section is now connected between two high impedances which act as shunt inductors. The overall effect is thus that of a high-pass filter (HPF).

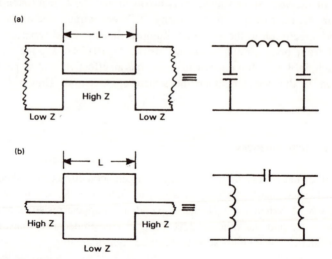

Figure 4.15 Filters: **(a)** low pass; **(b)** high pass.

Bandpass filters

An open circuit stub whose length is a half-wavelength is a high impedance at each end. (This is also true for integer multiples of $\lambda/2$.) Thus the half-wavelength stub of Figure 4.16(a) behaves as a high impedance to signals that

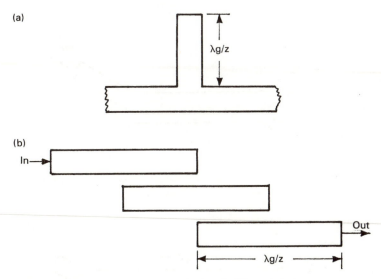

Figure 4.16 Bandpass filters: **(a)** single open circuit stub; **(b)** coupled resonators.

make it so. At frequencies on either side the stub impedance falls, so that less signal voltage will be developed. Figure 4.16(b) shows a series of half-wavelength strips (also known as resonators), edge- or parallel-coupled via the electromagnetic field. By slightly varying the length of each resonator, the bandwidth of the filter can be extended.

Proximity couplers

A transformer-type coupling between two circuits can be achieved in the manner shown in Figure 4.17(a). However, such a construction provides only loose coupling. Where a 3 dB coupling between circuits is needed, the 90° hybrid or *Lange* coupler of Figure 4.17(b) can be used. This consists of at least four inter-digitated fingers with *air bridge* connections to provide tighter coupling. Due to the length of the coupling structure, power coupled to the signal port is equally divided and transmitted to the coupled and direct ports, but with a phase difference of 90°.

90° hybrid branch line couplers

When input power is supplied to port 1 of the coupler shown in Figure 4.18(a), the signal can arrive at port 4 by two paths. One is $\lambda_g/4$ long and the other $3\lambda_g/4$ long. The signals at port 4 are thus anti-phase and self-cancelling, so that port 4 is isolated. The output power divides equally between ports 2 and 3, and since

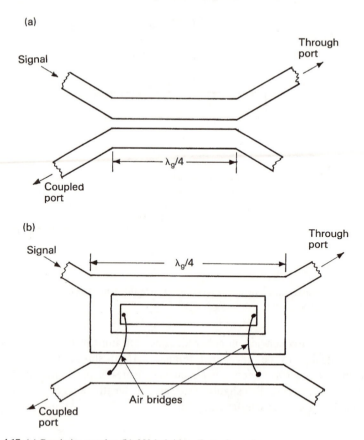

Figure 4.17 (a) Proximity coupler. (b) 90° hybrid or 'Lange' coupler.

these are separated by a strip $\lambda_g/4$ long there is 90° of phase difference between the signals. The alternative construction shown in Figure 4.18(b) behaves in the same way because the four ports are spaced by $\lambda_g/4$.

Hybrid ring or 'rat-race'

This device consists of an annular ring $1.5\lambda_g$ long, with four ports disposed as indicated by Figure 4.19. Signal power input to port 1 can circulate either clockwise or anticlockwise to reach ports 2, 3 and 4. Both paths to port 4 are $3\lambda_g/4$ long so that port 4 can provide an output. The paths to port 2 are either $\lambda_g/4$ or $5\lambda_g/4$ long, also providing in-phase signals so that port 2 is also an output. At port 3 the path lengths differ by $\lambda_g/2$ to produce anti-phase signals, so that port 3 is isolated. In a similar way, an input at port 3 will not couple with port 1.

(a)

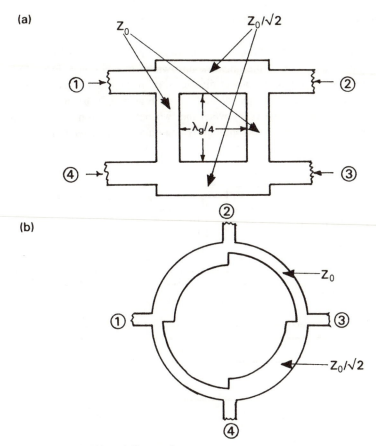

(b)

Figure 4.18 90° hybrid branch line coupler.

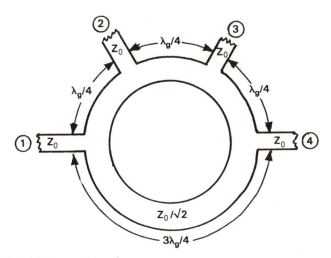

Figure 4.19 Hybrid ring or 'rat-race'.

Wilkinson power divider/combiner

The input and output limbs of this power divider/combiner are matched to Z_0, the characteristic impedance of the network into which it is coupled. From Figure 4.20(a), it can be seen that the power divides in proportion to the ratio of Z_1/Z_2, the impedances of the branches 'a' and 'b' in Figure 4.20(b). R is simply a lumped isolating resistor wired between the two output sections. The structure can be operated in reverse as a combiner by coupling identical sections as shown in Figure 4.20(c). In this case, the network becomes valuable as an adder for the

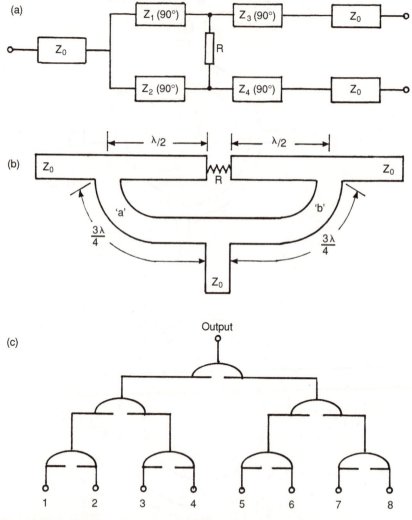

Figure 4.20 The Wilkinson power divider/combiner. (**a**) Circuit configuration. (**b**) One implementation of structure. (**c**) Divider used as eight-way signal combiner.

outputs of the several sections of a complex patch antenna structure. The device operates effectively beyond 30 GHz and has a frequency and phase response that extends to a bandwidth of about 5 percent of centre frequency. A similar configuration can be assembled for operation in UHF bands using lumped inductive and capacitive components.

The Rotamode directional coupler

This device combines the properties of a directional coupler with those of a cavity resonator. Typical applications include the combining of two signals for transmission over a common transmission line and as a bandpass filter. The coupler consists of a number of cylindrical cavity resonators coupled via iris apertures in the common wall as shown in Figure 4.21. When a signal is applied to the input stripline coupler, the potential difference between it and the cavity wall excites the cavity to induce electric and magnetic fields that interact with the output stripline coupler to provide the output signal. When the feeds to the two couplers are impedance matched and resistively terminated, the two input signals can be linearly combined, with the maximum isolation between the two driver circuits. Different-sized cavities are used to obtain bandpass filter characteristics.

Surface-mounted components

Although not specifically microwave components, the characteristics of these devices are very compatible with the planar technology of microstrip construction. A full range of these small, leadless devices is available for direct soldering

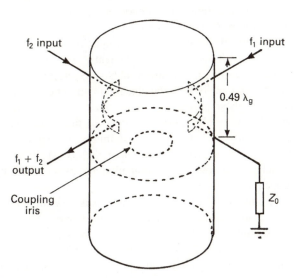

Figure 4.21 The Rotarnode directional coupler.

to the metallic conductor pads on the circuit boards, which do not need to be drilled for component insertion. These devices are smaller than their conventional counterparts and this leads to smaller sub-systems. Because of the relatively large area of the solder pads, highly reliable joints are produced with good heat-dissipating properties. The components are more efficient and their self-resistance, capacitance and inductance are much lower, so that these devices have better RF characteristics. The technique also lends itself to automated assembly, which in turn further improves the cost-effectiveness. Component marking is made difficult because of the very small size. Therefore from the servicing point of view, these should be kept in their packaging until needed.

4.9   ACTIVE DEVICES (7)

Solid state amplifiers

Suitably selected silicon bipolar and field effect transistors (FETs) are available for microwave applications. When equipped with beam lead terminations, they are compatible with microstrip structures. The combination of discrete components and microstrip circuits is sometimes referred to as *microwave integrated circuits* (MIC).

Bipolar devices are seldom used above about 2–3 GHz, while metal oxide semiconductor FETs (MOSFETs) are used from about 1 GHz up to around 30 GHz. The ability of MOSFETs to provide voltage and current gain, with relatively lower noise figures and higher efficiency, is a significant advantage.

The most important of the devices that are used as microwave amplifiers up to about 70 GHz are those constructed from a combination of elements from Groups III and V of the Periodic Table. The important elements are aluminium (Al), phosphorus (P), gallium (Ga) and arsenic (As).

The III–V system of semiconductor production allows the growth of crystalline compounds of two or more elements, typically gallium arsenide (GaAs) and gallium aluminium arsenide (GaAlAs). By accurately controlling the composition of the compound, both the electrical and optical characteristics can be manipulated. In these cases, the term 'band structure engineering' is particularly apt. The technology has developed to the point where integrated circuits in the normally accepted sense and microwave structures have been integrated into *monolithic microwave integrated circuits* (MMIC). These devices are therefore smaller, with low power dissipation and better reliability than their discrete component equivalents.

The crystalline structure of the III–V compounds is very similar to the familiar structure of silicon and germanium. Gallium arsenide has a higher energy band gap than either silicon or germanium, so that the bulk substrate is capable of being a better insulator. In addition, electron mobility is higher. Together, these features permit a higher frequency and speed of operation, with lower noise levels and improved linearity.

Developments in semiconductor material technology allow the production of very thin *heterojunctions* of GaAlAs and GaAs. The epitaxially grown layer is only a few atoms thick, so that the interface is almost a two-dimensional structure. The electrons which collect in this interface due to the electric field behave differently, because they virtually only have two degrees of freedom of movement. This results in an electron mobility that is a factor of three better than that for silicon, thus giving rise to devices known as *high electron mobility transistors* (HEMT). Electron mobility is related to the applied electric field by:

$$v = \mu\varepsilon \tag{4.4}$$

where v = average drift velocity cm/sec, μ = electron mobility cm^2/V.sec and ε = applied electric field V/cm. HEMT devices can operate at frequencies above 25 GHz, and several types are available with gain and noise factor parameters at 12 GHz that are better than 12 dB and 0.8 dB respectively.

Thermionic amplifiers

Although thermionic valves have virtually disappeared from communications systems, there is still one device in use for high-power amplification (PA) at transmitter output stages. This is the travelling wave tube amplifier (TWT). The general construction of this device is shown in Figure 4.22. A heater and cathode assembly generates an electron beam which is focused and accelerated towards a collector electrode by suitable potentials, the electron beam passing through a slow wave helix structure. The radio frequency input signal is applied to the cathode end of the helix and interaction between the beam and the RF wave creates an amplified signal at the output end. The electron beam concentration is maintained by the use of an external magnet structure in the manner shown in the diagram. To improve power efficiency, the device can be

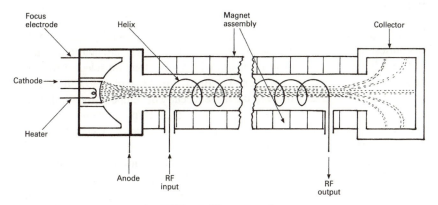

Figure 4.22 Travelling wave tube (TWT) amplifier construction.

equipped with a multi-stage depressed collector and the focus electrode can be used to blank the beam for pulsed operation. High-power amplification over the frequency range of about 2–40 GHz with a gain as high as 70 dB is possible. The power output can be as high as 500 W continuous rating, rising to 1 kW for pulsed operation.

Since the PA stage is often driven by multiple carrier frequencies simultaneously, its inherent non-linearity can lead to intermodulation distortion (IMD), particularly if the stage is fully driven. IMD can be avoided either by backing-off the output power level or including a suitable linearizing circuit. The latter method, which can lead to an improvement in PA efficiency and output power, uses either a feed-forward network or a pre-amplifier stage that generates a complementary and thus cancelling pre-distortion.

Power amplifier choices

The power supply for the TWT amplifier is more complex than that required for a solid state PA, but the thermionic device is much more robust under high voltage discharge conditions. Often, when employing portable communications equipment, it is necessary to consider the possibility of fault conditions that could lead to complete loss of service. In this case, it is common to provide a degree of redundancy in the system. With the PA stage, it is possible to combine the outputs of a number of identical stages in parallel in the following manner. If a power output of, say, 300 W is necessary, this can be provided from a pair of 150 W TWTs in parallel. If one device fails, then the power output drops by 3 dB and the service can continue but at reduced power. For a similar situation using solid state PA stages, the system might employ twenty 15 Watt output modules in parallel to provide the same level of service. In this case, if one stage fails, the loss of about 0.25 dB in output power would almost pass unnoticed.

Diode devices

Diode applications in microwave communications generally fall into two categories: mixers and single-port oscillators. Mixer stages are notoriously noisy and so it is most important to use non-linear devices that are selected for a low noise factor. For some time, the Schottky Barrier diode, with its low threshold of 0.3 V, has been popular. However, the more recently developed Mott diode is less noisy and is designed as a surface mounting chip. Without beam lead connections, these have less self-capacitance and inductance, which allows them to operate efficiently at least up to 50 GHz.

Common devices in the single-port oscillator group are the Gunn device and the IMPATT (Impact Avalanche and Transit Time) diode. Both devices have a significant negative resistance section in their V/I characteristics. When this negative resistance is placed in parallel with a small positive resistance, say that

Table 4.3

	Power output	Maximum frequency	Operating voltage
IMPATT diode	1 W	20 GHz	120 V
Gunn device	300 mW	45 GHz	12 V

of a resonant circuit or cavity, oscillations can occur. The origin of the negative resistance is the transfer of electrons from the main conductor energy band into a satellite band, depending on the magnitude of an applied electric field. This results in a pulse of current flowing through the device from cathode to anode.

Table 4.3 shows the typical peak range of values for both devices.

Hot carrier diodes

Although these devices are not specifically microwave types, many find applications in microwave systems. A *hot carrier* is an electron that has an energy level higher than that of the crystal structure, i.e. several kT above the Fermi level. A rectifying junction can be formed between a metal and a semiconductor (Schottky diode). If forward biased, majority carriers (electrons in N-type semiconductors) with an energy level greater than the Schottky barrier – the hot carriers – can cross the barrier and produce a current flow. The number of hot carriers increases with the forward bias so that the forward current rises rapidly. This feature considerably increases the forward sensitivity of the diode compared to that of the conventional PN junctions. The reverse biased current is negligibly small and the diode can switch state very rapidly. These properties make the device valuable for handling very low-amplitude, very high-frequency signals.

Gunn effect mechanism

When the applied voltage across the device creates an electric field in excess of about 35 V/cm, a high-level electric field domain is produced in the cathode region, which rapidly drifts to the anode. As the domain passes out at the anode the electric field falls rapidly, only to start to rise again almost immediately. A new domain forms when the field rises above the critical value, and the cycle repeats.

The equivalent circuit of the Gunn device is a negative resistance of about −5 ohms in series with a capacitance of about 0.2 pF. To make the circuit oscillate, the load connected to the device should have:

(1)   A series reactance that tunes the device to resonance.
(2)   A series load resistance less than the modulus of the negative resistance.
(3)   At frequencies other than resonance, the load resistance should be greater than the modulus of the negative resistance.

Provided that points (2) and (3) can be met, a variable reactance can be used to tune the circuit over an octave frequency range.

REFERENCES

(1)   Edwards, T.C. (1981) *Foundations of Microstrip Circuit Design*. London: John Wiley and Son.
(2)   (1971) *Microwave Engineers' Handbook*, Vol. 1. Artech House.
(3)   Slater, J.N. and Trinogga, L.A. (1985) *Satellite Broadcasting Systems: Planning and Design*. Chichester: Ellis Horwood.
(4)   (1982) *E-Plane Millimetre-wave Components and Sub-assemblies. M82-0097*. Mullard UK Ltd.
(5)   Connor, F.R. (1972) *Introductory Topics in Electronics & Telecommunications – Wave Transmission*, Vol. 3. London: Edward Arnold.
(6)   Mazda, F. (1993) *Telecommunications Engineers' Reference Book*. Oxford: Butterworth-Heinemann.
(7)   Lewis, G.E. (1997) *Communications Technology Handbook*, 2nd edn. Oxford: Butterworth-Heinemann.

Chapter 5

Digital signal processing

5.1 ANALOGUE AND DIGITAL SIGNALLING COMPARED

Wideband communications applications such as television traditionally use analogue signal processing, primarily for reasons of bandwidth conservation and the fact that such systems are well developed and understood. However, each application tends to become unique in certain ways. When the systems become concentrated into integrated circuits, these devices are dedicated to a particular application; relatively few are produced and so their cost is higher than would be the case for mass-produced devices. When the analogue signals are converted into digital form for processing and then back again for such purposes as display, the only dedicated chips are those associated with the interface between the two types of signal. The digital signal processing (DSP) area of the system then uses standard digital ICs that are very much more cost-effective.

The increased transmission bandwidth for digital signals is available on all communications links including satellite, cable and terrestrial networks where this overhead is in any case offset by the considerable advantages gained by changing to the digital concept. The systems become more flexible, systems integration can be achieved and computer control gives rise to the concept of *integrated services digital network* (ISDN), where many services including voice, video or data can be accommodated with equal performance.

The principal benefits of digital signal processing can be summarized as follows:

(1) More appropriate for linking devices that operate in the digital mode.
(2) Provides transmission speeds that are significantly higher than those commonly achieved with analogue processing.
(3) Provides for improved transmission quality in noisy environments. The noise effects can be reduced using signal regenerators and by using error detection/correction techniques.
(4) More compatible with the digital switching techniques used for distribution, and is a natural technique to apply on systems that are linked by optical fibres.
(5) Encryption/decryption can easily be adopted for security of information.
(6) Signal compression techniques (bit rate reduction) can be used to minimize the transmission bandwidth requirements.

(7)   For many applications, time or code division multiple access (TDMA or CDMA) can be used over satellite or cable links and this is more efficient in the use of the service than frequency division multiple access (FDMA).

(8)   The use of on-board microprocessor-controlled satellite switching becomes feasible and the signal can be regenerated before retransmission to improve the received signal quality. If this improvement is not needed, then regeneration allows smaller and simpler antennas to be used (1) (2).

5.2   SAMPLING AND QUANTIZATION

There are several ways of converting an analogue signal into digital form and all are effectively based on a sampling technique. It is shown by the Nyquist theorem that provided a complex analogue signal is sampled at a rate at least twice that of its highest frequency component, the original signal can be reconstructed from these samples without error. This arises because the two samples tend to produce a square wave at the original frequency. After low-pass filtering, the original signal frequency has been regenerated.

Figure 5.1(a) depicts the general principle for generating what is commonly known as pulse code modulation (PCM). The analogue signal is sampled at very precise intervals of time, to measure its amplitudes. Since only discrete levels are allowed in a digital signal, each of the amplitudes is quantized or allocated a value which is the integer part of the sampled value (i.e. the integer value of the level that the amplitude is just greater than). These values are then converted into a corresponding binary sequence for digital processing. For the waveform shown in Figure 5.1(a), the quantized and binary codes series would be:

4,	5,	5,	5,	5,	4,	3,	2,	2,	3,	4	... etc.
100,	101,	101,	101,	101,	100,	011,	010,	010,	011,	100	... etc.

It should be noted here that each of the eight levels shown can be coded using just three bits ($2^3 = 8$).

Any analogue signal that is reconstructed from such a series will obviously be an approximation of the original, the difference or error being referred to as *quantization noise*. It is shown in Appendix A4.1 that the signal-to-quantization-noise ratio (SQNR) for a dc signal such as video luminance is given by:

$$SQNR = (10.8 + 20 \log M) \text{ dB} \tag{5.1}$$

or: $$= (10.8 + 6n) \text{ dB} \tag{5.2}$$

where M = number of sampling levels, and n = number of bits per code sample. For the example shown in Figure 5.1(a):

$$SQNR = (10.8 + 20 \log 8) \text{ dB} = 29 \text{ dB}$$

(a)

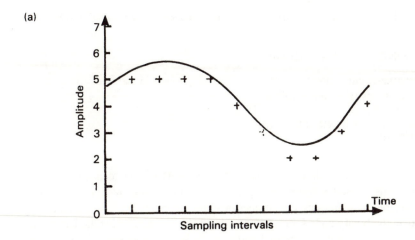

(b)

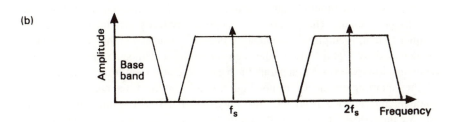

(c)

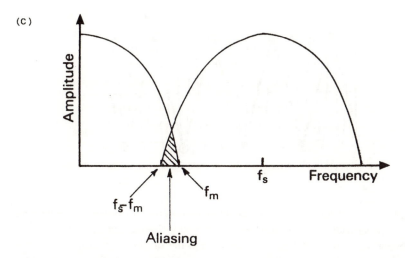

Figure 5.1 (a) Sampling an analogue signal. **(b)** Spectrum of sampled signal. **(c)** Introduction of aliasing.

It is further shown in Appendix A4.1 that the annoyance factor of the SQNR for an ac coupled signal is given by:

$$SQNR = (1.76 + 6.02n) \text{ dB} \tag{5.3}$$

Alternatively, equations 5.2 and 5.3 can be expressed in terms of the *effective number of bits* (ENOB) as follows:

$$ENOB = \frac{(SQNR - 1.76) \text{ dB}}{6.02} \tag{5.4}$$

from which it can be shown that an SQNR of 98 dB is equivalent to 16 bits.

Equations 5.1 and 5.2 show that quantization noise can be reduced to any low level desired by increasing the number of sampling levels and hence the number of bits in the binary code series. The overhead paid for this is that the bandwidth of the sampled signal is increased and this can be calculated as follows:

$$2nf_m \text{ Hz} \tag{5.5}$$

where f_m is the maximum frequency component in the signal, and n is the number of bits per sample. The process of sampling produces a frequency spectrum similar to that of amplitude modulation but with an infinite range of harmonics, as depicted by Figure 5.1(b). The reconstruction or demodulation circuit must contain a low-pass filter to separate the baseband component from the harmonics. If the sampling frequency is not high enough, or the filter cut-off not sharp enough, interference from the first lower sideband will result. Figure 5.1(c) shows the effect of using a sampling frequency less than $2f_m$, where it is impossible to distinguish between some of the components of the baseband and the lower sideband. Such interference is known as *aliasing*.

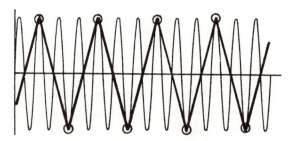

Figure 5.2 Sampling at too low a frequency introduces the new components of aliasing.

Figure 5.2 shows how these components that were not originally present can be created by sampling at too low a frequency. If aliasing occurs and it is impossible to increase the sampling rate, then the original signal must be low-pass filtered to remove the higher-order components that will create aliasing. Such devices are referred to as Nyquist filters. This filter must have a fairly sharp

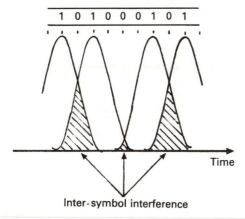

Figure 5.3 Inter-symbol interference.

cut-off frequency to avoid pulse deformation in the manner shown in Figure 5.3 where the spreading causes inter-symbol interference (ISI) which leads to further data corruption.

5.3 NON-LINEAR QUANTIZATION

Reference to Figure 5.1(a) shows that linear quantization produces proportionately more noise with smaller amplitude signals. In addition, large amplitude signals are better able to mask the effects of noise. This imbalance can be improved by using a non-linear form of quantization that behaves in the same way as companding. Such a characteristic, which is relatively easy to implement, is shown in Figure 5.4 and in the European Standard used, digital telephony is referred to as an A-law compander, 'A' being a constant chosen to suit the amplitude distribution on the signal to be processed and typically equal to 87.6.

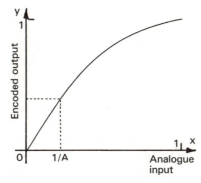

Figure 5.4 A-law companding.

The curve has a linear region to handle low-level signals and a logarithmic region for the larger amplitudes. Using normalized values, the law for this curve is specified by:

$$y = Ax/(1 + \ln A) \quad \text{for } 0 \le x \le 1/A \tag{5.6}$$

and

$$y = (1 + \ln Ax)/(1 + \ln A) \text{ for } 1/A \le x \le 1 \tag{5.7}$$

An alternative compander that finds favour in the North American standard is the μ-law device. This is defined by:

$$y = (\ln(1 + \mu x))/(\ln(1 + \mu)) \quad (0 < x < 1) \tag{5.8}$$

where μ is typically equal to 255.

It is neither truly linear nor logarithmic, but is a good approximation at the extremes. Whichever device is used at the transmitter, the complementary device must be used at the receiver to ensure an overall linear response.

In modern systems the compander stage is often incorporated within the same integrated circuit (IC) as the analogue to digital (A/D) and digital to analogue (D/A) converters. These devices are then often referred to as application-specific ICs (ASICs). Since the companding is now carried out in the digital domain, the two laws become modified as:

A-law: $y = 0.18(1 + \ln(A|x|)) \, \text{sgn}(x)$,   for $1/A < |x| < 1$

and

$$y = 0.18 \, (A|x|) \, \text{sgn}(x), \qquad \text{for } 0 < |x| < 1/A \tag{5.9}$$

μ-law: $y = 0.18 \ln(1 + \mu|x|) \, \text{sgn}(x)$ \hfill (5.10)

where: x = normalized analogue signal and encoder input or decoder output
         y = normalized digital signal and encoder output or decoder input
         A = 87.6
         μ = 255

5.4   QUANTIZING AC SIGNALS

The methods of sampling and quantizing previously described work well for signals that have a large dc component (such as the luminance signal of television). However, signals with both positive and negative excursions, such as audio, need an alternative approach. One possible way involves using an *offset binary* technique, where a constant is added to each sampled value. But in certain cases, such as with audio mixers, where it is necessary to add signals from different sources, the sum can overflow or exceed allowable peak values.

The commonly adopted solution involves using the two's complement method of representing a binary number. By convention, a leading zero indicates a positive number, while a leading one indicates a negative value. It will be recalled that the two's complement of a binary number is formed by inverting each bit in turn and adding 1. Thus the two's complement of 01010101 = 10101010 + 1 = 10101011. When reconstructing the analogue signal from a two's complement sample, the excess 1 should be removed before inversion. However, in practice, failure to do so causes such a minute error that it is often neglected. A quick method of finding the two's complement of a binary bit stream is to copy down the code from the right-hand side, up to and including the first 1, and then invert each remaining bit in turn.

Typically, then, an 8-bit two's complement code allows for $\pm 2^7 = \pm 128$ sampling levels. For ac signals, the RMS-signal-to-RMS-quantization ratio is more applicable. For this case, equation 5.3 shows that the SQNR is (1.76 + 6.02n) dB.

5.5 PULSE SPECTRA

Figure 5.5(a) shows a single rectangular pulse of amplitude V and time duration t. Such a pulse can be analysed by transforming it into a mathematical model in the frequency domain. In the time domain, the pulse is defined by:

$$f(t) = V \text{ for } |t| < t/2 \quad \text{and} \quad f(t) = 0 \text{ for } |t| > t/2$$

Transformation to the frequency domain by the Fourier transform:

$$F(\omega) = (Vt \sin(\omega t/2))/(\omega t/2) \tag{5.11}$$

where $\omega = 2\pi f$, the angular velocity.

A section of the spectrum for equation 5.11 is shown in Figure 5.5(b), and this is described generally as a sin x/x or sinc function. Figure 5.5(c) shows a series of such pulses which is typical of the situation at a receiver. As the zero crossings of the tails occur at the bit cell centres, the energy in the tails tends to be self-cancelling. This is particularly true if the receiver clock circuit is accurately timed. Weak synchronism between the receiver clock and the bit stream will lead to decision errors by the detector circuit, a situation which is often made worse by a relatively long string of zeros.

If the pulse stream were filtered before processing, some of the HF energy would have been removed and the tails of the spectrum would have less significance.

5.6 BASEBAND CODE FORMATS

The errors affecting data services via any form of communication links are chiefly characterized by added white noise, distortion and synchronism. For satellite links there is the further problem produced by the overall propagation delay and for geostationary birds this is in the order of 250 ms. The noise and distortion lead to the concept of a *bit error rate* (BER), while delay variation adds to the timing and synchronism problems and these in turn lead to further bit

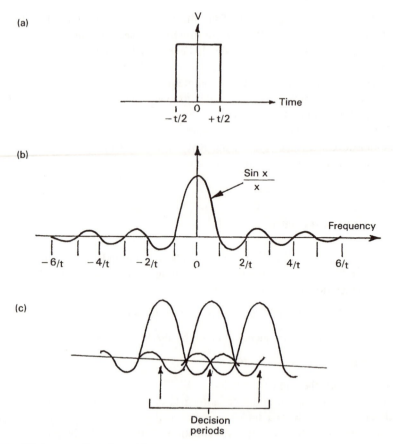

Figure 5.5 A rectangular pulse and its spectrum.

errors. Most terrestial transmitters and satellite transponders tend to be power rather than bandwidth limited so that Shannon's channel capacity rule becomes important:

$$C = B \log_2(1 + \text{SNR}) \text{ bits/sec} \tag{5.12}$$

where C = channel capacity, B = bandwidth, and SNR is the signal-to-noise ratio.

The balance between bandwidth and SNR can be used to good effect to maximize the channel capacity for an acceptable bit error rate suitable for the particular service.

Binary code formats are designed to insert extra bits into the data stream on a regular basis, in order to take advantage of this trade-off. A few of the many ways of achieving this are shown in Figure 5.6, the aim being to minimize the number of consecutive similar bits in the transmitted data stream. The receiver detector clock circuit can then be synchronized to a greater number of signal transitions and so improve its timing. An extra advantage may accrue because some formats have no dc component in their power spectrum, a feature that reduces the low-frequency response requirement of the receiver and allows ac coupling circuits to be used.

All the commonly adopted code formats can be generated and decoded using dedicated integrated circuits (ICs), the codes generally being produced from non-return-to-zero (NRZ) basic codes. The return-to-zero (RTZ) format is little used, as its half-width pulses represent an energy/bit penalty.

Codes of the nBmB type are often used to convert n bits/symbol into m bits/symbol (m > n), ensuring that, on average, the number of *ones and zeros* being transmitted are equal.

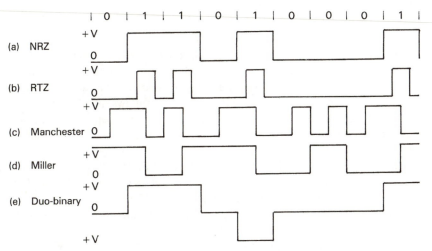

Figure 5.6 Some baseband code formats.

The bi-phase series of formats for which the basic Manchester code shown in Figure 5.6(c) is representative has the following features. A signal transition occurs at each bit cell centre, so that a zero is represented by 01 and a one by 10. This ensures that there are never more than two identical bits in series. Another variant of this is the *code mark inversion* (CMI) format, where 0 = 01 and 1 = 00, or 11 alternately. Although bi-phase codes have a 50 percent redundancy and double the transmission bandwidth, there is no dc component in the power spectrum, as depicted by Figure 5.7.

The Miller format, shown for comparison purposes in Figure 5.6(d), finds favour in the magnetic storage media and is not usually used for transmission purposes. A one is represented by a transition at mid-symbol and a zero by no transition. Except for two consecutive zeros when an extra transition is introduced at the end of the first zero, the Miller code has similar properties to the NRZ code (see Section 1.10).

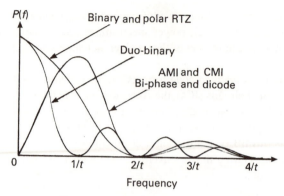

Figure 5.7 Power spectrum of some power formats.

The *duo-binary* code is a bi-polar, full-pulse-width code, as shown by Figure 5.6(e). It has a bit repetition rate that is half the frequency of the original signal. Zero is represented by 0 V and one by ±V. The V polarity is unchanged if the one follows an even number of zeros and reversed if it follows an odd number.

The more efficient codes use the least redundancy and there is, in general, a trade-off between the complexity of balancing the number of consecutive similar bits and the added redundancy.

The increase in bit rate that these codes produce represents a power penalty. For example, using a 3B4B format involves a bit rate increase by a factor of 4/3 which in turn requires a power increase of about 1.25 dB.

A simple form of error monitoring/detection takes the form of counting the running average of the number of ones and zeros. Any variation outside some predetermined bounds can be used to signal an error situation. With added redundancy, error detection/correction can be provided using *parity checks* or *Hamming codes*.

5.7 DATA ERROR CONTROL (FORWARD ERROR CORRECTION)

When data errors are detected in a bit stream, there are various corrective measures that can be applied. The actual method used often depends upon the source of the original data signal. For instance, had the source been analogue in form, then one of the error concealment techniques might be applicable. This possibility includes:

(1) Ignore the error and treat it as a zero-level signal.
(2) Repeat the last known correct value.
(3) Interpolate between two known correct values.

This latter method is really only suitable where a significant amount of data storage is available at the receiver, to allow time to regenerate the analogue signal after processing. In other cases there is the possibility of requesting a repeat transmission when errors have been detected. However, in general this is wasteful of both time and frequency spectrum. The ASCII code (American Standard Code for Information Interchange) is a commonly used method of representing alphanumeric characters in a digital system. This 7-bit code allows for $2^7 = 128$ different alphabetic, numeric and control characters. The commonly used word length is 8 bits (1 byte), so that space is available for one extra redundant bit.

Even and odd parity

A single-error detection code of n binary digits is produced by placing $n - 1$ information or message bits in the first $n - 1$ positions. The nth position is then filled with a 0 or a 1 (the *parity bit*), so that the entire code word (or code vector) contains an even number of ones. If such a code word is received over a noisy link and found to contain an odd number of ones, then an obvious error has occurred. Alternatively, a system might use *odd parity*, where the nth bit is such that the code word will contain an odd number of ones. In either case, a parity check at the receiver will detect when an odd number of errors has occurred. The effects of all even numbers of errors is self-cancelling, so these will pass undetected. The even or odd parity bits can be generated or checked, using Exclusive OR or Exclusive NOR logic respectively.

Such an arrangement of bits is described as an (n,k) code, n bits long and containing k bits of information. It thus follows that there are $n - k = c$ parity or protection bits in the code word. The set of 2^k possible code words is described as a *block code*. It may also be described as a linear code if the set of code words form a sub-space (part) of the vector-space (entirety) of all possible code words.

Hamming codes

Error correcting codes have been devised and are named after R.W. Hamming (3), the originator of much of the early work on error control. For a code word of length n bits, it is possible to identify n ways in which a single error can occur. Including the possibility of no error, there must be $n + 1$ different code patterns to be recognized.

Hamming showed that the number of parity bits c required for a single error correcting code was given by:

$$c \geq \log_2(n + 1) \text{ or } 2^c \geq (n + 1) \tag{5.13}$$

(Hamming also defined a 'perfect' code for the case where $2^c = (n + 1)$.)

Figure 5.8(a) shows how the message is expanded with redundant check bits. These are usually interleaved with the message bits and placed in

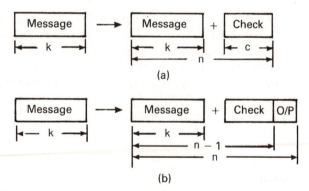

Figure 5.8 Hamming code formats: **(a)** SEC; **(b)** SEC/DED.

positions 2^0, 2^1, 2^2, etc. in the encoded bit pattern. The mechanics of the encoding and decoding process is explained in Table 5.1 for a (7,4) block code (block length n = 7, message length k = 4, parity bits c = 3).

The message bits to be transmitted (0011) are placed in the third, fifth, sixth and seventh positions respectively. The three parity checks are carried out, to determine the values (0 or 1) to be placed in positions 1, 2 and 4. In general, the xth parity check bit is given by the sum modulo 2 of all the information bits, where there is a 1 in the xth binary position. The code word to be transmitted is thus 1000011. If this is now received over a noisy link as 1000001, there is an error in the sixth position. The receiver decoder again carries out the three parity checks and generates the following results:

first check   0
second check   1
third check   1

Table 5.1

(Binary)	001	010	011	100	101	110	111
Position	(1)	(2)	(3)	(4)	(5)	(6)	(7)
	P	P	M	P	M	M	M
Check 1	*		*		*		*
Check 2		*	*			*	*
Check 3			*	*	*	*	*
Message			0		0	1	1
Parity bits	1	0		0			
Transmitted code word	1	0	0	0	0	1	1
Received code word	1	0	0	0	0	0	1
Recheck of parity	0	1		1 (reverse bit order)			
Syndrome = 110 = 6							
Error in position 6 – invert bit 6 to correct error							

The reverse of this series is called the *syndrome* (syndrome being a medical term for the symptoms of a disease) and this points to the bit error in position 110 (6). Correction is simply achieved by inverting the bit in error. An all-correct transmission would have yielded an all-zero syndrome.

By adding an overall parity (O/P) check bit as shown in Figure 5.8(b), the single-error correction capability is extended to double-error detection, the error patterns being indicated by the following conditions:

(1) No errors – zero syndrome and overall parity is satisfied.
(2) Single error (correctable) – non-zero syndrome and overall parity fails.
(3) Double errors (non-correctable) – non-zero syndrome and overall parity is satisfied.

Maximum likelihood decoding

The *distance* between any two n symbol code words is defined as the number of positions of bit difference. The *minimum distance d* between any valid code words is the minimum number of bit changes necessary to convert one code word into another. For the correction of all combinations of t or fewer errors, the minimum distance must be at least $2t - 1$, thus ensuring that if t errors occur then the received code vector will be nearer to the one transmitted than any other (i.e. $d \geq 2t + 1$).

This concept leads to a simple method of error correction. If a code word is detected as being in error, the decoder checks the distance between the received vector and all valid code words and selects the one exhibiting the minimum number of errors.

Cyclic codes

In certain transmission systems, the channel noise causes errors to occur not just randomly but in clusters or bursts. A sub-class of the linear block codes valuable in combating this problem is the group of *cyclic codes*. These have a form such that if a code vector such as 0110 is a valid code word, then so are all its cyclic translates such as 1100, 1001, 0011, etc. which are obtained by shifting the binary sequence one bit at a time to left or right. These codes can easily be encoded or decoded using ICs based on feedback shift registers. The *cyclic redundancy checking* (CRC) error detection concept is most effectively described in algebraic form using modulo-2 arithmetic. The basic rules are that $1 + 1 = 0$ and $+1 = -1$, so that addition does not involve a carry and produces the same result as subtraction.

Message and redundant check bits are expressed by the use of polynomials in terms of a dummy variable X, the lowest-order term X^0 representing the least significant bit (LSB) and the highest-order term X^n the most significant bit (MSB). Since the terms range from X^0 to X^n, there will be $n + 1$ bits in the message. The coefficients of the terms of the polynomial indicate whether a particular bit is 0 or 1. For example, the 5-bit message stream 11010 would be represented by:

$$1.X^4 + 1.X^3 + 0.X^2 + 1.X^1 + 0.X^0 \text{ or } X^4 + X^3 + X$$

The data stream is written with the MSB on the left when this is transmitted first. The degree of a polynomial is the power of the highest-order term, which in this example is 4. To generate the code for transmission, three polynomials are used: the message polynomial $k(P)$, a generator polynomial $G(P)$ which is selected from a group of *primitive polynomials* to produce the desired characteristics of block length and error detection/correction capability, and a parity check polynomial $c(P)$. The coded word length $n = k + c$, as for block codes.

During encoding, $k(P)$ is first loaded into a shift register and then multiplied by X^c to move the message c bits to the left, thus making room for c parity bits. The shifted polynomial is then divided by the generator polynomial to produce a remainder that forms the parity check polynomial $c(P)$.

$$(k(P).X^{n-k})/G(P) = Q(P) + c(P) \tag{5.14}$$

where $Q(P)$ is a quotient polynomial and $c(P)$ the remainder which is then loaded into the remaining shift register cells.

The transmitted code vectors for a (7,4) cyclic code ($k = 4, c = 3$) using the generator polynomial of $X^3 + X + 1$ are formed as shown by the following example:

$$\text{Message code} = 1101, k(P) = X^3 + X^2 + 1,$$

$$k(P).X^c = (X^3 + X^2 + 1)X^3, = X^6 + X^5 + X^3.$$

Now divide by $G(P)$.

$$
\begin{array}{l}
(X^3 + X + 1)\overline{X^6 + X^5 + X^3}(X^3 + X^2 + X + 1 \\
\quad \underline{X^6 + X^4 + X^3} \\
\quad X^5 + X^4 \\
\quad \underline{X^5 + X^3 + X^2} \\
\quad X^4 + X^3 + X^2 \\
\quad \underline{X^4 + X^2 + X} \\
\quad X^3 + X \\
\quad \underline{X^3 + X + 1} \\
\quad 1 = \text{REMAINDER}
\end{array}
$$

$X^6 + X^5 + X^3 + 1$ therefore divides exactly by $G(P)$, and so forms the transmitted polynomial 1101001. The first four bits 1101 are the original $k(P)$ while the remaining three bits 001 are $c(P)$, the parity polynomial. The full list of the $2^k = 16$ code words are shown in Table 5.2.

If a code word $T(P)$ is transmitted, and received without error, $T(P)$ divides exactly by $G(P)$, leaving a zero remainder. The last c bits are then stripped off to leave the original message code. If, however, an error occurs, then division leaves

Table 5.2

Message vector	Parity vector
0000	000
0001	011
0010	110
0011	101
0100	111
0101	100
0110	001
0111	010
1000	101
1001	110
1010	011
1011	000
1100	010
1101	001
1110	100
1111	111

a remainder polynomial that forms the syndrome. There is a one-to-one relationship between this and the error pattern, so that correctable errors can be inverted by logic circuits within the decoder.

The effectiveness of cyclic codes depends largely upon the generator polynomial. For a polynomial of degree n, the decoder is generally capable of detecting/correcting error bursts of n or less bits (some errors outside of this bound may be detectable), and odd numbers of random errors. A further advantage in cases where speed is not important is that CRC can operate with microprocessor-based coding, where the system characteristics can be reprogrammed.

Furthermore, the ITU-R (CCITT) have devised a number of standard polynomials for CRC control that include the above, plus $X^{16} + X^{12} + X^5 + 1$.

Golay codes

These are a sub-set of cyclic codes. The (23,12) versions using 11 parity bits are capable of correcting any combination of three random errors (including a burst of three) in a block of 23 bits. The codes are based on the generator polynomials:

$$G_1(P) = X^{11} + X^{10} + X^6 + X^5 + X^4 + X^2 + 1 \quad \text{and}$$

$$G^2(P) = X^{11} + X^9 + X^7 + X^6 + X^5 + X + 1$$

both of which are factors of $X^{23} + 1$. Encoding and decoding can be accomplished using ICs based on 11-bit feedback shift registers.

Bose–Chaudhuri–Hocquenghem (BCH) codes

This very important sub-set of cyclic codes is widely used for the control of random errors. For any positive integers m and t, such that $t \leq 2^{m-1}$, codes exist with the following parameters:

Blocklength	$n = 2^m - 1$
Parity bits	$c = n - k \leq mt$
Minimum distance	$d \geq 2t + 1$

which are capable of correcting t or fewer errors in a block $n = 2^m - 1$ bits. The generator polynomials used must be at least of degree mt. In general, the number of check bits c is almost mt, but if t is less than 5 then c = mt.

Values for n, k and t have been tabulated (4) for various polynomials. For example, when m = 5, n = 31, k = 26, c = 5; t is equal to 1, but when m = 5, n = 31, k = 11, c = 20, t rises to 5.

BCH codes can be processed either by digital logic circuits or by digital computer. The hardware solution is faster but the computer is, of course, more flexible.

Reed–Solomon codes

These are a sub-set of the BCH codes, which correct any combination of t or fewer errors and require no more than 2t parity bits. The parameters are n − k = c = 2t and d = 2t + 1. As with all cyclic codes, a generator polynornial is used for encoding, and the decoder again produces a syndrome that identifies the error pattern.

Two-dimensional Reed–Solomon codes

These form an extension of the R–S codes by using the interleaving technique. This involves generating two R–S codes from the data, and then cross-interleaving the coded bit patterns before transmission. Provided that the encoder and decoder are synchronized, relatively very long bursts of errors become correctable.

These have been developed as inner codes which can correct burst errors of a few bytes' length, while the outer codes can correct very long bursts. In one such code, the data is organized into a matrix of 600 bytes × 30 rows. The first or outer code is then used to add two check bytes to each of the columns to create 32 rows. Each row is then divided into ten blocks of 60 bytes and the second or inner code is used to add four check bytes to each block of 60 bytes to give an array of 640 bytes × 32 rows. The inner code is able to correct all single byte errors and tag all errors that are longer than this. The outer code can correct two inner code blocks of 60 bytes each, provided that they are tagged when passed to the decoder. It can therefore correct 120 bytes. However, since the inner code is interleaved to a depth of 10 bytes, the outer code, when using the inner code tags, can correct an error up to 1200 bytes long.

Interleaved or interlaced codes (*see also* Reed–Solomon codes)

This is a simple but very powerful way of dealing with either random or burst errors. Any cyclically coded (n,k) set of vectors can be used to produce a new code (αn,αk), by loading coded vectors from the original code into a matrix of n columns and α rows and then transmitting the bits column by column. The transmission sequence is then an interleaved or interlaced code, with an interleaving factor of α. If a burst of errors α or less in length occurs, there will only be one error in each affected word of the original code. As a lower bound, if the original code corrects t or fewer errors, the interleaved code will correct any combination of t bursts each of length α or less.

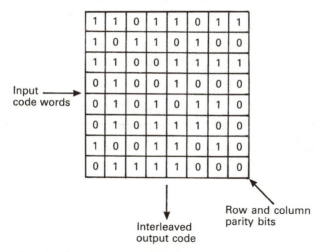

Figure 5.9 Interleaved coding.

Because the original code was cyclic, so will be the interleaved one. If the original generator polynomial had been G(X), the generator of the new code would be G(X^{α}). Therefore the interleaved code can also be encoded and decoded in a similar manner to cyclic codes.

Convolution codes

These codes, used for the control of burst errors, are produced by the complex process of convolution of the message stream with a generator matrix. Unlike cyclic codes, where the parity bits for any given block are contained within that block, the parity bits within a block of convolution code check the message bits in previous blocks as well. The range of blocks over which the check bits are operative is defined as the *constraint length m* for the code (a block code might be described as a convolution code for m = 1), the parity bits formed on the current block being dependent upon the message bits in the previous m − 1 blocks. The code structure as transmitted is represented by Figure 5.10(a) and has the following parameters:

Block length   = n
Message bits per block = k
Parity bits per block = c
Constraint length n_0 = m blocks = mn bits
Message bits within n_0 = k_0 = mk bits
Parity bits within n_0 = c_0 = mc bits

For convolution codes, n and k are normally small integers, often less than 5.

The encoder consists essentially of feedback registers and Ex-Or logic. For decoding, there are two strategies that can be used. Logic or algebraic decoding is restricted to the constraint length. This uses an encoder plus logic circuit to recalculate the parity bits and invert any correctable bits in error. The alternative is probabalistic decoding, where the decoder must be able to store more than m blocks. The sequential decoder then makes its decision on one block, based on

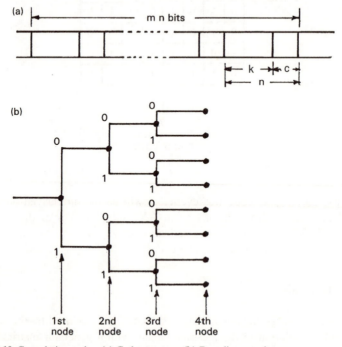

Figure 5.10 Convolution codes. **(a)** Code structure. **(b)** Decoding search trees.

more than m –1 previous blocks. The decoding follows a predetermined algorithm through a tree structure such as shown in Figure 5.10(b). When the decoder detects an error, it backtracks to the previous node and accepts the alternative branch.

The convolution code rate is expressed as a ratio such as 1/2, 3/4, 7/8, etc. For example, with a code rate of 1/2, then for every data bit entering the encoder, two bits leave it. The extra bit is the redundancy of FEC and in this case, each data bit has its own protection bit. The lower the code rate ratio, the greater the degree of redundancy and the better the level of protection.

Trellis modulation (5)

This is a transmission encoding and error correcting system that is often used in conjunction with convolution coding. One particular and popular implementation of this is the ITU-R (CCITT) V.32 encoder used with data and fax modems. For this version, the data stream is divided into 4-bit symbols which without FEC would produce a 16QAM signal constellation. Using trellis modulation, the 4-bit input to the V.32 encoder produces 5 bits output, which after mapping to the I and Q components generate a 32-point signal constellation. This would be expected to generate an SNR penalty because the new constellation points are closer together. However, the encoding process ensures that no two consecutive output symbols are within the surrounding neighbourhood of each other so that the Euclidean distances between such symbols are now further apart thus providing a 3 dB SNR advantage.

Of the four input bits, only b_3 and b_4 are passed direct to the encoder output stage unprocessed. Bits b_1 and b_2 are first differentially encoded and then convolutionally encoded to generate a set of three bits (constraint length 3). The differential encoding of b_1 and b_2 proceeds as follows:

Bit B_1 is produced by the sum modulo-2 of b_1 and the previous b_1.

B_2 is produced by differentially encoding the new b_1 and the previous b_1 and then taking the sum modulo-2 of the previous B_2 and the new b_2.

B_1 and B_2 are then used to generate the FEC redundant bit B_0.

Under certain signal conditions, the V.32 modem has the ability to dispense with FEC and to fall back to 16QAM operation. The convolution encoder is a 3-bit shift register interconnected by AND and logic which can be considered as a finite-state machine with a transition diagram in a trellis form. Hence the terminology. Higher levels of trellis modulation are possible.

Viterbi decoding algorithm (6)

The decoder calculates the Hamming distance function between each received code word and all the others in the code book. The word that meets the minimum distance requirement is selected as the most likely one to have been transmitted and is therefore often described as the *survivor*. The decoder stores the survivors and the associated distances to enable a tree search to proceed in the manner of Figure 5.10(b).

Since decoding represents an iterative process, the decoder can readily be fabricated on an ASIC to handle most of the standard convolution code formats.

For the more complex modulation processes such as QAM, where each transmitted signal symbol may represent several bits, the Euclidean distance in this case becomes more important. The closer the received symbol is to a point on the constellation, the more likely it is that this represents the transmitted code pattern.

Punctured codes (7)

At higher data rates, Viterbi/trellis decoding becomes more complex and hence more costly. *Punctured* convolution codes can achieve higher data rates without this penalty. The technique operates by selectively and periodically removing bits from the encoder output which effectively raises the code rate.

In practice, the output from an adaptive convolutional encoder is passed through an analogue gate circuit in blocks of parallel bits. The switching action of the gates is controlled by the *puncture* matrix, which defines the characteristics of the specific error protection for the bits in an information block.

The puncture matrix has to be available at the receiver decoder either as a hardware element or in software. The decoder then treats the punctured code in the same way as erased bits so that these do not affect the decoder decision making.

Variable length codes (Fano and Huffman)

Fano's algorithm
All the messages allowed in the code book are replaced by a variable length code that depends upon the probability of a message being transmitted. The probability of each message is calculated and the messages arranged in descending order of probability. The list is then divided into two groups of approximately equal total probability; the upper and lower groups are allocated the value 1 and 0 respectively. This process continues until all the messages have been assigned a unique code sequence. This principle is shown in Figure 5.11(a).

Huffman's algorithm
As with the Fano algorithm, the messages are again arranged in descending order of probability, but in this case, the two lower probabilities are combined to produce a new value. The lowest message is then designated 0 and the upper group 1. The

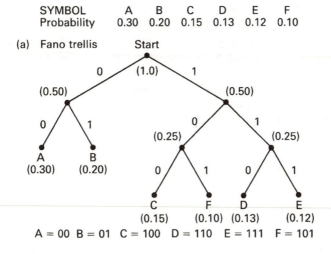

SYMBOL	A	B	C	D	E	F
Probability	0.30	0.20	0.15	0.13	0.12	0.10

(a) Fano trellis

A = 00 B = 01 C = 100 D = 110 E = 111 F = 101

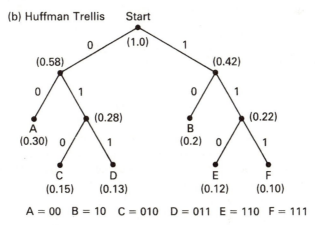

(b) Huffman Trellis

A = 00 B = 10 C = 010 D = 011 E = 110 F = 111

Figure 5.11 Variable length codes. (a) Fano. (b) Huffman.

upper group is then treated as a new list and the division repeated. Continuing this process results in the upper or most likely messages being allocated the shortest code words. This principle is explained in Figure 5.11(b).

Truncated codes

In any synchronous system, the decoder clock rate must be accurately locked to the transitions in the data stream. If this contains long runs of 1s or 0s, then the lack of transitions can allow the clock frequency to drift and introduce bit errors. Truncated codes were developed to minimize this effect and one particular coding scheme operates as follows.

An 8-bit code group produces 256 unique code words and this number rises to 16 384 for 14-bit codes. Of these, only the words that contain 10 or fewer 0s and with at least two 0s between successive 1s are selected. A further twenty-one words with the longest run lengths are discarded to leave 256, 14-bit code words. If one of the discarded code words is received, then an error must have occurred, so adding a further degree of error protection.

Both the encoder and decoder contain a look-up table to provide the one-to-one relationship between the 8- and 14-bit code groups. This particular scheme is known as 8 to 14 modulation (EFM).

The concept of mathematical combinations can be used to calaculate the number of code words that contain certain bit patterns. To find the number of code words containing r binary digits in n bits, proceed as follows.

$$_nC_r = \frac{n!}{r!(n-r)!}$$

Thus for three 1s and four 0s in seven digits,

$$_nC_r = \frac{7!}{3!(4!)} = \frac{7 \times 6 \times 5}{2 \times 3} = 35 \text{ code words}$$

Concatenated codes (*see also* Cellular telephones, Section 6.2)

These digital systems employ speech analysis and compression in the transmitter, followed by synthesis and expansion in the receiver. Typically, speech at a bit rate of 64 kbit/s is compressed into about 8 kbit/s so that the process requires a very significant degree of digital processing. In order to provide a flexible system with future upgrade capability, the technology uses highly integrated programmable DSP chips such as those from the Texas Instruments Inc. TMS 320 range.

Because of the mobility of the hand-held units, it is necessary to provide for a smooth hand-over (hand-off) between cells as the user moves around. To achieve this, the transmission multiplexed time frames not only include digitized speech, but also a range of control and synchronizing signals. Forward error control is therefore essential and involves the use of a number of concatenated techniques for maximum effect. Some of the bytes in each time frame use Reed–Solomon coding concatenated with convolution coding with extra CRC protection for the important part of the bit stream, while other bytes are unprotected. The bit stream is further interleaved across two time frames and the receiver employs a Viterbi decoder. The CRC bytes are calculated using the generator polynomial, $1 + X + X^2 + X^4 + X^5 + X^7$, with the LSB being transmitted first. The data is also transmitted in bursts because it is highly unlikely that a cluster of bit errors will occur in two successive bursts.

5.8 PSEUDO-RANDOM BINARY SEQUENCES (PRBS) (PSEUDO NOISE (PN))

For a series of binary digits to be in random order, each symbol must occur by chance and not be dependent upon any previous symbol. Over a long period, the number of occurrences of ones (n_1) and zeros (n_0) should be the same. In a similar way, runs of two, three or more of each symbol should be equi-probable. Such sequences can be generated using shift registers, as indicated by Figure 5.12, where the logic state of the switches controls the feedback paths, through modulo-2 adders placed between the serial shift register input and output, the state of the switches being set according to a *characteristic polynomial*.

Assuming a 4-bit register with the switches set, $S_1 = S_n = 1$, and $S_2 = S_{n-1} = 0$ (1001), then irrespective of the initial states of the shift register cells, the binary pattern shown in Table 5.3 will be produced. The bit pattern b_n is the

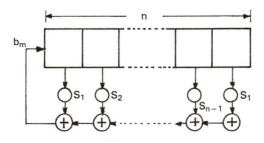

$\oplus$ = Modulo-2 adders

Figure 5.12 Pseudo-random binary sequence generator.

Table 5.3

		r_1	r_2	r_3	r_4	b_n
State	1	1	1	1	1	0
	2	0	1	1	1	1
	3	1	0	1	1	0
	4	0	1	0	1	1
	5	1	0	1	0	1
	6	1	1	0	1	0
	7	0	1	1	0	0
	8	0	0	1	1	1
	9	1	0	0	1	0
	10	0	1	0	0	0
	11	0	0	1	0	0
	12	0	0	0	1	1
	13	1	0	0	0	1
	14	1	1	0	0	1
	15	1	1	1	0	1

required sequence (010,110,010,001,111), generated on a periodic and cyclic basis. Selecting a new characteristic polynomial will create a new sequence.

There are 2^n possible states for the shift register cells, but the all-zero combination is not valid as this would bring the generator to a halt. Therefore the length of a sequence is $2^n - 1$, the period of repetition being independent of the initial conditions.

It can be shown for these sequences that $n_1 = 2^{n-1}$ and $n_0 = 2^{n-1} - 1$ so that if n is large then the sequence has near-random properties. A maximal length sequence is usually described as an m-sequence and finds many uses in communications systems.

Because of the pseudo-random properties, PRSBs can be used:

(1) as repeatable noise sources for testing digital systems:
(2) to add redundancy to a transmitted data stream, by coding logic 1 as the m-sequence and its inverse as logic 0;
(3) added to the data stream as shown by Figure 5.13, to act as a key to ensure secure data.

The major difficulties caused by points (2) and (3) are synchronism and a reduced data rate.

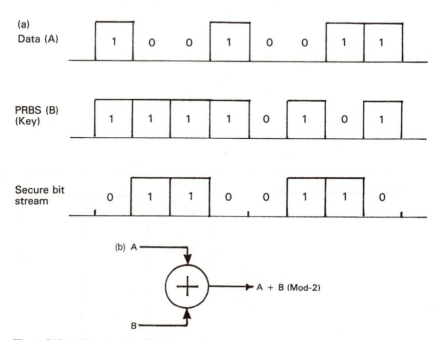

Figure 5.13 Addition (modulo-2) of data and m-sequence.

Fire codes

This class of burst error correcting cyclic codes was discovered by F. Fire for whom they are named. These are constructed systematically and can correct or detect a single burst of errors in a block of n digits, with small redundancy (n – k). If P(X) is an irreducible polynomial of degree m, and e is the smallest integer so that $X^e + 1$ is divisible by P(X), then an l-burst error correcting Fire code is generated by the polynomial. $G(X) = P(X)(1 + X^{2l-1})$, where $1 \leq m$ and $2l - 1$ is not exactly divisible by e. The number of parity bits is $m + 2l - 1$ and the code length is given by $n = LCM(e, 2l - 1)$, i.e. the lowest common multiple of e and $2l - 1$. A particularly popular Fire code that is capable of correcting any burst of length l or less and also detecting any burst of length $d \geq 1$ is generated by the polynomial $G(X) = P(X)(1 + X^c)$ where $c \geq 1 + d - 1$ and the length $n = LCM (e,c)$.

Gold code sequences (8)

These represent a family of pseudo-random sequences that were defined by R. Gold in 1967 as having a low cross-correlation between each other. As such they can occupy the same signalling channel without producing destructive inter-ference. Because of these properties, Gold codes find applications in code division multiple access (CDMA) or spread spectrum multiple access (SSMA) systems. Each code sequence is produced from a pair of PRBS generators, each with n stages, by modulo-2 addition. If all the $2^n + 1$ Gold sequences of period $2^n - 1$ are concatenated, the resulting sequence period becomes $(2^n + 1)(2^n - 1)$ $= 2^{2n} - 1$, the same as would be generated by a shift register with 2n cells. They are therefore the product of two m-sequences.

5.9   BIT RATE REDUCTION OR BANDWIDTH CONSERVATION

Digital modulation schemes

It was shown in Chapter 1 that binary PSK systems have a SNR advantage over both OOK and FSK modulation methods. Equation 5.12 relating to Shannon's channel capacity rule shows that it is possible to trade off SNR, bandwidth and channel capacity in order to obtain the advantages of any of these parameters according to the system designer's choice. Modulation schemes have been devised to use this trade-off to allow more bits per cycle of transmitted signal or symbol (bits/Hz) to be achieved at the expense of SNR and bandwidth. However, any scheme based on PSK will always have an advantage. This is a convenient point to clear up any misconceptions that may exist about the difference between bit and baud rates. Bit rate is the number of binary digits that are transmitted per second. Baud rate is the unit of modulation or signalling speed and represents the number of discrete signal events that occur in each second. For example, if a modulation scheme has four levels of changes per cycle or Hz, each event represents two bits (or one dibit) per symbol. Thus a bit rate of 1200 per second is equivalent to a baud rate of 600.

The ITU-R (International Telegraph and Telephone Consultative Committee's (CCITT)) standard for pulse code modulation (PCM), as used on telephony channels, operates at a sample frequency of 8 kHz and uses eight bits per sample (seven bits representing level plus one sign bit to represent polarity). The transmitted bit rate is thus $8 \times 8\,\text{kHz} = 64\,\text{kbit/s}$.

In order to minimize the bandwidth required, quaternary phase shift keying (QPSK) is used. Unlike bi-phase PSK, where each phase inversion represents one bit of information. QPSK uses four phase shifts as follows:

$$0° = 00,$$
$$90° = 01,$$
$$180° = 11,$$
$$270° = 10,$$

so that each phase now represents two bits, thus doubling the information content without the increased bandwidth penalty. However, the phase separation between each code symbol is halved relative to bi-phase PSK, which leads to a 3 dB SNR ratio penalty, and therefore companding is used in the system to recover some of this loss. Figure 5.14 indicates how this signal appears as a modulated RF waveform, while Figure 5.15(a) shows the signal vectors that are formed by this type of modulation.

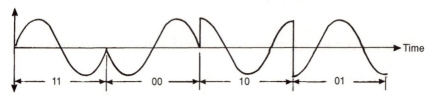

Figure 5.14 Typical QPSK radio frequency waveform.

QPSK modulation

For true QPSK operation, the vectors take up a position in phase with the I and Q axes (In phase and Quadrature) while the concept shown in Figure 5.15(a) is described as $\pi/4$QPSK because the vectors are phase shifted or offset by 45°. Both arrangements can be overlaid to provide eight-phase PSK where each signal vector represents three bits of data. Alternatively, both QPSK and $\pi/4\pi$QPSK can be used in opposite directions in the same system to provide for simultaneous

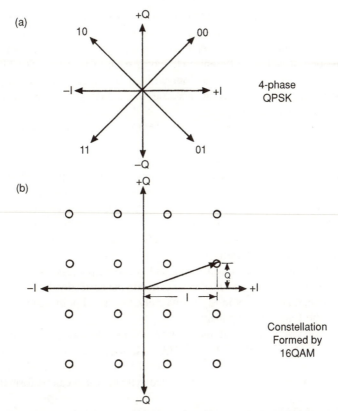

Figure 5.15 (a) QPSK constellation diagram. (b) Constellation formed by 16QAM.

duplex operation but with a useful degree of protection from mutual interference. For QPSK the system phase shifts are either 0, ± π/2 or π, while for the offset version (OQPSK) these are reduced to 0, ± π/4 or ± 3π/4. Thus for the latter case the modulation shift envelope is reduced and this helps to reduce the level of distortion caused by non-linear amplification in the later processing stages.

For most forms of PSK, the coding is usually based on a differential process (DPSK) because this eases the problems of demodulation. In this case, the data is carried in the phase differences between successive bits so that the decoder only has to compare the bit stream with itself, delayed by one bit period to generate an accurate output.

QAM modulation

Further bandwidth compression can be achieved by using an extension of QPSK. With this system, known as quadrature amplitude modulation (QAM), each of the vectors can be amplitude-modulated to one of several discrete levels. One example is shown for comparison with QPSK in Figure 5.15(b). This provides a number of vectors generated from I and Q components in the manner shown and each of the sixteen signal points in the constellation thus represents one of sixteen different code words each of four bits. The bit rate is thus now increased by a factor of four without invoking a bandwidth penalty, but at the expense of the SNR because the signal points are now closer together and easier to corrupt.

Figure 5.16 indicates the way in which 16QAM signals are demodulated. The carrier recovery circuit ensures that the local carrier oscillator is locked in frequency to the incoming signal. In-phase and quadrature versions of this signal are applied to the I and Q ring demodulator stages along with the input modulated signal. After bandpass filtering, the signal at point A has an analogue form but with discrete amplitudes. Synchronism for the data rate clock circuit is also derived from point A. The two data slicer circuits recover the original digitally formatted signal and this is then progressively decoded (points A, B, C and D) to provide the original bit stream.

Figure 5.17 shows how this encoding and decoding process works. The I and Q signal components in (a) and (b) each generate the corresponding signal points in the constellation diagram in (c). Conversely, the signal points can be decoded to provide the I and Q components.

A range of QAM levels of modulation are possible, ranging from 4QAM which is equivalent to QPSK, through 16QAM, 32QAM, 64QAM, 128QAM, to 256QAM which is currently the highest level in use. These provide two, four, five, six, seven and eight bits per transmitted symbol which can be formalized as follows.

For M-level QAM, $M = 2^k$ where M is the level and k the number of bits per symbol. Thus

$$k = 3.3222 \log M \tag{5.15}$$

It was shown in Chapter 1 that the BER depended on the E_b/N_0 ratio and this was extended to show that $E_b/N_0 = C/N \times B/R$ where C/N is the CNR, B is the bandwidth and R the bit rate involved. This equation can be rearranged and expressed in terms of decibels as $10 \log (E_b/N_0) = 10 \log CNR - 10 \log R/B$, where the last term is in units of bits/cycle or alternatively as bits/symbol.

Since each point on the constellation diagram represents a unique binary code, the decoding errors would be expected to double if the number of points were doubled. If binary PSK with two points in its constellation is used as a baseline because it provides the lowest bit error rate (BER) for a given CNR, then the following heuristic approach leads to a reasonably accurate assessment of the range of QAM systems (within 1 dB of values calculated from more precise formulae). Both QPSK and 4QAM have similar signal constellations with four signal points so that the possibility of error doubles. This represents a CNR penalty of $10 \log 2 = 3$ dB. Now the 16QAM constellation has eight times the number of signal points so that in this case the CNR penalty rises by $10 \log 8 = 9$ dB. Using this approach, the results can be tabulated (Table 5.4).

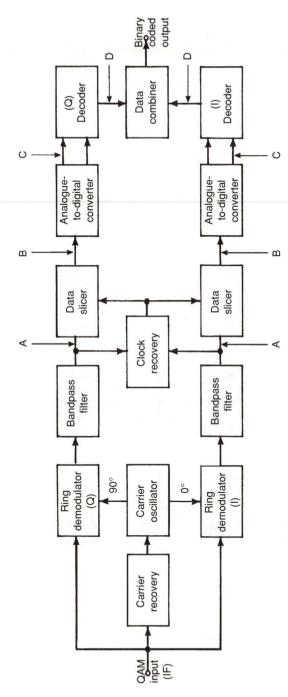

Figure 5.16 16QAM decoding sequence.

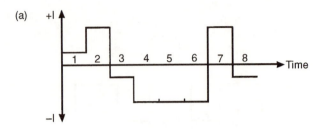

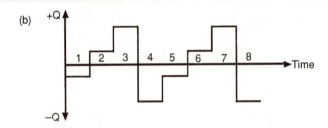

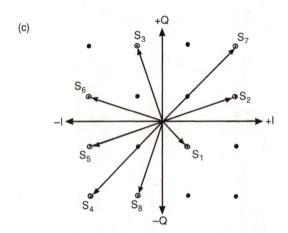

Figure 5.17 Decoding the I/Q bit stream. **(a) and (b)** I and Q channel bit streams. **(c)** Constellation summation of I and Q bits.

Table 5.4

Binary PSK	0 dB
QPSK	3 dB
4QAM	3 dB
16QAM	9 dB
64QAM	15 dB
256QAM	21 dB

Orthogonal frequency division multiplex (OFDM) modulation

This concept consists of generating a large number of carrier frequencies with equal spacing. Each is digitally modulated with a sub-band of frequencies and then filtered to produce a (sin x)/x or sinc x response as shown in Figure 5.18(a). The spectra of the individual neighbouring carriers thus overlap in the orthogonal manner shown. When these combine, the total spectrum becomes practically flat as shown in Figure 5.18(b). The channel capacity approaches the Shannon limiting value so that the spectrum behaves as a parallel transmitting bus.

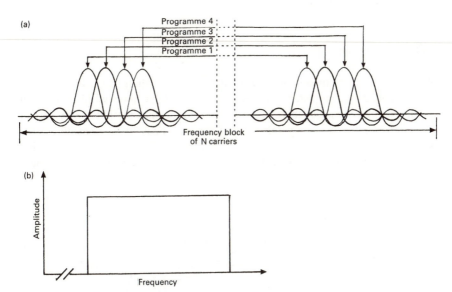

Figure 5.18 **(a)** Time domain of OFDM carriers. **(b)** OFDM frequency spectrum.

The allocated bandwidth is divided into N elementary frequencies and arranged to carry P programme channels. There are therefore N/P interleaved carriers which carry sub-band modulation in the manner shown. Either of PSK or QAM variants can be used for the digital modulation.

The individual carrier frequencies need to be accurately selected to ensure orthogonality and hence minimum mutual interference. The transmitter power output stages must be operated in a linear mode to avoid intermodulation distortion (particularly third order) between the carriers. Using Shannon's rule it can be seen that an increase in the number of carriers is likely to reduce the SNR if power output and bandwidth remain constant.

Because of the orthogonality of the carriers, several transmitters can use the same basic frequency without creating destructive co-channel interference. The system therefore lends itself to working as a single channel network.

Problems with PCM

Telephony by PCM can also be transmitted over satellite links, either by time division multiple access (TDMA) systems, or over digital data channels using the single channel per carrier (SCPC) concept. PCM can be used for other services such as high-quality music or television, but with these wider bandwidth signals the effects of bit errors can be a problem. With PCM, the effect of a single bit in error depends upon its weighting. While an error in the LSB will probably pass unnoticed, an MSB in error is likely to have a significant effect. Using companded PCM on music channels can cause the noise level to vary audibly as the signal level changes.

Delta modulation

Alternatively, delta modulation (DM) may be used, where the audio signal is simply coded by one bit, positive or negative, based upon whether a signal sample is greater or less than the previous value. Hence the alternative title of '1-bit PCM'. Because only one bit per sample needs to be transmitted, the sampling rate can be increased very significantly. This reduces quantization noise, simplifies the receiver anti-aliasing filter and at the same time reduces

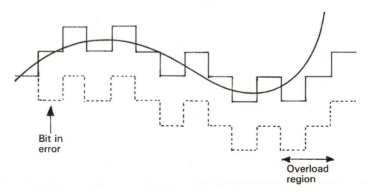

Figure 5.19 Delta modulation, bit error and overload.

the bandwidth required relative to standard PCM. A 1-bit error simply produces a step of the wrong polarity in the output signal, which then retains its correct general shape as shown in Figure 5.19. Such errors are then likely to pass unnoticed.

An overload effect can occur (also shown in Figure 5.19) when the input signal amplitude changes by a greater step than quantizing size during the sampling intervals, but this chiefly affects large-amplitude, high-frequency signal components, which in audio occur relatively infrequently.

Differential PCM (DPCM)

If the pattern of an analogue signal is known up to some point in time, then because of the correlation between successive values, it is possible to draw certain inferences about future behaviour. This can be achieved by a predictive or extrapolation process.

In predictive coding systems the signal is sampled at regular intervals, but as each sample time approaches the probable value of the next sample is predicted. The difference between the prediction and the actual value is coded as for PCM and transmitted. The receiver must make the same prediction and add the same correction. Figure 5.20(a) shows the basic principles of such a system. However, since the two predictors operate on slightly different signals, this leads to some

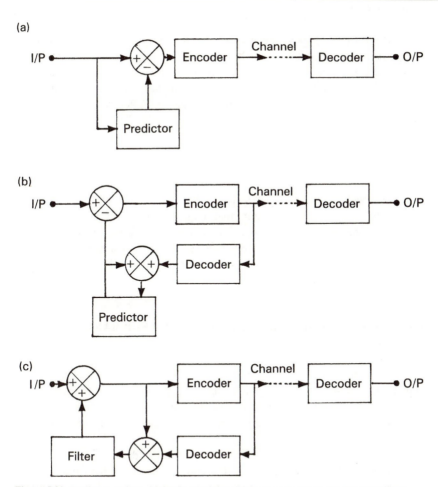

Figure 5.20 Predictive coding. **(a)** Basic principles. **(b)** Improved version. **(c)** Integrator/filter version.

errors. The system shown in Figure 5.20(b) is an improvement. Both predictors work on decoded signals and if no noise were added in the transmission channel, both would yield identical results. In the system illustrated in Figure 5.20(c), the predictor is replaced by an integrator/LPF, so making better use of the previous sample value because of the removal of the ripple due to sampling.

Although the predictions made under any system must contain errors, the advantages claimed for DPCM can be explained as follows. In standard PCM, no prediction is made; or in other words, the next predicted value is zero. Since an approximate prediction is better than no prediction at all and because of the good correlation between successive samples, DPCM must lead to a better SNR as well as a reduced bandwidth.

Adaptive systems

Both DM and DPCM systems can give better results if the quantization step size is made to vary in accordance with the time-varying amplitude of the input signal. Such adaptive circuits give a significant improvement in audio quality and behave as companded systems. In addition, pre-emphasis and de-emphasis can be applied to the analogue signals before encoding and after decoding to further improve the SNR.

Sub-Nyquist sampling

In certain special cases, alternate sampled values are suppressed, so that sampling effectively takes place at half the normal frequency. At the receiver, the missing samples can be replaced by interpolation or predictive coding. The overall effect reduces the bandwidth required by a factor of two. However, this concept requires the use of a very stable sampling frequency and accurate receiver filtering, plus the extra circuitry for interpolation.

5.10   QUADRATURE MIRROR FILTERS AND SUB-BAND CODING
    (8, 9)

It has been shown that to avoid aliasing when digitally processing an analogue signal, the sampling frequency must be at least twice that of the highest frequency component in the complex wave. If aliasing occurs then the original signal cannot normally be extracted (filtered) from the complex spectrum of the sampled signal.

In any wideband signal, many of the frequencies in the band are only rarely present. A good example of this is the television image, where much of the background remains unchanged from frame to frame and with only relatively small areas of movement. By dividing (filtering) the broad spectrum into narrower sub-bands, it will be found that many of these will contain only occasional information. If these sub-bands are sampled, then by using a variable length coding such as Huffman, which allocates the shortest code words to those values that have the highest occurrence probability (the stationary areas of the image), a useful bandwidth compression can be achieved.

Quadrature mirror filters (QMF) are basically multi-rate digital filters so that the sampling frequency is not constant throughout the system. Figure 5.21 shows the basic principle involved with the system containing *decimators* which *down-sample* the signal and *interpolators* that provide complementary *up-sampling*.

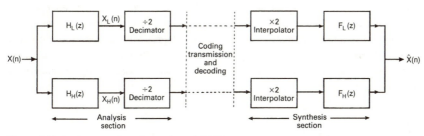

Figure 5.21 Basic generation of two-channel QMF system.

If a decimator has the digital sequence $X(n)$ as input, it will produce an output $Y(n) = X(Mn)$, where M is an integer that represents the down-sampling ratio. If $M = 2$, then $Y(n)$ will consist of every second sample. The decimator thus produces a compression in the time domain. In a practical system, before the signal is decimated, it will first be bandwidth limited to reduce the effects of aliasing using a *decimation filter*. At the receiver, the M-fold interpolator will replace the missing $M - 1$ values between adjacent samples. If $M = 2$, then the interpolator will either average successive values or insert zeros, the effect being a complementary expansion in the time domain.

The concept is closely related to sub-band coding. As indicated in Figure 5.21, the input sequence $X(n)$ is divided into separate channels using low- and high-pass filters with a response of $H_L(z)$ and $H_H(z)$ before down-sampling. This signal is then coded for transmission in any suitable manner, before being processed in a complementary manner at the receiver. Higher orders of filter can be produced by further sub-dividing each channel with low- and high-pass filters. It will be clear from the comments on sub-band coding that some of these channels may contain long strings of zeros, thus allowing significant bit rate reductions to be achieved. The combined response of decimator and interpolator can give rise to aliasing in the frequency domain, but the *synthesis filters* with response of $F_L(z)$ and $F_H(z)$ remove this from the respective channels. In a correctly designed system, the recombined output sequence $\hat{X}(n)$ will be a perfect reconstruction of the input $X(n)$, even under noisy transmission conditions.

The name quadrature mirror filter derives from the fact that the response of the filter $H_L(z)$ is a mirror image of that of $H_H(z)$ with respect to the normalized frequency $\pi/2$, which is a quarter of the sampling frequency.

5.11   TRANSFORM CODING (*see also* Chapters 6 and 7, H.261 codecs (Section 8.2) and Television, Chapter 10)

As with most areas of communications, there are a number of choices to be made when handling image processing and data compression. The concepts may be described as either *lossy* or *loss-less* and *symmetrical* or *asymmetrical*. The operations are considered to be lossless when the image can be reconstructed without error and in general, this limits the degree of data compression to a maximum of about 5:1. The systems are described as symmetrical when encoding and decoding can occur in real time and of equal duration, otherwise they are asymmetrical.

Discrete cosine transform

This technique is symmetrical and may be lossless if the compression ratio is restricted to about 4:1. This process is the one most commonly used for image signal transmission and operates in two stages. First, a linear transform is performed on the original image by splitting the space into N × N blocks of *picture elements* or *pixels*. The amplitude coefficient of each pixel is then mapped on to a transform space for coding and transmission. The *discrete cosine transform* (DCT) is related to the discrete and fast Fourier transforms (DFT and FFT) but retains only the *real* component (cosine) of the transform. This method is fast because it requires only the calculation of a few coefficients and is compatible with digital signal processing (DSP) ICs. When used with a suitable coding structure the DCT provides a high degree of image data compression. This transform technique thus finds applications in videophones, tele/video-conferencing, colour fax systems, interactive video discs, and high-definition television colour imaging.

Each block of pixel data is transformed using a two-dimensional matrix operation in the following manner:

$$[T] = [C].[D].[C]^T$$

where: [T]   is the transformed block,
         [C]   is the basis of the DCT matrix,
         [D]   is the original data block and
        $[C]^T$ is the transpose of [C].

The DCT coefficients are calculated from the relationship

$$F(u, v) = \frac{4C(u)C(v)}{N^2} \sum_{i=0}^{N-1} \sum_{j=0}^{N-1} f(i, j) \, CosA.CosB$$

The inverse transform relationship used at the receiver is given by

$$f(i,j) = \sum_{i=0}^{N-1} \sum_{j=0}^{N-1} C(u)C(v)F(u, v) \, CosA.CosB$$

where $A = \dfrac{(2i + 1)u\pi}{2N}$ and $B = \dfrac{(2j + 1)v\pi}{2N}$

In both cases:

- i, j and u, v = 0, 1, 2. ... N − 1 (N being the block size),
- i, j are the spatial coordinates in the original image plane,
- u, v are the corresponding coordinates in the transform plane,
- $C(u) = C(v) = 1/\sqrt{2}$ for u = v = 0 and
- $C(u) = C(v) = 1$ for u = v ≠ 0.

Such transforms are readily performed using dedicated ICs. The high degree of image data compression available arises not from the transform itself, but due to the fact that many of the transformed coefficients are either very small or zero, indicating little block-to-block variation. In addition, many of the remaining coefficients can be transmitted with lower precision without significantly affecting the received image quality. Since only a relatively few values need to be transmitted, any form of variable or run length coding can be used to advantage.

Depending upon the system requirements, a standard TV image can be reduced to a bit rate as low 64 kbit/s, but 2 Mbit/s is necessary to provide an acceptable quality of colour image.

Fractal Transform coding (10) (Fractal Transform is a trademark of Interated Systems Ltd)

The term fractal is a derivative of *fractured structure* and was coined to describe the way in which an image may he considered to be composed of many similar shapes and patterns of various sizes. Examples of this are snowflakes or the centre of sunflowers, where quite complex patterns can be defined by an origin, and motion and rotation instructions.

For encoding or compression, an image is divided into small blocks. These are searched for similar patterns that have been moved or rotated in order to determine the precise transforms that are occurring. The basis of this shape relationship is the matrix operation known as an *affine transformation*. An affine transformation is defined by the matrix

$$\begin{bmatrix} x \\ z \end{bmatrix} \rightarrow \begin{bmatrix} a & b \\ c & d \end{bmatrix} \cdot \begin{bmatrix} x \\ y \end{bmatrix} + \begin{bmatrix} e \\ f \end{bmatrix}$$

or

$$\begin{bmatrix} x = ax + by + e \\ y = cx + dy + f \end{bmatrix}$$

where a, b, c, d, e, f are real numbers that can include $\pm r \cos \theta$ and $\pm r \sin \theta$; r represents a scaling factor and θ represents a rotation, relative to the x and y axes.

In operation, this transformation represents a mapping from one shape onto another, point by point. For example, circles to ellipses, squares to parallelograms, right-angled triangles to equilateral triangles, etc. The affine transformation can thus describe a combination of rotation, scaling and translation of coordinate axes in n-dimensional space.

The compression/encoding process involves the use of an algorithm that is computationally intensive, which means that moving images cannot be processed in real time. By comparison, decompression/decoding can be performed in real time at 30 Hz frame rate using computer software only. The system is therefore most useful for asymmetrical processes that involve recording.

While it would take several minutes to encode a single colour frame, because video images can be encoded using inter-frame differences, a video signal can be encoded at an average rate of about two frames per second.

The following provides an indication of the degree of compression that can be achieved: a grey scale image can be compressed into about 3 kbytes, a colour image into about 10 kbytes, and a video frame using inter-frame differences into about 800 bytes.

Discrete wavelet transform coding (11)

These are mathematical functions that can be used to decompose data and signals into different frequency components to allow these to be characterized using different degrees of resolution. The processing integrates quadrature mirror filters and sub-band coding and can be used for data, image and audio compression, filtering to remove the effects of noise from measurements and in the mathematical solution of differential equations.

By contrast with Fourier transforms which resolve waveshapes into a range of sinusoidal frequencies with a relatively long duration, wavelets are localized in time and last for only a few cycles. The two important shapes of wavelets are the position in time and the duration. A wavelet transform therefore represents a signal as the summation of a number of wavelets of different position and scale.

For example, a sawtooth waveform can be represented by the sum of sixteen wavelets as opposed to the typical 256 samples required by Fourier analysis which finds difficulties with the discontinuity that occurs when the sawtooth changes direction. Discontinuities and edges show up very clearly in wavelet analysis and for this reason, the techniques could be valuable to the developing image compression technologies of the future. Because the system uses QMF, the decimation and down-sampling at each stage provide a very fast processing algorithm. The system is claimed to be symmetrical and to provide higher compression ratios with fewer losses than DCT processing, and is highly compatible with computer processing.

5.12 SPREAD SPECTRUM TECHNIQUES (12, 13)
(*see also* Section 13.2)

A spread spectrum system (SS) is one in which the transmission bandwidth is much wider than strictly necessary. FM is therefore an example of spread spectrum using analogue signalling. It can be shown that such a system has a significant SNR advantage over AM (12). Similarly, the bandwidth of a digital signal can be increased so that many bit periods are necessary to represent a single bit at baseband. Such a system has a processing gain expressed as the ratio of the transmission code rate to that of the original information bit rate. This leads to a reduction in the number of transmission errors which is equivalent to an increase in the system SNR.

These systems commonly use code division multiple access (CDMA) techniques where several transmissions simultaneously occupy the same channel and this leads to an improved spectrum utilization. At the heart of these systems is a PRBS or similar derived code (see Table 5.5) and there are two basic ways in which these are employed. For direct sequence spread spectrum (DSSS), either the original baseband bit stream is multiplied by the PRBS to produce a new bit stream or the PRBS and its inverse are used to represent logic 1 or 0 respectively.

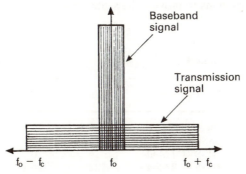

Figure 5.22 Spread spectrum signal spectra.

For the frequency agile or hopping systems (FHSS), the PRBS is used to make the RF carrier frequency hop around within the spread spectrum bandwidth. In both cases, only those receivers equipped with the correct PRBS can decode the transmissions. Basically the technique causes the energy in the original baseband signal to be spread across the much wider transmission bandwidth as shown in Figure 5.22. At the receiver, the low-level signal may even be swamped by noise but by the use of correlation decoding (see Appendix A4.2) the original baseband signal can be accurately reconstructed.

Barker and Willard codes

These shorter unique codes (Table 5.5) have been found by computer simulation to give an acceptable degree of correlation. They are less secure than the PRBS systems but are useful in noisy environments and are easy to implement.

Table 5.5

N	Barker	Willard
3	001	001
4	0001 or 0010	0011
5	00010	00101
7	0001101	0001011
11	00011101101	00010010111
13	0000011001010	0000011010111

Three other sequences can be generated from those shown in Table 5.5 by inversion or by reversal of the bit stream.

Table 5.6 provides a comparison of SNR in dB between BPSK and the various spread spectrum systems to provide the same BER.

Table 5.6

Bit error rate	10^{-3}	10^{-6}
Theoretical BPSK	6.5	10.5
DSSS @ 1 Mbit/s	8.5	12.5
FHSS @ 1 Mbit/s	16	20
FHSS @ 2 Mbit/s	22	26

REFERENCES

Because of the extensive nature of digital concepts, it has only been possible to give a brief description of the more common techniques in use. For a more expansive explanation the reader is referred to works such as those listed in the references below.

(1)   Halliwell, B.J. (1974) *Advanced Communication Systems*. London: Newnes– Butterworth Ltd.
(2)   Cattermole, K.W. (1969) *Principles of Pulse Code Modulation*. London: Iliffe Books Ltd.
(3)   Hamming, R.W. (1950) 'Error detecting and Error correcting Codes'. *Bell System Technical Journal*, Vol XXVI No. 2.
(4)   Shu Lin (1970) *An Introduction to Error-Correcting Codes*. New Jersey: Prentice-Hall Inc.
(5)   Chishtie, M.A. (1994) *Telecommunications Applications with the TMS320C5x DSPs*. Texas Instruments Corp, California.
(6)   Shu Lin and Costello (1983) *Fundamentals and Applications of Error Control Coding*. New Jersey: Prentice-Hall Inc.
(7)   Hagenauer, J. (1987) 'Rate compatible punctured convolutional codes'. Proc ICC '87, p. 1032, June.
(8)   Spilker, J.J. (1977) *Digital Communications by Satellite*. New Jersey: Prentice-Hall Inc.
(9)   Vaidyanathan, P.P. (1987) 'Quadrature Mirror Filter Banks, M-Band Extensions and Perfect-Reconstruction Techniques.' *IEEE ASSP Magazine*, pp. 4–20, July.
(10) Barnsley, M.F. (1993) *Fractal Image Compression*. AK Peters Ltd, Massachusetts.
(11) Stollnitz, De Rose, Salesin (1996) *Wavelets for Computer Graphics: Theory and Applications*. Morgan Kaufman, USA.
(12) Dixon, R.C. (1976) *Spread Spectrum Systems*. Wiley, New York.
(13) Lewis, G.E. (1997) *Communications Technology Handbook*. Oxford: Butterworth-Heinemann.

Chapter 6

Digital and digital/analogue communications systems

6.1 SYSTEMS OVERVIEW

When developing new communication services, the design engineer is faced with a wide range of possibilities that not only include the carrier medium and methods of modulation, but also the means of transmission (choice and compromise!). Today, it is possible to apply either analogue or digital techniques to almost any analogue system. Although digital systems are probably less well understood, they are invariably more flexible and are certainly much better suited to computer control. Because of the extensive expansion of digital networks, these systems are more economical, in spite of tending to be bandwidth hungry. Transmission via twisted pair telephone or coaxial cables is possible up to quite high frequencies. Even the *plain old telephone system* (POTS) is capable of accurately carrying data at more than 5 Mbit/s. Coaxial cable will easily support bit rates beyond 10 Mbit/s, while optical fibre is capable of supporting rates well beyond 100 Mbit/s. Broadcast video programmes are regularly carried over coaxial cables at carrier frequencies up to near 1 GHz. The major advantage of any cable network is that this is generally a lower noise level environment, particularly in the case of fibre networks.

New terrestrial radio-frequency broad- and narrow-casting systems have to share the existing heavily occupied spectrum so that for this means, it is necessary to adopt new technologies that multiplex several channels on to a single carrier or to employ clever frequency reuse methods. Because of the shared spectrum applications, there is a strong chance of intermodulation distortion and noise causing reception problems. The choice of AM or FM as the means of modulation has to be made against the trade-off between narrow bandwidth and lower noise levels. Again, by using digital methods that include error protection, the digital signal tends to have the best SNR and hence lower *bit error rates* (BER).

Practically any digitally based service that can operate within the terrestrial scheme of communications can function over a satellite space link. The services provided range from those specifically designed for computer-to-computer communications, through to the digital processing of services that are essentially analogue in origin.

The principal disturbance to space link signals is white noise, the effects of which can be mitigated by the use of a suitable error control technique. For digital transmissions, the most significant problems with *geostationary satellites* (Geo) arise from the long propagation delay of at least 250 ms overall, and Doppler shift. The latter can be a particular problem for high-speed signals and on mobile links. For *low earth orbiters* (LEOs) the delay is more acceptable at about 6 ms, but Doppler shift can still be a problem for mobiles.

A significant number of digital services operate through relatively large earth stations, with antennas of 5 m diameter or greater. In general, these provide point-to-multipoint communications, with the receiving stations acting as hubs for distribution purposes, these then act rather as *local area networks* (LANs).

Many new data services are developing for point-to-point communications, and these receiving stations can operate with antennas of about 1.2 m diameter or less. It is the latter type of system that this chapter will concentrate on. The systems described are considered as being representative of the much wider range of digital services available. Digital services are currently provided in the UHF, L, C and Ku bands. (The Ka band will probably come into use for inter-satellite links within the next few years.) Bit rates vary from 1.2 kbit/s up to many tens of Mbit/s. Many of the earlier, well-established services operate on the FDMA *single channel per carrier* (SCPC) basis, a significant application being the telephone voice services using various forms of PCM. The *satellite multiservice system* (SMS) operated by Eutelsat over the European Space Agency's ECS-2 satellite, for instance, divides a transponder's 72 MHz bandwidth into 3200×22.5 KHz frequency slots, each capable of supporting one 64 kbit/s digital PCM channel. A user can be allocated a single slot, or a contiguous multiple of slots, according to the baseband requirement. As will be seen, many of the satellite-delivered data services have their origins in the terrestrial telephone data services.

Some more recent and developing digital services use the *time division multiple access* (TDMA) system which when combined with *packet switching and digital speech interpolation* (DSI) (1) can more than double the capacity of a channel.

TDMA is the complex technique where a number of ground stations time-share a satellite space link in short bursts, often as short as 1 ms but sometimes longer. Time-sharing has to be accurately controlled and synchronized by one ground station of the system.

TDMA has much in common with terrestrial local area networks (LANs), where the data is organized into *packets* of bits. The make-up of a typical packet structure is shown in Figure 6.1, where:

(a)   Start flag indicates the beginning of the packet and can contain a *preamble* sequence of bits designed to aid synchronization.
(b)   Each packet carries the originating and destination addresses.
(c)   Control section holds the packet sequence number, which is needed if the message occupies more than one packet.

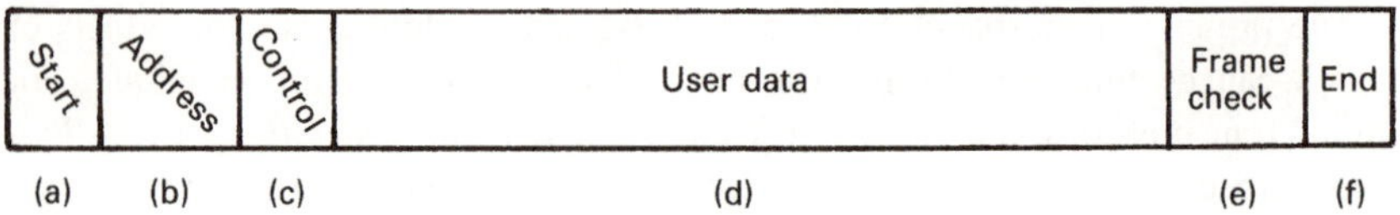

Start	Address	Control	User data	Frame check	End

| (a) | (b) | (c) | (d) | (e) | (f) |

Figure 6.1 Typical packet structure.

(d) The data bits may include their own error protection.

(e) Frame check provides error detection on the packet structure.

(f) An end flag signifies the last bit of the packet.

Services that handle data in this form are described as being *packet switched*, as opposed to the alternative of being circuit switched, where two communicating terminals can dominate a channel. Many of these services use the CCITT X.25 (ITU-T) Packet Radio standard and protocol which is closely related to frame relay. The X25 Recommendation defines a packet switching network interface rather than a complete network. Therefore any device that matches this requirement can be connected to an X25 network. The protocol at each node error-checks each received time frame, makes the necessary corrections and retransmits the packet to the next node which may or may not be the final destination. The node also makes a backward acknowledgement through the network to confirm that it has received the packet. X25 networks originally operated on 64 kbit/s leased lines, but can now handle data rates as high as 2.048 Mbit/s.

If the TDMA time slots are used on an unallocated basis, some form of *carrier sense multiple access* with *collison detection* (CSMA/CD) must be used. Basically, all the transmitting stations listen continually for a break before starting transmission. If two transmit simultaneously, each will detect the collision of data as noise and relinquish the channel for a random period before attempting to retransmit.

Between the extremes of FDMA and TDMA, there are a number of hybrid systems. These vary between using different transmission modes in each direction, to the use of several low-speed data TDMA carriers on one transponder. With the rapid developments in *digital signal processing* (DSP), *code division multiple access* (CDMA) provides a further convenient way of improving channel occupancy.

Digital speech interpolation (DSI) is used on TDMA systems and makes use of the time gaps that appear in all voice communications channels. The gaps are then allocated to other users waiting to transmit data.

Such schemes allow satellite communications to become integrated into a global system, thus giving rise to the *integrated services digital network* (ISDN) concept which is a communications network that has evolved because of the problems associated with analogue telephony systems. ISDN recognizes the considerable advantages that can be gained by changing to a system that allows for the end-to-end transfer of data in a digital format. Once such a transition has been made, the advantages gained include:

(1) greater reliability due to the use of digital integrated circuits;
(2) faster access speed due to the introduction of *dual tone multi-frequency* (DTMF) dialling instead of pulse dialling;
(3) allows for computer access to the system which gives rise to the concept of *computer-integrated telephony* (CIT), where the power of the computer can be combined with the communications power of ISDN;
(4) by introducing CIT, many new services such as video, data and high-speed facsimile can be introduced into the telephone system.

For reasons of economy, the service has to be compatible with the current analogue systems and introduced in an evolutionary manner.

Whichever way the space link is managed, the general ground receiver will be based on the double or triple superhet principle. The head-end electronics at the antenna act as a low-noise converter for a block of channels and provide the first *intermediate frequency* (IF), which is fed over land lines to the main receiver situated some distance away.

Comparative down-link budgets (TDMA and SCPC)

This comparison is based upon data obtained from references (2) and (3) for the EUTELSAT SMS service. The down-link service operates at 12.5 GHz in two possible extreme modes: TDMA at a transmission rate of 24.576 Mbit/s (74 dBHz), or FDMA (SCPC) at 64 kbit/s (48 dBHz). Both use QPSK to achieve a maximum bit error rate (BER) of 10^{-4}. Table 6.1 assumes that the EIRP over the -3 dB service area is at least 42 dBW. But due to power limitations, the

Table 6.1 Down-link power budget

		TDMA	*SCPC*
(a)	Transponder saturated EIRP (-3 dB contour)	42 dBW	42 dBW
(b)	Back-off for multi-carriers	0	6 dB
(c)	Operating EIRP (a–b)	42 dBW	36 dBW
(d)	Transponder power per carrier	42 dBW	16 dBW
(e)	Free space attenuation	208 dB	208 dB
(f)	Receiver antenna gain	47 dB	47 dB
(g)	Received signal power (d–e+f)	-119 dBW	-145 dBW
(h)	Receiver noise temperature	25 dBK	25 dBK
(i)	Down-link C/T ratio (g–h)	-144 dBW/K	-170 dBW/K
(j)	Boltzman's constant	-229 dBW/HzK	-229 dBW/HzK
(k)	C/N ratio (i–j)	85 dBHz	59 dBHz
(l)	Transmission rate	74 dBHz	48 dBHz
(m)	E_b/N_0 (k–l)	11 dBHz	11 dBHz
(n)	Degradation margin	4 dB	4 dB
(o)	E_b/N_0 (theoretical) (m–n)	7 dB	7 dB

transponder can only support 100 (−20 dB penalty) 64 kbit/s carriers simultaneously. The receiving ground station is assumed to be equipped with a 2 m
diameter antenna with an overall efficiency of 65 percent, yielding a gain of
47 dB.

References (2) and (3) show that there is no significant difference in signal
degradation due to the up-link at 14 GHz.

The down-link analysis of Table 6.1 shows that there is very little difference
in terms of E_b/N_0 (equivalent to SNR) between the two modes. FDMA is the
least efficient in terms of throughput of data because of the power limitation,
while TDMA makes full use of the available bandwidth at all times. However,
TDMA systems are more complex and thus more expensive to implement and
maintain.

With FDMA operation the up-link power needs to be set to achieve two
objectives:

(1)   to provide a transponder power output for down-link with an adequate
      SNR, and
(2)   to divide the on-board available power between the down-link carriers.

In the interests of objective (1) *intermodulation distortion* (IMD) is avoided by
backing-off the output power by between 6 and 10 dB. (No back-off is necessary
with TDMA.) However, both FDMA and TDMA can be combined within a
multiplex if necessary to conserve bandwidth or power. FDMA signals can be
either analogue or digital in format, while TDMA operates only with digital
signals. The functioning of a TDMA system needs to be synchronized by a ground-
controlled access station using a protocol similar to those used with LANs. (See
ALOHA, etc (Section 6.4).) The developing CDMA systems use spread spectrum
techniques which are characterized by the use of PRBS codes.

6.2   TELEPHONY SYSTEMS (4)

Modern telephony systems employ all the currently available techniques ranging
from analogue and digital formats, through all forms of modulation and all
methods of carrier or bearer means. As these networks have expanded, the range
of services has increased and computers and microprocessors have taken over
control. This has led to the introduction of the concept of *stored program control*
(SPC). Using SPC, all the necessary operational instructions are held in
programmable read-only memories (PROMs). Due to the high degree of
flexibility that this provides, systems of widely differing size and architectures
can be made to operate together in a compatible manner.

The principle motives for this development include:

● economy and flexibility,
● speed of operation,
● the ability to reconfigure the systems to meet developing needs,

- the ease with which new subscribers and subscriber services can be added,
- improved network management and control of fault conditions.

Traffic parameters

The utilization and provisioning of exchange equipment within a telephone system is based on the measurements of traffic flow through the network. The basic unit is the *Erlang* (E) which is defined as follows:

> One permanently engaged circuit has a traffic flow of 1 Erlang, a dimensionless unit. The volume of traffic is measured as the average traffic intensity of 1 Erlang for 1 hour or 1 Erlang hour.

If a total of n calls are made during a period of T seconds and each has a duration $h_1, h_2, h_3, \ldots h_n$ seconds, then the total use made of the system is given by:

$$\sum_{i=1}^{i=n} h_i \quad \text{call seconds (traffic volume for period T)} \tag{6.1}$$

$$\text{Average traffic E} = \frac{\sum_{i=1}^{i=n} h_i}{T} \text{ Erlangs} \tag{6.2}$$

The average time for which calls occupy the equipment, the *mean holding time* h, is given by:

$$h = \frac{\sum_{n=1}^{i=n} h_i}{n} \text{ seconds} \tag{6.3}$$

The average traffic E for the period T is = nh/T Erlangs (6.4)

The average rate at which new calls are made for period T (a calls/s) = n/T, so that

$$E = ah \text{ Erlangs} \tag{6.5}$$

If during the busy hour, C_A calls are attempted and C_B of these are blocked, then the probability of blocking $P_B = C_B/C_A$.

Trunking and scanning

These terms are usually applied to telephony channels carried via radio networks.

The frequency spectrum of a trunked network is divided into channels which are managed by a central controller. A caller obtains access to the network via the controller which allocates a free channel for the duration of the call. Once completed, the channel is returned to the control pool for future reuse.

Scanning or self-trunking is an extension of this technique. The equipment of the user making a call scans the available spectrum to locate a free channel. The user then calls the other party either over a calling channel or over a free one, to establish communications over a nominated channel. Without the central control, such a system is likely to crash under overload conditions, rather than degrade gracefully like the trunked network.

Digital systems and technologies (*see also* PCM, Section 5.2)

There are two classes of service available. A *basic rate access* (BRA) which is used by most subscribers and is known as 2B+D (B = bearer, D = diagnostic) and consists of two 64 kbit/s voice and data channels, plus one 16 kbit/s digital signalling channel, making a total of 144 kbit/s.

The second service is known as *primary rate access* (PRA) and consists of 30B+D (ITU-T standard 32 channel multiplex) channel groupings in Europe and 23B+D in the USA (Bell standard 24 channel multiplex), giving total signalling rates of 2.048 and 1.544 Mbit/s respectively. In both cases, the D channel forms a common signalling channel using the ITU-T *Common Channel Signalling System* No. 7 (CCSS-7).

As telephone usage has expanded, it has become economically necessary to maximize the use of the analogue equipment and system. By using the time-sharing concept of *time division multiplex* (TDM), considerably more subscribers can be catered for without completely re-engineering the analogue network.

The effects of aliasing, and interference with the 4 kHz spaced carriers of the analogue system, can be avoided by sampling the audio channel at the internationally agreed rate of 8 kHz, with quantization at eight bits per sample and using relatively simple filter-banks. Internationally there are two digital systems in operation, the American Bell/AT&T with twenty-four time slots (channels) and the European thirty-two time slots (channels) per frame, respectively. Both of the systems use time frames of 125 μs duration as shown in Figure 6.2 (a and b). The Bell/AT&T system uses twenty-four time slots each with eight bits capacity for message plus one extra bit for frame synchronism. This gives a total of 193 bits per 125 μs or a gross bit rate of 1.544 Mbit/s and is referred to as the D1 or T1 rate.

By comparison, the European system uses time slot 0 (TS-0) for synchronism and TS-16 for signalling and control. This leaves time for 30 audio channels. The bit rate in this case is 32×8 bits per 125 μs or 2.048 Mbit/s and this is referred to as the D2 or E1 rate. Interworking between the two rates with the same time frame duration is readily achieved using microprocessor control and semi-conductor memories.

The trunk network may be structured around copper coaxial or optical fibre cables. In the latter case, light wavelengths around 1300 and 1500 nm are used

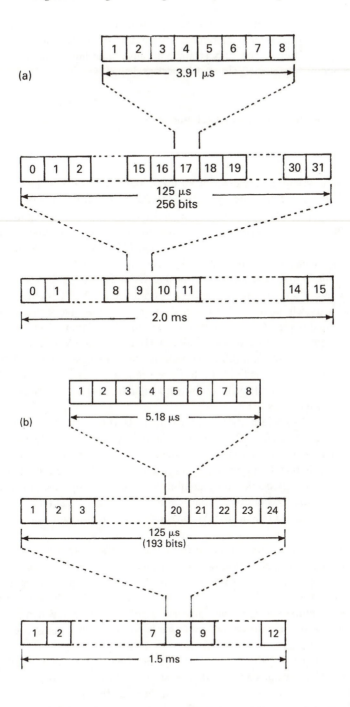

Figure 6.2 Time slot channelling for **(a)** European 30B+D system and **(b)** Bell/AT&T 23B+D system.

for carriers, with the speech modulated signals being organized as a *wavelength division multiplex* (WDM) hierarchy. Paired wires for the subscriber's *drop cables or final loop* are generally retained because sampling and quantization are more economically carried out at the local exchange.

Cordless communications and telephones

CT2 plus CAI (second-generation cordless telephone, plus common air interface)

This system was originally devised for use in the UK, but is now included in an ETSI (*European Telecommunications Standards Institute*) standard. CT2 is basically the portable cordless handset and the CAI provides a highly flexible way to interconnect handsets from different manufacturers and sub-systems into the PSTN or ISDN. The concept is variously known under a number of proprietary names but is covered by the generic title of *telepoint*.

The handsets may be used in either business, domestic or public access modes, with the latter normally only being able to originate a call. The digital approach provides a speech quality rather better than the CT1 analogue version, together with a limited degree of security and a capability for carrying data signals. The system operates in the band 864.1–868.1 MHz using FDMA with *time division duplex* (TDD) to provide a full duplex service over a single channel. Within the CAI, each channel is subdivided into three segments: a B-channel for 32 kbit/s speech or data, a D-channel for in-band signalling and a SYN-channel for synchronism purposes.

The 4 MHz bandwidth allows for 40 channels with 100 kHz spacing, using ADPCM (*adaptive delta pulse code modulation*) at a bit rate of 32 kbit/s. Digital speech packets of 2 ms duration are time-compressed into 1 ms and these are transmitted alternately in opposite directions for full duplex operation. An additional 6 kbit/s is needed for signalling and control purposes, plus a further overhead for duplex control, giving a gross data rate of 72 kbit/s. A handset maximum power output of 10 mW provides a maximum cell range of about 200 m.

Where permitted, calls are set up from either a base station or a handset, by selecting a free channel. A base station transmits a burst of 32 bits of D-channel information at 16 kbit/s, followed by 36 bits of SYN-channel data at 17 kbit/s. The latter carries a special marker bit pattern that is used by the handset for bit and burst synchronism. This burst provides a polling sequence which carries the identities (ID) of the base station and target handset. When a handset recognizes its ID, it responds.

Because the base station has to manage a large number of handset links, each calling handset transmits an extended burst of 720 bits. This is divided into 5 × 144-bit sequences each of which are further subdivided into 4 × 36 sub-multiplexes. Each sub-multiplex carries identical information which consists of a preamble and data. The remaining 144 bits provide the SYN-channel. Each burst carries data to identify the target base and particular handset. The handset stops transmitting the extended burst as soon as it detects the SYN bit pattern during its listening cycle and this confirms that the communication link has been established.

CT3 or DCT900 (third generation, Digital Cordless Telephone 900 MHz)

This development of CT2 technology utilizes similar operating frequencies and the TDD technique but exploits the advantages of TDMA. As indicated by Figure 6.3, the 16 ms time frames are divided into sixteen time slots, each of 1 ms duration. The latter are alternately used for transmission in opposite directions (TDD) to provide a full duplex service, with a gross bit rate of 640 kbit/s. By using TDMA, each time slot is capable of supporting eight speech channels or 32 kbit/s of digital data. A further advantage of TDMA accrues as a mobile handset moves from one cell to another; the change of base station and operating channels (hand-off) is virtually transparent to the user. Figure 6.3 also shows how each time slot is divided into segments for synchronism, indent, data and error correction purposes.

DCS 1800 (Digital Cellular System, 1800 MHz)

Apart from the operating frequency which is in the 1.8 GHz band, this system is compatible with the specification for GSM 900, but support-cells that are less than about 7 km radius. This concept forms one of the UK commitments to *personal communications networks* (PCN).

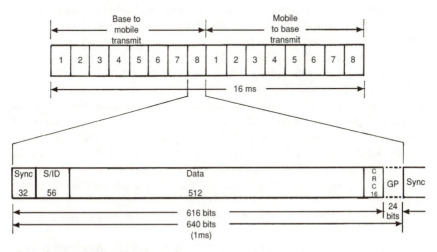

Sync = Sync word for bit and burst syncronism
S/ID = Signalling and identification
Data = Speech allocation
CRC = Cyclical redundancy check
GP = Guard period

Figure 6.3 Frame and time slot structure for CT3/DCT900.

DECT (Digital European Cordless Telephone)

This European standard, which uses TDMA/TDD, has much in common with CT3, but with a frame duration of 10 ms, divided into twenty-four time slots to accommodate twelve full duplex time division channels. Operation falls in the 1880–1900 MHz band and this provides enough spectrum for up to 120 simultaneous calls. The concept is designed for low-power operation and this restricts the cells to a maximum radius of about 200 m.

GSM-900 (Group Speciale Mobile-900 MHz, also Global System for Mobile Communications)

This cordless, cellular and frequency agile system represents a pan-European development backed up with ETSI standards. It operates in the paired bands, 890–915 MHz and 935–960 MHz with 200 kHz spaced carriers. As is common with other cellular concepts, GSM uses the lower frequency band for transmissions from the low-power mobile handset. The transmission system uses TDMA with TDD to provide seamless hand-off and a high frequency reuse factor, typically allowing up to twelve simultaneous communications links. With eight time slots per carrier, this allows 992 simultaneous users per cell.

The broadcast system uses a complex encryption technique, with interleaving and convolution coding to provide a high degree of system security and bit error control. Compared with an analogue system which requires a carrier-to-noise (C/N) ratio in the order of 30–35 dB for acceptable quality, GSM can offer a similar service with a C/N as low as 12 dB.

Signal modulation of the RF carrier uses Gaussian minimum frequency shift keying (GMSK) with a modulation index of 0.3 (MSK is a continuous phase modulation (CPM) version of FSK). The use of Gaussian-shaped pulses maximizes the bandwidth/spectral efficiency trade-off and improves the resilience to co-channel interference.

Each speech channel is sampled at 8 kHz and quantized to a resolution of 13 bits. This is then compressed by a factor of 8 in the full rate vocoder (voice coder) to give a bit rate of 13.4 kbit/s. Half-rate vocoders are available so that this can be reduced to 6.7 kbit/s. As indicated by the handset block diagram shown in Figure 6.4, signal processing utilizes both speech compression and synthesis. The vocoders are designed around high-speed digital signal processors (DSPs) and use a form of *linear predictive coding* (LPC) referred to as *residual excited* LPC. The algorithms for LPC attempt to model the human vocal chords in order to produce realistic synthetic speech with the minimum of memory.

An additional provision is made for an extra digital data channel with a capacity of 9.6 kbit/s.

Transmission power levels range from 20 W maximum for a base station down to 0.8 W minimum for a handset. A power saving circuit is also provided to allow the power level to be reduced by a maximum of fifteen 2 dB steps depending on a received signal level that gives an adequate bit error rate. Typically, a cell range varies from about 3 km to 35 km depending upon the local environment.

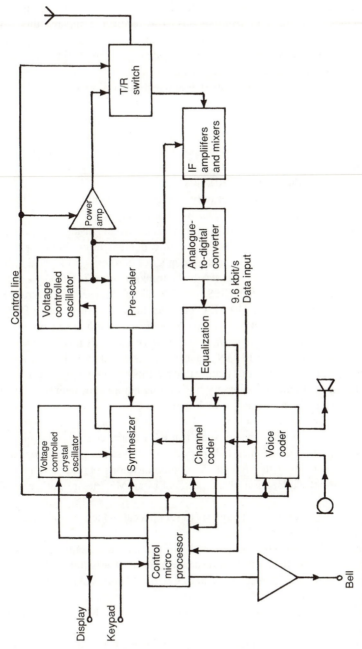

Figure 6.4 GSM-900 handset.

The specification provides for vehicle speeds up to 250 km/h (156 mph) and at maximum range this represents a time delay of around 15 µs. Because Doppler shift and multipath echoes can affect the received signal quality, each TDMA burst includes a number of *training bits*. The receiver compares this with a known training pattern and from this deduces the transfer function of the propagation path. An adaptive filter is then made to perform the inverse function, thus cancelling any unacceptable distortion.

Each 4.62 ms TDMA frame is divided into eight time slots with 557 µs of user capacity. These are interleaved so that the handset does not have to receive and transmit within the same time slot. Each block of 456 data bits is divided into four groups of 144 bits and these are loaded into alternate time slots, each with 20 training bits inserted between sub-groups of 72 data bits. The data packets are switched to a new carrier at about 217 Hz (frame rate). Altogether this produces a gross bit rate in the order of 270 kbit/s.

Since each handset transmits for only $\frac{1}{8}$ of the time ($\frac{1}{16}$ in the case of the half-rate vocoder), the average power consumption is very low.

GSM systems are structured in a hierarchical manner and installed on *intelligent networks* (IN); that is, networks with a significant element of computer control. Each base station (BS) serves a limited number of cordless terminals simultaneously and can switch up to twelve users to the trunks of a *public telephone network* (PTN). A switching sub-system (SSS) consists of a mobile service centre (MSC) plus the necessary database. The MSC provides the connections to the PTN and other MSCs. Each subscriber belongs to one *public land mobile network* (PLMN) and the relevant data is stored in a *home location register* (HLR) If a subscriber is currently outside his home PLMN, then the necessary data is held in a *visitor location register* (VLR). It is this feature that permits *roaming*. Each BS consists of a station controller and the necessary transcoding equipment, with the controller operating as an air interface for the mobile stations.

The operation and control of a GSM network is very largely managed by computer software. Unlike the conventional PTN where control is established at the beginning and end of each call period, GSM systems provide control and management signalling throughout the communications period. The following represents a brief explanation of the protocol as an MS tries to initiate a call.

- Phase 1. The mobile (MS) requests to set up a call which should result in the allocation of a control channel.
- Phase 2. The MSC checks the identity of MS and if authenticated it issues a new cipher key. If this fails, a disconnection release is initiated.
- Phase 3. The MSC agrees the ciphering with MS and provides the necessary synchronization.
- Phase 4. This represents the actual call set-up part of the message, including the called party's number.
- Phase 5. A traffic channel is assigned if available. If not, the call is placed in a queue. If the queueing capacity is exceeded, the calling MS is advised of the blocking situation.

● Phase 6. The radio link is established after the issue of *call connect* and *call acknowledge* signals.

Hand-off or hand-over occurs when MS moves from one cell to another. BSC periodically (every 480 ms) monitors the signal strength from a BS. It then employs a complex algorithm that considers the signal level relative to all neighbouring cells to make the hand-off decision. If the decision is made, hand-off occurs at the next time frame. The new BSC will then make a similar decision to check that the correct hand-off was made.

Mercury One-to-One (Ericsson Radio Systems Inc.)

This system is based on the GSM and DCS 1800 systems for personal communications within the UK, but with the addition of frequency hopping. This feature increases the capacity of the system cells and at the same time reduces the operating and infrastructure costs. Any calls in progress may be switched around the channels of each multi-channel cell at up to 217 times per second, instead of using a single pre-assigned channel. The operation averages the signal strength of all channels within a cell to configure the cell for maximum capacity, while maintaining an acceptable minimum signal-to-noise ratio in an adaptive manner.

6.3 NETWORK MANAGEMENT

Synchronous digital hierarchy (SDH)

Normally the high-capacity trunks and local networks are not fully synchronized so that the interfaces, particularly those for high-speed operation, find this a problem. With the SDH concept which was initially devised for use with optical fibre systems, the traffic in all parts of the network is transferred in synchronized packets. SDH therefore manages the transport or transmission link between communicating stations. This permits higher data speeds and better utilization of the network capacity. For example, an SDH system operating at 155 Mbit/s can provide for 1800 simultaneous telephone calls over each optical fibre. The service also allows for the integration of data, voice, video and television traffic. SDH also has the capability of *drop-insert*; this means that a network station can add only those signals required by that station, without control overhead bits.

The SDH is defined by ITU-T (CCITT) recommendations G707, G708 and G709, with the lowest multiplex data rate of 155.52 Mbit/s being described as STM-1 (synchronous transfer module-1). The multiplex is described in general terms as STM-N where N takes on the values 3, 4, 6, 8 and 16. Thus the upper rate is $16 \times 155.52 = 2488.32$ Mbit/s. The value 155.52 was chosen because it represents the convergence of different multiples of the CCITT and Bell/AT&T standard rates.

Each SDH frame can be represented as a 9 row by 270 column matrix as indicated in Figure 6.5. The first or top left-hand corner byte, known as the

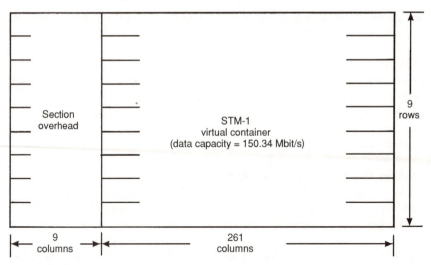

Figure 6.5 SDH STM-1 frame structure.

framing byte, provides bit rate clock synchronism and represents the start of a frame. Transmission then follows on a row-by-row basis. The 81 bytes described as section overhead, which are interleaved with the data, provide byte synchronism, system monitoring and frame delimiters.

The useful payload of each SDH frame is contained within the nine rows of 261 bytes. The overall bit rate is therefore given by:

$$270 \times 9 = 2430 \text{ bytes/frame}$$

$$8 \times 2430 = 19\,440 \text{ bits/frame}$$

At 8000 frames/s this gives $8000 \times 19\,440 = 155.52$ Mbit/s. The actual user channel capacity is given by:

$$261 \times 9 \times 8 \times 8000 = 150.336 \text{ Mbit/s} \tag{6.6}$$

SDH is thus used for the transmission of different bit rates framed in different VCs (*virtual containers*), with their control overhead bytes. The system further provides the means of worldwide unification of digital hierarchies and auxilliary channels, inserted by means of standard frame overheads.

Although initially designed for optical fibre applications, STM-1 can be handled over microwave links. Using either 32QAM or 64QAM, this yields a bandwidth between 30 and 40 Mhz.

Asynchronous transfer mode (ATM)

Conventional networks carry data in a synchronous manner and because empty slots are circulating even when the link is not needed, network capacity is wasted.

The ATM concept was developed for use in broadband metropolitan area networks (MAN) and optical fibre-based systems. It is supported by both CCITT and ANSI standards, and can also be interfaced to SONET (Synchronous Optical NETwork). ATM automatically adjusts the network capacity to meet the system needs and can handle data, voice, video and television signals. These are transferred in a sequence of fixed length data units called cells.

Common standards definitions are provided for both private and public networks so that ATM systems can be interfaced to either or both concepts. ATM is therefore a wideband, low-delay, packet-like switching and multiplexing concept that allows flexible use of the transmission bandwidth. Each data packet consists of five bytes of header field plus 48 bytes for user data. The header contains data that identifies the related cell, a logical address that identifies the routing, forward error correction (FEC) bits, plus bits for priority handling and network control. FEC applies only to the header as it is assumed that the network medium will not degrade the error rate below an acceptable level. All the cells of a virtual container follow the same path through the network and this was determined during call set-up. There is no fixed time slots in the system so that any user can access the transmission medium whenever an empty cell is available. ATM is capable of operating at bit rates of 155.52 and 622.08 Mbit/s and the cell stream is continuous without gaps. The position of the cells associated with a particular VC is random and depends upon the activity of the network. Cells produced by different streams to the ATM multiplex are stored in queues awaiting cell assignment.

Since a call is only accepted when the necessary bandwidth is available, there is a probability of queue overflow. Cell loss due to this forms the major ATM impairment but this can be minimized through the use of statistical multiplexers. Bit errors in the header which are beyond the FEC capability can lead to mis-routing. ATM is used to transport and route information over SDH facilities which in turn are used to manage the transmission system.

6.4   LOCAL AREA NETWORKS (LANs) (5)

The introduction of computer-to-computer communications completely changes the concept of a network. The communication of a computer with its peripheral devices forms the basic or primeval network, messages being passed over the data bus under the direction and control of the address and control buses. Many bus-expansion systems have been developed, each for a specific application. At a higher level, all the computer-associated elements on a particular site may be interconnected to form a *local area network* (LAN). By using the carrier services of radio and the PTTs, this concept can be expanded to cover an area as large as 50 km diameter. This gives rise to the term *metropolitan area network* or MAN. Further expansion makes use of the international radio and PTT networks to form a *wide area* (WAN) or global network. The actual description of a LAN, MAN and WAN is not easy to define as one definition tends to merge into another. At the basic level, communications is often at baseband, thus forming a *narrowband* system. However, many popular networks are *broadband* and use radio frequency multiplexing to increase the throughput of data. Networking requires the use of a *modem* or modulator/demodulator device to handle the data transfer. Different types of networks may be interconnected by using *gateways* placed at strategic points. The physical communications medium varies from twisted pair or copper coaxial cables, through radio links to optical fibres. The latter has the particular advantages of freedom from interference and electromagnetic effects and is capable of operating in very broadband networks.

Networking makes better use of expensive peripheral devices, as these can be shared between many users. The technique also increases the data rate at which information can be disseminated throughout an organization.

Network topologies

Bus or highway systems

All communicating elements of the system are connected to a common cable in the manner shown in Figure 6.6. Each node has a unique address and responds only to data that is sent to it. In network terminology, a node is defined as a connection, tap or branch point. As the cable acts as a transmission line, its two ends must be suitably loaded to prevent signal reflections, and because it carries no power, it is said to be inactive. The network is controlled by a common clock which must be positioned near to the middle of the cable. Its frequency then controls the rate of data transfers. If the network length is increased beyond some critical value, then the clock rate has to be reduced to maintain an acceptable bit error rate (BER). Each node is allowed direct access to the network, but in contention with all the other devices. Each transmitter device listens continually to the network. If a collision of data is detected, then

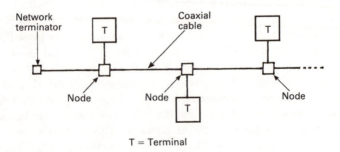

T = Terminal

Figure 6.6 Bus or highway network.

transmission ceases and the control protocol takes over. It is usually easy to extend this type of network, or add or remove a terminal without interrupting the data flow.

Ring networks

As the name implies, all the communicating devices are connected to a ring, with each device or terminal being equipped with an access node that has a unique address in the manner shown in Figure 6.7. Often no one node is responsible for network control and each has equal status. Transmission is normally unidirectional, although some bi-directional networks have been implemented. The ring usually carries power for the node interfaces and each node acts as a data regenerator, receiving the data on one side and retransmitting it to the next node in sequence. If the ring is broken, either under fault conditions or to modify the terminals, then the data flow ceases. Dual and braided rings which have two parallel signal paths have been devised to overcome this problem.

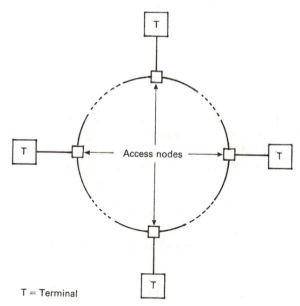

Figure 6.7 Ring network.

Star networks

Unlike the bus and ring networks, all the message switching and control is carried out at the central hub, as indicated in Figure 6.8. Since terminals can only communicate with each other via the hub, the configuration only finds favour where the data signals flow chiefly in one direction. Such an application would be the distribution of a television service.

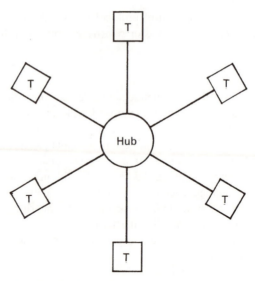

T = Terminal or node

Figure 6.8 Star network.

Protocols

Contention techniques

This allows each terminal exclusive use of a network, but in contention with all the other terminals under the control of a technique known as *carrier sense multiple access* (CSMA): carrier sense, because each terminal listens to the network to detect the absence or presence of a carrier; multiple access, because all terminals share the same transmission medium. Thus a device will not transmit its own data until it detects a gap in the transmissions. It is possible that two terminals waiting to transmit both detect the same gap and start to transmit together and cause a data collision. When this happens, both transmitters halt and *back-off* for a time before trying to retransmit. The control of this back-off period varies from system to system.

CSMA with collision avoidance (CSMA-CA)

This is based on an empty time slot system. Each node on the network is given a priority listing from a controlling node. If it has data to transmit, it does so only at its allocated time slot. If it has no data available, then this time slot is reallocated to the node with the next highest priority. Extra time slots can be allocated to those nodes that have a great deal of data to transmit.

CSMA with collision detection (CSMA-CD)

Data collisions can only occur during the short period after a transmission has started and before the signal has had time to reach all the other nodes on the network. This is the *collision window*. When a collision occurs, transmissions continue until all nodes on the network recognize the burst of noise as a collision. The back-off period varies from a random interval, to a period calculated from the node address. Thus all terminals will back-off for different periods of time.

ACK/NACK protocol (acknowledged/not acknowledged)
When the receiving station decodes a packet without error, it transmits an acknowledgement signal. If the transmitting station does not receive this acknowledgement, it decides that an error has occurred and automatically retransmits the data packet.

ALOHA (system devised for interworking of computer networks)
With the pure ALOHA protocol, terminals transmit as and when they have data ready for transmission and also continually monitor the network. If two terminals transmit together, they detect a collision of data and both back-off for a random time period before trying again. This is basically a collision detect-multiple access (CDMA) system.

Reservation TDMA
Each terminal is allocated a particular time slot of the time frame for its transmissions.

Selective spectrum ALOHA
An ALOHA protocol reserved for use with spread spectrum transmissions, when packets of data will not be affected by collisions.

Slotted ALOHA
As in pure ALOHA but each terminal transmission is restricted to allocated time slots.

SPADE (single channel per-carrier demand assigned multiple access)
A control station monitors the channel frequencies in use, then answers a request for interconnection by allocating a free channel to the two stations.

Comparison of advantages
Reservation TDMA is particularly useful when relatively long transmissions are required. Slotted ALOHA has an advantage over pure ALOHA in that once a terminal has accessed a time slot, it has sole use of this until the end of transmission. Selective spectrum ALOHA has the advantage that data collisions are not problematic but the system has to include forward error correction (FEC). An ACK/NACK system is not very useful over satellite links. Due to the overall time delay of about 250 ms, the following block may be transmitted before the lack of acknowledgement has been recognized and this will produce a data collision.

Proprietary networks

Cambridge ring

This network is constructed from two pairs of twisted pair cables and functions on the empty slot technique. Typically, four slots circulate unidirectionally around the network, being passed between repeaters placed at each node. As these are actively connected to the ring for the whole of the operational time, the necessary power is supplied over the ring. One of the nodes is allocated to a fixed monitor station which creates the empty slots at start-up, clears corrupted data packets and manages the error reporting function.

The success of this type of ring depends upon the cable characteristics. Any discrepancy in the lengths of the four wires can introduce a signal phase difference; the self-capacitance and attenuation can cause distortion, all leading to an increase in bit errors. To counter these problems, the repeaters are usually spaced intervals of less than 100 m. Provision is also made to introduce sections of optical fibre into the ring where it is necessary to traverse regions of high electrical interference. The raw data rate around the ring is 10 Mbit/s, but due to the addition of housekeeping bits, etc., the actual rate is nearer to 1 Mbit/s.

The basic data coding depends upon the voltage transitions on the cable pairs, which nominally carry a dc potential of 28 V. A logic 1 is signified by a change of state on both pairs of wires, while a logic 0 produces a change of state on one pair only. For a succession of zeros, the state changes alternate between pairs. The data is organized into *minipackets* each of 40 bits. These contain two data bytes, source and destination addresses, and response and control bits. Each circulating slot carries one minipacket. The address space for each node occupies eight bits allowing for 256 possible network stations. The all-zero pattern is reserved for the monitor and the all-ones indicates a minipacket that is broadcast to all stations. Communications around the ring are further organized into packets each containing up in 1024 data minipackets (2048 data bytes). Each packet is made up as follows: one header minipacket, one routing minipacket, up to 1024 data minipackets, plus a checksum minipacket. The checksum is a 16-bit pattern obtained from all the minipackets, computed modulo-2^{16} -1, with end-around carry.

Cambridge fast ring

In this development of the basic Cambridge ring, which also operates on the empty slot protocol, the raw data rate has been increased up 100 Mbit/s, a feature that has been achieved chiefly by improvements to the data handling at each node. Each node device is a serial–parallel–serial converter to match the serial network data requirement to the parallel needs of each terminal. Each node can support a small cluster, the devices of which are connected in a byte-wide ring fashion. The basic structure of the network still provides either for twisted copper pairs or optical fibre, but the nodes are now powered locally. The network modulation scheme also has the same characteristics in that transition occurs at each clock period. This allows synchronization to be achieved from the data stream. Each network, which has gateways or bridges to other networks, also contains a monitor station to maintain the slot structure, handle test and maintenance procedures and generally manage the network.

The size of each data packet has been increased to thirty-two bytes, a feature that helps to increase the data throughput. A packet is made up as follows: a start of packet bit always set to 1; a full/empty bit which signifies if the slot is in use or not; a monitor bit used by the monitor station to delete lost packets, and a start bit that is always set to 0. This is followed by the destination and source addresses, each of two bytes. Following the thirty-two bytes of data, each packet ends with twelve bits for CRC and four response bits, the latter being used to signify to the source, destination and monitor that the data has been received correctly or otherwise.

Ethernet system

This is a half duplex send-receive system based on a highway or bus. This is constructed from a length of 50 Ω coaxial cable which must be terminated at each end in a suitable load. The typical maximum cable length is 2.5 km, but this can be extended by interfacing other similar networks via suitable gateways. The maximum number of nodes or stations permitted on each sector is 1024. The raw data rate is 10 Mbit/s and each node on the network is driven by a separate 20 MHz clock. The Manchester code format is used to ensure that the clocks are synchronized to the data stream. The bit cell is divided into two, the second part containing the true bit value and the first its complement.

Network access control uses the *carrier sense, multiple access/collision detect* technique. All nodes listen continually to the network to detect a suitable time to transmit data. If two stations detect the same clear period, each will transmit and then detect a collision. Both will continue to transmit for a further 80 ns so that all nodes can recognize that a data collision has occurred. The transmitting nodes then back-off for a random period before trying to retransmit. If a further collision occurs both back-off for a longer period. After sixteen attempts, the node concerned logs a system failure.

The transmission frame format consists of a maximum of 1526 bytes made up as follows:

(1) A clock synchronizing preamble of alternate 1s and 0s consisting of seven bytes, followed by a similar eighth byte but ending with two 1s, the last 1 representing a start bit.

(2) Destination and source address fields each of six bytes. The first bit in each is described as a *multicast* bit. When this is set to 1 in the destination address, all terminals within a group or block must respond to the message. In the source address, this bit is always set to 0. Although only 1024 stations are permitted per network and these could be addressed by just ten bits, the forty-seven bits available could address more than 1.4×10^{14} unique nodes. This has been arranged so that stations in different networks have different

addresses and that owners of the patent rights can exert some control over the development of Ethernet. Twenty-three bits of the address field are allocated by Ethernet, leaving the remaining twenty-four bits for user allocation.

(3) The following two bytes are used to identify the data type and length.

(4) The data field is variable between the limits of forty-six and 1500 bytes.

(5) Each frame ends with four bytes of cyclical redundancy check. At the receiver, the bits following the start bit are stripped off and the CRC recalculated and compared with that transmitted, any disagreement being reported to the local microprocessor.

The Thin Ethernet or Cheapernet system operates at the same speed and in the same modes but uses the thinner 75 ohms coaxial cable. This restricts operations to a shorter network.

Fibre distributed data interface (FDDI) network

This network, which operates as a token ring, uses optical fibre as the transmission carrier. It has been designed so that it can be coupled through suitable gateways into Ethernet or other standard ring networks. The carrier wavelength is typically 1300 nm and this can easily accommodate the bit rate of 100 Mbit/s. Rings greater than 100 km circumference can be constructed and with up to 500 nodes per ring. The network consists of two separate fibres which connect to each node. This allows the network to be reconfigured under fault conditions at any node. A 4B/5B coding system is used to aid synchronization. Each 4-bit symbol is coded into five bits. Of the thirty-two bit patterns available, ten are discarded as having too few data transitions, six are used for control purposes and the remaining sixteen represent the original symbols. Expanding the data from four bits produces a baud rate of 125 Mbit/s. Although this coding is less rich in transitions than the Manchester coding which would require a bandwidth of 200 MHz for the same data rate, the slightly worsened synchronization is a good trade for the lower bandwidth. Unlike normal token rings, the FDDI ring node releases the token immediately it has transmitted its data. This utilizes the ring bandwidth and time more effectively so that many messages can be circulating simultaneously. This loses some of the error checking capability but this is recovered by making each node continually monitor the token rotation time. This therefore effectively defines a time slot for a node to transmit.

The FDDI-2 system has been designed to expand the flexibility of the concept and cater for both packet- and circuit-switched communications. This supports 64 kbit/s circuit-switched voice channels of an ISDN system. This is achieved by using a transport mechanism described as a *cycle* of 125 μs length. Of the 100 Mbit/s rate, 98.304 Mbit/s is available to share between packet and circuit switched applications. The remaining 1.696 Mbit/s is used for synchronization, header and cycle delimiting (housekeeping).

Internet/intranet

This is the term that is used to describe a global area network of information resources that are based in educational establishments, public libraries, government offices and corporate business premises. The resources are all stored in computer-controlled databases and linked via the normal telephone network. In addition to acting as information providers, the network provides users with e-mail facilities. There is basically no central control to the network and each information provider is responsible for its own data integrity.

The open system protocol (TCP/IP) that has developed to meet these needs is independent of the computer operating system and this is supervised by the National Science Foundation; this is probably the only controlling influence on the Internet.

Access to a particular database is via a menu-type search and a number of public domain software packages have been produced to facilitate this function. These *browsers* appear under such exotic titles as GOPHER (go for), ARCHIE, VERONICA and WAIS (wide area information services). The essential part of the protocol and search tools is the World Wide Web (WWW), often described as the glue that holds the resources together. The WWW is searched via a hypertext transport protocol (HTTP) which uses uniform resource locators (URL) as an address string. Web pages are ASCII text files that include special command codes and these files form a hypertext document. The ability to access a wide range of information resources is offset to some extent by generally large files and a rather slow telephone system, tending to make data transfers rather slow. Probably the weak point about the Internet is its lack of data security. It has been shown on many occasions that it is possible to hack into a database and illegally change the information on display.

By comparison, an intranet is a private corporate network that uses WWW technology to link local networks into a large corporate system. Thus personnel at one site have acceess to a wider global database. This extends the Internet concept on to ISDN systems for higher data rates and improved security. A guard system, often described as a *firewall*, is installed to prevent illegal access via the Internet so that sensitive data can be transmitted with confidence.

TCP/IP protocol

This represents the *protocol* by which the Internet manages communications between two computers on the system and each link is established via a three-way hand-shake concept. Computer A sends a synchronous packet to computer B. The packet contains a request for a particular port and also the return address for computer A. Computer B then sends a synchronous and acknowledge (Syn/Ack) packet in return to acknowledge computer A. The link is now half open. Computer A then sends an acknowledge packet (Ack) to computer B and when this is received the link is established. After computer B sends its Syn/Ack packet, it stores computer A's Syn packet in a buffer and waits for a predetermined period for a reply from computer A.

TCP takes the information to be transmitted by the application and passes it to the IP for transmission. IP is responsible for packet transmission from one computer to the other and TCP ensures that the messages are transmitted successfully (including error control).

The protocol has an inbuilt feature to prevent a fast data generator from swamping a slow line or receiver. Any loss of data is countered by adjusting the packet size according to the line conditions. Thus when faced with a slow link TCP/IP simply reduces the packet size to reduce the data throughout. This helps to ensure that data packets are delivered error free, in sequence and without duplication.

Each data packet consists of six fields: the destination address, request for specific port number, the message field, an end of message block, the checksum field and finally the source address.

Each device on the Internet has a unique global address that consists of four bytes referred to as a dotted quad (CO. B1. A0. 02 hex). This should not be confused with the e-mail address which is simply a nickname for a user at a computer (e.g. geoff@GLE.co.uk). There are four groups of addresses, described as Class A, B, C or D. Class D is reserved for multicast (broadcast) purposes such as the multicast backbone (MBONE) system that is capable of transmitting digital television. Class A applies to the very large networks, such as the USA military network MILNET. The class of address is defined in the first two bits of the address packet as follows: Class A – 00, Class B – 01, Class C – 11 and Class D – 10. (Note the Gray code relationship.)

For a Class C address, only the last byte is available to identify the particular computer on the network, i.e. one of 256 devices only.

For a Class B address, both bytes 3 and 4 are available to identify one of 65 536 devices on the network.

In Class C systems, the last six bits of the first byte and all the bits of the second and third bytes are available to identify the network on which the computer identified in the fourth byte can be found.

The system employs a device name server (DNS) which is basically a look-up table designed to convert between IP addresses and names, and vice versa. In addition, a router is used to link networks together. A router reads the address at the head of each packet, interrogates the DNS and uses this to re-route the packet to its next destination. The router also recalculates the checksum value and requests a repeat transmission in the event of an error.

Open system interconnect (OSI)

This concept has been developed to enable dissimilar and normally incompatible devices to exchange data by means of an agreed set of protocols. It is based on a defined system of interconnections and interactions between the seven

functional layers or levels of the model shown in Figure 6.9. The layers below
level 3 are related to system hardware and electrical interfaces, while the layers
above are technology independent and related mainly to software. Interaction
between terminals occurs at the same level, i.e. level 3 to level 3.

Level 1. This layer relates to the movement of data bits from the computer
terminal to the network, by defining the mechanical, electrical and functional
characteristics. For example, the RS232E interface.

Level 2. The data link control layer defines the way in which a terminal can
gain access to the network. The protocol arranges data bits into suitable and
acceptable-sized blocks, organizes error control and, in general, provides
reliable and accurate data transfers.

Level 3. The network layer is primarily responsible for setting up and
maintaining connections and moving data. In addition, it must add the
necessary destination and routing information to provide for the links across
other interconnected networks. For example, circuit or packet switching.

Level 4. The transport layer is basically responsible for network security
from end to end and the quality of service. It also defines how the various
nodes are to be addressed and the way in which connections can be made or
broken.

Level 5. This layer effectively operates as an interface between the transport
and application layers. It also allows control software to be written in a
network-independent manner. Together, levels 3, 4 and 5 are often described as
the network *subnet* level.

Level 6. This layer handles the interchange of data and information by
translating the data formats, codes and syntax applicable to the session and
application layers.

Level 7. This layer defines the services available to the user, such as file
transfer, access and management (FTAM), distributed databases, worldwide
messaging and electronic mail, together with the provision of a user-friendly
interface so that the system is transparent to the user.

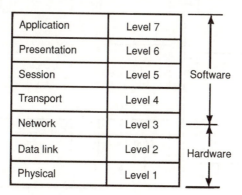

Figure 6.9 Open system interconnect seven-layer model.

IEEE-1394 or 'FireWire' bus system

The name FireWire is the intellectual property of Apple Computers Inc. originally established the basis for this easy-to-use, very fast and low-cost network concept as long ago as 1988. Since that time, the system has become an established IEEE standard that is supported by a worldwide Trade Association of more than ninety manufacturers and constructors. 1394, as FireWire is now generally known, is a cross between a network and a bus extension system which allows any device to be simply coupled into a communications network. The system was originally intended for the distribution of digital audio through the Apple computer, but over the years, it has expanded into many other areas and in the very near future it will be found to be the main mover of digital signals in the domestic communications and entertainment business. Such flexibility will hasten the convergence between the home PC and the television receiver. A very readable history of the development of this bus is included in the references (6).

1394 interconnections
Figure 6.10 gives an indication of the wide range of devices that can be linked together via 1394. Any devices fitted with the necessary interface can be coupled together through one of a number of ports via a simple cable without any consideration for the logical location on the network. The new services currently available include home video editing, photo-CD handling, image enhancement and at a later date, video and teleconferencing. Such is the adaptability that FireWire is also likely to find industrial applications. 1394 devices are fitted with

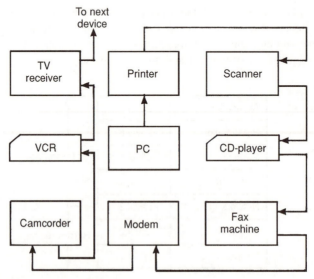

Figure 6.10 IEEE 1394 bus configuration.

one or three port interfaces which can be coupled together through a special cable unit. Any new device can be added to the network by simply plugging into a spare port anywhere on the network. The devices may be coupled in a daisy-chain format or in clusters, with the only restrictions being that there should be no more than sixteen hops between any two nodes and that no loops should be formed. The network is usually described in terms of a root, tree and branch or parent and child configuration with the root or parent being the nearest to the controlling device. The serial network is currently available for bit rates of 100, 200 and 400 Mbit/s, but development work will soon extend this to 800 Mbit/s or even 1.6 Gbit/s and beyond. As such, FireWire will be faster than the currently available optical fibre network, FibreNet which runs at 1 Gbit/s. Furthermore, since 1394 is currently compatible with MPEG-2 video data streams, it will also be compatible with the ATM (asynchronous transfer mode) system used for telecommunications which has a maximum data rate of 622 Mbit/s. FireWire is therefore seen as a possible method for delivering digital television signals directly to the home via a cable network.

1394 Cabling system and transmission techniques
The construction of the special screened cabling is shown in Figure 6.11. This consists of three individually shielded cable pairs, two screened and twisted signal pairs, plus two power lines, one designated as Ground (Vg) and the other Positive (Vp). The power line pair are capable of carrying up to 1.5 A at 8–40 V dc. For special applications, a cable without the power pair can be used where the device so coupled has its own power supply. The typical maximum cable length is 4.5 m but this might well be extended for special applications to about 25 m in the near future.

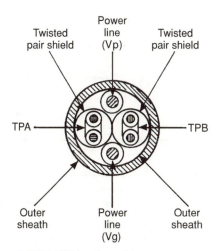

Figure 6.11 Section through IEEE 1394 interface cable.

Perhaps the most important feature of this network is its simplicity, at least as far as the user is concerned. Any new device may be plugged into a spare port without switching the power off and the system then automatically reconfigures and reprograms itself for the new situation. It is a genuine plug and play system.

The high data rates are achieved by using differential non-return-to-zero (NRZ) signalling on each shielded twisted pair (STP) which are biased with respect to earth at 2 volts dc maximum. At these high data rates it is important that the system maintains an accurate clock signal and this is achieved as follows. The data signal is carried on twisted pair TPA with a strobe signal on TPB. It is arranged so that the strobe signal changes state on every bit period that the data signal does not. In this way, either the data or the strobe signals change state at every bit period. As shown in Figure 6.12, at the transmitter the signal data stream and the clock signal are combined using Exclusive Or logic to create the strobe signal. At the receiver, the strobe and data signals can be combined Ex-Or to regenerate an accurate clock signal. The bus data streams are organized into two time division multiplex (TDM) formats, a one-way, low bit rate asynchronous stream used for control purposes and the high bit rate isochronous payload data for service distribution. An asynchronous steam is one in which the data is transmitted in blocks together with start and stop signals. Since the data rate is constant, the local clock can be regenerated from the data stream. By comparison, the data for an isochronous network is synchronized to the same master clock for the whole system. In this case, the current controlling node is acting as the cycle master. Both formats use variable length packets. Perhaps an important advantage of isochronous data transfer lies in the fact that this method needs less first-in-first-out (FIFO) memory before and after transmission across the 1394 bus. This significantly reduces the die size of the interface IC and hence ultimately reduces chip costs. This memory would need to be larger for non-isochronous data transfers due to their inherent wide range of changes of data rate and transport delay.

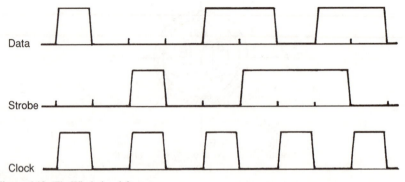

Figure 6.12 'FireWire' signal format.

FireWire protocols

The communicating protocols may be explained by their relationship to the ISO seven-layer model (International Standards Organization) that was developed for open systems interconnect (OSI). The general arrangement for FireWire (Figure 6.13) shows how the two lower levels of the ISO model are retained (Layer 1 – Physical layer, Layer 2 – Link layer) with the system control functions concentrated into Layers 3 through to 7.

The physical layer (PHY) has four main functions: to translate the symbols used by the link layer control (LLC) into the appropriate cable signals and vice versa, to define the mechanical and electrical connections for the bus, to provide the arbitration to ensure that only one node or device can transmit data at a given time and to ensure that all devices have fair and equitable access to the bus.

The link layer control (LLC) manages the data packet assembly and disassembly for both the asynchronous control data and the isochronous payload data. The former one-way packets which are transmitted to the transaction layer contain delimiting signals and their reception must be acknowledged (Ack). The isochronous data stream is transferred direct to the applications receiver.

In addition, LLC also handles address and error control, data framing and generates the packet cycle timing and synchronizing signals.

The resources manager layer acts as the transaction layer as regards control of the asynchronous data stream. A write operation sends data from the source to the receiver, while a read operation functions in the reverse direction. A lock operation is also possible in which data is sent on a round trip through the processing at both ends of the chain and can act as a test and control function.

The bus management layer is quite complex and operates in both the hardware and software of the individual node interface. It controls the operation of the physical, link and transaction layers. If there is a PC on the network this will most

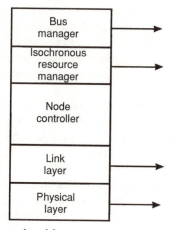

Figure 6.13 'FireWire' bus control model.

likely act as the bus manager which runs its own special applications program, but other arrangements are possible. A fully managed system includes either a PC or other similar smart device. It supports all modes of data transfer for up to sixty-four channels and is capable of power management and bus optimization. The PC can also create data rate maps and network topology diagrams.

A non-managed bus has a cycle master but is only capable of asynchronous data transfers for control functions. Such an application might be the direct data transfer between, say, a scanner and the hard disk or between the hard disk and printer without the direct involvement of a computer processor.

A limited bus management system falls some way between these two extremes. It has a limited power management ability, but can handle both asynchronous and isochronous data transfer for between eight and sixty-four channels.

A network includes up to sixty-three nodes or devices each with a 6-bit ID number. Multiple networks may be interconnected via bridges with up to 1023 separate buses each with a 10-bit ID. This combination allows for up to $63 \times 1023 = 64\,449$ (16 bits) nodes on the total system. Device addresses are 64 bits wide; 16 bits wide specify the nodes and networks and the remaining 48 bits are for memory addressing. Thus the network can uniquely identify $2^{48} = 2.8 \times 10^{14}$ bytes or 280 Tbytes of total memory.

Initialization process

At the end of this sequence, the root device will have been chosen and the node selected for this position remains in control as long as it is connected to the bus. Initialization occurs at power-up and whenever a node is added or removed through the generation of a reset signal. At the start of this operation, all the information about the network topology that is held in the node registers is cleared. The physical layer of each node first checks the connection status of its ports. Each port signals a 1 if it is connected, otherwise the device is in the disconnected mode. If there is more than one port set to 1, the device can be a branch. As this process continues, a tree structure begins to form so that a root node can be selected and all the remaining physical connections referred to it. Generally the last device selected in this process is designated as the root. However, if it is required that one particular PC should be designated as the root, then the process time can be forcibly extended to ensure that this result is achieved. After the tree has been formed, each node is allocated an ID for asynchronous traffic.

During the initialization process, the various management roles are allocated, most importantly that of the cycle master which is usually the root and has highest priority to bus access. The cycle master provides and maintains the clock signal for the isochronous data transfers. Some of the management roles may be allocated to devices other than the root. The isochronous resource manager allocates time slots to those devices with isochronous data to transmit.

Whenever hot plugging generates a reset signal, the isochronous resource and bus manager functions remain with the original devices (assuming that such a device was not removed).

The next stage of initialization involves allocating channels 0–63 and time slots to those devices that need to communicate. Only channels that are free can be allocated and this information is held in the channel available registers.

Following a reset action, the reallocation of time slots may leave one node short of its previous allotted capacity. Such a node then periodically makes requests for an increased allocation until this is granted through other nodes relinquishing their time slots. When configuration is completed, the nodes arbitrate for access to the bus. In addition, asynchronous and isochronous data also compete for access and this is all controlled via the cycle master which transmits a timing signal known as the cycle start, typically once every 125 μs.

System timing and arbitration

The system timing is based on a phase locked loop crystal oscillator in each node interface running at 24.576 MHz (98.304 MHz clocks may also be found). The clock in the interface of the node chosen as the cycle master is the one that is actually in use. The 24.576 MHz frequency is divided down to create 1 Hz (1 second) and 8 kHz timing control signals and it is from these that TDM multiplexing operates. The cycle status and control bits are contained within bits 20–24 of the third, fourth and fifth quadlets. The basic cycle duration lasts for 125 μs and repeats at the rate of 8000 per second. Of the total cycle period at least 20 percent is allocated to asynchronous control data, with the remaining maximum 80 percent for the isochronous payload data.

Nodes arbitrate for bus access on every cycle, but only one is allowed to transmit at a time. The nodes with reserved isochronous channels arbitrate first and when the node receives a cycle start signal it sends a request for access to the root. The root accepts the first request that it receives and this is always from the arbitrating node nearest to it. This is followed by a small isochronous gap after which the arbitration begins again and the next nearest node is granted access. This process continues until all the isochronous nodes that have data to transmit have been granted access. A longer gap called the sub-action gap then follows so that asynchronous arbitration can start. Both gaps are proportional to twice the number of connecting hops in the network. The sub-action gaps are needed to allow time for the acknowledge (Ack) signals. In order to allow fair access, each node is allowed to transmit only once during the asynchronous part of each cycle. The cycle time is ended with a longer idle period gap called the arbitration reset gap, after which the process restarts.

Data packet structures

All the serial data is first organized into quadlets each four bytes long (32 bits). Each packet must contain at least two bytes as a header and two bytes of data. The quadlets are time aligned for accuracy so that they may be loaded into the FIFO registers which are 32 bits wide and 64 quadlets deep. So that the quadlets consist of integer multiples of bytes, meaningless bits may be stuffed as padding. Cyclic redundancy checks (CRC) are included at the end of both header and

Table 6.2

Field name	Bit size	Comments
Data length	16	Indicates number of bytes in current packet
TAG	2	Data format*
Channel number	6	Indicates channel number with which data is associated
Transaction code	4	Code for current isochronous packet
Synchronism code	4	Carries the transaction layes specific sync code
Header CRC	32	All isochronous packets
Data block payload	–	All data block packets
Data block CRC	32	All data block packets

*The TAG field is used to define the data format. For example, 00 represents data formatted for normal 1394 operation and 01 is used to indicate that HyperLynx for MPEG-2 data is in use (4). The other two codes are currently not allocated.

payload data blocks. These basic elements are common to both asynchronous and isochronous packets but the headers for the two differ in length and content. Asynchronous packets must include at least four quadlets to specify destination ID, source ID and various control functions such as packet priority. By comparison, isochronous packet headers include the channel number plus control information and these can be as short as two quadlets because the destination and source addresses are inherent in the channel number. The isochronous packet structure is summarized in Table 6.2.

Operation of a typical interface (7 & 8)

The physical layer

This interface consists of little more than two VLSI, ASIC chips that act as the physical layer (PHY) and link layer controller (LLC). Typical of these are the Texas Instruments TSB11CO1 (PHY) and TSB12CO1 (LLC) which are provided in low-power CMOS technology, but with the inputs designed to allow for hot plugging. The former (PHY) is a 3-port device that includes the logic to perform the arbitration and bus initialization functions. The LLC transmits and receives correctly formatted isochronous data in real time. It carries reconfigurable FIFO memories for the data as well as the necessary configuration registers needed to operate the device. The essential part of the architecture of this chip is shown in Figure 6.14.

The crystal-controlled phase locked loop (PLL) clock provides three important frequencies via digital dividers: 98.304 MHz, 49.152 MHz and 24.576 MHz, with the 49.152 MHz signal being maintained to an accuracy of ±100 ppm (±4.9152 kHz) to control the outbound encoded strobe and data signals. This frequency is also needed at the LLC to resynchronize the received data.

Figure 6.14 shows the basic functions of the PHY layer with three identical ports. Data bits to be transmitted are received from the LLC over the two-pair

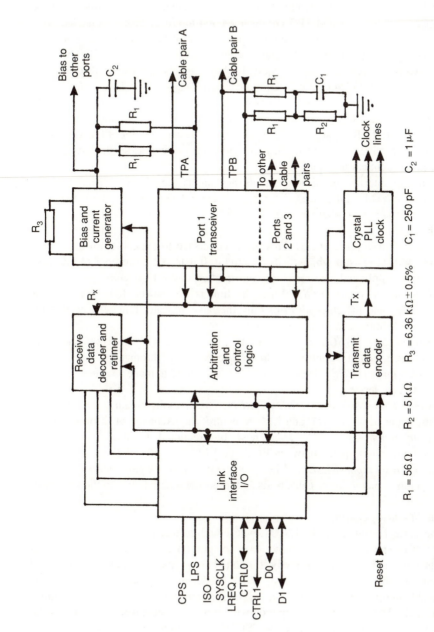

Figure 6.14 Architecture of physical layer control (Courtesy of Texas Instruments).

$R_1 = 56\,\Omega$ $R_2 = 5\,k\Omega$ $R_3 = 6.36\,k\Omega \pm 0.5\%$

$C_1 = 250\,pF$ $C_2 = 1\,\mu F$

cables TPA and TPB in synchronism with the 49.152 MHz clock. These bits are encoded and transmitted as outbound encoded data on TPA with the encoded strobe on TPB at 98.304 Mbit/s. During packet reception the transmitters of the transceivers for TPA and TPB are disabled and the receiver ports enabled. This is achieved by the use of a simple flip-flop control bit. Both the data and the strobe signals are differentially encoded and swing the signal equally about the 1.86 volts nominal bias level. Typically these signals are restricted to a swing range between 172 and 265 mV (about 220 mV ± 40 mV). These levels were chosen to allow interoperability between chip sets using either 3 or 5 V CMOS technology. Resistors R_1 are designed to achieve an optimum loading on the line drives of 112 Ω. R_2C_1 acts as a filter to ground the centre point of the TPB lines. R_3 sets the driver stage output currents and controls the bias level. Ports 2 and 3 act in an identical manner.

The link interface of this chip directs the data between the receive and transmit modes under the influence of a range of control signals, of which the most important are shown below.

Cable power status (CPS). This pin is connected to the cable power through the 400 kΩ resistor which feeds the circuit. It detects the presence of the cable power supply and also feeds this information to the LLC chip.

Link power status (LPS). When the link is not powered the SYSCLK is disabled and the chip performs only the basic repeater functions needed for network initialization and operation.

System clock (SYSCLK). This terminal provides the 49.152 MHz clock signal to which the data, control and link requests are synchronized.

Link request (LREQ). This signal from LLC is used to make a request for some particular service.

Control input/outputs (CTRL0/CTRL1). These bi-directional terminals communicate between PHY and LLC to control the exchange of information.

Data input/outputs (D0/D1). These bi-directional terminals provide the communicating paths between PHY and LLC.

Logic reset input (RESET). When this line is forced low, this causes a bus reset operation on the active cable ports and resets the internal logic to the start state.

The link layer control

The Texas Instruments TBS12CO1, whose architecture is shown in Figure 6.15, is a high-speed LLC that allows easy integration into an I/O sub-system. It transmits and receives correctly formatted 1394 packets and generates and evaluates the 32-bit CRC used to check header and payload data blocks. It is capable of operating as a cycle master and supports reception on two isochronous channels. The chip integrates directly with either physical layer chips such as the TSB11CO1 described above or the TSB21LV03 which is used for processing an MPEG-2 data stream. This LLC supports 100, 200 and 400 Mbit/s bit rates and its 32-bit bus is compatible with most other available 32-bit proprietary buses. The FIFO memories are software adjustable for performance optimization and

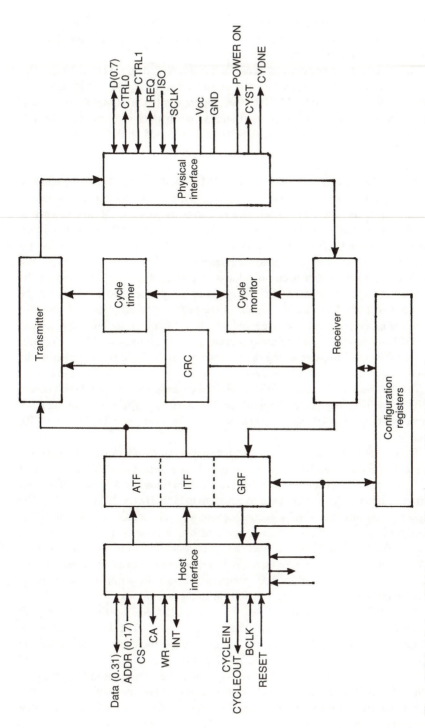

Figure 6.15 Architecture of link layer controller (Courtesy of Texas Instruments).

allow for variable length asynchronous transfer FIFO (ATF), isochronous transfer FIFO (ITF) and general receive FIFO (GRF). The physical interface I/O signals have been described above.

The transmitter retrieves data from either the ATF or the ITF and generates correctly formatted serial packets for transmission through the PHY interface. When data is present at the ATF interface, the transmitter arbitrates for bus access and then sends this data packet. Similarly, when data is present at the ITF interface the arbitration results in data being transmitted on the next isochronous cycle. When this chip is acting as cycle master, the transmitter automatically sends the cycle start packet.

The receiver accepts the data from the PHY interface and checks the address. If the data is addressed to this node and if the CRC is correct, the header is confirmed in the GRF. For block and isochronous packets, the rest of each is checked on a quadlet-by-quadlet basis through to the end of the packet and then confirmed in the GRF. The error code for the packet is thus contained in a status quadlet which is sent as acknowledgement for that particular packet. For isochronous packets that need no acknowledgement, the error code signals the transaction layer if the data CRC is correct or not. If the header is in error, the memory is flushed and the remainder of the packet ignored. When a cycle start message is received, it is detected and sent to the cycle timer but not placed in the GRF. At the end of an isochronous cycle, if the cycle mark enable (CyMrkEn) bit in the control register is set, the receiver inserts a cycle mark packet in the GRF to indicate the end of the cycle.

The transmit and receive FIFOs, both asynchronous and isochronous, are software adjustable to cater for individual applications. The maximum memory capacity is 509 quadlets and this can be shared between the ATF, ITF and GRF sections.

The cycle timer is used by all nodes that support isochronous data transfers and consists of a 32-bit register. The lower twelve bits form a modulo-3072 counter that increments once every 24.576 MHz clock periods (or 40.69 ns). The next thirteen higher-order bits are used to count up to 8000 Hz (or 125 μs) cycles. The higher seven bits then form a seconds count. A cycle source (CySrc) bit in the configuration register can be set to indicate which node is acting as the cycle master. The CYCLEIN input causes the cycle count to start to increment and the CYCLEOUT signal indicates that it is time to send the cycle start packet. The cycle monitor is only used by those nodes that support isochronous data transfers and monitors the chip activity and schedules the operations.

The host interface consists of a 32-bit parallel data bus together with an 8-bit address bus and BCLK represents the bus clock which is asynchronous to the system clock (SCLK). The CA and CS inputs denote the cycle acknowledge and cycle start signals respectively. The WR input is a read/write signal that is used in conjunction with CS. When both of these are driven high, a read from the chip is indicated. (Low inputs produce a write operation.) For speed of operation, this chip is interrupt driven and when the INT line is driven low this indicates that some particular service function needs to be performed.

Live insertion or plug and play

With many of today's computer-or microcomputer-controlled environments, it is unsafe to power down the system to modify its configuration without complete loss of service. Unless specific circuit design steps are taken, the removal or insertion of any module with power on could be destructive. In general, most ICs are protected at the inputs and outputs either by specially included shunt diodes or the parasitic diodes inherent in the fabrication process that is represented by the base to emitter or gate to source junctions of the input/output transistors.

When a circuit board is plugged into a slot, the contacts are made in a random manner due to the mechanical tolerances and the position of the operator. Furthermore, insertion or extraction under power is likely to induce arcing and electrostatic discharges. If either the ground or Vcc lines make contact simultaneously with a signal line, then the protective diodes can create a destructive current along the signal path or generate bus contention. To avoid this, the connectors are modified so that both Vcc and ground lines (leading ground and Vcc contacts) make contact before or break after any signal bus lines. In some large systems, each module can be equipped with a switch that is operated in conjunction with the circuit board clamp to ensure that the module being inserted or removed has its power lines disconnected from the circuit. In addition, the circuit may be modified to ensure that the bus lines are pre-charged to about half the logic voltages in order to minimize such disturbances.

For 1394 applications, the signal lines are fairly well protected by virtue of the bus driver transceivers at the inputs. In general, it is only necessary to include a series forward biased diode and resettable polymeric fuse in the positive power line to each interface to provide over-voltage and short-circuit protection. These devices normally have a very low series resistance which can be triggered into a high resistance state by a sudden rise in current. Once the overload condition has passed, the device reverts to its normal low-resistance state.

Low-power radio links (5)

There are a number of small segments of the VHF/UHF part of the frequency spectrum that have been allocated to the operation of unlicensed low-power radio communications systems that employ equipment that has been type-approved by a suitable test house. All these units must meet the EU standards provided by the EMC Directive. These are used for such applications as alarms, radio microphones, access control, industrial, medical and biological services and general telemetry and telecommand services that come under the heading of SCADA (supervisory control and data aquisition). Telemetry is the science of automatically collecting or recording data from distant measurements by radio signals. Similarly telecommand systems are used for the management of distant systems by remote control via a radio network. The data collection and control functions are carried out by transmitter-receiver modem units that may be powered from the electrical supply mains if available, batteries or even by solar panels or wind generators.

The radio units may operate in pairs at either end of a simple network or may even be arranged in a cluster that is scattered over an area which can be coupled into a LAN. In fact, the low-power radio concept has many useful advantages where network extensions are needed. The addition of wire-less radio modems can be used where normal wiring extensions are not even possible, such as across rivers, or through hostile environments and inhospitable regions. By linking these devices through serial interfaces, they can also be added very easily to personal computers.

The UK standards have been harmonized with those of Europe (EU) and these are included in the ETS-300 group of standards.

The section of the spectrum from 417.9 to 418.1 MHz which is covered by the MPT1340 standard in the UK is allocated to the use of industrial telemetry, telecommand and in-building security. A further section of 433.72–434.12 MHz is reserved for in-vehicle equipment and radio keys. Both are covered in the UK by the MPT1340 standards. The actual choice of frequencies employed within these bands is left to the discretion of the manufacturer, but the EIRP is restricted to 0.25 mW for 417.9–418.1 MHz and 10 mW for the 433.72–434.12 MHz segment. Transmission frequencies must, however, be maintained within $< \pm 50$ Hz.

The major part of this service is carried within the band 458.5–458.95 MHz and this is channelized so that specific frequency segments can be allocated to each of the units employed. To avoid overspill, each channel carrier is allocated within the above spectrum. This service is covered by the UK MPT1329 standard. There is provision for either 32×12.5 kHz or 15×25 kHz channels. Within this range there are three taboo channels; those centred on 458.825, 458.8375 and 458.900 MHz (covered by MPT1361) are allocated to fixed, mobile or transportable alarms or vehicle paging systems. The maximum frequency error for each carrier must not exceed ± 2 kHz for 25 kHz channels, ± 1.5 kHz for 12.5 kHz channels with hand-held devices and ± 1 kHz for 12.5 kHz for base station units.

The maximum carrier power is restricted to 500 mW but the EIRP is unspecified as directional aerials may be employed. The maximum path length for transmissions is also unspecified and may extend to 18–20 km under favourable propagation conditions. The adjacent channel inteference rejection ratio should be better than 90 dB for 25 kHz and better than 80 dB for 12.5 kHz channels respectively.

In the main, these wire-less radio modems operate in the half duplex mode although a few devices can employ full duplex working. The typical upper bit rate is 9.6 kbit/s using either FSK or PSK modulation. Units are now available that operate in the 2.4 GHz band using direct sequence spread spectrum (DSSS) techniques with bit rates as high as 2 Mbit/s with an EIRP of 100 mW. These are capable of working in either half or full duplex modes.

The transmitter/receiver units usually share a common synthesized PLL oscillator circuit for both modes using a mixing process to obtain the transmit and receive frequencies. To achieve the necessary adjacent channel rejection ratio, the receivers operate with a double conversion process typically employing IFs of 45 MHz and 465 kHz and the antenna is isolated between receive and transmit by using PIN switching diodes. Because these modems are intended for LAN working, each device has an address that can be programmed along with the selected channel numbers at installation time. Usually this is achieved by setting a series of DIP switches.

These modems can often either function in a transparent mode when the received data is automatically transmitted without delay, or operate in a store-and-forward mode when data is only transmitted upon interrogation from a base station.

6.5 FACSIMILE SYSTEMS (11, 12)

This service, originally developed to transmit photographic and documentary information over standard telephone cables, is now used over radio and satellite links. The many varied services available range from the transmission of weather maps and geological mappings from offshore oil platforms to the transmission of complete pages of a newspaper for remote printing. During the past forty years or so, a number of international standards have been formulated under the auspices of the International Telegraph and Telephone Consultative Committee (CCITT, but now ITU-T) (4). Table 6.3 lists the main characteristics and differences of the four groups of machines. Group 1 terminals are obsolete, with the major part of the service being carried by Group 3 machines which are capable of interworking with any Group 2 machines that remain in service. Because the cost of Group 3 machines has fallen dramatically in the past few years, the adoption of the very much faster and ISDN-compatible Group 4 machines have been very slow. The ultra-high-speed Group 4 terminals, which are capable of reproducing an A4-sized document in less than about five seconds, are available to work over digital networks (ISDN). While Group 4 machines are currently in operation, this CCITT standard still provides significant flexibility to allow for future developments (10).

The information in the document to be transmitted usually lies in dark markings on a light background. This can be analysed by segmenting the document into elemental areas small enough to resolve the finest detail needed. The document for transmission is scanned sequentially by a light beam, in a series of very narrow strips. The magnitude of the reflected light from each *picture element* (pel or pixel) is then used to generate an electrical signal. In earlier machines, this was accomplished by a photocell/electron multiplier tube, but this has now been superseded by an array of semiconductor devices, either photodiodes or charge-coupled image sensors. As fax service terminals are

Table 6.3 Standard FAX groups

	Group 1	Group 2	Group 3	Group 4
Generic title	Low speed	Medium speed	High speed	Ultra high speed
Transmission speed (A4 document)	6 min.	3 min.	1 min.	2–4 sec.
Modulation	FM	AM/PM-VSB	DPSK	Digital (64 kb/sec)
Carrier frequency	1700 Hz ± 400 Hz	2100 Hz	1800 Hz	
White level	1500 Hz	Max. Amp.		
Resolution				
Vertical	3.85 l/mm	3.85 l/mm	3.85 l/mm	7.7 l/mm
Horizontal		5.3 l/mm	7.7 l/mm	15 l/mm
		5.3 pel/mm	8 pel/mm	16 pel/mm
Image signals	Analogue Audio tones		Digital	Digital
Handshake signals			300 b/sec FSK (CCITT V21)	ISDN-compatible (CCITT V29/33)
Redundancy reduction	None	None recommended	READ	Modified READ

transceivers, this signal can now be used to construct an accurate facsimile of the original document, either locally or at a distance.

Table 6.3 also shows the several methods of sub-carrier modulation in use. These are necessary in order to accommodate the signal within the 300–3400 Hz bandwidth of the telephone channel and to allow ac coupling to be used. Both Group 3 and Group 4 terminals tend to be constructed around very large-scale integrated (VLSI) application-specific integrated circuits (ASICs) with embedded microprocessors so that they should be capable of being programmed to cooperate with each other. Unlike the Group 3 terminals which were designed to work over the standard telephone lines, the Groups 4 units were originally designed to operate over the wider bandwidth, leased lines service. However, a high-speed modem is available so that Group 4 terminals can operate over the voice channels of the *public switched telephone network* (PSTN). The increase in transmission rate achieved by the Group 4 terminals is due to an improved data compression algorithm and the availability of the higher data rates on CCITT V29 and V33 systems. These provide for basic data rates of 9.6 or 14.4 kbit/s respectively.

Because the Group 4 machines are ISDN compatible, this design has been extended to provide a PC fax service by the addition of a *fax card* (circuit) to the standard bus system of a personal computer. This concept not only allows for computer-to-computer communications, but also for services that include e-mail (electronic mail), store-and-forward or store-and-retrieval messaging and even optical character recognition (OCR). The system is compatible with the International Organization for Standardization's (ISO) seven-layer *open systems interconnect* (OSI) standard.

To ensure that the receiving terminal reproduces or *writes* the same corresponding pel that the transmitter has produced, a *phasing signal* or *white burst* is transmitted, always at the beginning of each page and often at the beginning of each line. It is also important that the writing and reading rates are synchronized. To this end, all timing signals are derived by division from a crystal-controlled oscillator.

It is not always necessary for the facsimile to be the same size as the original. Certain terminals have the facility to enlarge or reduce. However, if distortion in the document is to be avoided, the page aspect ratio should remain constant. The compatibility of aspect ratios is reflected in the factor or index of cooperation (FOC or IOC), which is based on the ratio of scan line length to vertical scanning density (width).

$$\text{FOC} = \text{Effective scan length} \times \text{vertical scan density} \qquad (6.7)$$

{Effective scan length = actual length + 5% to accommodate the phasing signal}

The IOC ratio was originally defined for drum-scanned systems, hence,

$$\text{IOC} = \text{FOC}/\pi \qquad (6.8)$$

Provided that the machines working together have the same ratio, the document shape will be retained even though its actual size may be different.

The standards for resolution, which define the finest detail that can be reproduced, are also shown in Table 6.3, from which it can be seen that the resolution of Group 2 terminals is about 20 pels/mm^2 (3.85 × 5.3). As the pel size is reduced, the vertical scan density increases to produce a higher value of IOC (FOC). A Group 3 machine at minimum resolution produces slightly more than 30 pels/mm^2, so that an A4 page of 210 mm × 297 mm would be resolved into about 1.9 million pixels. If all these have to be transmitted, the coding system used must be very efficient to minimize the transmission time and/or the bandwidth required.

The study of a typical document will show that it contains considerable redundant information which need not be transmitted. Redundancy reduction can work in two dimensions:

(a)   Many sections of each scan line are continuously white and so hold no information to print. Omitting these produces a horizontal economy known as one-dimensional coding

(b)   On average, one scan line bears a close resemblance to each of its neighbours. This fact can be exploited by only transmitting information on how the current line differs from the previous one, thus producing a vertical economy.

The use of both horizontal and vertical coding (two-dimensional) is often referred to as *relative element address designate* (READ). Its use can reduce the transmission time by a factor of about ten.

Originally, frequency modulation of the sub-carrier was used because of the noise reduction properties. However, the need to increase speed, and hence bandwidth, caused the adoption of a modified form of AM for Group 2 terminals.

A normal double sideband AM signal can be filtered to remove a part of one sideband, leaving a *vestige* of it to provide a vestigial sideband (VSB) signal. This reduces the AM bandwidth and still leaves a signal that can be processed in a normal AM system. The use of VSB saves about 30 percent on bandwidth to support a corresponding increase in transmission speed.

A further saving of bandwidth can be effected by the introduction of a phase modulation component. Assume that white represents a peak positive voltage and black zero volts. A series of transitions between black and white thus represent a particular frequency. If alternate white peaks are now inverted to produce a negative voltage (see alternate mark inversion – AMI), the fundamental frequency will be halved. When this signal is used to modulate the sub-carrier, the negative peaks produce a carrier phase reversal, producing a *white* signal without any change of frequency or amplitude. This form of modulation, known as AM/PM-VSB, has a reduced bandwidth such that the transmission speed can be doubled.

An alternative time-saving method causes the system to scan more rapidly when no black/white transitions are detected, i.e. in a white area. This *skipping white spaces* requires a feedback network in the scanner mechanism and is used successfully in the *Pagefax* system which is used to transmit whole pages of newsprint. In transmission, Pagefax occupies twelve telephony channels (48 kHz). The document service, *Docfax*, as transmitted over the INMARSAT satellite links, occupies a normal telephony channel, and is transmitted FM/SCPC for both analogue and digital terminals.

The facsimile terminal

Figure 6.16 shows the basic organization of a facsimile terminal. The document to be transmitted is illuminated in a series of very narrow strips, each of which is scanned from side to side sequentially. The light reflected from the document surface is focused on to a photo-transducer to generate the electrical signal. This is then modulated on to the sub-carrier and filtered to ensure that the signal lies within the spectrum of a telephone channel. A line amplifier is used to achieve the correct signal level and impedance match for the transmission medium.

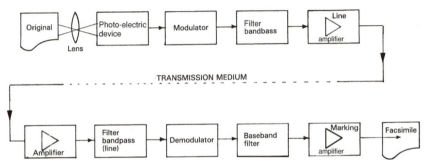

Figure 6.16 Basic fax system.

The recording (*writing*) path is practically complementary. The received signal is first amplified and then filtered to remove any line noise. Demodulation restores the baseband signal, which then passes through a *marking amplifier* to produce the facsimile document. Figure 6.17 gives an indication of how the facilities can be extended using microprocessor control. Semiconductor technology provides the basis of better resolution and faster transmission. An array of 5000 photodiodes can be used to produce a horizontal resolution of 16 pels/mm. The use of semiconductor stores and companding can increase transmission speeds up to 9.6 kbit/s. As an example, a Group 3 machine scans each pixel in about 2 µs, whereas the line signal can only be changed every 140 µs. The scanned signal is therefore stored for signal processing, coding and companding before transmission. Microprocessor control also introduces the possibility of encrypting the data stream in the digital fax terminal for security and privacy. The proven technology of *auto dialling and auto answering*, often found in local area networks (LANs), can also be applied.

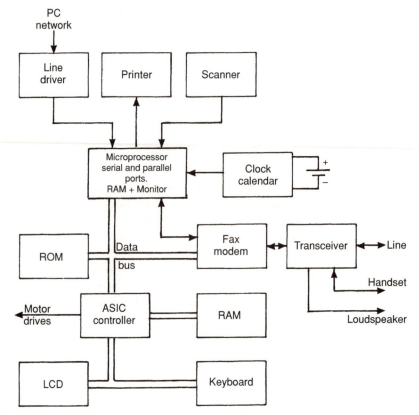

Figure 6.17 Integrated fax terminal.

Recording (writing) methods

Of the many ways of creating the facsimile from the received signal, only the electrolytic, electrostatic and thermal methods have been popular in the most generally used fax systems.

The electrolytic method uses a special paper, impregnated to render it conductive. Current flows from a scanning stylus, through the paper to a fixed back contact. This causes the paper to discolour in proportion to the magnitude of the current density.

Variants of the electrostatic method which is common in office photocopiers may also be used in fax machines. Styli attached to a flexible belt are driven across standard paper to leave a charged pattern on it. The styli voltage varies between + 600 V for black and −450 V for white. The charged paper passes over a magnetic roller bristling with magnetized iron particles and holding a black toner powder in the interstices of the bristles. The powder is attracted to the positively charged areas and repelled by the negative regions. The powder thus forms a facsimile of the original document. Passing the paper over a heated roller causes the toner to bond permanently to the paper.

The thermal method employs a special thermosensitive paper, which discolours when its temperature exceeds about 50°C. Full black is produced at about 110°C. The paper is passed over an array of minute heating resistors which are made using thin-film technology. This provides a heating element with very little thermal inertia. The elements can thus respond rapidly to the changing signal. More than 2000 elements may be mounted in an array, giving a horizontal resolution of 8 pels/mm, a figure which for Group 4 machines can double to 16 pels/mm. One end of each element is connected to a critical voltage, while the signal voltage is supplied sequentially to the other end. The paper temperature is made to vary between 60°C and 110°C, to produce a copy with varying tonal shades if required in the original. Unless stored in a controlled temperature environment, these copies are likely to degrade with time.

Copying on to standard paper is also carried out using thermal transfer technology. A special meltable ink film is carried on a base film and this can be transferred to the copy paper by the heated thermal heads. Colour printing is also possible using this technique, by transferring coloured inks (yellow, cyan or magenta), successively overlaid, to provide a range of colours.

Two further methods may be found in weather fax recording systems. A photographic unit which uses photosensitive paper, stored either in cassettes or as separate sheets, for automatic feeding, provides the facsimile. The exposure light may be a laser or a high-brightness lamp source. The unit contains facilities to complete the photographic development, and this normally follows on automatically after exposure. The method has the advantage of a high grade of reproduction with a grey scale of up to sixteen levels. However, as the process is essentially a wet one, the equipment is not very suitable for portable operation and the cost of the unit and the paper is high.

A dry silver paper process that can produce results almost as good and with a grey scale of about eight levels is also available. The recording process uses a laser to make the exposure. The paper cost is the highest of all methods and can provide some storage problems. If stored at too high a temperature, the facsimile quality becomes degraded.

Handshaking and synchronizing

Handshaking is the term used to describe the sequence of signalling used between communicating terminals prior to the transmission of fax signals. This procedure is carried out to check mutual compatibility and status, to issue control commands and, in some cases, to monitor line conditions. It is a way of identifying each machine's capability, whereupon one will select a particular mode, which in turn will be acknowledged by the other. Following the handshake procedure, the originating station transmits a start signal, the nature of which depends upon the group. A white burst may be transmitted for thirty seconds, or one of two audio tones. This will be followed by a phasing burst and then the document signal proper. Stop may be signified either by loss of carrier for five seconds, or another tone burst.

After the transmission of the document, further handshaking confirms satisfactory reception and indicates whether more pages are to be sent or not.

Applications involving satellite links can present some problems. Handshaking inherently implies a duplex link for communications, and the propagation delay needs to be taken into consideration. In addition, interference and signal fading can introduce a signal corruption.

Weather chart recorder

Many of these machines (9) are receive-only fax terminal developed to the World Meteorological Organization (WMO) standards for the reception of weather charts from the various satellite sources. The terminals, which are microprocessor controlled, are capable of either local or remote operation and can process either AM or FM signals automatically. They can thus work with signals from either polar-orbiting or geostationary weather satellites. Printout is usually produced on electrosensitive paper and the units are made suitable for either fixed, ship-borne or other forms of mobile operations. The organization of the signal controlling section is displayed in Figure 6.18.

Image signal input

The satellite image data is fed to the signal programmable interface adapter (PIA). This circuit also contains a multiplexer which switches the buffer, either to the data source or to a test reference, the switching action depending upon the status of the front panel control (local or remote). The digital control bus which is managed by the microprocessor (MPU) program directs these inputs via the control input/output (I/O) PIA to the multiplexer.

Carrier detection

The buffered signal is applied to the carrier detect and dropout delay circuit. This also contains a tone detector which supplies a *flag* indicating when a carrier is present. The MPU is thus signalled via the signal PIA to start whenever a polar orbiter carrier is present and stop when the carrier drops out for more than three seconds. The dropout delay circuit is included to avoid a noisy carrier prematurely stopping the system.

Image data AGC

The level of the data signal is maintained by an AGC loop, under the control of the MPU via the real-time controller.

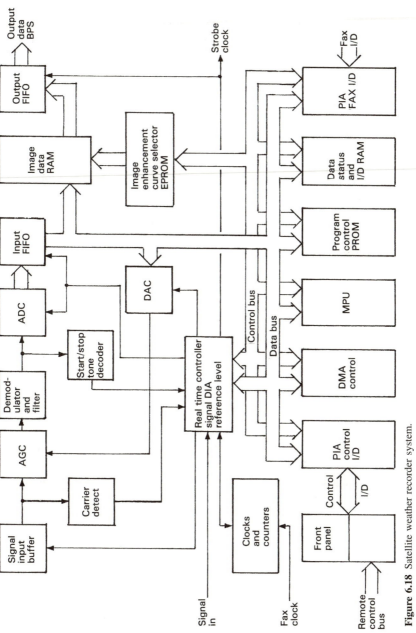

Figure 6.18 Satellite weather recorder system.

Demodulator circuit

A full-wave demodulator and sub-carrier filter is used to recover the baseband signal. This is applied to the 8-bit analogue-to-digital converter (ADC) and the tone decoder stages. The data signal is now converted into the 8-bit parallel form and temporarily stored in the input first-in-first-out (FIFO) buffer. At the appropriate time, the MPU reads the input FIFO and transfers its contents to the various nodes over the data bus.

Tone decoder

In the geostationary satellite mode, the start/stop signals are carried as tones of 300 or 450 Hz respectively. This stage generates a flag to signal the MPU via the signal PIA, to start or stop its run routine.

AGC operation

When the MPU is flagged to start and the data is present on the 8-bit data bus, the AGC routine is entered. The MPU compares the data with a reference based on peak white, and calculates a gain control value. This is sent to a digital-to-analogue converter (DAC) as an 8-bit word, where it is converted and filtered to provide an AGC voltage, to adjust the loop gain. The MPU repeats this routine until it decides that the signal level is within a predetermined tolerance.

Sync detection

When the AGC has been set, the MPU enters its sync detection routine, which differs according to the signal format selected. The MPU therefore examines the front panel control settings to decide which sync software routine to run. It then looks for the appropriate sync words in the data stream. Once detected, the clocks and counters are reset via the control bus and the signal PIA, to provide the correct frame and line sync timings.

Clocks and counters

The main fax clock provides an input at the very precise frequency of 3.949440 MHz. This is divided down to generate the sampling and data strobing references. The division ratios, which are dependent upon the image data format selected produce frequencies of either 7.2 or 14.4 kHz, for polar orbiter or geostationary reception respectively. These frequencies are further divided down to produce either 2 or 4 Hz for the line blanking interval. The output data to the recorder is fixed at 4114 words per line, of which a 185-word period represents the blanking period. Thus each printed line requires 3929 data words which are strobed out and counted.

Image enhancement

Although the recorder carries manual controls for the adjustment of *brightness* and *contrast* of the printout, it also has a facility for image *enhancement*. This may also be controlled manually or automatically by the MPU. An electrically programmable read-only memory (EPROM) carries a selection of enhancement curves, and when one is selected a copy is mapped into the image data random access memory (RAM). Under the direct memory access controller (DMAC), the data in the input FIFO is transferred over the data bus to address the image data RAM, where each address corresponds to a point on the enhancement curve. This point, once addressed, is dumped as data into the output FIFO, from where it is strobed as enhanced output data to the fax printer.

Control input/output

Control of the MPU unit and the fax recorder is undertaken via the control I/O PIA and handled by the MPU to give the required response. The MPU can be programmed manually from the front panel, or remotely via an 8-bit parallel bus through the control I/O PIA.

Fax input/output

The fax I/O bus is used to carry handshake and status signals between the recorder section and the control unit.

REFERENCES

(1) Bhargava, Haccoun, Matyas and Nuspl (1981) *Digital Communications by Satellite (Modulation, Multiple Access and Coding)*. New York: John Wiley and Son Inc.
(2) European Space Agency. *ECS Data Book esa BR-08*.
(3) European Space Agency. *ECS Data Book esa BR-08 Appendix*.
(4) Davies, C. Texas Instruments UK Ltd, Private communication to author.
(5) Chiplin, S. and Fretter, M. Pascall Electronics Ltd, Ryde, I.O.W., UK. Private communication to author.
(6) Wickelgren, I.J. (1997) Facts about FireWire. 'Spectrum' *IEEE Journal*, April, 1997 pp. 19–25.
(7) Texas Instruments (1997) IEEE 1394 Circuits, Product Information.

(8)   Texas Instruments, IEEE 1394-1995 Link-Layer Controller for MPEG-2 Transport. *TSB12LV41* (MPEG2Lynx).

(9)   Knowles, K.A., Muirhead Data Communications Ltd, UK. Private communications to author.

(10) McConnel, K.R., Bodson, D. and Schaphorst R. (1989) *FAX: Digital Facsimile, Technology and Applications*. London: Artech House.

(11) Mazda F. (1993) *Telecommunication Engineer's Reference Book*. Oxford: Butterworth-Heinemann.

(12) Lewis, G.E. (1997) *Communications Technology Handbook*. Oxford: Butterworth-Heinemann.

Chapter 7

Satellite weather, environmental, mobile and navigation services

7.1 WEATHER SYSTEMS

The satellite weather services were set up under the auspices of the World Meteorological Organization (WMO) to provide a permanent World Weather Watch (WWW) and to carry out experiments within the Global Atmospheric Research Programme (GARP). The total system at any one time involves the services of six geostationary satellites, plus at least four polar orbiters.

Of the geostationary satellites, two are operated by the USA and are known as Geostationary Operational Environment Satellites (GOES); one, the Geostationary Meteorological Satellite (GMS), is operated by Japan; one is operated by the Russian Federation and is referred to as Geostationary Operational Meteorological Satellite (GOMS); one is operated by the Indian Satellite Research Organisation (ISRO) and known as INSAT; while that operated by the European Space Agency (ESA), Eumetsat, belongs to the Meteosat series. These satellites are supported by about 9000 earth stations, 7000 ships and 850 balloons from more than 150 countries. Unlike the other satellites, GOES-H also monitors the earth's magnetic field, and the intensity of the solar winds and the radiation belts around the earth. It also acts as a relay link in the 406 MHz band, for the international search and rescue service, COSPAS-SARSAT.

The geostationary satellites are spaced about 70° longitude apart, in order to provide a wide coverage up to about 75° latitude. The actual orbital positions are:

> GOES-F at 135°W (Pacific Ocean Region W) (POR)
> GOES-H at 75°W (Atlantic Ocean Region) (AOR)
> METEOSAT at 0° (Greenwich Meridian)
> GOMS at 70°E
> INSAT at 74°E (Indian Ocean Region) (IOR)
> GMS at 140°E (Pacific Ocean Region E) (POR)

with at least one in-orbit spare satellite.

The view from these satellites takes in a full earth disc that covers about one-quarter of the surface; however, near to the horizon the view may become distorted, but this can be compensated for by computer enhancement.

The polar-orbiting satellites provided by the USA are of the TIROS and NIMBUS series (1) and are operated by the National Oceanographic and Atmospheric Administration (NOAA). The satellites provided by the Russian Federation are of the Meteor series. All these have a period of about 100 minutes, at an altitude of between 700 and 1500 km (2). Due to the earth's rotation, each orbit crosses the equator about 25° longitude further west than the previous orbit. The on-board instruments see the earth surface as a series of strips, which are scanned from side to side. A particular location is thus viewed at least twice a day, once during a north-to-south pass and again, about twelve hours later, during a south-to-north pass. Because of the width of each scan, there is an overlap of tracks, so that some areas are viewed on successive orbits. The two systems together provide a complete worldwide coverage to detect weather patterns as they develop.

A radiometer that measures the magnitude of earth radiation (heat, light, etc.) is carried on each satellite; sensors convert this data into electrical signals for transmission. To provide the most useful images for meteorological purposes, the radiation waveband is restricted by the use of filters. The Meteosat data that is transmitted (3) covers the following bands or channels:

    0.4–1.1 μm – visible range (VIS)
    5.7–7.1 μm – water absorption range (WV)
    10.5–12.5 μm – infrared range (IR)

to provide three distinct images.

Visual range (VIS). These images show only the reflected light from the earth and so are only available for the daylit hemisphere. In the reproduced image, space appears black and snow and clouds white. Other areas are shown as varying shades of grey. (See Figure 7.1.)

Water vapour (WV). These images do not provide an earth surface view but only represent the upper atmosphere. White areas represent low temperatures, which can be equated with high humidity. The darker areas represent a lower level of atmospheric humidity. (See Figure 7.1.)

Infrared (IR). Infrared radiation is proportional to temperature, so these images are available during both daylight and darkness. Since space and high clouds are cold, these regions are depicted as white. Hot deserts appear very dark. The grey scale is thus temperature dependent. (See Figure 7.1.)

Each geostationary meteorological satellite spins on its axis at 100 rpm, and its radiometer scans the earth in the east-to-west direction. After each revolution, the on-board sensors are deflected in small steps in the south-to-north direction. This dual action causes the earth to be scanned in a series of lines, a full image being generated at half-hourly intervals. Each image data is gathered during 1/20 of each revolution, which represents a one-line sampling period of the earth radiation. Each sample contains 2560, 32-bit words, each of which contains visual, infrared and water vapour data. The corresponding bit rate can be calculated as follows:

Figure 7.1 Earth's disc seen from Meteosat (15 January 1993; Courtesy of *Earth Observation Quarterly*, ESA, March 1996). (Top) Visible channel. (Left) Infrared channel. (Right) Water vapour.

Time for 1 revolution	$= 1/100 \times 60\,\mathrm{s}$	$= 600\,\mathrm{ms}$	
Radiometer sample period	$= 600 \times 1/20$	$= 30\,\mathrm{ms}$	
Total number of bits per sample	$= 2560 \times 32$	$= 81\,920$ bits	
Bit rate	$= 81\,920/0.030$	$= 2.730\,666\,\mathrm{Mbit/s}$	(7.1)

The raw data for each line of the image is stored in memory and then transmitted in somewhat less than 570 ms at 166.7 Kbit/s, using digital split phase modulation (SP-L). This is a version of the Manchester code, in which a transition occurs at each bit cell centre. Effectively, $1 = 10$ and $0 = 01$. On Meteosat, the carrier frequency is 1686.833 MHz, linear polarized at an EIRP of 19 dBW per transponder. If the line store fails, provision is made to bypass the 'stretched mode' and transmit the raw data in a 'burst mode' at the same rate that it was gathered (2.73 Mbit/s).

To provide a global service, the data is initially processed at centres in Melbourne, Moscow or Washington, the final reports being produced either in Washington (US) or Bracknell (UK).

The data for each image is gathered in twenty-five minutes and a further five minutes are allowed to reset the vertical scanning mechanism, thus providing a new image every thirty minutes. The maximum earth resolution is either 2.5 or 5 km depending upon the image mode. After the raw data has been received and stored at the earth station meteorological centre, it is processed before being retransmitted, through the satellite, in both analogue and digital form for dissemination to the various users. Processing is necessary to remove the defects in the radiometer, sensors and filter characteristics, to correct any inaccuracies in synchronism and to ensure registration of the three views. Processing also allows other derived images to be transmitted, such as cloud motion vectors and cloud top heights. Apart from earth imaging, the geostationary satellites provide two further services to meteorology: the dissemination of processed raw data to other areas of the world, and data collection via data collection platforms (DCPs). These are small automatic or semiautomatic units that monitor environmental data and use the satellite to transmit this back to a central ground station. These platforms may be carried in ships or aircraft, or be fixed on land sites. Some are self-timed to transmit their data by an internal clock while others may transmit their data upon interrogation from a central station. An 'alert' DCP automatically transmits a message if one of its measuring parameters exceeds a preset level. This gives early warning of risks of serious disturbances. DCPs are interrogated over one of two channels and transmit within the frequency range 402–402.2 MHz.

The DCPs are supported by a system of three geostationary satellites designed by NASA to act as data relays. Because these can *see* the polar orbiters for longer periods of time than an earth station, they increase the system coverage with fewer ground installations. The tracking and data relay satellites (TDRS), as these are known, provide a service to LAND-SAT, the NASA space shuttle, C-band satellites and a number of LEOs. The system operates on several carrier frequencies, using the S band for data rates up to 250 kbit/s and the Ku band for higher data rates. The down-link to the earth station is by Ku band (13.5–15.2 GHz) using a spread spectrum technique that provides a multiplex for up to thirty spacecraft signal channels simultaneously. In addition, the ARGOS system is used to locate, collect and disseminate marine environmental data from fixed or mobile DCPs. The geostationary satellite stations fall into two classes: primary data user stations (PDUS) which receive the processed data in digital form for high-resolution images, and secondary data user stations (SDUS) which receive the data in analogue form to the WEFAX standard (4). Down-link frequencies for both Meteosat PDUSs and SDUSs are either 1691 or 1694.5 MHz, linear polarized. In general, the two channels lie in the range 1690–1697 MHz.

The PDU stations, on the whole, are much the more complex of the two. SDU stations provide images that are easily displayed on CRTs or fax machines, using a facility known as automatic picture transmission (APT). This is also used by the polar orbiters, the image data being continuously transmitted. With the latter satellites, reception is continuous while it is more than about 5° above the horizon. Typically, such data can then be received over a circular area of about 2500 km radius from the antenna.

Normally, the polar-orbiting satellites work in pairs separated by 90° longitude, so that each earth point is scanned every six hours. The TIROS-N series of satellites carry advanced very high-resolution radiometers (AVHRR) whose outputs are focused on to five sensors to gather data covering the following channels:

0.58–0.68 μm
0.725–1.1 μm
3.58–3.93 μm
10.3–11.3 μm
11.5–12.5 μm

The data is digitized by an on-board computer, partly to linearize each line scan to compensate for the curvature of the earth and partly because the data will be received by fairly simple ground stations, without processing capability. After processing, the data from two channels is selected and synchronizing signals that will identify the image edges are added. This composite signal is then converted back into analogue form and used to amplitude-modulate a 2.4 KHz sub-carrier. This DSB AM sub-carrier, in turn, is used to frequency-modulate a final RF carrier that is typically in the range 137.15–137.62 MHz. The transmitter power output is approximately 39 dBm (5 W) and the transmission is right-hand circular (RHC) polarized.

The APT facility is accomplished by continuous transmission at 120 lines per minute, to give an earth resolution of 4 km. The APT video format, before D/A conversion, is shown in Figure 7.2, the receiver locking on to the required channel after identifying the appropriate sync pulse sequence. Sync for channel A is seven cycles of 1040 Hz square wave, while sync B is seven pulses of 832 pps, as explained in Figure 7.2.

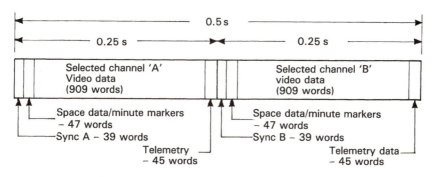

Note: 1) Equivalent data rate 41.6 kbyte/s
2) 10 bits per word
3) APT frame of 128 lines
4) Any two of the five AVHRR channels may be selected for transmission
5) Sync A is 7 cycles of 1040 Hz square wave
6) Sync B is 7 pulses of an 832 pps pulse train
7) Telemetry data carries calibration information

Figure 7.2 APT video line format in digital form.

Later TIROS-N satellites also include a high-resolution picture transmission (HRPT) facility. This is a digital service that provides for an earth resolution of 1.1 km. The outputs of all five AVHRR data channels are time-multiplexed (commutated) for transmission by split-phase (SP-L) modulation at a bit rate of 665.4 kbit/s on a carrier of 1698 or 1707 MHz. RHC polarization is again used, at a level of 39 dBm.

Primary data user stations (PDUS)

These stations consist essentially of receiver, digital processor and image handling sections, and usually operate from antennas of 4 m or more in diameter. This then usually involves a fairly long run of coaxial cable, between the head-end electronics and the main receiver. The usual trade-off between antenna size/gain and system noise temperature is possible. The initial specification quoted in the literature (5) calls for an antenna of 4.5 m diameter with a gain of 33 dB at 1.7 GHz and a G/T ratio of 10.5 dB/K. This would allow the use of RF transistors with a noise temperature of about 200 K. Technical developments now allow the use of an antenna of less than 2 m diameter, which when combined with a low-noise head amplifier/down-converter stage and a personal computer (PC), as exemplified by the Feedback WSR 524/528/538 systems, means that a very effective weather station can be assembled for quite a modest cost.

The receiver block diagram of Figure 7.3 owes its origins to a design developed for the European Space Agency (ESA) by the University of Dundee (6). In this double conversion superhet receiver, both the local oscillators work on the low side of the signal frequency. This avoids frequency inversion following the mixer stages. The first local oscillator uses a cavity-tuned microwave transistor circuit, phase-locked to the 30th harmonic of a reference, which comprises two separate crystals – one for the reception of each channel frequency. The two frequencies, 1553.9 and 1557.4 MHz, produce a first IF of 137.1 MHz from the two data dissemination channels. The value of 137.1 MHz was chosen because it falls in the VHF weather satellite band and thus provides some protection from IF break through due to terrestrial services. The front-end design is also suitable to feed L band WEFAX data into an existing 137 MHz band receiver. The RF bandpass filters (BPF) are designed to give good rejection of the image channel frequencies on 1416.8 and 1420.3 MHz. The isolator not only helps to minimize the first local oscillator radiation by the antenna, but also acts as a buffer between the two RF amplifiers and the mixer, to improve circuit stability. The adoption of a stage of first IF amplification on the head-end unit provides a convenient way of driving the main receiver, via a long coaxial cable feed.

The second local oscillator uses a 63.2 MHz crystal, the oscillator output being doubled to 126.4 MHz to produce a second IF of 10.7 MHz. This value, which is internationally recognized as a standard IF, ensures little interference from IF

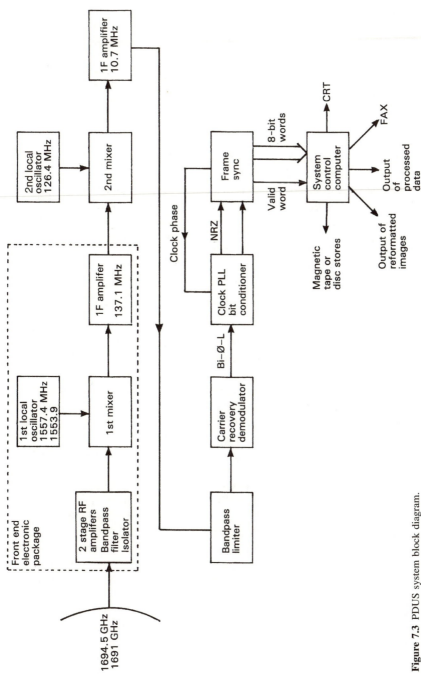

Figure 7.3 PDUS system block diagram.

breakthrough and gives good rejection at the second mixer image channel. The frequency here is calculated from the optimum intermediate frequency formula:

$$f_{(IF1)} = \sqrt{(f_{(Sig)} \times f_{(IF2)})} \tag{7.2}$$

where $f_{(IF1)}$ is the first IF, $f_{(Sig)}$ is the signal frequency and $f_{(IF2)}$ is the optimum second IF.

The digital PCM data is transmitted as PSK modulation, using a split-phase or bi-phase code format (a version of the Manchester code) at a bit rate of 166.67 Kbit/sec; 8-bit bytes or words are organized into frames of 364 bytes, which are in turn organized into subframes of four or eight frames, depending on the transmission format (5).

The first stage of demodulation uses a carrier recovery phase lock loop (PLL), which locks on to the residual carrier component in the received signal, now centred at 10.7 MHz. Phase deviations are converted into bipolar voltage swings at the loop detector output. This is in bi-phase format, where a transition at each bit cell centre is used to define the binary value as follows:

1 = transition from 1 to 0   and

0 = transition from 0 to 1,   both occurring at the bit cell centres

If two or more similar bits occur in sequence, then extra transitions are introduced at the trailing edges of the appropriate bit cells. These transitions, combined with the fact that the bi-phase signal does not contain a spectral component at the clock rate, complicates the decoding process. However, ICs are available from most chip set manufacturers that can encode and decode these signals using the non-return-to-zero (NRZ) code as a basis. Basically, the decoding process which yields the original information in PCM form is one of filtering, squaring and dividing. If the bi-phase bit stream is passed through an LPF with a cut-off at the bit rate B_r and then squared, the signal will contain a strong component at $2B_r$. This can then be filtered from the unwanted products using a narrowband PLL. The clock rate is then generated by one bi-stable. A second bi-stable is used to produce a 90° phase shifted clock, this being used to clock the serial NRZ data into the frame synchronizer circuit. Here the data is run into a 32-bit shift register which is used to search for sync words and then divided up into 8-bit words. The presence of a particular 24-bit sequence indicates the start of a 364-byte frame. The presence of this sequence, plus an 8-bit identity (ID) code, signifies the start of a sub-frame. The output from the sync circuit can then be passed to a system control computer.

The first function of the control is to *decommutate* the signal into the separate components representing the transmissions from each of the radiometer channels (VIS, WV or IR). The data can then be reformatted and sent to such display devices as CRTs or fax. For archive purposes, the data is stored on magnetic tape or disc. Since computer processing is involved, various forms of derived information may be generated, such as image enhancement using false colours or computer enlargements of sections of the image. In addition, information from other sources such as weather radar can be merged. Further derivations then include the retransmission of cloud motion vectors, cloud analysis, sea surface temperatures, and even animated images.

Secondary data user stations (SDUS)

These rather simpler ground stations conveniently divide into three sections: the antenna and head-end electronics, the main receiver and the data storage/display sections. The double superhet concept shown in Figure 7.4 is typical for the system.

The output from the spacecraft is 19 dBW EIRP (worst case 18 dBW) per transponder. The average free space attenuation will be in the order of 165 dB, so that the PFD at the antenna will be about $-146\,dBW/m^2$. Antennas smaller than 2 m in diameter can give good results, and since these have a beamwidth of about 5–8°, no servo-controlled steering systems will be needed.

The head-end electronics consists of low-noise amplifiers and first converter stages, a G/T ratio of 2.5 dB/K being typical. The RF section is tuned to a centre frequency of 1693 MHz with a bandwidth of 4–6 MHz. A crystal-controlled oscillator chain producing 1556 MHz yields a first IF of 137 MHz. The WEFAX system also uses APT (the frame format is shown in Figure 7.5), so that the main receiver section can be used with polar-orbiter signals. Any image channel interference is likely to arise from terrestrial line-of-sight communications systems. For antenna elevation angles of about 5°, a rejection ratio of 80 dB will provide adequate protection from a transmitter 25 km away. This ratio can be relaxed somewhat for higher elevation angles. At angles of about 30°, 60 dB will give a similar protection (4).

The main receiver RF/IF stages can follow typical VHF/FM design, the RF stages tuning over a range 136–138 MHz and with a second IF bandwidth of 30 kHz. A wider bandwidth will only increase the noise level and impose a higher specification on the head end.

The second mixer stage will usually include a voltage-controlled and tuned oscillator, which in the interests of frequency stability will be included in an AFC loop.

The received signal is frequency-modulated, and a standard FM demodulator with a threshold of 12 dB will give satisfactory results. However, a threshold improvement of 2–4 dB can be useful under adverse conditions, providing a margin for non-optimum performance or slight antenna misalignment.

The demodulated signal is a 2.4 kHz sub-carrier with DSB AM. Therefore, if the index or factor of cooperation is correct, the buffered signal can be used to drive a fax machine direct. After further decoding, the signal can be displayed on the CRT of a computer monitor or standard TV receiver.

The demodulated signal is also suitable for recording on magnetic tape. However, if an audio recorder is to be used, it is important that the record and

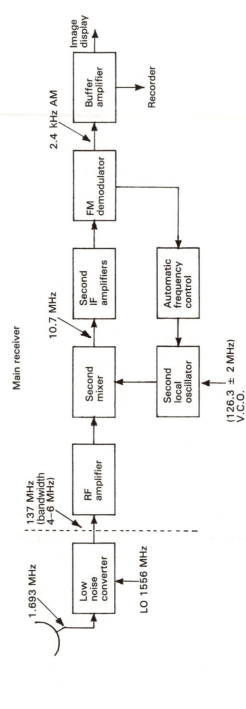

Figure 7.4 SDUS receiver block diagram.

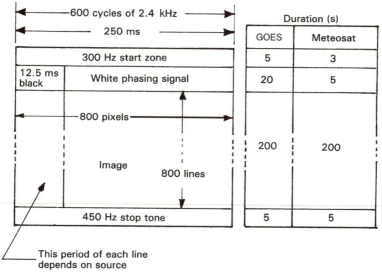

Figure 7.5 WEFAX frame format (APT).

replay tape speeds are within fairly close range agreement. It is recommended that tape-synchronous playback machines are used. The frequency of the supply driving the motor is recorded on an additional tape track and this signal is recovered on playback to synchronize the motor.

A practical SDUS

The complexity of SDU stations can vary considerably, from kit-form receiver/ decoders, suitable for use as a peripheral device for a home computer, costing around £150 (7), to the very complex systems used by national meteorological centres. These are typically available either as a straight VHF system or with an add-on L band front end. The basic arrangement of this system is indicated by Figure 7.6. The main VHF receiver processes either a VHF signal from a polar-orbiting satellite, or a VHF first IF signal from the L band converter, via a switching circuit. The antennas consist of a parabolic dish for the 1693 MHz feed, or a helical or quadrifilar antenna for VHF. Both systems utilize a low-noise RF pre-amplifier mounted in the antenna. The L band first converter is separately mounted at the prime focus point on the antenna.

The APT receiver produces an IF typically of 10.7 MHz, which after amplification and filtering is demodulated using a phase locked loop (PLL). The 2.4 kHz sub-carrier is then decoded. The receiver is equipped with enough digital memory to hold at least three frames of data to provide a dynamic display. After conversion to analogue format, the data is available in either digital or analogue form. The raster timing generator is needed because the main display medium

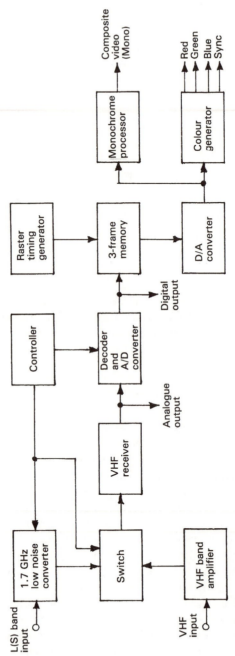

Figure 7.6 A typical secondary data user's receiver.

may be either a standard monochrome or colour TV receiver. As the image data is basically a stepped variation of grey scale, the colour generator analyses each grey level and converts it into a suitable *false colour*; for instance, by displaying hot areas in red, the image details will be highlighted.

TV studio applications

Television broadcasters have become prime users of the satellite weather services, often using a combination of PDU and SDU systems plus weather information feeds from the national weather centres. In general, the digital data provided for the PDUS terminals is the more superior because of the fewer processing stages. This fact also makes this data the more up-to-date version. Since the land and sea features of each weather map that is transmitted fall on identical pixels each time, it is possible for any TV station to store its own basic maps. The locally processed images can then be overlaid on to these in a preferred *in-house* style. The weather data provided by the national weather centre will in general also include information collected from weather radar systems. The local television weather forecaster then has historic, current and predictive data on which to base a weather forecast, for either local or national broadcasting.

Typical of these systems is the CloudFile 2000 kit produced by Feedback Instruments Ltd, of Crowborough, UK (8) which is shown in Figure 7.7. This employs a 3 m diameter dish with a compound GaAs FET low-noise amplifier (LNA) mounted at the prime focus point. This feeds a low-noise down-converter (LNC) stage via a short length of 50 Ω coaxial cable which is mounted at the back of the dish. The amplifier covers the frequency range of 1680–1700 MHz, has a gain of 30 dB, a noise temperature of 100k and together with the antenna has a G/T ratio better than 12 dB/k. The input frequencies to the converter stage of 1691 and 1694.5 MHz produce an output first IF of 137.5 MHz. Both the LNA and LNC are designed around microstrip technology for low-noise and high-stability operation. Again 50 Ω coaxial cable is used to feed the main receiver and the dc feed and control signals to the head end are carried over a separate multiway cable. If the receiver feeder is longer than about 50 m then an additional low noise line amplifier may be needed.

Although the receiver is intended for operation from the geostationary satellites, because the first IF is at 137.5 MHz it can be driven from a polar-orbiter signal. The second IF runs at 10.7 MHz and the synchronous demodulator includes a matched filter that converts the output directly to NRZ format. This signal is then input to the frame synchronizer stage so that 8-bit words can be extracted from the serial data stream. The output from the receiver to the display monitor is via an interface with an embedded control microprocessor. As can be seen from Figure 7.7, the CloudFile system is intended to run in conjunction with a Pentium-based IBM-compatible PC, with 32 Mbit of RAM, 1 Gbyte hard disk drive, a 3.5″ floppy disk drive, keyboard and SVGA monitor.

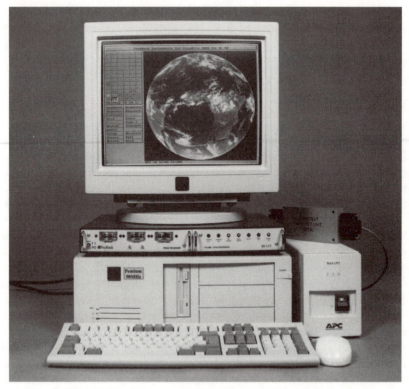

Figure 7.7 CloudFile 2000 Weathersat system (Courtesy of Feedback Instruments, UK).

The output images are displayed under software control as either visible, infrared or water vapour files using false colours, image enhancement and overlaid latitude and longitude grid lines. Features include density slicing in order to obtain measures of air and earth temperatures. The images may be zoomed or panned and the contrast range can be stretched. The memory can store 800 images so that the output can be displayed as sequences of events covering forty hours of a changing weather pattern. By sampling the image data frames, it is possible to produce a weather sequence covering a very much longer period.

7.2 ENVIRONMENTAL SATELLITE SERVICES (9)

Because the data is supplied from low earth polar orbiters equipped with scanning systems, these have much in common with the meteorological services. Typically the orbits are at an altitude of between 750 and 850 km with an inclination of about 98.5° and a period of 100 minutes. The sensors are chosen to collect data acquired by scanning the earth's surface over a range of about 450–950 nm. This represents the visible colours through into the infrared region. High-resolution images can be generated from the received data to an accuracy of less than 20 m. The scanning systems commonly use the synthethic aperture radar (SAR) concept that was originally developed for radio astronomy. For this application, the outputs from a number of small antennas were coupled in parallel. The antennas were so positioned that the total received signals were phase coherent. In one example, eight 13 m diameter dishes were located along an 8 km track to synthesize a very large antenna. Even larger structures have been produced in recent years. For satellite use, the bird illuminates an area in a strip fashion, but since it is moving, it automatically generates the SAR effect.

A new generation of spectrometer sensors has been designed to capture more than 11 Gbytes of data per hour. These devices can simultaneously record data from 102 channels between 430 and 1270 nm. The 2D spatial images are overlaid with a series of spectral images at different wavelengths to produce a 3D volume image. The term *voxel* has been coined to describe this 3D pixel concept.

Spatial and spectral resolutions of 1–10 m and 2–20 nm respectively have been recorded from these devices.

The sensors can be used to obtain earth data on agronomy, atmospheric physics, botany, geology, hydrology, marine biology, pollution and vulcanology. Such data allows the commercial development of such activities as farming, fishing, forestery, gas, land development, minerals, oil and water.

As an example of the speed and accuracy of the recording and reporting of environmental happenings, it is now possible to detect oil tankers washing out their empty tanks while under way.

LANDSAT

This US series of satellites is operated by Earth Observation Satellite Corporation (EOSAT) and is intended to be financially self-supporting through the sale of the remote sensing information. The on-board sensors are designed to provide images that can be used for a wide range of operations. These include land use and mapping, soil erosion, crop management, volcanic activity, mineral deposits and environmental disasters. The sensors have the following earth resolutions:

visual images	20 m
cartographic images	15 m
infrared thermal images	100 m

The data that is collected on board is stored using high-density magnetic tape recorders. To save wear and tear on the recorder mechanism and spacecraft power, the tape machines transmit the stored data in reverse. This avoids having to rewind and then replay. The data is relayed to the ground stations either directly on command from a control station, or via the tracking and data relay satellite system (TDRSS). For the relay of the stored data, modulated X-band carriers are used, with data rates of 15 Mbit/s for visual and IR images, and 85 Mbit/s for cartographic data.

The accuracy of the processed data is validated by on-the-ground observations of closely monitored areas. For example, SPOT has an area near Avignon, France that is used as a calibration range, while the ERS group have used a site 70 km west of Munich, Germany for a similar activity.

SPOT (Système Probatoire d'Observation de la Terre)

This series of French satellites is owned by a public company of which MATRA and Centre National d'Etudes Spatiale (CNES) are major shareholders. The on-board sensors provide typical environmental information with a resolution of 10 m for colour images and 20 m for the wideband coverage data. A unique feature involves the ability to provide 3D images from the received data. The collected data is stored on a high-density magnetic tape recorder using *three-position* modulation, a technique that provides three data bits for every two flux reversals. The relayed data is PCM encoded at 25 Mbit/s on to 20 watt carriers of either 8.025 or 8.40 GHz.

ERS-1 and ERS-2 (European Remote Sensing)

This series of satellites is owned and managed by the European Space Agency (ESA) and is basically intended to provide information about the marine environment. The features being monitored include mean sea height to an accuracy within 10 cm, wave movement, sea and cloud temperatures, ice flows and icebergs, the ozone layer and climatology in general.

Figures 7.8 and 7.9 provide just two examples of the type of information that has been obtained via the ERS-2 satellite.

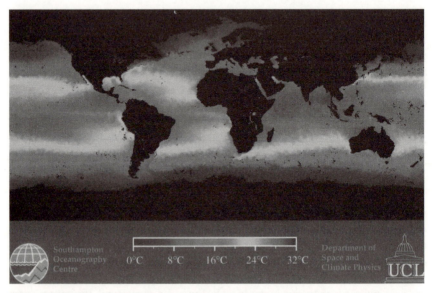

Figure 7.8 Global sea-surface temperature (May 1993) (Courtesy of *Earth Observation Quarterly*, ESA, March 1996 (University College London and Southampton Oceanography Centre)).

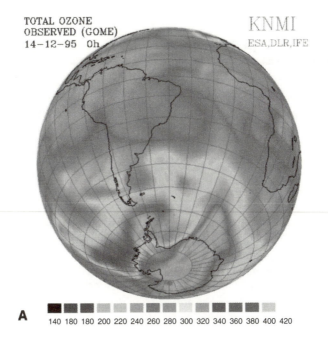

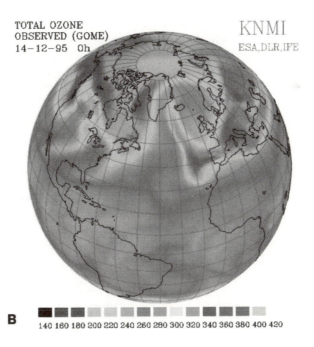

Figure 7.9 Ozone atmospheric distribution (14 December 1995) (Courtesy of *Earth Observation Quarterly*, ESA, March 1996).

7.3   MOBILE SYSTEMS

One sector that was quick to adopt radio as its main means of long-distance communications was the shipping industry. The need for an easy and reliable method, not only for day-to-day operations but also in times of distress, has long been recognized. However, until the advent of satellites, the shipping services had to depend heavily on the vagaries of HF radio for long-distance communications which was later supported by VHF radio for local inshore links.

INMARSAT Standard A system

Satellites have made great changes to the services provided for mobile operation, not only at sea but also for land and air applications. Geostationary and polar-orbiting satellites play complementary roles to provide these services, of which probably the best developed is that provided by the international consortium INMARSAT (International Maritime Satellite Organization) (10). This organization provides four operational satellites in geostationary orbit and positioned at 15.5°W and 54°W (Atlantic Ocean Region – AOR), 64°E (Indian Ocean Region – IOR) and 178°E (Pacific Ocean Region – POR). These provide a wide range of services up to about 75° latitude, north and south. At these low angles of radiation and reception, multipath transmissions, particularly by reflections off the sea surface, can create communication problems. Hence the need for robust signal modulation and coding techniques. A Network Coordination Station (NCS) is located in each area and is responsible for communications management throughout that region. All four NCSs are connected via terrestrial links to the Network Control Centre (NCC) in London. Thus the organization virtually acts as a worldwide extension to the national post, telephone and telegraph organizations (PTTs), any service provided by a PTT being continued over the INMARSAT network.

Basically, the system is divided into three sections: a coast earth station (CES), linked to the national PTT network; a space link provided by the satellite acting as a frequency translator; and a ship earth station (SES) mounted on each mobile platform. Each CES employs an antenna of 10–13 m diameter for communication with the satellite and transmits and receives in the 6 and 4 GHz bands (C band) respectively. The satellite down-link to the SESs provides an EIRP of 18-dBW, right-hand circular polarized (RHCP). The system power budget is so balanced that the mobile station can be very much smaller and less complex that a CES. Some typical features are given below.

Antenna diameter	Antenna gain	Antenna beamwidth	Noise temperature
1.2 m	23 dBi	10°	400 k
0.9 m	20 dBi	16°	200 k

The SES operates in the L band, all signals being RHCP, with a typical up-link EIRP of 36 dBW. The operational frequencies are as follows:

Service	Transmit (MHz)	Receive (MHz)
Maritime	1626.5–1645.5	1530–1544
Aeronautical	1645.5–1660.5	1545–1559

A critical element of the system operation is the frequency errors arising from oscillator instability and Doppler shift. To simplify the specification of each SES, AFC compensation loops are provided within each CES and in the satellites' C to L and L to C band transponders.

The services provided include narrowband FM (NBFM) telephony with 2:1 companded audio and a frequency range of 300–3400 Hz, digital data, analogue and digital facsimile, and electronic mail at data rates of up to 2.4 kbit/s, transmitted using FM and SCPC. Telegraphy channels provide for 50 baud (50 bit/s) telex, which is transmitted in a single channel per burst mode on a TDMA carrier. High-speed computer data at 56 kbit/s is included using QPSK (4-phase). Over the space link, this uses a differential code where a logic 1 is signified by a change of state and this is followed by a 1/2 convolution coding of constraint length 7, the transmitted bit rate being 112 kbit/s. In addition, other services included are meteorological and search and rescue.

A typical ship earth station (SES) (11)

Each SES system can be subdivided into two sections, the above-deck equipment and below-deck equipment (ADE and BDE). The former comprises the 0.9 m diameter antenna and its steering mechanism, the transmitting high-power amplifier (HPA) and the receiver LNB, together with a diplexer. All are mounted within a glass fibre radome, for weather protection. The antenna gain in the transmit mode is 22 dBi. The HPA provides an output of 14 dBW or 25 W, to give a total EIRP in the preferred direction of 36 dBW. Antenna pointing is controlled and stabilized against pitch and roll by gyroscopic motors, and in azimuth and elevation by control signals provided via an embedded computer control system. The gyroscope motor platform is clamped to the anntena mount by a solenoid action which can be released for service purposes. The HPA is only energized in the transmit mode, and to avoid accidents, the access door for service within the radome is barred during periods when the HPA is in the transmit mode.

The HPA driver and receiver RF stages include frequency conversion so that the RF link between ADE and BDE operates at a much lower frequency. This is achieved by the use of the fourth harmonic of a 365 MHz oscillator (1460 MHz) as follows:

The received frequency range of 1535–1543.5 MHz is converted to 75–83.5 MHz by subtraction and the transmits range of 176.5–185 MHz is converted to 1636.5–1645 MHz by addition.

The 365 MHz local oscillator is locked to a 5 MHz crystal which also provides the master timing signals for all the digital functions. The main receiver operates as a dual conversion superhet and handles both the FM and PSK carriers. The level of the AGC line voltage is also used as the source of the drive signals to control the orientation of the antenna system. When a ship makes a request for transmission, a CES replies by transmitting a 2600 Hz tone on its FM carrier. This is detected by the receiver and causes the channel select oscillator to change, to produce a 10.7 MHz IF with 2600 Hz tone. After demodulation and filtering, this tone is used to signal to the system computer that the CES has established a link. The ship then replies with its own 2600 Hz tone which has been derived from the master oscillator. This signifies to the CES that a two-way link has been established, and it now transmits a 425 Hz tone for 1.5 seconds to signal 'go-ahead with dialling'. The dialling technique used is the standard dual tone multi-frequency (DTMF) system. When the CES receives an answer from the called number, it transmits a tone of 2900 Hz for 150 ms to signal the start of the charge period. When the handset is replaced, the system computer arranges for the transmission of the 2600 Hz tone for two seconds to terminate the call.

Although these systems were initially devised for the larger ocean-going ships, the relatively small size, and the low weight and power consumption make such equipment also suitable for smaller vessels, such as those used by the fishing industry. A land-based version is also available, mounted on a rugged four-wheel-drive, cross-country vehicle and designed for such things as survey operations off the beaten track.

INMARSAT Standard B system (12)

The Standard A system is somewhat limited in the facilities offered and the size of the vessel on which it can be installed. To overcome some of these problems, the Standard B system was developed. This provides a telephony service using digital speech processing and coding plus TDMA, BPSK and Offset-QPSK modulation. The mobile station uses a 0.9 m diameter antenna, with a G/T ratio of −4 dBk and a transmit lower-power HPA (25 W) which also runs in Class C. One of two digital communications data rates (9.6 and 16 kbit/s) are user selectable. The system uses adaptive predictive coding with FEC (forward error correction) and a 1/2 rate convolution code, plus Viterbi soft decoding at the receiver. The system provides for fifty-six simultaneous telephone channels. The telephony mode is voice operated to allow faster and simpler operation of this lower-cost SES.

INMARSAT Standard C system

The Standard C system which has developed into a very flexible one, uses the same transmission frequencies as Standard A and was designed to extend digital services to smaller vessels and land vehicles over the INMARSAT system. To keep the total power requirement as low as possible required that the transmission output power is generally restricted to about 1–20 W (13 dBW). The usual Shannon–Nyquist SNR trade-off thus implies that operation at a low CNR means that the system has to operate at a low bit rate and a narrow bandwidth. The resulting design is a low-cost, flexible, go-anywhere, satellite communications system that is capable of interconnecting with a mobile terminal to practically any PSTN system.

The system shown in Figure 7.10, Model TT-3020C by Thrane & Thrane, Denmark, is a good example of the degree of flexibility that can be achieved. This system is fully compliant with INMARSAT C for SOLAS/GMDSS with distress calling and also includes a built-in GPS receiver with an eight-channel option. It is small (car radio sized), economically priced, lightweight and rugged, with a low power consumption. It is capable of providing two-way data, telex, fax and X25 e-mail services worldwide. The receiver provides for position and status reporting and instant fleet tracking capabilities back to base headquarters.

The omni-directional antenna has a G/T ratio of 23 dBk and with 25 W power input provides an EIRP of 14 dBW at 5° elevation, with coverage extending from +90° down to –15°. The operating frequencies are as follows:

Receive MHz	*Transmit MHz*	*GPS MHz*
1525–1559	1626.5–1660.5	1575.42

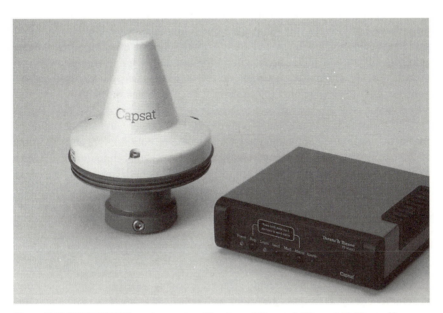

Figure 7.10 INMARSAT-C receiver system (Courtesy of Thrane & Thrane Ltd, Denmark).

The channel spacing is either 1.25, 2.5 or 5 kHz, the modulation employs BPSK at a data rate of 600 bit/s, equivalent to 1200 symbols/s.

The system has a sleep mode power saving circuit that reduces the normal operating power consumption of 81 W down to 30 mW in six stages over a total period of ten hours inactivity.

Semiconductor memory is provided in two sections, 512 kbytes of flash EPROM for system memory and 256 kbytes of SRAM for user data. The receiver contains interfaces for connections to serial data and GPS I/O, parallel I/O for a printer, and a link to the ArcNet system.

In general the system coding method uses a 1/2 rate Viterbi code which can be interleaved for added error protection to give a bit error rate (BER) better than 10^{-3}. The system frequency tuning is synthesizer controlled in steps of 5 kHz. The transmission coding and system protocol is based on the CCITT X25/X400 standards, with the data organized into packets with 0.264 s duration frames.

The service facility for reporting the mobile terminal position and status is carried in 32 bytes contained within three packets. Both position and data reports can be initiated either by polling or interrogation from a base station. Poll commands instruct the terminal how and when it should respond. There are three types of polling signals available, for individual, group or area responses. In the last two cases the polling terminal arranges for queuing control. An *enhanced group call* service is also available for messages fed into the Standard C system via a terrestrial PTT network. This allows messages to be routed to mobiles according to a priority. A single message can be received simultaneously by a number of mobiles anywhere within global range, or by mobiles just within a specific region.

The FleetNET system, which operates over INMARSAT C, allows individual companies to communicate with all their associated mobiles in a broadcast manner, or individually by using a unique addressing technique. In addition, navigation sensors can be added to the mobile terminals. This allows them automatically to transmit regular position reports to the home base station.

SafetyNET is exclusively available to the maritime user. This is used for the transmission of safety-related information such as weather warnings for specific areas.

Since the Standard C terminals require very little power and can operate in an automatic mode, they are sometimes used for the remote sensing and reporting of terrestrial situations. This supervisory control and data acquisition (SCADA) mode allows the terminals to be positioned to gather data from such situations as volcanic, geothermal, pressure ridges and plate movement, thus providing advanced warning of developing environmental disasters

INMARSAT Standard D system

This represents the smallest and cheapest portable satellite communications system. It is designed to pass messages with up to 138 characters to a pager-type handset. It forms an ideal terminal for the transfer of point-to-multipoint broadcast information, such as financial data, credit card listings and disaster alerts. Access to the satellite up- and down-links are via the PTTs and the system uses QPSK modulation with FEC.

INMARSAT Standard E system

This system provides maritime distress alerting services that are transmitted from emergency position radio beacons (EPIRBS) and relayed through the Inmarsat CESs. The system covers virtually the whole of the world ocean regions and is fully compliant with the GMDSS and GPS systems. This provides an emergency location accurate to within 200 m.

INMARSAT Standard M system (13)

This system has been devised to provide a cost-effective means of introducing satellite phone, fax and data communications between the public switched telephone networks and mobile users on land and at sea. The system operates with antennas as small as 70 cm in diameter and uses modern digital technology and signal processing in order to minimize channel bandwidth and conserve power. The modulation employs offset-QPSK (O-QPSK) with SCPC which allows the use of Class C power amplifiers for energy conservation. The digital voice codec operates at 6.4 kbit/s which includes a basic voice rate of 4.8 kbit/s plus an overhead for error control, with a TDM time frame of 20 ms. The operation of the speech codec can be summarized as follows (14). The speech channel is sampled and digitized and then processed through a fast Fourier transform (FFT) stage to determine the fundamental frequencies involved. A comb bandpass filter then selects out the successive harmonics so that the energy in each can be assessed. Only harmonics above a predetermined threshold are retained. At the receiver, the fundamentals and harmonics are used to reconstruct the original speech to an acceptable degree of accuracy.

Radio frequency specifications

	Land	*Maritime*
G/T ratio	− 12/dB/k min.	− 10 dB/k min.
EIRP	19–25 dBW	21–27 dBW
Rx range MHz	1530.0–1559.0	1530.0–1545.0
Tx range MHz	1631.5–1660.5	1631.5–1646.5
Polarization Rx and Tx	RHCP	RHCP

INMARSAT aeronautical mobile systems

This developing service operates by using the satellite as a relay link between the aircraft and a ground station, which in turn provides the interconnection to the terrestrial PSTN system. The service, which operates in the L band, provides both passengers and aircrew with an almost global voice and data communications link. Two digital voice channels are provided at 9.6 kbit/s for passenger use, a single channel 4.8 kbit/s for crew use, and 600 bit/s for a digital data massaging service. Due to the high aircraft speeds, Doppler shift could be a problem. The RF modulation and coding schemes are devised so that provided that the Doppler shift does not exceed ±100 Hz, the system can provide a high-quality service. The aircraft antennas, which are encased in an acrofoil-shaped housing, are mounted externally and take on the appearance of *shark fins*. To provide all-round coverage and maintain constant contact with the satellite, the antennas are of the steerable, planar, phased array types. Currently there are three variants involved in this service but they all use O-QPSK modulation.

Aero-H (high gain). This service provides two-way digital voice, G3 fax and data for the flight and cabin crews, plus passenger facilities at data rates of 4.8 and 9.6 kbit/s. The system has global coverage and operates in two modes, packet and circuit switched. The bandwidths employed are 10 kHz and 17.5 kHz for packet and circuit modes respectively. This service is also used for airline operations and air traffic control.

Aero-I (intermediate gain). This service is intended for regional operation in short- and medium-haul aircraft and provides for telephony, G3 fax and real-time data. The data rate is 4.8 kbit/s and the data is organized into X25 format. The service can support six simultaneous telephone calls.

Aero-L (low power). This is a low-gain system offering real-time two-way air to ground data transfers at 600 bit/s in the X25 format.

Global maritime distress and safety systems (GMDSS)

The meteorological and other polar-orbiting satellites often perform a dual role by providing a relay for emergency and navigation signals. These satellites are sun-synchronous in that they pass over the same point on the earth's surface at the same time each day. The operating frequencies being used are all in the VHF or low UHF bands, 121.5, 243, 401 and 406 MHz, which include the common international distress frequencies. (The distress calling frequencies of 500 and 2182 kHz are still active, but are now largely by-passed by the new system.) The services are virtually international, but are generally within the SARSAT/ COSPAS agreements. (SARSAT = Search And Rescue SATellite; COSPAR = Cosmicheskaya Systema Poyska Avarinich Sudov, which roughly translates to 'Space System for the Search of Ships in Distress'.)

This service, which is expected to be globally operational by 1999, will be made mandatory for all sea-going vessels under the SOLAS (Safety Of Life At Sea) Convention. It already has the support of the United Nations via the work of the International Telecommunications Union (ITU) and the International Maritime Organization (IMO), two of the organizations that have been responsible for the development of the technical standards involved.

The important emergency part of this system is based on a small beacon transmitter that, when activated either manually or automatically, continuously emits an AM signal at a power output of 100 mW. This signal is picked up by a polar-orbiting satellite and repeated in real time to be received by a local user terminal (LUT) ground station. The beacon transmitters are generally known as emergency position indicating radio beacons (EPIRB) or search and rescue beacon equipment (SARBE). The position of the emergency is determined by the LUT using the Doppler shift affecting the beacon signal received at the satellite. The satellite processes the beacon identification, emergency and user category codes, adds a time code and then retransmits the message.

Each LUT is capable of providing coverage over an area of about 2500 km radius and, depending upon conditions, produces a position accurate to within 5–10 km.

PRODAT data service

The European Space Agency (ESA) developed a satellite communications system known as PROSAT, to be available for land, air and maritime mobile operations. The maritime version is referred to as PROMAR. Included in the scheme is a low-cost digital data-only service that is known as PRODAT.

This system operates through existing ESA ground stations and INMARSAT communications satellites and provides a low-speed, low-power and narrow bandwidth service. It was initially intended to work alongside and support the HF communications radio systems that were commonly used by aircraft. Since this mode suffers from the vagaries of variable propagation, the satellite system provides a more consistent and reliable service. The flexible system design allows for communications mobile to ground, mobile to mobile, and ground to mobile.

The ground station transmits to the satellite in the 6 GHz band using TDMA with differential binary phase shift keying (DBPSK). Each TDM frame is 1.024 seconds long and is divided into 64-bit slots each slot representing a channel sending data to a user at 47 bits/s. The other bits in each slot are used for coding and error control. This signal is then relayed to the mobile by a transponder of 24 dBW output using a 1.5 GHz link.

PRODAT uses a two-dimensional Reed–Solomon (R–S) interleaved code that is capable of correcting both random and burst errors. In addition, if the burst errors are too long for correction, an automatic request repeat (ARQ) for retransmission can be generated, acknowledgement of accurate reception being given during the transmission of the following block. Each block is numbered, due to the delay that occurs over the satellite link. Quadrifilar helix antennas with 0 dBi gain and a hemispherical radiation pattern are mounted externally to the aircraft and housed within a low-drag aerofoil casing.

The aircraft transmissions use the 1.6 GHz band to the satellite, which in turn relays the signal to ground using a 6 GHz carrier. The down-link uses CDMA with suitable collision detection. The *spread spectrum* signal is generated by the addition of a PRBS sequence to the channel signal. The system allows for thirty-two simultaneous channels using the same carrier frequency and occupying a total bandwidth of 650 kHz. The CDMA signal is decoded at the ground station using correlation detection and the appropriate PRBS code, before being directed to the user terminal.

7.4 SATELLITE NAVIGATION SERVICES

Transit system

Satellite navigation has its roots in astro-navigation, whereby navigators located their positional fixes using the light from the sun or fixed stars. This concept was the source of many errors due to the uncertainty of clear day or night light and the use of mechanical instrumentation. The former problem was resolved by switching to radio signals from satellites which are unaffected by day- or night-time conditions. At the same time this allowed the introduction of a computer for rapid processing of the received data.

The first operational system to be employed but which is now virtually obsolete (described here for reference only), was the US Navy Navigational Satellite System, known as the Transit System, which was available for water and land-based mobile vehicles.

The space link part of this system consisted of five satellites in polar orbit, at an altitude of about 1100 km, with periods of about 107 minutes. The radiated RF power was of the order of 1 watt. The transmitted data included a time code and precise details of the orbit parameters, a fix being obtained by decoding the data and measuring the Doppler shift in the received carrier frequency. The information was then evaluated using a computer-controlled system.

The satellite's precise orbit was not circular, but affected by minor perturbations. These would lead to errors in the calculated positions. To ensure that the data was as accurate as possible, ground control stations monitored each satellite transmission and used a computer to establish the true orbit. Updated, corrected information was then transmitted back to the satellite, twice in each 24-hour period.

A satellite continuously transmitted messages of precisely two minutes' duration on frequencies of 150 and 400 MHz, although only the latter was used for civil navigation. Each message consisted of 156 words of 39 bits, plus one 19-bit word, making a total of 6103 bits at an equivalent rate of 50.858 bit/s. The first three words defined universal time (UTC) and the next 25 words, used for navigation, defined the minor perturbations and the fixed parameters of the current and future orbits. The remaining words were used for military purposes and were not available for civilian use. The primary bit pattern shown in Figure 7.11(a) had a duration of 19.7 ms (Binary 1 was the inverse). This bit pattern was used to provide PSK at ± 60° of the 399.968 MHz carrier. This form of

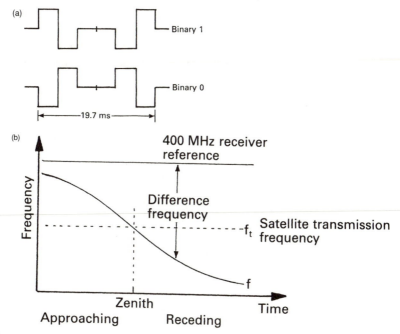

Figure 7.11 (a) Transit system logic format. (b) Doppler frequency relationship.

modulation was chosen so that the Doppler shift in the received carrier frequency could be easily and continuously measured.

The received frequency was different to that transmitted due to the Doppler effect, which depended upon the relative velocities of the satellite, the receiver and the axial velocity of the earth. A simple mathematical formula (15) shows that the Doppler shift is given by:

$$f_t - f_r = f_t(2v/c) \tag{7.3}$$

where: f_t = transmitted frequency
f_r = received frequency
v = relative velocity of source and receiver
$c = 3 \times 10^8$ m/s

As the satellite rises towards its zenith, approaching the receiver, the received frequency would be higher than that transmitted. At the zenith the relative velocities are momentarily zero, so that received and transmitted frequencies are identical. As the satellite recedes, the received frequency falls; this effect is shown in Figure 7.11(b). To avoid the problem of dealing with positive and negative Doppler shifts, the satellite navigation receiver compared the received frequency with a highly accurate and stable local frequency of 400 MHz. The difference frequency thus varied around 32 kHz during each satellite pass.

During each acceptable pass, the Doppler shift was measured and counted over periods of thirty seconds and stored in the system memory. By the end of each pass, the Doppler count had been used to compute a curve similar to that shown in Figure 7.11(b). This uniquely related the receiver position to the orbit. The computer then used this, together with the data from each two-minute message, to compute and display the position. Between such fixes, data from the ship's log (speed) and compass (bearing) were input to the computer which then continually updated the position by dead reckoning (DR). The DR navigation concept relies on knowing the time elapsed, the vehicle speed and course to calculate each new position, which was of course itself a source of error.

Orbits that produced angles of elevation between about 15° and 75° produced fixes that even under worst-case conditions were within 500 m accuracy. Orbits outside of this range produced unacceptable errors due to the non-spherical nature of the earth's surface. At an altitude of 1100 km, the minimum free space attenuation was in the order of 145 dB. At elevation angles below 15°, the propagation path length increases by a factor of more than 2.4. This produced an additional attenuation of $(2.4)^2$, or about 7.5 dB.

Global positioning system (GPS) (16)

NAVSTAR (17)

This highly complex navigation system, initially developed by the US Department of Defense for military purposes, can also be used in a restricted form by civilian operators. Unlike the Transit system, which uses the Doppler shift of UHF signals as the measurement domain, NAVSTAR uses the propagation delay of the signals transmitted in the L band by each satellite. This system provides three-dimensional (3D) fixes that are accurate under certain circumstances to better than 3 m. State-of-the-art versions of NAVSTAR are capable of computing seven-dimensional information, 3D position, 3D velocity and precise time. All this is achievable because of the highly accurate space-borne clocks carried on each satellite and by the use of computer control and data processing. The system provides for both military and civilian applications and serves all means of transport. When used in conjunction with meteorological data, the system allows air- and sea-borne travellers to make best use of tail winds and tides and permits an accurate tracking of great circle routes (shortest distances) in order to save time and fuel. Extensions to this satellite system can improve collision avoidance and safety in all weathers and provide for enhanced search and rescue operations.

The space segment

This consists of eighteen operational satellites plus six in-orbit spares. These are located in three circular orbits inclined at an angle of 55°, at an altitude of about 19 652 km (10 611 nautical miles) and with a period of twelve hours. The orbits are spaced from each other by 120° of latitude. Each satellite crosses the equator in a northerly direction at two points spaced by exactly 180°, giving a fixed sinusoidal ground track. Satellites with different phases, but in the same orbit, have different ground tracks which are displaced by an amount due to the earth's rotation between crossings. Thus if a satellite crosses the equator northerly at 0° and 180° longitude, another satellite in the same phase but delayed by six hours (sidereal time) crosses the equator northerly at 90°E and 90°W longitude. Southerly crossing will thus occur 90° longitude later.

Eighteen operational satellites ensure that there are always at least six birds in view and up to a maximum of eleven, depending upon the user's location and altitude. The satellites, and hence their signals, must be observed simultaneously and without excessive interference. Each satellite carries a very accurate atomic clock that transmits digitally coded time signals on a frequency of 1227.60 Mhz (L_2). Other transmission frequencies are 1381.05 and 1575.42 MHz (L_1), but only the latter is used for navigation purposes. The L_1 and L_2 carriers are modulated by two pseudo-random binary codes (PRBS) to form the C/A (Clear or Course acquisition) and the P (Precision) codes. The latter is reserved for military purposes and when encrypted is known as the P(Y) code.

Each satellite employs a shaped beam antenna to provide a near-uniform power distribution down to an elevation of 5°. Thus the propagation path length ranges from 19 652 km up to about 25 340 km under worst-case conditions. The minimum received signal power is at least −163 dBW for the L_1P(Y) code and −160 dBW for the C/A code. The signal level for both code versions borne by the L_2 carrier is −166 dBW. The maximum received signal power level for either carrier is −150 dBW.

The time taken to acquire a navigational fix ranges from a few seconds for an update, to a few minutes for the time to first fix (TTFF), but these times vary considerably with the complexity and speed of the receiver/processor.

The coding system
The two carrier frequencies are related as follows:

$$L_1 = 1575.42 \text{ MHz} = 154 \times 10.23 \text{ MHz}, \quad \text{and}$$

$$L_2 = 1227.6 \text{ MHz} = 120 \times 10.23 \text{ MHz}$$

The L_2 signal is generally only modulated by the P code, whilst the L_1 carrier may be modulated by both the P and C/A codes. Both of these codes are formed by the modulo-2 addition of a PRBS and the 50 bit/s binary data stream. The L_1 in-phase carrier component is modulated by the P code while the quadrature component is modulated by the C/A code. The P code is formed from the product of two PRBS of 15 345 000 and 15 345 037 chips and both sequences are reset once a week. The natural period of this combined sequence is 267 days. The P code is transmitted as psuedo-random signal with a clock rate of 10.23 Mbit/s. Because this long code is difficult to acquire, the C/A code is normally accessed first and then processing is handed over to the P code system. The data is organized into 6 s sub-frames and 30 s frame periods. The basic period or epoch extends for 1.5 s.

The C/A code is shorter with 1023 bits per millisecond or 1.023 Mbit/s. Each satellite transmits on the same carrier frequency of 1575.42 MHz but is identified by its unique Gold code which provides BPSK modulation and direct sequence-spread spectrum (DS-SS) transmission. The relationship between this carrier and those of the INMARSAT-C system is shown in Figure 7.12(a). Each Gold code is formed by the product of two 1023 bit PRBS generated in 10-stage shift registers and formed from the generator polynomials: $G_1(X) = 1 + X^3 + X^{10}$ and $G_2(X) = 1 + X^2 + X^3 + X^6 + X^8 + X^9 + X^{10}$. Since this code has a 1 ms period, there are 20 C/A epochs for every data bit. Since each Gold code is 1023 bits long and repeated 1000 times per second, it produces a chip rate of 1.023 Mbit/s. Modulation raises the nominally 100 Hz wide baseband up to a transmission bandwidth of about 2 MHz. The 50 bit/s data is therefore synchronized to both the C/A and P epochs. The transmission power level is, at −163/dBW, well below the system general noise level.

The spectra for the two codes are shown in Figure 7.12(b). As an indication of the accuracy of positioning, one bit of the C/A code is equivalent to 300 m whilst that for the P code is about 1/10 of this. Significantly better accuracy can be achieved with both codes by using a phase measuring technique in the receiver.

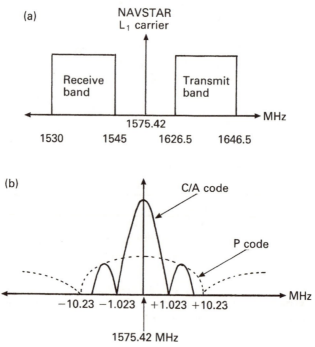

Figure 7.12 (a) NAVSTAR L1 frequency relative to INMARSAT-C frequencies. (b) Spectra of NAVSTAR C/A and P codes.

There are two data formats that have to be handled by the receiver. The first is the binary mode GPS data which allows the the user to initialize the system and read the data output from the receiver. As described above, this is packetized and carries FEC bits that allows corrupted data to be discarded. The second format is described as National Maritime Electronic Association (NMEA) messaging that is universally recognized. This is compatible with many marine display systems and outputs data in ASCII code format that is easily read by the terminal processor.

The command segment

Because of the variations in earth geometry and the vagaries of propagation, each satellite additionally transmits data about the parameters of the present and future orbits of all the satellites. This *almanac* allows the receivers to calculate accurate positional fixes and to be prepared with the correct code as a new satellite appears over the horizon. Information for the almanac is collected by ground stations for processing in the system central computer at the master control station in Colorado, USA. Four other ground stations located in Ascension Island, Diego Garcia, Kwagale and Hawaii ensure that any satellite is never out of contact with a ground station for more than two hours, the regular updating period. To allow a significant margin of error the almanac remains valid for up to four hours.

The user segment

In order to obtain a fix in three dimensions it is necessary to obtain data from three satellites. However, positional accuracy will not be uniform across the earth's surface, due in the main to:

- Changing propagation conditions in the ionosphere and the use of a minimal number of satellites.
- Gravitational effects and *relativity*. The latter feature causes the earthbound clocks to appear to run slow.
- The effects of multipath reception can give rise to noise and phase disturbances in the demodulation stages.

To overcome these problems a fourth satellite is always used to provide a cross-reference. Many current receivers use five or more satellite channels simultaneously, four to provide an accurate fix and the others to provide quick access to the correct codes as a new satellite appears above the horizon. The mobile antenna needs to have a hemispherical response to signals with an elevation as low as 5° above the horizon.

To descramble/despread the received signal the receiver has to generate a copy of the satellite code and multiply this with the incoming code. When the code patterns agree, the correlation detector ensures that the energy spread throughout the 2 MHz bandwidth becomes concentrated into the original 100 Hz baseband, with the significant coding gain. It is this feature that allows accurate reception of signals well below the noise level. The recovered data is then automatically entered into the mobile terminal computer. This then solves the necessary four simultaneous equations in an iterative manner, before presenting the results to the user on a suitable display.

The navigation message which carries the data that the mobile receiver needs to be able to calculate its position includes:

- satellite status information,
- time synchronous data for the transfer between the C/A and the P codes,
- parameters for computing the clock correction,
- the ephemeris table that gives the predicted position and movement of the satellite,
- correction for the signal propagation delay,
- almanac information that defines the approximate ephemeris of the other satellites,
- any special messages.

Each sub-frame of data starts with a telemetry word (TLM) and the C/A to P code hand-over word (HOW). The first eight bits of the TLM represent a preamble that is used for synchronization purposes. The following five blocks carry information for clock correction, ephemeris, almanac and messages. The first nineteen bits of the HOW are used to represent spacecraft time and the following three bits to identify the particular sub-frame.

Both clock and ephemeris correction parameters are updated every hour from the control segment. The clock correction block also carries an 8-bit word that identifies the age of the data. This gives the more sophisticated receivers the opportunity of selecting a satellite with the most up-to-date information. The almanac data, which is too long to contain within a single frame, is carried in a series of rolling frames.

GPS time differs somewhat from UTC which has to periodically adjusted to account for leap-seconds. Such an adjustment of GPS time would disrupt the continuously available navigation data. The difference between the two times is maintained to within $100\,\mu s$ and the difference published at periodic intervals.

The sources of navigational errors include the following: deviation of the satellite clock, ephemeris errors, atmospheric, ionospheric and propagation delays, multipath propagation and the effects of ground reflections, group delay errors due to signal processing, receiver noise and vehicle dynamics which involve changes of position and velocity. Typically these may add up to an error as high as $20\,m$.

In order to frustrate the use of the system by enemy action, ground control can deliberately introduce timing and position errors into the data stream. This is described as selective availability (SA) which reduces the accuracy for civilian and unauthorized users to about $100\,m$ for about 90 percent of the time. This value is suitable for general navigation but inadequate for weapon guidance. The addition of encryption to the P code also introduces a further restriction to control the system use.

The system power budget

The approximate system power budget for the C/A code part of the system is given in Table 7.1 (Courtesy of J.I.R. Owen (18)).

Compared with the receiver thermal noise level of –137 dBW in the C/A code bandwidth, the input signal-to-noise ratio is –20 dB. It is only after the spread spectrum modulation is removed from the C/A code that a positive SNR is produced. The 1.023/Mbit/s C/A code enables a processing gain of about 52 dB to be achieved, resulting in a SNR of about 30 dB in the carrier tracking loop. Processing gain is the ratio of the received signal bandwidth to the detection bandwidth, in this case, the carrier tracking loop bandwidth and a value of 6 Hz are assumed here.

An SNR of about 16 dB is necessary to ensure tracking of the carrier in order to read the navigation data accurately. Assuming a receiver power input of –156 dBW, the approximate noise power (interference) needed to halt tracking and jam the system is given by:

Receiver power + processing gain – 16 dBW = jamming level

In this case, $-156 + 53 - 16 = -120\,\text{dBW}$

The receiver

Because of the very low level of input signal, the use of a double-superhet receiver is practically mandatory. Conversion to a first IF in the range 100–200 MHz gives good image frequency rejection while high gain can readily be established in a second IF of 5–20 MHz. Since all the satellite frequencies are multiples of the basic chip rate of 1.023 MHz, it is useful to use the same concept in the receiver. Thus a carrier frequency of

1540 × 1.023 MHz = 1575.42 MHz,   and first IF of

120 × 1.023 MHz = 122.76 MHz or 160 × 1.023 MHz = 163.68 MHz

requires a local oscillator frequency (LO) of 1452.66 or 1411.74 MHz.

Table 7.1

Transmitter power output	14.2 dBW
RF losses	1.25 dB
Antenna gain (worst case)	13.5 dB
EIRP	26.5 dB
Atmospheric and polarization losses	2.0 dB
Path losses (worst case)	184.4 dB
Received signal power	–160.0 dBW
Receiver antenna gain	–3.0 dB
Down lead losses	1.5 dB
Total received power	–164.5 dBW
Noise power spectral density	–202.5 dBW/Hz
Received SNR	–38.0 dB

By using such related frequencies, the locally generated signals can be synchronously locked. This avoids spurious beats and harmonics that could cause interference problems, leading to a reduction in processing accuracy. The decoding/despreading action is carried out in two stages, one section generating the correct Gold code tracking while the other synchronizes the locally generated carrier to the incoming signal. This, due to the relative velocities of the transmitters and receivers, is affected by Doppler shift modulation. Processing at this stage is therefore usually accomplished by using either a phase or delay lock or Costa's loop circuit.

The code tracking loop decoding sequence functions by comparing the recent past and the predicted future codes. This results in the 2 MHz wide IF signal being reduced to its original 100 Hz baseband, but still in the BPSK format. After demodulation this can be processed to yield the navigational information.

Processing algorithm

A typical algorithmic process to provide a solution to the GPS positioning problem is as follows:

(1)   Estimate an initial position and time.
(2)   Select four satellites.
(3)   Obtain pseudo range values from received data.
(4)   Compute values for pseudo range matrix.
(5)   From the matrix compute the range errors.
(6)   Update estimated position.
(7)   Compute positional error.
(8)   Update estimated position.
(9)   Repeat from 3 if error is greater than some specified tolerance, otherwise repeat from 1.

Step 8 ultimately provides an accurate fix.

Builder-2 GPS Development System (19)

This system is designed around a two-chip set (GP2010 and GP2021) that operates from a dc level of 3–5 volts and processes the C/A code only. It requires an interface to link it to a display PC which may be either a portable or a desktop machine. The 1575.42 MHz signal which is derived from an active antenna coupled to a suitable low-noise amplifier (LNA) provides an input level of 15 dBm. Although the system is capable of tracking twelve satellites, any unwanted channels can easily be de-activated.

This is a triple conversion system based on a 10 MHz temperature-controlled master oscillator and a common phase locked loop (PLL) with a frequency divider network. The basic RF processing is shown in Figure 7.13. The first IF of 175.42 MHz is produced by subtraction at the first mixer. After dividing the basic 1400 MHz frequency by 10, subtraction again provides the second IF of 35.42 MHz. Accurate filtering at this frequency, which is necessary to provide

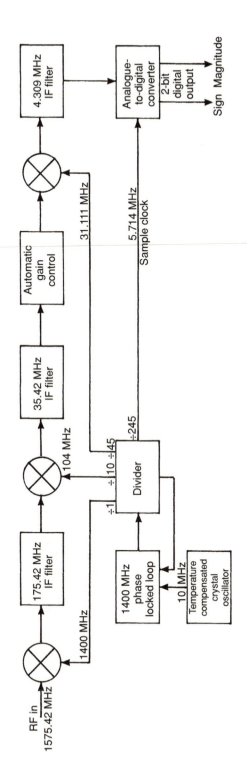

Figure 7.13 Basic RF processing (GPS GP2010) (Courtesy of GEC Plessey Semiconductors).

part of the processing gain, is achieved by using a surface acoustic wave filter (SAW). This is followed by two stages of gain-controlled amplication before being applied to the third mixer along with the 31.111 MHz derived from the oscillator by division by 45. The third IF of 4.309 MHz is again produced by subtraction. The filtered output from this stage is in analogue form and this is digitized by sampling using a 5.714 MHz signal derived by dividing the PLL signal by 245. The dual bit stream at the output of the D-to-A converter then provides the input to the correlator chip GP2021.

The microprocessor interface is compatible with most 16- and 32-bit processors from the Motorola, Intel and ARM60 ranges, thus providing for a very flexible operation.

As shown by Figure 7.14, the 2-bit input signal, sign and magnitude, is used to generate a bipolar signal (+1, −1) from the NRZ polar signal decoded by the receiver section. A clock generator circuit divides down the output from the master clock to provide all the necessary timing signals, including the memory control logic. The real-time clock frequency is controlled from a 32.768 kHz crystal circuit and this provides a 24-bit output from fixed division ratios. The first divider creates a 1 Hz output which is counted into seconds, minutes and hours to cover a maximum of 194 days, the counted time being stored in three 8-bit registers. The circuit includes a watch-dog timer which is used as a power saving device. The clock continues to run in the power-down mode, but register access is barred during this period. This helps to reduce the time to first fix (TTFF) to around one minute.

A dual UART circuit is included to provide for serial communications and the baud rate for each can be independently set. The serial data is organized in a common format, with start and stop bits, parity or non-parity bit, with the LSB following the start bit.

The microprocessor interface handles the data interchange between the GPS system and the display processor via the address and data bus system. This section is split into two parts, for use with either an ARM60 processor or the Intel or Motorola devices.

Figure 7.15 shows just one of the twelve correlator circuits on the GP2021 chip. The sign and magnitude bits are latched into each of the selected tracking modules in turn, together with a timing control signal. The timebase generator creates two interrupt signals to allow for the precise time for measurement and accumulation. The ACCUM_INT signal controls the data transfer between the correlator/accummulator and the microprocessor, while the MEAS_INT signal is used as a software switch that effectively provides 50 ms intervals for data accumulation.

The tracking modules identify each satellite in turn, either GPS or INMARSAT, by their unique Gold code.

The status registers contain the flags associated with the accumulated and measured data for each of the twelve channels.

This part of the chip contains twelve identical modules that generate the data used to track the satellites (see Figure 7.16). This performs the search operation

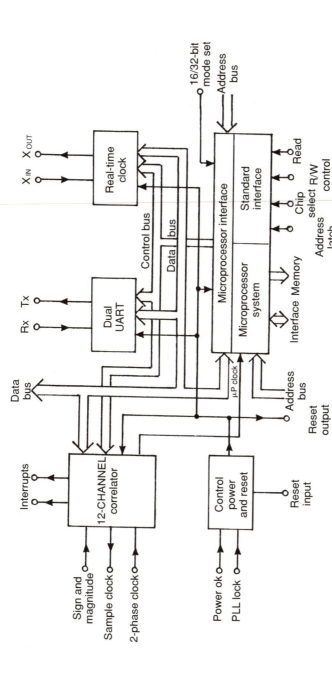

Figure 7.14 Block diagram of twelve-channel correlator ASIC (Courtesy of GEC Plessey Semiconductors).

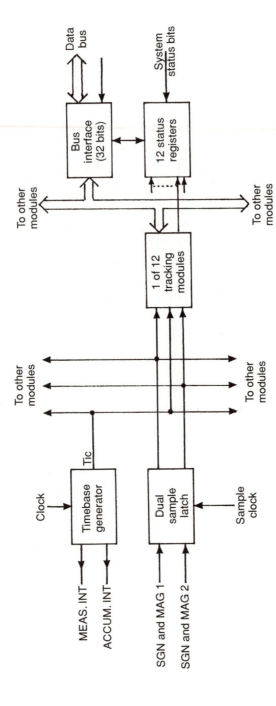

Figure 7.15 Correlator block diagram (Courtesy of GEC Plessey Semiconductors).

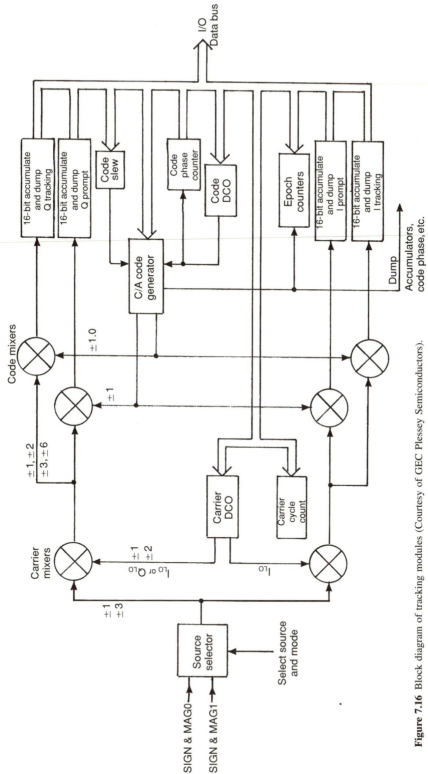

Figure 7.16 Block diagram of tracking modules (Courtesy of GEC Plessey Semiconductors).

using a correlation detection process (see Appendix A4.2) until the correct sequence is acquired.

The input signal may be provided via two receiver units to give better sky coverage and hence a faster access. The source selector stage redirects the Sgn and Mag 1 and 2 signals to the In-phase and Quadrature arms of the mixer stages respectively.

The maximum carrier frequency deviates from its nominal value due to Doppler shift and clock errors, while the maximum code phase is defined by the fixed code length. All code phases are searched at a given frequency before advancing to the next carrier frequency to repeat the code phase search.

The carrier DCO is used to synthesize the local digital oscillator signal so that it returns the input signal back to baseband in the mixer stage. Its nominal value is adjusted to counter the errors mentioned above. The frequency count is contained within a 26-bit register, this fine resolution being needed to ensure that the DCO will remain in phase with its satellite signal for an adequate time. The carrier DCO outputs are four-level, eight-phase sinusoids with the following sequence over one cycle:

$$I_{LO} = -1, \quad +1, \quad +2, \quad +2, \quad +1, \quad -1, \quad -2, \quad -2$$
$$Q_{LO} = +2, \quad +2, \quad +1, \quad -1, \quad -2, \quad -2, \quad -1, \quad +1$$

the sequences being three steps out of phase.

The carrier mixers multiply the digital input by the carrier DCO to generate the baseband signal. The code mixer multiplies the I and Q baseband signals from the carrier mixer with both the Prompt and Tracking local replica codes from the C/A code generator. This produces four separate correlation results. These are then integrated in the Accumulate and Dump blocks over the 1 ms code phase period. The code phase counter counts the number of half-chip periods of the generated codes and stores this value in a register.

The code slew count is used to slew the generated code by a number of half-chips ranging from zero to 2047. During the slewing process the accumulators for the channel being slewed are inhibited so that the currently stored value is valid.

The epoch counters keep track of the number of code phases over a one-second period. These counters can be pre-loaded to synchronize them to the data coming from the satellite. Figure 7.17 shows a typical screen display of the system channel status, the various parameters being defined on each screen for ease of use.

GLONASS (GLObal NAvigation Satellite System) (Russian Federation)

This system operates in a very similar manner to NAVSTAR, in that it employs spread spectrum ranging techniques, but uses multiple L band carriers in the range 1602.5625–1615.5 MHz. The system employs twenty-four operational satellites in three inclined orbits. Again, two levels of location accuracy can be achieved using a C/A code of 511 kbits and a P code of 5.11 Mbits. The code repetition rate is also 1000 times per second but with a basic bit rate of 50 kbit/s.

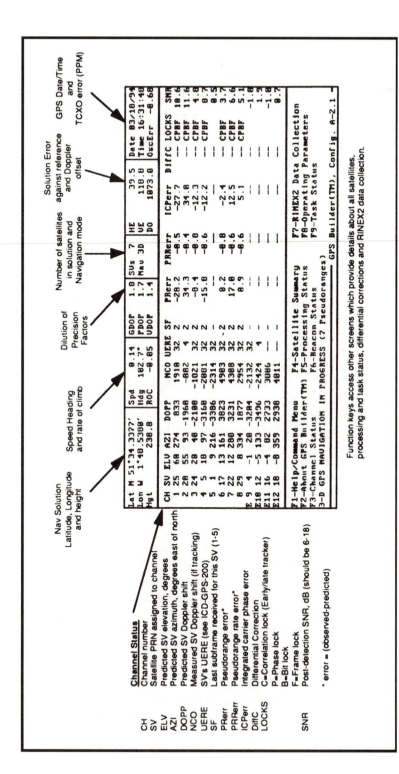

Figure 7.17 Typical screen display of channel status (Courtesy of GEC Plessey Semiconductors).

Differential GPS (DGPS)

This technique greatly enhances the accuracy of fixes without affecting the integrity of the military part of the system. It requires the additional use of a fixed GPS receiver located to within a surveyed positional accuracy of better than 1 m. The computer in this reference receiver compares its accurately known position with that obtained from GPS so that it can calculate a correction factor. This is then transmitted to all suitably equipped mobile GPS receivers, where it can be applied to the raw GPS fix to calculate a position, accurate to within 5 m. This extra feature requires that the GPS receiver must be equipped to receive the correction factor transmissions either via satellite or over a conventional radio link.

Wide Area Augmentation System

The DGPS system has been extended within North America to provide a very accurate location method for Air Traffic Control (ATC). A series of twenty-four DGPS ground stations are spread across the area. Each station compares its precisely known geographical location with that obtained from the GPS system. It then calculates the positional error that arises due to the vagaries of propagation conditions. This error is then passed to a ground control station for onward transmission to the aircraft via a geostationary satellite. On-board equipment then combines the data received from the GPS bird with that provided from the WAAS to determine its more accurate position.

The system provides a fix that is accurate to within 7.5 m which is considered to be good enough to allow it to replace the microwave landing system that is currently extensively employed for airport aircraft landing control. Such a system could be much more widely in operation by the year 2010.

The WAAS concept can also be applied to the control of railway rolling stock. In this case the system can be simplified to a two-dimensional problem because the train must be somewhere along a known track.

INMARSAT Overlay System

The navigation payload of the INMARSAT-3 generation of satellites provides a service to extend and complement the current GPS/GLONASS systems. This overlaid service operates by means of the transmission of navigation signals through a dedicated satellite repeater channel. The data provided by this service improves the accuracy of satellite navigation for air traffic control and monitoring purposes. INMARSAT provides the space segment for the service and the civil aviation authorities are responsible for implementation and operation.

This variation of WAAS includes three signal components as follows:

● Global Navigation Satellite System (GNSS) Integrity Channel (GIC) which provides information about the GPS and GLONASS satellite integrity and status in real time to ensure that the user does not employ a faulty satellite for navigation.

- A ranging global integrity channel (RGIC) provides the user with additional ranging information to give improved resolution.
- A wide area differential GNSS signal provides a differential correction signal for both GPS and GLONASS birds.

This additional information can improve the positional accuracy to about 3–5 m and provide a clock that is accurate to within 10 ns. Such accuracy can provide for much smaller aircraft in-flight separation distances and allow the system to be used for automatic landing under relatively poor weather conditions. It also allows the facility for automated operations on runways that are not equipped with the expensive microwave instrument landing system (ILS).

As indicated in Figure 7.18, navigation signals are transmitted from GPS and GLONASS satellites [1] and received by the users [2]. These signals are also received by the Integrity Monitoring Networks [3]. The monitored data is sent to Regional Integrity Network Central Processing [4]. At this point, the data is processed into message types and forwarded to the Navigation Earth Stations (NES) [5] and [10]. At the NES the spread spectrum navigation signal is precisely synchronized to a reference time and the C band up-link signal [6] is modulated with the integrity message data. The spread spectrum navigation signal is frequency-translated through the navigation payload on the INMAR-SAT-3 bird [7] and transmitted to the user [8] in the L band. An identical signal [9] is also transmitted at C band. This signal is used for maintaining the navigation signal timing loop, which is done in a very precise manner in order for

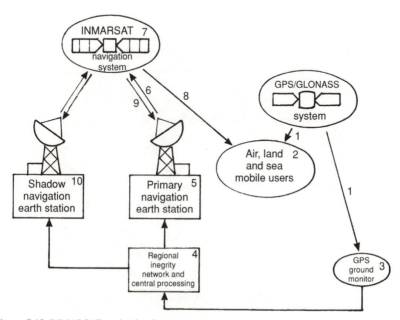

Figure 7.18 INMARSAT navigational support system.

the user to process the signal as though it was generated on board the satellite. The NES and central processing facility may be co-located. The shadowing NES [10] functions as a 'hot standby' receiving identical data from the central processing facility and maintaining a timing loop so as to assume operational status in the event of a failure at the primary NES.

Developing systems

Because all the systems described operate in very similar frequency ranges and have many features in common, the use of an embedded microprocessor allows many of the services to be integrated into one common receiver. In particular, the introduction of low-cost, high-speed digital signal processing (DSP) chips, such as the transputer, allows many of the hardware problems to be resolved by software. Receivers capable of operating from both NAVSTAR and GLONASS systems have several advantages through the availability of twice the number of satellites. The reliability increases by a factor of 100 percent, the basic resolution is reduced to 10–15 m and when using DGPS, the positional error can be as low as 90 cm. Furthermore, both systems can be integrated with INMARSAT-C terminals. By using the combined results of processing from all three systems with a new faster software algorithm, it is expected that a positional accuracy of ±1 mm will ultimately be achieved.

The hand-held portable system shown in Figure 7.19 (courtesy of Magellan Systems Corp. USA) can track all satellites in view (twelve channels), has an accuracy as low as 15 m and is available at low cost so that it may be used for

Figure 7.19 The Magellan NAV DLX-10 hand-held receiver (Courtesy of Next Destination Ltd, UK).

virtually any outdoor activity. This particular model can display up to six different graphics or navigation displays, that include up to 1000-way points in seven legs, and facilities to retrace any of these tracks. This model is DGPS compatible and is supplied with a detachable quadrifilar helix antenna. When used in conjunction with digitized maps, these GPS devices form a valuable aid for all forms of travel.

The rapid expansion in the use of ASIC devices has allowed the production of a GPS instrument that is capable of simultaneously tracking twelve satellites. From these it extracts the data from the CA code, while decoding the encrypted P code from eight of these birds. The receiver then uses differential phase measurements between the L_1 and L_2 signals to obtain an enhanced degree of accuracy. This newly developed system can be integrated with the augmentation signals described above, to produce an on-board instrument that provides milli-metric accuracy suitable for use with an instrument aircraft landing system. By the addition of multiple antenna inputs, the receiver can also generate attitude information to make the system suitable as a very accurate blind flying aid.

7.5   RADIO DETERMINATION SATELLITE SERVICE (RDSS) (20)

This commercial system is used to report accurate information about the location of mobile units back to a transport operator's headquarters. It is suitable for use on road vehicles, railway trains, aircraft or boats and can provide positional fixes accurate to less than 10 m. In addition, provision is also made to allow for short, two-way messages to be passed between headquarters and the mobile user. The system operates through either low earth orbiters (LEO) or geostationary satellites, using either the standard LORAN-C (LOng Range Aid to Navigation), Transit or GPS positioning services.

In 1986 the US GEOSTAR Corp, was granted a licence and the first system became operational in 1987. In the same year, a European consortium, LOCSTAR, signed a licensing agreement as the first step to a global expansion of the service. Since that time many more countries, including Australia, Brazil, China and India, have adopted the concept.

Development progressed in stages. The original System 1 operated through spare transponders of the ARGOS system LEOs, known also as NOAA 9 and 10. This provided basic positional reporting and allowed for only a one-way data service. System 2 went through a number of enhancement stages during 1988 and 1989, providing a more accurate location service plus two-way messaging. System 3, which provides for satellite ranging and navigation, came into service during 1991 and provides a positional fix accurate to less than 7 m, plus two-way messaging. System 4 came into operation during 1994 and provided for a worldwide network that allowed *roaming* and *visiting*, with many millions of users.

The 1987 World Administrative Radio Conference for Mobile Services (known as MobWARC'87) agreed to the international standards jointly proposed by the International Telecommunications Union (ITU), the Federal Communications Commission (FCC), the International Radio Consultative Committee (CCIR) and the International Civil Aviation Organization (ICAO). Such was the demand for this service that almost 100 MHz of spectrum was allocated in the following frequency bands:

1610–1626.5 MHz,	L band user up-link
2483.5–2500 MHz,	S band user down-link
5150–5216 MHz,	C band satellite to ground station link
6525–6541.5 MHz,	C band ground station to satellite link

The system uses two radio channels, one for data and messages from the mobile to the central control station (in-bound) and the other in the reverse direction (out-bound). Each message sent over the system carries the unique identity code (ID) of the user, thus ensuring that only the addressee receives that message. Because RDSS uses spread spectrum, burst transmission techniques, many users can communicate simultaneously with the geostationary satellite. The Gold spreading codes form the basic protection from data collision in this CDMA-controlled system. The GEOSTAR control centre transmits interrogation signals through the satellite to all users many times per second. When received by a mobile, it replies with its own unique ID together with the digital data that it has waiting. The mobile transmitter then automatically shuts down while the control centre stores the messages in its computer. Once stored, the control centre transmits an acknowledge signal and then forwards the message to a prearranged destination.

The basic packet structure consists of about 130 000 time slots or chips. Each packet has a maximum length of 128 bytes of which 105 are allocated to messages. A packet consists of header, address, data or text, CRC error check, and trailer, with small variations between in-bound and out-bound messages. Messages that cannot be contained within a single packet require the addition of a sequence number.

The user terminal automatically counts from the start of a frame and, if prompted, it transmits a prearranged chip sequence. This prevents other users from accessing the same slot. Generally a three-chip separation is allowed between all users existing in the same frame. If any user terminal is blocked in any given frame it has a better than 99 percent chance of access within the next frame. A tier of priority is provided in the protocol, so that a terminal with an emergency can obtain rapid access.

BPSK is used for the primary coding format at a basic rate of 15.6 kbit/s. The use of a 1/2 rate convolution code with constraint length 7 doubles this to a transmission rate of 31.2 kbit/s. Burst lengths vary between 20 and 80 ms, and the use of a Gold spreading code expands the bandwidth to 16.5 MHz. The typical transmit power level is in the order of 50 watts (17 dBW).

As an example of the value of RDSS to transportation generally, a fully operational System 3 installation can handle 4 million out-bound and more than

20 million in-bound messages per hour. For added security and privacy, the system also provides for message encryption. A typical user terminal consists of a main receiver/processor/transmitter, a keyboard/display unit, receive/transmit antennas, plus the option of a hardcopy printer. During the development period of the system, the size and power requirement of the terminal has reduced markedly and hand-held units are now available.

The antennas used vary from a 42 cm monopole for LORAN reception to microwave patch and helical devices for the L and S bands.

7.6   TRACKING AND TAGGING SYSTEMS

These systems have been designed to automatically identify, track and record the movement of virtually any item in a reliable, flexible and accurate manner. These include vehicles, animals, persons or even components in a production environment. Some systems can also be adapted to handle electronic cash transactions.

Automatic debiting systems

These are typically used for the control and pricing of the tolling of major trunk road accesses. This involves the setting up of roadside units at all major access and exit points to detect the entry and exit of each vehicle. In addition, a further network is required to link all the roadside units to a central controlling computer to manage the billing system. This more solid link may form part of a network which is based on either copper, optical fibre or radio. However, the contactless link between vehicle and roadside unit provides greater difficulties. There are many ways in which this link can be enabled, ranging from buried inductive loops to satellites. However, in Europe, the band 5.795–5.805 GHz has been set aside for these systems. Additionally, in some cases, a further band from 5.805 to 5.815 GHz may also be available. The complete system must provide secure and high-speed data links, but because of the special needs, it can operate in the half duplex mode. The antennas for both roadside units and vehicles can be constructed using microwave patch structures, and those for the roadside units are probably more effective if mounted on an overhead bridge or gantry. Circular polarization is preferred because of the high degree of multipath reflections that are generated by the odd shape of vehicles. The roadside unit provides an RF output of about 2 W EIRP and this is enough to provide a range of about 10 m at vehicle speeds up to 160 km/h. The roadside to vehicle unit transmits using ASK at 250 kbit/s, which includes overhead for error control using CRC. This method reduces the cost of the on-board detector/receiver stages. The vehicle to roadside unit transmits at the same rate but uses PSK in the interests of a low error rate. Synchronous data transmission is achieved by using one of the self-clocking Manchester codes.

Radio tags

These are intended for attachment to the item that is to be tracked and there are two basic concepts available, active and passive. The active devices are powered by a long-life battery, whereas the passive devices are signal powered.

Mitsubishi types

These are credit-card-sized devices that operate in the contactless mode and incorporate an on-chip microprocessor for processing, encryption and control. Because of the provision for encryption, these are highly secure devices that can also be used for electronic cash applications. The memory component is based on SRAM technology which is backed up by a long-life (typically five years) battery. The communications link uses OOK (ASK) for simplicity, with the card reader transmitting at 455 kHz and the card at about 227 kHz over a maximum range of about 0.5 m.

Racam DSS 1000

This system uses a ferroelectric memory (FRAM) and does not need a back-up battery because it is powered from the card reader signal. It thus forms a credit-card-sized transponder with a memory capacity of 256 bits. This concept uses much less power than an EEPROM-equipped device and can be reprogrammed from the power supplied via the inductively coupled radio signal. The communications link operates at 125 kHz and uses FSK to provide a range of about 0.25 m. The cards can be used for security and access control and also for electronic cash transactions.

TIRIS (Texas Instruments Registration and Identification System)

This system, which is based on RF technology, requires no direct line-of-sight path between the tag and the reader. In fact, the tag is readable even when embedded in a packing case, or covered with mud, ice, snow or most non-metallic materials. The credit-card-sized tag carries the integrated semiconductor electronics and the frame antenna. In some cases, a ferrite antenna may be employed. It is powered from the transmitted reading signal and can be read as it moves past the reader at normal speed at distances of up to about 3 m.

The tag reader can be interfaced to a computer or programmable controller to collect data about any process to which the tag is attached. The system consists of three elements, the tag, reader and antenna, with the tag acting as a transponder. In operation, the reader transmits a power burst that is received by the tag. This is rectified and the dc component used to charge a capacitor which in turn provides the power for the tag. This causes the tag to return its specific data back to the reader as FSK using the frequencies 124.2 and 134.2 kHz.

Each tag carries its own unique code that is factory programmed, plus the capability of storing from four up to sixteen pages of 64-bit words which include the ID code plus data and CRC check. The transmit power is 20 W maximum and the reader can handle up to ten tags per second. When used with an RS-232 or RS-422 interface, the reader can provide either hardcopy printout or download its data to a host computer.

Star-Track

This is an automatic vehicle location and data collection system that is based on the global positioning system (GPS) linked with mobile data communications technology. The GPS is used to fix the vehicle latitude and longitude and the mobile data network (typically Mobitex) is used to provide the back-haul link to the vehicle base. Apart from location information, the mobile data link provides the base station with data about both the driver and vehicle status and serviceability. Mobitex is a packet-switched system that is ideally suited to a service with small to medium volumes of data and is currently in the process of being implemented worldwide. When not needed for vehicular information, Mobitex can be used as a voice service to replace the more expensive mobile telephone. At the base station, a computer-controlled system collates all the incoming data and presents this information to the controllers on a screen-displayed map.

Trafficmaster

This system is designed to provide in-vehicle information for drivers via a portable, dashboard-mounted display unit. The LCD display is backlit for night-time use and displays a map of the area of interest with cursor to indicate the direction of any traffic problem and the traffic speed at that point. Alternatively, the display may be used as a radio pager unit or present textual information about the general road conditions within an area.

Overhead infrared (IR) sensors are mounted on bridges or gantries and typically spaced 3 km apart, and used to measure the traffic speed. An inbuilt microprocessor calculates the three-minute rolling average of the traffic speed. If this speed is below some threshold (typically 50 km/h), this data, together with the sensor's unique location code, is transmitted at three-minute intervals, via a radio network, to a computer-controlled centre.

The control centre collates all the received data and then transmits any necessary information back to the vehicles via a radio paging network. Each driver has the facility to interrogate the system before starting out on a journey. Any information about possible hold-ups in the area of interest is then displayed as a text screen.

REFERENCES

(1) Turner, J. *The Down Link Signal Characteristics of TIROS-N Satellites*. National Meteorological Office, UK.

(2) Turner, J. (1985) *Orbital Parameters and Transmission Frequencies of Meteorological Satellites*. Oct. National Meteorological Office, UK.

(3) European Space Agency (1981) *Introduction to the Meteosat System*, SP-1041.

(4) European Space Agency (1980) *Meteosat WEFAX Transmissions*.

(5) European Space Agency (1984) *Meteosat High Resolution Image Dissemination*.

(6) Baylis, P.E., Mather, J.R. and Brush, R.J. (1980) *A Meteosat Primary Data User Station*. Research carried out for ESA by the University of Dundee, Scotland.

(7) Kirsch, R. (1986) *Maplin Magazine*.

(8) Christieson, M. *CloudFile 2000 System Manual*. Feedback Instruments Ltd, UK.

(9) *Earth Observation Quarterly*. Journal of ESA, ESTEC. Noordwijk, Netherlands.

(10) Häkan Olsen, International Maritime Satellite Organization (IMARSAT), London. Private communication to author.

(11) Marconi International Marine Co. Ltd (1992) *'Oceanray' Satellite Communications Terminal, Ship's Manual*.

(12) INMARSAT-B System Technical Summary, 1996. Inmarsat, London.

(13) INMARSAT-M System Technical Summary, 1996. Inmarsat, London.

(14) Griffin D.W. and Lim J.S. (1988) 'Multiband Excitation Vocoder'. *IEEE, Transactions on Acoustics, Speech and Signal Processing*, Vol 36, No 8, August.

(15) Appleyard, S.F. (1980) *Marine Electronic Navigation*, London: Routledge and Kegan Paul Ltd.

(16) Mattos, P.G. (1989) 'Global Positioning by Satellite'. *Electronics + Wireless World*, Feb., p. 137.

(17) Spilker, J.J. (1978) 'GPS Signal Structure and Characteristics'. *Journal of the Institute of Navigation* (USA), Vol. 25, No. 2, Summer.

(18) Owen J.I.R., DRA, Farnborough, UK. Private communication to author, 1996.

(19) GPS Builder-2 Development System Product Information Notes. 1997. GEC Plessey Semiconductors Ltd, UK.

(20) Pierce, J. and Finley, M., eds (1989) *Understanding Radio Determination Satellite Service*. Geostar Corp., USA.

Chapter 8

Global business systems, ancillary services and hybrid systems

8.1 MAJOR CORPORATE BUSINESS SYSTEMS

In the main, the major owners of the satellite space segments are organizations such as INTELSAT (International Telecommunications Satellite Organization), EUTELSAT (European Telecommunications Satellite service, an arm of the European Space Agency), PASAT (Pan American Satellite Inc.) and Société Européenne des Satellites (SES). These then lease the day-to-day operation to other suitably qualified and certified organizations.

The up-link ground stations are usually equipped with antennas ranging in diameter from 13 to 18 m for C band and 9 to 13 m for Ku band. The leassees then operate the down-link ground stations with antennas that may range in diameter from 3.5 to 13 m. The individual transponder channels may then be sub-leased to other end users. The services provided include television, voice and digital data and these are often linked into the national PSTN or ISDN. In fact, apart from the propagation delay which only becomes apparent during two-way interviews, the high grade of these services makes the satellite channels practically transparent to the end users.

The wide range of antenna sizes in operation allows for a correspondingly wide range of LNAs/LNBs to be used to meet the system overall G/T ratios. The parameters and standards for the complete ground stations, including up-link, down-link and footprints (specified down to a minimum elevation angle of 10°) are closely specified in the literature (1). The power budget calculations and the comparison of the relative merits of TDMA and SCPC have been explained earlier.

Services are provided in both the C and Ku bands and the latter is probably most popular outside of the USA. The transponder bandwidths are in the order of 36–72 MHz and these may be occupied by either analogue or digital signals. All forms of analogue modulation are catered for, typically using FDMA/SCPC. Most of the digital services carried use QPSK/2–4PSK or QAM modulation with TDMA/SCPC protocols. The developing digital television services will employ multiple channels per carrier within a complex multiplex. The bandwidth for these services is usually allocated in contiguous blocks of 64 kbit/s depending upon the user requirement up to a maximum of 8.488 Mbit/s. This, however, can be extended up to 24.576 Mbit/s for special cases using differential encoding and demand assignment (DA). FEC using 1/2 or 3/4 rate convolutional coding plus Viterbi decoding is commonly employed to produce a bit error rate better than 10^{-3}. A form of spread spectrum transmission is commonly employed using scrambling to act as a form of energy dispersal to obtain full channel occupancy. Even so, it is still allowed for the originator to include encryption within his own domain.

A number of operators have been licensed to operate fixed and mobile ground stations through most satellites. These organizations lease the transponders on a permanent basis to provide such services as satellite news-gathering services with news feeds on an international basis; videoconferencing and other corporate communications services; even a private racing network service with sound and video distribution to bookmakers throughout Europe. Although the racing network uses a B-MAC system developed by Scientific Atlanta Inc. for vision with Dolby ADM for sound, all other forms of modulation and television formats can be handled.

The INTELSAT system

This organization is the oldest and largest international group involved with satellite communications and was formed in the USA in 1964. Since that time, the organization has developed a rolling sequence of new satellites. Currently the Series IV are the oldest in regular operation and are due to be replaced by the Series IX which should start to be delivered in orbit in about the year 2000. Since each Series IX satellite will have the equivalent capacity to replace two Series IV birds, this will significantly reduce the pressure on the IFRB (International Frequency Registration Board) to provide extra geostationary locations.

Almost all of the satellites use both the C and Ku bands with frequency reuse through alternative polarizations (the exception being INTELSAT K). The up-link frequencies in use are 6 GHz and 14–14.5 GHz for the C and Ku bands respectively. The equivalent down-link frequencies are 4 GHz for the C band and 11.45–12.75 GHz (FSS Fixed satellite) and BSS (Broadcast satellite)) for the Ku band. Most of the satellites employ either steerable high-gain spot beam antennas or broad coverage contoured beams with about 2 dBW lower EIRP for a more flexible earth coverage. The down-link channels employ FDM for television distribution and TDM for telephony and digital data. Four-phase PSK modulation is used for the digital data channels at a rate of 120.832 Mbit/s. Other modulation methods may be employed for both the analogue and digital channels. The transponder bandwidths are in general 72 MHz wide.

In general, the available on-board power, the number of transponders and the channel capacity has increased with each new series of bird, with the exception of the Series VII. This pioneered a number of new techniques such as the introduction of solid state power ampliers (SSPA) for the C band down-link channels, which then extends through to the Ku band transponders of later birds.

Furthermore, the Series VII replaced the concept of using the transponders as frequency changers by introducing on-board switching so that each up-link signal could be switched through to any down-link channel.

The INTELSAT K birds employ only Ku band for their down-link services. This allows for the simultaneous up-linking of either point-to-point, point-to-multipoint or multipoint-to-multipoint services. A total available transponder power of 3.155 kW is divided between the Ku band channels, each providing an output of 18 dBW (60 W). This with the antenna gains brings the EIRP up to 47–50 dBW, a level suitable for direct-to-home (DTH) broadcasting services. Each transponder uses both vertical and horizontal polarizations as frequency reuse.

The EUTELSAT system

Although the European Telecommunications Satellite Organization was founded during 1977, EUTELSAT owes its origins to the interest and work inspired by the earlier European Space Research Organization (ESRO) and the European Launcher Development Organization (ELDO) which were formed in 1962 and 1964 respectively. The European Space Agency (ESA) developed from the former (1975), while the latter gave birth to Arianne 1, the European launch vehicle which itself has now developed into a successful fifth-generation launch system. During 1983 Arianne 1 successfully launched Europe's first communications bird Euteesat 1-F1. Kourou in French Guiana was chosen as the launch site for the European satellites because it is only about 4° north of the equator, a fact that maximizes the slingshot effect which allows a heavier load to be placed in orbit for a given energy input. By the end of the 1980s there were five Eutelsats in operation covering all of Europe and the northern coastal parts of Africa. All the Eutelsat birds are located at 7°, 10°, 13°, or 16° East.

The service is linked to all the European PTTs via two earth stations, Guadalajara (Spain) and Fucino (Italy). These act as reference and timing stations for all the earth stations in the network, including the TDMA synchronism. The system provides for telephony that includes DSI, telecommunications, television, and digital business services. The television transmissions allow for DTH using antennas with a dish diameter of about 1.2 m. The business system allows either open or dedicated networks, with users having access to data rates of 2.048 Mbit/s which can provide for videoconferencing and similar operations. Various other data rates are available in multiples of 64 kbit/s for rapid file transfers. The closed part of the system provides for broadcast, point-to-multipoint corporate users such as stock exchanges.

The up-link stations employ antennas with a diameter ranging from 14 to 20 m and transmit in the 14 GHz band. The down-link frequencies fall in the 11–12 GHz band. The television channels use FDMA analogue transmissions in PAL, SECAM or NTSC while the digital system employs TDMA at about 120 Mbit/s.

Eutelsat II birds have a total power availability of 3 kW which can power sixteen transponders that can all operate simultaneously to provide individual RF power outputs of 50 W. The EIRP ranges from 47–50 dBW for spot beams to 39–44 dBW for the wide area coverage.

The third-generation European satellites, designed for an operational lifetime of fifteen years, are known as HOT-BIRD. HB1 is currently in operation and by the year 2000, HB2, HB3, HB4 and HB5 should all be co-located at 13° East. At that stage, eighty-two transponders will provide for 800 digital television channels covering the FSS and BSS bands. The transponder power amplifiers are to be TWT devices providing outputs of either 115 or 135 W. Again, on-board switching is provided to couple any up-link input to any down-link output.

HB5 and HB6 will include a system referred to as SKYPLEX which will allow each bird to receive up-link digital broadcast signals from multiple ground stations simultaneously and then rebroadcast them on a common carrier using the TDM system.

The PASAT system

The privately owned Pan-American Satellite organization is the smallest of the three described here, but probably has the densest array of transponders. These provide a worldwide service to all continents from birds located over the oceans to maximize the coverage. Five satellites are currently in use and three more are on order or being built. Each bird carries sixteen C band and twenty-four Ku band transponders. The TWTA power amplifiers provide an RF input to the antennas of 30 W (15 dBW) and 63 W (18 dBW) for the C and Ku band transponders respectively. On-board cross-strapping or switching can link any C band input to any Ku band output and vice versa. The EIRP from the wide area coverage antennas ranges from 40 to 47 dBW. The system operates successfully using up-link antennas of 2.3 m diameter, with 1.8 m diameter for reception.

Future developments

While technology changes take a considerable time to perfect, each new launch invariably sees some new feature that has to be tested in the harsh environment of space. Depending upon the viewpoint, changes can therefore appear to be quite slow or even dramatic. Where current satellites have been designed and built to provide for perhaps twenty analogue television channels, the next generation will need to be able to power and switch more than ten times this number of multiplexed digital channels.

Inter-satellite communications links can quite considerably increase the path range of communications. Radio frequency links have aready been used to advantage in a number of services and this concept could well develop further. By moving to the 80–100 GHz frequency range, small, lightweight and high-gain antennas become available for inter-satellite links, in an environment that does not suffer from rain fade problems. Links using optical or infrared wavelengths can be used and these do not have the same bandwidth/power limitations as RF.

User interactive services are also necessary for many applications but the problem of providing a return path via satellite for, say, a television services subscriber is fraught with difficulties. The usual approach is to utilize the telephone network but this is very limited in its data-carrying capacity. In addition, there are many areas of the world in which it is difficult or not even economic to install telephone cables. A proposition has already been placed before the ITU and the American FCC in which the DTH subscriber return up-link might be provided over the Ka band.

By receiving down-link signals in the Ku band, it is conjectured that a low data rate digital signal could be up-linked through to the service originator by using the same receiver antenna but energized at Ka band. The switch from, say, 10 to 30 GHz means that the antenna would have an extra gain of $(30/10)^2 = 9$ or about 9.5 dB for the interactive leg of the system. The application to use this concept proposes sixteen co-located birds which could also provide business and home videoconferencing, database transmissions and even telephony. The major disadvantages are the propagation delay involved and the fact that the Ka band is much more susceptible to rain fade problems than the Ku band signals.

8.2   SATELLITE NEWS GATHERING (SNG)

Basically there are two situations where the use of mobile TV camera equipment is needed. One is the large international event, well publicized beforehand, which can be covered readily with relatively large earth stations with 3 or 4 m diameter antennas and using standard TV satellite transmissions. Alternatively, emergency-type news situations may require the rapid movement of equipment and operating staff over very great distances. Satellite equipment to support such an operation requires a much higher degree of portability. The equipment should be capable of being packed into flight cases for transit with the operating crew using scheduled airlines or be installed in a light motor vehicle. Both the C and Ku bands are available to provide such a service and, of the two, the Ku band is probably the more attractive as there are fewer terrestrial microwave telephone networks to produce mutual interference problems. In any case, signals transmitted over the Ku band can easily be retransmitted or networked over the C band, where the need arises.

For operation in remote areas, primary power consumption can be a critical factor. The antenna size/gain and high-power amplifier (HPA) power requirements form one compromise. The antenna size, beamwidth and side-lobe response also has to be taken into consideration. With satellite spacings of 2° or less, it is important that the side-lobe response should be well within the CCIR $29-25 \log \theta$ dB level. Portability limits the HPA perhaps to 300 W maximum. A typical 600 W HPA weighs something like 135 kg and needs about 5 kW of primary power.

The use of digital processing with some form of bandwidth compression can also be considered. This, combined with forward error correction, could mean that the transmit EIRP required to produce a satisfactory link performance might well be reduced. If the bandwidth is reduced, then so is the noise power contained within it. Thus the signal power can be reduced to maintain the same SNR for a given channel capacity (Shannon's theorem). Reducing the EIRP requirement automatically improves portability.

A digitally encoded broadcast standard analogue colour TV signal would require a bit rate of around 180 or 220 Mbit/s for NTSC or PAL respectively. A bit rate reduction could impair the displayed picture quality, unless use is made of the high level of redundancy contained in the signal. The average information in the TV picture varies relatively little from frame to frame, except in the areas containing movement. This suggests that a compromise might be made between link margin, data rate and picture quality.

It has been conjectured that, in terms of link margin, the standard FM satellite link of 30 MHz is roughly equivalent to a bit rate of 60 Mbit/s. Thus a reduction to 8 Mbit/s or even 2 Mbit/s would yield an improvement in link margin of 60/8 to 60/2, or about 9–15 dB. With operation towards the edge of the satellite coverage area and in bad weather, the SNR might well be degraded. However, using FEC techniques the digital signal would be less affected, any deterioration in the display quality being largely restricted to moving edge definition.

Two equipments that meet these operational and portability criteria are the Ranger (2), manufactured by Alcatel Multipoint Ltd, Witham, Essex, UK, and the Mantis (3) manufactured by Advent Communications Ltd, Chesham, Bucks, UK. Both are available in various configurations to meet a range of different conditions. Depending upon the actual configuration, they are designed to be packed into four to seven flight cases for transportation purposes, and deployed and operated by a one- or two-person crew. Ranger may be equipped with either a 0.9, 1.5 or 2.4 m diamond-shaped antenna, as indicated by Figure 8.1, while Mantis employs either a 1.5 or 1.9 m diameter circular antenna (see Figure 8.2). The Ranger antenna is of the offset fed type, while Mantis uses a prime focus feed. Both antennas are sectionalized for ease of transportation, with the panels being accurately aligned and securely clamped when deployed. Both more than adequately meet the CCIR side-lobe response requirements applicable to all satellite operators.

Both systems provide a minimum EIRP of 69 dBW with the smaller antenna and a single 350 W HPA. The addition of a phase-combined second HPA raises the power output to 700 W (a 3 dB increase). This, together with the larger antenna, then raises the EIRP to a maximum of almost 75 dBW.

The equipments (see Figure 8.3) include a receiver used for both antenna alignment and link monitoring. Both transmit and receive signals are processed in a double conversion mode, with transmission in the range of 14–14.5 GHz. The corresponding receive band covers the range 10.95–12.75 GHz. Transmis-

Figure 8.1 Ranger satellite news-gathering equipment (Courtesy of Alcatel Multipoint Ltd, Witham, Essex, UK).

sion uses standard frequency modulation, plus energy dispersal for the vision channel, and a choice of sub-carriers, including dual, for sound. Using alternative modulators, provision is made to handle digital signals from 64 kbit/s to 2.048 Mbit/s, plus those from a video digital coder/decoder (codec). Provision is made to transmit either analogue NTSC, PAL or SECAM standard TV signals, using frequency modulation or MPEG digital signals as QPSK modulation. Provision is also made for the use of video compression codecs at bit rates of 1.5–8 Mbit/s.

Both systems are capable of handling radio broadcasts, data transmissions, telephony and video signals and can be deployed in less than twenty minutes.

Referring to Figure 8.3, the signal input to the digital video encoder may be either composite video or RGB, plus audio, from either an electronic news-gathering (ENG) camera or a video tape recorder (VTR). These signals are

Figure 8.2 Mantis satellite news-gathering system (Courtesy of Advent Communications Ltd, Chesham, UK).

converted into a common digital data stream with a very low bit rate, from 1.544 Mbit/s for the North American and 2.048 Mbit/s for the European standard, up to a maximum of 8 Mbit/s. The codec is capable of working between the 625/50 and 525/60 line standards without using an analogue video standards converter.

The data compression technique (4) consists essentially of transmitting only the frame-to-frame changes in the picture information. Picture areas containing movement can be predictively encoded using DPCM, followed by a statistically matched variable length code format. This data signal is then used to QPSK-modulate a 70 MHz carrier. Alternatively, when the network demands a higher picture quality, the analogue video signal can be used to frequency-modulate a 70 MHz carrier in the conventional manner. Either 70 MHz modulated signal is then up-converted and amplified to provide an output at 14–14.5 GHz from the antenna via the orthomode transducer (OMT).

The down-link signals in the range 10.95–12.75 GHz, which are handled in two sub-bands, are filtered and down-converted by the LNB to provide a first IF of 950–1750 MHz.

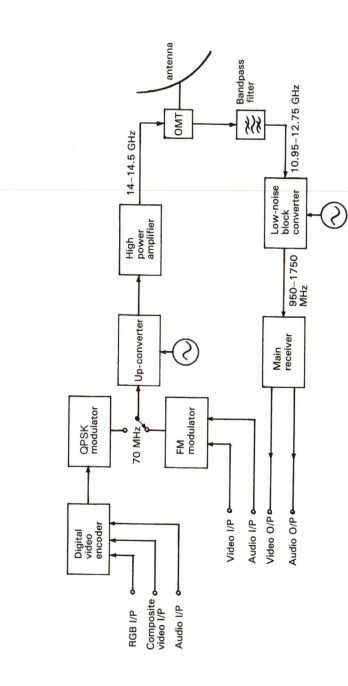

Figure 8.3 Block diagram of basic SNG system.

As an alternative to the mobile SNG concept described above, the complete system may be enclosed within a 30 m^3 road transport truck body, with typically a 2.6 m Gregorian offset-fed antenna mounted on the roof, in a folded configuration for transportation. Such an antenna typically has a gain of 50 dB in the transmit mode and 49 dB for receive, with adequate side-lobe rejection to meet the standards set by all satellite operators.

This size of body also provides for a limited-facility outside broadcast (OB) service. This, together with its own 15 kW diesel powered generator, allows the system to provide a very flexible service to network stations, in any TV format. Two HP As can be provided so that these can function either in parallel for increased output or with one as a redundant spare. The maximum EIRP is then better than 77 dBW for the 14.0–14.5 GHz transmission band.

Videoconferencing

A videoconference is a *meeting* between two or more groups of people in different locations, which is organized via a two-way sound and vision link. The locations may be in very different parts of the world, in which case satellite and cable systems can play a vital role in the provision of the link. Currently, the space links for these services are provided by such organizations as EUTELSAT and INTELSAT, with the large earth stations and back-haul links being provided by the PTTs. In addition, corporate telecommunication organizations provide ISDN and similar services over wide area wideband cable systems.

The extent to which this service has grown is indicated by the number of standards that have been formulated by the ITU. Of these, the following are probably the most important.

H261. Describes how the codec should compress the video signal and recommends the algorithms by which it can be achieved. This also recommends the common image format (CIF) which includes the number of scan lines, the pixel density (pixels per line), and the frame rate. The CIF consists of 288 lines each of 352 pixels in each frame, with a repetition frequency of 30 frames per second. The standard also defines a quarter CIF (QCIF) of 144 lines and 176 pixels at the same 30 Hz frame rate. The QCIF standard was designed for picture telephone applications. Although the standard defines the coding scheme, it leaves room within the codec for various levels of implementation, ranging from inexpensive low quality, up to complex technologies with higher quality images.

H320. Defines the parameters for audio and video codecs and protocols for services over ISDN lines. The design caters for desktop videoconferencing where point-to-point links can be established between two computers over local or wide area networks (LAN or WAN) or over an ISDN.

H323. Provides for audio and video codec and protocols for Internet (IP) based LANs. This is an adaption of H320 codecs to the IP environment, but still needs the bandwidth available from the LAN.

H324. As for H320 but intended for operation over the plain old telephone system (POTS). The low-bandwidth analogue lines produce a significant bottleneck with their low transmission rate.

H325. The design covers high-speed services using the asynchronous transfer mode (ATM) of data exchange.

T120. Covers the protocols for data exchanges.

The major claims made for the effectiveness of these services lie in the reduction of travel for personnel and the speed with which international videoconferences can be organized. Typically, up to six persons can be comfortably catered for at each end terminal or studio. The essential elements of this system, which is based on closed circuit TV (CCTV), are shown in Figure 8.4 (5). The system consists of one or two *face-to-face* cameras and one or two colour TV receivers for the incoming signals. A local colour monitor is also provided and the terminal is often housed in a roll-away cabinet. The TV system for each end terminal, as described here, is generally either PAL, NTSC or SECAM encoded, although the more recent developing systems will cater for compressed digital video signals. A high-resolution *graphics* camera is also incorporated. Additional provision can be made for an alphanumeric keyboard to insert text data as the need arises, together with a video printer and interface for a VTR. A digital interface is also available to connect a fax machine or a graphics tablet via the data port.

Local control over the system is via a conventional infrared remote control, similar to that used on many TV receivers. This can also be used to control the *focus* and *zoom* functions on the graphics camera.

The central element in each terminal is a codec (5) which codes and decodes the vision, sound and data signals that may be transmitted over land lines or directly from a VSAT terminal. The unit also provides for security of information by using optional encryption/decryption of the data stream.

The main information channel is the face-to-face vision sub-system. Here it is usual for each camera to provide a full frame view of up to three persons, sitting side by side. The middle strip of each frame from each camera output is selected and then electronically stacked, to provide a three-over-three, full frame view for transmission. This *split screen* approach avoids the corners of the camera images, where resolution and distortion are not of the best. The decoder receives this stacked image and generates two half-sized images which are then centrally positioned in each video frame, with the top and bottom sections blanked to black level. These are then displayed either on two adjacent monitors or on one single large-screen receiver to provide an image of the distant studio.

The codec usually has two modes of operation: fast for high-resolution graphics, and slow for moving picture face-to-face operation.

A number of different video compression techniques have been applied to videoconferencing and are described in the literature (6). These range from transmitting every nineteenth pixel, which requires up to two seconds to transmit a single frame, up to the MPEG compression techniques with bit rates ranging from about 384 kHz upwards.

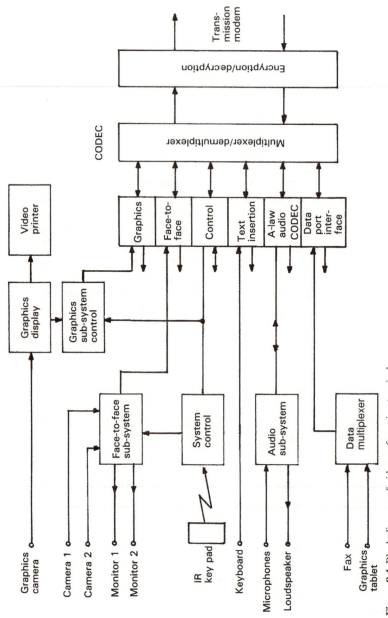

Figure 8.4 Block diagram of videoconferencing terminal.

The audio channel, which can provide for stereo as well as mono signals, uses A-law companding and PCM coding, for *sound-in-vision* (SIV). This is a time multiplex used to avoid the necessity for separate sound and control channels. The audio signal is sampled at a rate synchronized to the line frequency of the local camera, and the derived data words are inserted, one in each line blanking period. The sound sub-system also includes an *echo cancelling* unit. Echoes can be caused by the outputs from the terminal loudspeakers which may be retransmitted by the terminal's microphones. This unit samples the incoming audio signal, compares it with the studio sound and estimates the echo component, which is then subtracted from the outgoing audio signal.

Sound in vision

To improve flexibility of operation, the codec may be installed at a switching centre. In this case, the video signal may be delivered over a land line. In order to avoid the use of separate sound and data channels, a time multiplex, known alternatively as sound-in-vision (SIV) or sound-in-syncs (SIS), can be used. The land lines used to carry the video signal would be those normally used to carry thirty-two 64 kbit/s (2.048 Mbit/s) PCM channels in Europe, or twenty-four 64 kbit/s channels plus eight framing bits (1.544 Mbit/s) in the USA. For this application of SIV, the audio signal is low-pass-filtered, and sampled at 7.8125 kHz (1/2 line rate) and quantized using eight bits. These are then inserted into a 2 μs time slot during each alternate line sync pulse period. The instantaneous bit rate is thus 4 Mbit/s, with an average rate of (8 × 7.8125 kHz)/2 = 31.35 kbit/s. On the alternate lines, four bits can be transmitted for identification purposes, leaving four bits spare for the control of auxillary applications.

Desktop videoconferencing

This development allows the personal computer (PC) to be connected into a corporate LAN either from a home terminal via an ISDN link, or directly into a business network. It only requires the installation of a plug-in card to the PC bus system and the addition of a small camera such as that shown in Figure 8.5 (7). This device provides a high-resolution image from a 1/4″ CCD sensor and a 4 mm, F = 1:3.8 lens. the camera operates adequately from light levels as low as 10 lux and has an automatic white level balance. An electronic shutter with speeds ranging from 8 to 20 ms is also provided. The 5 V power requirements can be provided from the host computer and the camera produces a standard video output level of 1 V into 75 Ω and mono audio at a level of 327 mV.

Bandwidth compression

Any videoconferencing codec has to respond to two basic situations: the transmission of moving pictures of reasonable quality and high-quality images of

Figure 8.5 Miniature desktop videoconferencing camera (Courtesy of Premier Electronics Ltd, Waltham Cross, UK).

documents. The codec for analogue TV systems operates on the components of the video signal, i.e. the luminance and the two colour difference signals (for example, Y and U, V in the PAL system). Operating in this way makes the codec readily adaptable for processing NTSC and SECAM signals. Because all these formats differ chiefly only in the way that the colour difference signals are processed and transmitted, all the variants can be handled by the use of suitable video interfaces. While an RGB interface might also be provided, the data compression only operates on the video components (Y and U, V). Provision also has to be made for the processing of audio and data signals. A block diagram of the encoder section of a typical codec is given in Figure 8.6. Its companion decoder is essentially complementary.

Redundancy in the video image

Bit rate reduction techniques make use of the high level of redundancy contained in the information of a television picture. The literature (8, 9, 10) explains very

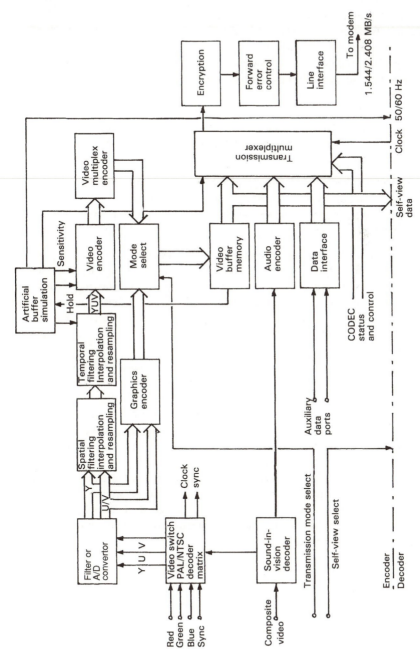

Figure 8.6 System block diagram for typical encoder section of video codec.

clearly how this is related to the picture definition and quality. Even in its analogue form, the picture has been derived by a sampling process. Horizontal scanning represents sampling in the vertical sense, as this divides the image into very narrow strips, the smallest definable strip being represented by the number of lines per picture height. A series of separate images or frames can represent a moving scene, the movement between images going undetected. The frame rate therefore represents a sampling of images per unit time. Digitization of each scan line would introduce horizontal sampling.

The definition or degree of fineness of detail contained in an image is measured in terms of pixels and the rate at which these can change in intensity. This therefore leads to a response that can be evaluated using three kinds of frequency:

- Horizontal frequency f_x, as cycles per picture width, c/pw
- Vertical frequency f_y, as cycles per picture height, c/ph
- Temporal frequency f_t, indicating how fast the image intensity is changing as a function of time

These components can be represented in three-dimensional space by three frequencies mutually at right angles to each other. Obviously, the greater the number of pixels used and change per unit time, the greater the bandwidth needed for transmission. For bandwidth compression to be effective this detail must be minimized in some way, such as by combining pixels. This can be achieved if each frame is digitized and the image data stored in a semiconductor memory.

In both the analogue and digital senses, filtering amounts to the combination or averaging of information, in this case from a number of different pixels. Horizontal or vertical (spatial) filtering is achieved by combining pixels from the same or adjacent lines respectively. Temporal filtering is achieved by combining only those pixels that occupy the same position in successive frames. By including more than one kind of pixel in the same filtering process, horizontal-temporal or vertical-temporal filtering can be achieved. The general term for this is *spatio-temporal* filtering. From this, it can be seen that there are two distinct areas where redundancy can occur: from line to line or *intra-frame*, or from frame to frame or *inter-frame*. Both can be invoked to reduce the bandwidth required, by transmitting the stationary area detail less often and/or by signalling the position of the moving areas.

The H.261 codec (4, 11)

International collaboration through the Motion Picture Experts Group (MPEG) and Joint Photographic Experts Group (JPEG) committees of the CCITT has led to the development and design of a codec that is ISDN compatible. It can be used for audio visual services at bit rates between 64 kbit/s and 2.048 Mbit/s. This has been achieved by allowing each codec to apply pre- and post-processing of the local television signal. Either 625/25 or 525/30 standard formats generate a *common image format* (CIF) signal for the transmission channel. The CIF is based on non-interlaced lines (sequential or progressive scanning). 625 line systems use 576 active lines per picture (frame), so that 288 lines form one field. Therefore 625/25 codecs only have to perform a conversion to meet the 30 Hz picture rate and 525/30 codecs already operate at the correct frame rate so these only have to convert between 240 and 288 active lines. The advantage of the CIF is that all transmissions are to a common standard, a feature that means that the core codec design is to a world standard and this considerably aids interconnectability.

The CIF is formed by sampling the video signal luminance component at 6.75 MHz (chrominance at 3.375 MHz) to produce 352 eight bit samples per line. This is equivalent to an analogue bandwidth of about 3.4 MHz, so that the processed image is only about 30 percent below that of full studio quality.

A lower image resolution is acceptable for applications such as video phones and for these cases a second standard is incorporated in H.261. This is described as the *quarter common image format* (QCIF).

The coding scheme and data compression algorithm are based on *differential PCM* (DPCM) and *discrete cosine transform* (DCT) with *motion compensation*. Conceptually, the 1D (one-dimensional) DCT is equivalent to taking the Fourier transform and retaining only the *real* or cosine part. The 2D (two-dimensional) DCT can be obtained by performing a 1D operation on the columns of a matrix, followed by a second 1D operation on the rows. The sampled YUV (luminance and chrominance) components of the video signal are processed separately but in the same way. The basic processing technique for each component is shown in Figure 8.7 which indicates how the previously coded image data is subtracted from the current one to produce a *difference* image (point 1). The image is divided into blocks of 8 × 8 pixels which are then DCT-processed using the transfer functions quoted in Chapters 5 and 9.

The coefficients in each block represent the amplitudes of the various spatial frequencies present, the top left-hand element in this matrix representing the average or dc level for the whole block. The matrix values are then scanned in a zigzag fashion as indicated in Figure 8.8 to produce a serial bit stream. At this stage only the dc component and a few low spatial frequencies have any significant magnitude. The following quantizing stage sets all the very low values to zero and truncates the others to a set of preferred levels, further reducing the number of values that need to be transmitted.

Motion compensation is achieved by minimizing the frame-to-frame differences that have to be transmitted. This operates by taking four blocks (16 × 16 pixels) from the current image which has been reconstructed via the inverse DCT processor, and searching over ±15 pixels vertically and horizontally to find the best match. The variable length store is then adjusted so that the best match section of the image is used for subtraction at point 4. The vertical and horizontal translations derived from this *block matching* are later included in the transmission multiplex as motion correction or displacement vectors. While the

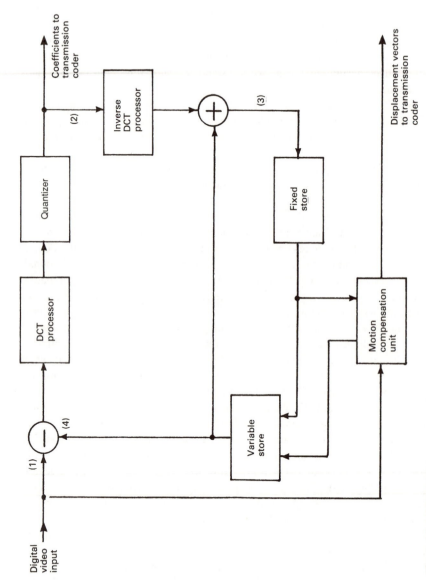

Figure 8.7 MPEG/H261 image processing.

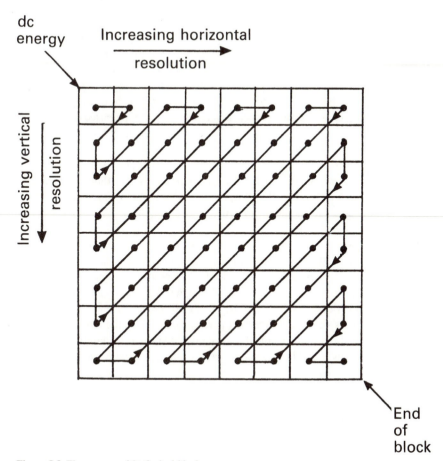

Figure 8.8 Zigzag scan of 8×8 pixel block.

data bits are acquired at a variable rate and need to be transmitted at a constant rate, buffer stores are needed at both the encoding and decoding stages. Control signals are therefore added, to ensure that the receiver decoder uses up the data bits at the correct variable rate. At the receiver, the decoder uses the DCT coefficient values and the displacement vectors with a *block matching* technique, to reconstruct the image in a manner similar to that at point 3 in Figure 8.7.

Data compression for transmission is achieved by using run-length coding (RLC) which functions in the following manner. The quantized ac coefficients usually contain many runs of consecutive zeros and these are indicated by two 4-bit nibbles as follows. The upper four bits indicate the number of consecutive zeros before the next coefficient, while the lower four bits indicate the number of significant bits in the next coefficient. Following this code symbol are the significant bits of the coefficient, whose length can be determined from the lower four bits of the code symbol. At the receiver, the inverse RLC decoder translates the coded bit stream into an output array of ac coefficients. It takes the current code and inserts the number of zeros indicated by the RLC. The coefficient entered into the array has the number of bits indicated by the lower four bits of the RLC and a value determined from the number of the trailing bits.

A further degree of bit rate reduction can be achieved by using a modified Huffman code. In this case, shorter code words are used for frequently occurring symbols and longer codes for the occasional ones. This can be based on a look-up table stored in a read-only memory (ROM) or alternatively operated in an adaptive manner for specific images. This involves creating a table based on the frequency count of each symbol in the image. This data table is then stored in a random access memory (RAM) for use in a similar way. Although the digital processing in the video channel is fast, the propagation delay has to be matched in the audio channel to maintain lip-sync.

JPEG compression

An A4 (210 mm × 297 mm) colour image scanned at 300 dpi (dots per inch) and using a 24-bit pixel creates an image file of about 25 Mbytes and lossless compression can reduce this to about 6–10 Mbytes. The new standard for JPEG lossless compression was due to be finalized before 1998 and provides compression ratios that are at least 20 percent better than the earlier standard. JPEG 2000 is a further enhancement that is aimed at providing a unified standard that covers both lossy and lossless compression and will cope with a wider range of original input images.

The lossless JPEG system operates on the basis that pixels in close proximity to each other tend to have a high degree of correlation. Pixel values are stored in a raster format of lines that make up the image. The values are scanned and a prediction process is used to estimate the value of a pixel based on the previous stored value. Then instead of storing the pixel value, the difference between the predicted and actual value is stored. Since encoding and decoding will use the same algorithm, it is highly likely that the decoder will make the same predictions. By operating an entropy coding system such as Huffman on the difference data, the image can be stored with fewer bits per pixel.

The major problems occur with vertical edges because these represent regions where neighbouring pixels are uncorrelated. To counter this, the predictor considers pixels on either side of the detected edge before making its decision. The new standard has been achieved by creating more accurate prediction algorithms to improve the entropy coding efficiency. Also, feedback has been introduced during the compression process to allow the algorithm to learn about the statistics of the particular image and so be able to adjust the encoding process accordingly.

Primary code format

The primary coding for the transmitted bit stream is alternate mark inversion (AMI) in the USA and high-density bipolar 3 (HDB3) in Europe. In both cases, a *zero* is coded by the absence of a pulse and a *one* by alternate positive and negative pulses of 50 percent duty cycle. Such a format is most suitable for cable and other forms of transmission, because their frequency spectra contain no dc component. However, a long string of zeros can lead to loss of clock synchronization and consequent data errors.

This problem can be minimized by the use of the bipolar N-zero substitution (BNZS) format, typical codes being B6ZS or B8ZS, where a string of six or eight zeros is substituted by bipolar pulses that infringe the 'alternate ones' rule. The decoder recognizes these substitutions as code violations and produces the necessary corrective action.

The HDB3 code is similar to the B3ZS, where code violations are added for strings of four consecutive zeros. Transcoder chips are available that can work with either AMI, HDB3, B6ZS or B8ZS, simply by changing a 2-bit code on a pair of control lines.

For ISDN transmission, the data can be contained in a multiplex as shown in Figure 8.9. The multiplexer stage organizes the digital data components into frames, which are in turn assembled into 16-frame multiframes and 8-multiframe super-multiframes for both European and USA transmission standards. A European frame structure is shown in Figure 8.9. Although the US frame structure is similar, it only contains twenty-four 64 kbit/s time slots. Whereas the European frame is synchronized from time slot zero, the USA frame is synchronized by the 193rd bit in each time slot. For cross-system working (e.g.

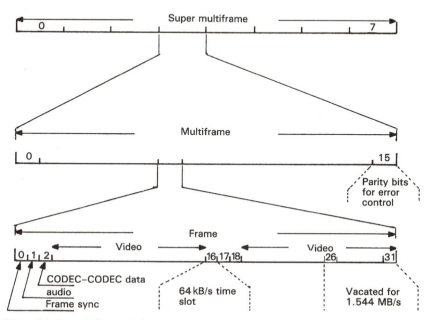

Figure 8.9 Transmission multiplex structure.

NTSC to PAL), the European time slots 26–31 are vacated to allow a remultiplexer to transform the frame formats.

Optional facilities

Although many satellite links provide encryption for data security, it may be necessary to add such protection for land line carriers. This can be provided for within the codec. Forward error correction (FEC) in Europe commonly uses a BCH code (4095, 4035), whose sixty parity bits provide for the correction of up to five random errors plus one burst of up to twenty-six errors in each block of data. The parity bits are inserted into the last eight time slots of each multiframe. For the USA, a shorter FEC code is used, the parity bits for which are transmitted in frame time slot 2.

Developing technology

Briefcase SNG terminal
A small, light, go-anywhere system was developed through cooperation between Columbia Broadcasting System (CBS), Teleglobe Canada and Skywave Electronics Ltd. The latest version of the unit weighs only about 12 kg, and is capable of providing good-quality speech and still pictures plus data into any PSTN (public switched telephone network) over a satellite channel. It operates in the full duplex mode over INMARSAT-C links of 1.5–1.6 GHz to a hub earth station which itself operates in the 4 and 6 GHz bands. The antennas consist of two flat patch microwave arrays, providing circular polarization with a gain of more than 17 dBi. Together with a 10 W RF power amplifier stage, the system produces an EIRP of 27 dBW in a 5 kHz bandwidth. This allows two terminals to operate simultaneously over a single 25 kHz INMARSAT channel. The antennas are fixed to the lid top which is orientated in azimuth and elevation using locking hinges. During deployment the antenna is aligned using the satellite beacon signal. Speech transmissions employ *amplitude companded single sideband* (ACSSB) and the digital modulation scheme uses DMSK at 2400 bit/s.

Power for the terminal may be provided by locally rechargeable NiCd batteries or by 110/230 V 50/60 Hz mains supplies.

When deployed, the terminal can also receive calls, but with the distant operator dialling first the hub terminal code, followed by the briefcase terminal code.

WorldPhone (Nera Telecommunications)
While described as portable satellite telephone, this unit, shown in Figure 8.10, could more accurately be described as the interface to a worldwide communications system for voice, fax, data and e-mail from a portable computer. Interfaces

Figure 8.10 The Nera Worldphone (Courtesy of NERA Telecommunications, Windsor, UK).

to a cordless base station or PABX is provided and data can be sent and received at 2.4 or 4.8 kbit/s. The unit is basically designed to operate through the third generation of INMARSAT birds but it is flexible enough to be able to operate through the ICO system. With battery pack the WorldPhone weighs 2.4 kg and is no larger than a laptop PC. The lid, which acts as the antenna, is detachable and can be used up to 90 m from the base unit. The system can be activated in less than two minutes by aligning the antenna to the satellite beacon signal. Compressed and encrypted data can be sent via the use of a laptop PC coupled through the RS232 interface. The battery pack, which is rechargeable from any AC supply, allows for up to three hours of continuous operation or up to fifty hours on standby. The unit is also capable of being operated from any vehicle battery supply ranging from 10 to 32 V dc.

8.3 PERSONAL COMMUNICATIONS NETWORKS (PCN) AND TELEPHONY SYSTEMS

The developing nations of the world need to be assured of an equitable share of the new telecommunications capabilities if they are to be able to expand their economies in a controlled manner. The availablity of a global information infrastructure (GII) holds the key to many of the problems faced by the so-called third world countries. The provisioning of a new communications system under such conditions poses many questions for the engineering fraternity and, as usual, choices and compromises have to be made.

These regions are often epitomized by small high-density cities, small townships and very small villages and hamlets all scattered across many hundreds or even thousands of miles. The surrounding terrain varies; it may be plains, hills and mountains, forests, deserts, or swamps, in fact all those regions that make life very difficult, both physically and economically, for the communications engineer. Terrestrial radio and television can readily be provided in the VHF/UHF bands for the denser populated areas, with medium-frequency radio broadcasting for the more scattered regions. However, these services are to some extend restricted by the spectrum capacity, the availability of local power supplies and the accessability of the head-end infrastructure for servicing purposes. For cable television and telephony services, the prospect of laying cables or overhead lines through some of these terrains is fraught with difficulties. The one common solution for most of these regions is to resort to satellite-delivered services. While satellite radio and television distribution is well tried and tested, the telephony systems lag some way behind and it is in this field that much new development work is in progress. Telephony via GEO satellites such as the INMARSAT service is not readily available to individual isolated users and in any case requires connection to a PTT or other similar network with the necessary back-up infrastructure. The GEO birds also need quite significant up- and down-link power, levels that are not commonly found in telephony networks. Furthermore, it is necessary to contend with the round trip propagation delay.

Many of the developing communications concepts can be tested in space using microsatellites. These are small satellites that have been developed as a result of cooperation between the Amateur Radio Satellite Corp. (USA), the University of Surrey (UK) and Surrey Satellite Technology Ltd (UK), which form part of the PACSAT Communications Experiment (PCE). The satellites occupy a low earth polar orbit with a period of 90–100 minutes, so that any earth station is covered at least three times every twelve hours. The satellite carries a full-scale *store-and-forward* messaging system, with messages and data being stored in an on-board RAM disk memory. Some of the satellites carry an on-board *charge-coupled-device* (CCD) image sensor for earth scanning, but other sensors are employed. The stored messages and data are transmitted using a packet technique for distribution to the many scattered outposts, helped by the fact that the system software is PC compatible. Due to their relatively very low cost, micro-satellites thus form a very useful concept for testing new ideas under actual space conditions.

Communication via LEOs is already well tried and tested and the low path length losses and propagation delay make these a useful technology for telephony. However, birds with an altitude of about 700–1500 km fly across a given earth location in a few tens of minutes so that many satellites are needed in the same orbit plane to provide a continuous service. Medium earth orbiters (MEOs) that fly at an altitude of about 10 000 km have been tested and these need fewer birds but with a somewhat higher power level to provide for continuous operation.

As a result of the expanding needs for telecommunications, many new proposals are currently being evaluated or established, and taken together these show the extent of the compromises involved. The following sections describe the important features of these developments set out in alphabetical order and not in any particular perceived order of merit.

Astrolink

This proposal is based on five GEO satellites to provide voice, data and video services at data rates from 384 kbit/s up to 8.448 Mbit/s. The power budget is so balanced that the downlink user will be able to receive error correctable digital signals, from dishes ranging from 65 to 120 cm in diameter and operating in the 20–30 GHz band. The five birds will use inter-satellite communications links to obtain global coverage.

Celestri

This proposal, made by a consortium led by Motorola, Matra and Marconi, is intended to provide broadband services for mobile users and will employ a constellation of one GEO plus seventy LEO satellites. The LEOs will interwork with the GEO bird via a space link and the system is expected to become operative by 2003. Apart from a satellite telephone network, the system is intended to provide for videoconferencing, interactive TV, fast Internet access, software distribution and electronic books.

Echostar

Initially this proposed system will operate in the 20–30 GHz band using just two GEO satellites. It is intended to provide voice, video and data communications with bit rates ranging fromn 384 kbit/s to 1.544 Mbit/s.

Galaxy or Spaceway

This system is also intended to operate in the Ku and Ka bands from nine Hughes GEO birds. The service will provide video, audio and data communications direct to the home (DTH) with the receiver employing 66 cm diameter dishes. The data rates range from 384 kbit/s to 6 Mbit/s. Global coverage will be achieved by using inter-satellite links.

GE Star (GE Americom)

This is also a nine GEO satellite system operating in the 20–30 GHz band, but is designed to provide video and audio teleconferencing to small ground stations. The power budget is so balanced that the down-link receiver can operate with an antenna of 65 cm diameter. Data rates will range from 384 kbit/s up to 40 Mbit/s.

Globalstar

This LEO satellite system is funded by American, European and Asian partners and is intended to start operation in 1999. The sequence of birds will occupy a circular orbit at an altitude of about 1400 km which gives them a period of approximately 113 minutes. The orbits will be inclined at an angle of 48° and will initially include eight birds in three planes, later expanding to eight birds in each of six planes.

ICO (*see also* Odyssey)

This intermediate circular orbit (ICO) system will employ ten operation satellites with a design lifetime of twelve years, in two orbits inclined at 45° to the equator with an altitude of 10 355 km and a period of six hours. Each orbit will also include two spare birds. INMARSAT is the largest shareholder and sponsor of the system.

The system has been designed to have the advantages of both LEOs and GEOs without too many of the disadvantages. At this altitude, each bird travels across the earth at the low rate of 1° per minute so that any ground user will be able to see at least two birds at any one time. The system will include twelve satellite access nodes (SAN) that are distributed globally and linked together via the so-called P-Net, which also provides gateways to the public terrestrial and cellular networks.

The user's dual mode handset will be able to select either satellite or terrestrial mode and will be able to receive or initiate calls. The maximum handset transmit power is in the order of 0.25 W. The system uses a form of path diversity via multiple satellites which provides an adequate service with a link margin as low as 7 dB. The TDMA mode of access has been selected because it generally provides a greater traffic-handling capacity. ICO is intended for either voice or data communications at bit rates of either 2.4 or 4.8 kbit/s.

The handsets operate in the bands 1980–2010 MHz and 2170–2200 MHz and the feeder links between the SANs and P-Net to the satellites operate at 5100–5250 MHz and 6925–7055 MHz.

Iridium system (element 77 in the atomic table)

This proposal, originally made by Motorola Corp., is now under construction for a large international consortium. The network should commence operations during 1999. The system was initially based on seventy-seven LEOs at an altitude of about 780 km. The sixty-six satellites in the latest design will be located in six circular orbit planes and with eleven birds to each plane. The orbit planes are inclined at an angle of 86.5° and the satellite period is 100 minutes. The system is equipped with inter-satellite links to provide global communications. Like the GSM system with which it shares a number of features, Iridium employs CDMA. It operates on a cellular basis with calls being switched between satellites, then ultimately to a ground station to be patched into the terrestrial telephone system. The narrowband service will operate in the Ka band and utilize bit rates of 2.4 and 4.8 kbit/s for digital voice, fax and data. The service also provides for receive-only pagers that can display up to 220 alphanumeric characters. The system will depend upon smart cards for authentication and security. This service should prove to be more economical than the present terrestrial telephone system, particularly in low population density and remote rural areas.

Millennium

This is another Motorola proposition but aimed at providing point-to-point and point-to-multipoint communications in real time. The services include voice, fax, video and data at bit rates ranging from 384 kbit/s to 51.84 Mbit/s using four GEO satellites equipped with intersatellite links and operating in the Ka band. The power budget is designed to allow the receiver users to operate with antennas of about 70 cm diameter.

M-Star

During 1996 Motorola lodged a filing to use 1.5 GHz of the 40–50 GHz part of the spectrum to provide services for corporate and private users of intranets, LANs and WANs. The system calls for twelve LEO birds in orbits inclined at 47° and with six satellites in each plane. With an altitude of 1350 km, the period would be about 110 minutes. With a user antenna size of 65–150 cm, the system could support bit rates ranging from 2.048–51.84 Mbit/s.

Odyssey (*see also* ICO)

This proposition had the support of a North American (USA and Canada) consortium and provides for a total of twelve LEOs in three circular orbits inclined at 55° at an altitude of 10 400 km and with a period of about 360 minutes. The ground station to satellite links operate within the Ka band and the user section employs the L band to support data rates of 4.8 or 9.6 kbit/s. Because of the similarities between the two systems and to make better use of the joint research and development facilities, Odyssey has now merged with ICO.

Orion

This system is designed to support high-speed digital services using eight GEO satellites and with user antennas of about 2 m diameter. While the user bit rate ranges from 64 kbit/s to 2.048 Mbit/s, the on-board transponders are capable of operating at 155 Mbit/s.

Sativod

This Alcatel proposition is based initially on thirty-two LEOs located at an altitude of 1626 km to provide broadband communications services with dishes as small as 35 cm diameter. The system is ultimately expandable to sixty-four satellites. The user frequencies fall in the 1–14 GHz range while the feeder up-links operate in the Ka band. The up-link can support a total of 60 Mbit/s which is shared between users at 16 kbit/s up to 2.048 Mbit/s.

Teledesic

This extensive system of LEOs includes 840 satellites, plus eighty-four inorbit spares, in twenty-one orbit planes, located at an altitude of 700 km. The aim is to provide an almost global coverage in a cellular fashion. It is anticipated that the service will start in 2002 and will eventually cover almost 99 percent of the earth's surface. The system will operate in the Ka band using antennas with a diameter of 30–150 cm. Bit rates will range from 16 kbit/s to 2.048 Mbit/s for digital data, including fast Internet access, with 4.8 kbit/s allocated to digital telephony.

Telenor

This represents a major down-linking gateway to several satellite systems and is operated by the Norwegian telecommunications organization Telenor. The ground station is located close to the polar ice cap and within 200 km of the North Pole. At this location it is possible to *see* many of the world's GEO, LEO, MEO and polar-orbiting satellites. It is therefore ideally suited to down-linking digital information at data rates of up to 105 Mbit/s from any of these birds. The station operates in a store-and-forward mode so that the received data can be up-linked to any GEO satellite for onward transmission to the final addressee at a bit rate of 45 Mbit/s. The service typically provides for environmental and earth observation data and is used by both NASA and Eumetsat. Additionally the station can be used for satellite telemetry, tracking and control (TTC), because it can retain contact with LEO birds when other monitoring stations are unsighted. For this service, the station can transmit corrective positioning data to any satellite in sight.

Voicespan

This American AT&T proposition calls for twelve GEO satellites operating in the Ka band to provide for a wide range of services ranging from basic telephony to advanced multimedia transmissions. The available bit rates range from 32 kbit/s to 1.544 Mbit/s. Antenna size will depend upon the nature of the service being used and ranges from about 1 to 2 m in diameter.

8.4 SMALL SYSTEM SATELLITE SERVICES

The technical developments of the past decade have had a marked effect on both satellite-borne equipment and ground station characteristics. Improvements in semiconductor technology now provide amplifier devices that operate up to higher frequencies, with higher gain and lower noise factors. Improvements to high-power amplifiers (HPA) for ground stations and the travelling wave tube (TWT) and solid state RF power amplifiers for satellite transmissions contribute to the need for smaller antennas. Due to the availability of suitable integrated circuits (ICs), the efficient modulation schemes and coding techniques of a decade ago have now become a practical reality. The traditional system design trade-offs using Shannon, Hartley and Nyquist criteria still apply. The above improvements give an adequate SNR (particularly with digital processing) to allow the use of low-power transmissions using small antennas. The new systems are capable of providing significantly high data rates with acceptably low bit error rates. As an example of the extent of development, hand-held telephones and radio-paging devices have now been demonstrated to be practical and economical.

Very small aperture satellite systems (VSAT)

VSAT systems are usually considered to be those designed to operate with antennas that are the equivalent of 1.8 m diameter or less. The relatively low gain provided by these has to be countered by very careful design. Reference to the rules of communications (Shannon, Hartley, Nyquist) will show that systems operated in this way suffer from a reduced signal-to-noise (SNR) ratio and hence an increase in error rate. However, an acceptable error rate can be achieved by reducing the information transmission rate. VSAT systems are therefore essentially designed to provide digital services at a reduced basic data rate of 9.6 kbit/s, a value that can rise to 1.544 or 2.048 Mbit/s under special circumstances. Second-generation VSAT terminals operate as transceivers, working through a satellite and a higher-powered ground or hub station equipped with an antenna of 3.5 m diameter or more. The larger antenna and greater power level is necessary to maintain an adequate overall SNR. The hub station provides the link to other network users, via either a second satellite link or the terrestrial PSTN or other suitable network. Due to improving technology, third-generation VSATs are able to operate directly in VSAT-to-VSAT mode, without the intervention of a hub station.

VSAT networks form a valuable global link or bridge between isolated terrestrial local area networks (LAN) with which they have much in common and can easily be integrated. They thus add considerably to the communications capability of international corporate users, even to the extent of providing private video/telephony conferencing. For example, several large international marketing organizations operate large in-store networks serving several thousand stores. These are used for the fast validation of credit cards, inventory and stock control and many other functions that need to be addressed by such large organizations. Motor industry manufacturers also operate systems with similar features, but add the facilities to include video training programmes for the staff in more remote areas, plus the provisioning of the rapid availability of technical information for service staff. Other organizations have established networks that are linked worldwide to the ISDN system. These allow for the use of contiguous 64 kbit/s channels to provide a full range of services, even to the extent of being able to rent any spare communications capacity to outside organizations.

VSAT systems operate in both the C and Ku bands but the latter probably carries the greater part of these services. The systems may use any of the techniques of modulation, access and control that apply to both satellites and LANs.

Terminals are divided into two basic sections as indicated by Figure 8.11. The outdoor section comprises of an antenna with a low-noise block converter (LNC) and high-power amplifier (HPA). The electronics units are usually contained within a single casing and mounted in the manner shown in Figure 8.12.

The HPA, which is a semiconductor device, commonly produces an RF power of some 1–20 W depending upon the number of amplifiers coupled in parallel. This assembly also carries the orthomode transducer and waveguide filters which are necessary to separate the transmit and receive signals. Both transmitter and receiver function on the dual conversion, double superhet principle. The local oscillator is normally a crystal-controlled phase lock loop, with frequency synthesis to select the correct frequencies for up- and down-link operation. The typical first IFs are around 1 GHz for the Ku band and 600 MHz for the C band, while the second IF within the indoor unit is commonly either 70 or 140 MHz.

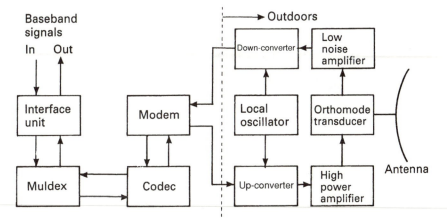

Figure 8.11 Typical VSAT earth station.

The typical figure of merit (G/T) for the front end is in the order of 18–29 dBK, depending on the combination of antenna size, low-noise amplifier characteristics and frequency band in use.

The indoor section contains the second stage of frequency conversion, plus the modern, codec and muldex (multiplexer/demultiplexer), these elements providing complementary functions in the transmit and receive modes. The interface unit processes the baseband signals and matches the various input devices to the digital processing stages. The muldex combines/distributes a given transmission channel between several inputs. The codec and modem stages handle the forward error correction (typically a 1/2 or 3/4 rate convolution code that produces a BER of better than 10^{-7} for an E_b/N_o ratio of about 8.5 dB) and convert the source code, usually pure binary, into the channel code of either BPSK or QPSK, with the latter being preferred because it doubles the channel capacity without increasing the bandwidth requirement.

The outdoor components of the Alcatel Multipoint Ltd VSAT terminal shown in Figure 8.12 may be equipped with antennas ranging from 1.8 to 3.7 m in diameter, with the larger dishes being necessary for operations through the INTELSAT or EUTELSAT systems. This system is designed to operate in the point-to-point communications mode in either mesh or star networks. For operations with the Alcatel FASTAR network the hub station must be equipped with an antenna of about 5 m in diameter. In this case the basic network provides 20 × 9.6 kbit/s SCPC trunks from VSAT to hub and a single TDM frame of 20 × 9.6 kbit/s time slots in the reverse direction. The VSAT to hub channels consist of one random access signalling channel and nineteen SCPC DAMA (demand assigned multiple access) message channels. The reverse direction time slots are similarly allocated, one for signalling and nineteen DAMA for messages. The system control operates on a modified SPADE protocol. A VSAT accesses the hub via its signalling channel f_1 requesting connection. The hub informs the

Figure 8.12 Outdoor unit of VSAT terminal (Courtesy of Alcatel Multipoint Ltd, Witham, Essex, UK).

calling station of the assigned channel via its signalling time slot t_1 of the TDM frame. The VSAT then transmits on frequency f_x and receives on time slot t_x. For VSAT-to-VSAT links, two DAMA channels need to be allocated by the hub, f_x and t_x as described above, and f_y and t_y for the relay between the hub and the called VSAT.

Using the system software, FASTAR can be programmed to provide the higher data rates of 19.2 or 64 kbit/s, but with fewer DAMA channels.

The system shown in Figure 8.12 can operate either in SCPC or MCPC mode. A single channel per carrier terminal may operate in the permanent (pre-assigned) or DAMA mode accessing the satellite as and when necessary. By comparison, a multiple channel per carrier installation must occupy a permanent satellite. For low bit rate systems (16–128 kbit/s) up to eight channels can be offered per terminal with the data being digitally compressed to 8 or 16 kbit/s. Higher bit rate systems (128 kbit/s to 2.048 Mbit/s) where 32 kbit/s ADPCM or 64 kbit/s PCM are needed (videoconferencing or high-speed data transfers) are also an option. As a hub station this equipment operates with an output power of either 300 or 600 W.

Demand assigned multiple access (DAMA)

This concept is also known as bandwidth-on-demand and can improve the efficiency and data throughput of time-varying satellite mesh networks. Low-speed lightly loaded routes often use FDMA to minimize the delays, but this is not particularly spectrum efficient. With a number of simultaneous active services available, the system becomes either bandwidth or power limited and either will degrade the quality of service. Both SCPC and MCPC network configurations can provide the same functions as DAMA, but with the dedicated assignments they tend to become more costly. These limitations can be relieved by using either DSI (digital speech interpolation) or TASI (time assigned speech interpolation) whereby the gaps in normal voice conversations can be filled with other transmissions to allow almost double the network occupancy.

DAMA systems can use any LAN-type protocol but of these, polling is probably best suited to satellite systems. In this case, each user is interrogated in turn to check the availability of data for transmission. If this is not ready, the next user is polled. Once a transmission starts it continues until the user is out of data, but this creates the major problem of network hogging – a station with a lot of data tends to monopolize the network. The number of VSATs that can be supported by a pool of DAMA channels is determined in the same way as the number of telephones that can be supported by the lines of a telephone exchange. The Erlang* loading of each VSAT is calculated and summed to give the network loading. The network size is adjusted for the grade of service required in terms of probability of queuing for a channel. Typically, twenty DAMA channels will support 500–1000 VSATs with 2 percent queuing probability. Thus some VSATs can support a single terminal while others support a network of telephones and

---

*Erlang, the unit of traffic intensity. One permanently engaged circuit has a traffic flow of 1 Erlang. If the average number of simultaneous calls in progress in a given period over a given network is E, the traffic intensity on that network is E Erlangs. (Erlang-hour = one Erlang of traffic intensity maintained for one hour.)

computers. A VSAT supporting a local network may need simultaneous access to more than one DAMA channel.

TSAT (12)

This later generation of VSAT systems is so called because it was designed to operate at the ITU/R (CCITT) T1/E1 data rates of 1.544 Mbit/s (North America) or 2.048 Mbit/s (Europe). Unlike the VSAT which normally operates in a *star* mode of connection, the TSAT is capable of operating in a *mesh* configuration, connecting each location to all others without the need of a hub station. Not only are these systems faster with a higher data capacity, they are also significantly cheaper. The networks were originally conceived by SPAR Aerospace Ltd of Canada. They are ISDN compatible in that they provide both basic rate access of 2B + D (64 kbit/s) and primary rate access of 23B + D (1.544 Mbit/s) or 30B + D (2.048 Mbit/s) (the B channel is used for voice and data services and the D channel for signalling purposes).

System access protocols

Generally, the traffic loading on a VSAT terminal tends to be very variable, so that the systems tend to be bandwidth rather than power limited. The access problems are very similar to those of LANs and therefore the protocol, which can be critical, needs to be carefully chosen bearing the following points in mind:

- Average acceptable transmission delay
- Range of data rates involved
- Acceptable message failure rate
- Message format – fixed or variable length

The SPADE (Single-channel Per-carrier DEmand assigned and multiple access) system requires a control station to monitor the channel frequencies in use, then to provide access to a free channel when available.

The pure ALOHA protocol requires that all stations continually monitor the network and then transmit data as and when it is available. If two terminals transmit together, they detect a collision of data and then both back-off for a random period of time before trying again. This is basically a collision detect–multiple access (CDMA) system.

Reservation TDMA: Each terminal is allocated a particular time slot of the time frame for its transmissions.

The slotted ALOHA protocol is a combination of ALOHA and Reservation TDMA. Selective spectrum ALOHA is reserved for use with spread spectrum transmissions when packets of data are not normally affected by collision.

With the ACK/NACK protocol (acknowledged/not acknowledged), when a receiving station decodes a packet without error it transmits an acknowledgement signal. If the transmitting station does not receive this acknowledgement, it decides that an error has occurred and automatically retransmits the data packet.

Reservation TDMA is particularly useful when relatively long transmissions are required. Slotted ALOHA has an advantage over pure ALOHA in that once a terminal has accessed a time slot, it has sole use of this until the end of transmission. Selective spectrum ALOHA has the advantage that data collisions are not problematic but the system has to include some form of forward error correction (FEC). The ACK/NACK system is not very useful over GEO satellite links. Due to the overall time delay of about 250 ms, the following block may be transmitted before the lack of acknowledgement has been recognized and this will produce a data collision.

8.5   HYBRID SYSTEMS

Telemedicine and Medisat (13)

In 1996 the following scenario took much of the world's population by surprise. Doctors at the Walter Reed Army Medical Center in Washington supervised a surgical operation to save the badly injured leg of a young boy in Mogadishu, Somalia. The cooperative operation took place via the satellite-based links provided by INMARSAT through a system known as Camnet.

The Camnet system combines the use of high-definition video screens, very small video cameras, PC technology and a suitable satellite communications link to provide almost worldwide coverage. In suitable cases, the communications link might well be provided by radio, telephone line or cell phone. The doctor in the field wears a headset that contains a microphone and earphones for audio with a solid state colour video display screen and a sub-miniature video camera for vision. In the prototype built by Nera, the headset was linked to a belt pack that contained the necessary batteries, camera controls and computer. In later versions, the cabling was replaced by a low-power wireless link to improve mobility. The camera, which weighed less than 25 g, had a single optimally fixed focus and aperture setting, but later cameras could be equipped with a zoom control that is adjustable by either the headset wearer or the distant viewer.

The camera captures all the necessary X-ray and other images and transmits these over the high-speed data channels of a suitable satellite link. The images may be displayed on a single screen or a stereoscopic pair close to the eye of the operating doctor. These can also display information or diagrams that are input from the remote surgeon. This system can help to avoid moving seriously ill or injured patients over unfriendly terrain, thus aiding their recovery.

The Medisat system is also a PC-based system designed by Aries Communications Ltd to provide a real-time telemedicine service. This not only carries live video and audio links but also provides a telemetry link which can be connected to medical sensors to transmit the patient's vital parameters back to base. The whole system weighs less than 10 kg and can be carried as hand baggage on board an aircraft. When this kit arrives on site, a sick or injured person can quickly be linked to highly qualified medical help virtually anywere in the world.

The yacht video system (14)

Round the world yacht racing has a wide appeal to many people, in particular the major corporate organizations that sponsor these races. There is therefore a great demand for continuous media coverage as these events develop. To meet this demand, British Telecommunications Ltd (BTL) have developed the Yacht Video System (YVS) which provides time-delayed live video and audio material of acceptable quality for broadcasting purposes. The system employs video compression, satellite communications and digital data using a store-and-forward technique combined with an unusual form of error control. Of all the forms of radio communications available, only satellite delivery meets all the needs of the system. Since BTL is the UK signator to the INMARSAT international treaty, this was chosen as the supporting organization. The INMARSAT-A system provides voice, telex, fax and voice band digital data facilities together with a simplex/duplex option for high-speed data (HSD) at 56 or 64 kbit/s. FM is employed for the low-rate bands, while QPSK with FEC is used with the HSD link. The HSD channel in simplex mode provides for the yacht-to-shore communications, while the audio channel provides the reverse link back to the yacht. This latter is used to control the error correction system. The practically standard INMARSAT SES (ship earth station) on board each yacht includes an antenna of 0.9 m diameter with computer control to maintain satellite aiming under the most hazardous of conditions, all enclosed in a water-tight compartment and radome.

The compression ratio needed to squeeze the video and audio signals into a 64 kbit/s channel would create an image that was not suitable for re-broadcast purposes. This problem was resolved by using a store-and-forward technique. The video material with a bandwidth of about 3.5–4 MHz (VHS quality) is collected by fixed and mobile cameras operated by the crew over a period of time. This is then edited into a video clip of about 2.5 minutes' duration using a simple on-board editing system and video cassette recorders. The prepared clip is then played through a modified H.320 video and audio codec to provide a bit rate of 768 kbit/s (compression ratio of about 80:1). The processed data is then stored as a file ready for transmission. The slow data rate transmission back to the UK base involving the 64 kbit/s channel occupies about thirty minutes which is equivalent to a further lossless compression ratio of 12:1. This means that the data rate is no longer real time but the compression problem has been bypassed.

The data for transmission in both directions is formatted into blocks. The video clip from yacht to shore consists of eight bytes of alternate 1s and 0s to provide clock sync, two bytes of unique framing code, two bytes for block number, one byte for block type, one byte spare for future developments, 8000 bytes for video and audio and two bytes for a checksum. The 16 bit checksum is used to detect when packets are received in error. The return link uses a similar format but without the preamble clock sync bytes and with only fifty-six bytes for the data field. These latter bytes are used to request the repeat retransmission of up to twenty-eight blocks. The ARQ error control system thus operates on a selective repeat basis.

Automotive communications and guidance (15)

Road travellers in most of the industrialized parts of the world suffer from the same basic problems. Road congestion leads to accidents which in turn lead to further congestion. The problem is intended to be relieved by building more roads, but this is almost always defeated by a further increase in road traffic density. The overall result of this vicious circle is an increase in the amount of fumes and noxious gases released into the atmosphere, which aggravate global warming and human breathing difficulties. Assuming that traffic densities are not going to fall, some form of traffic management is essential. Electronic control and communications could play a large part in the relief of one of our major problems. Any help to allow drivers to bypass congested roads can only help to speed up the general traffic flow and reduce journey times. A number of systems have been devised for specific routes and these have been described elsewhere.

However, there are new and much wider-ranging systems now under development. These involve the use of an embedded PC to control features that include GPS receivers, CD-ROM digitized maps with zoom control, GSM cellular phone networks, messaging services and even vehicle security tracking. The driver's route and important traffic information is displayed on a dashboard-mounted LCD solid state screen, with audio prompts provided via the in-car public broadcast radio system. Dead-reckoning navigation can be added to the GPS facilities by using gyro-chips. These are solid state devices that incorporate a quartz crystal oscillator that generates a dc voltage proportional to the rate of rotation around its longitudinal axis. Similar acceleration sensors that are linked to the road wheel rotation can give an indication of the vehicle's speed so that a continual along-track correction calculation can be made.

The current FM radio broadcasts already carry a wide range of information via the radio data service (RDS) system and the developing digital audio broadcasting (DAB) service is set to extend this option.

The motor vehicle itself is undergoing a revolution in its own control system. In fact, it already has a standard control area network (CAN) that behaves exactly as the communication LANs already described elsewhere. As might be expected, the system has room for expansion to include driver guidance as well as vehicle management using an embedded PC (car PC) for overall control via cabling or optical fibre. The motor vehicle is a highly intolerant environment as far as electronic systems are concerned. Not only are these subjected to a high degree of physical vibration but they must also operate in a region of intense electromagnetic interference. By using optical fibre for the carrier medium of CAN, the effects of many of these problems can be minimized. Because the length of the fibre needed to support such a network is short, low-cost, wide-bandwidth, easily connected plastic optical fibre forms an ideal carrier medium.

The D2B system based on Conan technology has been designed by Communications and Control Electronics Ltd to integrate such features as multimedia, audio, video, navigation travel information and much more. This allows devices connected to the network to communicate with and control each other, by exchanging instructions and status codes. The network is based on a unidirectional ring structure which has a high capacity and provides a maximum data rate of 4.2 Mbit/s, with the data stream bi-phase encoded to ensure good lock of the system clocks. The network is easily extended as and when necessary.

Each major unit connected to the system is referred to as a *device* such as car radio. This can then be subdivided into *sub-devices* such as tuner unit, audio amplifier stages, video controller, etc. and all sub-devices can be uniquely addressed. Thus the system can function on a resource-sharing basis with the audio stages linked with the radio receiver, telephone or GPS receiver, in a very flexible manner. By using this technique, high-priority messages can be allowed to override lower priority ones; for example, a traffic announcement or a telephone call would take priority over the sound output from the CD player.

Figure 8.13(a) shows the way in which the data structure is organized into frames to provide both source and control signals. Each of the forty-eight frames is subdivided into two subframes each of forty-eight bits plus two control bits. The control bits from each of the ninety-six subframes are used to form the 192-bit control frame. At the typical frame rate of 44.1 kHz (CD and CD-ROM bit rates), the source code capacity is 44.1 kHz $\times$ 96 = 4.433 Mbit/s. Using the same basic data rate, the control channel capacity is 44.1 kHz $\times$ 4 = 176.4 kbit/s, equal to about 920 control messages per second.

Figure 8.13(b) shows the control frame data structure. The first two bits form an arbitration field that ensures that the frame is used by one device only. The two address fields provide the obvious functions. The Type and Length fields refer to the data bytes. The CRC code allows the system to check the integrity of any control message. The ACK/NAK bytes provide a response to any data error that calls for a retransmission after a defined time delay. Spare space is provided within this structure for future developments. Vehicle navigation, anti-collision radar and cellular data systems are already a proven technology and these can be combined to provide the *road-train* concept. Greater traffic densities and shorter journey times can be achieved by allowing a stream of vehicles to travel at the same speed and with a closely controlled separation distance. This has already been demonstrated to be feasible by employing vehicle-mounted anti-collision forward- and reverse-looking radar and along-track roadside guidance systems

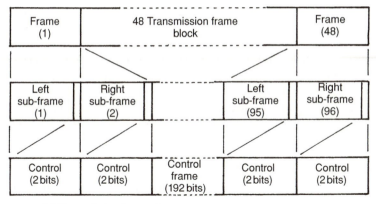

(a) Transmission frame structure

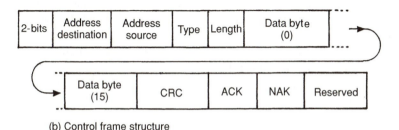

(b) Control frame structure

Figure 8.13 Automotive network data structure. **(a)** Transmission frame structure. **(b)** Control frame structure.

using microwave radio. Road vehicles of the future will be equipped with GPS to ensure accurate location and tracking information. The roof will carry the conformal antenna for all forms of radio telecommunications. Much of the mechanics of the vehicle is already controlled and monitored via the several on-board microprocessors. In the very near future, provided that the owner is a member of a suitable organization, the car's integrity will be continually remotely monitored. At some point in a journey, the vehicle may start to fail for some reason, but the exact state of its serviceability will already be known to the headquarters via the base station. The first indication that the driver might receive that problems are developing, is that a warning message will be transmitted and displayed giving instructions to pull into a nearby service area. Here the driver will be met by a service technician armed with the necessary spare parts to effect the repairs. In the future? The technology is available today!

Internet and telephony developments

Because access to the Internet is charged by the Information Provider (IP) at local call rates and it is a digital service provided over an analogue network, there is a demand to allow the IPs to provide a voice service as well. Technically, there is no useful advantage to be gained from such a change. The quality of voice over the Internet is questionable, largely because of the lack of bandwidth, and the additional use would further load the system. Out-of-sequence packets, lost packets and network time delays cannot be guaranteed and all of these contribute to a lowering of service quality.

The major problem associated with the Internet is its slow data transfer rate. Even with the latest 56 kbit/s modems it takes a long time to transfer image and graphics data. The move to an ISDN 64 kbit/s line offers little improvement. Corporate users of the intranet concept tend to use the ISDN primary rate access of 2.048 Mbit/s or employ VSATs.

Many new systems have been proposed that use satellites, both LEOs and GEOs, to provide fast downstream data transfers, with the user demand link, which needs a relatively low data rate, being provided over the POTS network. For example, the Teledesic Corp. proposes to deploy Boeing satellites in a global broadband *Internet in the sky* network by 2002. This is intended to emulate the Internet with guaranteed quality of service and ease of access. In a similar time scale, others are intending to start direct telephone services via groups of LEOs using the current type of cellular handsets.

Power line telephony

The major costs for establishing any new telephony network is the installation of the basic infrastructure such as the carrier medium. For more than twenty years, it has been possible to use the power distribution wiring to carry additional signals, but with the major problems of electrical isolation and the removal of the ac component of the power supply from the superimposed signals. It has recently been reported that these problems have been resolved and such a system should appear in the marketplace in the very near future.

At least one major power supply distributor has installed optical fibre cables along the main high-voltage distribution cables and these are capable of carrying large quantities of data and telephony signals. There are two options open for these systems. The fibre can be carried over either of the live lines or the earth conductor, but with the latter being preferred because of the reduced possibility of damage from very high-voltage spikes that could destroy the cable insulation.

Mobility aids for the blind (16)

The eyes are probably the most important sensory organs possessed by human beings, so that blindness is the most difficult affliction to overcome. It was from this recognition that the European Union (EU) established the MoBIC project to attempt to provide improved mobility for such persons using the most modern technology. The current state of development, while very promising, shows that there are many obstacles that the unsighted person meets in very ordinary circumstances. As a result of the testing that has been carried out in Europe, there is great hope that the life of the blind can be significantly improved, even if, at the present time, the costs are high. While many of the elements of a useful system are available at reasonable cost, a few key items await mass production in other areas of navigation and guidance.

The MoBIC project identified many of the important information items that would be necessary for a blind person to navigate his or her way around a busy town area. The display of such information has to be of an audible, vibratory or tactile nature and in some cases capable of being converted into Braille characters.

The system as designed consists of two units. There is an indoor unit on which the user can carefully plan in advance a journey into the real world. The basis of this unit is the home PC equipped with a CD-ROM player to create digital maps with zoom facilities on which are featured the various obstacles that might be encountered. Such maps can be printed out a a hard copy, but using either embossed features or Braille characters where necessary. The journey plan is converted into coordinates suitable for use with the GPS system and then downloaded into a portable computer that forms part of the outdoor unit. This information might include bus and rail timetables, shop locations, the location of important obstacles such as street or road works, opening hours of civic offices, etc.

Figure 8.14 gives an indication of the way in which many of the current technologies can be integrated into a valuable guidance system for the blind. The initial experiments involved carrying the system in a back-pack, but miniaturization quickly reduced this to a specially equipped waistcoat. Among others, Rockwell have now developed the Trekker PC system that can be carried as a belt or shoulder-strap package. The system includes a head-up VGA display panel worn as a headband and a mouse pad mounted on the computer and uses off-the-shelf standard peripherals such as those based on the PCMCIA (Personal Computer Memory Card Interface Association) interface. The software is based on the industry standard Windows and the computer hardware is Pentium based to provide the equivalent of a high-powered notebook processor. This part of the kit weights about 6 kg and contains 16 Mbytes of RAM and 1.2 Gbytes of hard disk memory, with PCMCIA slots and serial and parallel ports for expansion. The keyboard may be a simple three- five- or eight-key pad that is wired to an interface connector or coupled via a low-power radio link. The battery pack uses rechargeable Lithium-Ion technology for light weight, small size, better energy density with no memory effect, and is more environmentally friendly than earlier types of battery. The user load might be reduced by downloading a local route map and other important data on to a PCMCIA memory card which is then plugged into the roaming unit.

Hand-held GPS receivers are available at an acceptable cost but do not have a small enough resolution. Newly developed carrier phase GPS receivers have a positioning accuracy down to about 1 m but are still too expensive. The cost of the standard DGPS receiver system is similarly too high. However, commercial

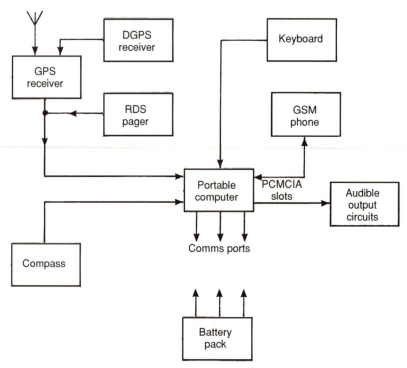

Figure 8.14 The outdoor guidance unit.

DGPS data is freely available in the UK via at least one FM transmission on the Radio Data System (RDS). It is thought that the developing digital audio broadcast (DAB) networks might also carry this data. The integrated compass needs to be of the flux gate type that produces an electrical signal for its output. Some of the guidance software is already well tried and tested with video games of the dungeons and castles types.

Maps as geographic data files have already been standardized for road engineers and others but do not show such features as street furniture, lampposts, bus stop signs and the like. There is also a need to allow the user to know beforehand something about the nature of the underfoot surface and whether there are footbridges or underpasses involved along the route. There is also a need to include some emergency commands for the user in difficulties – answers to questions such as, where am I, where is the next obstacle along the route, which way am I facing now?

Finally there is also a need to train and test the user of this kit – how to explore an area on the indoor unit, how to plan a route, then practical training with the outdoor unit.

Further aids to the unsighted may be made available by installing talking street furniture that produces an output when interrogated by an infrared beam. These might include talking timetables, etc., which could be integrated into the system and operated in a similar way to the familiar remote control of the TV set.

REFERENCES

(1) Akroyd, B. (1990) *World Satellite Communications & Earth Station Design.* London: BSP Professional Books Ltd.

(2) Player, J.K. and Baker, D.W., Multipoint Communications Ltd, Essex, UK. Private communication to author.

(3) Advent Communications Ltd, Chesham, Bucks, UK. HP5 1LF. Private communication to author.

(4) Clark, R.J. (1985) *Transform Coding of Images.* London: Academic Press Ltd.

(5) Nicol, R.C. and Duffy, T.S. (1983) 'A codec system for world-wide video-conferencing'. *Professional Video* (now *Broadcast Systems Engineering*).

(6) Carr, M.D. and Clapp, C.S.K. (1984) 'The integration of television standards conversion into a conditional replenishment codec for visual teleconferencing'. *International Teleconference Symposium*, London.

(7) Coffey, D., Premier Electronics Ltd, Waltham Cross, EN8 7JU. UK. Private communication to author.

(8) Annegarn, M.J.J.C., Arragon, J.P. *et al.* (1987) 'HD-MAC: a step forward in the evolution of television technology'. *Philips Technical Review 43*, No. 8.

(9) Barratt, L.H. and Lucas, K. (1979) 'An introduction to sub-nyquist sampling'. *IBA Technical Review 12*. London: Independent Broadcasting Authority, UK.

(10) Lever, I.R. (1979) 'Analogue to digital conversion'. *IBA Technical Review 12*. London: Independent Broadcasting Authority, UK.

(11) Kenyon, N.D. (1985) *British Telecom Technology Journal*, Vol. 2, No. 5.

(12) Garland, P.J., SPAR Aerospace Ltd, Canada. Private communication to author.

(13) Livewire Digital Ltd, Epsom, Surrey, KT19 9QN, UK. Private communication to author.

(14) Woolf, C.D. and Tilson D.A. (1995) 'Yacht Video System for the Whitbread Round the World Race'. *British Telecomms Technology Journal*, Vol. 13, No. 4, October.

(15) Van De Water, A., Communications and Control Electronics Ltd, Guildford, GU2 5RF, UK. Private communication to author.

(16) Gill, J., Petrie, H. *et al.* (1997) *Mobility of Blind and Elderly People – Interacting with Computers.* RNIB, on behalf of the MoBIC Consortium.

Chapter 9

Analogue television systems

9.1 REVIEW OF CURRENT SYSTEMS

It is intended in this section only to review the principles and characteristics of the current systems in order to understand why and how certain developments are occurring. For a complete understanding of three systems, NTSC (National Television Standards Committee), SECAM (Séquential á Mémoire) and PAL (Phase Alternation Line-by-line), the reader is referred to some of the standard works of reference (1, 2, 3, 4).

All the variants of the colour TV systems in service are based on the concept of the brightness or luminance (Y) component signal of the earlier monochrome systems, plus chrominance (colour) information. In all three systems, the Y component is formed from the weighted addition of red (R), green (G) and blue (B) gamma-corrected camera voltages that represent the three primary colour signals, i.e.:

$$Y' = 0.299R' + 0.587G' + 0.114B' \tag{9.1}$$

Because the human eye is only about 50 percent as sensitive to colour information as it is to brightness changes, three colour difference signals are generated for transmission purposes, $(R' - Y')$, $(G' - Y')$ and $(B' - Y')$. When the Y' component is added to each of these at the receiver, a colour signal voltage is regenerated that represents the original colours.

Of the three colour difference signals, $(G' - Y')$ is always of the lowest amplitude and will thus be affected the most by noise in the transmission channel. Since the Y' component contains a portion of all three colours, $(G' - Y')$ can be regenerated at the receiver from the Y', $(R' - Y')$ and $(B' - Y')$ components. These three components are therefore all that is necessary for the transmission of colour TV signals. Thus the two colour difference signal components to be transmitted are of the form $(B' - Y')$ and $(R' - Y')$. These are modulated on to sub-carrier frequencies and in order to conserve bandwidth, the spectral components of modulation are interleaved with the luminance spectrum. In a limited way, this interleaving, which influences the choice of the actual sub-carrier frequency, represents a form of analogue bandwidth compression. The major differences between the systems lie in the way in which the chrominance information is modulated on to the sub-carriers.

Historically the NTSC system of the USA was the first system to enter operational service. This was made compatible with the North American monochrome service that was based on a 525-line image format. The line and field rates were nominally 15.75 kHz and 60 Hz respectively. To accommodate the 3.579545 MHz sub-carrier and minimize the interference beats between this and the sound carrier, these frequencies were marginally offset to 15.734254 kHz and 59.94 Hz respectively. (These changes were insufficient to cause a monochrome receiver to lose timebase lock.) The colour sub-carrier therefore lies exactly halfway between the 227th and 228th harmonic of the line timebase frequency. The chosen colour difference components amplitude-modulate quadrature (QAM) versions of the same carrier frequency, to produce I (in-phase) and Q (quadrature) components, with the double side band, suppressed carrier (DSBSC) mode being employed. Like the Y' component, both I and Q signals are formed by weighted addition of the R', G' and B' primary components.

$$I = 0.596R' - 0.275G' - 0.322B' \quad \text{and}$$

$$Q = 0.211R' - 0.523G' - 0.312B' \tag{9.2}$$

As indicated in Figure 9.1, both the I and Q components contain a fraction of both $(R' - Y')$ and $(B' - Y')$. This was arranged to combat the effects of non-linearity, where amplitude distortion might cause a change of colour saturation. More importantly, however, phase distortion would produce an actual change of hue (colour).

Consistent with the technology then available, the NTSC system provided very adequate colour images and maintained compatibility with the previous monochrome service.

The later-developing European colour TV industry recognized these possible problems and devised the SECAM system in France and the PAL system in West Germany, almost in parallel. Due to technological advances made during the intervening time, both of these systems provided better-quality pictures and so became competing European Standards.

The SECAM system adopted the technique of transmitting the two colour difference signals sequentially, on alternate lines, using frequency modulation of two different sub-carrier frequencies, thus ensuring that there would be no cross-talk between these two components. However, the two frequencies needed to be very carefully chosen to minimize the effect on monochrome areas of the image because unlike both NTSC and PAL, both of which use DSBSC, the sub-carrier amplitudes do not fall to zero when both the $(R' - Y')$ and $(B' - Y')$ components are absent, as in the grey picture areas.

The two colour difference signals of SECAM are designated as $D_R = -1.902(R' - Y')$ and $D_B = 1.505(B' - Y')$ which are pre-emphasized before being used to frequency-modulate the two sub-carriers of 4.40626 MHz and 4.25 MHz respectively. The magnitude of the coefficients are chosen so that total deviation is restricted to 3.9–4.75 MHz for both sub-carriers. The negative

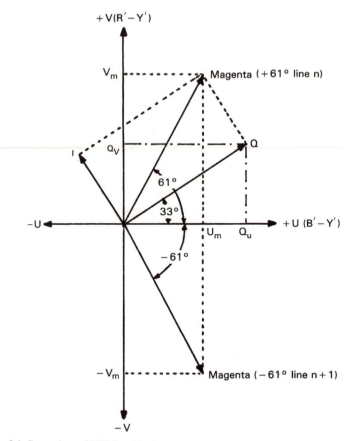

Figure 9.1 Comparison of NTSC and PAL chrominance phasors.

coefficient of D_R results in the two difference signals deviating their carriers in opposite directions. This was adopted in order to minimize the possible effects of differential phase errors, but practice has shown this to be unnecessary. The later specifications for SECAM therefore use negative coefficients for both D_R and D_B. The sub-carriers are maintained to an accuracy within ±2 kHz and represent the 282nd and 272nd harmonics of the line timebase frequency.

For the PAL system, the two colour difference components are scaled or weighted so that the total signal of luminance plus chrominance does not produce over-modulation. The two modulating colour difference components are thus:

$$U = 0.493(B' - Y') \quad \text{and} \quad V = 0.877(R' - Y') \tag{9.3}$$

Like the NTSC system, PAL utilizes analogue QAM, DSBSC, but uses an alternating phase inversion, line by line, of the V or $(R' - Y')$ component. In this way phase errors on successive lines tend to average out and cancel, thus improving the colour performance.

Figure 9.1 shows how the NTSC and PAL chrominance components differ. Both the I and the Q signals contain an element of each colour difference signal due to the rotation of the reference phase. The figure compares the phasors for a magenta hue that forms the basis of the two chrominance signals.

The relationship between the sub-carrier and line timebase frequencies is much more complex due to the problem of *line crawl*. The precise value of 4.43361875 MHz represents 283.75 times line frequency plus an offset of 25 Hz. This results in an eight-field sequence before the colour sub-carrier phase and line frequency (SC-H) repeats itself. For all three systems, the sub-carrier frequencies have to be carefully chosen, not only for reasons of frequency interleaving but to avoid patterning due to beat frequencies between the luminance and chrominance signal components.

After some forty years of development, the increased size and brightness of the modern picture tube is causing other system impairments (*artefacts*) to become apparent, such as *cross-colour/luminance* effects that arise due to the imperfect separation of the interleaved spectra. Luminance information can reach the chrominance channel and create false colours, and in a similar way chrominance information can create high-frequency patterning in the receiver luminance channel. These effects can be minimized by the use of modern comb filter techniques or by digital processing of the composite video signal. However, the sampled nature of the image signal creates aliasing problems that are not so easily solved. As stated earlier, the response of the image could be expressed in terms of three kinds of frequency, as indicated by Figure 9.2(a). Considering the horizontal frequency f_x as a continuous function of time and hence analogue, the remaining two frequencies f_y and f_t represent the two-dimensional vertical and temporal sampling frequencies respectively. Figure 9.2(b) represents these spatio-temporal spectra for a period when $f_x = 0$.

A sampling operation always generates repeated sideband pairs, related to the baseband and disposed around multiples of the sampling frequency. Figure 9.2(b) translates such spectra into two dimensions simultaneously, where the *quincunx* areas (four corner and centre points of a square) represent the repeating spectra. The diagram is scaled for a 625-line system using 575 active lines per frame, giving a vertical resolution of $575/2 = 287.5$ c/ph (cycles per picture height) with a 25 Hz temporal or frame frequency. Even if the spectral groups do not overlap to produce aliasing, the human eye will act as an imperfect filter. The approximate response of the eye is enclosed by the dotted line. This includes some of the repeat spectra that give rise to the aliasing effect.

Referring to Figure 9.2(b), area A is responsible for *large area flicker*, which is essentially a peripheral vision effect. It is related not only to the signal but also to the display viewing angle. Area B represents the *vertical aliasing*, which is responsible for the visibility of the line structure and the *Kell effect* (5).

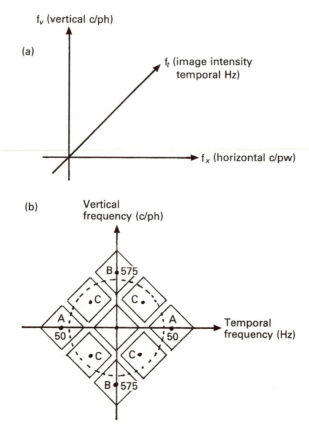

Figure 9.2 (a) Three-dimensional presentation of image response. (b) Two-dimensional spectra for $f_x = 0$.

This describes the loss of vertical resolution relative to that in the horizontal plane. Area C, the *temporal aliasing*, only exists in interlaced raster structures and is responsible for the apparent inter-line flicker or crawl. This effect also causes wheels to appear to rotate in reverse, and increasing the frame rate only increases the frequency at which this occurs.

9.2 IMPROVED PROCESSING OF CURRENT SYSTEMS

The past decade has seen a number of new technological developments introduced into the current systems in order to improve image quality. Some have been more successful than others in removing the alias-based artefacts.

The areas where picture quality can be improved are chiefly those that generate intermodulation and other distortions through non-linearity, namely the IF amplifier, vision demodulator and colour separation/decoder stages. The use of integrated circuit versions of high-gain IF amplifiers combined with surface acoustic wave (SAW) filters, followed by synchronous or phase lock loop demodulators, is now common.

The luminance/chrominance separation can be improved by the use of charge-coupled devices (CCDs) and gyrator circuits in IC form. (A gyrator is a two-port, non-reciprocal device whose input impedance is the reciprocal of its load impedance; for instance, a gyrator terminated with a capacitance behaves as an inductance of $Z_{in} - R^2/Z_L$, where R is the gyration resistance.) Such an approach produces better results with NTSC than with PAL systems because of the simpler relationship between the sub-carrier frequency and the harmonics of the line scan frequency.

The comb filter, which is based on a delay line and adder, has been a feature of the PAL system since its inception. The initial difficulties of producing delays of the order of 64 μs was resolved by using an ultrasonic glass delay line, as these were then the only suitable devices. However, comb filters can now also be constructed in digital form and this feature becomes increasingly attractive as digital processing encroaches further into this analogue field. The comb filter effectively averages the information in at least two adjacent lines and the number of such lines increases with the order of the filter. However, the use of a filter with too high an order leads to loss of vertical resolution.

The digital filter, which is constructed from semiconductor amplifiers and delays, also acts as an averaging device because its output depends not only on the present input pulse but also on the previous ones. The major advantages of such filters are that they are very stable and can be reprogrammed.

The wideband luminance signal passes through its processing channel somewhat faster than the relatively narrowband chrominance signal and this would create mis-registration of the two components. The inclusion of an additional luminance delay of around 700 ns provides some correction for this.

Scan velocity modulation (SVM)

This technique can be used with advantage on receivers with modern picture tubes. Figure 9.3(a) depicts the way that a part of the luminance signal is tapped off at its delay line, differentiated and then amplified before being applied to an auxiliary coil on the scanning assembly. Figure 9.3(b) shows how a luminance transient is enhanced by this technique. A luminance signal of the form $V_1 = A$ Sin.ωt, when differentiated, becomes:

$$V_0 = \omega t A \; Cos.\omega t \qquad (9.4)$$

where t = CR, the time constant of the differentiator. This circuit will thus increase the slope of luminance transients to define changes of image intensity more clearly.

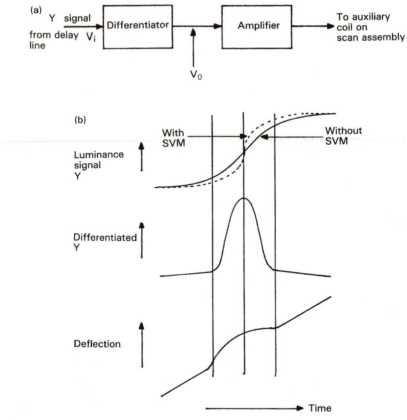

Figure 9.3 Scan velocity modulation: **(a)** principles; **(b)** SVM waveforms.

Colour transient improvement (CTI)

This technique uses the same principles as SVM but is applied to the chrominance channel. Figure 9.4(a) shows the block diagram of an integrated circuit (TDA 4560) that was specifically developed to provide this feature. Figure 9.4(b) shows the standard approach to matching the different time delays by the addition of a luminance delay line (i, ii, iii), while iv and v indicate how the enhancement of the chrominance component, by differentiation, improves the combined edge response. This particular IC formed part of a chip set that was designed to provide multi-standard decoding.

Hybrid processing

Other developments have led to hybrid processing using a combination of analogue and digital techniques using application-specific ICs (ASICs) in

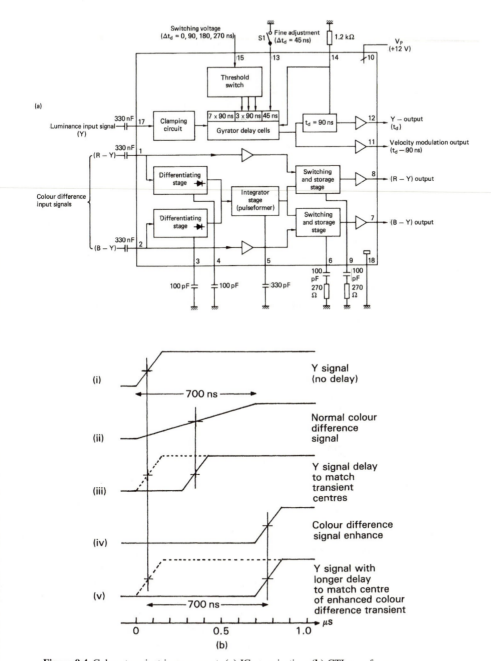

Figure 9.4 Colour transient improvement: **(a)** IC organization; **(b)** CTI waveforms.

suitable circuit areas. Such an introduction had many advantages, as it led to the use of microprocessor control of the many features available in modern receivers such as teletext, picture-in-picture, computer RGB monitor, freeze frame, video printer, etc. The use of semiconductor memories as frame stores allows the same line or frame to be displayed twice in the same line or frame period, effectively doubling the scanning frequencies and removing flicker.

Taking this concept of the digital processing further, it was obvious that the earlier digitization takes place, the lower would be the signal degradation due to the analogue processing circuitry. ICs are just becoming available that will provide direct conversion to baseband from UHF channel frequencies, thus removing other sources of distortion and interference.

Super-NTSC

This system, devised by Faroudja Laboratories in the USA, recognizes that luminance-to-chrominance cross-talk arises because of imperfect interleaving of spectral components at the encoder and imperfect separation at the decoder. In this system, the source image is produced with a resolution of 1050 lines and progressively scanned at a frame rate of 29.97 Hz. This is then converted into a sequential (interlaced) scan using a frame store. The luminance component is split into two and the high-frequency part accurately comb-filtered between 2.3 and 4.2 MHz, the frequencies largely responsible for the cross-talk. The chrominance component that covers much the same frequency range is comb-filtered in an adaptive manner, the filter coefficient being changed in accordance with the steepness on chrominance transients. Luminance transients that coincide with chrominance ones are also enhanced to improve the horizontal resolution. The basic principles of this concept are shown in Figure 9.5. A conventional NTSC receiver gains from this pre-processing, but the Super-NTSC receiver also has complementary comb filtering, plus a frame store which allows line doubling to greatly enhance the reproduced images.

PAL+

A number of PAL derivatives have been designed and tested in order to provide a compatible system that minimizes the cross-colour effects. At the same time, it was hoped to stimulate viewers into investing in new receivers that would be an introduction to an enhanced viewing experience. To date, the only system to go into limited operation is PAL+ which is based on a wide-screen display with an aspect ratio of 16:9. To achieve compatibility with standard PAL receivers, PAL + transmits only 432 active lines together with a helper signal which allows the wide-screen receiver to expand the image to a full 576 active lines. The standard PAL receiver then displays a 16:9 letterbox image with black bars at the top and bottom. The helper signal for the PAL+ system is buried within the 144 blanked lines, with a control signal carried in line 23.

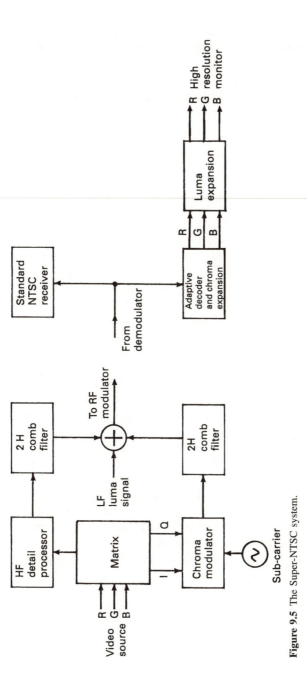

Figure 9.5 The Super-NTSC system.

In order to reduce the letterbox effect for normal viewers, a halfway development state allows the standard PAL receiver to overscan the 16:9 image and display it in 14:9 format. Furthermore, Sony has produced a receiver with interpolation filters that generates four lines for every three PAL+ lines and so avoids the use of the helper signal (also bypassing the Patent problems). The coding algorithm is very complex and this can make the system somewhat sync-sensitive with low-level signals. In addition, encryption can create synchronism difficulties, particularly over satellite links.

9.3   ITT DIGITAL TELEVISION SIGNAL PROCESSING (6)

For the past decade ITT (Intermetall Semiconductors Ltd) have been continuously developing the digital signal processing (DSP) concept for the control of TV receivers. The earlier Digit 2000 system represented a significant advance, both in the application of DSP to TV receivers and also in the quality of the resulting images. The Digit 2000 TV sets comprised of up to twelve LSI/VLSI integrated circuits to provide for the processing of NTSC, SECAM or PAL video signals; mono, stereo or dual channel audio; deflection system generators; automatic picture control; plus teletext, with the overall control exerted via a microcomputer.

As the system has developed, the memory element has expanded and the density of the chips increased to such a point that the Digit 3000 system uses a maximum of five VSLI ICs to provide even more features. In addition to the composite video input, these now include provisions for S-VHS luminance and chrominance, high-definition TV (HDTV), MAC signals from a satellite tuner, ISDN terminals, home PC, and Internet access; in fact the system encompasses what is now described as multimedia systems. User control is completely digital.

The VLSI chips are now fabricated using very high-density CMOS technology, with the smallest circuit element being based on macro-cells. These can be flexibly combined in different ways to provide new ICs that are capable of wider uses in such as industrial or automotive applications. The next stage of development is likely to be the replacement of the tuner unit and IF strip plus demodulator with a direct conversion unit so that digitization takes place very much earlier in the TV signal processing stage.

Because of the high degree of integration that has developed, the operation of the system is perhaps most easily explained by using the basic Digit 2000 receiver.

Referring to Figure 9.6, the television signals are processed in the analogue format from the antenna through to the demodulator stages. Thereafter the processing is digital. This allows the use of advanced methods of video processing, which includes adaptive noise and ghosting reduction, aliasing and flicker suppression. Auxiliary processing allows for teletext and computer monitor applications, together with the additional inputs from video disc or cassette machines.

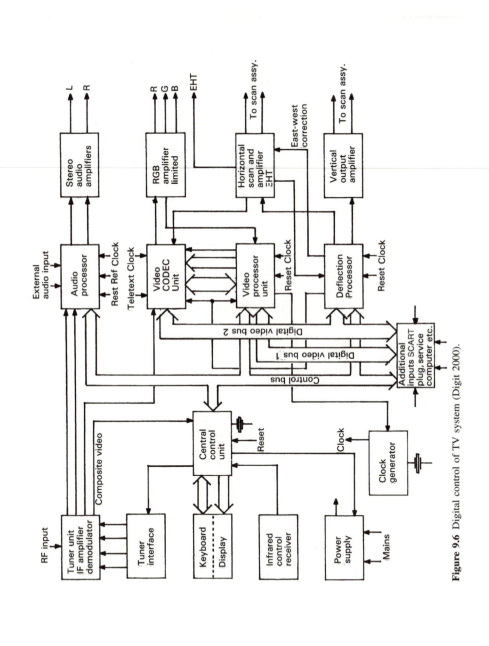

Figure 9.6 Digital control of TV system (Digit 2000).

RF/IF processing

Channel selection is controlled by frequency synthesis, with tuning steps of 62.5 kHz which are derived from division by 64 from a 4 MHz crystal-controlled oscillator. Automatic channel search is included, with AFC for fine tuning, functions that are carried out under software control from the microprocessor in the central control unit (CCU). The local oscillator frequency (f_o) is divided by 64 to produce a value within the operating frequency range of a PLL. This signal is compared with the required channel value, an action which causes up/down signals to be generated and fed to the tuner interface. These have a repetition frequency of 976.5625 Hz, of variable pulse duration and derived from 62.5 kHz/ 64. These two pulse streams produce a charge/discharge action on an integrating capacitor, which generates a tuning voltage proportional to the average of the two. The IF/demodulator circuitry uses integrated circuit technology for analogue processing. However, all of the tuning and alignment facilities normal in such circuits are carried out digitally. Initial alignment is carried out using a production line computer, to optimize the receiver performance. All of these tuning values are then digitally stored in an EEPROM. Subsequent servicing can involve the use of a service computer or handset to modify these values as necessary in order to re-establish the original performance, an operation that is often described as using an *electronic screwdriver*. The demodulated output signals are multiplexed audio and composite video.

User controls

Operation is controlled from either a front panel keyboard or an infra-red remote control sub-system. The latter uses a space duration 10-bit code, with start and stop bits to convey instructions. Logic 0 or 1 is determined by the time duration between very narrow pulses. Provision is thus made for $2^{10} = 1024$ different commands. These are usually split between $2^4 = 16$ differently addressed sub-systems, each capable of responding to $2^6 = 64$ different commands.

Audio channels

Provision is made for either the Zweiton (German) L + R/2R stereo multiplex, or the US Zenith Corporation's multi-carrier L + R/(SAP) FM multiplex. (SAP = secondary audio programme, carrying the L-R signal component.) Either multiplex is converted into a serial bit stream using *pulse density modulators* (PDM), the pulse density being proportional to the signal amplitude. The maximum pulse rate of 7.1 MHz means that no anti-aliasing filters need to be incorporated at the inputs. The serial data is converted into 16-bit parallel words for further processing. This includes de-emphasis, tone, volume, loudness, stereo width and balance controls, plus the generation of pseudo-stereo from a mono signal. The final conversion to analogue format is carried out by two *pulse width modulators* (PWM). Such outputs only require simple filtering to provide the necessary drive to analogue power amplifiers.

Central control unit

This control unit is based on a microprocessor and is designed to work as an interface between the user and the receiver. The original factory alignment and tuning data is stored in the EEPROM and these values are used as references. Control is exercised over the three-wire serial inter-IC control bus. (This includes Ident, Clock and Data lines.) The programmability of the microprocessor allows different set manufacturers to design receivers around the chip set to meet their own particular specifications. Control signals to the various digital processors are passed over the serial bus, and these cause parallel data to be transferred as needed over one or other of the parallel data buses.

Video codec and processing units

These two ICs work in conjunction to decode the composite video signal into its luminance (Y′) and colour difference components (R′ − Y′) and (B′ − Y′). The signal is first converted into a pseudo 8-bit parallel Gray code (actually only seven bits are generated). The Gray code is particularly suitable at this stage. Each successive value changes only in one bit position and this feature assists the noise reduction which is carried out next. This signal is then passed over a parallel bus into the video processing stage, where it is converted into a simple 8-bit code for the luminance channel and an offset binary code for chrominance processing. In the luminance channel, the signal is filtered, the contrast level set and then delayed to obtain optimum luminance/chrominance registration for the display. The delay is achieved quite simply, by halting the movement of the luminance signal for a programmable number of clock pulses. The Y′ signal is then passed back to the codec unit, still as eight parallel bits. The chrominance signal is decoded into (R′ − Y′) and (B′ − Y′) components and also passed back to the codec unit, but in two 4-bit time-multiplexed groups. The three components of the video signal are then converted into analogue format and matrixed to produce the R, G, B primary colour signals.

In addition to inputs from external audio and video sources, interfacing is also provided for such auxiliary inputs as a SCART or Peritel socket and connection to the service computer.

Video memory controller

Figure 9.7 illustrates how the addition of a video memory controller (VMC) and six dynamic RAMs (DRAM) can be used to create a flicker-free picture. The 8-bit luminance and 4 + 4-bit time-multiplexed colour difference signals from the VPU are input to the VMC. The 8-bit groups are reorganized into 24-bit parallel

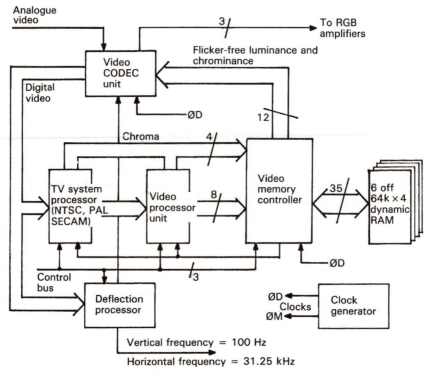

Figure 9.7 Flicker-free image sub-system.

groups by an encoder, for storage in the six 64k × 4-bit DRAMs. This field data memory is organized into a 64k × 24-bit array. The read-out process is practically complementary, except that the field data is read out twice in each normal field period and then passed to the video codec unit for processing into RGB signals. The overall effect is to double both the horizontal and the vertical scanning rates to remove flicker. A freeze frame effect is simply achieved by halting the write to memory process.

Although this process yields good results with the normal video signals, a much faster rise time is needed in the analogue RGB stages when the receiver is used for teletext or as a home computer monitor. For these applications, an RGB double-scan processor chip can be used to good effect.

Picture-in-picture processing (PIP)

The image data for the primary channel is processed as previously described (analogue video in Figure 9.7). For PIP operation, an appropriate processor and two 16k × 4-bit DRAMs are added. The latter are used to store the data for a

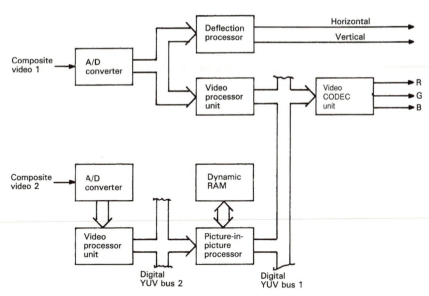

Figure 9.8 Picture-in-picture processing.

secondary channel, whose image will be overlaid on that of the primary image. The data for this second channel is obtained via the receiver, video processor unit and TV system processor unit, the derived data being passed over data bus 2 (Figure 9.8) to the PIP processing section. A sampling process selects every third pixel and every third line, to produce data for a 1/9th normal-sized picture. This data is stored in the memory, to be read out during the appropriate part of each normal line and field scan period.

Closed caption transmissions

A simplified *teletext* type of service has been devised in cooperation with the American National Captioning Institute to provide a service for viewers with impaired hearing. Although this was specifically designed to operate with NTSC receivers, the service can be applied to any PAL or SECAM receiver that is equipped with a control microprocessor. It is thus compatible with the DIGIT 2000/3000 system for which ITT have produced a single chip decoder, the CCD 3000.

An area of the screen is allocated for the display of up to eight rows, each containing up to thirty-two characters. Apart from where characters are displayed, this area is transparent. For NTSC, the data is transmitted during line 21 of field 1 (odd) in NRZ format. The data stream, at 503 kHZ, consists of a *clock-run-in* sequence followed by a *start code* consisting of two logic 0s and logic 1. This is followed by two 8-bit bytes that represent two ASCII characters.

A simple parity check is provided by a single bit in each byte. The actual usable data rate is thus 16 bits per 1/30 s or 480 bit/s. The received codes, including control codes, are decoded and stored in memory (a RAM plus a ROM character generator), to be displayed on the CRT under the control of the system microprocessor. A wide range of *fonts* and many of the normal teletext type of *attributes* are permitted.

9.4   MULTIPLEXED ANALOGUE COMPONENT (MAC) SYSTEMS
   (7, 8)

The opportunity to introduce a new system of delivering television signals into the home, occurs rarely in the history of television engineering. It gives a chance to introduce new concepts that overcome the display problems of the earlier systems and to provide an image quality in keeping with the capability of the latest display technology. The opportunity presented by direct-to-home (DTH) broadcasting via satellites also extends the influence of *pay* or *subscription* TV services.

The use of frequency modulation for the space link has already been justified. Therefore a review of the effect of FM noise on the current television formats can usefully be made here. Figure 9.9 shows the disposition of the chrominance component within the luminance spectrum with the triangular spectrum for FM noise superimposed. It can be seen that the chrominance component lies in the noisier region. Demodulation returns the chrominance signal to baseband together with the noise element. The colour response of the human eye is approximately triangular and complementary to the FM noise spectrum. Therefore the colour noise appears in the most annoying region, being particularly troublesome in the highly saturated colour areas of the image.

Under the aegis of the European Broadcasting Union (EBU) and the Eureka-95 programme supported by the European Union (EU), the 1980s produced a great deal of development work based on a hybrid solution referred to as the multiplexed analogue component (MAC) system. This employs a combination of analogue and digital processing for the vision and sound signals respectively. The

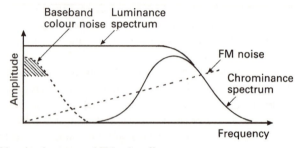

Figure 9.9 Video signal spectra and FM noise effect.

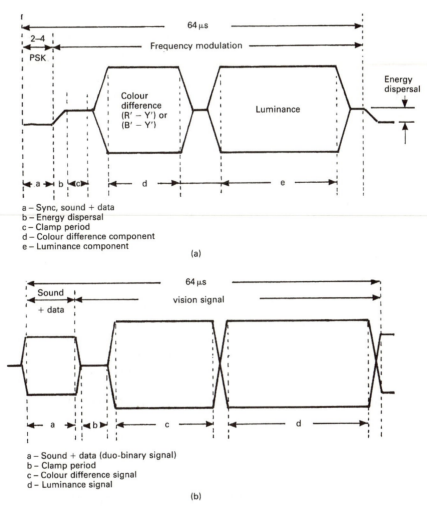

a – Sync, sound + data
b – Energy dispersal
c – Clamp period
d – Colour difference component
e – Luminance component

(a)

a – Sound + data (duo-binary signal)
b – Clamp period
c – Colour difference signal
d – Luminance signal

(b)

Figure 9.10 MAC line multiplex. **(a)** C-MAC. **(b)** D/D2-MAC.

Y and U, V components of video are time-compressed for separate transmission, thus automatically resolving the cross-luminance/chrominance problem. This concept gave rise to perhaps twelve variants, each with some different properties, but only two formats have survived into practical service.

The format of the video line time multiplex, which is shown for two of the variants in Figure 9.10, is typical of almost all versions. The active line period for the current systems is about 52 μs. For MAC systems, the luminance signal is time-compressed by a ratio of 3:2 so that it occupies about 35 μs. The two colour difference signals are compressed by a ratio of 3:1, with a corresponding duration of approximately 17.5 μs. By transmitting the compressed Y signal on each line with one of the compressed U (C_B) and V (C_R) signals alternately on odd and even lines, the active line period is still 52 μs. As the action of the conventional line sync pulse can be replaced by a digital control, there is a period of about 10 μs which is available for digitized sound, data and digital control signalling.

Of the two systems remaining in service, B-MAC is used via satellite to provide a racing service for UK bookmakers and D2-MAC is used for DTH television in the Nordic countries.

B-MAC

This version time-multiplexes the digital sound and data information at baseband into the 10 μs horizontal line blanking interval. The bandwidth is limited to about 6 MHz and so B-MAC is suitable for distribution over both satellite and cable links.

C- and D-MAC systems (7)

Both of these systems were designed to use similar line multiplexes as indicated by Figure 9.10 but with different methods of modulation for the sound and data channels. The carrier is frequency-modulated by the analogue vision signal components for 52 μs and then digitally modulated during a further 10 μs by a multiplex of the sound channel and data. The C-MAC variant employs a form of QPSK for its digital modulation, while D-MAC uses duo-binary PSK modulation at a data rate of 20.25 MHz. This is reduced by a factor of two to 10.125 MHz for D2-MAC.

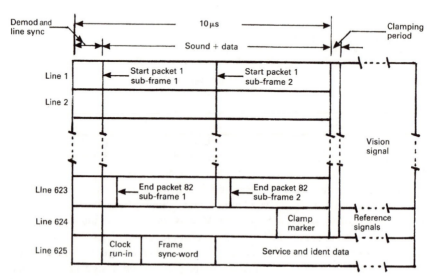

Figure 9.11 C- and D-MAC packet multiplex.

For duo-binary PSK modulation, logic 0 and 1 are represented by zero phase shift and ±90° respectively, except for the following rule. If there is an odd number of 0s between two successive 1s, the polarity or phase of the second 1 is reversed. If there is an even number of 0s, then the phase of the second 1 is the same as that of the first. The frequency spectrum for this code format has a dc component, but the first zero crossing occurs at 1/2T, instead of 1/T which is common for many binary codes and is therefore half the bandwidth. This bit stream is then filtered to remove many of the harmonics to leave a waveform that virually consists of a series of hemi-sinusoids. Demodulation is simply carried out by using full-wave rectification followed by slicing at about the half-amplitude level.

For the European 625 line services, the following EBU standard was adopted for the C/D-MAC/packet systems:

Frame frequency	25 Hz
Line frequency	15.625 kHz
Interlace	2:1
Aspect ratio	4:3
Y compression ratio	3:2
U, V compression ratio	3:1
Luminance bandwidth	5.6 MHz
Chrominance bandwidth	2.8 MHz
Transmission baseband	8.4 MHz (luminance 5.6 × 3/2 = 8.4)
	(chrominance 2.8 × 3 = 8.4)
Sound channel	40–15 000 Hz
Sampling frequency	32 kHz
Dynamic range	>80 dB

Figure 9.11 indicates how the the frame multiplex is structured for both the C- and D-MAC systems. The data is organized into packets, each of 751 bits as shown. For the D2-MAC variant, the number of sub-frames is reduced to one per line to reduce the bit rate. Each packet contains a header and a data section. Each header consists of ten address bits to identify any one of 1024 different services and eleven protection or parity bits for a Golay 23, 12 cyclic error correcting code. This can correct any three errors in up to twenty-three bits. Packet zero is allocated to service identification. Figure 9.11 also shows how the digital line and field synchronism is achieved.

Figure 9.12 shows clearly how the luminance, chrominance and digital data are assembled into a frame multiplex.

Comparison of MAC system characteristics

From the point of view of transmitter power, C-MAC, which required only one carrier frequency, was the most efficient. With more than 3 Mb/s of digital

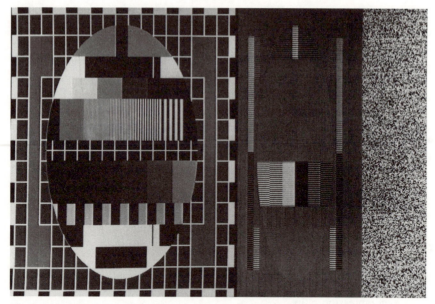

Figure 9.12 C-MAC signal displayed on a PAL TV receiver (Courtesy of IBA, UK).

capacity, the system could easily support as many as eight audio channels simultaneously. However, the wide bandwidth made this system unsuitable for use with many cable TV networks.

D-MAC allowed simpler and cheaper receivers to be developed, with decoders that are compatible with D2-MAC.

The D2-MAC variant has the same basic characteristics as D-MAC, but with only half the data capacity. However, using the technology available, it was the only member of the family whose signal could easily be recorded on a domestic video recorder.

Hi-Vision or MUSE (9, 10)

This system, known as MUSE (Multiple Sub-Nyquist Sampling Encoding), was derived from the high-definition TV system developed by the Japan Broadcasting Corporation (NHK) Technical Research Laboratories. The broadcast version known as Hi-Vision currently provides the only HDTV system being broadcast anywhere in the world. It is also used by the Sony Corporation of Japan as the basis of the high-definition video system (HDVS) used in video production facilities, producing an image quality that is the equal of 35 mm film but at a very much lower production cost. The basic parameters of the system are:

Scanning lines per frame	1125
Active lines per frame	1035
Field frequency	60 Hz
Line frequency	33.75 kHz
Interlace	2:1
Aspect ratio	16:9
Video bandwidth	30 MHz

For transmission through a single satellite channel as Hi-Vision, the signal is passed through a bandwidth compression system that reduces the baseband requirement to about 8 MHz. The chrominance signal is time-compressed by a factor of 4:1 and the colour difference signals transmitted line sequentially. This information is time-multiplexed along with control and sync information during the horizontal line blanking interval. The luminance component is not compressed and is transmitted in interlaced form. The line multiplex is shown in Figure 9.13, the three intervals representing 12, 94 and 374 sampling points at the 16.2 MHz rate.

The bandwidth reduction is mainly achieved by the use of spatial and temporal filtering, sampling and sub-sampling. The video signal is sampled at the high rate of 64.8 MHz, which produces 1920 sample points per line. These are stored in a four-field memory and then resampled at the lower rate of 16.2 MHz. This results in the selection of every fourth pixel data. The field sub-sampling pattern and sequence is shown in Figure 9.14.

At the same time, the image data is compared inter-frame and intra-frame to detect minor movement within a frame to generate a motion compensation signal. In addition, camera operations such as pan and zoom can create whole image movements which can be compensated for by the application of signals known as *motion vectors*. The motion compensating signals are then multiplexed into the vertical blanking interval for control purposes.

The stereo sound channel is sampled at 32 kHz and transmitted as four-phase DPSK within the vertical blanking interval multiplex. The composite signal has

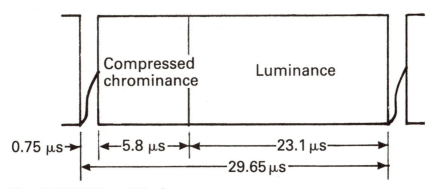

Figure 9.13 MUSE line multiplex format.

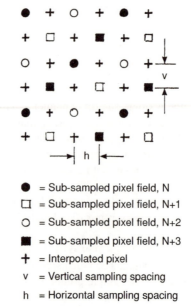

● = Sub-sampled pixel field, N
▢ = Sub-sampled pixel field, N+1
○ = Sub-sampled pixel field, N+2
■ = Sub-sampled pixel field, N+3
+ = Interpolated pixel
v = Vertical sampling spacing
h = Horizontal sampling spacing

Figure 9.14 MUSE raster sub-sampling format.

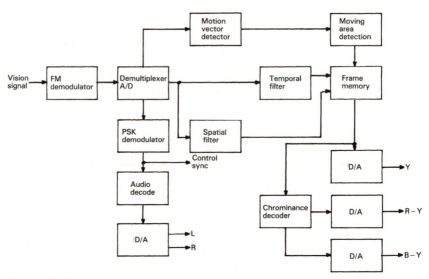

Figure 9.15 Block diagram of a MUSE decoder.

a baseband width of about 8 MHz and this is then transmitted by frequency modulation over the space link. A block diagram of a receiver decoder is shown in Figure 9.15. After conventional processing, the FM signal is demodulated, demultiplexed and converted into a digital format. The audio, sync and control signals are separated from the video components, which are two-dimensionally filtered and then stored in the four-field memory, with a capacity of about 10 Mbits. The digital data is then clocked out and motionally corrected, the missing pixels being regenerated by intra-frame and inter-frame interpolation. The colour difference signals are decoded and the Y, (R−Y) and (B−Y) components restored to analogue format. A conventional matrix then recreates the primary RGB signals.

This system therefore represents a revolutionary approach to higher-definition TV via satellite.

REFERENCES

(1) Carnt, P.S. and Townsend, G.B. (1969) *Colour Television.* London: Iliffe Books Ltd.
(2) Hutson, G.H. (1971) *Colour Television Theory.* London: McGraw-Hill.
(3) Weaver, L.E. (1982) *The SECAM Colour Television System.* Tektronix Inc., USA.
(4) Slater, J. (1991) *Modern Television Systems – to HDTV and Beyond.* London: Pitman Publishers.
(5) Kell, R.D. *et al.* (1934) 'An Experimental Television System' *Proc. IRE. 22,* pp. 1246–1265.
(6) Thorogood, J. ITT Semiconductors Ltd, UK. *'Digit 2000/ Digit 3000' VLSI Digital TV System.* 6250-11-4E/6200-230-1E. 1986/1996. (Intermetall Semiconductors GmbH).
(7) EBU Technical Document (1984) *Technical Specification for C-MAC/Packet System. SPB 284.* 2nd revised edition. C/D-MAC/Packet Family Specification, Tech. Doc. 3258, 1987.
(8) Annegarn, M.J.J.C. *et al.* (1987) 'HD-MAC: A Step Forward in the Evolution of Television Technology'. *Philips Technical Review* **43**, No. 8.
(9) Takashi, Fujio *et al.* (1985) 'HDTV Transmission Method (MUSE)'. *14th International Television Symposia,* Montreux.
(10) Kimura, E. *et al.* (1984) 'HDTV Broadcast Systems by a Satellite'. *International Broadcasting Convention, IBC '84* (UK).

Chapter 10

Digital television systems

10.1 BACKGROUND TO DIGITAL DEVELOPMENTS

While the 1980s were notable as a decade in which the drive for better television images and higher definition followed the evolutionary analogue approach, the 1990s became dominated by convergence with computer technology. The television receiver technology is now being driven towards that of the home personal computer (PC). This has resulted in the development of the digital multimedia concept which represents a new revolutionary approach. PC engineering is now almost a globally standardized business through the acceptance of the de facto standards derived for both hardware and software. By comparison, worldwide television services have only developed in an economical way because of the acceptance of standards developed through the appropriate bodies of the International Telecommunications Union (ITU) (originally the CCIR or CCITT but now known as the ITU-R and ITU-T bodies).

To provide an HDTV service with a resolution greater than 1000 lines and an aspect ratio of 16:9 requires a base bandwidth in the order of 30 MHz. This automatically precludes the use of such a system as a terrestrial service. The only spectrum available for such a wideband service lies in the Ku and Ka bands of the satellite communications allocations. Hence the development of MUSE.

The bandwidth required to process the luminance component of a 625/25/2:1 image using a 4:3 aspect ratio can be calculated as follows:

$$625 \times 625 \times 4/3 \times \tfrac{1}{2} \times 25 = 6.51 \,\text{MHz} \qquad (10.1)$$

To establish an HDTV service using the European format of 1250/25/2:1 with a 16:9 aspect ratio yields a total bit rate in excess of 1.1 Gbit/s. Thus the need for a common image compression technology is well established.

For the current analogue service, using a sampling frequency of 13.5 MHz and a resolution of eight bits per sample yields a bit rate of 108 Mbit/s for the luma channel alone. The inclusion of the two chrominance components, each with a resolution of four bits per sample, adds a further 108 Mbit/s to give a total bit rate of 216 Mbit/s.

10.2 DEVELOPMENT OF DIGITAL TELEVISION

Standards are deemed to be necessary to ensure that equipment built by many different manufacturers will function in a cooperative manner. This leads to mass production which creates an economy of scale that ensures that both suppliers and users gain from the implementation of any new service. De facto standards arise to meet an immediate need because no alternative exists. As these become more widely accepted and the technology spreads throughout an industry, these limited agreement standards may well form the eventual basis of an international standard. The ultimate ambition of the television industry must be to develop a true worldwide standard. This failed dismally with analogue processing but due to the convergence towards a multimedia system with open receivers, the current digital approach may be the best possible achievement in the real world. Multimedia now encompasses television, audio, telephony, publishing, compact disc both audio and video, computing, internet-working, plus communications functions that at present may not have even been considered.

The major stumbling block towards the development of a common television standard is related to the lack of terrestrial frequency spectrum and the different ways in which the NTSC and PAL systems developed in North America and Japan, and in Europe. The adopted channel bandwidths of 6 and 8 MHz for NTSC and PAL systems respectively is not an insurmountable problem, but the different ways in which the transmission environments developed is much more intractable. In the USA many privately owned transmitter sites radiate only a single channel local television programme together with feeds from affiliated major networks as and when needed. In Europe, where television started up in the public domain and under governmental control, each station radiates typically four or more programmes to provide a national service. Furthermore, there is a significant difference in the way in which the available frequency spectrum was employed. In North America, with great transmission areas to cover, there was an incentive to maximize the use of the VHF band which for a given power level provided a greater service area. The result of this was that the UHF bands were largely left for inner city, local area use. Thus there is a significant difference in the demands on the frequency spectrum.

It will be seen from the descriptions of the MAC and MUSE systems that the main interests of the 1980s developments were aimed at ultimately providing a high-definition television (HDTV) system. All the hype and hope of the times produced very little in the way of harmony, but with the advent of digital television, there now appears, at last, a chance of developing a near-universal system that meets the needs of the TV industry and the viewers. Using the newly developed techniques, it is claimed that image resolution is now only limited by the picture tube or display device itself.

Modulation schemes that allow each transmitted symbol to represent several binary digits are now available. For example, digital 16 quadrature amplitude modulation (16 QAM) is based on the PSK system. This employs eight vectors each capable of being modulated to one of two amplitudes and spaced by 45° (four vectors and four amplitudes are also possible). Each vector may now represent one of sixteen unique code words to generate four bits per transmitted symbol. However, relative to bi-phase PSK, reducing the vector spacing from 180° to 45° represents a noise penalty of 6 dB. Technical developments now allow up to 256 QAM to be used in suitable low-noise transmission media. This provides up to eight bits per symbol to be transmitted with the attendant bandwidth reduction.

Because digital signals are generally more robust than analogue ones under noise conditions, lower transmission power can be used. It is generally agreed that a CNR of 45 dB is necessary to achieve good image quality in an analogue system. With the current digital technology, similar image quality can be achieved with a CNR of less than 20 dB, and with a more uniform spectral power distribution. This adds a further incentive to broadcasters because it reduces their transmitter power bill by a very significant factor. It has long been recognized that if any new TV service (HD or otherwise) is to be economically viable, it must be built on the back of the already installed customer/viewer base. It was this that generated the dichotomy of whether to introduce the service in a compatible or non-compatible manner. The first viewpoint considers the immediate financial aspects, but in the long run it might be easier and cheaper to forego the advantages and the problems of compatibility that have been so troublesome to the industry in the past.

A clear indication of the convergence mentioned above can be found from the outputs of the study groups set up by the ISO/IEC, ITU-R and ITU-T (CCITT and CCIR), a brief history of which is included in the references (1). These groups operated under the acronyms of:

JBIG or Joint Bi-level Image Group	(black and white images)
JPEG or Joint Photographic Expert Group	(still colour images)
MPEG or Motion Picture Expert Group	(colour and moving images)

The important MPEG group developed in a progressive manner. Phase I or MPEG-1 was associated with early image compression work, while Phase II, which became known as MPEG-2, developed the current standards for high levels of compression for full motion video. MPEG-3 has been amalgamated into MPEG-4 which is now responsible for the investigations into future image compression for multimedia technology. Such is the impetus that MPEG-5 has now been established.

While European development followed one particular path towards the solution, the North Americans adopted quite a different approach. Throughout the 1980s the US Federal Communications Commission (FCC) insisted that any new service should be compatible with the NTSC receivers then currently in use. This led to various ingenious proposals, many of which used augmentation channels in which the necessary extra information would be transmitted. Then in early 1990, the FCC decided that this approach was wasteful of frequency spectrum and decreed that a simultcast technique would be used. This would allow a station to transmit HDTV in parallel with its current NTSC service using an alternative 6 MHz channel. Compatibility was thus no longer a constraint.

On any broadcast network, transmission frequencies can only be reused if mutual channel interference is avoided, and this feature gives rise to the term 'taboo channels'. This interference arises primarily due to the power distribution throughout each channel, being particularly high in the region of the carrier and sub-carrier frequencies. If a more uniform power distribution could be achieved, some of the taboo channels might be available for the new HDTV service.

The Advanced Television Test Centre (ATTC) was set up to test all of the competing systems and the initial twenty-three proposals were reduced to a short list of three. Ultimately, a Grand Alliance of all the contestants came together to formulate one common standard. It was hoped that this would become a world standard so that the USA could once again reestablish leadership in the consumer electronics marketplace.

This non-compatible change allows a digital TV service to be launched without disenfranchising the current NTSC viewer. (HDTV would then be implemented at a later stage.) Over a period of perhaps fifteen years the current NTSC system will atrophy and viewers will gradually change over to the new system, allowing the present carrier frequencies to be re-allocated to other services.

The committee of the world's eight broadcasting unions, the Inter-Union Technical Committee (IUTC), has adopted a world standard approach to HDTV for the production and exchange of HD television programmes. The recommendation, referred to as HD-CIF, Rec 709 (Common Interchange Format), is based on 1080 lines, each with a sampling rate of 1920 pixels and a dual field rate of 50 or 60 Hz.

True to the history of communications, while the finally chosen system has much in common with the European ideas of a new digital TV system, the final result will again be one of compromise.

10.3 EUROPEAN DIGITAL TELEVISION SYSTEM

The Digital Video Broadcasting (DVB) (Spec. ETS 300 468 DVB-SI) specification for Europe has developed into a broad-based concept so that all services can, as far as possible, use a receiver with a common core, initially driven via a set-top box (STB) decoder adaptor. Ultimately, this will combine to form an integrated receiver decoder (IRD). There are four main receiving systems that need to be serviced:

- Satellite delivery – DVB-S
- Cable delivery – DVB-C
- Terrestrial television – DVB-T
- Satellite master antenna systems (SMATV) – DVB-CS

In addition, future provision has been made for the introduction of an interactive television service described as multi-media distribution system (MMDS) which is referred to as DVB-MS.

The luminance and colour difference signals, Y, (R – Y), (B – Y), are sampled at 13.5 and 6.75 MHz respectively and quantized to ten bits per sample. This high degree of resolution ensures that the images are of a high quality for studio and production origination. The serial bit rate at this stage is thus 270 Mbit/s and represents a multiplexed sequence of Y, (R – Y) (C_R), (B – Y) (C_B) components.

The MPEG-2 encoding stage (2) which provides the data compression follows next. Basically the compression process relies on removing redundant information from the original images while making the overall system as lossless as possible. This redundancy appears in each frame (inter-frame) and between frames (intra-frame). Inter-frame or temporal compression uses data from more than one frame, while intra-frame or spatial compression reduces the redundancy in one frame only. Both of these compression techniques are adjusted by a rate control system to provide either a constant bit rate or a variable bit rate that keeps the image quality constant.

The overall lossiness of the system can be minimized by pre-processing the original signal. This involves reducing each 10-bit sample to eight bits and using a chroma structure that is suited to the application. The standardized sampling frequency of 13.5 MHz was chosen as a compromise to suit both 525/60 and 625/50 systems. It is the sixth harmonic of 2.25 MHz which is the lowest common frequency to provide a static sampling pattern in both systems. The luma component is sampled at 13.5 MHz and the two chroma difference signals at 6.75 MHz, with the two groups of sampling points being co-sited. This format is referred to as the 4:2:2 system. By reducing the chroma sampling frequency to 3.375 MHz, the format becomes known as the 4:1:1 system. For MPEG-2 it was decided to change the system to 4:2:0 so that the total number of samples remained the same, but the chroma samples are obtained by interpolation between two adjacent lines and are not co-sited with the luma samples. This approach provides a better-quality image and at a lower bit rate. The image pixel data is then organized into a two-dimensional (2D) matrix using a Discrete Cosine Transform (equation 10.2), followed by scanning the transformed matrix in such a manner that long runs of near zero values are obtained. (See Chapter 8, H.261 codecs.)

Encoder:

$$F(u, v) = \frac{2}{N} C(u)C(v) \sum_{x=0}^{N-1} \sum_{y=0}^{N-1} f(x, y) \, CosA.CosB$$

Decoder:

$$f(x, y) = \frac{2}{N} \sum_{u=0}^{N-1} \sum_{v=0}^{N-1} C(u)C(v)F(u, v) \, CosA.CosB \quad \text{where,}$$

$$A = \frac{(2x + 1)u\pi}{2N}, \quad B = \frac{(2y + 1)v\pi}{2N} \quad \text{and}$$

$$C(u) = C(v) = 1/\sqrt{2} \text{ for } u = v = 0 \quad \text{and}$$

$$C(u) = C(v) = 1 \text{ otherwise.} \tag{10.2}$$

Table 10.1 Forward and reverse DCT processing of 8 × 8 pixel block

139	144	149	153	155	155	155	155	
144	151	153	156	159	156	156	156	
150	155	160	163	158	156	156	156	
159	161	162	160	160	159	159	159	Original
159	160	161	162	162	155	155	155	8 × 8 block
161	161	161	161	160	157	157	157	
162	162	161	163	162	157	157	157	
162	162	161	161	163	158	158	158	
314.91	−0.26	−3.02	−1.30	0.53	−0.42	−0.68	0.33	
5.65	−4.37	−1.56	−0.79	−0.71	−0.02	0.11	−0.30	
2.74	−2.32	−0.39	0.38	0.05	−0.24	−0.14	−0.02	DCT
1.77	−0.48	0.06	0.36	0.22	−0.02	−0.01	0.08	processed
0.16	−0.21	0.37	0.39	−0.03	−0.17	0.15	0.32	block
0.44	−0.05	0.41	−0.09	−0.19	0.37	0.26	−0.25	
0.32	−0.09	−0.08	−0.37	−0.12	0.43	0.27	−0.19	
0.65	0.39	−0.94	−0.46	0.47	0.30	−0.14	−0.11	
315	0	−3	−1	1	0	−1	0	
−6	−4	−2	−1	−1	0	0	0	
−3	−2	0	0	0	0	0	0	
−2	0	0	0	0	0	0	0	Quantized
0	0	0	0	0	0	0	0	coefficients
0	0	0	0	0	0	0	0	
0	0	0	0	0	0	0	0	
−1	0	−1	0	0	0	0	0	
139	145	150	154	154	153	154	153	
145	150	154	157	157	155	156	156	
150	155	158	161	160	157	157	155	
159	161	161	163	161	158	159	158	Reconstructed
159	160	161	163	161	157	156	155	8×8 block
163	162	160	162	161	157	157	158	
162	161	159	162	161	157	157	157	
164	162	160	163	162	158	159	160	

(Courtesy of General Instruments Corp. VideoCipher Division (3))

The transformation itself does not generate any compression, but this is achieved at the next stage. By using adaptive quantization of the matrix coefficients the number of significant values can be reduced. The effect of this processing is clearly shown in Table 10.1.

When this is followed by a form of entropy and run-length coding where, for example, the values 7,7,7,7 would be coded 7,4 (i.e. 7 four times), there is quite a considerable reduction in the data that needs to be transmitted.

Each frame or field has thus been partitioned into luma and chroma blocks of DCT components. These are now sliced on a line-by-line sequence to generate the serial bit stream for further MPEG processing.

The audio signal does not respond well to entropy and run-length coding, therefore a psychoacoustic modelling is used. This is based on the concept that if a particular frequency component cannot be heard, then there is little point in transmitting it. MPEG audio processing will be described later.

The video and audio bit streams are then MPEG and run-length encoded to achieve the necessary compression, before being organized into packets of 188 bytes (4). These packets are then combined into the transport bit stream which consists of a multiplex of a range of programmes referred to as a bouquet. As an indication of the level of commonality that has been achieved with this new standard, the programme stream multiplex output shown in Figure 10.1 can also be used for the Digital Video or Versatile Disk (DVD) system. The data input to this stage includes all the control and service information necessary for the decoder to unlock the whole programme structure. At this stage the packets are 188 bytes long and start with the synchronism byte 01000111 (47 Hex). In order to break up long runs of 1s or 0s and balance the spectral loading of the transmission channel, the bit stream, with the exception of the sync byte, is scrambled (the energy dispersal) by combining it with a pseudo-random binary sequence (PRBS). This also ensures that there are enough signal transitions to provide adequate receiver clock recovery. The PRBS is repeated every eight packets so that the receiver is aware of its pattern and to enable the decoder to locate this sequence, the sync byte is also inverted once in every eight bytes.

The (204,188) Reed–Solomon outer code then adds sixteen extra bytes as CRC so that the packet length is now 204 bytes. This additional redundancy allows up to eight errored bytes in a packet to be corrected. The outer interleaver stores twelve consecutive packets in memory and then reads these out byte by byte from each packet in turn so that the data becomes evenly spread over a longer period. If the data stream is errored for a limited period, the longer bursts of interference are divided over many small periods so that these errors can be corrected. The next two stages do not apply to all delivery methods. An inner punctured convolutional code with a rate varying from 1/2 (unpunctured) to 7/8 with a constraint length 7 can be selected to suit the noise conditions of the particular service. Puncturing involves dropping error protection bits from the data stream in a controlled manner to achieve the new code rate. The inner encoder employs Trellis modulation which requires the use of Viterbi decoding at the receiver. The packet data stream is further interleaved before being applied to the modulator stage. For the DVB-S system, the modulated carrier frequency will typically be either 70 or 140 MHz. The error protection for the transport stream is adapted to suit the physical carrier medium by varying the channel coding. As shown in Figure 10.1, the cable delivery systems with their generally more robust carrier medium do not employ either the inner coding or interleaving stages, but pulse filtering is used to restrict the signal frequency spectrum. It is only the terrestrially delivered signals that use the total available error protection.

The modulation systems employed for the three modes of delivery are as follows: DVB-S (satellite) uses QPSK, DVB-C (cable) uses 64 QAM, and DVB-T (terrestrial) uses COFDM.

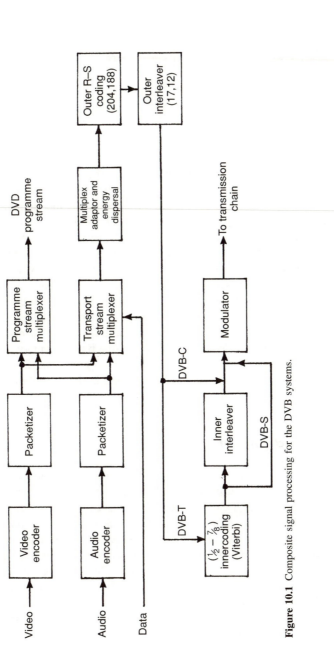

Figure 10.1 Composite signal processing for the DVB systems.

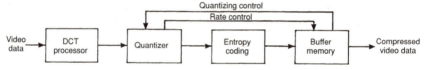

Figure 10.2 Intra-frame coding.

Intra-frame compression (I-pictures)

These frames represent virtually complete pictures because they are compressed to remove only the spatial redundancy from a particular frame. The I pictures or frames are thus independent of the other frames and are therefore also referred to as anchor frames. With reference to Figure 10.2, the digitized ten bits per sample video input signal has previously been reduced to eight bits resolution. The signal is then processed through the DCT transform stage which converts the amplitude coefficients into frequency values. As shown in Table 10.1, when the matrix is scanned in a zigzag fashion, this generates many low-level values that, when quantized and rounded, create long runs of zeros. Because this creates a variable data rate, the bit stream is stored in a buffer memory. If the buffer tends to overflow, a rate control signal causes the quantizer stage to change its resolution to lower the bit rate. Controlled in this way, the buffer memory operates at the nearly full state for most of the processing time. The quantizing scale factor is continually passed to the memory for inclusion in the control data stream.

Inter-frame compression (P-pictures)

The processing system that removes the inter-frame or temporal redundancy is shown in Figure 10.3. A predicted P-frame uses the nearest I- or P-frame as the prediction reference. It can therefore in turn act as a reference to future P- or B-frames. Because P-frames have a greater degree of data compression than I-frames, any errors can propagate throughout a group of pictures (GOP) to create problems. B-frames are obtained by bi-directional, forward and backward comparison and have an even greater degree of data compression making them unfit for use as a reference frame. Figure 10.3 shows how the current and predicted frames are compared so that only the differences need to be coded for these frames. A good predictor would simply be the previous frame. Due to the use of the inverse quantizer and DCT transform, the fixed store holds a full resolution image from the previous picture. The motion compensation/estimation stages predict the present frame and at the same time generate a motion vector that describes how parts of the frame are moving. If the predictor frame was the previous one then there would be no movement and this vector would be zero. Any motion vectors needs to be added to the coded data stream via the

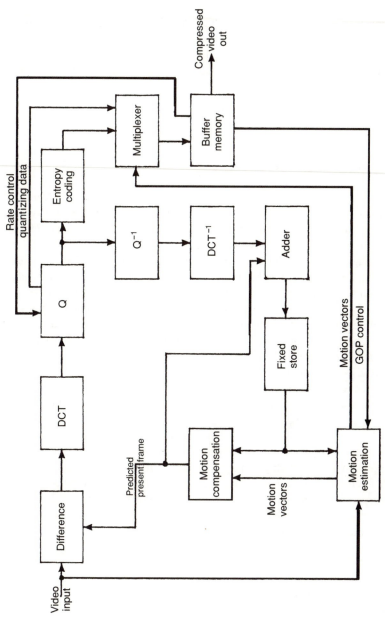

Figure 10.3 MPEG video compression for P-pictures.

multiplexer. In order to reduce the motion information to a minimum, the estimation is performed on a 16×16 pixel macroblock which coincides with the chroma signal. A single vector can thus be used to describe the motion in both the luma and chroma channels. In this way, the bit rate overhead needed to describe motion is just nine bits per macroblock. The operation of the entropy coding and buffer blocks was described in the I-frame compression stage. However, if it is detected that a pixel block ends in a long run of zeros, an end-of-block code can be appended after the last non-zero value to further increase the compression ratio.

Groups of pictures (GOP)

If bit errors occur in the transmission process, the errors will propagate throughout the image. To overcome this, complete frames are periodically added to the sequence. These are the I or anchor frames because they make no reference to other frames in the transmission sequence.

The major problem with moving areas within an image is that these reveal background information that has previously been hidden from view, thus making prediction very difficult. This is overcome in MPEG-2 by using information from a future frame and, to achieve this, the real-time frame sequence has to be shuffled. Each I-frame is therefore followed by a future forward predicted P-frame and stored for comparison in a memory to detect image motion and background information. These are then followed by a number of B-frames (bi-directional) which can be created by forward and backward motion compensated differences using the macroblocks as a basis.

If the real-time frame sequence is $I_1, B_1, B_2, P_1, B_3, B_4, P_2, \ldots$ then in order to decode a B-frame the two frames used in its prediction must already be stored in the decoder memory. Thus the transmission sequence must be $I_1, P_1, B_1, B_2, P_2, B_3, B_4, \ldots$ In practice, the distance between I-frame sequences controls the reconstructed image quality. Three common GOP sequences are likely to be encountered and these are described in terms of the factor M, N, where M and N are the periodicity of the I- and B-frames respectively. System 6,3 would be employed in studios and production areas, 12,3 for standard definition broadcast television and 15,3 for lower quality services.

MPEG-2 packet structures

The basic MPEG packet of 188 bytes consists of at least four header bytes, the first of which is a sync byte (47H). The following 184-byte payload contains the system control or programme data. The appended Reed-Solomon (204,188) FEC bytes make a total of 204 bytes as shown in Figure 10.4(a). It is these basic

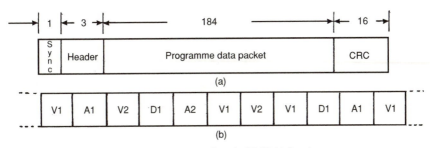

Figure 10.4 (a) MPEG-2 data packet structure (bytes). (b) Multiplexed transport stream.

packets of video (V), audio (A) and data (D) that are interleaved in the manner shown in Figure 10.4(b) to produce the total multiplex of programmes. Figure 10.5 shows that the header consists of eight fields of various bit lengths and gives their nominal operational values in hexadecimal.

MPEG profiles and levels

The specification was future proofed by allowing for applications using very high bit rates and high pixel densities. However, these are practically bounded by what is currently technologically possible and these are described in terms of twelve profiles and levels. This has the advantage of allowing for a scalability of receiver decoder complexity and hence cost. These standards are optimized for all services, including both 50 and 60 Hz environments and eventually HD. Production areas will, in general, operate in the 'MPEG-2 MP @ ML' (main profile at main level). The data shown in Table 10.2 represents just three columns from the 4 × 5 matrix that contains the twelve variants.

The specification also permits the introduction of a telecommunications concept that is used in SDH (synchronous digital hierarchy) and ATM (asynchronous transfer mode): the use of statistical multiplexing whereby a

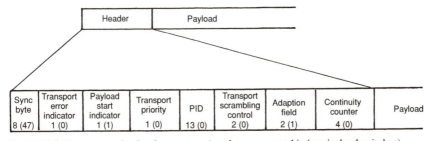

Figure 10.5 Transport packet header structure (numbers represent bits/nominal value in hex).

Table 10.2

Level	Profile		
	Simple	Main	Profile
High 1920		4:2:0 1920 × 1152 80 Mbit/s I,P,B, frames	
High 1440		4:2:0 1440 × 1152 60 Mbit/s I,P,B, frames	
Main	4:2:0 720 × 576 15 Mbit/s I,P, frames	4:2:0 720 × 576 15 Mbit/s I,P,B, frames	4:2:0 720 × 608 50 Mbit/s I,P,B, frames
Low		4:2:0 352 × 288 4 Mbit/s I,P,B, frames	

channel may actually borrow, at any given time, extra bit rate from another with spare capacity. For example, six channels may be allocated a total capacity of 36 Mbit/s (6 Mbit/s per channel). At a given instant, there may be a great deal of movement in one channel that requires a higher bit rate, while another may be carrying captions. Statistical multiplexing allows such a channel to steal extra bit rate for the duration of this excessive motion. Managed in this way, it may well be possible to implement the provisions of the 1997 MPEG-2 standards which include the possibility of HDTV within a standard definition (SDTV) multiplex.

Possible MPEG-2 problems

Course quantizing errors following the inverse DCT stage at the decoder creates errors in the reconstructed sampling values which lead to contouring at the block boundaries. This *blockiness* becomes more noticeable on the chroma information because this signal was originally coded in larger 16 × 16 pixel macroblocks. Truncated high-frequency coefficients following the DCT processing stage can cause *ringing* at image component edges which is particularly noticable on graphics and captions. The sudden change in lighting levels that occurs through the use of flash photography at certain outdoor functions can cause prediction problems when the coefficients for whole frames change suddenly. Noisy image sources create variable DCT coefficients that can overload the encoding and decoding systems. In order to minimize these and other effects, the original input image signal can be pre-processed by filtering to remove noise, lowering the entropy of the source material by down-sampling or by increasing the I-frame rate. The problems for the domestic receiver are likely to be rather less important than those found in the production areas. Editing can become difficult because of the long period between I-frames. Telecine transfers between film and video tape or disk has to counter the problems that arise from the different frame rates (film at 24 f/s and video at 25 or 30 f/s).

The basic MPEG-2 packet structure is shown in Figure 10.4(a) where the header consists of at least four bytes and the main part of the packet, called the payload, consists of a maximum of 184 bytes. To this is appended the Reed–Solomon (204,188) cyclic redundancy check block to produce a transmission packet of length 204 bytes. The payload part of the packet may carry either programme data signals or an extension of the header control bytes. Figure 10.4(b) shows how the individual packets of video (V), audio (A), or data (D) from the several programmes are interleaved to produce the transmission multiplex.

The most important part of the header sequence is the 8-bit sync byte and the 13-bit PID (Programme ID) field. The 13 bits can represent a total of 8191 values of which only 0, 1 and 8191 are currently assigned. The 4-bit continuity counter counts sequentially from 0 to 15 to detect any lost or repeated packets. The 2-bit scrambling control field is used to signify the PRBS in use.

The Adaption field, which is transmitted periodically, points to an extension of the header into the payload section and the important fields here include a 1-bit discontinuity indicator which flags a continuity counter mis-count or a timebase discontinuity, a 48-bit programme clock reference, an 8-bit splice count-down field which specified the number of packets with the same PID value before a splice point, and a 1-bit random access indicator field which signals the start of a video or audio field in the same packet PID stream.

Programme and packet control

In addition to the shuffling of the individual frames, each transmission multiplex may consist of up to six programmes. Each of these may in turn carry a number of elementary streams associated with video, audio and data, so that this forms a highly complex multiplex. Thus the information carried in the packet headers and adaption fields are particularly important to the decoder. The actual decoding process is carried out via a mapping scheme that carries Programme-Specific Information (PSI) which must also he transmitted within the multiplex. Each transport stream has a Programme Associated Table (PAT) which is also PID0 (Packet ID zero). This is the table that identifies the PID numbers for the table that defines each programme. Each programme also has a number of Programme

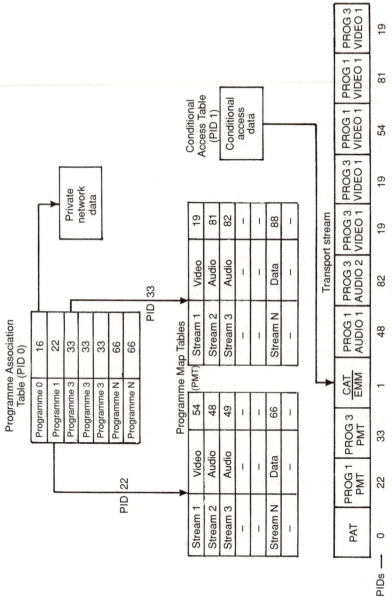

Figure 10.6 Programme-specific information table.

Map Tables (PMT) which states the PID number for each elementary stream in a specific programme. The Conditional Access Table (CAT), which is also always PID1, carries information about the scrambling system and indirectly the Entitlement Management Message (EMM) system that refers to the programme availability for any given user. PID 8191 is reserved for null packets.

The programmes are numbered sequentially and programme zero (PID0) is always the Network Information Table (NIT). This includes the Service Description Table (SDT) which describes the service details which can include information for the compilation of the Electronic Programme Guide (EPG).

Figure 10.6 shows how this information is used by the decoder in the following order:

The PAT (PID0) is recovered to identify the PIDs for the PMT.
The PMTs are recovered to indicate the use of the other PIDs. In the diagram shown, the PAT indicates that PID22 and PID33 mark the PMTs for programmes 1 and 2 respectively.
PID48 is stream 2, audio 1, for programme 1.
PID82 is stream 3, audio 2, for programme 3; etc.

Timing and synchronism

Because of the shuffling of frames and the differences used in the encoding of the elemental video and audio streams, it is important that the decoder should be able to achieve synchronism between sound and vision from signals that could potentially differ in time by almost one second. The system clock reference (SCR) provides a number of clock pulse sequences. A 33-bit Presentation Time Stamp (PST) is inserted by the encoder into the data stream to identify specific video frames and audio sequences. The receiver decoder recovers the SCRs and transfers the data to the video and audio decoders to update their local clocks. The receiver decoders then check the incoming PTS markers against the SCR before displaying a picture. If any timing error is detected, this is used to modify the speed of the recovered clock until synchronism is achieved.

Coded orthogonal frequency division multiplex (COFDM) modulation scheme

This concept consists of generating a large number of carrier frequencies with equal spacing. Each is then digitally modulated with a sub-band of frequencies and then filtered to produce a (sin x)/x (or sinc x) response as shown in Figure 10.7(a). The spectra of the individual carriers thus overlap in the orthogonal manner shown. When these combine, the total spectrum becomes practically flat

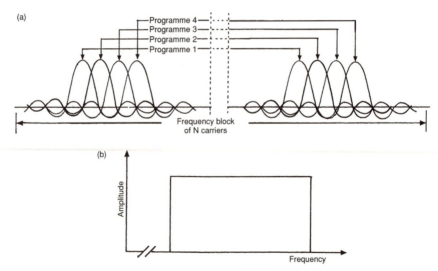

Figure 10.7 (a) Time domain of OFDM carriers. (b) OFDM frequency spectrum.

as shown in Figure 10.7(b). The channel capacity approaches the Shannon limiting value and the spectrum behaves as a parallel transmission bus.

The allocated bandwidth is divided into N elementary frequencies and arranged to carry P programme channels. There are therefore N/P interleaved elementary carriers which carry sub-band modulation in the manner shown. Either variants of QPSK or QAM can be used for the digital modulation.

In a practical system, each of the carriers will carry an equal share of the total bandwidth to be transmitted so that although the overall transmission bit rate can be very high, the individual carriers bit rates will be relatively very low. The coded variant of OFDM (COFDM) uses fast Fourier transform (FFT) processing and convolutional coding at the modulator stage. When this is combined with complementary FFT processing and Viterbi decoding at the demodulator, the overall bit error rate is very low.

Since the COFDM spectrum has noise-like properties and the signal can be transmitted at relatively low power levels, it produces very little adjacent channel interference and does not suffer from multipath transmission effects.

To minimize the effects of inter-symbol interference (ISI) and improve the overall bit error rate (BER), a short guard interval is inserted before each symbol. To achieve the maximum bit rate the guard interval should be as short as possible, typically less than 25 percent of the useful symbol period (about $250 \mu s$). The carrier spacing is inversely proportional to the symbol duration. Thus with a guard interval of about $250 \mu s$ and a symbol time of 1 ms there can be 8 000 carriers in an 8 MHz channel.

In the European DVB-T system, the fast Fourier transform (FFT) processor size is made either $2^{11} = 2048$ or $2^{13} = 8192$ points and this in turn sets the

Table 10.3

Parameter	2k mode	8k mode
Number of carriers	1705	6817
Symbol duration	224 μs	896 μs
Guard interval	7–56 μs	28–224 μs
Carrier spacing	1116 Hz	4464 Hz
Total carrier spacing	7.61 MHz	7.61 MHz
Carrier modulation	QPSK, 16-QAM, 64-QAM	QPSK, 16-QAM, 64-QAM,
Code rate	1/2–7/8	1/2–7/8

maximum number of carriers. The two versions are referred to as 2k or 8k systems. An 8k processor will be able to demodulate either version but the 2k decoder will only handle its own specific system.

A number of carrier frequencies are allocated to system synchronism and are thus not available for signal modulation. This discrepancy can be seen in Table 10.3. Two types of synchronizing carriers are used and these are referred to as continual and scattered pilots. The former are spread randomly across all the carriers associated with the same symbol while the latter are disposed across the whole spectrum.

Transmission parameter signalling (TPS) adds further information to the bit stream. This carries information about the mode, the guard interval, the modulation and the code rate, all helping the receiver to achieve a fast acquisition of the signal. This data is transmitted by using binary PSK. Figure 10.8 shows the general processing used for this form of modulation, while Table 10.3 shows the important parameters of both the 2k and 8k systems.

Modulation schemes and bit error rates

A rigorous analysis of the various forms of digital QAM is particularly complex. However, an intuitive comparative approach can provide solutions that are within about 1 dB of the mathematical calculations and very close to the results obtained

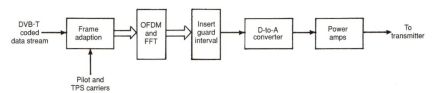

Figure 10.8 DVB-T COFDM signal processing at the transmitter.

from practical testing (5). It has been theoretically and practically demonstrated that a BER = 2×10^4 provides good-quality television images and that the service threshold is as low as one errored bit in 10^{-3}. The general case for digital QAM can be expressed as follows.

For m-QAM, where m = 2k, k is the number of bits per symbol and m is the number of points in the signal space or constellation.

It is shown in the literature (6) that to achieve a BER above the service threshold level (1×10^{-3}) using PSK with synchronous demodulation requires an SNR of approximately 6 dB. PSK has been chosen as the baseline for this approach because it represents a simple digital modulation with the minimum bandwidth. By comparison, QPSK has a signal constellation that contains four points, with each point representing two bits. The chances of making a decoding error with this mode is therefore now twice as great. Hence for the same BER, the SNR will need to be increased by 3 dB. Now 4QAM has the same number of signal points in its constellation as QPSK and therefore has the same SNR penalty for a constant BER. Thus 4QAM requires a minimum SNR of 9 dB and every increase of one bit per symbol demands an extra 3 dB improvement in signal quality. For 16QAM with its four bits per symbol, this will require a further 6 dB of signal or an SNR of 15 dB. By the same reasoning, an SNR of 21 dB will be needed for 64QAM.

For COFDM, the dichotomy that arises around the use of the 2k or 8k modes can also be treated in an intuitive manner. The 8k mode has four times as many carriers as the 2k mode but for the same total bit rate and bandwidth, the individual carrier bit rate will only be one-quarter of that found in the 2k mode. Thus for the same signal power and bandwidth, the E_b/N_o ratio should be the same in each case so that white noise will affect both modes equally. The implementation losses at both the transmitter and receiver are similar so that neither mode has a significant advantage. The fabrication process for 8k chip sets is somewhat more complex, but still well within the current bounds of manufacturing capabilities and tolerances. It is when the effects of multipath transmissions, echoes and reflections of the type that produce ghosting with analogue television signals are considered that it is found that the 8k mode is much more robust. This arises chiefly because of the longer guard intervals and the lower individual carrier bit rates which lead to lower levels of inter-symbol interference (ISI) so that the delayed signals tend to be additive and constructive.

10.4 AMERICAN DIGITAL TELEVISION SYSTEM (3, 7)

The US Federal Communications Commission's (FCC) final choice for DTV approaches that of an open system. The basic principle is the same as that in Europe, to introduce digital television (DTV) with more channels in the same bandwidth and at the same time employ less transmitter power with a better energy distribution throughout each channel. The use of lower power means that the taboo channels can be used without the fear of mutual interference with current services. The migration to HDTV can then take place in an orderly manner. The standard provides for a range of image formats, using 16:9 aspect ratio, 4:2:0 chroma sampling and with one exception, progressive field/frame scanning. The line structure/sampling points range from HDTV at 1080/1920, 1080/1440, 720/1280, to a 525-line system compatible with the current NTSC service. Although the basic frame rate is 30 Hz, provision has been made for twenty-four frames per second to accommodate film formats. The exception to this is the 1080 $\times$ 1920 $\times$ 60 Hz frame rate format which will use sequential scanning because this signal cannot at present be squeezed into the 6 MHz bandwidth. The sound programme will be distributed using the Dolby AC-3 system which is basically a five-channel surround system that will be described later.

The main signal compression and processing is achieved by using the MPEG-2 standard as in Europe so there is a significant degree of commonality between the two systems. The major differences occur in the format of the baseband data stream and the type of modulation used for transmission purposes. The latter employs a form of vestigial sideband (VSB) (8) modulation which with MPEG-2 compression allows the TV signal to be accommodated within a 6 MHz bandwidth as shown in Figure 10.9(a). As shown, the -3 dB bandwidth of the signal is symmetrically disposed within the 6 MHz transmission band and a low-level pilot carrier (0.3 dB of the total power) is positioned at the lower band edge.

This concept has been extensively tested over both terrestrial and cable systems and shows that there is negligible interference with or from other services and at the same time it provides significantly better pictures than the NTSC system which it will eventually replace.

Figure 10.9(b) shows the baseband signal format for the 8T-VSB mode of operation. The symbol rate of 10.762 MHz is used for all modes of the digital VSB system. Although 8-VSB provides three bits per symbol, the 8T variant uses two bits per symbol for the data and reserves the extra bit for the Trellis encoder redundancy. Thus 4-VSB would have a similar baseband format. The system data error threshold is approximately 10 dB.

The data signal consists of 832 symbol segments with the first four symbols being used for segment sync. The segment is compatible with the 188-byte format used for MPEG-2 processing. The major difference for the US system is the addition of a 20-byte Reed–Solomon parity code for error control. This is capable of correcting up to ten errored bytes per packet. The MPEG-encoded bit stream occupies discrete and defined levels within this format. The carrier pilot is formed by the addition of a dc level to the baseband data stream to aid the carrier recovery at the receiver. Thus with the aid of this and the segment sync group which is extracted at the receiver using a correlation detection method, both carrier and segment sync lock can be achieved with an SNR as low as 0 dB.

(a)

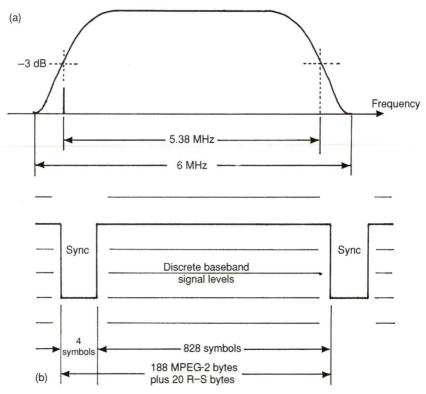

Figure 10.9 (a) VSB RF signal spectrum. (b) Baseband data segment (8T-VSB = 2 bits/symbol).

One in every 313 segments is reserved for data frame sync and the format for this is shown in Figure 10.10(a). Synchronism is achieved by using a group of pseudo-random binary sequences (PRBS). Using this method, frame lock can be achieved with an SNR of 0 dB. This sync segment can also be used as a *training* sequence to control adaptive equalizers in the receiver that counter the effects of signal path distortions. Long time equalizers are controlled via the 511-symbol PRBS and short time equalizers by the 63-symbol PRBSs. The middle 63-symbol PRBS is inverted on alternate frames to produce frame sync in the manner shown in Figure 10.10(b). The twenty-four symbols of Level ID are used to signal the mode of VSB in operation. Of the remaining group of 104 symbols, ninety-two are reserved for future system expansion while the last twelve are used for continuity of the 8T trellis decoder by repeating the symbols from the previous segment. Figure 10.10(b) shows how the segment and frame sync symbols are organized and used to control the frame structure. It should be pointed out here that the time durations shown for segments and frames are not directly related to the image structure because these consist of time-compressed image data bits.

(a)

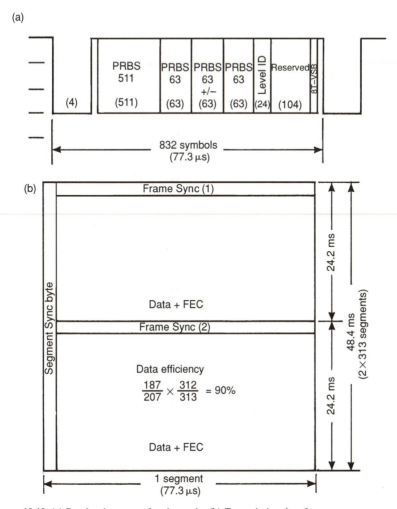

Figure 10.10 (a) Baseband segment framing code. (b) Transmission data frame.

Figure 10.11 shows the block diagram of the transmission signal processing. The MPEG coded and compressed data stream is first randomized (energy dispersal) to ensure an even distribution of power throughout the 6 MHz bandwidth. The Reed–Solomon encoder adds a further twenty bytes to the data stream for FEC and the data is then interleaved to spread burst errors over fifty two data segments. The transmission multiplexer has three inputs: the Trellis-coded signal data, plus segment and frame syncs. The pilot dc level is added after multiplexing and then passed through a root-raised-cosine filter and the VSB modulator. The output at this stage is typically a VSB signal with a carrier of 44 MHz, which after distribution will be up-converted to the final radiating frequency.

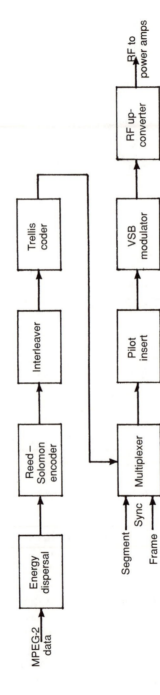

Figure 10.11 Transmitter block diagram (8T-VSB).

Table 10.4 VSB modulation system parameters

Parameters	8-VSB	8T-VSB	16-VSB	Units
Bandwidth	6.0	6.0	6.0	MHz
Symbol rate	10.762	10.762	10.762	Msymbol/s
Bandwidth efficiency	3	3	4	Bits/symbol
Trellis coding rate	None	2/3	None	–
RS–FEC	207 187	207 187	207 187	–
Segment length (inc sync)	832	832	832	Symbols
Segment sync duration	4	4	4	Symbols
Frame sync duty cycle	1/313	1/313	1/313	Segments
Payload data rate	28.9	19.3	38.6	Mbit/s
Pilot power	0.3	0.3	0.3	dB
CNR @ threshold	22.3	15.0	28.5	dB

A summary of the system modes and parameters is shown in Table 10.4. In particular it is interesting to compare the values for the payload data rate with those shown for the CNR @ threshold values. This shows how the SNR requirements vary as the bit/symbol rate is changed.

REFERENCES

(1) *Compressed Video Standards*. International Broadcast Engineer, 1997 Year Book. pp. 61–62.
(2) Brunton, L., Tektronix UK Ltd, Marlow, Bucks. Convergence Seminar Tour 1997.
(3) Medress, Dr M., Video-Cipher Div, General Instruments Corp, California, USA. Private communication to author.
(4) Noah, J.O., Tektronix Inc., USA (1997) 'A Rational Approach to Testing MPEG-2'. *IEEE Journal* 'Spectrum', May.
(5) Morello, G. *et al.* (1997) 'Performance Assessment of a DVB-T Television System'. *Proceedings of the International Television Symposium*, Montreux, pp. 298–310.
(6) Schwartz, M. (1979) *Information Modulation and Noise*, 2nd edition. McGraw-Hill Kogakosha Ltd, Tokyo.
(7) Taylor, J., Zenith Electronics Corp., Illinois, USA. Private communication to author.
(8) Citta, R. and Sgrignoli, G. (1997) 'A TSC Transmission System: VSB Tutorial' *Proceedings of the International Television Symposium*, Montreux, pp. 281–297.

Chapter 11

Television receivers and distribution systems

11.1 DELIVERY SYSTEMS

The choices to be made about the delivery systems, satellite, terrestrial or cable, have been discussed earlier, in particular in connection with MPEG-2 TV transmissions. This chapter then deals with the implications of satellite delivery either direct to home (DTH or DBS) or as a feed to a cable system head end (television receive only – TVRO systems). The choices about operating frequencies have followed the traditional developments in telecommunications; the low bands are exploited first and as the technology develops this is followed by a progressive move to the higher bands. Generally this move is forced by the popularity of the services provided and then the resulting spectrum congestion that seems to occur naturally.

C band systems are still popular in North America but suffer from congestion and interference from microwave telecommunications systems and involve the use of comparatively large antennas with their attendant wind-loading problems. The frequencies in use are 5.925–6.425 GHz and 3.7–4.25 GHz for the up- and down-links respectively. The typical down-link power flux density (PFD) is in the order of 36–40 dBW.

The Ku band is now widely established but, in certain highly populated areas of the world, is becoming congested. The down-link ground receivers employ antennas of around 50 cm to 1 m diameter to handle PFDs that range from about 45 to 50 dBW. The Ku band was initially divided into two segments: the FSS (fixed service systems for cable system feeds) and the DBS (direct broadcasting by satellite – now known as DTH), but these have now merged. The up-link frequency bands are 12.75–13.25 GHz (FSS) and 14.0–14.5 GHz (DTH). The corresponding down-link frequencies are 10.7–11.7 GHz and 11.7–12.75 GHz.

The Ka band allocation for television extends from 17.7 to 21.2 GHz and 27.5 to 31.0 GHz for down- and up-link respectively. These higher frequencies and shorter wavelengths means that the antennas and head-end electronic sub-systems can be made relatively very small. The development to date suggests that this band will be used extensively for digital television services which have a significant power advantage over similar analogue transmissions. In fact it may well be possible to provide the end user, the viewer, with a low bit rate digital return channel to control interactive services.

Implications of digital television broadcasting

The change to compressed digital television transmission brings many advantages; in particular, it allows the transmission agencies to include perhaps six simultaneous standard definition television programmes in a single 8 MHz channel. The resulting saving in frequency spectrum is then available for other newly developing services. With the change to digital processing the transponder bandwidth then becomes a virtual transport container for a multiplex of digital data allocated to many different functions. The total transponder capacity can be shared in a mix of multiplexes between standard or high-definition TV programmes and compact disc quality audio or telecommunications channels.

Digital transmission systems with FEC can provide television images of higher quality than is currently available from analogue processing and with typically 10–15 dB less transmitter power output. However, this saving is likely to be claimed by the transmitting authority and used to reduce the cost of the primary electrical energy. Any LNB experiences a wide range of ambient temperatures that can affect the stability of the local oscillator. For an LNB currently used for analogue services, this temperature drift might well represent 2 MHz in 10 GHz or 0.02 percent and have negligible effect on receiver performance. However, such a drift with digital signals might well create intermittent operation as the receiver drifts in and out of the range of the system FEC control. This could be particularly noticeable during periods of rain fade or during signal outages when the sun falls behind the satellite. Thus the viewer will still need an antenna of the same size and perhaps even an enhanced head-end electronics unit to maximize the picture quality advantage.

Table 11.1

Noise figure	0.7–1.2 dB
LO stability	>±25 kHz
LO phase noise	−75 dBc/Hz @ 1 kHz offset
Conversion gain	60 dB (flat within ± 0.5 dB)
1 dB compression level	+3 dBm
Power input	15–24 volts @ 350 mA
VSWR	2.0:1 to 2.4:1

The main parameters for a modern LNB that uses a phase locked loop (PLL), crystal-control local oscillator are shown in Table 11.1.

11.2 OUTDOOR ELECTRONICS UNIT

The importance of using low-noise techniques for the first signal processing stages of a system was stressed in Chapter 2. Since the signal levels received from a satellite are very small, typically 10 pW or less, the performance of the

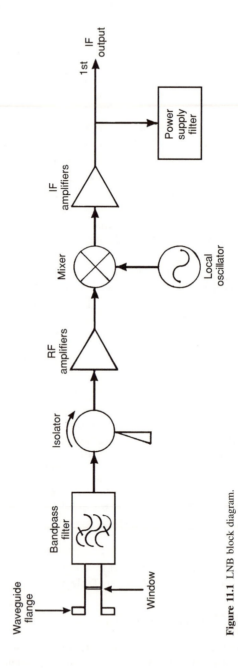

Figure 11.1 LNB block diagram.

outdoor or head-end unit is particularly critical. This section, the block diagram of which is depicted in Figure 11.1, is often known as the low-noise block converter (LNB), because it down-converts blocks of channels to the first IF. The unit consists of several low-noise amplifiers (LNA) and a low-noise converter (LNC). Figure 11.1 shows the typical configuration of an LNB for use at the Ku band.

The circuit is constructed from thin film microstrip on a ceramic or similar substrate. The discrete components used are normally of the surface mounting type, for low component loss. The unit is housed in an aluminium casing that is hermetically sealed to provide weather protection, the waveguide input being sealed with a quartz glass or plastic window, the former material being preferred because it is much less prone to embrittlement due to ultraviolet radiation. This feature is particularly important because the ingress of moisture can cause corrosion of the side walls of the waveguide, which in turn creates a surface roughness that increases the degree of attenuation. Also, it is not unknown for insects to nest within the warm waveguide, which also adds to the signal losses. A waveguide cavity type of bandpass filter may be used to minimize image channel interference and reduce the local oscillator radiation. The latter is further assisted by the use of an isolator, which also helps to improve the impedance matching between the waveguide and the input stage of the LNB. The three or four stages of RF amplification, the mixer and the local oscillator all use HEMT GaAs devices, selected for their high gain and low noise characteristics. The first stage is biased to provide low-noise operation while the others are biased to provide higher gain. The local oscillator typically employs a dielectric resonator for high-frequency stability. Since the LNB has to drive the main receiver via a significant length of coaxial cable, it is usual to include an IF output circuit that consists of two or three stages of amplification. Again, the first stage is biased for low noise with the major part of the IF gain being provided in the later stages. Power to the LNB, together with the necessary control signals, is provided over the coaxial cable. It is therefore most important that these supplies should be well filtered, to avoid unwanted feedback. By careful selection of the components and by precise tuning of the strip-line circuit elements, it is possible to produce an LNB with a noise factor of less than 1 dB, equivalent to a noise temperature better than 75 K. Such is the rate of semiconductor development that individual RF transistors are now available with a gain of 12 dB at 12 GHz and with a noise factor of less than 1 dB. Other microwave circuit concepts that are in use include fin-line waveguide structures which are formed by punched sheet metal with the active components mounted directly within the tuned slots. Further developments in GaAs semiconductor technology include the production of monolithic microwave integrated circuits (MMICs) that significantly reduce the LNB power requirements and heat dissipation, provide a noise factor of about 0.75 dB and make for an even smaller unit. A typical MMIC using HEMT technology consists of two or three RF amplifiers, double balanced mixer, local oscillator with dielectric resonator and three IF amplifiers. In a typical TVRO application and using a 10 GHz local oscillator frequency, these devices are capable of producing

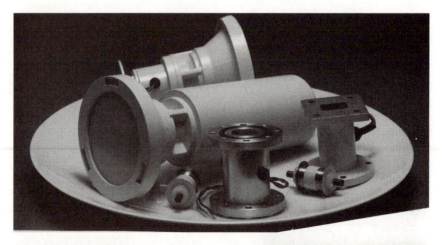

1.-Low Noise Polar Converter LNP4505
A fully integrated environmentally sealed unit comprising a state-of-the-art LNB, a low loss ferrite polariser and a high performance broadband feedhorn. V/H polarisation is selected by voltage switching via the RF signal cable.
2.-Feedhorn/Polariser PS45818F
Comprising a broadband feedhorn and polariser the PS45818F is a high quality environmentally sealed unit. By using a metal cover plus 'O' ring seal this innovative design avoids the problems of water ingress and plastic creep.
3.-Broadband Polarisers
Racal-MESL offer a selection of discrete ferrite polarisers, used for linear (V/H) channel selection. Racal's unique technology ensures very high reliability and low insertion loss. A variety of flange fixings are available along with a universal polariser which allows V/H *and* circular depolarisation.
4.-Polariser Inserts "Bobbins" PS45801
These miniature ferrite polarisers for V/H channel selection are designed for insertion into customer specific feedhorns. For customers with suitable microwave assembly and test capabilities this insert can be procured as a stand alone item.

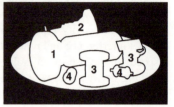

Figure 11.2 Head-end waveguide components (Courtesy of Racal-MESL Ltd).

a conversion gain in excess of 60 dB over the band 10.7–12.7 GHz. Figure 11.2 shows a collection of current head-end devices (courtesy of Racal-MESL Ltd) together with their important features.

Mixer stages

The mixer stage is the noisiest in the receiver, and for this reason it should always be preceded by some low-noise RF amplification. The noise source is largely due to the non-linearity which creates harmonic distortion, and a conversion loss that represents a noise factor equal to the loss ratio. The oscillator itself has two components of noise, amplitude and phase, of which the latter is probably the most significant as far as mixers are concerned. This generates two sidebands displaced equally about the centre frequency which create their own sum and difference frequencies in the mixing process, thus transferring the phase noise to the wanted output signal by *reciprocal mixing*. This interfering component reduces the adjacent channel rejection ratio for the system. The magnitude of the phase noise is measured with reference to the level of the wanted local oscillator frequency at some frequency offset in dBc/Hz. The typical values of offsets are 1 kHz, 10 kHz and 100 kHz, which produces descreasing values of interference. One particular system produced the following results: −50 dBc/Hz at 1 kHz, −75 dBc/Hz at 10 kHz and −95 dBc/Hz at 100 kHz.

Various mixing circuits have been adopted. These include sub-harmonic mixing using two inverse parallel diodes, with the oscillator operating at a sub-harmonic. This improves oscillator stability, but tends to be noisier and have a greater conversion loss. An alternative method that uses two diodes in a balanced mixer configuration gives a better isolation between the RF stages and the local oscillator.

A very useful mixer stage that is capable of being produced as an IC using GaAs technology is the double balanced Gilbert cell with differential inputs and

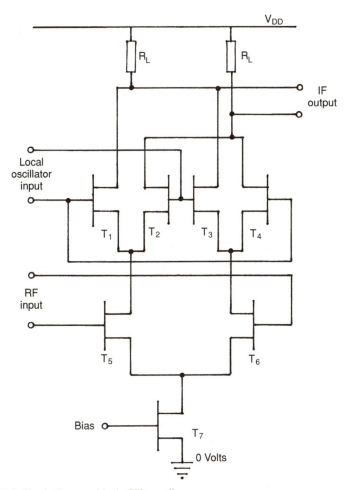

Figure 11.3 Circuit diagram of basic Gilbert cell.

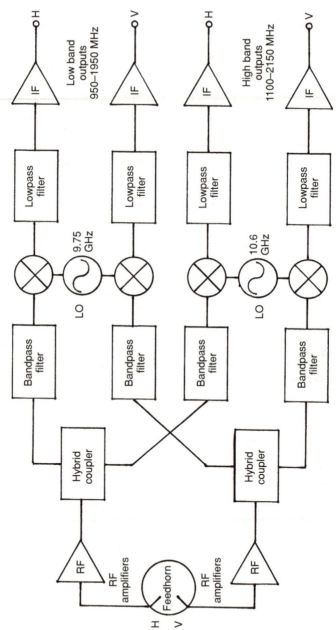

Figure 11.4 Block diagram of quad outlet Ku band LNB.

outputs that is shown in Figure 11.3. This provides a useful conversion gain of better than 3 dB, with a noise factor of less than 10 dB at a 1 dB compression point of 3 dBm. In practice the constant current transistor T_7 would be replaced by an inductor (which also behaves as a constant current device to ac signals), and the two load resistors R_L by resonant circuits to make better use of the dc supply voltage. By utilizing a pair of Gilbert cell mixers driven by quadrature versions of the same local oscillator signal and by combining the two IF signals at the output, a very useful image rejection characteristic of better than 25 dB can be achieved.

Figure 11.4 shows the block diagram of an LNB designed to cover the full range of the Ku band to drive a cable television system head end. After amplification, both the RF signals for vertical and horizontal polarizations are separated into high- and low-band frequency components via the hybrid couplers and bandpass filters. These signals are mixed with the outputs from either the 9.75 or 10.6 GHz local oscillators, low-pass filtered and then amplified to provide the first IF drive to the main cable system receivers via coaxial cables.

Voltage standing wave ratio (VSWR) or return loss

Impedance mismatching can occur at both ends of the LNB, leading to signal loss and degradation of SNR. It is shown in the literature (1) that this can be quantified by either the VSWR or the return loss.

The reflection coefficient r due to a mismatch is given by:

$r = \sqrt{(\text{Power reflected/Power received})}$, or

$\quad = (\text{Voltage reflected/Voltage received})$ at a load

Alternatively, in terms of the mismatch impedances:

$$r = |(Z_O - Z_L)/(Z_O + Z_L)| \text{ and is complex.}$$

Return Loss $= r^2$, or in dB,

$$-10 \log r^2 = -20 \log r \text{ dB} \tag{11.1}$$

$$\text{Also VSWR} = (1 + r)/(1 - r) \tag{11.2}$$

G/T ratio

The equation for the system noise factor that is derived in Appendix A2.1 shows that the antenna with its gain, and the LNB with its noise factor, will have a significant effect on the overall system noise performance. In fact, this is conveniently expressed as a figure of merit in the gain/temperature (G/T) ratio. This is perhaps most easily explained by a numerical example.

A 1.2 m diameter antenna of 65 percent efficiency has a gain of approximately 41 dBi. It may be pointed towards a signal source with a background noise temperature of 40 K. When used with an LNB that has a noise factor of 1.8 dB, or equivalent noise temperature of 150 K, the total noise temperature is 150 + 40 = 190 K = 22.8 dBK. The system G/T ratio is thus (41 − 22.8) − 18.2 dB/K. Thus a particular value of G/T ratio can be achieved by using a low-noise LNB with a small antenna or with a lower-cost, noisier LNB and a larger antenna.

Intermodulation and non-linear distortion

Because the LNB is processing a number of carrier frequencies simultaneously, any non-linearity will produce *intermodulation distortion products*, shown in Figure 11.5 for the two input frequencies f_1 and f_2. Except in the case of very wideband amplifiers, the second-order terms $f_2 − f_1$, $2f_1$, $f_2 + f_1$ and $2f_2$ will be well outside of the system passband. However, the third-order terms $2f_1 − f_2$ and $2f_2 − f_1$ can create problems.

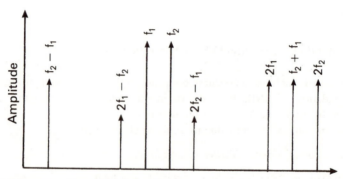

Figure 11.5 Spectrum of intermodulation products.

Figure 11.6 shows the characteristic for an amplifier with a nominal gain of 10 dB. With increasing input level, the amplifier starts to distort and will eventually saturate. Over the linear part of the characteristic, the gain slope is 1 dB/dB. Assuming that the amplifier is initially saturated due to over-driving, the output signal spectrum then contains fundamental plus harmonic components. If the input level is reduced slowly, the harmonic components will reduce faster than will the fundamental. In fact, the third-order term will reduce with a slope of 3 dB/dB as shown in Figure 11.6. The slopes of the linear and third-order characteristic coincide at a point known as the third-order intercept (TOI), the theoretical point where the intermodulation product and the signal are of equal amplitude. If this point is known, then the third-order signal-to-intermodulation-noise ratio can be evaluated for any input signal level as follows:

$$\text{SNR (third order)} = 2(\text{TOI} − P_{in}) \text{ dBc} \tag{11.3}$$

where TOI is the third-order intercept and P_{in} is the power level of the input.

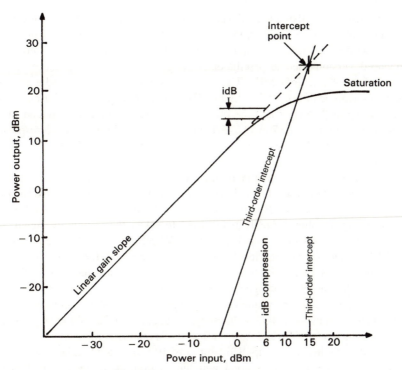

Figure 11.6 Graphical representation of intermodulation products.

Figure 11.6 also shows the 1 dB compression point, which is a way of representing the degree of non-linear distortion. This point represents the input signal level that produces an output at the fundamental frequency, that is, 1 dB less than it would if the amplifier were completely linear.

For the amplifier characteristic shown in Figure 11.6, the third-order intercept occurs at 15 dBm and the 1 dB compression point at 6 dBm. The higher the value of these two parameters, the lower will be the degree of non-linearity.

A further useful parameter, which is chiefly related to the mixer performance, is the *spurious free dynamic range* (SFDR). This is defined as the amplitude range between a fundamental frequency and the first spurious noise component due to distortion and is measured in units of dBc relative to the level of the fundamental signal.

Control of multiple LNBs and polarity switching (2)

Due to the rapid expansion of television services in the Ku band, particularly in Europe, there was a progressive merging of the FSS and DTH sub-bands. This resulted in three distinct stages of LNB development. The first LNB, which is now referred to as the Standard version, used a local oscillator running at a frequency of 10 GHz to convert the band of 10.95–11.7 GHz into an IF range of 950–1700 MHz. When the band was extended from 10.7 to 11.8 Ghz, the Enhanced version used an oscillator running at 9.75 GHz to produce an IF ranging from 950 to 2050 MHz. The Universal version was introduced when the band was extended from 10.7 to 12.75 GHz. This employed two local oscillators, one running at 9.75 GHz and the other at 10.6 GHz, to produce low and high bands extending from 10.7 to 11.7 GHz and 11.7 to 12.75 GHz. The corresponding ranges of IF are therefore 950–1950 MHz and 1100–2150 MHz respectively.

The first stages of development required only a switching action between vertical (V) and horizontal (H) polarizations. This was achieved by switching the dc feed provided over the IF signal coaxial cable between the 13 and 17 V levels, with the higher value normally being used to select the H polarity signal. In practice, these levels range between 11.5–14 V and 16–19 V. The circuit within the LNB employs a voltage level detector to determine if the supply is above about 16 V. This then operates a switching stage constructed from either a semiconductor or electromagnetic relay to select the output from the RF amplifier connected to the wanted polarity signal probe as shown in Figure 11.7. Being fabricated using CMOS technology, the unbiased RF amplifier stage is cut off. The change of DC level does not affect the operating parameters of the LNB because the amplifiers are supplied from 5 to 10 V dc via a regulator stage.

To meet the needs of the second switching action, the dc feed is modulated with a 22 kHz tone, whose presence is normally used to select the high band. This ac signal is provided at a level of +600 mV, ±200 mV which when rectified and voltage doubled provides a dc level of about 1 V which is then used to operate the switching action. Two possibilities exist here: either the voltage supply to one oscillator is disconnected, or the switching action selects the wanted output from a parallel IF amplifier chain as shown in Figure 11.7.

A further problem has arisen in Europe with the introduction of television services from the EUTELSAT HOT BIRD series of satellites located at 13°E. To receive these signals and those transmitted via the ASTRA bird at 19.2° requires either a motorized antenna system or some form of compromise. It has been found that two LNBs can be mounted in tandem at the prime focus feed point of a single antenna and by pointing the dish at about 16°E, both signals can be received with adequate picture quality. However, there is now a need to introduce an extra switching action to select the wanted LNB. It will be interesting to see how this situation develops when television signals become available from the 28°E and 28.2°E locations. The following system, which was devised and patented by EUTELSAT, operates by modulating the 22 kHz tone signal to obtain the additional control. This system is referred to as Digital Satellite Equipment Control (DiSEqC).

This system can operate with a master/slave control protocol much as a local area network does (3, 4). Figure 11.8(a) shows how the 22 kHz tone is pulse width or duration modulated. Each bit lasts for 1.5 ms and the tone burst occurs

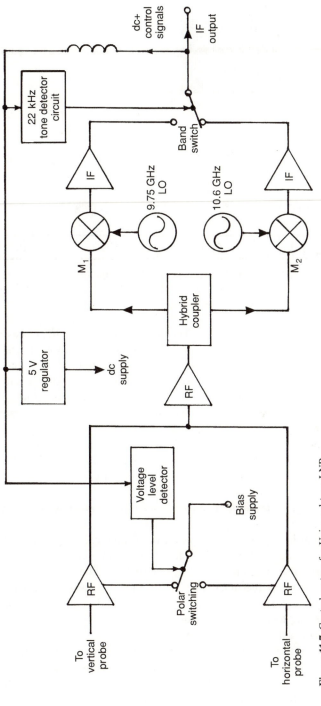

Figure 11.7 Control system for Universal-type LNB.

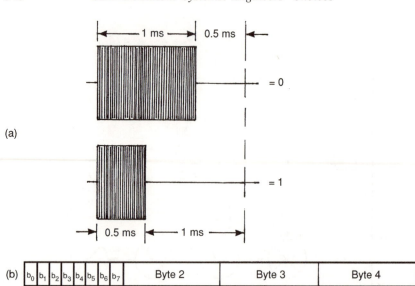

(a)

(b) | b_0 b_1 b_2 b_3 b_4 b_5 b_6 b_7 | Byte 2 | Byte 3 | Byte 4 |

Figure 11.8 EUTELSAT digital signalling control system. **(a)** Bit pattern. **(b)** Byte format.

for 1/3(1) or 2/3(0) of this duration. The system uses a 4-byte sequence to provide a much wider range of control features and allow for future expansion. (See Figure 11.8(b).) Bits b_0 to b_4 of byte 1 form a unique framing code that signifies the start of a transmission. b_5 is set to 1 for a command from the master to a slave unit and set to 0 for a command in the reverse direction. b_6 is set to 1 if a reply in necessary, otherwise it is set to 0. b_7 is set to 1 to indicate a repeat transmission because no reply was received from the slave unit.

Byte 2 forms a device address with the first four bits indicating a group of devices and the second four bits the actual device within that group. If the latter four bits are set to 0, then the command is broadcast to all units.

Byte 3 describes the command function.

Byte 4 can provide further commands such as antenna position, skew setting etc.

The system has three levels of protocol. Simple control is shown in Figure 11.9(a), where the 22 kHz tone is used to select either one LNB or the other. A 9-bit period burst (12.5 ms) will select one LNB while a burst of nine 1 bits (12.5 ms) will select the other one. The version 1.0 switch is a unidirectional system which can select any one of four LNBs and control such functions as polarization and local oscillator frequency.

The version 2.0 system is bi-directional with command lines being wired in series as shown in Figure 11.9(c), allowing for return messages from the controlled devices. This provides for such functions as variable skew control, control of a motorized antenna, etc., but in this case there needs to be a provision for the extra wires to carry the motor currents.

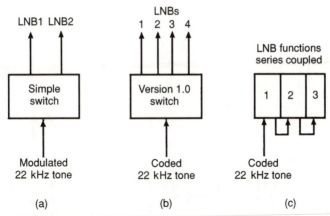

Figure 11.9 EUTELSAT digital satellite equipment control. (**a**) Simple 'either-or' system. (**b**) Version 1.0 controlling four LNBs. (**c**) Version 2.0 series control of functions.

Adjustment of polarization skew

For linear polarized waves the pick-up probe within the waveguide should be parallel to the plane of the electric wave in the received wavefront. If the receiving site is either east or west of the satellite location then the received plane of polarization will differ from that of the satellite transponder. Thus it is necessary to align the probe with the received polarization angle for maximum received signal level. Mechanical rotation of the LNB will be made at the time of installation and should be made against a weak signal for best results. For installations with a motorized antenna system, this plane will vary as different satellites are tracked across the horizon, it is then common to provide a polarization skew adjustment at the receiver. Typically this involves either an electromechanical rotation of the pick-up probe or the variation of a control current through a ferrite device that operates on the Faraday effect principle. The mechanical system is now not generally found outside of earlier C band systems. The ferrite device only requires a two-wire control for forward and reverse currents, varying typically within the range of ±50 mA. This device has a very low loss of around 0.15 dB at 11 GHz. Most modern receivers incorporate an automatic skew adjustment to compensate for variation as the antenna scans across the horizon.

11.3   TV RECEIVER DRAKE SERIES ESR 800XT AND 2000XT (5)

This series of North American receivers is designed for both C and Ku band operation to provide *direct-to-home* (DTH) television services in NTSC, PAL and SECAM formats. All receivers are microprocessor controlled for system operation, tuning and antenna positioning via an infrared remote control unit and

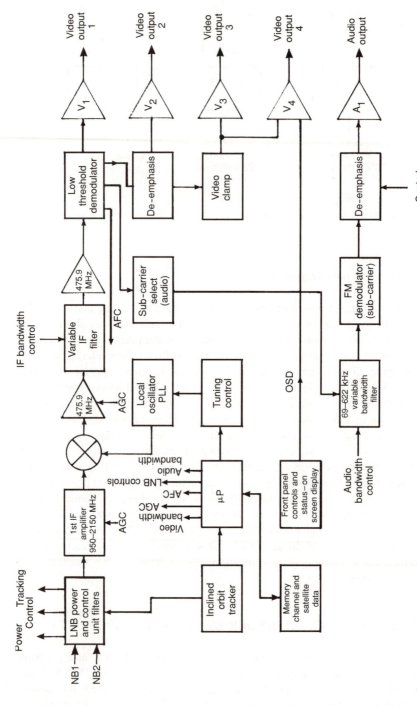

Figure 11.10 Simplified block diagram of DRAKE satellite TV receivers – ESR2000XT and ESR800XT (Courtesy of R.L. DRAKE Inc.).

the I²C bus. Both systems employ a built-in antenna positioner with an automatic satellite finder circuit, and the ESR2000XT can be equipped with further antenna control that allows the receiver to track satellites with an inclined orbit.

In addition, on-screen graphics and menus in six of the world's most popular languages are provided to aid the setting up and tuning of the receivers. Figure 11.10 shows a simplified block diagram that represents the operation of both versions.

Power and control signals to the LNBs are provided over the coaxial first IF signal cable and therefore filtering is included at the receiver input circuits to prevent spurious interference. The first IF tuning range extends from 950 to 2150 MHz and the tuned RF amplifier section is capable of handling input signal levels ranging from −60 to −30 dBm without overload. Tuning for the RF and local oscillator stages is microprocessor controlled, using frequency synthesis with a PLL, with user tuning data being held in a semiconductor memory. The microprocessor also provides outputs to drive the front panel status lamps and, together with a character generator, provides the on-screen graphic signals that are gated through the video amplifier output stages.

The second IF amplifier stage, which operates at 479.5 MHz, uses surface acoustic wave (SAW) filters to provide much of the selectivity for switchable bandwidths of 18 or 27 MHz. These stages, which use conventional gain control (which also provides the drive for the signal level indicator) and limiting, are followed by an FM demodulator that employs a PLL which achieves a video-carrier-to-noise threshold level of 6 to 3 dB. The AFC circuit is also driven from this stage via the microprocessor.

Most of the baseband signal processing is carried out within a very large ASIC chip, an STV0030 that handles the separation of video and audio signals, demodulates the audio signal from the sub-carriers, carries out the necessary de-emphasis and noise reduction, and adapts to all known conditions in analogue video and radio transmissions. The 5–9 MHz audio sub-carriers provide either mono or stereo signals that are compatible with Wegener companding. This processing stage has programmable bandwidths that range from 69 to 622 kHz and the audio is demodulated using a PLL circuit with a low threshold level to provide a wide frequency range audio output signal.

The receivers are equipped with either three (800XT) or four (2000XT) rear panel mounted SCART connectors to provide for connections to VCRs, alternative decoders, service computer system, etc. Both receivers include event timers to allow for recordings to be made from satellite transmissions. Provision is also made for two card readers in the conditional access module to cater for such encryption services as VideoCrypt and EuroCrypt.

Following demodulation, the video signal is split into three paths. One provides a raw video output that is unclamped and non-de-emphasized with a bandwidth of 20 Hz to 10 MHz for further processing. The de-emphasized and unclamped wideband signal which is fed to the decryption circuit for decoding also has the same bandwidth. For video output 3, the energy dispersal component is removed by clamping. Video output 4 is similarly processed but is gated with the on-screen display signal generated from the microprocessor stage. For these latter two outputs, the bandwidth is restricted to 20 Hz to 5 MHz.

The channel programme memory capacity for both receivers is extensive: 800 channels with the ESR800XT and 2000 channels with the ESR2000XT. Both are capable of a selection of up to 400 favourite channels when any programme can be selected with just two keystrokes. With such a large memory, the act of programming a receiver becomes somewhat tiring and error prone. Fortunately it is possible to link two receivers together via the SCART sockets and programme one from the other. Alternatively, it is also possible to programme a receiver direct from a PC via the DRAKE Data Transfer Unit. This is an extremely valuable feature for any busy service department.

11.4   TV RECEIVERS PACE MICRO TECHNOLOGY SERIES MSS1000 (6)

This series of UK-designed receivers is equipped for handling both PAL and D2-MAC signals to provide a DTH service, including controlled access to encrypted signals (see Figure 11.11). The receiver has provision for dual LNB inputs covering both Ku and C band transmissions and incorporates facilities to add the necessary module to control an antenna positioner device. The receivers are controlled via the normal infrared handset and the antenna band and polarity functions are selected by signals transmitted over the coaxial feed cable. The conditional access module carries two card slots to cater for encrypted services (VideoCrypt and EuroCrypt). An extensive semiconductor memory holds all the data to allow any of up to 500 channels to be selected by the minimum of keystrokes. The receivers also contain an eight-event timer to allow for the recording of satellite-delivered signals and on-screen menus are provided in multiple languages. The audio channel provides for Wegener Panda 1 Stereo processing together with satellite-delivered radio channel reception, plus Dolby Pro-logic surround sound for the home-cinema concept.

The main control microprocessor is a Z8 device, but the receivers also employ an additional microprocessor for control over the front panel displays, remote control commands, the conditional access module and the dish position if fitted. All of these devices communicate with each other and the control system via data and address buses. Most of the video signal processing is carried out in a large VSLI, ASIC device that is often referred to as a 'Nicky' chip. The broadband tuner unit covers the range 750–2100 MHz and with the local oscillator that runs high, produces a second IF of 479.5 MHz. The local oscillator therefore tunes over the range 1230–2580 MHz. The main PLL used to control the local oscillator frequency is contained partly within the microprocessor and partly within the Nicky chip. The local oscillator frequency is divided by 128 and these samples are further divided in a pre-scaler to bring the step size within the range of the AFC system.

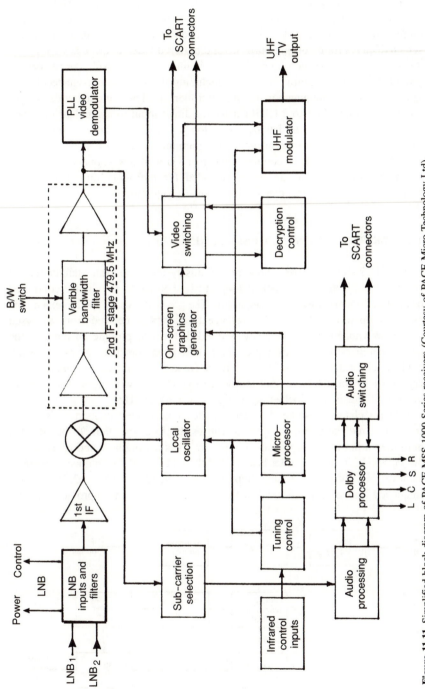

Figure 11.11 Simplified block diagram of PACE MSS 1000 Series receivers (Courtesy of PACE Micro Technology Ltd).

The second IF bandwidth can be switched between 27 and 15 MHz so that noise can be minimized under interfering conditions (rain fade, etc.). Multiple outputs are provided for clamped or unclamped video, video with gated-out on-screen displays for recording purposes and buffered video to drive any additional decoder that may be incorporated. A maximum of four SCART connectors are provided for these satellite receivers, including the main television receiver, a video recorder, an antenna positioning controller, etc. The audio and video output are also modulated on to a UHF carrier for direct input to a standard receiver.

The PACE Link system has been developed as a service aid to minimize the tiresome task of programming and reprogramming the 500 channels on these receivers (7). This simply couples a receiver via a SCART connector to a PC, when the original data can be downloaded for reprogramming purposes or transferred to another receiver for its original programming.

11.5 FREQUENCY SYNTHESIS TUNING (8)

Figure 11.12 shows the basic principles of this system. The local oscillator signal is provided by the phase locked loop (PLL) consisting of voltage-controlled oscillator, dividers, filter and comparator. The pre-scaler (n) is used to extend the range of operation. The basic reference frequency is derived from a crystal oscillator whose output frequency is divided down to provide an input to the phase comparator. An example from television practice gives a useful explanation of the principle. The reference frequency is provided from a 4 MHz crystal oscillator, whose output is divided by 1024 in two stages. The receiver local oscillator is thus locked to multiples of 3.90625 kHz.

When a channel number is selected, the control logic converts this into a frequency and the phase comparator causes the local oscillator to be adjusted until the output from the variable divider (m) is equal in phase and frequency to 3.90625 KHz If the pre-scaler has divided the local oscillator frequency by 16 to achieve this, the actual tuning steps will be $3.90625 \times 16 = 62.5$ kHz. This frequency is small enough to allow the receiver AFC system to provide the final

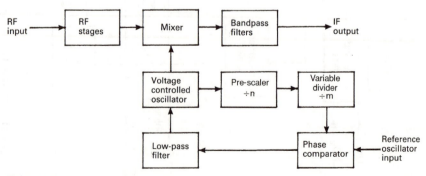

Figure 11.12 Frequency synthesis tuning.

tuning accuracy. Thus by choosing suitable reference frequencies and division ratios, any step size can be generated. Often for a communications receiver, the step size is as low as 10 Hz and this gives the operator the impression of almost continuous tuning.

The output from the local oscillator can be fed to a frequency counter that has been offset by the IF value. The counter output can then be used to provide a digital read-out of the tuned frequency. Because the division ratios are scaled in binary, it is possible to adapt this concept to digital tuning. Receivers equipped with microprocessor control can make use of the I^2C bus which consists of two lines forming a ring network to which all the controlled and controlling chips are connected in a master/slave fashion. One line provides for serial data up to 100 kbit/s and the other carries the clock signal.

A further digital extension provides for scan tuning. In this mode, the receiver scans the particular waveband automatically and stops when a signal with the predetermined characteristics is located. The tuning of a frequency synthesis tuned receiver is very stable due to the fact that all the injection frequencies are obtained from the same high-stability crystal oscillator. Problems that can occur include excess noise in the form of jitter from the oscillator and spurious beat notes that can be generated from the high-speed divider circuits.

Direct digital synthesis (DDS) is a technique that is rapidly gaining in popularity. This concept can provide a system with lower phase noise than the direct analogue synthesis (DAS) method that is described above and, in addition, is more compatible with microprocessor control. Essentially this system consists of a register/accumulator type of memory, an address bus, a semiconductor memory look-up table and a digital-to-analogue converter (DAC), all controlled by an accurate clock circuit. The required tuning frequency is entered into the register and this binary number is used to address the memory whose contents represent the binary code associated with this frequency. When this output is converted into an analogue form it represents the tuning frequency. As an example, the output frequency is given by:

$$f_{out} = \text{Input data value } (f_{clock}/2^n) \tag{11.4}$$

where n is the number of address bits.

Thus if the system uses a 16-bit address system and a clock frequency of 327.68 MHz, the system will tune in steps of

$$(327.68 \times 10^6)/2^{16} = 5 \times 10^3 \text{ Hz}$$

up to the clock frequency. Higher frequencies can be generated by mixing the output step values in a frequency converter stage.

11.6 THRESHOLD EXTENSION DEMODULATORS

Part of the noise advantage of FM derives from the fact that the FM demodulator has a noise power improvement figure of about 15 dBs over AM, between the input carrier to noise (CNR) ratio and the output SNR, provided that the input level is above some *threshold* value. This improvement exists over the linear part of the demodulator characteristic that has a slope of 1 dB/dB. When the CNR falls below this level, FM rapidly loses its noise advantage.

It is shown in the literature (9) that the usual definition of this threshold level is a kind of 1 dB compression effect. It is the value of input CNR at which the output SNR is 1 dB less than it would be over the linear region. Below the threshold level, the onset of noise produces *clicks* in audio systems and *sparklies* on vision. Modern threshold extension circuits have reduced this level from about 14 dBs down to about 3 dB of CNR, providing a significant margin to relax the system specification in other areas. Recently, threshold extension demodulators using a combination of analogue and digital techniques have been used to build devices with a theoretical threshold of 0 dB.

Basically, there are three circuit configurations that can be used and these all function on the same principle. The detection bandwidth is reduced without reducing the signal energy, thus enhancing the SNR by a factor that is practically equal to the frequency reduction ratio.

Frequency modulation feedback (FMFB)

Figure 11.13 shows this demodulator as a type of frequency changer. Assuming that the mixer input is the carrier frequency f_c, plus the instantaneous deviation f_d, $(f_c + f_d)$, the output from the discriminator is a voltage v, proportional to f_d. When this is filtered and applied to the VCO with a nominal frequency of f_o, it will produce a change of frequency, say kf_d. The second mixer input is thus $f_o + kf_d$. The difference signal at the mixer output is therefore $f_c + f_d - f_o - kf_d$. Now $f_c - f_o$ is a new intermediate frequency f_i so that the mixer output becomes $f_i + f_d - kf_d = f_i + f_d(1 - k)$. Since k must be less than unity the deviation has been reduced to allow the use of a narrow bandwidth filter, thus reducing the detection bandwidth and hence the noise power.

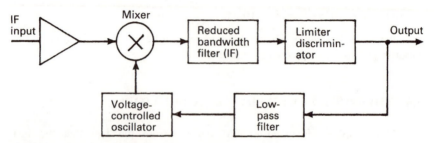

Figure 11.13 Frequency-modulated feedback demodulator.

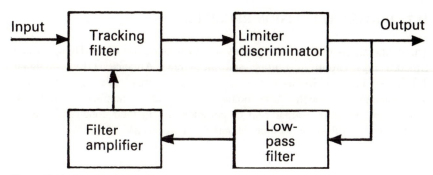

Figure 11.14 Dynamic tracking filter demodulator.

Dynamic tracking filter demodulator

The circuit configuration shown in Figure 11.14 is similar in form to the PLL. However the *tracking filter* is an active device with a narrow bandwidth and with a centre frequency that is made to track the relatively slowly deviating FM carrier under feedback control. Since the detection noise bandwidth is just the tracking filter bandwidth, the SNR at the output is improved by as much as 9 dB.

Phase locked loop demodulator (PLL)

Figure 11.15 shows how the basic PLL is modified by the addition of a secondary feedback loop filter. Due to the feedback, the VCO is made to follow the deviations of the input FM carrier. Its driving voltage is thus dependent upon the deviation, and so represents the modulation component. The circuit therefore functions as an FM demodulator. The addition of a narrow bandwidth secondary feedback loop in the form of an active filter again reduces the detection bandwidth to improve the SNR.

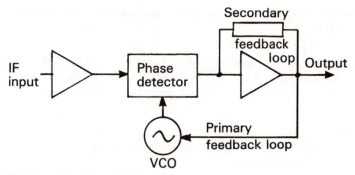

Figure 11.15 Phase locked loop (PLL) demodulator.

11.7 DIGITAL TELEVISION RECEIVERS

The deliberations of two large groups of researchers, the DVB (Digital Video Broadcasting) Group in Europe and the Grand Alliance (DTV – Digital Television) in the USA, have been responsible for many new and interesting developments. Although these bodies arrived at a number of different conclusions, there is a great deal of commonality in their conclusions, as is shown by the following sections about digital receivers.

The European receiver (10)

As the transmitted signal has an analogue form due to the filtering effect of the transmission and propagation channels, the front end of this receiver follows conventional techniques up to and including the IF amplifier stages which are AGC controlled. A block diagram that represents the general outline of the three variants is shown in Figure 11.16. After IF amplification the signal is demodulated into its in-phase (I) and quadrature (Q) components and these are then converted into a digital format. The demodulator stage is designed for either COFDM (T), QPSK (S) or QAM (C). These have been chosen to counter the propagation anomalies most commonly found in each transmission signal path. The cable system will be the least noisy while the terrestrial system will be the least robust. Operated in this way, equal input signal-to-noise ratios should provide equal bit error rates at the three outputs. The energy dispersal component is removed following de-interleaving so that the bytes in each packet are returned to their original sequence. The transport demultiplexer separates out the audio, video and data streams and the programme demultiplexer separates out the various programmes. Finally, the packets are decoded to provide the video, audio and data bit streams associated with each particular programme stream.

The Digital Video Broadcast integrated receiver decoder (DVBird) receiver (11)

A small consortium of members of the European DVB Group was formed to develop the basis of a digital receiver. This small group consisted of silicon manufacturers, set-top box makers and programme providers and their remit was to:

● validate the standard and test it in its various modes,
● promote the concept throughout manufacturers' design teams by disseminating the resulting know-how,
● prepare for competitive development towards a single chip solution.

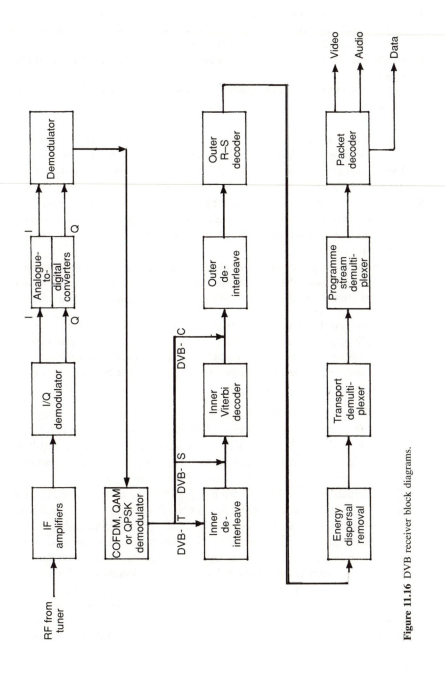

Figure 11.16 DVB receiver block diagrams.

Summary of the major DVB signal features:

- A concatenated channel coding based on the Reed–Solomon (188,204) scheme with a convolutional code of constraint length, k = 7 and normal code rate of 1/2. This can be increased by puncturing.
- Block interleaving to spread the coded bits over the whole of the COFDM spectrum
- QPSK, 16QAM or 64QAM constellations with a wide range of bit rates to allow an SNR trade-off against robustness.
- COFDM multiplex with the above complex symbols transmitted on a large number of carriers generated by fast Fourier transform (FFT). Provision for two options, either 1705 (2k) or 6817 (8k) carriers with a nominal symbol length increased by a guard interval factor ranging over 1/32, 1/16, 1/8 and 1/4.
- Coherent demodulation facilitated by including pilot symbols which are inserted periodically. These are inserted on carriers programmed within the receiver to allow it to estimate the channel frequency response and to provide time synchronism.
- Facilities for frequency synchronism by including a small sub-set of carriers that always transmit the same symbol. Analysing the phase rotations caused by these allows the receiver to perform a robust frequency synchronism.

The outcome from these deliberations produced a four-chip set that has at the input the A/D converted analogue signal from the IF amplifier, and provides the MPEG-2 transport stream at the output. But perhaps most significantly, it produced a programmable FFT device that could integrate both the 2k and 8k modulation systems.

IC1. This chip generates the I/Q data stream from the A/D converted input at a bit rate of 18 MHz. It retrieves the amplitude and phase information of each carrier from either the 2k or 8k FFTs. It also generate an AGC control voltage that is applied to the receiver analogue front end. Course time synchronization is provided through the repetitive nature of the guard intervals.

IC2. The inputs here are the FFTs from IC1. It uses the pilots inserted into the DVB signal to estimate and correct the channel frequency response, first from the pilots and then from the remainder of the signal by interpolation. The transmission parameter signalling (TPS), which includes the code rate, constellation in use, etc., is transmitted on the dedicated sub-set of carriers. This chip also estimates the channel SNR so that the Viterbi decoder does not have to rely too highly on bits modulated on to corrupted carriers.

IC3. This chip performs the decoding for the concatenated coded bit stream, using the convolutional Viterbi decoder and the Reed–Solomon decoder. It also performs the bit and byte de-interleaving to create the MPEG-2 bit stream for demultiplexing.

IC4. This device acts as a dedicated controller for the other three chips and performs time and frequency synchronism. It is basically constructed around

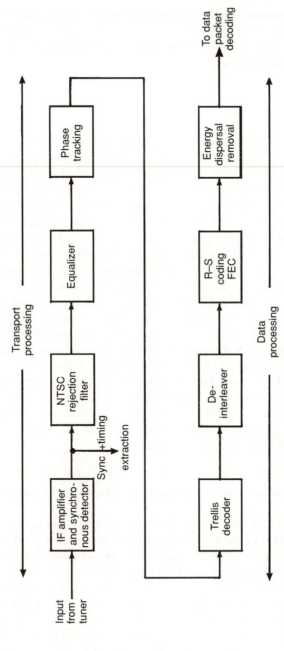

Figure 11.17 US DTV receiver signal decoding.

a DSP core with some memory and hard-wired functions. The time and frequency errors are obtained from the pilots and the time estimate error is used to tune the sampling rate. Communications between IC4 and the other chips are carried out over a dedicated high-speed serial bus, and it functions as master over the other slaves. IC4 also handles the synchronism for the whole receiver. The main communications with the rest of the receiver are carried out over the popular I^2C bus.

The USA DTV receiver (12)

The DTV signal, which uses the existing 6 MHz NTSC RF channel allocation, is converted by the tuner section into a standard intermediate frequency of 44 MHz before being processed through an AGC-controlled IF stage. The pilot carrier is extracted by a synchronous demodulator using a narrowband frequency and phase locked loop (FPLL). This also provides an output derived from the segment timing, for synchronism purposes. This can be achieved by using correlation detection because only the data component was randomized during the transmission coding stage, leaving the sync component correlated. The signal is next filtered to remove any adjacent or co-channel NTSC interference and then equalized to minimize the effects of any propagation distortions such as multipath effects. The equalizer uses the known frame sync component as a timing signal so that it can function in an adaptive manner. The phase tracker removes any phase noise that might remain after the action of the FPLL.

In the terrestrial mode the trellis decoder uses the maximum likelihood Viterbi scheme to correct any data errors and produce a sliced data output. De-interleaving follows to reinstate the correct order of the data bytes. During this process, any contiguous burst errors become spread out over many packets so that the Reed–Solomon decoder can correct any burst errors of ten bytes or fewer in a data packet. The final de-randomization puts the data back into its original format of video, audio and ancillary data.

The effects of concatenating two methods of forward error correction (13)

It was shown in Chapter 1 that the BER was proportional to the carrier-to-noise ratio (CNR) and the energy per bit per watt of noise power per Hz as follows: $E_b/N_o = CNR \times B/R$, where B is the bandwidth and R the bit rate. It was also shown that if the CNR is increased then the BER will be reduced. It has also been shown that packing more data into a given bandwidth also increases the BER. For example, the use of QPSK instead of pure binary PSK incurrs a 3 dB SNR penalty for the same level of BER. The DVB television broadcast system puts the FEC techniques to very good use. An inner convolutional coding scheme with possible code rates ranging from 1/2 to 7/8 provides good correction ability to random errors. It will be recalled that the 1/2 coding system generates two bits output for every data bit input to the encoder, thus every data bit has its own unique parity bit. Reducing the error correctability of the code by reducing the number of parity bits increases the data throughput but at the expense of an increased BER. It is shown in the literature (13) that the above equation can be modified as follows: CNR = E_b/N_0 × number of bits per symbol × overall code rate, which for the QPSK parameters in use simplifies to:

$$CNR = E_b/N_0 \times 2 \times 1/2 \times 0.92 \tag{11.5}$$

It is further shown that the change of code rate from 1/2 to 7/8 imposes a 4.3 dB CNR penalty on the system. As a comparison, with the code rate set at 1/2, the system just fails at a CNR 4.1 dB, but with a 7/8 code rate it is necessary to increase the CNR to 8.4 dB to compensate.

The DVB system aims the provide a BER of 2×10^{-4} at the output of the inner FEC receiver stage and it is shown that this threshold level can just be achieved with a CNR of 4.5 dB. By using data interleaving, any burst errors that would normally be uncorrectable become spread out over many bytes at the decoding stage. These errors now come within the correction range of the Reed–Solomon (R–S) decoder. If the error correctability before de-interleaving has been met, then the expected BER at the output of the outer R–S decoder has improved to 1×10^{-11}. At a typical nominal bit rate of 10 MHz for the MPEG-2 system, this represents one bit in error every 2.77 hours.

The homodyne receiver (14)

The concept of the direct conversion receiver, or the homodyne, is probably even older than that of the superhet which dates from around 1936. In this case, the local oscillator frequency has the same value as the carrier of the wanted modulated RF signal. By beating the two frequencies together in a conventional mixer stage, the normal sum and difference components are generated. However, the sum frequency is now well outside the receiver passband and is of little consequence. The difference frequency is just the modulation component from the carrier, so that demodulation has been simultaneously achieved.

Historically, the major problems that have been faced by this concept all relate to local oscillator stability. Since the LNB of a satellite receiver acts as the normal superhet first conversion stage, the stable homodyne frequency of around 2 GHz needed to process the second IF at the indoor receiver can now be accurately produced. Figure 11.18 shows the basic principles of such a receiver front. The Maxim MAX2102 integrated device, designed to tune across the whole of the DVB system band, not only performs this function and produces a very compact receiver, but also provides a very high degree of image channel rejection. As shown, the circuit consists of a double balanced mixer stage driven by the second IF signal from the LNB and an external voltage-controlled local oscillator (VCO) based on a PLL that includes a pre-scaler stage. Because of the use of quadrature versions of the local oscillator signal the two outputs from the

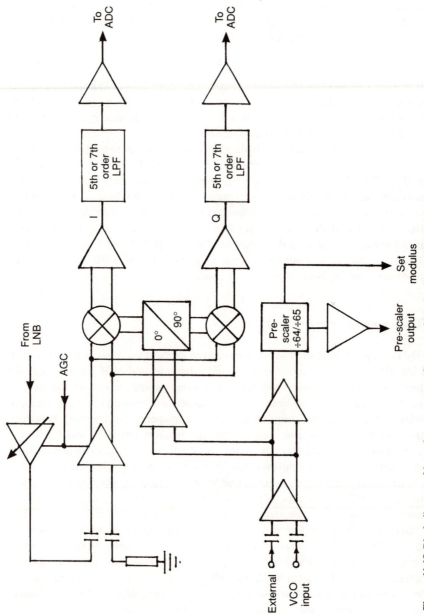

Figure 11.18 Block diagram of homodyne converter (Courtesy of Maxim Integrated Products Ltd).

mixers represent the I and Q components of modulation. After A/D conversion and low-pass filtering these are ready for DVB decoding. The pre-scaler is programmable via the receiver microprocessor and its output signal is available to synchronize the local oscillator synthesizer.

The typical major parameters for this design includes: noise figure 13 dB, third-order intercept 6 dBm, worst-case VSWR 2.3:1, baseband width (−3 dB) 94 MHz.

The reference receiver (15)

The MPEG standard is very extensive and runs to several hundred pages in length. It is possible that different chip makers might interpret the standards in different ways so that receiver decoders might function differently under the same fault conditions. Because of the large amount of programme control data that has to be transmitted to decode the signals, the clock recovery circuits might become critical, even though the standard calls for a time sync tolerance of less than 500 ns with a very low level of jitter. It will therefore be important that transponder monitoring stations, cable system head-end service units and the larger service departments should have some form of standard against which to quantify the quality of service. To meet this demand, a number of manufactures have produced *reference receivers* and Comatlas (15) in particular now manufacture receivers against which the quality of satellite, cable and terrestrial transmissions can be measured; typical of these is the CAS3143A designed for DVB-S applications.

The input to the receiver is direct from an LNB and covers the frequency range 950–2150 MHz with an input level ranging from −65 to −25 dBm (about 30 pW to 3 mW). A facility is provided so that several receivers can be looped through and fed from a single LNB. The digital signal symbol rate ranges from 3 to 30 Mbauds. The outputs may be either the Viterbi decoded serial bit stream, the parallel MPEG-2 transport stream or I/Q outputs from the QPSK demodulator when the signal constellation can be displayed on an oscilloscope.

This receiver performs all the MPEG-2 decoding, including QPSK demodulation, Viterbi decoding, inner de-interleaving, R–S decoding, descrambling and MPEG-2 packet decoding. Its 4-row by 20-character LCD display unit with scroll facility can be used to indicate the channel bit error rate, the Viterbi decoding error rate, the carrier frequency, RF input level, uncorrectable MPEG block errors and many other system dynamic parameters. These receivers can also be coupled to any PC via the serial RS232 port to provide a large screen display and for hardcopy printouts. In addition, the receivers can be programmed via the PC keyboard.

11.8 TELEVISION DISTRIBUTION TECHNIQUES

Apart from the single user television receive-only (TVRO) applications, there are two other important distribution concepts: the satellite master antenna TV systems (SMATV), serving a single site such as a hotel or block of flats, and the full community antenna TV system (CATV) or cable system. The latter is already well documented (16) and will only be considered here in a limited way.

SMATV system

Figure 11.19 shows one half of a typical simple SMATV system, designed for operation with the Fixed Satellite Services (FSS) band to provide for up to eight satellite TV channels. A line amplifier stage is needed because the antenna site, and hence the LNB, will most probably be more than 50 m away from the power splitter unit. Due to the extra loading imposed by the system and the need to ensure a high grade of service, the SMATV antenna will need to provide an extra 3–4 dB of gain. For example, if an antenna of 0.6–0.8 m diameter would provide an adequate TVRO service, then for a SMATV system at the same site an antenna of about 1.2–1.5 m diameter should be installed. After signal splitting, using an active device, each output can be fed to separate receivers, each tuned for the vision and sound parameters of that transponder channel. Where a channel is carrying encrypted signals, the wideband unclamped video output will be used to drive the necessary decoders. The baseband signals are then remodulated on to separate UHF carriers and combined for distribution to standard UHF TV receivers.

The two LNBs for each of the X and Y linear polarizations can be fed from the same antenna using an orthomode transducer. The complete system will thus be twice as extensive as that depicted in Figure 11.19. For distribution of signals from the DTH section of the Ku band, the LNB feeds may also need to accommodate left- and right-hand circular polarizations for D2-MAC as well as both linear polarizations for the other transmissions.

Larger SMATV systems for multi-channel distribution

The tree and branch configuration shown in Figure 11.20(a) works adequately for small networks distributing up to about five programmes to about twenty homes. For cable networks larger than this, it is necessary to adopt the switched star network configuration where each subscriber has direct access to the head end via the main switching centre. The basic principle for this is shown in Figure 11.20(b). With the expansion of co-located satellites that are virtually all dedicated to television services, each subscriber might well have up to 150–200 digital programme channels available. With such a large number of channels, it is no longer economical or even technically feasible to distribute all these over a single cable to each subscriber. For these services it is best to distribute the satellite-delivered signals over the network at the first IF from the head-end LNBs direct into each subscriber's receiver decoder unit. This then leaves the subscriber with the facility of selecting high or low band channels and vertical or horizontal polarization in the same way as the single antenna system user.

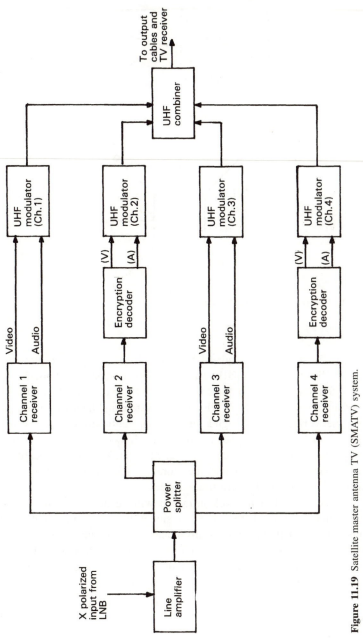

Figure 11.19 Satellite master antenna TV (SMATV) system.

(a)

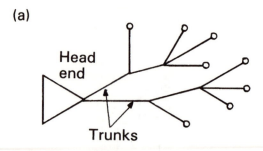

(b)

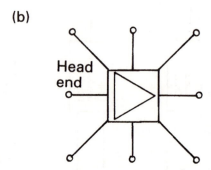

Figure 11.20 Networks: (a) tree and branch; (b) star.

Figure 11.21 shows how a quad LNB can deliver such services covering the whole of the band 10.7–12.75 GHz using a combination network known as a *tree-star* configuration. The four outputs from the LNB are combined with the signals derived from a terrestrial VHF/UHF antenna system and then fed over a parallel backbone network looped through a series of star multi-way switches which then feed the subscribers' drop cables as shown. Each switch unit then receives the control signals of voltage-level change or 22 kHz tone over the drop cables in the normal manner. Each drop cable therefore carries the four normal satellite options plus the VHF/UHF terrestrial services.

As the size of such a network grows, it will be necessary to increase the antenna diameter to provide the additional signal strength. For example, a typical combination of an EIRP level of 50 dBW and 75 cm diameter dish will provide an adequate digital signal for a network of four receivers. Increasing the network to sixteen or sixty-four receivers will require an antenna of about 90 cm and 1.2 m diameter respectively.

CATV considerations

Metallic coaxial cables or optical glass fibres may be used for the new distribution systems the final choice being a compromise based on the cost-

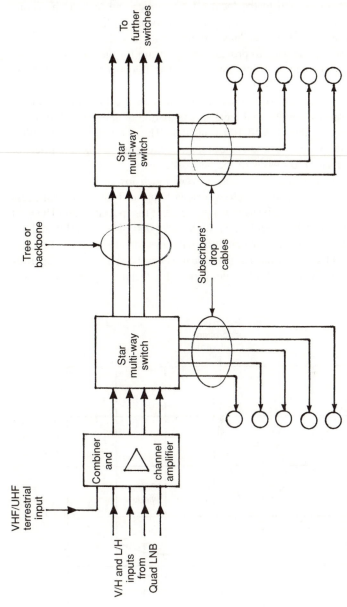

Figure 11.21 Multi-channel television distribution network.

effectiveness of the system as a whole. Coaxial cables are leaky to RF, radiating and receiving unwanted signal energy. Although the cable bandwidth may be as high as 500 MHz, certain carrier frequencies have to be avoided (the taboo channels). These are related to the local off-air service and include the actual local carrier frequencies and their images, plus the local oscillator frequencies of receivers tuned to such channels. This produces such a restriction that several parallel cables have to be used to provide the spectrum for the required number of channels. Coaxial cable attenuation increases with frequency, and at 400 MHz may vary between about 3 dB/100 m for a trunk cable and 15 dB/100 m for a subscriber's drop cable. By comparison, a typical coaxial cable suitable for the new digital TV services might well have an attenuation of about 35 dB/100 m at 2150 MHz, falling to about 23 dB/100 m at 950 MHz (a range of 12 dB/100 m over the bandwidth in use). These values may entail the use of line amplifiers or repeaters about every 750 metres of the network.

The attenuation of optical glass fibre is very much lower, but is dependent upon the fibre technology and the light wavelength in use. Typical losses are less than 1–2 dB/km, but this may be as low as 0.2 dB/km for special fibres. The total signal bandwidth available could be as high as 25 000 GHz (25 THz) and the attenuation and two most common operating windows for a mono-mode fibre are shown in Figure 11.22. This means that repeaters can be spaced as far apart as 50 km or more in an optical fibre network. The technology, constructional

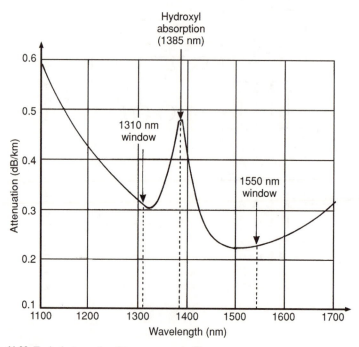

Figure 11.22 Typical attenuation for a mono-mode fibre.

features and properties of optical fibres are well documented (17), but some of the important features and advantages are as follows:

(1) Low-cost, abundant supply of raw material (silica, sand) with falling production costs.
(2) Very much wider bandwidth and lower attenuation.
(3) Glass, being an electrical insulator, does not generate and is not influenced by electromagnetic interference.
(4) Very many fewer repeaters are needed in the system.
(5) There is no standing wave/impedance mismatch problem associated with fibre jointing.
(6) Light beams have no electrical impedance.

Due to the very small diameter of these fibres, multi-fibre cables can be readily constructed to maximize the transmission-bandwidth-to-installation-costs ratio. Such cables need to include metallic strength members to avoid cable laying stresses that could lead to fibre fracture. In addition, the cables have to be sealed against water ingress which would cause an early deterioration of the fibre characteristics.

Light energy is launched into the fibres from either a light emitting diode or a laser and detected at the far end by either a photodiode or a transistor. In practice, the actual devices used depend largely upon the length of the network.

Types of optical fibres

Optical fibres are constructed in a bi-cylindrical manner as indicated by Figure 11.23, the glass used for the inner core having a higher refractive index than that for the outer cladding. The behaviour of a ray of light energy directed into the core can be predicted from Snell's Law which states that $n_1 \sin \theta_1 = n_2 \sin \theta_2$, where n_1 and n_2 are the refractive indices of the two media forming a refractive layer and θ_1 and θ_2 are the angles of incidence and refraction to the normal, respectively. For two practical media, a critical angle θ_c will be found when total reflection occurs at the interface and this is given by $\sin \theta_c = n_{cl}/n_{co}$, where n_{cl} and n_{co} are the refractive indices of the cladding and core respectively. For example, if the cladding and core refractive indices are 1.4 and 1.5 respectively, then the critical angle is about 69° to the normal. Any ray directed into the fibre at an angle greater than this will therefore be trapped and transported to the far end.

Multi-mode step index fibre
De facto standards of 50 μm core and 125 μm cladding have been established for telecommunications purposes. As indicated by Figure 11.23(a), several modes can propagate simultaneously. The scattering and absorption losses for this form of fibre are higher than those of the alternatives, making this type suitable chiefly for short-haul, bandwidth-restricted, low-cost applications only.

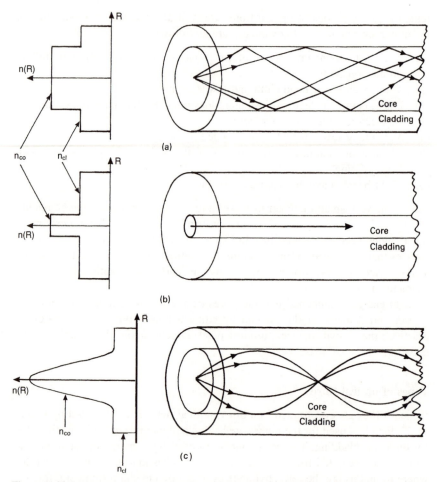

Figure 11.23 (a) Multi-mode step index fibre. (b) Mono-mode step index fibre. (c) Graded index fibre.

Mono-mode step index fibre

Typically the inner core is made less than 10 μm diameter so that only one mode of wave can propagate in the way shown in Figure 11.23(b). The outer cladding diameter must be more than ten times this value to minimize losses. These fibres are very suitable for wide bandwidth, long haul networks.

Graded index fibre

In this type the core glass has a radially graded refractive index. As indicated by Figure 11.23(c), the rays tend to take a sinusoidal path through the core with the fastest components taking the longest path. As the rays can be considered to represent the different modes travelling through the fibre, they all have the same transit time. Thus the losses are relatively small. Telecommunications de facto standard diameters have been agreed for core and cladding diameters of 50 μm and 125 μm respectively. The best grades of this type are suitable for long-haul, wide-bandwidth systems.

Wavelength division multiplexing (WDM)

By selecting a number of lasers each with different wavelengths of radiation, and then combining their outputs in a wavelength multiplexer or combiner, it becomes possible to launch several rays of energy into each fibre simultaneously, with each representing a different signal. All these signals will then travel along the fibre to the far end where they can be separated using tunable optical filters and then demodulated. It is possible to select lasers whose radiation wavelengths differ by as little as 0.4–4 nm, to produce a system often referred to as dense wavelength division multiplexing (DWDM).

In order to increase the density of the data being carried over a fibre, it is possible to combine WDM with TDM, a concept that is usually referred to as wavelength and time division multiplex (WTDM). If the basic system bit duration is T and the output from the lasers can be sampled four times during this period, then the outputs of four different channels can be sampled sequentially. These outputs may then be carried in sequence over a single fibre to be demultiplexed at the receiving end.

During 1995, as a result of the European RACE research programme, it was demonstrated that it was possible that more than 200 simultaneous video and audio signal channels could be routed to more than 200 destinations using WTDM. The test used the internationally agreed standard of synchronous digital hierarchy (SDH). A total of 40 Gbit/s was divided across sixteen WTDM channels at 2.48 Gbit/s, each separated by a wavelength of 4 nm using the 1500 nm window. The system was shown to be able to support 128 component video signals or thirty-two HDTV signals, plus sound and ancillary control signals.

Operated in this way, it has been demonstrated in Japan that it is possible to transmit twenty-two WDM channels, each wavelength spaced by 0.4 μm and carrying a bit rate of 5.3 Gbit/s, over a 9500 km fibre. The system employed 980 nm pumped erbium-doped fibre amplifiers to counter the losses.

In the medium-term future, broadband cable networks are most likely to remain as hybrids, with fibre as the main carrier medium with copper coaxial drop cables for the last 100 metres or so. Further into the future, distribution systems are highly likely to be completely fibre based.

Fibre jointing methods

There are two basic methods of forming joints between sections of optical fibres. The first is simple. It involves accurate abutment of the two ends and then the

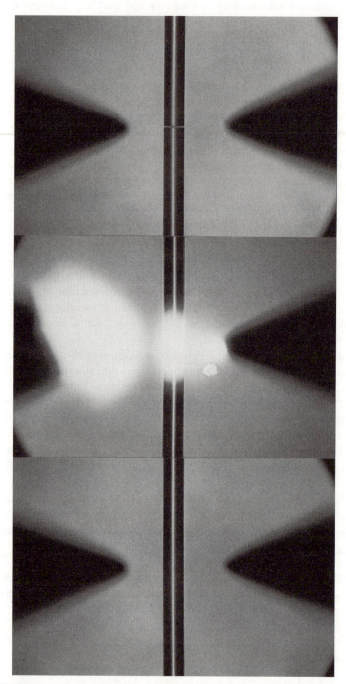

Figure 11.24 Fusion spliced optical fibres (Courtesy of BICC Research and Engineering Ltd).

sealing of the joint with an ultra-violet light-curing adhesive. Such joints may produce losses of less than 0.5 dB. The major problem of joint losses arises from the small eccentricity of the core and cladding glasses. Joints made by the alignment of the outer glass diameter may thus be suspect.

An alternative, but more effective, method is provided by the *fusion splicer* (18). Here light is injected into one of the two fibres and extracted from the other by making use of the micro-bend effect. The two ends are then manipulated under microprocessor control, to maximize the light transfer. At this point, an arc is struck between a pair of electrodes that causes the glass to fuse. Joints made in this manner have a loss in the order of 0.05 dB. Figure 11.24 (19) shows this jointing technique very clearly.

The erbium-doped fibre amplifier (or Raman amplifier)

Before the development of this amplifying technique, all optical fibre signal losses had to be countered by demodulating the light signal and then regenerating and amplifying it by using conventional electronic methods. The Raman amplifier consists of a loop of about 20 m of silica fibre doped with the tri-valent element erbium which is linked into the optical fibre signal path in the manner shown in Figure 11.25. The low-level signal to be amplified is combined with a high-level pump signal using a coupler. The combined signal then passes through the length of doped fibre. The pump source uses a wavelength of either 980 or 1480 nm which requires a few tens of milliwatts to provide about 50 mA of drive current. As the two signals pass through the doped section, the weak signal extracts energy from the pump signal through stimulated emission and ionic excitation of the molecular structure. The wanted signal thus becomes coherently amplified (without change of wavelength). Experimental amplifiers have been shown to have gains as high as 40 dB with commercial devices at about 10 dB less. These are low-noise amplifiers capable of handling bit rates of 100 Mbit/s with a noise factor typically about 2 dB above the theoretical quantum level of 3 dB. Since the noise bandwidth is commonly much greater than that of the

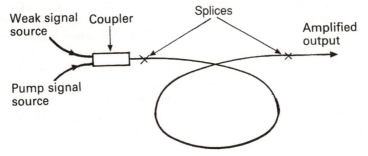

Figure 11.25 Erbium-doped fibre amplifier.

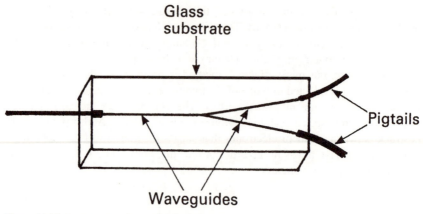

Figure 11.26 Optical multiplexer/splitter/coupler.

signal, the detector stages are usually equipped with tunable optical filters to improve the SNR.

Optical waveguides can be constructed within a glass substrate so that optical signal paths can be split or combined in a variety of ways. Figure 11.26 shows a simple one- to two-way coupler or splitter. The waveguide pattern is formed on a special glass substrate using photolithographic and masking techniques, similar to those used in semiconductor fabrication. The final waveguide is formed by an ion exchange process that takes place in a molten salt bath when thallium ions are exchanged for those of sodium and potassiuim ions contained within the glass. Fibre pigtails are then attached to the ports using index matched adhesive. At the typical operating wavelength of 800–1550 nm, the through loss is only in the order of 0.2 dB and the 3 dB split of one signal into two paths can be achieved within ±0.1 dB.

Network configuration and switching

The traditional cable systems of the past have been based on the *tree and branch* configuration where it is particularly difficult to provide for subscriber-to-subscriber interactivity. This concept therefore gave way to the *switched star* network where, by including suitable switches at each system node, complete flexibility is provided for interactive services.

For copper cable systems each switching unit in the system has to be based on a matrix formed by the incoming lines and the outgoing subscribers' feeds. This leads to two possible switching methods: either by switching at baseband, which requires demodulation at the switch and final distribution at baseband, or by remodulation on to a new carrier. The preferred method uses a frequency translator type of switch. The incoming VHF distribution signal is frequency-changed to a UHF carrier for direct feed to a standard TV receiver. Matrix

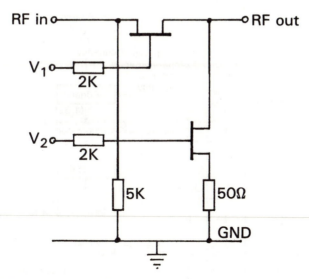

Figure 11.27 GaAs semiconductor RF switch.

switches are still required at each cross-point, but these can be fabricated using GaAs semiconductor technology, in the manner shown by Figure 11.27. By providing simultaneous negative and positive voltages at V_1 and V_2, a fast switching action is generated, with a loss at 500 MHz of less than 0.7 dB in the ON state and an isolation greater than 50 dB when OFF.

One recent development of the splitting device shown in Figure 11.26 is its conversion to function as an optical switch. By adding a flip-flop semiconductor heating device at the dual end, a single-ended input signal can be rapidly switched to either output. This switching action exploits a thermo-optic effect whereby the refractive index of the fibre falls significantly with a rise in temperature to cut off the light path. Such switches can be constructed as 1×2 as shown through to an 8×8 configuration in a single device. These switches thus make a very useful addition to an optical fibre distribution network.

Frequency agile switching

The technique shown in Figure 11.28 represents one way in which a frequency agile switching system can be implemented. The channel switch for TV is based on a matrix formed by the six trunk cables and the three feeds to each subscriber, the cross-point switching and channel selection being performed in two stages, which involves a two-digit programme selection. These digits define the wanted channel and cable respectively.

In the example represented in Figure 11.28, UHF channel 21, with a vision carrier at 471.25 MHz, has been selected. This signal has been delivered to the switch at 54.06 MHz. Within the switch unit, two groups of highly accurate reference frequencies are generated from transmitted pilot signals. These are five

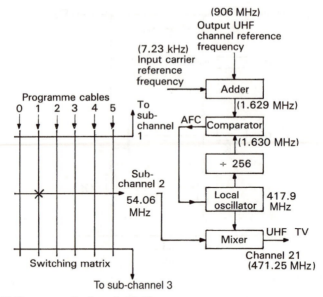

Figure 11.28 Frequency agile channel switching.

square wave switching signals in the range 343–723 kHz and three sine waves in the range 906 kHz to 2.38 MHZ. The two groups are used as references for the input and output frequencies respectively. In the example shown, the references 723 and 906 kHz are selected and added to produce one input to the AFC comparator at 1.629 MHz, the local oscillator frequency, divided by 256, providing the second input. The frequency error causes the AFC system to retune the varicap diode tuned local osillator to 417.9 MHz. The mixer thus translates the input VHF signal to the desired channel value of 471.25 MHz, for delivery to the subscriber's receiver.

Now that the correct frequency translation has been set up, a semiconductor cross-point switch closes to select the wanted cable.

The multimedia broadband cable concept

Due to the deregulation that is taking place in the telecommunications industry, cable TV operators are now able to offer the customer/subscriber many other services. Bandwidth to provide full duplex interactive telephone-type services and television is readily available using optical fibre as the transmission medium. The networks are completely computer controlled, not only for the management system, conditional access and customer billing, but also to control an interface to the public switched telephone network (PSTN) and the integrated services digital network (ISDN). These networks are capable of supporting all current and proposed future TV formats, including HDTV and video-on-demand. A data capacity is also available for such services as TV surveillance, business data communications, home computer users, teleconferencing, fast Internet access and other multimedia operations. The primary distribution is over a trunk network of optical fibres. Because of the low loss, distribution amplifiers are only required at the switching points. The switching points form the hub of a star switched network, each serving perhaps 100 or more homes or business premises. Initially the switching had to be performed electronically but fibre developments are such that optical switching has already been shown to be a viable proposition. The trunks may consist of up to eight or more fibres, each carrying up to fifty digital TV or radio channels, with provision for reverse communications.

11.9 SYNCHRONOUS DIGITAL HIERARCHY (SDH) AND ASYNCHRONOUS TRANSFER MODE (ATM)

Normally, the high-capacity trunk system of a telecommunications system and the local networks are not fully synchronized so that the interfaces, particularly those for high-speed operation, find this a problem. With the SDH concept, which is a standard recognized by the ITU-T, the traffic in all parts of the network is transferred in synchronized packets. This permits higher data speeds and better utilization of the network capacity. For example, an SDH system operating at 155 Mbit/s can provide for at least 1800 simultaneous telephone calls over each optical fibre. The service also allows for the integration of data, voice, video and television traffic. SDH also has the capability of *drop-insert*; this means that a network station can add only those signals required by that station, without control overhead bits.

The SDH is defined by ITU-T recommendations G707, G708 and G709, with the lowest multiplex data rate of 155.52 Mbit/s being described as STM-1 (synchronous transfer module-1). The multiplex is described in general terms as STM-N where N takes on the values of 3, 4, 6, 8 and 16. Thus the upper rate is $16 \times 155.52 = 2488.32$ Mbit/s. The value of 155.52 was chosen because it represents the convergence of different multiples of the CCITT and Bell/AT&T standard rates.

Each SDH frame can be represented as a 9-row by 270-column matrix as indicated by Figure 11.29. The first or top left-hand byte, known as the *framing byte*, provides bit rate clock synchronism and represents the start of a frame. Transmission then follows on a row-by-row basis. The eighty-one bytes described as section overhead, which are interleaved with the data, provide byte synchronism, system monitoring and frame delimiters.

The useful payload of each SDH frame is contained within the nine rows of 261 bytes. The overall bit rate is therefore given by:

$270 \times 9 = 2430$ bytes/frame

$8 \times 2430 = 19\,440$ bits/frame

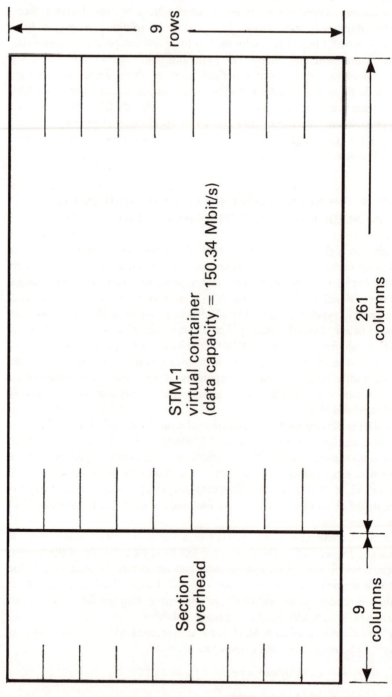

Figure 11.29 SDH STM-1 frame structure.

At 8000 frames/s this gives $8000 \times 19\,440 = 155.52\,\text{Mbit/s}$. The actual user channel capacity is given by:

$$261 \times 9 \times 8 \times 8000 = 150.336\,\text{Mbit/s}$$

SDH is thus used for the transmission of different bit rates framed in different virtual containers (VCs), with their control overhead bytes. The system further provides the means of worldwide unification of digital hierarchies and auxillary channels, inserted by means of standard frame overheads.

Although initially designed for use over an optical fibre network, STM-1 can be handled over a microwave link. Using either 32QAM or 64QAM, this yields a bandwidth between 30 and 40 MHz.

The ATM concept, which was designed for use with broadband wide area networks, is also supported by both ITU-T and ANSI standards and can be interfaced to the SONET (Synchronous Optical NETwork). ATM automatically adjusts the network capacity to meet the system needs and can handle data, voice, video and television signals. These are transferred in a sequence of fixed length data units called cells.

ATM is a wideband, low-delay, packet-like switching and multiplexing concept that allows flexible use of the transmission bandwidth and is capable of working at data rates as high as 622.08 Mbit/s. Because ATM is compatible with SDH data rates, it is used to transport and route users' information over SDH facilities. Thus the combination of ATM and SDH is likely to be the future prime means of transport for digital compressed video such as MPEG-2.

Each data packet consists of five bytes of header field plus forty-eight bytes for user data. The header contains data that identifies the related cell, a logical address that identifies the routeing, forward error correction (FEC) bits, plus bits for priority handling and network management functions. FEC applies only to the header as it is assumed that the network medium will not degrade the error rate below an acceptable level. All the cells of a virtual container follow the same path through the network that was determined during call set-up. There are no fixed time slots in the system so that any user can access the transmission medium whenever an empty cell is available. ATM is capable of operating at bit rates of 155.52 and 622.08 Mbit/s and the cell stream is continuous and without gaps.

The position of the cells associated with a particular VC is random and depends upon the activity of the network. Cells produced by different streams to the ATM multiplex are stored in queues awaiting cell assignment. Since a call is only accepted when the necessary bandwidth is available, there is a probability of queue overflow. Cell loss due to this forms one ATM impairment. However, this can be minimized through the use of statistical multiplexers. Bit errors in the header which are beyond the FEC capability can lead to misrouteing.

Cells in frames (CIF)

This concept is set to provide a further link between wired local area networks (LAN) such as Ethernet and optical fibre systems. It can handle a wide range of traffic, including the Internet, which it does much faster than the TCP/IP protocol which is used over the plain old telephone system (POTS). This arises because the variable length frames of fast LANs can easily be switched. CIF uses the Ethernet or Token ring frames but adds four bytes as CIF/ATM frame header. Each frame carries thirty-one ATM cells which are passed from CIF switch to switch. For Ethernet there is a maximum 1500-byte length limit to the frame. The adding or dropping of the 4-byte header is carried out under software control at the network nodes.

11.10   ASYMMETRICAL DIGITAL SUBSCRIBERS' LINE (ADSL)

There is already a very large installed base of twisted pair cables between telephone exchange buildings and many millions of subscribers' premises. These represent the installations that provide the normal voice traffic using copper or aluminium wires of various gauges, ranging from 0.32 to 0.9 mm in diameter. Any particular subscriber's link may consist of more than two of these so that the overall attenuation may well vary from link to link.

It has been shown experimentally that these installations, originally designed for low voice frequencies (300–3400 Hz), are capable of carrying much higher frequencies, providing that the line characteristics are suitably countered. Figure 11.30 shows approximately how the line attenuation varies up to 1 MHz. While this figure is high, about 0.075 dB/kHz, the characteristic is fairly linear and easily equalized. But most importantly, over this same range, the group delay which represents the ratio of phase change per unit Hz is almost constant. This

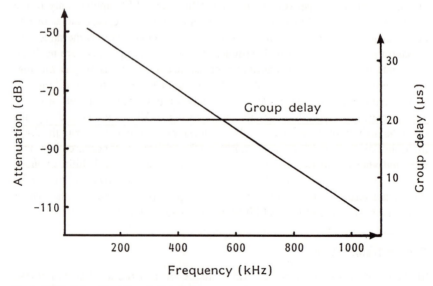

Figure 11.30 Subscribers' line characteristics.

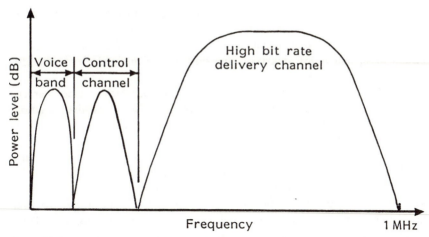

Figure 11.31 Channel allocation of ADSL multiplex.

means that because the phase change introduced by the line is proportional to the signal frequency, there will be little pulse distortion and consequently few bit errors in a digital transmission. These features simultaneously allow the use of high bit rate digital transmissions and conventional telephony over the same local loop.

Figure 11.31 shows the general allocation of the frequency spectrum above the normal voice band. A low bit rate control channel operating at either 9.6, 16 or 64 kbit/s provides for the subscribers' demands, together with a high bit rate channel for the delivery of selected television programmes or other services. It is this asymmetrical bit rate allocation that gives the system its title. Organizing the system in this way is cost-effective. The hardware costs for the individual user are relatively low, while the high costs of the high bit rate end are shared by the many subscribers. ADSL systems can provide instant video-on-demand using the voice channel and also TV with VCR-like characteristics – fast forward, fast rewind, freeze frame, pause, etc. by demands via the control channel. The system is also capable of delivering TV programmes for recording on the subscriber's VCR during night time or other off-peak periods.

Using MPEG-1 digital compression with suitable channel coding, video signals of various grades can be transmitted direct to the home. A bit rate of 2.048 Mbit/s can provide VHS-quality video together with digitally coded stereo sound. At 6.144 Mbit/s with MPEG-2 compression, the video quality is equal to that of a broadcast transmission.

There are various ways of allocating the high bit rate downstream channel; four times 1.544 Mbit/s and 6.176 Mbit/s suit North America while three times 2.048 Mbit/s and 6.144 Mbit/s cater for Europe, but other combinations are possible. It should be noted that these bit rates are compatible with ISDN, but the higher bit rate systems, due to the attenuation, will tend to have a shorter network penetration.

Analogue filters with high stop-band attenuation are used at each end of an ADSL network in order to combine or separate the telephony and the additional services with the minimum of mutual interference. In practice, it is necessary to be able to separate ADSL signals of a few millivolts in amplitude from a few tens of volts of ringing tone.

Because of the make-up of the local loop, many of which include overhead sections, there are many connections that can give rise to resistive variations which tend to be temperature and moisture dependent. In particular, overhead line vibrations and other variables can give rise to signal drop-outs that last for several milliseconds. ADSL networks are therefore designed to ride out such breaks without resetting.

Cross-talk between the individual pairs in a multi-pair cable is not significant and neither is cross-talk between other ADSL users. Impulsive noise from ringing tones and switching signals could be troublesome, but by using a suitable transmission technique with FEC, this has little significance in a well-maintained network.

Digital adaptive equalizers adjust automatically to suit individual line characteristics. These include temperature- and moisture-dependent variable parameters and continuous interference. Provision is made so that at each new acquisition, the line amplifiers and equalizers are reset under a short training sequence to establish the maximum signal-to-noise ratio.

In order to maximize the channel capacity a form of bit rate reduction coding known as 2B1Q is employed. With this, each pair of binary input digits is converted into one of four quaternary symbols. Further, to minimize the effects of both radiated and induced radio frequency interference, ADSL employs a balanced feed of RF signals to the line.

Several different forms of modulation have been tested on practical ADSL networks and the following modes have been shown to be most effective:

Quadrature amplitude modulation (QAM). The binary data stream is first split into two sub-streams and each separately modulated on to orthogonal (quadrature) versions of the same carrier. These two modulated signals are then added before transmission to line.

Carrierless amplitude/phase modulation (CAP). As indicated by Figure 11.32, the bit stream is again split into two components and then separately passed through two digital filters that have an impulse response differing by 90°. The outputs are then added, passed through a digital-to-analogue converter and filtered before being passed to the transmission network.

Discrete multi-tone modulation (DMT). This preferred method has a lot in common with CODFM (coded orthogonal frequency division multiplexing) in that the main channel is divided into many sub-channels. Each serial digital input signal is first encoded into parallel format and then passed through a fast Fourier transform (FFT) processor to convert the frequency domain samples into time domain values with a sliding time-window effect. These values are transcoded into a serial format, then digital-to-analogue converted before

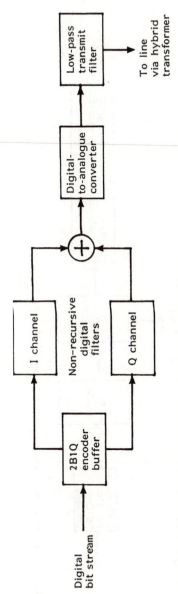

Figure 11.32 Carrier amplitude modulation processing of the ADSL signal.

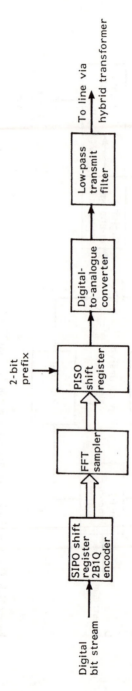

Figure 11.33 Discrete multi-tone modulation processing of the ADSL signal.

transmission. The general processing is shown in Figure 11.33 which shows that two or more prefix bits are added to the bit stream. When these are dropped at the decoder, the bit stream is typically broken up into 512-bit blocks to improve the definition of the FFT window. The line characteristics for each narrow sub-channel are practically constant so that the minimum of pulse smearing is created, thus improving signal quality. Any impulsive noise that is input as interference is spread over many sub-channels by the FFT processor window so that this form of interference is less likely to create data errors. The number of bits transmitted in a sub-channel can be varied adaptively depending on the signal-to-noise ratio in any channel. This not only improves the signal quality on a particular line, but also minimizes the effect of cross-talk from other lines. The specification includes error control in the form of Reed–Soloman coding with the possibility of adding interleaving. These features make the DMT scheme more robust under noisy conditions.

The ADSL concept is also of particular interest to Internet users who feel very much constricted by the slow rate of the POTS networks. Typically, the maximum signal speed using standard modems cannot currently exceed 56 kbit/s. Even by using the ISDN lines at the maximum rate of 2.048 Mbit/s, this does not compare favourably with cable system modems that can achieve 6 Mbit/s. Internet activity can reach this desirable state by using ADSL. The technology has been chiefly developed in North America and Europe, but has been tested worldwide. Standards are covered by both the American National Standards Institute (ANSI) and the European Telecommunications Standards Institute (ETSI).

11.11   MULTI-CHANNEL MULTIPOINT DISTRIBUTION SYSTEMS (MMDS) (20, 21)

Around the world, there are many areas where it is impossible to receive either television pictures or stereo radio satisfactorily, and in the main, a significant number of these are located in valleys. Often these are areas of small communities which make it uneconomic for such services to be provided via the national systems. A number of ingenious receiver/retransmitter systems, such as passive reflectors mounted on mountain tops, have been installed in an attempt to alleviate the problem. These installations are often privately owned and sometimes illegally operated. Additionally, there are many areas of towns and cities where it is not economical or even feasible to bury some section of a cable network. A system known variously as Multi-channel Multipoint Distribution Services or Multi-channel Microwave Distribution Services (MMDS) (often referred to as wire-less cable systems) has been developed to provide broadband services which can provide an effective solution to these problems. A further set of acronyms are also in use: MVDS for Microwave Video Distribution Service and M³VDS for Millimetre-wave Multi-channel Multipoint Video Distribution System.

In its original form, MMDS operated in the 2.5 GHz band where there is almost a complete absence of Sporadic-E radiation, to provide an educational service to rural areas or to retransmit either national or satellite-sourced TV signals. Such a service has also been successfully established to provide an extension to the twelve-channel cable network in County Cork, Ireland. The frequency range from 2.5 to 2.686 GHz provides for twenty-three PAL-I system channels. These are operated using carrier frequency offset, plus vertical and horizontal polarizations to minimize interference. The twenty-three channels are utilized in such a way as to provide service from at least eleven TV transmissions for all cable subscribers.

MMDS is essentially a local wideband rebroadcast system for the delivery of video, including teletext; sound, including stereo; and data, over a restricted area. High-power MMDS using transmitter output powers of 10–100 W can provide a service extending more than 40 km. Low-power MMDS (1–10 W output) can provide coverage for up to 10 km, depending on the power output, transmitter antenna height, and the terrain, as a line-of-sight path is necessary. Low-power MMDS tests have been carried out to show that, for a transmitter RF output power of 1 W at 2.5 GHz, TV pictures of excellent quality can be obtained at distances in excess of five kilometres and with no interference to other services. Reference to system power budgets and signal-to-noise ratio calculations show quite clearly that a service can be achieved with a relatively low level of technology and with cost-effective equipment.

System power budget

The transmission power budget for such a system can be calculated as follows.

For the sake of convenience, it is assumed here that both transmit and receive antennas are 50 cm diameter, with an efficiency of 55 percent at 2.5 GHz, so that each has a gain of approximately 20 dBi.

It is further assumed that a television receiver requires an input signal of 1 mV into 75 Ω for adequate picture quality. This represents an input signal power of 13.33 nW. If the receiving antenna is considered to act as a correctly matched signal source, then it must receive twice this amount of power, i.e. 26.66 nW or −75.75 dBW. For signal propagation path lengths of 10 and 40 km, it can be calculated that the attenuation will be 120.4 dB and 132.5 dB respectively.

The general expression for the transmitter output power is given by:

$$P_T = P_R - G_R - G_T + A \qquad (11.6)$$

where: P_T is the transmitter output power in dBW,
   P_R is the received signal power in dBW,
   G_R is the receiver antenna gain in dBi,
   G_T is the transmitter antenna gain in dBi, and
   A is the propagation path attenuation in dB.

Thus for 10 and 40 km path lengths, the required transmitter output powers are 4.65 dBW (nearly 3 W) and 16.75 dBW (less than 50 W) respectively.

Practical tests have shown that it is possible to operate an MMDS system without mutual interference to other services in both the 2.5 and 28 GHz bands.

The 2.5 GHz band is not available in some areas because of occupation by previously allocated services such as troposcatter communications and so other parts of the spectrum have been evaluated. The Ku band was ruled out due to possible interference with the reception of satellite services. Most of the new development work is concentrated in the band between 27.5 and 30 GHz and most of the worldwide developing systems will in fact employ this band. The choice between the two parts of the spectrum is therefore based on the fact that 2.5 GHz provides a well-proven technology, while the Ka band provides systems that operate with much smaller antennas. Gallium Arsenide semiconductor technology is now so well advanced that there is virtually no major hardware cost advantages for either sector.

System signal-to-noise ratio

It is assumed here that the input signal is provided for an AM television channel of 8 MHz bandwidth.

It can be shown theoretically that the received SNR is given by:

$$SNR = G/T + EIRP - BC - NB - A \text{ dB} \tag{11.7}$$

where: SNR is the received SNR in dB,
             G/T is the gain to noise temperature ratio in dB/K,
             EIRP is the effective isotropic radiated power from the
                transmitter = $P_T + G_T$ dBW,
             BC is Boltzmann's constant, 1.38×10^{-23} J/K or -228.6 dB/K/Hz,
             NB is the noise bandwidth, 8 MHz or 69 dBHz, and
             A is the propagation path attenuation in dB.

Suppose that the chosen LNB has a noise factor of 6.5 dB, which can be shown to be equivalent to a noise temperature of 1005 K. Assume further that the antenna is looking along a typically noisy earth surface of 290 K. Then the total noise temperature is 1295 K or 31.1 dBK.

The G/T ratio for this combination is given by:

$$G/T = G_R - N_T \tag{11.8}$$

where: N_T is the equivalent noise temperature in dBK,
             G/T = 20 dBi − 31.3 dBK = −11.1 dB/K. A relatively low level of
             the state of the art.

The received SNR for both 10 and 40 km paths thus becomes:

$$SNR = -11.1 + 24.65 + 228.6 - 69 - 120.4 = 52.75 \, dB, \quad or$$

$$-11.1 + 36.75 + 228.6 - 69 - 132.5 = 52.75 \, dB$$

If a lower SNR is acceptable, then the path lengths can be increased.

Figure 11.34 shows the basic principles of the operation of an MMDS system. At the transmitter, the incoming signals are either up- or down-converted as required, filtered and then amplified at 2.5 GHz. Earlier high-powered MMDS transmitters used one Driver/Power amplifier stage per channel. However, recent GaAs FET developments now allow the low-power systems to combine channels into blocks for delivery via a single Driver/Power amplifier stage. The provision of power supplies for rebroadcast transmitters at isolated sites has always been a problem. However, it is now possible to use the latest technology of battery operation, with recharging being achieved from either a wind or solar generator. At the receiver, the LNB down-converts the 2.5 GHz signals to frequencies that allows direct input to standard receivers.

The antennas used at 2.5 GHz for both transmit and receive are often around 50 cm diameter, or of similar rectangular area. Because of the relatively low microwave frequencies involved, the reflectors can be perforated to reduce windage and lightly corrugated to increase the mechanical stiffness, without introducing significant surface error losses. The small reflectors can easily be

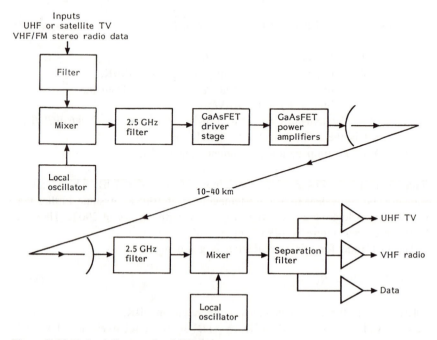

Figure 11.34 Notional diagram of an MMDS system.

Figure 11.35 A mesh-constructed dish antenna.

fabricated from stainless steel for good corrosion resistance. Such antennas and their mountings are less expensive than Yagi arrays of a similar gain. A 50 cm diameter dish typically has a beamwidth of 15° so that pointing accuracy is no problem, neither is antenna movement with wind. A wedge of more than 2.5 km wide can be covered with a beamwidth of 15° at a range of 10 km. This represents a very significant spread of signal energy. Figures 11.35 and 11.36 clearly show the simplicity of the reflector antenna types that may be used. The received signal is focused on to a dipole structure fabricated in microstrip and coupled directly to the LNB via a coaxial cable. For transmission purposes, one or more such antennas can be fed in parallel to provide the required radiation pattern.

There are many ways in which the retransmission bandwidth might be used, the simplest being a block translation of the incoming channels. However, in the interests of good spectrum management, it might be an advantage in some cases

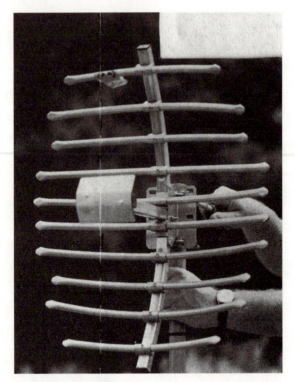

Figure 11.36 An alternative dish antenna.

to demodulate and then remodulate the signals before retransmission in the local TV standard.

Wherever MMDS operates, the equipment could be community owned. Alternatively, it is fairly simple to include encryption for delivery on a subscription basis. In fact, a very useful and simple security system was developed in America. This is known as the Comband system. Two video channels are multiplexed into a single channel bandwidth, effectively doubling the system capacity. Since each subscriber requires a special demultiplexer to recover the signals, this acts as a simple controlled-access system.

Digital power budget option

Reference to the digital power budget shown in Table 11.2 shows the viability of including a digital service within the frequency multiplex. It is thus possible to provide end users with a digital return channel, giving them a full duplex data service. Since only 10 mW of RF power is required, this could easily be provided by a fairly simple Gunn Diode transmitter circuit.

Table 11.2

Transmission output power (10 mW)	−20.0 dBW
Transmitter antenna gain	20.0 dBi
Attenuation at 2.5 GHz over 10 km	120.4 dB
Receiver noise temperature	31.1 dBK
Received signal power/noise temperature ratio	−151.5 dBW/K
Boltzmann's constant	−228.6 dB/K/Hz
Received SNR power ratio/Hz	77.1 dBHz
Transmission bit rate (7 Mbit/s)	68.5 dBHz
Equivalent digital SNR (E_B/N_O)	8.6 dB

It can be shown that such a performance will provide a bit error rate (BER) of better than 10^{-4} for any method of digital modulation, either OOK, FSK or PSK. To put this error rate into perspective, recall that the teletext page consists of twenty-four rows each of forty 8-bit characters, making a total of 7680 bits per page. Thus an error rate of 1 in 10^4 is equivalent to less than one error per page, at almost 7 Mbit/s. Reducing the bit rate will automatically reduce the error rate. By comparison, the NICAM digital stereo signal is transmitted at the very much lower bit rate of 728 kbit/s so that such a BER falls well within the system forward error correction (FEC) capability.

11.12   THE FUTURE OF TELEVISION

With the advent of a number of television broadcasting agencies offering the viewer in excess of 200 stations, it is right to question the impact that this might have on both the viewers and the system providers. Will the viewers watch for longer periods? Will more programmes mean greater demands on the programme providers to produce better quality television? Past experience does not support either proposition. Then what will be the impact for the engineering fraternity?

The introduction of multi-channel multiplexed television programmes provides a further drive towards integration and convergence with the computing and general media services – multimedia! The rapid expansion of the Internet into everyday life has reached such a stage that the general complaint is that the service is now too slow, in spite of the fact that 56 kbit/s modems are now very cost-effective. ADSL has been shown to offer a way to overcome this particular problem and perhaps at the same time, bypass the ISDN system. Near-video-on-demand offers a very poor spectrum-efficient way of using the extra channels. Perhaps using as many as six channels to show the same movie with different start times is not really an engineer's answer to such a problem. Video-on-demand using the ADSL concept is much more spectrum efficient. The integration of computer hard disk technology with the television system adds some further useful impetus to the video-on-demand concept as does the use of laser scanned video and audio (video disc and compact disc). These systems lend themselves readily to the downloading of programmes into domestic VCRs during off-peak periods.

The availability of IEEE 1395 networks will simplify the domestic user's interconnection problems, but will these actually make life easier? Service engineers could certainly gain much work from the problems these new technologies might introduce.

With such a large number of programme channels available, the conventional printed guide becomes very viewer unfriendly. There is therefore a need by the programme providers to attract viewers to their specific offerings by creating an electronic programmme guide (EPG) which advertises the pay-per-view or premium rate channels. Such a guide could be produced with current technology – even teletext systems are now available that will store 2000+ pages. This concept would allow the viewer to select a programme direct from the screen using a cursor, even allowing the selection to be recorded on the home VCR. Down-loading of video games for use with the home computer is already available via the Internet. With built-in timed self-destruct, these games could readily be rented along with cable TV or broadcast offerings.

REFERENCES

(1)   Hewlett-Packard Inc. (1964) *Applications Note No. 16: Waves on Transmission Lines.*

(2)   Bone, A. and Cockerill, M., PACE Micro Technology Ltd, Shipley, West Yorks, UK. Private communication to author.

(3)   Woolman, J., Grundig International Ltd, Rugby, UK. Private communication to author.

(4)   Whitlock, N., Cambridge Industries Ltd, Theale, UK. Private communication to author.

(5)   Morgan G. and Jackson, B., R.L. Drake Company, Ohio, USA. Private communication to author.

(6)   Cockerill, M. and Bone, A., PACE Micro Technology Ltd, Shipley West Yorks, UK. Private communication to author.

(7)   McCrae, G., Kesh Electronics, County Fermanagh, NI. Private communication to author.

(8)   Salter, J. (1983) *'SP5000' Single Chip Frequency Synthesis.* Plessey Semi-conductors Ltd, UK.

(9)   Beech, B. and Moor, S. (1985) 'Threshold Extension Techniques'. *IBA Report 130/84* Independent Broadcasting Authority UK.

(10) Moller, L.G. and Danmark, T. (1997) 'COFDM and the choice of parameters for DVB-T'. *Proceedings of International Television Symposium*, Montreux, pp. 270–280.

(11) Combelles, P. *et al.* (1997) 'Results from the DVBird Project'. *Proceedings of International Television Symposium*, Montreux, pp. 235–239.

(12) Citta, R. and Sgrignoli, G. (1997) 'ATSC Transmission System'. *Proceedings of International Television Symposium*, Montreux, pp. 281–297.

(13) Reimars, U. (1994) 'Future Digital Transmission'. *Television*, Journal of the Royal Television Society, Sept. pp. 29–34.

(14) Bramble, S., Maxim Integrated Products UK Ltd, Theale, UK. Private communication to author.

(15) Dubreuil, A. and Gautier, I., Comatlas, Cesson-Sevigné, France. Private communication to author.

(16) Maynard, J. (1985) *Cable Television*. London: Collins Professional and Technical Books Ltd.

(17) Senior, J. (1985) *Optical Fiber Communications: Principles and Practice*. London: Prentice-Hall International Inc.

(18) Andrews, P.V., Grigsby, R. *et al.* (1984) 'A Portable Self-aligning Fusion Splicer for Single-mode Fibres'. *International Wire and Cable Symposium*, Nevada, USA. (BICC Research and Engineering Ltd, UK.)

(19) Grigsby, R., BICC Research and Engineering Ltd, UK. Private communication to author.

(20) Henry, D.G., DGH Communications Systems Ltd, Ontario, Canada. Private communication to author.

(21) Evans, W.E., E.B Systems Ltd, Winnipeg, Manitoba, Canada. Private communication to author.

Chapter 12

Television sound and radio channels

12.1 DEVELOPMENT OF ANALOGUE SYSTEMS

Throughout almost fifty years of television engineering development the sound channel tended to be neglected, at least as far as the receiver design and construction were concerned. Although broadcasters invariably tried to radiate a high-quality signal, the set manufactures somehow failed to find a significant marketplace for television with hi-fi sound. The cabinet of the typical vision receiver could in no way match the acoustic properties of even a simple design of loudspeaker enclosure. The big improvements in audio quality provided through the introduction of the compact disc system created a new enthusiasm for better audio quality, including stereo and even surround sound, to enhance the total viewing experience. This has been further encouraged by satellite television, where the overspill of national boundaries and the increasing number of polyglot communities have produced a demand for parallel bilingual sound channels.

The Zenith GE pilot tone system, which has been used for many years for terrestrial VHF/FM radio, provided the basis for a number of television variants that could provide a satisfactory service provided that the sound channel was delivered through a separate hi-fi audio system.

The Leaming system

In this variant of the Zenith GE system, the two audio stereo channels (L and R) were first added and subtracted. The difference signal (L-R) was then used to amplitude-modulate a 38 kHz sub-carrier using DBSSC. In order to regenerate an accurate sub-carrier at the receiver, a 19 kHz pilot tone was added, together with the sum signal (L + R), to form the baseband frequency multiplex. This could be companded to improve SNR, before being used to frequency-modulate the final RF carrier. The receiver decoder had to contain a *whistle filter* to remove the beat note between the pilot tone and the line timebase frequency.

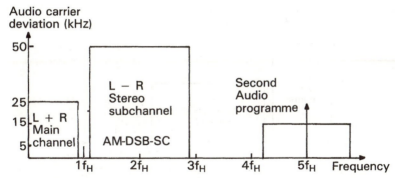

Figure 12.1 BTSC multi-channel stereo sound spectrum.

Broadcast Television Systems Committee (BTSC) Multi-channel Television Sound (MTS) system

This variant uses a pilot tone and sub-carrier locked to the horizontal timebase frequency to avoid the beat note problem. The baseband frequency multiplex is shown in Figure 12.1. In addition to the sum and difference signal components, a separate audio programme (SAP) channel is provided. This represents a 12 kHz wide audio band, which is frequency modulated on to a sub-carrier at five times the line frequency. Both the L-R and SAP components are companded. The SAP channel may provide an alternative language version of the main programme, or may be completely unrelated to it. In certain cases, a further *professional channel* can be located at 6.5 times the line frequency. This narrowband (3.4 kHz) channel is provided *for talkback* during outside broadcasts. The decoder phase adjustment can be critical and such errors can impair the channel separation.

Japanese FM-FM system

The sub-carrier of this system is locked to the second harmonic of the horizontal timebase. The sub-carrier channel may carry either the (L-R) stereo component or a mono second language signal as frequency modulation. An amplitude-modulated 55 kHz sub-carrier is used to convey to the receiver decoder the necessary control signals for automatic switching between bilingual and stereo operation. The composite baseband multiplex, which is shown in Figure 12.2, is then used to frequency-modulate the final RF carrier. The system offers good mono/stereo/bilingual compatibility, is easy to implement and the decoders are relatively simple. However, the rather wide bandwidth can give rise to adjacent channel interference problems.

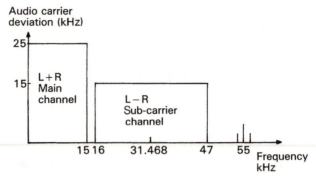

Figure 12.2 Japanese FM-FM system spectrum.

12.2 MULTI-CARRIER CHANNEL OPERATION

It was demonstrated (1) that as many as eight or ten FM sub-carriers could be added to the normal video/sound channel spectrum without any significant effects on the video SNR or the demodulator threshold. Wegener Communications Inc. devised a standardized sub-carrier band plan for such operation. This allows not only for the programme audio channel, but also for non-related signals, such as data communications. The main criteria are that the FM modulation index should be between 0.14 and 0.18 and that the sub-carriers should be spaced by 180 kHz. Provided that the total sub-carrier deviations are small compared to that produced by the video signal, their contribution to the total bandwidth is insignificant.

Each 180 kHz slot can be allocated to 15 kHz of audio, or further subdivided for either 7.5 or 3.5 kHz of audio, or even for data, using FSK or QPSK, etc. One Dolby ADM channel can be accommodated in two adjacent 180 kHz slots. For NTSC applications, the sub-carriers are typically disposed between 5.2 and 8.5 MHz. The equivalent distribution on PAL systems lies between 6.3 and 7.94 MHz.

Wegener 1600 stereo system

This stereo system is a sub-set of the Wegener band plan. The left (L) and right (R) audio channels each frequency-modulate (FM) separate sub-carriers spaced by 180 kHz. These FM sub-carriers are then used to frequency-modulate the final RF carrier, a technique often referred to as FM^2, two commonly used sub-carriers being 7.02 and 7.20 MHz. Companding of both audio channels is employed to improve signal-to-noise ratio and a sub-carrier deviation of ±50 kHz is allowed.

Two different companding standards are in use. PANDA I is a broadband, 2:1 companded linear system which under certain conditions suffers from system noise. It is therefore only satisfactory for high-level audio signals. PANDA II, which is now more common, resolves the problem by splitting each audio channel into two at 2.1 kHz and then applying companding with a ratio of 3:1 to each segment.

Warner Amex system

This is a dual sub-carrier system, in which sum (L + R) and difference (L – R) audio signals are generated and used to frequency-modulate separate sub-carriers. This multiplex is then in turn used to frequency-modulate the main sound carrier.

Zweiton (Germany) dual channel stereo system

Unlike the Zenith GE variants that transmit the sum (L + R) and difference (L – R) components within a baseband multiplex, this system transmits the sum component on the main carrier and the additional difference information on a sub-carrier. This is done because the conventional decoding matrix that is used for sum and difference components, shown in Figure 12.3(a), typically only achieves about 35 dB of channel separation. This is insufficient for dual language operation. In addition, the noise due to an interfering signal (N), which will affect each channel equally, tends to concentrate in one channel output. This can be simply explained as follows, assuming that the two inputs are $\frac{1}{2}$(R+L) + N and $\frac{1}{2}$(R–L) + N respectively:

For the sum channel:

$$(\tfrac{1}{2}(R+L)+N) + (\tfrac{1}{2}(R-L)+N)$$
$$= R/2 + L/2 + N + R/2 - L/2 + N$$
$$= R + 2N \tag{12.1}$$

For the difference channel:

$$(\tfrac{1}{2}(R+L)+N) - (\tfrac{1}{2}(R-L)+N)$$
$$= R/2 + L/2 + N - R/2 + L/2 - N$$
$$= L \tag{12.2}$$

The noise is thus shown to have concentrated in the right channel.

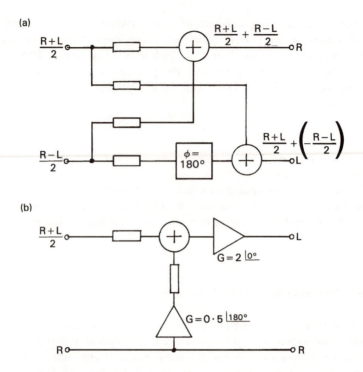

Figure 12.3 Stereo decoder matrices. **(a)** Zenith system. **(b)** Zweiton system.

By transmitting the stereo signals as R + L and 2R, and by using the decoding matrix shown in Figure 12.3(b), the new conditions are as follows:

For the left channel:

$$2(\tfrac{1}{2}(R + L) + N) + (-\tfrac{1}{2}(R + N))$$

$$= R + L + 2N - R - N$$

$$= L + N \qquad\qquad (12.3)$$

The right channel is simply:

$$= R + N \qquad\qquad (12.4)$$

Thus the noise is now equally distributed across the two channels.

This state is achieved by the use of two carriers: one placed at 5.5 MHz as normal, and the second at 5.742 MHz above the vision carrier (Figure 12.4). This latter may carry a second language. In order to minimize any cross-talk, its level

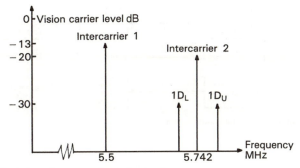

Figure 12.4 Dual channel spectrum for audio signals.

is maintained 7 dB below the level of the main sound carrier. Compatibility with mono receivers is assured because the main carrier conveys the sum (L + R) signal. There are thus three modes of transmission: mono, stereo and bilingual. Mode control is automatically effected by additional signalling on the second carrier. This is frequency-modulated with a deviation of ±2.5 kHz, with an identification signal consisting of a 54.6875 kHz pilot sub-carrier, which is unmodulated for mono transmissions and amplitude-modulated to 50 percent by tones of 117.5 and 274.1 Hz for stereo and dual language sound respectively. Both the sound carriers and the control signals are multiples or sub-multiples of the line scan frequency.

The basic operation of this decoder can be explained with the aid of Figure 12.5. The modulation recovered from the two sound carriers is dematrixed as necessary and then de-emphasized. An ID decoder identifies the particular mode of transmission and generates logic-switching signals. These allow the audio switch unit to provide the appropriate outputs. As most receivers designed for this system have headphone listening facilities, the switch unit provides dual outputs.

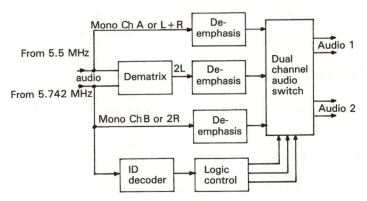

Figure 12.5 Block diagram of Zweiton dual channel stereo decoder.

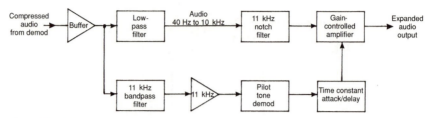

Figure 12.6 Pilot tone controlled audio expander.

The system is relatively economical to implement and has the necessary mono/stereo/bilingual flexibility. Under conditions of adjacent channel interference, however, a buzz on sound and/or a patterning on vision can be produced.

Gorizont sound channels

This Russian Federation C band satellite system transmits SECAM TV with the main sound channel frequency-modulated and located 7 MHz above the vision carrier. It also carries a radio programme on a sub-carrier of 7.5 MHz. The TV sound channel, which has a baseband extending to 10 kHz, is non-linearly companded. The low-level audio components thus produce almost the same deviation as do the high-level ones. An 11 kHz pilot tone is added to convey the control information to the receiver expander, the pilot tone being amplitude-modulated at syllabic rate. Figure 12.6 shows how the received audio component is processed. The audio and pilot tone are separated using filters; the pilot tone is demodulated and its varying dc voltage used to control the gain of a voltage-controlled amplifier, thus restoring the original dynamic range. An 11 kHz notch filter is needed to prevent unwanted whistles due to the pilot tone. The separation filters are rather critical. Any high-frequency audio component reaching the pilot tone detector will generate a false control, allowing accentuation of sibilants ('essing'). The time constant circuit is also fairly critical. If this is too long, the expansion will not be sufficient; if too short, the audio level will fluctuate.

12.3 DIGITAL DEVELOPMENTS

Dolby adaptive delta modulation (ADM) digital audio system (AC-1)

Delta modulation (DM) uses only one bit per sample to indicate whether the analogue signal level is increasing or decreasing in amplitude. This effective bit rate reduction technique allows the use of a higher sampling frequency, which in turn leads to a simpler filter arrangement in the decoder, without the risk of aliasing. Unlike PCM, a single bit in error produces the same signal effect wherever it occurs. When a bit error is detected in a DM system, the introduction of an opposite polarity bit will reduce the audible effect to practically zero. The only major disadvantage is that an overload can arise when the signal amplitude being sampled changes by more than the step size. Dolby Laboratories Inc. (2) have devised an adaptive delta modulation (ADM) system that has been adopted for use with the B-MAC system used over the Australian DBS service. This uses a variable step size to overcome the overloading and variable pre-emphasis to further improve the overall SNR.

At the encoder of the ADM system, a pre-emphasis section analyses the frequency spectrum of the audio signal to determine the optimum pre-emphasis characteristic. After pre-emphasis, the signal is passed to a step size section, which continually evaluates the signal slope to select the step size. The pre-emphasis and step size information is coded into two low bit rate control signals. The main audio signal is then digitized and delayed by an extra 10 ms. This allows the control signals to reach the decoder in time to process the audio signal in a complementary manner.

The digital data is formatted into blocks for transmission, when provision is made for synchronization. Two types of format are provided for: one for bursty systems such as sound-in-syncs or B-MAC, and the other for continuous channels.

The basic function of the ADM decoder can be explained by Figure 12.7. After demodulation, the signal is filtered to separate out the components. The audio data for each channel typically runs at a bit rate of 200–300 kbit/s and the control data at 7.8 kbit/s (half line rate). The audio data is clocked into a multiplier stage as a bipolar signal, with the step size data acting as the multiplying constant. It is then converted into analogue format using a leaky integrator. The de-emphasis control signal functions in a similar way, but instead of being used as a gain varying element, this amplifier stage functions as a variable, single-pole frequency, de-emphasis network. The decoder, which is available as an IC from several sources, is simple and relatively insensitive to component tolerances.

Dolby AC-2 or Dolby-Fax (3, 4)

The AC-1 system is not too well suited to the high quality needs of a studio environment where the sampling rate would need to be much higher. At audio frequencies exceeding about 15 kHz there is also a problem of making the step-size changes adequately track the waveform envelope. These problems and the need to pass high-grade audio signals across the ISDN system between originating studios and mixing centres resulted in the development of the Dolby AC-2 system. This system employs an aural perceptual coding and masking concept that not only provides a very high audio quality, but also achieves a bit rate reduction ratio that ranges from about 4 to 12. (Reference to the Fletcher-Munsen or NPL curves will show how the human ear becomes very much less sensitive to sound energy at frequencies below about 200 Hz and above about 8 kHz.)

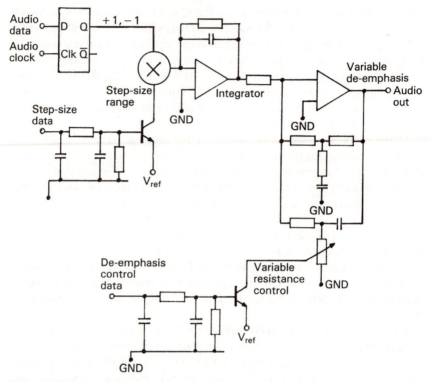

Figure 12.7 ADM decoder.

The four-step encoding process involves:

- Analogue-to-digital conversion to create PCM samples.
- Analysis of the PCM signal components for frequency spectral content.
- Compare this analysis with a model of the human hearing process.
- Code the most audible part of the spectrum with greatest accuracy and hence the highest number of bits. Ignore those components below the threshold of audibility and code the remainder according to amplitude or significance.

Instead of using a digital filter bank to generate a set of sub-bands, the AC-2 system employs an adaptive transform coding (ATC) which is based on the fast Fourier transform (FFT). This translates the time-varying signals into their frequency-varying equivalents. The system can achieve a lossless data compression ratio of about 6 and by using a Reed–Solomon FEC algorithm can provide protection against random burst errors of up to one in 10^5.

At the sampling rate of 48 kHz with 18-bit resolution, a data throughput of 256 kbit/s can be obtained, a figure that is compatible with the basic ISDN access rate of multiples of 64 kbit/s. A frequency response extending from 20 Hz to 20 kHz flat to within ±0.2 dB and a dynamic range of better than 108 dB with

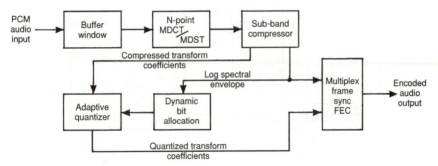

Figure 12.8 Dolby AC-2 audio digital encoder.

cross-talk below –120 dBc can be achieved. These parameters are achieved with an encode/decode delay of less than 40 ms.

Figure 12.8 summarizes the way in which the audio signal is processed using the AC-2 technology. The PCM input stream is organized into frames of N-length samples in the buffer stage. Because the frames overlap each other by 50 percent the first N/2 samples in each frame are the last N/2 samples from the previous frame so that N input samples are spread across two frames. The buffered frames are then multiplied by a window function that reduces the effect of the frame boundaries. Windowing also helps to improve the frequency analysis action of the encoder.

The time to frequency domain transformation is based on evenly stacked time domain aliasing cancellation (TDAC) functions which consist of alternating modified discrete cosine and sine transforms (MDCT and MDST). Using this technique, only N/2 non-zero transform coefficients are generated. The TDAC components are then compared with an auditory model by grouping adjacent coefficients into sub-bands for further compression. The fixed point coefficients of a sub-band are then converted into a floating point format where the exponents represent the quantized peak log amplitude for that sub-band. This then controls the dynamic bit allocation in a feed-forward manner. This allocation process then provides the step-size information for the adaptive quantizer. Each sub-band mantissa is thus quantized to a bit resolution defined by the sum of the fixed and dynamic allocation. In the final stage, the exponents are multiplexed and interleaved with the mantissa bits for transmission over the network for processing by the decoder which functions in a complementary manner.

Dolby AC-3 system (5)

Like the AC-2 system from which it was derived, Dolby AC-3 is an ATC system that uses a frequency linear, critically sampled filter-bank based on TDAC. The prime advantage of this is that it maximizes the masking effect, minimizes the

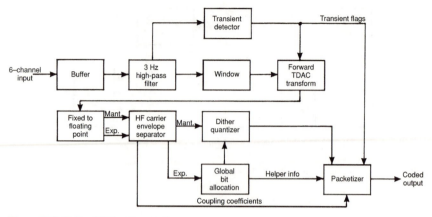

Figure 12.9 Dolby AC-3 audio encoder.

data rate and improves the perceptual effect of virtually noise-free decoding. In the presence of transients, the block length of the filter-bank can be dynamically reduced to limit quantization noise. AC-3 is described as a 5.1 channel system designed for surround sound applications such as the movie cinema. It thus provides five full bandwidth channels for Left (L), Right (R), Centre (C), Left surround (L_s) and Right surround (R_s) with a limited bandwidth low-frequency sub-woofer channel.

The important system parameters include:

- Sampling rates, 32 kbit/s, 44.1 kbit/s, 48 kbit/s.
- Resolution, up to 20 bits.
- Frequency response, 20 Hz to 20 kHz flat within ±0.2 dB.
- Dynamic range, better than −120 dBc at 1 kHz.
- Data rates, from 192 kbit/s for two channels, 384 kbit/s for 5.1 system up to 640 kbit/s for multiple channels.
- Encode/decode delay, ranging from 140 ms at 48 kHz, to 210 ms at 32 kHz sampling rates.

Figure 12.9 shows the general principles involved in the encoding process (the decoder processing is virtually complementary). The data for up to six channels is collected in the input buffer stage and organized into 512 samples per block for the proceeding stages. The transient detector stage detects the presence of signal transients and this information is used to adjust the block size of the TDAC-based filter-bank which helps to minimize the quantization noise associated with very sudden changes of amplitude. Windowing is applied as with the AC-2 system and the time domain signals are filtered with the TDAC filter-bank. The complete 5.1 channel ensemble is treated as a single entity and only the sub-woofer component is treated differently. The remainder of this part of the circuit and the fixed to floating point conversion stage performs much as in the AC-2 system.

The carrier pre-combination stage carries out some quite complex processing based on the number of channels being processed and the basic bit rate. It is shown in the references (5) that the total bit rate for multiple channels is approximately proportional to the bit rate for one channel and the square root of the number of channels. Thus if 128 kbit/s is needed to code a single channel, it will take $128\sqrt{5.1} = 289$ kbit/s to handle a 5.1 channel system. This stage also separates out the high-frequency sub-band signals into envelope and carrier information and generally codes the envelope component with greater precision than the carrier information. The mantissa and exponent outputs from this stage are in the form of matrix arrays, while the coupling coefficients are just a series of scalar values.

The global bit allocation stage allows the coding to be adjusted to suit the inter-channel masking effect in relationship with the absolute hearing threshold to the number of bits required to code each mantissa. To minimize the bit rate, this operation is carried out globally over the ensemble of channels.

The results of the bit allocation process are used to quantize the TDAC mantissa data, a dither component being added to provide a zero-centred quantization level. The dither component is generated via a pseudo-random binary sequence process.

The packetizing stage converts each block of the six channels of time signals into a series of arrays and scalar values, including the TDAC exponents and mantissas. This information is then packed into a single block that carries a header plus the necessary timing and synchronizing signals.

Dolby Pro-Logic and surround sound (the home cinema)

The Dolby surround sound system operates on the premise that two micro-phones placed to the left (L) and right (R) of a sound stage will respond not only to the direct L and R components of sound, but also to signals arriving from the centre, sides and rear of an auditorium. Thus just two suitably phased signals L_t and R_t can be used to represent the total sound information. If L_t and R_t are suitably processed, then the left, right, centre (C), left rear and right rear (S) signal components can be regenerated to provide a surround sound effect. The original analogue concept developed for cinema applications was known as the SR system. This was eventually digitized and then referred to as SR-D, where blocks of digital data were encoded into the gaps between the film sprocket holes. The concept is referred to as a 5.1 system catering for L, R, C, S, plus a band-limited bass signal. This concept has carried over into the broadcast and domestic market as Dolby Pro-Logic and by using a suitable decoder, it is possible to re-create a very accurate representation of the original sound stage.

Figure 12.10 indicates the basic principles involved in decoding the Pro-Logic signal. The two components L_t and R_t are passed through a level control stage and input digital buffer before being applied to an adaptive matrix. This stage

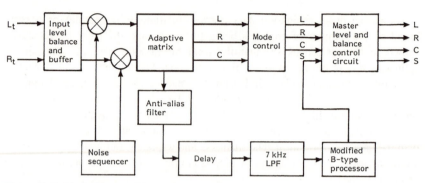

Figure 12.10 Block diagram of Dolby Pro-Logic decoding.

determines the dominance of the signal components being processed. This is achieved by full-wave rectifying the L, R, L – R and L + R elements and then taking a logarithmic difference to generate a set of control voltages. These are bipolar DC signals of varying levels that are vector representations of the sound space. These voltages are then used to control the gain of a number of voltage-controlled amplifiers. The surround component of the signal is anti-alias filtered at the matrix, delayed, low-pass filtered and then processed through a modified Dolby B-type decoder to provide the surround component. When enabled, the noise sequencer stage injects pink noise into each channel in turn, to allow the user to check and adjust the system balance controls.

MPEG audio

This system has been developed for use with MPEG-coded video signals and achieves CD audio quality with a bit rate reduction that employs the masking effect. This was originally based on a four-layer format depending upon the sampling and bit rates. However, this has now merged into Layer I and Layer II versions.

As with the video signal, the audio is compressed to form elementary streams (ES) which are then formatted to form packetized streams (PES). These are then multiplexed into transport streams of 188-byte length packets. A single programme transport stream can then be combined into a multi-programme transport stream for transmission.

As run-length or entropy coding does not work very effectively with audio signals, MPEG makes use of the masking effect to create bit rate compression. The psychoacoustic model assumes that if a frequency component in the signal cannot be heard then there is no need to transmit it due to the masking effect. The system thus makes use of the threshold of audibility feature shown in the Fletcher-Munsen or NPI curves.

AES/EBU PCM samples are divided into thirty-two sub-bands which are then analysed for redundant and irrelevant information and because only those samples above the threshold of audibility are coded, a useful bit rate reduction is achieved. If any bit periods are unused, these can be dynamically allocated to other sub-bands. This process is somewhat similar to the fast packet protocol that is used with ATM networks. Both encoding and decoding circuits are usually controlled via microprocessors or dedicated DSP chips.

Layer I and Layer II systems are based on 384 or 1152 (3 × 384) samples respectively. The 384 or 1152 samples are divided into twelve or thirty-six groups each of thirty-two samples and these provide the input to the 32-sub-band filter-bank. Data is not compressed or lost at this stage. The output from the filter-bank is amplitude-scaled to generate a scaling factor and quantized if above the threshold level for the band. It is at this stage that data compression is achieved. Finally the twelve or thirty-six groups of samples are multiplexed into the standard 188-byte frames.

The important system performance parameters include the following:

- Sampling rates: 32 kHz, 44.1 kHz or 48 kHz
- Resolution: 16, 18, 20 or 24 bits
- Frequency response: 20 Hz to 20 kHz, flat within ±0.25 dB
- Pre-emphasis/de-emphasis: provision for either 15 μs, 50 μs or J17 time constants
- Dynamic range: up to −120 dBc at 1 kHz
- Data rates: up to 2 Mbyte/s
- Encode/decode delay: ranges from 107 to 161 ns at 48 and 32 kHz sampling respectively

Because of the complexity of the signal processing, it is important to provide a reference receiver to manage the quality of service, particularly in the studio or production environments. Dolby Inc. have designed two encoder/decoder units, the DP503 and DP524, that meet these requirements and can process AC-2, AC-3 and MPEG Layer II signals.

The AES/EBU (Audio Engineering Society/European Broadcasting Union) interface

This standard interface provides for the interconnection of either professional or consumer equipment via a serial digital communications link. The concept allows audio and video data to be mixed on a recording medium and even share the same encoding/decoding circuits. By passing the signals in digital format, there is no degradation as would normally occur when using analogue transmission with A/D and D/A conversions at each end. The system handles PCM sampling rates of 32, 44.1 or 48 kHz, all software controlled via the bit stream. The resolution range includes 16, 18, 20 or 24 bits to allow headroom for signal degradation during subsequent mixing, processing or recording.

The equipment can provide for either 4 × 15 kHz audio channels on a 2.048 Mbit/s ISDN stream using 14-bit linear PCM or 5 × 15 kHz or 10 × 7 kHz channels using instantaneous companding with 10 bits resolution. A similar wide spread of single channel bit rates are included in the specification, ranging from 32 × 11 kbit/s in a transmission network to 48 × 24 kbit/s in a studio feed.

Communications are standardized on a single twisted pair cable using XLR connectors as previously used for analogue audio signalling, although an additional cable screen may be provided.

The transmission bit stream is divided into two sub-frames each of 32 bits duration. The sub-frame period is thus dependent on the sampling rate. Sub-frame A is reserved for the left-hand channel stream, while sub-frame B carries the corresponding right-hand channel. Alternatively, both sub-frames may be allocated to a mono channel and the necessary information about this is included in the housekeeping bits multiplexed into the data stream.

The first four bits of each sub-frame act as a preamble and time sync. Three different preamble sequences are used to select either the start of Sub-frame A, Sub-frame B or a special frame that contains the beginning of a 192-bit house-keeping sequence. These are referred to as the Sync X, Y or Z preambles. The following four bits (LSB first) are described as auxillary bits and these can be used either to provide an extra four bits of precision for the sampled code words or to provide a low-grade parallel voice channel. The following twenty bits (again LSB first) represent audio data. Thus under software-controlled conditions, each sub-frame might contain twenty-four audio sample bits. The last nibble in each sub-frame carries further housekeeping bits. Of these, the first or 'V' acts as a validity flag to indicate if the sample is suitable for conversion back into analogue format. The next 'U' bit is allocated to the user's own messages and forms one bit of a 192-bit long sequence derived from each frame. The penultimate 'C' bit is a channel status bit; like the 'U' bit, it can be used to create a 24-byte sequence over successive frames and signifies if the system is in the professional or consumer mode, mono or stereo mode, the sample rate or quantization word length, etc. The final 'P' bit acts as even parity for the sub-frame (excluding sync). If parity fails the system can employ either error concealment or muting. As a second function, because of even parity, this bit has the same value as the bit at the start, thus ensuring that the sync pattern is always received with the same polarity.

The 24-byte (192 bits) channel status data contains the following information:

Byte	0	Professional/consumer
	1	Channel usage
	2	Word length
	3	Vectored target byte for byte 0
	4 & 5	Reserved for expansion
	6–9	Four ASCII characters plus one bit odd parity, origin channel

10–13 Four ASCII characters plus odd parity, destination channel
14–17 Local address code
18–21 32-bit binary time code
22   Data reliability flags
23   CRC for bytes 0–22

If the consumer interface is identified, byte 1 can identify the data source, either CD, DAT or other digital source. This can also invoke the Serial Management Copy System Agreement which will only permit one digital copy of a CD, a pre-recorded DAT tape or a digital broadcast to be made.

12.4 DIGITAL SOUND CHANNELS ON ANALOGUE TV SYSTEMS

Wegener SDM 2000 digital audio transmission system

This concept, based on Dolby ADM, is intended to provide stereo radio/audio programmes with a quality equivalent to 14 bits resolution for redistribution over an analogue cable TV network. The system utilizes the band space of two Wegener sub-carriers to carry two digitally encoded audio signals in a total bandwidth of about 250 kHz. A total of 512 kbit/s data stream is modulated on to a carrier using QPSK to have the required bandwidth. This leaves space for additional channels that may be allocated as one 19.2 kbaud synchronous data, plus fifteen remote control commands and one encryption control command if necessary.

D-MAC sound and data channels

The MAC system was basically devised to separate the transmission and processing of the luma and chrome components of the video signal by using time compression, to combat the cross-colour effects associated with the analogue services. At the same time, this gave an opportunity to improve the sound channel quality by changing to a bursty transmission of digital signals. By using a digital code to replace the traditional analogue sync pulses, there was enough space within the vertical blanking interval to include a range of audio options plus a digital data service.

Currently only the D2-MAC variant has survived, mostly for use via satellites within the Scandinavian region. The bit stream is interleaved to minimize the effects of burst errors and randomized by mixing with a pseudo-random binary sequence for energy dispersal. The D-MAC specification provided for a *duo-binary* PSK signal format with the full bit rate of 20.25 Mbit/s but this was reduced to 10.125 Mbit/s for the D2-MAC version.

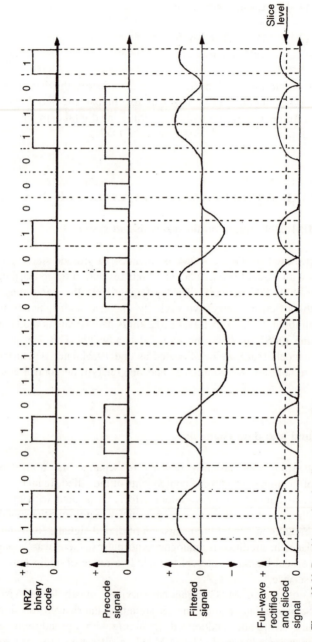

Figure 12.11 Duo-binary signal coding and decoding.

The coding process is carried out from the NRZ format as shown in Figure 12.11. This first replaces each binary 0 with a signal transition at the bit cell centre, and a binary 1 with no transition. This new signal is then passed through a filter with a cut-off bandwidth at the half-Nyquist value (about 5.06 MHz for D2-MAC). This generates an analogue type of signal with a small DC component. Due to filtering, adjacent transitions of opposite sense tend to cancel and leave the signal with an average zero value. A series of two or more 1s or 0s produce positive and negative peaks respectively, the duration of each peak being proportional to the number of successive similar bits. As shown in Figure 12.11, the original data signal can be recovered very simply by full-wave rectification, followed by slicing at the half-amplitude level.

The total transmission signal bandwidth is about 13 MHz and the audio channel provides for one high-quality stereo channel, plus a lower grade audio channel and a limited data service.

Vertical Interval Multiple Channel Audio System (VIMCAS)

An important feature that has to be considered when planning to add stereo audio to an established mono television network is the cost of modifying all the transmitters. An Australian organization, IRT Ltd, have developed a *bolt-on* black box system that neatly side-steps this problem. Known by the acronym VIMCAS, this system can be used for satellite and terrestrial television and video recorders without modification to the original system.

Basically the system transmits time-compressed and companded audio signals during spare line periods of the field blanking interval. Each line can support an audio base bandwidth of approximately 4.7 kHz, so that six lines can provide for a pair of stereo channels 14 kHz wide. Alternatively, multiple lines can be used for dual language or data transmissions. Figure 12.12 shows the general principles involved. Each audio channel signal is band limited and compressed while in the analogue form. The signal is then sampled and quantized and loaded into a digital memory. At the time of the appropriate video line, the memory is read out at a very much higher rate to achieve time compression. This is then converted back into analogue form and gated into the video signal. The time-compressed audio signal now has a bandwidth of about 2.5 MHz, so that it is well within the capacity of the video signal channel. Reference to Figure 12.12(b) shows that decoding is achieved in a complementary manner. Any additional channels require dedicated A/D converters and digital memories but can share the final D/A converter, because these are used on a gated basis.

Where several contiguous lines are used for wideband audio, there is a duplication of signal at the end and beginning of successive lines. This is done to ensure that the signal at the beginning of a line, which is most likely to be corrupted by interference or distortion, can be discarded. In operation, the system has been found to be very flexible, it being possible to mix wide and narrowband signals without cross-talk. Scrambling can be provided in the digital domain of

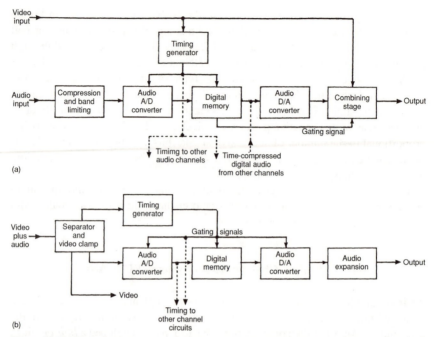

Figure 12.12 Block diagrams for the Vertical Interval Multiple Channel Audio System. **(a)** Encoding. **(b)** Decoding.

processing, or simply by alternating the line sequences. With video tape recording, the signals are not affected by head switching and wow and flutter are said to be negligible due to the method of synchronism in use.

NICAM-728 stereo audio system (6)

The system which is known as NICAM-728 (Near Instantaneous Companded Audio Multiplex – 728 kbit/s), has been adapted to suit all PAL or NTSC systems. It provides almost CD quality stereo audio to be delivered direct to the home along with a television signal and is also capable of including a data service such as teletext.

The NICAM signal structure

In the interests of compatibility, NICAM transmissions retain the standard 6 MHz monophonic FM audio channel and place the digital signal on a second sub-carrier located at 6.552 MHz or 9 × 728 kHz above the vision carrier. For the PAL systems that use 5.5 MHz sound carriers, the NICAM sub-carrier is located at about 5.85 MHz above the vision carrier. The sub-carrier, which is maintained at a level of −20 and −10 dB relative to the peak vision and sound carriers respectively, is differentially encoded with the digital signals for both channels of the stereo pair using quadrature (4 phase) PSK modulation. Using this scheme, each carrier resting phase represents two data bits and so halves the bandwidth requirements. Because the data is differentially encoded (DQPSK) it is only the phase changes that have to be detected at the receiver decoder. The bits-to-phase-change relationships are as follows:

- 00 = −0°   phase change,
- 01 = −90°   phase change,
- 11 = −180° phase change,
- 10 = −270° phase change.

By using this Gray code scheme, only one bit change is needed for each step phase shift, making the signal more robust in noisy conditions. Pre-emphasis/de-emphasis to CCITT Recommendation J.17, which provides 6.5 dB boost or cut at 800 Hz, is applied to the sound signal either when in the analogue state, or by using digital filters in the digital domain.

The left- and right-hand audio channels are simultaneously sampled at 32 kHz, coded and quantized separately to 14 bits resolution and transmitted alternately at a frame rate of 728 kbit/s. Using the formula of $(1.76 + 6.02n)$ dB for bipolar signals shows that where $n = 14$ bits per sample this yields a quantization noise of about 86 dB.

The NICAM compander processes the 14-bit samples in the manner shown in Figure 12.13 and the protocol for discarding bits can be summarized as follows:

> The most significant bit (MSB) is retained and the four following bits are dropped if and only if they are of the same consecutive value as the MSB. If this leaves a word longer than ten bits, then the excess bits are dropped from the least significant bit (LSB) region.

A single even parity bit is added to check the six MSB bits in each word. The data stream is then organized into blocks of thirty-two 11-bit words in the two's complement format. This is used because it provides for both positive and negative signal values. A 3-bit compression scaling factor is calculated from the magnitude of the largest sample in each block and this is then encoded into the parity bits for that block. At the receiver, the scale factor can be extracted using a majority voting logic circuit. At the same time, this process restores the original parity bit pattern.

Two blocks of data are then interleaved in a 16×44 (704 bits) matrix, to minimize the effects of burst data errors. Adjacent bits in the original data stream are now 16 bits apart. A transmission frame multiplex is then organized in the manner shown in Figure 12.14 with additional bits being used as follows:

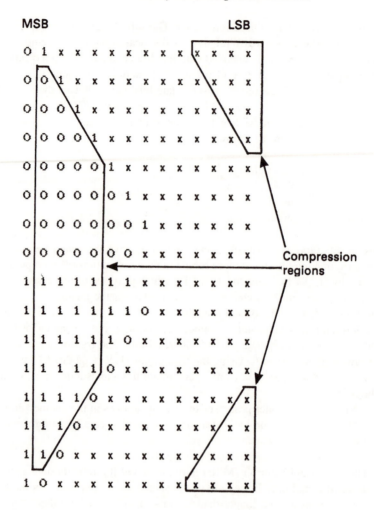

X = Don't care

Figure 12.13 NICAM 728 companding coding scheme.

- Eight bits (0100 1110) are used as a frame alignment word (FAW).
- Five control bits are used to select the mode of operation (C_0–C_4), either:
  - Stereo signal composed of alternate channel A and B samples
  - Two independent mono signals, transmitted in alternate frames
  - One mono signal plus one 352 kbit/s data channel on alternate frames
  - One 704 kb/s data channel. Plus other concepts so far undefined.
- Eleven data bits are entirely reserved for future developments.

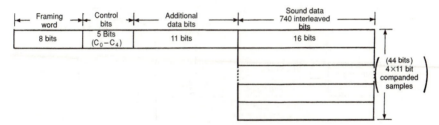

Figure 12.14 NICAM 728 frame multiplex.

Following the interleaving of the 704 sound data bits (64×11-bit samples), the complete frame, with the exception of FAW, is scrambled for energy dispersal, by adding it Fx-Or to a pseudo-random binary sequence (PRBS) of length $2^9 - 1$ (511). This 10-bit sequence (1000010001) is created by the generator polynomial, $X^9 + X^4 + 1$. At the decoder, the PRBS generator is reset on receipt of every FAW code.

To limit the signal bandwidth, the data stream is passed through a spectrum-shaping filter that removes much of the harmonic content of the data pulses. This, combined with the effect of a similar filter in the receiver, produces an overall response that is described as having a full or 100 percent cosine roll-off.

The data stream is finally divided into bit pairs to drive the DQPSK modulator of the 6.552 MHz sub-carrier.

The NICAM receiver (7)

The NICAM sub-carrier appears at either 32.948 MHz (39.5–6.552 MHz) or 6.552 MHz depending upon the adopted method for sound IF channel processing. As indicated by Figure 12.15, this component is amplified and gain controlled within the normal receiver IF stages. The spectrum-shaping filter forms part of the system overall pulse shaping and has an important effect upon the noise immunity. The overall filtering effect ensures that most of the pulse energy lies below a frequency of 364 kHz (half bit rate).

The QPSK decoder recovers the data stream and the framing word detector scans this to locate the start of each frame and reset the PRBS generator. This sequence is then added Ex-Or to the data for descrambling. The de-interleaving circuit is also synchronized by the arrival of the FAW code word.

Error control follows standard practice, but since this is buried within an IC, the process is transparent to outsiders.

The operating mode detector searches for the control bits C_0–C_4, to automatically set up the data and audio stage switches, the data outputs being those for the 352 or 704 kbit/s, options.

The NICAM expansion circuit functions in a complementary manner to the compressor, but using the scaling factor to expand the 10-bit data words into 14-bit samples.

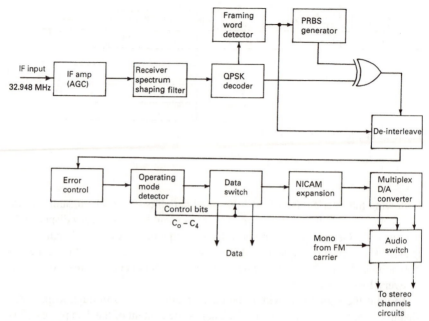

Figure 12.15 Decoding the NICAM stereo signal.

Finally, the data stream is converted back into analogue format for delivery to the audio amplifier stages. These are designed to a very high standard, because NICAM-728 has an audio quality that approaches that of the compact disc systems.

The DQPSK decoder

This complex stage is commonly embedded within an application-specific IC (ASIC) NICAM processor device. Figure 12.16, which represents this, is very much simplified. The two main sections are associated with the recovery of the carrier and bit rate clock. The first section relies on a voltage-controlled crystal oscillator running at 6.552 MHz and two phase detectors to regenerate the parallel bit pairs, referred to as the I and Q signals (in-phase and quadrature). A second similar circuit, which is locked to the bit rate of 728 kHz, is used to synchronize and recover the data stream. Parallel adaptive data slicers and differential logic circuits are used to square up the data pulses and decode the DQPSK signals. The bit pairs are then converted into serial formal. The practical decoder incorporates a third phase detector circuit driven from the Q chain. This is used as an amplitude detector to generate a muting signal if the 6.552 MHz sub-carrier is absent or fails. This mute signal is then used to switch the audio system over to the normal 6 MHz mono FM sound signal.

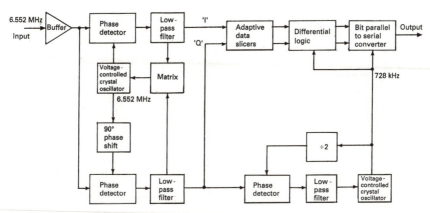

Figure 12.16 Decoding the DQPSK signal.

Apart from Europe where NICAM-728 was adopted as a stereo standard, the system has been installed in many other parts of the world, including adapation to suit the 525-line NTSC market.

12.5   SATELLITE-DELIVERED DIGITAL RADIO (ASTRA DIGITAL RADIO (ADR))

The Wegener Corporation showed that it was possible to incorporate up to ten FM sub-carriers spaced by 180 kHz, within the spectrum of the satellite-delivered sound and vision channel. They further demonstrated that some of these channels could be digitally modulated. These concepts have been further developed by the Société Européenne des Satellites (SES), the satellite provider for the ASTRA services.

The ASTRA digital radio (ADR) system

Figure 12.17(a) shows the frequency spectrum associated with the television baseband signal as applied to the ASTRA system before the introduction of ADR. The monophonic sound channel was placed at 6.5 MHz above the vision carrier and two Wegener-type stereo channels positioned at 7.02 and 7.20 MHz. At further 180 kHz intervals a group of stereo radio service sub-carriers was included. The component at 8.64 MHz is used for network control. As the provision for stereo audio became a standard feature of satellite TV receivers, the mono channel virtually became redundant. The new frequency spectrum for ASTRA satellites Series 1 birds is shown in Figure 12.17(b) with the original two stereo channels at 7.02 and 7.20 MHz being retained, leaving the spectrum to

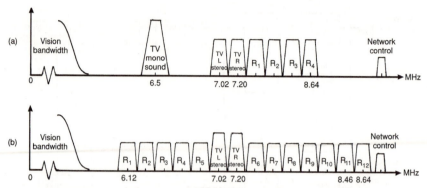

Figure 12.17 (a) Sound channel spectrum before ADR. (b) Reallocation of spectrum after introduction of ADR.

support twelve stereo radio channels each spaced by 180 kHz. Thus it becomes possible to provide twelve stereo (or twenty-four mono or any mix of the two) audio channels with each TV channel on the sixteen transponders of all the satellites. The basic parameters of the ADR system are shown in Table 12.1.

Of the 192 kbit/s audio rate, 9.6 kbit/s is reserved for service use. This can provide on-screen display information such as channel number, station name, music title, artist, etc. related to the programme being received. Encryption to the CCITT V.35 standard provides for pay channels which are switched on via a smart card system.

MUSICAM (MPEG Layer II) audio processing

The Musicam system exploits the masking effect whereby only those sounds above some threshold level of hearing convey useful information. This threshold is sensitive to the level of nearby frequency components in the signal and also to

Table 12.1 ADR transmission parameters

Audio frequency range	20 Hz to 20 kHz
Sampling frequency	48 kHz
Dynamic range	>90 dB
SNR	>96 dB
Modulation	DQPSK
Audio coding	MUSICAM (MPEG-Layer II)
Data rate	192 kbit/s total
Error control	CRC for data and scale factor
Bandwidth	130 kHz (180 kHz carrier spacing)
Encryption	IDR/IBS implementation of CCITT v.35

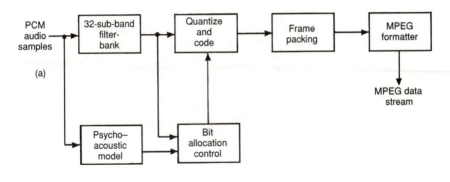

(a)

MPEG data
stream

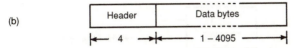

(b)

Figure 12.18 **(a)** MPEG audio processor/encoder. **(b)** MPEG audio bit stream frame format.

the actual frequencies involved. A simplified block diagram of the processor is shown in Figure 12.18(a). The PCM audio samples are filtered into thirty-two sub-bands. A model based on the perception of human hearing is then used to generate a set of data that is used to control the quantizing and coding process. Successive samples of each sub-band data are grouped into blocks in which the maximum level in each sub-band is used to calculate a scale factor. In this way, it is possible to code only those signal components above the individual threshold levels using just two or three bits to ensure that the quantization noise is inaudible. The re-quantized and coded signal words together with the scaling factor are then packed into MPEG frames in the manner shown in Figure 12.18(b). The formatter stage inserts the ancillary data bits and the error control checks. The signal is then passed to the digital modulator stage. At the receiver, the data from the set of code words is decoded to recover the different elements of the signal to reconstruct the quantized sub-band samples. An inverse filter-bank then transforms the sub-bands back into digital PCM code at the original 48 kbit/s sampling rate.

The ADR receiver

Figure 12.19 shows the several ways that the receiver can be linked to a satellite TV system which allow for radio reception even when the TV set is switched off. In Figure 12.19(a), the ADR set is coupled via a loop-through to the normal

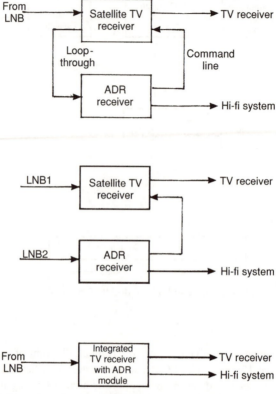

Figure 12.19 (a) Separate receivers but with loop-through control. (b) TV/radio fed via separate LNBs. (c) Combined TV/radio receiver.

satellite receiver, dividing the signal into its two constituent parts and avoiding the need for using a separate LNB as shown in Figure 12.19(b). Later-developed receivers will incorporate the ADR receiver module into the main system as implied by Figure 12.19(c). Whichever way the system is deployed, the receiver/ decoder will rely heavily on microprocessor control and phase locked loops. Figure 12.20 shows how this processing may be achieved. The input to the receiver is via an LNB which provides the first IF signal at 950–2150 MHz with the band switching, channel switching and polarization selection under the control of the microprocessor. The satellite tuner section down-converts this to the second intermediate frequency typically at 480 MHz before being amplified under the control of the AGC system. The serial digital signal is formatted into 8-bit parallel words before being input to the QPSK demodulator. Note that this stage is driven by a crystal-controlled oscillator running at 24.576 MHz and that all the other frequencies that are derived from this are all multiples of the bit rate of 192 kbit/s or sub-multiples of 24.576 MHz. The demodulated I and Q signals

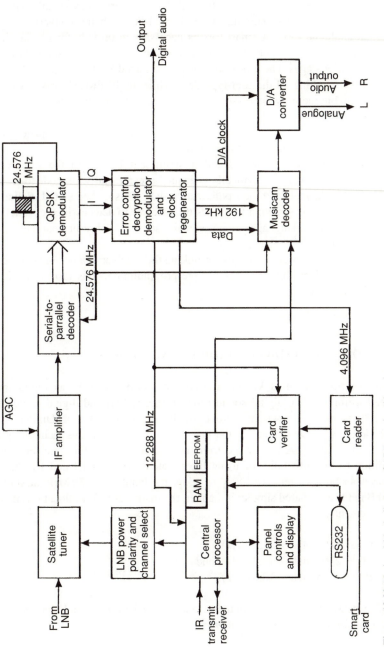

Figure 12.20 Notional block diagram of ADR receiver/decoder.

are then input to an ASIC which carries out error control, decryption and demultiplexing as well as regenerating all the necessary clock signals. The data stream is then decoded back into PCM formal before being converted into its original analogue form. A smart card is necessary to provide for pay-per-listen programmes and this function is controlled via the central processor and the card reader/verifier stages. The processor carries embedded RAM and EEPROM, with the former handling all the user-type data, while the EEPROM provides for the programmable memory necessary for channel tuning, etc. Because the ancillary data (9.6 kbit/s) carries information about each programme, additional interfaces are provided which allow this to be displayed either on the front panel of the receiver or on the remote control handset.

The central processor adds another significant feature to the receiver; at power-up the receiver automatically goes into a search and scan mode to identify all the ARD channels and their polarization data. This is then stored in memory for future use. This system also allows the receiver to detect which channels are transmitting dual language mono signals so that the user can select the appropriate one.

The RS232E interface provides for linking the receiver to a personal computer and not only does this provides for pre-programming, it is also valuable for service purposes.

12.6   DIGITAL RADIO BROADCASTING (DRB)

This concept, which is known around the world variously as digital radio broadcasting (DRB), digital sound broadcasting (DSB) and digital audio radio (DAR), is better known in Europe by its registered title of Digital Audio Broadcasting or DAB. Such is the international interest in this technology that three ranges of the frequency spectrum have been allocated for these services. In addition to the possibility of using the vacated VHF Band I and III channels (European broadcasters are likely to adopt the band 217–230 MHz at start-up) and Band II in a shared simulcast manner, the main frequency allocations include the segments:

● 1452–1492 MHz – (1.5 GHz),
● 2310–2360 MHz – (2.3 GHz), and
● 2535–2655 MHz – (2.6 GHz).

The possibility of using simulcast techniques within Band II has generated some quaint terminology, as follows:

● In band/On channel (IBOC) – the DSB signal is broadcast on the same channel frequency as occupied by the normal FM signal, hopefully without creating mutual interference.

- In band interstitial (IBI), or In band/Adjacent channel (IBAC) – the DSB signal occupies the normally taboo FM channels.
- New band (NB) – the DSB signal occupies an entirely new frequency allocation.

The DAB system (8, 9)

This system, which derived from the European Union (EU) Eureka 147 development project, is accepted by the ITU-R organization as one of the world standards for digital broadcasting. It is also covered by the European ETSI standards in document ETS 300/401. DAB is sometimes referred to internationally as Digital System A. The project developed from the perceived need to find a system that could deliver CD quality audio into moving vehicles with little or no multipath distortion effects. As the system has developed, it has been shown to be capable of delivering a much wider service to listeners, not only those that are mobile, but also as a possible future replacement for conventional sound broadcasting needs. The service can be delivered by terrestrial transmissions, satellites or even via cable networks. It can radiate high-quality signals into even the concrete canyons of built-up city areas. Bit rate reduction is achieved by using the MPEG II (Musicam) algorithm and the data stream is heavily error protected before transmission. The system can provide a range of services as follows

- Audio, stereo, mono or bi-lingual.
- Programme-associated data, programme type, transmitter identification, date, time, etc.
- Independent data for road maps, pictures and even differential GPS data.

Coded orthogonal frequency division multiplex (COFDM)

The OFDM concept consists of generating a large number of carrier frequencies with equal spacing. Each is digitally modulated with a sub-band of frequencies and then filtered to produce a (sin x)/x response. The spectra of the individual neighbouring carriers thus overlap in an orthogonal manner. When these combine, the total spectrum becomes practically flat and the channel capacity approaches the Shannon limiting value so that the spectrum of carriers behaves as a parallel transmission bus. The use of COFDM allows typically six programmes to be multiplexed into a single channel. Furthermore, other transmitters can occupy the same nominal carrier frequency to form a single frequency network (SFN) because overlapping transmissions do not generally create multipath effects. Small low-power transmitters can be employed in local areas where the loss of signals occur (in the concrete canyons) as gap filling stations. The system allows for a wide area seamless transfer of services for the same programme multiplex even if radiated from different transmitters, either satellite or terrestrial.

The allocated bandwidth is divided into N elementary frequencies and arranged to carry P programme channels. There are therefore N/P interleaved elementary carriers which carry sub-band modulation allocated to each programme. In practice, either 4 or 8 phase PSK or even 64-QAM modulation may be employed.

The system performance can be further improved by employing COFDM and it is this form that is actually in use. A fast Fourier transform (FFT) processor is used in conjunction with convolution error coding at the modulator stage. When used with a complementary FFT processor and Viterbi decoding at the demodulator, the overall bit error rate is very low. Since the COFDM spectrum has noise-like properties and the signal can be transmitted at relatively low power, it produces very little adjacent channel interference. In addition, co-channel interference from transmitters radiating exactly the same data will actually reinforce the primary signal provided that the delay is within some specific limits. This is achieved because transmitted symbols are separated by a small guard interval.

The transmission system

The multiplex of bit rate reduced audio together with its service information, programme-associated data and independent data provides a 2.048 Mbit/s data stream which is distributed to all the transmitters in the network. The multiplex configuration information (MCI) is transmitted within the programme-associated data group and this is used to ensure correct decoding. This concept can also give warning to the receiver about impending changes and so ensure a seamless changeover. The correct synchronization of the signals for each transmitter is important, hence one possible delivery system would involve the SDH (synchronous digital hierarchy) system of the telecom companies. The data is time stamped before delivery to the distribution network so that the precise time for the transmission of each packet is accurately known. This time reference may easily be obtained from an incorporated GPS (global positioning system) receiver.

Generating the transmission signal

The COFDM generator converts the 2.048 Mbit/s data stream into I and Q signals using a DSP (digital signal processing) chip. An adjustable delay is arranged via software control to ensure synchronism with other transmitters in the network. The data is modulated using DQPSK on to the individual carriers of the COFDM system. Although the gross bit rate is high, the actual rate per individual carrier is relatively low when shared between all the carriers. This feature provides much of the multipath immunity. This output is then modulated on to a relatively low RF carrier which can then be up-converted to the final transmission band. Before

Table 12.2

System parameters	Transmission mode			
	1	*2*	*3*	*4*
Max separation of TX sites (km)	96	24	12	48
Max receiver frequency (mobile Ghz)	0.375	1.5	3.0	1.5
Number of carriers	1536	384	192	768
Guard interval (μs)	250	62.5	31.25	125
Carrier spacings (kHz)	1	4	8	2

final radiation, the RF signal is bandpass filtered to remove any spurious components that might create interference with other DAB transmissions. The radiated power is relatively low; for example, using Band III VHF, the total radiated power may be around 1 kW.

Four modes of operation are defined in the standards as shown by Table 12.2.

Because all the same transmitters within a network radiate the same group of programmes within the same multiplex bandwidth, typically 1.5 MHz, DAB makes much better use of the frequency spectrum. By comparison, four VHF/FM stereo transmissions occupy at least 2.2 MHz of bandwidth.

The signal parameters for Mode 3 operation are shown in Table 12.3.

Typically each carrier of the OFDM system is unaffected by delayed signals up to 1.2 times the guard period. For the 12 km path for Mode 3 operation, this represents a signal arriving from an extra path distance of around 10 km.

For a mode 1 system operating with 1536 individual carriers, there are thus 256 carriers per programme. The carriers are spaced by 1 kHz so that with a 250 kHz guard band the occupied bandwidth is 1.537 + 0.25 = 1.787 MHz. Operating with QPSK modulation there are two binary bits per transmitted symbol. The symbol duration lasts for 1.246 ms which includes 1 ms symbol period plus 246 μs guard period. The bit rate per carrier is therefore 1.605 kbit/s, making a total transmission bit rate of about 2.465 Mbit/s. 1.2 times the guard period of 250 μs gives a figure of 300 μs which corresponds to a delay signal

Table 12.3

Frame duration	24 ms
Sync signal duration	250 μs
Total signal symbol duration	156.25 μs
Useful signal symbol duration	125 μs
Guard period	31.25 μs

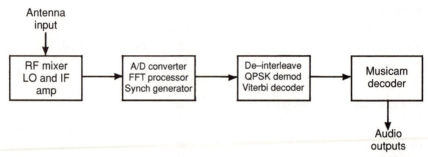

Figure 12.21 Notional block diagram of a four-chip DAB receiver.

path length of about 90 km. (From Table 12.2 the maximum transmitter site separation for Mode 1 is 96 km.)

Due to the Doppler shift introduced by moving vehicles, Mode 1 systems are limited to about 350 MHz maximum carrier frequency. By comparison, Modes 2 and 3 are limited to about 1.5 and 3 GHz respectively. It has been shown in tests that a Doppler shift of about 1/20 of the carrier frequency introduces a need for an extra 4 dB of CNR and that in general, the DAB system provides error-free decoding with a CNR value above about 10 dB.

Design of the DAB receiver
Among the many proposals that have been made that might create consumer confidence and enthusiasm for this new system, the following are the result of listening to many learned discussions. It is thought that the listener is unlikely to accept the new system unless the extra cost is somewhat below £300 within the first two to three years of production. Figure 12.21, based on the superhet principle, summarizes one possible approach. The front-end tuner, which may well operate on the homeodyne principle, needs only to be frequency switchable between channels and so could easily be produced today using surface mount technology and a dedicated ASIC chip. Eventually, the whole of this stage could be integrated into a single chip that is software controlled. If a relatively low or zero IF is chosen, then this signal could be conveniently converted into digital format at this very early stage, thus removing much of the filtering normally associated with such analogue amplifiers. Since a modern DSP chip using a 50 MHz clock can easily handle the conversion of an IF signal up to 12.5 MHz, either the superhet or the direct conversion technique can be used. A second DSP can handle all the data packet decoding, error control and demodulation. Finally, dedicated MPEG Layer-2/Musicam chips are already available. Judging by the rapid progress being made in ASIC fabrication developments, such a receiver might well be produced at most as a two-chip design before the end of this century.

12.7 THE JPL DIGITAL SYSTEM

This system, which is often referred to internationally as Digital System B, has been developed by the Jet Propulsion Laboratory (JPL) of America, under the sponsorship of the Voice of America (VOA). It is capable of delivering full CD-quality stereo audio at 384 kbit/s together with a range of lower qualities at slower bit rates right down to 32 kbit/s. The system uses convolutional encoding followed by interleaving for a high degree of error protection. Once again, DQPSK modulation is employed with the data pulses being filtered to ensure bandwidth efficiency. In order to synchronize the demodulation and de-interleaving process, a unique sync word is included within the data multiplex. The receivers for this system are designed to be resilient to fading, echoes and multipath effects by the inclusion of the following features.

- Convolutional encoding at either the 1/2 or 2/3 rate can be selected by the service provider, with the 1/2 rate being preferred for use under the most difficult conditions.
- Viterbi maximum likelihood decoding is well established for high-integrity error control systems.
- Because of the multipath effects in built-up areas and within buildings, it is suggested that space diversity reception will be necessary. This involves using more than one aerial on each receiver.
- The receiver circuitry will include an equalizer that automatically chooses between the direct and reflected signals.

12.8 THE SOFTWARE-CONTROLLED RECEIVER

The case for employing digital instead of analogue signal processing has already been made. Using chips that are standard production items that have been manufactured in large quantities significantly reduces system development costs. Furthermore, the modern technique of fabricating special ICs (ASICs) that are based on a library of cells that have been tried and tested in other circuits means that these new devices can be quickly brought to market almost as soon as a need has been established. The superhet receiver has a long-established history in the field of communications and the major problems associated with digitizing such a circuit concerns the high rate at which it is necessary to convert the analogue signal into a digital format. In the past this has been achieved by using a relatively low IF, but the introduction of a homodyne method that works well up to at least 2 GHz further simplifies the problems. In addition, it is also now possible to control the frequency changer stage by employing a digital version of the phase locked loop oscillator.

Analogue-to-digital converters (ADC) are now available with an input bandwidth of at least 200 MHz and a spurious free dynamic range (SFDR) of more than 80 dB at full-scale conversion. By simultaneously adding a dither signal to the input in the form of a psuedo-random binary sequence (PRBS) to minimize the non-linearity errors and noise of conversion, the SFDR can be improved by a further 25 dB.

Many of the digital systems employ the fast Fourier transform (FFT) and its inverse. In general, the greater the number of points included in the algorithm, the greater the information content of the signal and hence the higher the bit rate. Such chips are now available in a programmable version that is capable of handling FFT processing ranging from 2 to 8192 points. These find applications in digital filters and spectral analysis. By including PIN switching diodes within the chips, it becomes possible to select a range of function variations via a microprocessor under software control. The change of tuning range, change of demodulator characteristic, variable selectivity, variable filter bandwidth etc. can all be obtained by programming instructions.

There are many instances in which multiple receivers are needed in communications networks; cellular phone networks and cable TV head ends are just two examples. The principle involves broadband conversion to down convert many channels in a single step, signal conversion to a digital format and then by using digital filters, create the separate channel inputs to the individual demodulators. Finally the signals are converted back into analogue form. Such a development could have a significant cost and power consumption reduction, with reduced size. While the receiver front end would be more expensive, it would certainly be less than the cost of, say, 100 individual channel receivers. It has been suggested that the break-even point occurs when processing signals from between six and ten channels.

Such a receiver could easily be reprogrammed to handle different standard signals and this is much easier and cheaper than managing station and frequency planning in hardware.

The WiNRADIO/Visitune system receivers (10)

The two receivers in this range are constructed on full length ISA cards for inclusion within a standard PC which can accept up to a maximum of eight such receivers. These are designed for professional automatic station monitoring, system surveillance and data logging, spectrum monitoring and audio recording. The modulation and services include AM, SSB narrow- and wideband FM, WEFAX weather maps, and packet radio (HF and VHF), plus a number of useful maintenance features such as a real-time spectrum analyser, audio oscilloscope and recorder.

In use, the PC monitor displays a virtual receiver front panel and the Visitune spectrum display of the band of interest. Clicking the mouse button on a particular signal peak selects that station and the receiver front panel then displays the frequency, signal modulation and local and world standard time. If the receiver is in the scanning mode, it also displays the scanning step size and rate. The spectrum screen displays the signal strength in dB against frequency, the start and end of the frequency span, the step size and the sweep mode.

The two receivers (WR-1000i and WR-3000i) cover the tuning ranges of 500 kHz to 1.3 GHz and 150 kHz to 1.5 GHz respectively. Both employ digitally controlled PLL frequency synthesizers in a triple conversion configuration and the three IF ranges and their bandwidths are software selectable according to the tuning range. The receiver sensitivities are better than 5 μv for AM, 2.5 μv for SSB, 2 μv for narrow FM and 4 μv for wide FM. The scanning speed is fifty channels per second and the tuning steps are 100 Hz to 1 MHz depending on the frequency range, with 10 Hz used for SSB.

The receivers can be tuned either from the front panel as described above or directly from an extensive and user-editable database of more than 300 000 worldwide stations.

REFERENCES

(1) Mountain, N. (1985) 'Satellite Transponder Operation with Video and Multiple Sub-carriers'. *Proc. 14th. International TV Symposium*, Montreux.

(2) Todd, C.C. and Gundry, K.J. (1984) 'A Digital Audio System for DBS, Cable and Terrestrial Broadcasting'. *Proc. IBC '84*, 10th International Broadcasting Convention, Brighton.

(3) Day, A., Dolby Laboratories Inc., Wootton Bassett, UK. Private communication to author.

(4) Fielder, L.D. and Davidson, G.A. (1991) 'AC-2: A Family of Low Complexity Transform Based Music Coders'. *Dolby Technical Papers, Pub No. S92/9398*.

(5) Davis, M.F. (1993) 'The AC-3 Multichannel Coder'. *Dolby Technical Papers, Pub No. S93/9951*.

(6) *NICAM-728 System Specification*. BBC Engineering Information Department, 1986.

(7) Texas Instruments (1989) *NICAM-728 Stereo TV Sound Decoder*.

(8) Weck, Ch., *et al.* (1988) 'Digital Audio Broadcasting'. *Proc. IBC '88*, IEE Pub. No. 293, p. 36.

(9) Pommier, D. *et al.* (1988) 'Prospects for High Quality Digital Sound Broadcasting'. *Proc. IBC '88*. IEE Pub. No. 293, p. 349.

(10) WiNRADIO Communications Ltd, Melbourne, Australia. Courtesy of Broadercasting Communication Systems Ltd, Chelmsford, UK. Private communication to author.

Chapter 13

Information security and conditional access

13.1 INTRODUCTION TO SECURE COMMUNICATIONS

Due to the broadcast nature of many communication systems, some form of security becomes essential in very many applications. These include such areas as computer-to-computer data signals, as used by banks and businesses. TV programme providers need to be able to obtain revenue from their services. Even the POTS, the Internet and the ISDN systems can gain much from an improved degree of data security. When these networks are used for the exchange of electronic funds, such security is essential. However, security will only be gained at the expense of a lower data throughput. In many digital applications, the use of *code division multiple access* (CDMA) provides an economical way of sharing the resource. It will be recalled that CDMA involves translating the pure binary code into an alternative bit pattern. Commonly, either a *pseudo-random binary sequence* (PRBS) or a Gold code and their inverses are used to represent logic 1 and 0 respectively. The smallest duration of the code sequence, the PRBS clock period, is usually referred to as a *chip*. Each data bit is normally an integral number of chips in length so that the data transitions all coincide with clock pulse edges. As all stations transmit simultaneously, only the receiver that is equipped with the correct PRBS can, by use of correlation detection, decode the data that is intended for it. As many bits are now required in the transmission band to represent one bit in the baseband, this *addressability* leads to a reduction in the actual data transfer rate.

13.2 SPREAD SPECTRUM TECHNIQUES (*see also* Section 5.12)

Theoretically, all systems where the transmitted frequency spectrum is much wider than the minimum required is a spread spectrum system (1, 2). CDMA and FM are therefore digital and analogue examples respectively. These can be shown to have an SNR advantage that is gained due to the modulation/demodulation process. It was shown that FM has an SNR advantage over AM of $3\beta^2F$, where β is the deviation ratio and F the ratio of peak deviation to baseband width. In a similar way, the digital system has a processing gain proportional to the ratio R_c/R_i, where R_c and R_i are the actual transmitted code rate and the original information rate respectively. This trade-off of improved SNR for an increase in bandwidth is a good example of the use of the Hartley/Shannon laws of information theory.

With either of the two basic spread spectrum techniques, the receiver has to be equipped with the correct PRBS to be able to decode the original data. The use of the direct sequence (DS) or the frequency hopping (FH) system depends on the choice between the rate of data throughput and system security. In the DS system the baseband code bits are simply exchanged for the PRBS or its inverse, while in the FH system the pseudo code is used to drive a frequency synthesizer to create the carrier hopping. But in both cases the system processing gain is the ratio of the RF bandwidth to message bandwidth.

Because of the relatively slow response of the frequency synthesizer, FH systems tend to have the slower code rate, typically around 200 kbit/s, as opposed to as high as 200 Mbit/s for DS systems. The longer the code sequence, the greater the degree of security but the longer the time needed for synchronism. The security of the longer code can be achieved by using a second PRBS to select a truncated version of the first, but with a shorter sync time.

For an FH system with a carrier frequency of f_o, a chip duration of t_c, a chip frequency of $1/t_c$ and a sequence of L chips long, the resulting spectrum is centred on f_o and consists of discrete spectral lines at $1/Lt_c$ intervals. The envelope distribution is given by $E(f) = (t_c/2)(\text{sinc } x)^2$, where $x = \pi f t_c$ and sinc $x = (\sin x)/x$. Theoretically, more than 90 percent of the transmitted energy lies within the band $(f_o - f_c)$ to $(f_o + f_c)$.

There are also several hybrid spread spectrum systems in use that combine the various merits of both systems. For maximum processing gain, DS systems must have a very high chip rate, while FH systems must have a large number of channels. The overall gain of the hybrid system is then the sum of the DS and FH system gains.

13.3 SCRAMBLING AND ENCRYPTION

In general, the terms *scrambling* and *encryption* tend to be used synonymously. In this text, however, the term 'scrambling' will be taken to mean the rearrangement of the order of the original information, while 'encryption' will imply that the original information (often referred to as *plain* or *clear text*) has been replaced by some alternative code pattern (known as *cypher* or *encrypted text*). Scrambling alone is not considered to be secure, because a study of the signal behaviour can lead to the design of a suitable descrambler. The encryption operation is quite simple when all the characters to be secretly transmitted are in a binary electronic form. When a second binary sequence is added to the first, using modulo-2 arithmetic, the resulting sequence carries no obvious information. The original sequence can be revealed by performing the inverse operation at the receiver. The rules for modulo-2 addition and subtraction can be stated as follows:

$$0 + 0 = 0 \qquad\qquad 0 - 0 = 0$$
$$0 + 1 = 1 \qquad \text{and} \quad 0 - 1 = -1 \quad \text{(ignore minus)}$$
$$1 + 0 = 1 \qquad\qquad 1 - 0 = 1$$
$$1 + 1 = 0 \quad \text{(ignore carry)} \qquad 1 - 1 = 0$$

Thus both addition and subtraction are equivalent to the logic operation of exclusive OR (Ex. Or).

For example, it is required to secretly transmit the binary character 10001110 and an 8-bit key, 10101010, is chosen for encryption. The transmission/reception process then becomes:

Character to send:	10001110	
Key	10101010	
Sum modulo-2	00100100	(this is transmitted and received)
Key	10101010	
Sum modulo-2	10001110	(the original character)

In the general case, keys are produced using PRBS or Gold code generators. Such keys have several advantages, including:

● They are practically random and easy to generate and change.
● The longer the key, the more difficult becomes unauthorized decryption.

The *one-key* system just described has a significant disadvantage. The key has to be transmitted in some way, to all authorized users, before the message. This results in a time delay, but perhaps more importantly there is a risk that the key might fall into the wrong hands. Furthermore, if it is possible to obtain the system response to a spoof code input, the correct key can be generated by combining this modulo-2 with the false input. Multiple key systems have been devised to reduce these risks and improve security.

In a *two-key or public key* system, one key is made public for encryption while the second is kept secret and is used as a *modifier*. This key can be used to rearrange the logic used to set up the PRBS generator and is therefore sometimes known as the *keystream*.

A very high degree of security can be achieved using a *three-key system*. Two secret keys, primary and secondary, are user programmable and stored in a digital memory. The third non-secret key, which acts as a modifier, can be generated as a new PRBS at the start of each transmission. This technique provides a very high degree of security and is at the same time very flexible.

Three commonly used encryption algorithms are the Diffie Hellman, the RSA Public Key Exchange System (named after the authors, Rivest, Shamir and Adelman), and the Federal Information Processing Data Encryption Standard (FIB:DES) (3, 4).

The most important rules of any encryption system can now be stated:

- The number of possible keys should be very large to prevent a pirate from testing all possible keys in succession.
- Any fixed encryption operation should be very complex, making it impossible to deduce the operation from a few plain text/cypher text pairs.
- If security is to be based on secret information, then this must be created after the system is built; then if it is subsequently revealed, it will not jeopardize the entire system security.

For *soft encryption* the single key is embedded in the decoder. By comparison, the more secure *hard encryption* technique involves the use of a combination of several keys, shared between the encoder and the decoder.

The encryption/decryption process can be expressed mathematically as follows.

The encryption function E, when performed on plain text characters P, using key K, results in cypher text C. Thus the encryption process is given by:

$$E(K).P = C \qquad (13.1)$$

The decryption function D(K) is the inverse of E(K) or $(EK)^{-1}$. Therefore the decryption process is given by:

$$E(K)^{-1}.C = D(K).C = P \qquad (13.2)$$

The Diffie Hellman algorithm (5)

This shared key system requires that each end of the communications link shall contain a limited degree of computing power to calculate the shared *secret key* S. The system contains two numbers, P which is a prime, and X, both of which may be public. The two communicators A and B both choose random values (a) and (b) respectively that lie between 0 and P − 1.

The secure link is established as described by the following four stages:

(1) A computes X^a mod P which is sent to B
(2) B computes X^b mod P which is sent to A
(3) A then computes $S = (X^b \text{ mod } P)^a \text{ mod } P = X^{ab} \text{ mod } P$
(4) B then computes $S = (X^a \text{ mod } P)^b \text{ mod } P = X^{ab} \text{ mod } P$

Both A and B now know the secret key S that is to be used for the encryption process. Provided that a, b and P are large, it is extremely difficult to find the secret numbers by taking logarithms, even though X^a mod P and X^b mod P have been openly transmitted.

Rivest, Shamir and Adelman (RSA) public key system (5)

This secure system relies upon the choice of two large prime numbers, P and Q, both chosen at random and used to calculate a modulus N number from the product (PQ). Mod-N can be made public without jeopardizing P and Q. The encryption key (E) and the decryption key (D) are then evaluated from the formula:

ED mod (P − 1)(Q − 1) = 1

The cypher text C is then obtained from the plain text M by:

$C = M^E \mod N$

The message is recovered from the received text by using:

$C^D \mod N = M$

For example, if P = 3, Q = 11, then N = 33 and (P − 1)(Q − 1) = 20. Thus when ED mod 20 − 1, E = 7 and D = 3 are possible values. If M = 4, then $C = 4^7 \mod 33 = 16$ and this is the code that is transmitted. For decryption, $16^3 \mod 33 = 4$, the original code.

Any pirate attack on this system requires the factoring of mod-N to discover the two prime numbers P and Q or taking discrete logarithms of $C = M^E \mod N$. Both operations are equally complex and require the same number of steps. The fastest known algorithm that will achieve this is quoted as having the following number of steps S:

$S = \exp(\ln(n)\ln(\ln(n)))^{1/2}$, where n = modulus value

Assuming that a computer is available that will perform the steps at a rate of one million per second, then for 256 binary digits which give a modulus $n(2^{256})$ of 1.158×10^{77}, the time taken to break this code is in the order of 170 days. The problem is very similar for the Diffie-Hellman scheme and considering that dedicated high-speed processors are now available that will provide calculations for encryption keys to 1024 bits within 40 ms, these two schemes look to have a secure future.

Data Encryption Standard algorithm (DES)

This algorithm translates blocks of 64 bits of plain text into similar block sizes of cypher text, using 56-bit keys. Each plain text block is divided into left (L) and right (R) groups, each of 32 bits, and then processed as shown in the flow chart of Figure 13.1(a).

Successive R groups are combined with successive keys using a very complex function f, which is fully described in the literature (3). Each processed R group is then added modulo-2 to the corresponding L group, the 16-bit groups being formed according to the formulas:

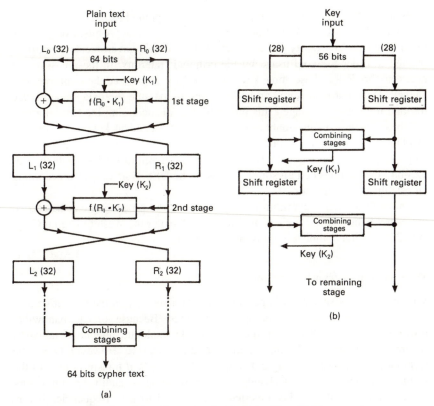

Figure 13.1 (**a**) Operation of Data Encryption Standard algorithm. (**b**) Key generator.

$$L_j = R_{j-1} \tag{13.3}$$

$$R_j = f\{R_{j-i} . K_j\} \oplus L_{j-1} \tag{13.4}$$

After processing using 16 keys, the L and R groups are recombined, but in the reverse order (R, L).

The initial 56-bit key group is divided into two 28-bit sub-groups and processed through shift register sequences. A new key is formed by combining the sub-groups after one or two left shifts. After 16 keys have been produced, each group of 28 bits is ready to repeat. Using 56-bit keys as described, the probability of a pirate deciphering the code is as follows: $P = 1/2^{56} = 7.206 \times 10^{16}$ or about 1.4×10^{-17}, very unlikely. Alternatively, $2^{56} = 7.206 \times 10^{16}$.

A pirate makes one attempt every nanosecond, then on average it will take about 3.6×10^{16} ns, or more than 1.140 years, to decipher the message. The DES algorithm has been shown to be vulnerable to attack using massive parallel computer processing. But in many cases it must be cheaper to pay the system access charges than to rent such computing power.

By using the DES algorithm repeatedly in overlapping blocks, it is possible to encypher plain text blocks that are very much longer than 64 bits. Longer keys provide enhanced security but in some of these cases, governmental control is exerted in order to avoid usage by the criminal fraternity. In these cases, it is necessary to lodge these long keys with a duly authorized law enforcement agency. This control feature can be bypassed by passing the data stream twice through the encryptor stage. This has the effect of increasing the key length to 112 bits. Systems using double or even triple independent keys are also now available. For less secure applications, DES systems using 40-bit keys can be employed. The International Data Encryption Algorithm (IDEA), which uses 128-bit keys and has certain similarities with the DES system, is also becoming an established competitor.

Although the DES algorithm is very complex, the processing can be carried out using dedicated ICs such as the Intel 8294A (6) or the Western Digital Corp. WD 2001/2 in a completely transparent manner.

Voice system encryption/scrambling

Within the ISDN service, it is possible to obtain security in the 64 kbit/s voice channels by using any of the above schemes. Because of the bandwidth restrictions (300–3400 Hz) of the voice-grade analogue telephone network, secure communications become more difficult to achieve. However, two basic techniques are possible, using either *spectral* or *temporal* transpositions. In the former, a range of contiguous bandpass filters separate the audio signal into sub-bands. These are then either inverted or translated to new frequencies before being reassembled into a *new* analogue signal within the same frequency range but now completely unintelligible. The intended receiving terminal must be equipped with a complementary filter/processor unit.

For temporal transposition, the audio signal is converted into digital format using sampling, quantization and delta modulation. The data stream is then divided into blocks of typically 100 ms duration which are reversed in time and then concatenated before being converted back into an encrypted analogue signal. This new signal may then be transmitted over either a telephone or a radio network. A further level of security is possible by subdividing each block into segments which may be shuffled and then relocated within the original block period. The shuffling sequence may be controlled either from a look-up table stored in ROM (Read-only memory) or by a PRBS generator. The synchronizing of a pair of scrambled telephones is carried out using a handshaking technique to establish the scrambling sequence before the start of voice transmission.

Security on the Internet and ISDN systems

Internet access over the plain old telephone system (POTS) is open to hackers and pirates and is far from secure. Corporate users normally employ *firewalls* that are positioned between their local network and the telephone system to provide added security. These networks are then referred to as intranets. The barrier is used to intercept and monitor accesses via the Internet and prevent illegal access to sensitive areas of the main database. Passwords and personal identity numbers (PIN) form the major part of this access control but sensitive data is only passed over the POTS system when encrypted.

In addition, it is now recognized that there is a need for security of home shopping via the Internet system, particularly with regard to financial transactions. This type of operation usually employs to services of a third party, the bank or financial controller. For purchases over the Internet, it is first necessary to register with the paying authority so that all future transactions do not include the transfer of any credit card details. Purchases are then made using names and addresses only which can be encrypted.

The ISDN system automatically provides for encryption so that data transfers are as secure as is needed. Basically, the 16 kbit/s D channel is used for common signalling and control, while the 64 kbit/s B channels are used for data transfers, but data can, in certain circumstances, be passed over the D channel. The network can therefore be hijacked for unauthorized use through the D channel. The system security can be improved by the addition of a filter network to monitor and log the activity of the D channel. When unusual accesses are detected, the line can be shut down to prevent data transfers over the D channel and the source of the attempted access logged for future reference. Such a filter has been developed by Rohde & Schwarz of Germany and can simply be added to any ISDN system without interfering with its normal operation.

13.4 SMART CARDS

These devices consist of credit-card-sized plastic cards with semiconductor electronic circuits fabricated in HCMOS or similar technology and built into the slim structure. Typically, a purpose-developed 8-bit microprocessor is accompanied by up to 20 kbytes of ROM, 8 kbytes of EEPROM, 512 bytes of RAM and registers that may be 512 bits long. The operating system ensures that all volatile data held in the RAM is transferred to the EEPROM at power-down. Often each chip is security-coded at manufacture for traceability. The microprocessor is designed to manage the access control protocol, and calculate the subscriber's debit/credit rating and billing arrangements. As constructed, these can be used to control access to premises, personal banking and commercial actions, the Internet and other local area networks and computer systems. The ROM carries the simple applications programs, operating system and security logic (encryption and PIN number). The RAM holds the data associated with the calculations for a single transaction, data which is lost on power-down. The EEPROM considerably extends the card life because its data is cleared and updated at every access or transaction and is particularly useful for electronic purse-type applications. The encryption systems commonly used include DES or RSA, and either provides a cheap and secure control element. If the card is to be used to control the transfer of sensitive data, the RSA algorithm can be used to transport DES keys.

There are two types of card in general use. One carries contacts to the dedicated IC embedded in the card surface and the other makes contacts via an inductive pick-up loop and radio frequency signals, but the former is currently most common. There are commonly eight gold-plated contacts on each card and five or six of these provide for the following features:

- SDA – serial data address and bidirectional input/output (I/O)
- SCL – serial data clock that is used to synchronize all data I/O
- Vcc – power supply positive
- Gnd – ground, power negative and screen
- Mode – writing either page or multiple bytes to the memory
- PRE – write protect enable, not used on all cards

The protocol is based on the I^2C system bus. When one type of device is inserted into the card reader, it is challenged with a random number. The card then uses its private key encryption number to derive a new key, which it presents to the reader. If this is accepted as correct, the user is granted access. A further extension of this technique, adopted by the GSM mobile phone system, involves the user manually inputting a PIN and if this is accepted, the user can proceed to the next stage. Further systems employ the user's fingerprints or eye structure as an ID. Typically, after three false access attempts, the user is automatically locked out.

For TV access control, the decoder often contains one of the system keys embedded in a ROM. The second key is provided by a smart card which is either periodically replaced or recharged, while the third key is transmitted over the air or cable system in the form of a receiver address. In addition, the card reader often carries an edge contact system that indicates to the decoder that a valid card has been inserted.

13.5   CONDITIONAL ACCESS (CA) AND THE TELEVISION SERVICES

Scrambling in the amplitude and time domains provides the two basic methods of denying the user of a video signal its entertainment value. The most elementary method that has been used, without success, is the suppression of line or field sync pulses. This fails chiefly because modern TV receivers, with their flywheel sync/PLL-type timebases, require only little modification to produce a locked picture direct from the luminance signal.

Two basic levels of service have to be provided for. In some countries, a *must-carry* rule applies to both the cable and satellite network providers. This means that the system must distribute national programmes without restriction. If scrambling is applied to all channels, then the descrambling key has to be freely available. Therefore for premium services such as subscription or pay-per-view television, an extra level of security is needed.

It has been shown subjectively (7) that, under conditions of adjacent and co-channel interference, a scrambled picture has a 2 dB SNR advantage. This is because such interference produces patterning that would apply to the scrambled picture. Descrambling then breaks up the patterning and makes it much less visible.

Video inversion

Simple video signal inversion, which is not secure, can be successfully combined with a PRBS to provide very high security. The PAYTEL (UK) system (8) inverts alternate groups of lines in a continuously variable manner. This is effectively a three-key system, with digital data regarding the scrambling sequence being transmitted with the signal and changing with every programme. This is used in conjunction with a unique key held in each descrambling/decoder unit and the subscriber's *smart card*. The decoder key is well hidden within the decoder electronics and the user smart-card electronics can be reprogrammed on a monthly basis, the card being programmed to work only with one decoder. The card alone provides access to the must-carry programmes. Typically, this smart card with a limited degree of computing ability can thus keep track of the debit/credit rating of the subscriber.

Line translation

This technique causes the line blanking period to be varied in a pseudo-random manner over a period of several frames. It requires the use of a line store, but those based on charge-coupled device (CCD) technology are relatively inexpensive. To some extent, the degree of security depends upon the number of time shifts permitted within the blanking interval; systems using as few as three shifts have been shown to be insecure. The key to the PRBS for the time shifting, which is transmitted within the field blanking period, can readily be changed. The technique can be raised to the security level of a two-key system by combining the PRBS key with a PIN number that is user programmable.

The Scientific Atlanta B-MAC system, as used on the AUSSAT DBS service, uses this technique in conjunction with a three-key algorithm. Because there are no conventional sync pulses in the MAC system, it becomes very difficult for a pirate to detect where one line ends and another begins. In any case, the sync point is continually jumping around.

Line shuffle

The lines of a normal video signal are transmitted in sequence, from 1 through to 525 or 625. If a frame or field store is available at each transmitter and receiver, this order can be scrambled in a pseudo-random manner. The concept is capable of providing a very secure system, but full field or frame stores still tend to be costly. However, the concept could well return to favour with digital television.

Line segmentation

In this technique each video line is divided into segments, and it is these that are scrambled. By varying the *cut point* in a pseudo-random manner, a very high degree of security can be achieved using only two segments per line (two cut points per line systems have been demonstrated). A single 8-bit binary word can identify any one of 256 cut points. The concept is particularly economical to implement on video signals that are digital at some stage of processing. The chief constraints imposed by this method are related to the linearity and frequency response of the equipment in the transmit/receive chain. Due to these imperfections, *line tilt* can arise with analogue signals. This is a gradual drift in the black or dc level of the signal. Under normal conditions it might pass unnoticed, but as the descrambling process changes the positions of each segment, a step appears as indicated in Figure 13.2. Since the cut point varies in

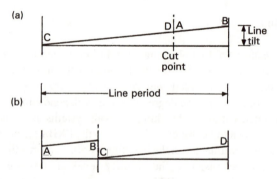

Figure 13.2 Effect of line tilt and line segmentation (**a**) before descrambling, (**b**) after descrambling.

a random fashion, a visible pattern of low-frequency noise can be displayed. Additionally, if such a signal is processed over a *Vestigial Side Band* (VSB) cable network, any receiver mistuning will distort the skew symmetry in the demodulator frequency response, giving rise to accentuation or attenuation of the low video frequencies. This generates overshoots or undershoots in the signal in the manner shown in Figure 13.3, again giving rise to a noise pattern on the display.

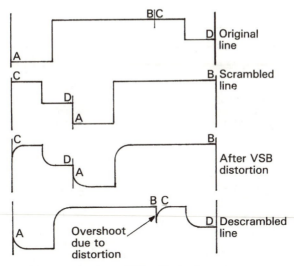

Figure 13.3 Effect of line segmentation on VSB cable signal.

Controlled access for digital television

Conditional access (CA) systems are designed to give the broadcaster a
system and service management tool which in turn provides the income to run
the system. Such systems should include control of subscribers' programme
tiering or bouquet, pay-per-view or video-on-demand, over-the-air or cable
addressing and the allocation of the services to accredited viewers. With the
introduction of digital television, this problem becomes rather complicated.
Encryption is particularly easy but with a large number of programme
providers, the use of a common key system would be unacceptable unless
there is some means of distinguishing between members of the individual
customer base. Whose specific CA system is going to be built into the set-top
boxes (STB) or integrated receiver decoders (IRD)? How many card reader
slots will the STB accommodate? Will the subscriber become locked into the
output from one or two programme providers (similar to the problem faced by
many computer system users)?

With so many programmes being available via digital TV, there is likely to
be an increase in the pirate production of faked smart cards and even the
possibility of introducing viruses into the control systems. To some extent,
smart cards can be made hacker-proof by erasing part of the programming
path to make the fixed data inaccessible. However, this feature is unavailable
to systems that make use of the downloading of subscription renewals over
the air. This involves leaving the receiver in the standby mode overnight
where the power loss and heat generated are not always user friendly or
acceptable. Choices and compromises are once again involved.

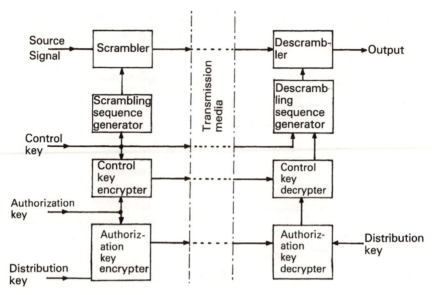

Figure 13.4 Conditional access system for television.

EBU controlled access system (9)

The European Broadcasting Union (EBU) devised a control standard for conditional access to the MAC systems which is capable of adaptation for digital TV. It uses an extension of the DES three-key algorithm and its general principle is indicated in Figure 13.4. A PRBS is defined by a *control key* that, for free access to any must-carry signals, is fixed and publicized, so that a receiver can automatically descramble such programmes. Where access is controlled, the control key is encrypted by an *authorization key* which is in turn encrypted by a *distribution key*.

Decryption of the authorization key is effected by the use of the distribution key, which may be transmitted over the air or input via a smart card. The encrypted version of the control key is decrypted by the use of a combination of authorization and distribution keys. This then enables the selection of the correct PRBS to descramble the signal. Subscriber billing can also be built into this system. This is managed via the system control computer, using reprogrammable data on the smart card, or through the distribution key.

Piracy and analogue TV

Probably a more insidious form of illegal operation involves the transmission of narrowband digital signals within the sidebands of an FM analogue television transmission. A typical TV transponder has a bandwidth somewhat in excess of

30 MHz and at the band edges the signal contains very little power. A relatively low-power digital transmission from a VSAT terminal with a bandwidth up to about 30 kHz is easily hidden beneath the *noise* of the television signal. In an attempt to further hide these illegal transmissions, energy balancing at both band edges can be employed, one used for the up-link and the other for the down-link. With digital TV transmissions, the broadcast spectrum will be filled with signal energy right up to the band edges and so this type of illegal operation is likely to dissappear.

13.6 CONTROLLED ACCESS SYSTEMS IN OPERATION

Over the past decade there have been a number of CA systems that were developed for specific distribution networks only to atrophy through lack of support. Through technical interest, some of these are described here.

MAC scrambling and encryption system

Scrambling using the double cut and rotate principle for luminance and chrominance was included in the MAC specification. The cut-point positions in each component of the video signal were controlled by a PRBS generator with an 8-bit control word used to uniquely define up to 256 cut points. A 60-bit linear feedback shift register was used to generate a PRBS with a very long cycle time. This sequence was reset to a different starting point every 256 frames by using a control word transmitted during line 625.

The scrambling sequence was encrypted using a shared-key system to provide controlled access in the manner indicated in Figure 13.4. The data periods in the MAC packet system provided ample capacity for system management by over-the-air addressing. This allowed for programme tiering, parental lock-out, decoder authorization for specific services and pirate lock-out. The audio channel digital data stream was also encrypted in a similar way using the same PRBS generator.

Videocode and Digicrypt

These two similar systems were developed by Space Communications (Sat-Tel) Ltd for use with PAL systems. It used a line shuffling technique based on a sequence of 32 or 128 lines respectively. Each encoder and decoder therefore had line storage for 32 or 128 lines. In addition to line shuffling, provision was made to displace randomly the line start by ±1.5 μs. An encrypted key was transmitted in the vertical blanking interval (VBI) during lines 6, 7, 8, 9, 319, 320, 321 and 322, to instruct the decoder of the precise sequence in use.

Videocrypt/PALcrypt

This system, which also used cut and rotate, was developed for use with the PAL DTH services and employed a code that could be changed every ten seconds. The cut point was calculated by the system control computer with the cut and rotate being performed in a one-line memory with the signal in the digital domain. This avoided the problems of chroma sub-carrier phase errors when each line was rejoined. In most cases, the audio channel was transmitted in the clear.

The public key system was controlled partly by data transmitted during the VBI and partly by a code held in a smart card which had to be changed periodically.

Sat-Pac

This scheme was designed by Matsushita of Japan for use with PAL systems in Europe and Scandinavia. The method of encryption involved inverting alternate fields of the video signal and shifting the dc level of the blanking signals. This ensured that the sync pulses and colour burst were buried within the video signal level. The composite blanking signals were then transmitted on an FM sub-carrier of 7.56 MHz. A second sub-carrier at 7.02 MHz was used to carry data to enable/disable viewers' decoders according to their subscription levels.

VideoCipher II (10)

This North American system developed by General Instruments Inc. includes all the necessary elements for the secure delivery of high-quality vision, plus stereo audio, to both CATV and DTH subscribers. It also carries all the signals necessary for system control and management, including tiering of authorized access, impulse pay-per-view, on-screen menus to aid subscriber choice, and parental lock-out, together with text and message services. Video security is achieved partly by removing all line and field sync pulses, inverting the video signal and positioning the colour burst at a non-standard level.

The two analogue audio channels are filtered, sampled and digitized at the standard CD rate. Each sample is added modulo-2 to a PRBS generated by the DES algorithm, forward error coded (FEC) and interleaved for transmission over a satellite channel. The FEC coding can detect and correct all single errors, and detect and conceal all double errors using interpolation. Together with addressing and control information, this multiplex is transmitted during the sync pulse period of each line. Since this multiplex becomes part of the 4.2 MHz video signal, no additional audio sub-carriers are needed. This effective bandwidth reduction results in an overall 2 dB improvement in video CNR, relative to the unscrambled signal.

Video scrambling operates on the cut and rotate principle. The active period of each line is sampled and quantized at four times the colour sub-carrier frequency and stored in a multiple line memory. The line data is then split into segments of variable length, under the control of the DES algorithm, and the position of the segments interchanged. This data is then read out of memory and converted back into an analogue format for transmission. To ensure system security with flexibility, a multi-level key hierarchy is employed. Each decoder has a unique public address and a number of DES keys stored within its microprocessor memory. To receive scrambled/encrypted programmes for each billing period, the decoder first receives a message with the monthly key, together with service attributes (tiering, credit, etc.) This is transmitted over a control channel to the decoder with that unique key. So that only the authorized decoder can process the encrypted signal, this data is added to the decoder memory.

Every programme is encrypted with a different programme key and only those decoders equipped with the monthly key can decipher these programmes. By changing monthly keys the programme provider can automatically authorize/ cancel a complete set of decoders with a single transmission.

At the programme-originating centre, the file of decoding and address keys is itself DES encrypted for added security. The system is so engineered that if a decoder is stolen, cloning will not allow access to programmes because pirate decoders are easily de-authorized over the air.

The VideoCipher II system has been adapted for use with the newly developed European and North American digital television systems.

Eurocypher

This system, developed by European Television Encryption Ltd in cooperation with General Instruments Corp., is modelled on the VideoCipher II management and access system with enhanced security, but modified to be used with the MAC scrambling and encryption system.

An access control module within the decoder has a unique address and its memory holds a series of keys necessary to decode the signals. Other keys, which are changed on a regular basis, are transmitted over the air to provide the final level of access control.

This system was adapted for use with those PAL transmissions that employed encryption using the cut and rotate principle and, like the VideoCipher II system, can also be used with the new digital television services.

Eurocrypt

This system, which was developed by CCETT (Centre Commun d'Etudes de Télédiffusion et Télécommunication, France) and France Telecom Labs, has much in common with VideoCipher II, but was intended for use with the

D2-MAC system (either cable or satellite delivery), where the primary specification provided for scrambling on a cut and rotate basis.

Controlled access was via a smart card which was capable of being programmed over the air and which thus ultimately carried all the necessary keys for security, services and management. The final element in the key system was the control word that was transmitted within the signal multiplex, and changed every ten seconds. Eurocrypt can also be adapted to function with the newly developed digital television systems.

B-Crypt

The algorithm for this system was devised by GPT Video Systems Ltd for use with videoconferencing and to overcome the restrictions imposed on the use of the DES algorithm. Like DES, this system operates with two 56-bit codes, one of which forms a crypto-variable key calculated by the system and the second an initialization code. The latter is a random number that is changed and transmitted every 32 ms. The overall encryption key, which is a combination of both codes, is never transmitted over the link.

REFERENCES

(1) Dixon, R.C. (1976) *Spread Spectrum Systems*. New York: John Wiley & Sons.
(2) Lewis, G.E. (1997) *Communications Technology Handbook*. 2nd edn. Oxford: Butterworth-Heinemann.
(3) 'DES Algorithm' (1977) *FIBS: PUB* 46. Washington, DC: National Bureau of Standards, Data Encryption Standards.
(4) McArdle, B.P. (1986) 'Using the Data Encryption Standard'. *Electronics and Wireless World*. London: Business Press International Ltd.
(5) Denning, D. (1983) *Cryptography and Data Security*. Addison-Wesley.
(6) *8294A Data Encryption Unit*, Intel International Corp. Ltd, Swindon, UK. Applications note.
(7) Edwardson, S.M. (1984) 'Scrambling & Encryption for Direct Broadcasting by Satellite'. *Proc. IBC '84*. International Broadcasting Convention, Brighton, UK.
(8) Dickson, M.G., Paytel Ltd, Reigate, Surrey, UK. 'How the PAYTEL System Works' Private communication to author.
(9) Mason, A.G. (1984) 'Proposal for a DBS Over-Air Addressed Conditional Access System'. *IBA Experimental Report 132/84*. Independent Broadcasting Authority.
(10) Katznelson, R.D., VideoCipher Division, General Instruments Corp., San Diego, USA. Private communication to author.

Chapter 14

Installation and maintenance of small satellite systems

14.1 SYSTEM CHOICES

In this context, small systems are defined as those intended to provide services for cable TV head-end reception, DTH or TVRO direct to home users, SMATV systems and small business VSAT systems. In the early stages of development for these services, the C band was extensively employed, particularly in North America and Russia. In Europe, where these developments tended to occur somewhat later, the Ku band was used almost from the start. While in the past the GEO birds provided most of the mainline communications services, there might well be a move to make use of the lower-cost, but perhaps less convenient, LEOs and MEOs in the near future.

While not a satellite system, troposcatter communication, which was developed from the radar research of the 1950s, has much in common with operations from the low earth orbiters. In the 1960s the oil companies developed a need for the rapid transmission of geological data from offshore oil rigs back to the research headquarters, and troposcatter techniques were virtually the only useful option.

The troposphere is a region of the ionosphere that is continually in a state of turbulence which produces local variations in the refractive index. Waves passing through this region tend to scatter in random directions. When the wavelength of the signal is small compared with the irregular eddies, the scattering tends to take place in a forward-directed cone-shaped region. This gives enhanced over-the-horizon propagation which can cover distances up to 2000 km at frequencies as high as 3 GHz. Troposcatter links can therefore provide reliable communications in the 2.5 GHz region, a band that is shared worldwide with microwave cookers (radio gastronomy?). The system requires the use of two high-gain directive antennas, both of which are aimed at a point in space at an altitude of about 1–2 km, roughly halfway between the two sites. Typically, for every watt of transmitted power, about a picowatt of energy is received at the distant antenna. Apart from the power inefficiency, the scattered energy simply adds to the general ionospheric background interference. Thus as communications technology has developed, the choice of options has changed and therefore as these links reach the age of retirement, they are tending to be replaced by the more efficient and environmentally friendly GEO satellite systems.

14.2 INITIAL SURVEY

The installation of a small dish satellite-receiving ground station can produce problems that involve several different classes of regulations. These may range from structural engineering, town planning/use of land regulations, to safe working practice, both on site and during transportation. A very useful code of practice that relates to these cases and many other associated problems is to be found in the literature (1, 2, 3).

The site survey should include a check to ascertain a clear view of the chosen orbit, in particular in the direction of the satellites of interest. It is not only important to ensure that there are no obstructions such as buildings, trees, etc., but also that there are no plans for such construction in the foreseeable future. Nearby roads that are used by high-sided vehicles can also be a problem. Generally, because of the great path length between the terminal and the satellite, there is no advantage to be gained from a roof mounting unless it is necessary to clear some obstruction. In such a case it will be necessary to consult structural engineers to ensure that the roof is strong enough to support the load. A ground site will need to be prepared that is capable of supporting the antenna structure and this may lead to considerations of site access.

Having located a suitable site, then because it is important to maximize the signal- or carrier-to-noise ratio (SNR/CNR), it is important to check for any local sources of terrestrial microwave interference. This is particularly so for C band installations. This can be done by temporarily inter-connecting the system, using the LNB without its reflector antenna, and scanning the surrounding area for signs of microwave transmissions. On a spectrum analyser or television receiving system, a no-interference situation will be indicated by a simple random noise display. Interference will produce a display with horizontal banding as the test set or receiver is tuned across the frequency band. If interference is found, it may be possible to resite the antenna, making use of the shielding effects of a building or even a mound of earth. It is much more economical to spend time at this stage than to become involved in an expensive filtering operation when the antenna has been finally installed. Interference and poor CNR are much more likely to be encountered at the higher-latitude sites, as the antenna boresight is *looking* along a noisy earth. Limiting locations are in the order of 75° of latitude and longitude difference between the orbital and earth station positions.

A very useful suite of programs designed to run on a PC under the Windows operating system is available (4) and will prove to be an invaluable tool at this stage of the installation development. Satmaster Pro for Windows carries out all the necessary calculations for both domestic and professional (including VSAT and SNG) installations. It quickly performs link power budget analysis, rain fade and atmospheric anomalies, earth magnetic variations and very much more. The calculations provide for both single and multiple channels per carrier system and multi-level modulation schemes such as the QPSK and QAM variants. The facility also exists to obtain hardcopy printouts of the footprints and technical data obtained from the programs which can then be included in reports. As with all Windows applications, the suite is user friendly and operates with pull-down menus and dialogue boxes. Certain areas of the database are user editable so that personally obtained information can be recorded.

14.3 MECHANICAL CONSIDERATIONS

The extent of the site preparations needed depends upon the particular application. CATV, SMATV and multi-service digital systems demand an antenna of about 1.5–3 m in diameter and one per satellite. Small dish business systems will generally work effectively with antennas of less than 1.5 m diameter, while domestic DTH systems will need to employ antennas ranging from 0.6 to 0.9 m diameter depending on the station latitude. The operational application will largely define the type of mount to be used. For the larger fixed antenna, the 'A' frame type of mount is most suitable. However, its concrete base positioning must reflect the limited degree of azimuth adjustment available once construction is complete. For smaller installations, the azimuth/elevation mount is the simplest to set up, but if signals from more than one satellite are required then two servo steering motors may be needed. In some cases, a polar mount system that requires only one drive system is more flexible but more difficult to set up. The king-post/pedestal component of these mounts must not only be very rigidly fixed but must also be very accurately vertical.

There will be considerable stresses set up on the mounting, due to the wind loading and aerofoil effects on the dish. An adequate safety factor must be allowed for. This should take into consideration the following problems.

- Metal fatigue can arise from excessive vibration and flexing.
- Aluminium can be subject to acid attack if exposed to a sulphurous atmosphere.
- Electrolytic corrosion results from the contacts between dissimilar metals.
- Galvanized steel will corrode if the zinc coating is damaged.

The whole structure should be adequately protected by paint and at the same time effectively earthed.

A further important electrical consideration at this stage is the distance between the head end and the main receiver. If this exceeds about 100 m, then almost certainly a line amplifier will need to be provided at the LNB first IF output.

14.4 ANTENNA/LNB COMBINATION

Just as the mechanical considerations are crucial to the system's effective operation, so is the actual choice of antenna/LNB combination. This is effectively the first stages of the system and so greatly affects the overall signal performance. Mistakes made at this stage will result in either an over-engineered

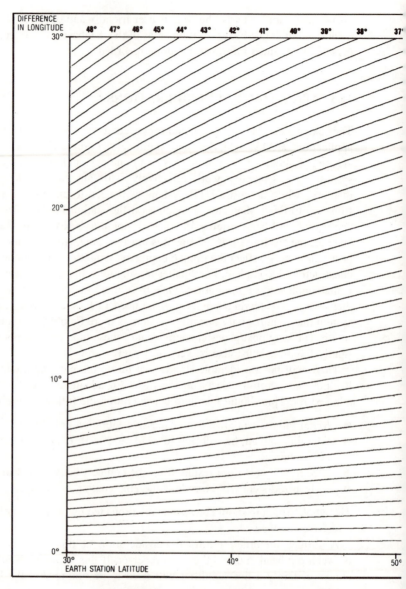

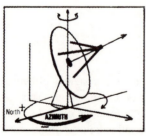

AZIMUTH ANGLE

The azimuth angle is the angle by which the antenna, pointing at the horizon, must be rotated about its vertical axis. Rotation must be in a clockwise direction, starting from geographical North, to bring the radiation axis of the antenna into the vertical plane containing the satellite direction. The azimuth angle is between 0° and 360°. The values given on the chart are added to or subtracted from 180°, depending on whether the station lies to the East or to the West of the satellite meridian.

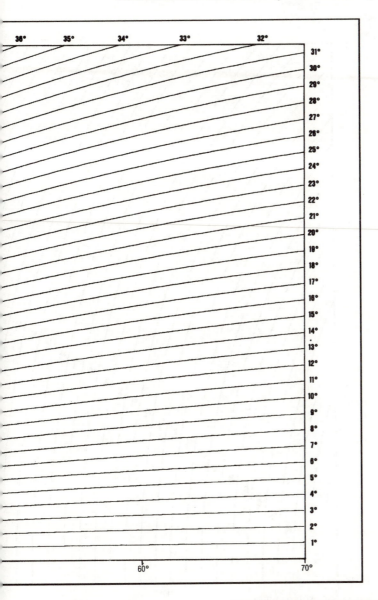

Figure 14.1 Azimuth angles (Courtesy of European Telecommunications Satellite Organization (EUTELSAT)).

EXAMPLE 1		
Coordinates of the site		
Latitude		42° North
Longitude		14° East
Longitude of satellite		7° East
Difference in longitude		7°
Reading given on the chart for (7 ; 42)		10.4°
Position relative to satellite meridian		East
		↓
Azimuth angle:		180° + 10.4°
		= 190.4°

EXAMPLE 2		
Coordinates of the site		
Latitude		52° North
Longitude		3° West
Longitude of satellite		13° East
Difference in longitude		16°
Reading given on the chart for (16 ; 52)		20.0°
Position relative to satellite meridian		West
		↓
Azimuth angle:		180° − 20.0°
		= 160.0°

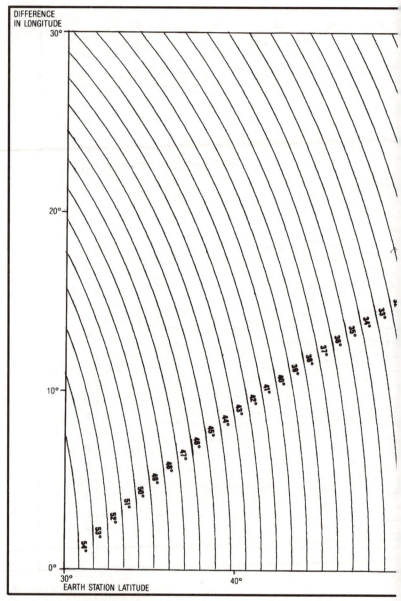

ELEVATION ANGLE

The elevation angle is the angle by which the radiation axis of the antenna must be rotated vertically, from its horizontal position, to align it with the direction of the satellite. The elevation angle is between 0° and 90°

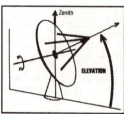

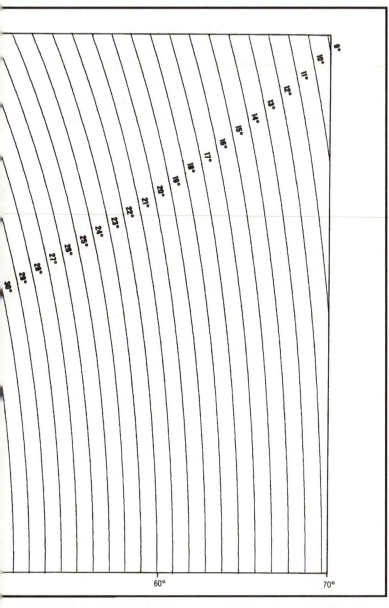

Figure 14.2 Elevation angles (Courtesy of European Telecommunications Satellite Organization (EUTELSAT)).

EXAMPLE 1	
Coordinates of the site	
Latitude	40° North
Longitude	33° East
Longitude of satellite	7° East
Difference in longitude	26°
Reading given on the chart for (26; 40)	36.6°
Elevation angle	= 36.6°

EXAMPLE 2	
Coordinates of the site	
Latitude	48° North
Longitude	7° East
Longitude of satellite	8° West
Difference in longitude	15°
Reading given on the chart for (15; 48)	33.0°
Elevation angle	= 33.0°

system or one that gives poor performance. In either case, this results in a dissatisfied client and/or expensive reworking. A theoretical evaluation is critical if this is to be avoided.

- Consult the published footprints for the satellites of interest to determine the available signal levels.
- Calculate the azimuth/elevation angles and the range, as set out in Appendix A3.3, or consult the graphs of Figures 14.1 and 14.2. In particular, calculate the worst-case path length or range.
- For the worst-case range r, calculate the free space losses L_s for the frequency range involved, using:

$$L_s = \{\lambda/(4\pi r)\}^2 = 20 \log \{\lambda/(4\pi r)\} \text{ dB, or,}$$

$$L_s = (32.44 + 20 \log f + 20 \log r) \text{ dB}$$
$$\text{where f is in MHz and r in km} \tag{14.1}$$

- Make allowances for additional losses due to pointing errors and rain fade. Typically, 2–3 dB is adequate, except for the case where the same rain storm can affect both up- and down-links simultaneously, when these allowances should be doubled.
- Using the receiver's required CNR as a basis, calculate the down-link power budget to evaluate the G/T ratio. The antenna/LNB combination's gain and noise figure/noise temperature will dominate the system's noise performance, so that a CNR or 2 dB above the demodulator threshold can be aimed for.
- The G/T ratio can be provided in many ways, ranging from a large antenna with an inexpensive LNB to a small antenna with a very low-noise LNB. The final compromise will be based on what is technologically and economically possible.
- The antenna diameter can now be calculated, or obtained from Table 14.1.

Table 14.1 Gain (dBi)

Diameter (metres)	P/F fed $\eta = 55\%$	O/S fed $\eta = 70\%$	Beamwidth (degrees)
0.5	32.6	33.7	3.5
1.0	38.6	39.7	1.7
1.5	42.2	43.2	1.2
2.0	44.7	45.7	0.9
2.5	46.6	47.6	0.7
3.0	48.2	49.2	0.6
3.5	49.5	50.6	0.5
4.0	50.7	51.7	0.45
4.5	51.9	52.9	0.4

P/F = prime focus feed; O/S = offset feed

Down-link power budgets

The power budgets given in Chapter 6 can be rearranged to analyse the antenna/ LNB characteristics, Table 6.1 being suitable for dealing with digital systems. Rearrangement of the budget for a TV system yields the following relationship:

Received CNR = G/T + EIRP − Boltzman's constant − noise bandwidth
− free space attenuation − other losses

Assuming a satellite EIRP = 46 dBW

Bandwidth = 27 MHz = 74.3 dBHz

Range = 39 000 km

Required CNR = demodulator threshold (8 dB) + 2 dB
= 10 dB

Free space attenuation A = 205 dB

Rain and pointing losses = 3 dB

Boltzman's constant = −228.6 dB/K/Hz

10 dB = G/T + 46 dBW + 228.6 dB/K/Hz − 74.3 dBHz − 205 dB − 3 dB

G/T = 17.7 dB/K

If the chosen LNB has a noise factor of:

1.5 dB = 10 log (1 + T/T_0)

which is equivalent to a noise temperature of 120 K, and we assume an antenna noise input of 60 K, then:

Total noise 180 K = 22.6 dBK

Thus required antenna gain = 22.6 + 17.7 = 40.3 dBi.

From Table 14.1, it will be seen that this can be provided by an antenna of less than 1.5 m diameter of either type. Other factors being equal, however, the offset feed type will give an extra 1 dB of protection.

14.5 ALIGNMENT OF THE ANTENNA ASSEMBLY

Having derived suitable parameters for the various elements of the system, the antenna can then be installed in accordance with the code of practice. For the reception of linear polarized signals the next stage involves the four adjustments of azimuth or bearing, elevation/declination, focus of the LNB feed, and the polarization skew. The data obtained from Figures 14.1, 14.2 and 14.5 will be found to be useful.

The initial pointing accuracy in the first two stages depends upon obtaining the values of latitude and longitude for the antenna site to within 0.1°. The calculated values of the azimuth/elevation angles thus obtained can be finally rounded to the nearest 1/4° or 1/2°, depending on the beamwidth of the antenna.

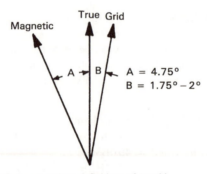

Figure 14.3 Relationship between various definitions of 'north'.

Because the direction of the azimuth bearing depends upon the fixed stars, it is necessary to locate the true north bearing. Magnetic north varies with time and place. For instance, in the south-east of England during 1996, the magnetic north was about 4° west of true north, and this will probably decrease by about 0.2° per year in the near future. The magnetic north pole is located close to longitude 101° W, latitude 76° N, near to Bathurst Island, off the northern coast of Canada. As a result, the *magnetic declination*, or deviation between true and magnetic north bearings, varies worldwide, the error ranging from zero to more than 40° east or west of true north. The deviation for any particular location is best obtained from aeronautical navigation charts.

Even if due allowance is made for this, the magnetic compass can be grossly misleading near to iron structures. Errors of more than 20° have been noted near to steel-framed buildings, and correspondingly smaller errors close to antenna mountings. In the UK, Ordnance Survey maps are available (similar are available in most other countries) and these can often be used to derive a bearing from some prominent local landmark. However, because of the projection used for such maps, the direction of grid north can vary from true north. Figure 14.3 shows the relationship between these northerly directions, with typical differences for the south-east of England.

Solar transit

Alternatively, use may be made of the sun's *meridian passage* or *transit* – the time when the sun is due south. Nominally, the sun is due south of the Greenwich meridian at 12.00 hours Greenwich Mean Time (GMT), or Universal Time (UT). Here due allowance needs to be taken for any local summer daylight saving arrangements. In the UK, for example, British Summer Time (BST) = GMT + 1 hour. Since the transit occurs approximately every 24 hours, the sun traverses the skies at the rate of 360°/24 = 15° per hour, or 1° per 4 minutes.

This simple relationship does not take into consideration the cyclic variations in the solar transit. This can be as much as ±15 minutes from GMT, depending on the time of year. Thus an error of +3.75° can easily be made. In astronomy, this effect is described by the *equation of time*. The due south time, or solar transit time, is tabulated in such as Reed's or Whitaker's nautical almanacs. These show the sun's bearing from Greenwich at 12.00 hours GMT for each day of the year, and this is referred to as the *Greenwich hour angle* (GHA). From this data, the due south time can easily be calculated. For example, if the table for a particular day gives a large number such as 358° for GHA, this means that the sun is 2° east of the meridian at 12.00 hours. The local noon, and hence the due south direction at this longitude, occurs eight minutes early, at 11.52 a.m. A small number, such as 3°, indicates that the local noon is later by twelve minutes, so that the sun will be due south at 12.12 p.m. The difficult problem of finding an accurate direction thus becomes the simpler one of finding an accurate time. The solar transit time can also be used to calculate the time that the sun will occupy the same azimuth bearing as a wanted satellite.

Having calculated the local noon time, the difference between the local longitude and the satellite's azimuth has to be traversed by the sun at 1° per 4 minutes. Assuming that the satellite azimuth is 20° west of the ground station, the sun will be on the same bearing after 20 × 4 = 80 minutes after the local noon time. Such information can be useful for the local calibration of a magnetic compass.

The elevation angle can be set using an *inclinometer* set against the vertical edge of the antenna aperture plane, remembering to take into consideration the typical 28° difference between the boresight and aperture plane when installing an offset fed antenna. The actual offset angle will be quoted in the manufacturer's literature or even stamped on the metalwork of the frame.

Polar mounts

In relation to polar mounts, some alternative terminology may be encountered. The elevation due south and the azimuth adjustment are sometimes known as the *axis inclination* and *east/west steering angle* respectively. The information for setting up a polar mount can be derived from Appendix A3. The total declination angle, for the given latitude (ϕ), can be calculated (α + β) from the graphs of Figure A3.5. This angle should then be set on the declination adjustment. Next, the elevation angle can be calculated from equation A3.12, $90° - (\alpha + \beta + \phi)$. This allows the angle of the aperture plane to be set. The whole antenna should then be directed due south, by rotation around the vertical axis of the king-post/pedestal. Once this adjustment has been locked, the antenna will swing around its declination bearings to track all the geostationary satellites that appear above the local horizon. These adjustment points are clearly shown in Figure 14.4.

Figure 14.4 Adjustment points for modified polar mount. (**a**) Elevation angle adjustment.
(**b**) Declination angle adjustment. (**c**) Pivot axis. (**d**) Jackscrew and motor for azimuth adjustment.

Focus adjustments

The focal point of a parabolic reflector can be calculated from the dimension of
the dish, using the formula:

$$F = r^2/4d$$

where: F = distance of focal point from centre of dish
        r = radius of antenna aperture plane
        d = depth of dish

This gives the approximate practical position at which the LNB feedhorn, or the sub-reflector, needs to be initially placed before final adjustment for maximum antenna gain.

Polarization skew

In the case of reception of linear polarized signals, the waveguide pick-up probe needs to be positioned parallel to the plane of the signal electric field. Only if the receiving antenna and the satellite share the same longitude will the polarization angle be the same as that at which the signal was transmitted. For receivers located east or west of the satellite, this angle will rotate as shown by Figure 14.5, which can be used to obtain the initial setting of the polarization skew adjustment.

Fine-tuning of the antenna assembly

The final tuning of all of these above adjustments should be made with reference to the received signal level. A signal strength meter driven from the receiver AGC circuit is suitable, but not very convenient as the receiver may well be situated a long way from the antenna. The AFC system can produce some misleading effects, so this should be switched OFF during these adjustments. However, the FM capture effect can lead to similar problems. A small readjustment can suddenly produce complete loss of signals that do not return when the original adjustment position is reset. This is caused by the receiver demodulator suddenly running out of the capture effect *hold range*. For the peaking of the polarization skew, it is often best to tune up on the wrong polarization where it is usually easier to see the minimum response, rather than the maximum level on the right polarization. In any case, it is often an advantage to choose a weak signal for the final tweaking because small changes in response can more easily be seen. The final tuning of VSAT antennas is usually carried out with the system in the receive mode and by reference to the satellite transponder beacon signal. Because of the reciprocal nature of the antenna properties, non-reflector types are also best tweaked in the receive mode. In this way, the frequency selectivity and response can be optimized and the standing wave ratio minimized for both the receive and transmit modes.

Satellite tracking meters and spectrum analysers (5)

Normally, the oscilloscope provides a window in the time domain, but when used with a spectrum analyser it can provide a window in the frequency domain. This

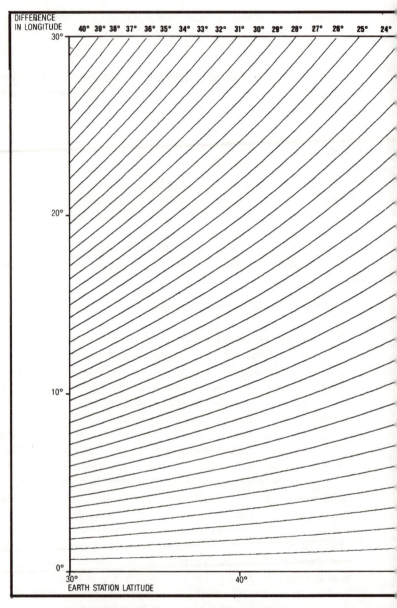

DIFFERENCE IN LONGITUDE

40° 39° 38° 37° 36° 35° 34° 33° 32° 31° 30° 29° 28° 27° 26° 25° 24°

30°

20°

10°

0°

30°   40°

EARTH STATION LATITUDE

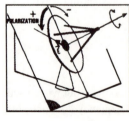

POLARIZATION ANGLE

This chart allows us to determine the angle between the polarization plane of a linear polarized wave emitted by the satellite and the vertical plane containing the antenna axis (once the antenna is pointing at the satellite).

The values given on this chart correspond to a situation where the polarization plane is perpendicular to the orbital plane. In this case, the position of the polarization plane will be obtained by rotating from the vertical plane in a clockwise direction (for an observer positioned behind the antenna and looking towards the satellite) if the station lies to the East of the satellite meridian, and in an anti-clockwise direction if the station lies to the West of that meridian.

If the polarization plane of the emitted wave is not perpendicular to the orbital plane, a further rotation will be necessary ▮ the position thus obtained. ▮ the EUTELSAT 1 satellites this ▮ be 3.5° or 93.5° in a clock▮ direction, depending on the ▮ rization used (Polarization ▮ Polarization X, respectively) ▮ the TELECOM 1 satellites it ▮ be 22° in an anti-clock▮ direction.

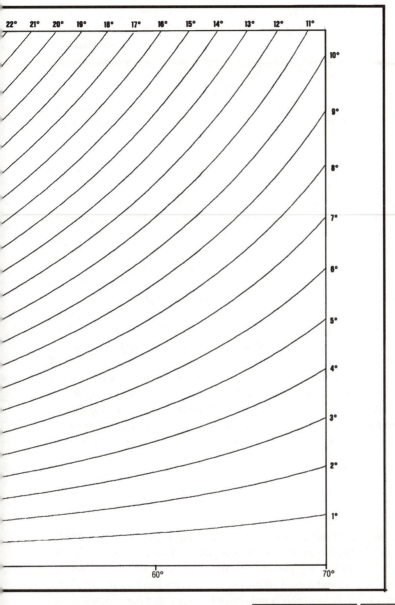

22° 21° 20° 19° 18° 17° 16° 15° 14° 13° 12° 11°

10°

9°

8°

7°

6°

5°

4°

3°

2°

1°

60° 70°

Figure 14.5 Polarization angles (Courtesy of European Telecommunications Satellite Organization (EUTELSAT)).

EXAMPLE 1	
Coordinates of the site	
Latitude	50° North
Longitude	8° East
Longitude of satellite	13° East
Difference in longitude	5°
Reading given on the chart for (5; 50)	4.2°
Position relative	
to satellite meridian	West
	↓
Polarization angle	− 4.2°

For the EUTELSAT I satellites the polarizations will therefore be as follows:
Pol. X :   93.5° − 4.2° = 89.3°
Pol. Y :   3.5° − 4.2° = −0.7°

EXAMPLE 2	
Coordinates of the site	
Latitude	59° North
Longitude	6° East
Longitude of satellite	8° West
Difference in longitude	14°
Reading given on the chart for (14; 59)	8.4°
Position relative	
to satellite meridian	East
	↓
Polarization angle	+ 8.4°

For the TELECOM 1 satellite the polarization will be:

− 22.0° + 8.4° = − 13.6°

makes it particularly useful for setting the antenna adjustments. However, until recently this expensive instrument was chiefly restricted to laboratory use. The Swires Research TVA97 and SA97 Spectrum and Television Signal Analyser utilizes the system LNB for most of its microwave signal processing, and this considerably reduces the cost. These are battery operated and provide power for the LNB, which makes them readily portable and suitable for on-site use. Because the TVA97 provides alternative displays of the frequency spectrum and the received TV signal, it can display the image as it will be seen, sparklies, ghosting and all. The SA97 unit is a spectrum analyser with a wide frequency range, extending to beyond 2 GHz. It contains an LCD display but this is supported by a memory unit which allows the screen displays to be saved and later downloaded into a PC for future analysis.

There are now many hand-held inexpensive instruments available, designed specifically as aids to antenna alignment and adjustment. They are basically portable receivers designed to operate with IF inputs in the range 950–2150 MHz, sometimes in two bands and giving various indications of received signal strength. They are commonly operated from rechargeable batteries and suitable for one-person operation. The main receiver section is sometimes broadband-tuned to remove this variable from the exercise.

In operation, the antenna is first approximately positioned according to the azimuth and elevation calculations and the meter plugged into the LNB. This action provides power for the LNB and a signal input to the instrument at the same time. At this stage the instrument usually gives some audible indication of the presence of a satellite signal, an audio channel being helpful in identifying a particular transponder transmission. As the antenna adjustments approach optimum, the pitch or loudness of the audio tone may increase. Additional indication may be given on bar graph or analogue-type meters. The receiver section also often has an automatic gain reduction facility that adjusts sensitivity as the received signal level increases.

Weather-proofing

Before leaving the antenna site, ensure that all mounting assembly nuts and bolts are securely locked. Weather-proof all external electrical connections, including the coaxial cable connectors and power leads to the polarization selector device. The exposed lead screws and pivot bearings of the steering mechanism should be adequately protected with grease. It is important to ensure that the window to the LNB waveguide input is correctly sealed and not damaged.

Polar mount steering drives

There are various ways of applying remote control to the polar mount steering mechanism, and these have a bearing on servicing. The basic drive assembly consists of a geared, fractional horsepower DC motor, driving a jack lead screw, to swing the antenna around its mounting axis. See Figure 14.4. The simplest arrangement involves using a variable resistor transducer attached to the motor drive, so that its resistance value is proportional to the antenna position. The remote control unit also contains a similar-valued variable resistor which is attached to a calibrated angular scale. The two resistors form part of a bridge circuit which, when balanced, indicates that the antenna points in the direction indicated by the remote control. The balance condition is used to halt the motor drive. An alternative version that employs a similar transducer uses the voltage developed across it to indicate the antenna position. This voltage is converted into a digital value that can be compared with a preset value stored in the control system memory to drive the steering system.

Two further variants use a pulse-counting technique to control antenna position. Permanent magnets attached to the motor drive gears energize either reed relays or Hall effect devices to generate a pulse train. The number of pulses generated, in respect to some preset reference value stored in memory, then indicates the antenna position.

It is important that a periodic inspection be made of the weather-proofing of this part of the structure. Although the motor drive mechanism usually contains a slipping clutch that operates in the event of jamming and failure of the limit switches, mechanical damage can occur.

Coaxial cable problems

The coaxial cable between the LNB and the main receiver carries signals typically in the range 950–2150 MHz. At these frequencies a quarter-wavelength varies between about 3.5 cm (1.4″) and 8 cm (3.2″). Thus any sharp bends in the cable run, or tight clipping that distorts the cable cross-section, can give rise to an impedance change, leading to a mismatch. In addition, the use of incorrect cable end connectors or poor fitments can further create mismatches. Such problems create multiple reflections along a cable run, leading to destructive additions of the forward wave energy. It has been noted that for short cable runs (less than about 10 m) these problems can result in a Ku band system producing a very poor signal-to-noise ratio on just one channel within a transponder bandwidth. This has almost always been overcome by using a longer length of cable and taking greater care with the installation.

14.6   SURFACE-MOUNTED DEVICES

In the two decades following WARC '77 which set out the standards to be used for television broadcasting via satellites, greater improvements in system performance were achieved than were probably anticipated at that time. The fixed satellite services (FSS) were thought then to be capable of supporting only services that used antennas of 3–4 m in diameter. Within ten years, the

Figure 14.6 Surface-mounted devices (Courtesy of Texas Instruments Ltd UK).

technological advances, particularly in LNBs and receiver demodulator threshold performance, showed that adequate services can be provided with antennas less than 1.2 m in diameter. A further significant improvement occurred in the next ten years when the Société Européene des Satellites (SES) introduced the ASTRA high-powered transponders. At this stage, antenna diameters were reduced to about 80 cm. In spite of this, a significant contribution to these improvements was made by the use of *surface-mounted devices* or *components* (SMD/C). The important properties of these devices were described in Chapter 4. Figure 14.6, provided courtesy of Texas Instruments Ltd UK, shows how the introduction of surface mount technology and ASICs has allowed the volume of multiple page-store teletext decoders to be very significantly reduced.

Allied to the use of SMDs are the changes in soldering technology that have occurred over the past two decades. What was at one time seen as an acquired practical skill is now seen as the application of a section of chemical science, a feature that has also made a significant contribution to the improvements in system performance.

The use of smaller circuit boards also leads to a further small improvement in RF performance. The printed circuit boards (PCBs) or substrates used with SMDs normally carry no through-holes for conventional components; the component lead-outs are soldered directly to pads or lands provided on the metallic print. This feature has led to the development of new soldering techniques which impart further advantages. In manufacture, surface mounted technology readily adapts to automated assembly, and the soldering methods used lead to improved connection reliability, both of which mean a reduction of costs. The particular technique employed in manufacture has a bearing on the way in which SMDs can be handled during servicing.

> *Wave soldering:* The components are attached to the solder resist on each PCB, using an ultra-violet light or heat-curing adhesive. The boards are then passed, inverted, over a wave soldering bath with the adhesive holding the components in place, while each joint is soldered.
>
> *Reflow soldering:* A solder paste or cream is applied to each pad on the circuit board through a silk screen, and components are accurately positioned and held in place by the viscosity of the cream. The boards are then passed through a melting furnace or over a hot plate, to reflow the solder and make each connection.
>
> *Vapour phase reflow soldering:* This more controlled way (6) of operating the reflow process uses the latent heat of vaporization to melt the solder cream. The boards to be soldered are immersed in an inert vapour from a saturated solution of boiling *fluorocarbon liquid*, used as the heating medium. Heat is distributed quickly and evenly as the vapour condenses on the cooler board and components. The fact that the soldering temperature cannot exceed the boiling point of the liquid (215°C) is an important safety factor.

Solders and the effects of component heating

Electronic components experience distress at all elevated temperatures (7). For example, in wave soldering, most baths have an absolute limit of both temperature and time – normally, 260°C for no more than 4 s. As the damaging effects of heat are cumulative, manufacturing and servicing temperatures have to be kept to a minimum. The use of a low melting point solder is therefore crucial. The common 60/40 tin/lead solder (MP = 188°C) is not suitable for SMD use. The lowest melting point tin/lead alloy (eutectic alloy) solder has a melting point of 183°C, and this also is not suitable. Components often have silver- or gold-plated lead-outs to minimize contact resistance. Tin/lead solder alloys cause *silver leaching*; that is, over a period of time the solder absorbs silver from the component and eventually causes a high-resistance joint. This can be avoided by using a silver-loaded solder alloy of 62 percent tin, 35.7 percent lead, 2 percent silver and 0.3 percent antimony. Such a solder has a melting point of 179°C. Tin also tends to absorb gold with a similar effect, and this is aggravated by a higher soldering temperature. This latter alloy is thus particularly suitable. The fluxes used as anti-oxidants are also important. An effective flux improves the solderability of the components, the rate of solder flow and hence the speed at which an effective joint can be made. The flux used for SMD circuits should either be a natural organic resin compound, or one of the newer equivalent synthetic chemical types.

Servicing SMD circuits

For the larger centralized service department, a soldering rework station might well be cost-effective. This might include a small portable vapour phase soldering unit, such as the Multicore Vaporette (7), which is particularly suited for small batch work as commonly found in such establishments. For the smaller service department, much ingenuity might be needed when dealing with SMD circuits.

The method used to remove suspect components may vary with the number of leads per device. For a device with only two or three leads, a fine soldering iron, in conjunction with a *solder sucker or solder braid*, can be successful. For multi-pin ICs, two methods are popular. One involves directly heating the soldered connections with a carefully temperature-controlled hot-air blast. The other method uses an electrically heated collett or special extension to an electrical wire stripper, to heat all pins simultaneously. When the solder flows, the component can be lifted away. In a simpler way, all the leads can be severed using a pair of cutters with strong, fine points. The tabs can then be removed separately. This is not quite so disastrous as it appears. Any suspect component that is removed, and subsequently found not to be faulty, should *not* be reused: the additional two heating cycles are very likely to lead to premature failure. As the desoldering of even a few leads can be difficult, it is important that the circuit board should be firmly held in a suitable clamp.

Even after all the solder has been removed, a problem of removing the component may still exist if an adhesive was used in manufacture. Although care should be exercised when prising the component off the board, damage to the printed tracks is unlikely. The adhesive should have been applied only to the solder resist. After component removal, boards should be examined under a magnifier to check for damage to the print.

Before commencing to fit the new components, the solder pads should be lightly pre-tinned, using the appropriate solder and flux. Each component will need to be precisely positioned and firmly held in place while the first joints are made. For multi-leaded components, secure two diagonally opposite leads first. The soldering iron used should not exceed 40 watts rating and should not be applied to a joint for more than three seconds. The heat from the iron should be applied to the component via the molten solder and not direct as indicated, in Figure 14.7(b). The final joint should have a smooth 45° angled fillet. Figure 14.7 also shows three incorrectly made joints: (a) has used too little solder, and this produces a high-resistance connection; (c) has been made with the application of too little heat, which will also lead to a high-resistance connection; in (d), too much solder has been applied and this has probably resulted in excessive heating of the component.

Some SMDs are too small to value-code in the conventional way. These should therefore be stored in their packaging until actually needed, to avoid mixing components that are difficult to identify.

Experience suggests that the most over-stressed discrete components in a system are the capacitors, particularly the electrolytics. If these are operated at

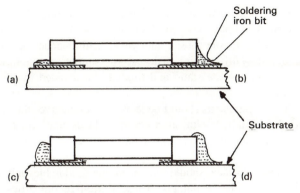

Figure 14.7 Soldering chip-type SMDs.

too high a temperature, the eletrolyte tends to dry out or leak. In the first case, this leads to a significant reduction in capacity with the attendant loss of performance. In the latter case, the leakage can create corrosion on the circuit board to generate open circuit tracks. When replacing a capacitor it is therefore important to ensure that not only are the capacitance value, voltage rating and ESR (equivalent series resistance – typically 2×10^{-2} Ω) correct, but also that the temperature rating will not be exceeded. Typically, for television and satellite receiver applications, a 105° rating is specified but upgrading this to 125° will improve reliability. Again, if these devices are operated at too low a dc voltage, the dielectric material will start to decay. At first this causes the capacitance value to rise with the thinner dielectric, but this quickly punctures and becomes a short circuit. Modern circuit boards tend to be liberally populated with these devices and experience has shown that when one fails the others are quite likely to follow suit in quick succession.

14.7   CONTROL OF STATIC IN THE SERVICING ENVIRONMENT

MOSFETs, CMOS and Group iii/v (GaAs, etc.) semiconductor devices can easily be damaged by the discharge of static electricity. A discharge from a pd as low as 50 volts can cause component degradation and, since the effect is cumulative, repeated small discharges can lead to ultimate failure. It is therefore important that sensitive devices, such as LNBs, should be serviced in a workshop where static electricity can be controlled much better than on site. Bipolar transistors are rather more robust in this respect.

The basic work station should provide for operators, work bench, floor mat, test equipment and device under service to be at the same electrical potential. Operators should be connected to the work bench via a wrist strap. Since static electricity is often generated by friction between dissimilar materials, the operator's clothing also needs to be considered. The wearing of wool and man-made fibres such as nylon creates considerable static. One very useful garment is a smock made of polyester fabric, interwoven with conductive carbon fibres. This has through-the-cuff earthing. The use of compressed air to clean down boards can actually generate static and this can be avoided by the use of an ionized air blast.

Static-sensitive components should be stored in conductive film or trays until required and then handled with short-circuited leads until finally in circuit. Soldering-iron bit potentials can also be troublesome unless adequately earthed.

The work bench surface should be clean, hard, durable and capable of dissipating any static charge quickly. These static-free properties should not change with handling cleaning/rubbing or with ambient humidity.

The use of an ionized air ventilation scheme can be an advantage. Large quantities of negatively and positively charged air molecules can quickly neutralize unwanted static charges over quite a significant area.

14.8   SERVICING THE LNB

This section of the receiver system can be the most difficult to repair. Fortunately, to date, these units are proving to be very reliable. Servicing of S/L band units is probably no more complex than repairing the tuner units of UHF television receivers. However, as the operating frequencies rise, both the cost of the test equipment and the level of expertise needed increase in proportion. Manu-facturers' service departments can usually justify the necessary spectrum analyser and signal generator needed for signal tracing and circuit alignment. However, the smaller department is left with the choice of returning faulty units to the manufacturer, or using its inherent skill and ingenuity to provide a local service. Each LNB is hermetically sealed and weather-proofed and the waveguide aperture is closed with a window that is transparent to signals. This may be made of glass or a plastic such as Mylar or Terylene. The latter materials can degrade and crack with ageing, probably due to exposure to ultra-violet radiation, and therefore need periodic replacement. It is important to keep moisture out of any waveguide-type structure, as corrosion gives rise to a surface roughness, which increases the attenuation.

The covers of most units are screwed in place and include gaskets that are not only part of the weather-proofing but are also RF conductive. Those must be treated with care or replaced, if a unit is opened for service work. Some units are enclosed in a Duralumin tube, one end of which is spun sealed. If it is thought economically viable, these can be opened by carefully removing the spun edge with a small chisel. The unit can be resealed, after servicing, using a silver-loaded epoxy adhesive. This material is very suitable for metals, and has a resistivity of about $500\,\mu\Omega.\mathrm{cm}$, which ensures RF sealing. The curing time of these adhesives can be improved by raising the temperature to about $50°\mathrm{C}$.

It should be noted that when the covers of the LNB are removed, the waveguide-like structure is changed. This gives rise to a change of circuit conditions so that the performance may change as a result. Also, it is not easy to inject or extract signals from a microwave circuit board without disturbing the operating conditions. Such coupling problems may be alleviated by using waveguide-to-coaxial cable adaptors. These consist of a short section of guide, blanked off at one end and containing a pick-up probe.

Signal generators from the Marconi series, which are capable of providing both AM and FM signals, cover the frequency range of 1–8 GHz and are suitable for workshop use. Marconi Gunn Device Oscillators, covering 8–11.5 GHz, are readily available and suitably portable for on-site use. Gunn devices are very suitable for portable operation as they are capable of producing up to 10 mW of output power from battery supplies. However, if used as a resonant cavity oscillator, Gunn devices tend to have a power output that is frequency dependent, due to variation of circuit Q factor.

Because of the restricted bandwidth covered by Ku band LNBs (much less than one octave), the distortion component of a lower-frequency signal generator can be made use of in an emergency. A signal source may be stated to have a total harmonic content of typically −40 dBc (40 dB below the carrier or fundamental level). This distortion will predominantly be third order, and might have a level of −50 dBc. With the carrier set to 10 mW, the third harmonic level would be 0.1 μW and this is of the same order as the RF input signal to a Ku band LNB. Thus a C band signal generator might, with care, be used to provide a Ku band input.

The LNBs used for data services are sometimes separated into low-noise amplifier plus low-noise converter stages, and housed in separate casings. To some extent, this eases the servicing problems. Because the data services commonly operate SCPC in a relatively narrow band, this imposes additional restrictions on such parameters as oscillator drift and phase noise.

Each LNB is supplied by power over the coaxial feeder cable of typically 15–20 volts. There will be contained within the unit, two voltage stabilizer circuits to provide collector/drain voltages and gate bias. This part of the circuit should include a transient suppressor for protection, typically a PN silicon device capable of responding to an overvoltage in about 1 picasecond. The first RF stage will generally be biased for a low current/low noise state, while succeeding stages will be biased for high gain.

The transistors used in the LNBs are very expensive, and any that are found to be faulty should be replaced by identical types. The device parameters actually form part of the circuit tuning. Resolder components with care because too much solder on a joint can affect its RF performance. Internal RF interstage screens should not be disturbed unless absolutely necessary. If they need to be removed, then silver-loaded epoxy adhesive can be very effectively used in the refitment.

Soldering to ceramic-based circuit boards can be difficult. The heat loss from the soldering iron bit is greater than that experienced with lower-frequency boards. To avoid static electricity problems, the soldering-iron bit should be earthed direct to a convenient earthy connection on the LNB.

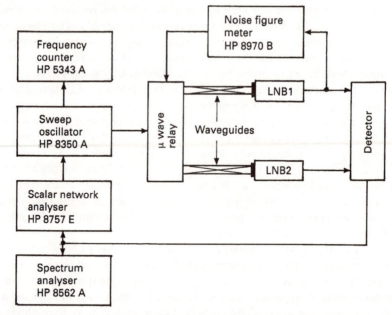

Figure 14.8 LNB test bench (Courtesy of MCES Ltd and Hewlett-Packard Ltd).

The system diagram of the test and alignment bench developed for the repair of Ku band LNBs is shown in Figure 14.8 (courtesy of MCES Ltd and Hewlett-Packard Ltd (8)). The test signal source is provided from the sweep generator via a microwave relay to a pair of waveguides which are provided to meet the needs of two different types of waveguide coupling. The waveguides are also provided with rotational flanges to cater for both horizontal and vertical polarizations. The sweep generator may operate in its basic mode or as a spot frequency generator for alignment purposes. The generator output level is capable of being varied over the range −75 to 7 dBm, but the typical amplitude used for basic alignment is in the order of −60 dBm. This ensures that LNBs are tested for sensitivity with a relatively low-level input. Increasing this level allows such parameters as third-order intercept and intermodulation products to be evaluated.

The detector stage routes the IF output from the LNB under test back to the display section. This consists of a scalar network analyser to monitor the overall gain across the passband and a spectrum analyser to test for harmonic distortion, instability and spurious responses. The frequency counter is included so that the local oscillator frequency can be accurately set to within 100 kHz in 10 GHz.

The noise figure meter is capable of working with LNBs producing outputs up to 1.8 GHz and measuring and displaying gain and noise figures to within 0.01 dB. This instrument provides a standard reference noise level input to the LNB under test via the relay and waveguide. The IF output is routed back as shown and the noise contribution made by the LNB (the excess noise ratio)

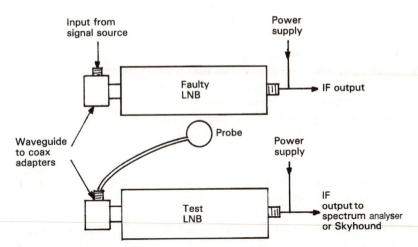

Figure 14.9 Fault-finding in an LNB.

obtained by subtraction of the original noise level from the new measured value. Because the temperature of the waveguide can affect the noise figure, this is continually monitored to allow correcting data to be entered into the final calculation. A typically good Ku band LNB after repair would be expected to yield a gain of at least 58 dB, flat over the passband to within 3 dB, and with a noise figure of less than 1.5 dB. Just as the LNB can be used as a front end to a spectrum analyser or alignment meter, a working LNB can in an emergency be pressed into service as an aid to fault finding. The basic arrangement is shown in Figure 14.9. The inputs to the two LNBs are provided via waveguide adaptors and both are powered through their IF outputs. However, the test LNB can be powered from a spectrum analyser or an antenna alignment meter. The signal input to the test LNB is via a coaxial cable terminated in a small loop aerial of about 1 cm diameter, or a dipole probe of about 1 cm length. The presence of a signal in the faulty LNB can be detected by probing along the circuit board with the aerial, the point at which the signal is lost indicating the faulty stage. Fault-finding in the IF section of the LNB then follows a procedure typical of UHF TV servicing.

A further useful source of Ku band test signals has been produced by converting an LNB from its normal down-converting mode into an up-converting unit. This is basically achieved by reversing the inputs to the mixer stage. The units that appear to be most amenable to this conversion are those that are housed in cylindrical aluminium casings. The general procedure for carrying out this conversion is as follows.

● Remove the circuit board from the casing and cut the tracks as follows:
   (1)   Mixer output to IF input amplifier;
   (2)   IF output stage to coax connector;

(3)   Waveguide probe to first RF amplifier input;
(4)   RF output amplifier to mixer input;
(5)   Input to the last RF amplifier.
● Then using thin coaxial cable, link the following points:
(1)   IF output socket to first IF amplifier input;
(2)   IF output stage to mixer input;
(3)   Mixer output to last RF amplifier input;
(4)   Last RF amplifier output to waveguide probe.

An input signal ranging from 1 to 2 GHz applied to the old IF output socket will now generate radiation from the waveguide over the range 11–12 GHz. The output from this source might create interference to nearby installations or overload a test LNB placed in front of the output waveguide. A simple form of attenuation can be produced by glueing a small ball of steel wool into the mouth of the guide. Some experimentation with this method and careful handling of the circuit board will be needed, but a cheap and fairly stable Ku band signal source can be created.

Fault conditions

Faults in the LNBs can be subdivided into three groups: those attributed to weather and electrostatic discharges (ESD – lightning), those that produce a complete failure, or partial failures that are made obvious by sparklies and noise. The effects of ESD are cumulative so that these faults may not be immediately associated with this phenomenon. Because the LNBs employ FET devices that are susceptible to this problem, several distant strikes can have the same effect as a more local one. Take care when the covers are removed because even body static can induce the final strike.

Complete failures are most likely to be associated with the power supplies. When connected to a bench power unit, the current drawn by a correctly operating LNB should be in the order of 200–300 mA. If the current is very low or zero, this can indicate a faulty voltage regulator or an open circuit line connection. A high current could indicate a partial short circuit probably through corrosion or a leaky large value capacitor. With universal LNBs the failure of both V/H polarization and H/L band switching can cause a complete or partial failure.

The typical LNB has three RF and three IF amplifier stages and it is unlikely that all will be simultaneously faulty. It is therefore possible to compare voltages on a high impedance meter to obtain an indication of the activity of each stage. For RF stages the drain voltage will typically lie in the region of $3\,V \pm \frac{1}{2}\,V$, while the gate voltage should be around $-\frac{1}{2}\,V$. Note that the V/H switching should cause one or other of the first RF amplifiers to be turned off. The IF amplifier voltages will usually be somewhat higher than their RF counterparts but again these voltage levels should be much the same for all three stages. The local oscillator stages are difficult to check because the output is normally fairly small. This circuit may be off-tune or non-functioning and either way the LNB will not work. Usually there is a very low value of resistor in series with the drain lead and a volts drop across this will indicate whether the circuit is drawing current or not. If the gate electrode is shunted to ground by a resistor of about 500 Ω and the drain voltage does not change, then the transistor is most likely to be at fault. An off-tune oscillator is difficult to diagnose with the covers off and virtually impossible with the covers on without a spectrum analyser. Small but noted tweaks of the tuning screw can be made to check the effects (half a turn may be enough to take the signals completely out of range). This adjustment has a typical range of about 150–200 MHz and turning the screw clockwise increases the frequency at about 50 MHz per complete turn.

Sparklies and analogue systems

With NTSC, PAL and SECAM systems, the video noise problems appear to be most annoying in saturated areas of colour (often red) and the colour level tends to fade. Since these problems are much less visible with MAC systems, it would appear that the future digital transmissions will also be more resilient to this problem. Digital systems are well known for providing good images as the SNR degrades, only to crash suddenly when some low threshold is reached.

Sparkly problems are most prevalent at the edges of the service area and can be most troublesome under storm conditions. If this trouble is a persistent one, there are three typical ways in which improvements can be achieved: increase the antenna diameter, fit an LNB with a lower noise factor or install a receiver with a lower demodulator threshold level. Certain manufacturers provide an add-on filter unit that can be looped-through at IF on the main receiver; this reduces the effects of sparklies but at the expense of reduced video bandwidth.

For sparklies that develop during normal service, attention should be directed towards the coaxial cable and its connector. The ingress of moisture at this point can significantly affect the cable attenuation.

14.9 SERVICING THE MAIN RECEIVER

An overview

The pre-demodulator stages of receivers for either analogue or digital services will normally incorporate a significant amount of analogue signal processing. This section may either be based on the single or double conversion superhet principle, or even employ the direct conversion homodyne system, depending on the operating frequency range. The well-tried and tested method of signal injection/signal tracing can be used to isolate a faulty stage. For Ku band systems, the first IF will be fairly high and the circuit often employs discrete components. Any repair or component replacements in this stage are thus likely to involve realignment using a swept frequency signal generator and spectrum analyser. This operation may be particularly critical with certain TVRO receivers, where the IF bandwidth is preselectable for different services. The work of fault-finding in analogue stages is generally well documented (9). Post-demodulator processing may be either analogue or digital, the latter being well described in the literature (10).

Faults causing gain reduction in pre-demodulator stages lead to a poor SNR in analogue systems, the cause of which can readily be located by signal tracing. However, in digital services the same effect leads to an increase in bit errors, and the cause of this is not so easily traced.

Analogue section

The front end of these receivers may involve one or more stages of frequency conversion, prior to demodulation. Faulty stages can be readily isolated using the well-tried method of signal tracing/injection. Loss of gain in these IF stages leads to a worsening of SNR for analogue services and an increase in bit error rate on digital services. For systems like the TVRO receivers, the first IF will typically be tunable over the range 950–2150 MHz, with the circuits consisting of discrete components. Faulty component replacement in such stages will involve checks of alignment, a swept frequency signal generator and spectrum analyser being almost obligatory to obtain satisfactory results. Second or subsequent IF stages are commonly based around integrated circuits, which introduce their own particular servicing problems. The first line of approach should be the comparison between input and output signals, followed by a check of dc levels. Take particular note of the pins on which identical voltages exist because these can point to short circuits which may be either on the chip or in an external component. If the chip is socket mounted, its removal will usually remove the element of doubt. If not, and if disconnecting the external feeds does not clear the way, then the chip may need to be treated as described under SMD devices. After any servicing in the IF stages, it is important to check that gain and bandwidth are maintained across the tuning range.

The digital receiver

It was explained earlier that the digital equivalent of an SNR measurement was related to the *Energy per bit per Watt of noise power per Hz of bandwidth* (E_b/N_o), which in turn is related to the bit error rate (BER). If a data signal is applied to the vertical input of an oscilloscope whose timebase is locked in a particular way to the data rate, the resulting display becomes a series of superimposed signal transitions that create an *eye* diagram (11). Figure 14.10 represents such a display and shows how the pattern is formed and the principle of measuring the *eye height*. The height H and width W of the eye are a function

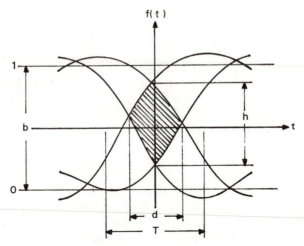

Figure 14.10 Details of 'eye' display.

of the slopes of the data transitions; these, in turn, are dependent upon the degree of noise and distortion to which the signal has been exposed.

The eye height is defined as the ratio of the difference in levels between worst-case 0s and 1s, to the difference in levels between a long sequence of 0s and 1s. From Figure 14.10, this can be expressed as:

$$H = h/b \times 100\% \tag{14.2}$$

The eye width W and jitter J are also significant in the interests of a low BER. The greater the width of the eye, the lower will be the error rate after the resampling process. W is defined as the ratio of eye width to data bit period. The system noise margin and sensitivity to timing errors is related to the vertical height and horizontal width of the eye respectively. From Figure 14.10:

$$W = d/T \tag{14.3}$$

Jitter, which is usually expressed as an error in time, is chiefly due to inter-symbol interference; it also affects the error rate and can be evaluated as:

$$J = T(1 - W) \tag{14.4}$$

A non-symmetrical appearance of the eye about the centre line indicates that non-linearities are present in the system under test. The slope of the vertical sides of the eye between the 10 and 90 percent amplitudes are related to the rise and fall times and this gives an indication of the system frequency response.

The principle of an eye pattern display unit can be described with the aid of Figure 14.11 (11). A clock signal is derived from the data signal and its frequency divided by four. This signal is then low-pass filtered to obtain a

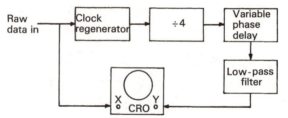

Figure 14.11 Principle of an 'eye' display unit.

sinusoid at 1/4 of the bit rate. This sinusoid and the original data stream are applied to the X and Y inputs respectively of an oscilloscope. By adjusting the phasing of the sinusoid, the displayed Lissajous figure becomes an 'eye'.

As an alternative, an oscilloscope can be used directly to provide an assessment of the eye height. If the raw data is applied to the Y input and the timebase set to run at a much lower frequency, the data transitions will be displayed in the manner shown in Figure 14.12. Overshoots and undershoots generated by signal distortion give rise to the two brighter bands, which give the method its descriptive title – the 'tram-line' method. A reasonable approximation to the eye height can be obtained as:

$$a/b \times 100\% \tag{14.5}$$

When servicing a digital receiver, a before and after check of the eye height on the just demodulated signal can give a useful assessment of any

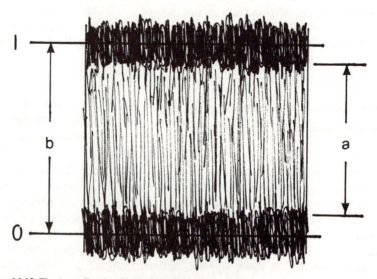

Figure 14.12 The 'tram-lines' method of corrupted data display.

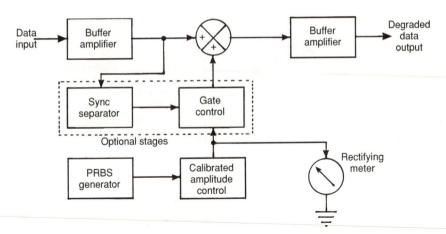

Figure 14.13 Decoding margin test unit.

improvements made. In general, a good eye height value would be around 75 percent. In practice, most digital receivers will work, with very few errors, down to an eye height of about 25per cent before the system crashes.

The decoding margin

Figure 14.13 shows the basic principles of a simple test unit that was developed for use with the teletext systems that are broadcast intermittently within the vertical blanking interval of the television signal. The output from a PRBS generator is combined with the received signal in a controlled manner. The amplitude of this *noise* component is slowly increased until decoding just fails. Once this control and the corresponding meter have been calibrated, the test unit gives an indication of the *in-hand* distortion or decoding margin for the system. If the data stream is a continuous one, then the sync and gating sections of this device will not be needed.

Other BER testers (BERT) range in complexity from laboratory instruments to relatively simple hand-held devices suitable for field use. These latter instruments usually provide a system test input from a long PRBS and then compare this with the response at the output to calculate the measured errors.

Distortion testing with multi-level modulation systems

The constellation analyser is an instrument that is capable of distinguishing between the various causes of bit errors in multi-level (QAM or QPSK) signalling systems. The CRO display is a plot on the real and imaginary axes, representing the in-phase and quadrature signal components, respectively. The

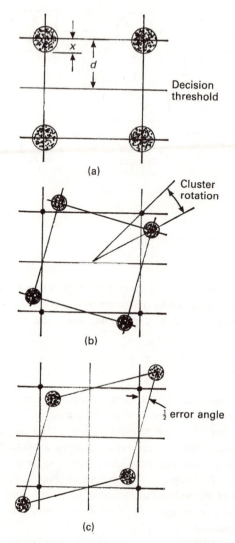

Figure 14.14 Constellation diagrams. (**a**) Equivalent to eye closure. (**b**) Lock angle. (**c**) Quadrature angle error.

coincident points in the signal vector space produce a bright-up effect on the CRT face. An N-level signal produces an N-point square of bright regions, the constellation, where each point represents a particular phase/magnitude relationship from the complex modulated signal. Repeated display of the data stream integrates the effect to produce patterns similar to those shown in Figure 14.14. The overall summation of noise and distortion produces an effect similar to that shown in Figure 14.14(a), where the ratio x/d × 100% is equivalent to the eye height. The angular rotation from the ideal position as shown by the cluster at (b)

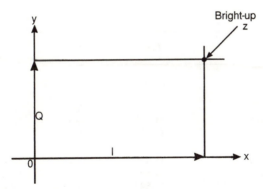

Figure 14.15 Generation of signal constellation points.

represents the effect of phase angle errors between the data stream and the decoder clock recovery circuit. This is described as the lock-angle error. An error between the I and Q phases can arise either at the transmitter or in the receiver decoder section and this is described as a quadrature error. The total angular error can be evaluated by doubling the angle measured in (c). In a practical situation, a constellation would display the summation of all errors, but these can be separated by careful analysis.

Figure 14.15 shows how the constellation points are produced by a three-dimensional effect on the CRT screen, each point being created from the I and Q components coincident with a bright-up pulse that is synchronized to the data symbol rate.

The digital receiver

Test equipment required for servicing in the digital control section includes logic probes, frequency meters/counters and oscilloscopes. It is important to point out here that, even when displaying a relatively low bit rate signal, the CRO bandwidth should be sufficient to encompass at least the tenth harmonic, if the Y amplifiers are not going to further distort the data signal.

The equipment needed for fault tracing in this section depends on the nature of the data signal. While the signal is in serial form, it can be traced with an oscilloscope and its quality evaluated via an eye height measurement. When the data is in a parallel form, a logic analyser is more appropriate. For the system control stages, a logic probe will be found to be most effective. Problems related to frequency synthesis tuning systems should lead to an investigation first of dc levels, then of an accurate measurement of the main clock signal and its divided versions. Strange control faults can often arise because of corrupted data being held in microprocessor memory. There is normally a switch included in the system reset circuit to clear the EPROM memory completely to allow

Table 14.2

No.	Name	Freq.	Pol.	LNB	Aud.
64	ASTRA 60	10.877	Vert	N/A	StA
65	ASTRA 62	10.906	Vert	N/A	StA
66	SKY RADIO	11.318	Vert	N/A	StB
67	RADIO 538	11.318	Vert	N/A	StC
68	VIRGIN	11.377	Vert	N/A	StB
69	SUNRISE	11.479	Vert	N/A	Mo4
70	HOLLAND FM	11.479	Vert	N/A	Mo5
71	RADIO ASIA	11.597	Vert	N/A	Mo4
72	RAD SWEDEN	11.597	Vert	N/A	Mo6

reprogramming. But with so many channels now available this becomes a daunting task.

Table 14.2, which is an extract from the listings of a system known as PACE Link (12), gives a good example of why this approach is often avoided. However, there are now some useful aids available to the service engineer which allow the receiver tuning data to be downloaded into a PC. The PACE Link system has been developed to enable the receiver tuning to be edited via the keyboard using an interface coupled between the decoder/scrambler SCART socket and the PC serial port. The software provides a wide range of facilities specifically for PACE Ltd receivers. The features include reading the current memory contents, editing an entry, interchanging and updating channel settings, and uploading the new set-up data into the receiver, together with preview and printout of the data tables. These features are also helpful when installing a new receiver. Before clearing the memory of any suspect system, it is only necessary to download the current tuning data, edit the data table and reload the new channel information. At least at this stage, the engineer knows that the memory is not corrupted. Other similar system designs are available for other makes of receiver and a number of simple DIY EEPROM-based circuits have been described in the technical journals (13).

Fault-finding in the microprocessor control section

When a microprocessor control system fails, the parallel nature of its data organization and the high degree of interdependence between the inputs and outputs can make the task of fault-finding difficult. All the elements of the system are interconnected via the data, address and control buses, so that a fault in one section can be reflected into several other areas. Typical bus line faults include short circuits between adjacent lines, or one or more lines jammed at logic 0 or 1 due to a short circuit to earth or positive supply rail. Various test methods are described in the literature (14), some of which are only suitable for a large service organization.

The logic analyser is the digital equivalent of the oscilloscope, but with parallel inputs. Modern instruments are available that will store as many as a hundred 32-bit words of data. These may be displayed, either as binary or hexadecimal characters, or as a series of waveforms, representing the high/low activity states of the various lines.

When a prototype system has been constructed and proved to function correctly, it can be made to execute a sequence of instructions in a repetitive manner. By monitoring each node of the system, data can be acquired about the correct logical activity. *Signature analysis*, as developed by Hewlett-Packard Ltd, converts each node data into a unique four-character hexadecimal code that represents the 'signature' at a correctly functioning node. System documentation is then prepared, which includes a circuit diagram with all the correct node signatures appended. In servicing, a faulty component can then be identified as a device that produces an error output from correct input signatures.

Portable diagnostic aids based on a PROM that carries a stored test program may be plugged into a system test socket, or clipped 'piggy-back' fashion to the microprocessor, they can be valuable field service tools. Such devices are operated in some prescribed manner, so that the various elements of the system may be tested. Their status may be displayed either on LED/LCD, seven-segment indicators or, as in the case of a TV system, directly on the receiver screen.

Even without such aids, fault-finding is still possible (15). The microprocessor IC is normally mounted in a socket, so that it can be removed to enable the bus lines to be checked for short circuits. An adaptor socket that isolates the microprocessor from the data bus can be interposed between this IC and its own socket. Forcing the microprocessor into a non-operation (NOP) or *free-running* mode causes it to issue every possible address value, in a continuous cycle. By comparing the pulse repetition frequency on adjacent lines, using a double-beam oscilloscope, the 2:1 relationship between correctly functioning address lines can quickly be established.

The data bus lines can easily be checked for short circuits by the use of a logic probe. To examine its activity, the microprocessor needs to be forced into *a single-step* mode. It then becomes possible to check the validity of data transfers.

The status of the system clock waveform, or any derivatives, can easily be checked using an oscilloscope or logic probe.

Once the control section of the system has been proven to function correctly, attention can be directed towards the other elements in a systematic manner.

Fault-finding in the new developing MPEG-based receivers is still very much an unknown factor. Since these are most likely to be constructed around high-density ASIC chips, it will be important to obtain a thorough understanding of the way in which the signal elements are processed so that the signal inputs and outputs can be compared to enable an accurate diagnosis to be made. Analogue signal processing will remain dominant up to the first demodulator stage and there will still be faulty power supplies to contend with.

The manufacturers (18) have the services of complex test sets that exercise the MPEG decoders to provide outputs to PCs that include all the special programme code and control groups. However, because it is likely to a few years before cut-down versions of such equipment becomes available to the general workshops, the service engineers nearest to the customers will have to get by using their inherent skills and ingenuity.

14.10   SERVICE SUPPORT DATABASES

When television receivers were constructed around many discrete components, device reliability was relatively poor. Failures occurred in a regular manner, giving rise to the stock faults. Indeed, many service departments established a sound reputation for quick and reliable repairs. With the introduction of dedicated ICs, system reliability improved very considerably. However, the stock faults still occur but repeat with a much lower frequency, making a good memory an additional requirement for the service engineer. Fortunately there are now a number of computer system databases available that have been designed to aid service personnel in the repair of equipment. While these can provide almost instant access to many of the stock faults, it must be emphasized that these should be used in conjunction with system circuit diagrams and data sheets. Two of these databases have been tested and found to be invaluable to the busy workshop.

SoftCopy (16)

This has been published by SoftCopy Ltd, Cheltenham, UK in cooperation with the journal *Television* which is published by Reed Business Publications, and is updated annually. The program, which has been designed to run on a relatively low-level IBM-compatible PC, contains more than 7000 different fault condition entries and is very easy to use. There is additional space within the system memory to incorporate the results of personal experience. The database covers most of the faults on CD players, camcorders, satellite TV systems and VCR machines as well as television receivers, plus many descriptive articles that have been published in the journal back to 1986. These provide good background reading to obtain an understanding of the operations of many of the popular items of equipment. It is thus a tool that should be found useful in any busy service department. Because of the relatively low processing needs, this database can also be installed to run on a laptop computer for use by field service engineers.

Euras (17)

By comparison, the database provided by EURAS International Ltd, Bristol, UK, is supplied on a CD-ROM which to some extent increases the processing needs. However, this is updated three times annually on a subscription basis. The fault-finding and repair hints represent the knowledge gleaned from manufacturers, dealers and repair centres, and cover about 500 000 entries from more than 600 manufacturers. Unusually, the database information is covered in most European languages. Again, the system memory provides space to record personal knowledge gained over a period of time. Because of the greater available memory space on the CD-ROM, the publishers have provided the appropriate circuit diagram segment with each repair hint.

Unattended operation

Some systems, such as those providing cable TV head-end and SMATV system feeds, are designed for unmanned operation. On these, a monthly maintenance check is advisable because this can considerably reduce the incidence of service failure. In addition, it is useful to keep a log of the system parameters. The most important checks should include:

- that the noise levels on both the video and audio channels are unchanged;
- the AFC voltage level – if this is drifting towards the edge of its hold range, a readjustment might avoid a later service failure;
- relative signal levels – variation in such levels may give an indication of component ageing, receiver drift or slight antenna misalignment problems due to weather conditions;
- system running temperature and installation weather-proofing.

14.11   CABLE SYSTEM MAINTENANCE (18)

Whether the services are analogue or digital and the carrier medium copper cable or optical fibre, many of the system parameters are very similar. For example, the frequency and amplitude response, group delay, attenuation, distortion and noise all affect the quality of service provided. All systems also suffer from similar basic failure modes and problems. These range from contractors for other services either digging up underground cabling or severing overhead lines, to weathering and ageing effects and other man-made problems. Because the broadband copper cable networks cover a frequency range of almost five octaves (45–850 MHz) and attenuation rises very significantly with frequency, these need to be compensated by introducing correction in the form of pre-emphasis. For digital systems, the important feature is probably the maximum distance reached by a particular bit rate and again these are contrary factors. Many of the parameters depend upon the velocity ratio or factor which for coaxial cable ranges from about 0.66 to 0.75. This factor is dependent upon the cable construction and the dielectric constant which ranges from 1 for free air to about 0.5 for PVC insulators.

All cable systems suffer to some extent from RF leakage, both egress and ingress. By comparison, the former is the easiest to measure and is well correlated with values for the latter. Leakage occurs chiefly due to the ageing, weathering and man-made causes. Points of common leakage are associated with tap points and distribution amplifers. RF leakage out of a system can be detected by using a hand-held unit equipped with a short loaded monopole antenna with the receiver being operated in the scanning mode to locate the radiation due to troublesome frequencies.

Carrier frequency leakage occurs if any suppressed carrier modulators are not correctly balanced and some carrier component leaks into the output stages. While such energy does not usually create interference, it represents a loss of transmission power which can lead to a degraded quality of service or bit errors in a digital network.

A power budget similar to that calculated for satellite systems can be derived for optical fibre networks and this demonstrates the difference in dB between the source output level and the receiver sensitivity. It therefore shows the total margin allowable for fibre, splice, connector and splitter losses, together with the overhead required to counter temperature changes and ageing effects.

Time domain reflectometry (TDR) provides the means of testing both copper and optical fibre networks. Just as a radar signal reflects off a surface to provide a return signal that can be used for identification and location, electromagnetic energy also reflects from a mismatched impedance in a conductor and from discontinuities in optical fibres. The time taken for the reflection to return to the source depends on the velocity of propagation, the velocity ratio of the transmission medium and its length. If these factors are known or can be measured, then not only can data about the cable parameters be determined, but also the distance to a fault can be accurately calculated. TDR instruments are designed for fault location, length measurement and transmission path characteristics. When the lines are suitably terminated, testing can be carried out from just one end of the system. The common factors that create a change of impedance along a cable include the ingress of water which changes the dielectric constant, a cracked or damaged screen which changes the capacitance, and high-resistance connections. TDR testing will indicate open or short circuits, badly made crimps or connections, water in a cable, amplifier faults and even illegal taps. Line amplifiers tend to isolate the network into sections so that TDR cannot usually locate faults beyond an amplifier. Frequency domain reflectometry (FDR) using a swept frequency source is often more sensitive to problems close to the subscriber's end of the line and is often used to test the drop cables.

The difference between the methods used for optical fibres and copper cables lies in the nature of the energizing pulse. For optical TDR (OTDR), a short, high-density pulse of light is input to the fibre, while the copper cable system is energized with a short-duration electrical pulse. After transmission, the test set enters a monitor mode to detect and time the arrival of the backscatter. By including a CRT type of display together with a microprocessor control circuit within the instrument, it is possible to measure the relative amplitudes of the forward and reflected pulses to obtain the attenuation. The time delay between the two pulses is indicative of the distance to any discontinuity. Portable instruments are available that will calculate most of the important system parameters, store the results on floppy disk or hardcopy printer, and even interface to a PC. OTDR instruments generally have a dead band which represents the accuracy to which a distance measurement can be made and this varies from about 1 to 20 m. The maximum optical range can exceed 200 km. The more sophisticated instruments can take measurements at any of the most common optical windows of 850 nm, 1310 nm, 1550 nm and 1625 nm.

REFERENCES

(1) *Code of Practice for the Installation of Satellite Television Receiving Antennas.* (1998). London: Confederation of Aerial Industries.

(2) Mazda, F. (1993) *Telecommunications Engineers Reference Book.* Oxford: Butterworth–Heinemann Ltd.

(3) Ackroyd, B. (1990) *World Satellite Communications & Earth Station Design.* Oxford: Blackwells Scientific Publishing Ltd.

(4) Stephenson, D.J. (1998) *Satmaster PRO for Windows.* Cricklade, UK: Swift Television Publications.

(5) Kaplan, J., Swires Research Ltd, Basildon, Essex. UK. Private communication to author.

(6) Frodsham, S., Commercial Chemicals Division, 3 M UK Ltd, Bracknell, UK. Private communication to author.

(7) Cato, R.I., Multicore Solders Ltd, Hemel Hempstead, UK. Private communication to author.

(8) Ayriss, J.F. and Glenton, J.A., MIC Colour Engineering Services Ltd, Manchester, UK. Private communication to author.

(9) Trundle, E. (1996) *TV and Video Technology*, 2nd edn. Oxford: Butterworth-Heinemann Ltd.

(10) Sinclair, I. and Lewis, G. (1996). *Digital Techniques & Microprocessor Systems.* Oxford: Butterworth-Heinemann.

(11) Bennet, W.R. and Davey, J.R. (1965) *Data Transmission.* London: McGraw-Hill.

(12) Bone, A., Pace Micro Technology, Shipley, W. Yorks, UK. Private communication to author.

(13) *Television.* Reed Business Information, The Quadrant, Sutton, Surrey, UK.

(14) Day, S. (1981) 'Techniques for Fault finding in Microprocessor-Based Systems'. *IBA Technical Review No. 15.* Independent Broadcasting Authority, UK.

(15) Williams, G.B. (1986) 'Simple Test Equipment for Microcomputers'. *Electronics and Wireless World.* Business Press International Ltd.

(16) SoftCopy Ltd, Cheltenham, UK. Private communication to author.

(17) EURAS Imternational Ltd, Bristol, UK. Private communication to author.

(18) *Proceedings* (1997) Tektronix Convergence Symposium, Tektronix, UK.

Appendix 1

A1.1 GEOSTATIONARY ORBITS

The gravitational force of attraction between two bodies is proportional to the product of their masses M, and inversely proportional to the square of the distance r between their centres of mass, the constant of proportionality being G, the Universal Gravitational Constant of $6.67 \times 10^{-11}\,\text{Nm}^2/\text{kg}^2$.

Thus the gravitational force acting between a geostationary satellite and the earth (see Figure A1.1) is given by:

$$F_g = GM_eM_s/r^2 \text{ Newtons} \tag{A1.1}$$

where M_e and M_s are the masses of the earth and satellite respectively.

$$(M_e = 5.98 \times 10^{24}\,\text{kg})$$

The force acting on a body, constrained to circular motion, is proportional to its mass, the radius of the circular path and the square of the angular velocity. Thus the force acting on a geostationary satellite against gravity is given by:

$$F_c = M_g r\omega^2 \text{ Newtons} \tag{A1.2}$$

where r is the radius of the circular path and ω is the angular velocity.

The satellite continues in circular orbit around the earth when their separation and velocity are such that equations A1.1 and A1.2 are equal, so that:

$$GM_eM_s/r^2 = M_s r\omega^2 \quad \text{and}$$

$$r^3 = GM_e/\omega^2$$

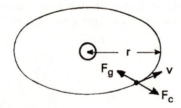

Figure A1.1 The geostationary orbit.

Now, since the satellite is geostationary, its angular velocity ω is the same as that of the earth, $2\pi r$ radians per sidereal day.

$$\omega = 2\pi/(23.9345 \times 60 \times 60)\,\text{rad/sec}$$

$$= 7.30 \times 10^{-5}\,\text{rad/sec (approx.)}$$

$$r^3 = (6.67 \times 10^{-11} \times 5.98 \times 10^{24})/(7.3^2 \times 10^{-10})$$

$$r = 42\,143\,\text{km (approx.)}$$

Assuming a mean earth radius of 6378 km, the satellite average height above the equator is 35 765 km.

$$\text{Satellite velocity} = 2\pi(42\,143 \times 10^3)/(23.9345 \times 60 \times 60)$$

$$= 3.073\,\text{km/sec (approx.)}$$

A1.2   ELLIPTICAL ORBITS

Satellites using these orbits, shown in Figure A1.2, obey Kepler's law of planetary motion fairly accurately. Rephrased for satellite applications, these state:

● The satellite moves in an elliptical orbit with the centre of the earth at one focus.
● The radius vector sweeps out equal areas in equal time.
● The square of the period of revolution is proportional to the cube of the semi-major axis, giving rise to the equation:

$$T = 2\pi\sqrt{(a^3/GM_e)} \tag{A1.3}$$

where T is the orbit period in seconds, a is a semi-major axis in metres,

$$M_e = 5.98 \times 10^{24}\,\text{kg}$$

$$G = 6.67 \times 10^{-11}\,\text{Nm}^2/\text{kg}^2$$

The velocity of the satellite is greatest at the perigee and least at the apogee. For this reason, the satellite is in communications range for fairly long periods at the greatest distance from earth. Using values taken from the OSCAR-10 satellite

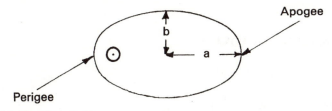

Figure A1.2 The elliptical orbit.

(Orbiting Satellite Carrying Amateur Radio) gives an orbital time of approximately 11.66 hrs.

Semi-major axis	26 100 km
Semi-minor axis	20 800 km
Apogee	35 500 km
Perigee	3 960 km

Observations taken from satellites in these orbits show that equation A1.3 needs only a small correction, to account for the earth's elliptical shape and anisotropic density.

A1.3   MICROWAVE FREQUENCY BAND CLASSIFICATION

As stated in Chapter 1, the frequency ranges used for satellite communications are commonly known by the American Radar Engineering Standard. In Europe, however, another classification may be used, and this can give rise to some confusion.

Table A1.1 Frequency ranges (GHz)

Band	American	European
P	0.2–1.0	0.2–0.375
L	1.0–2.0	0.375–1.5
S	2.0–4.0	1.5–3.75
C	4.0–8.0	3.75–6.0
X	8.0–12.5	6.0–11.5
J	–	11.5–18.0
Ku	12.5–18.0	–
K	18.0–26.5	18.0–30.0
Ka	26.5–40.0	–
Q	40.0–50.0	30.0–47.0
V	–	47.0–56.0

A1.4   FM/AM NOISE ADVANTAGES

Noise power proportional to v^2

$$\text{Noise power (AM)} = \int_0^{f_1} 1^2.df = f_1 \, W$$

Noise power (FM) $= \int_0^{f_1} v^2.df$ $[v = 1 \times f_1/f_2,$ and therefore
$$v^2 = \{f_1/f_2\}^2]$$

$$= \int_0^{f_1} (f_1/f_2)^2.df \ (f_2 \text{ is a constant})$$

$$= 1/f_2^2(f_1^3/3) = f_1^3/3f_2^2 \, W$$

Ratio AM noise/FM noise $= \dfrac{f_1 \times 3f_2^2}{f_1^3} = 3(f_2/f_1)^2$

$$= 3M^2 \ \{M = f_2/f_1, \text{ the deviation ratio}\}$$

Factor of improvement, SNR $= 3M^2$

When $M = 5$, the noise improvement $= 10 \log.25 = 18.75\,dB$.

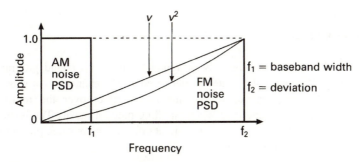

Figure A1.3 AM/FM noise power spectral density.

A1.5 DE-EMPHASIS

$$v_0 = i/(j\omega c)$$

$$i = v_i/(R + 1/j\omega c)$$

$$v_i = iR + i/(j\omega c)$$

$$v_0/v_i = (1/j\omega c)/(R + 1/j\omega c) = 1/(1 + j\omega cR)$$

$$= 1/(1 + j\omega t) \ [t = CR]$$

$$|v_0/v_i| = 1/\surd(1 + \omega^2 t^2)$$

$$20 \log |v_0/v_i| = 20 \log(1 + \omega^2 t^2)^{-1/2} = -10 \log(1 + \omega^2 t^2)$$

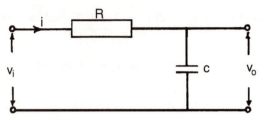

Figure A1.4 De-emphasis network.

To give the circuit response at any frequency; for example, the response at 10 kHz with a time constant t = 50 μs is:

$$-10 \log(1 + (2\pi)^2 \times 10^8 \times 50^2 \times 10^{-12}) \, \mathrm{dB}$$

$$= -10 \log(1 + 9.87) \, \mathrm{dB}$$

$$= -10.36 \, \mathrm{dB}$$

J.17   Pre-emphasis

This standard, which was originally designed for use with sound programme links, is now often applied to satellite-delivered sound channels. As shown in Figure A1.5, the response curve has maximum effect over the mid-range frequencies, and this is beneficial when handling modern music. The levelling-off at HF is also helpful in minimizing sibilant effects that are often present with single-order pre-emphasis circuits.

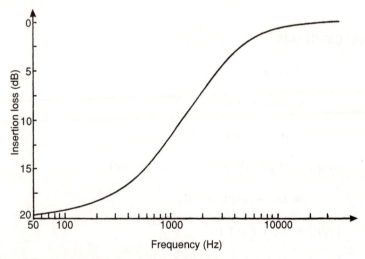

Figure A1.5 J17 pre-emphasis characteristic.

The response curve represents an insertion loss given by:

$$10 \log \frac{75 + (\omega/3000)^2}{1 + (\omega/3000)^2} \text{ dB}$$

where $\omega = 2\pi f$ and f is the corresponding frequency.

The curve is practically symmetrical about 1.2 kHz and provides about 6 dB boost relative to LF at 800 Hz.

The receiver de-emphasis circuit obviously needs to have a complementary response.

A1.6 SIGNALS IN THE PRESENCE OF NOISE

This section is not intended to be definitive, but is offered more in the revisionary sense. The reader should refer to such texts as are listed in the bibliography (1, 2, 3) for a more detailed analysis of signal behaviour in the presence of noise.

White noise has a normal or Gaussian distribution; that is, it has an amplitude

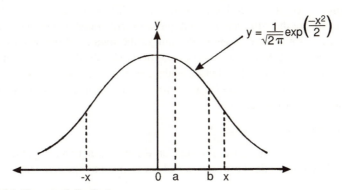

Figure A1.6 The normal distribution.

distribution described statistically by the curve of Figure A1.6. The curve is drawn for the function:

$$y = 1/\sqrt{(2\pi)} \exp(-x^2/2)$$

The following points should be noted:

- When $x = 0$, $y = 1/\sqrt{(2\pi)}$ or approximately 0.4.
- The curve is symmetrical about the y axis.
- The area under the curve is unity (1).
- y approaches zero as x tends to infinity (∞).
- For this normal distribution, the area under the curve represents the

probability that x(P(x)) falls within a range of values. For example:

$$P(x) \; -\infty < x < +\infty \; = \; 1$$

$$P(x) \text{ is negative} \; = \; P(x) \text{ is positive} \; = \; 0.5$$

In general, the probability that x lies between a and b is given by the area bounded by a, b and the curve. For convenience, the probability values are tabulated.

The following is an extract from tables such as those given in reference (1).

Value of x	0	0.5	1.0	1.5	2.0	2.5
Area between 0 and x	0	0.1915	0.3413	0.4332	0.4772	0.4938

Thus:

Probability that x lies between 0 and 1 = 0.3413
Probability that x lies between 1 and 2 = 0.1359
Probability that x is greater than 1.5   = 0.5 – 0.4332
                                         = 0.0668

Because of symmetry, the mean (μ) or average value of the function is zero. In a practical situation this is unlikely, and it is important to know the dispersion or deviation from the mean that the values take. The most effective parameters in these cases are the *variance* (σ^2) and the *standard deviation* (σ). The variance of the distribution is the average of the sum of the squares of the deviation from the mean value, while the standard deviation is simply the square root of the variance. For the normal distribution with $\mu = 0$, $\sigma^2 = 1$ and $\sigma = 1$.

In the case where the mean is non-zero, the probability is given by the area under the curve of the function:

$$y \; = \; 1/\sqrt{(2\pi\sigma)}.\exp(-x^2/2\sigma^2)$$

which is much less easy to use. For such cases, other functions are tabulated (3). The probability that x lies between $-x$ and $+x$ is given by the *error function* (erf) where:

$$\text{erf}(x) \; = \; 2\left[\frac{1}{\sqrt{\pi}} \int_0^x \exp.(-y^2) \, dy\right]$$

The probability that x lies outside this range is given by the *complementary error function* (erfc) where:

$$\text{erfc}(x) \; = \; 1 - \text{erf}(x)$$

It is shown (2, 3) that the probability of error P_e is given by:

$$P_e \; = \; \frac{1}{2} \text{ erfc}\left[\frac{x}{\sigma\sqrt{2}}\right]$$

Table A1.2 Normal error function tables

$$\text{erf } x = \frac{2}{\sqrt{\pi}} \int_0^x \exp(-y^2) \, dy$$

x	erf x	x	erf x	x	erf x	x	erf x
0.00	0.000 000	0.50	0.520 500	1.00	0.842 701	1.50	0.966 105
0.01	0.011 283	0.51	0.529 244	1.01	0.846 810	1.51	0.967 277
0.02	0.022 565	0.52	0.537 899	1.02	0.850 838	1.52	0.968 413
0.03	0.033 841	0.53	0.546 464	1.03	0.854 784	1.53	0.969 516
0.04	0.045 111	0.54	0.554 939	1.04	0.858 650	1.54	0.970 586
0.05	0.056 372	0.55	0.563 323	1.05	0.862 436	1.55	0.971 623
0.06	0.067 622	0.56	0.571 616	1.06	0.866 144	1.56	0.972 628
0.07	0.078 858	0.57	0.579 816	1.07	0.869 773	1.57	0.973 603
0.08	0.090 078	0.58	0.587 923	1.08	0.873 326	1.58	0.974 547
0.09	0.101 281	0.59	0.595 936	1.09	0.876 803	1.59	0.975 462
0.10	0.112 463	0.60	0.603 856	1.10	0.880 205	1.60	0.976 348
0.11	0.123 623	0.61	0.611 681	1.11	0.883 533	1.61	0.977 207
0.12	0.134 758	0.62	0.619 411	1.12	0.886 788	1.62	0.978 038
0.13	0.145 867	0.63	0.627 046	1.13	0.889 971	1.63	0.978 843
0.14	0.156 947	0.64	0.634 586	1.14	0.893 082	1.64	0.979 622
0.15	0.167 996	0.65	0.642 029	1.15	0.896 124	1.65	0.980 376
0.16	0.179 012	0.66	0.649 377	1.16	0.899 096	1.66	0.981 105
0.17	0.189 992	0.67	0.656 628	1.17	0.902 000	1.67	0.981 810
0.18	0.200 936	0.68	0.663 782	1.18	0.904 837	1.68	0.982 493
0.19	0.211 840	0.69	0.670 840	1.19	0.907 608	1.69	0.983 153
0.20	0.222 703	0.70	0.677 801	1.20	0.910 314	1.70	0.983 790
0.21	0.233 522	0.71	0.684 666	1.21	0.912 956	1.71	0.984 407
0.22	0.244 296	0.72	0.691 433	1.22	0.915 534	1.72	0.985 003
0.23	0.255 023	0.73	0.698 104	1.23	0.918 050	1.73	0.985 578
0.24	0.265 700	0.74	0.704 678	1.24	0.920 505	1.74	0.986 135
0.25	0.276 326	0.75	0.711 156	1.25	0.922 900	1.75	0.986 672
0.26	0.286 900	0.76	0.717 537	1.26	0.925 236	1.76	0.987 190
0.27	0.297 418	0.77	0.723 822	1.27	0.927 514	1.77	0.987 691
0.28	0.307 880	0.78	0.730 010	1.28	0.929 734	1.78	0.988 174
0.29	0.318 283	0.79	0.736 103	1.29	0.931 899	1.79	0.988 641
0.30	0.328 627	0.80	0.742 101	1.30	0.934 008	1.80	0.989 091
0.31	0.338 908	0.81	0.748 003	1.31	0.936 063	1.81	0.989 525
0.32	0.349 126	0.82	0.753 811	1.32	0.938 065	1.82	0.989 943
0.33	0.359 279	0.83	0.759 524	1.33	0.940 015	1.83	0.990 347
0.34	0.369 365	0.84	0.765 143	1.34	0.941 914	1.84	0.990 736
0.35	0.379 382	0.85	0.770 668	1.35	0.943 762	1.85	0.991 111
0.36	0.389 330	0.86	0.776 100	1.36	0.945 561	1.86	0.991 472
0.37	0.399 206	0.87	0.781 440	1.37	0.947 312	1.87	0.991 821
0.38	0.409 009	0.88	0.786 687	1.38	0.949 016	1.88	0.992 156
0.39	0.418 739	0.89	0.791 843	1.39	0.950 673	1.89	0.992 479
0.40	0.428 392	0.90	0.796 908	1.40	0.952 285	1.90	0.992 790
0.41	0.437 969	0.91	0.801 883	1.41	0.953 852	1.91	0.993 090
0.42	0.447 468	0.92	0.806 768	1.42	0.955 376	1.92	0.993 378
0.43	0.456 887	0.93	0.811 564	1.43	0.956 857	1.93	0.993 656
0.44	0.466 225	0.94	0.816 271	1.44	0.958 297	1.94	0.993 923
0.45	0.475 482	0.95	0.820 891	1.45	0.959 695	1.95	0.994 179
0.46	0.484 635	0.96	0.825 424	1.46	0.961 054	1.96	0.994 426
0.47	0.493 745	0.97	0.829 870	1.47	0.962 373	1.97	0.994 664
0.48	0.502 750	0.98	0.834 232	1.48	0.963 654	1.98	0.994 892
0.49	0.511 668	0.99	0.838 508	1.49	0.964 898	1.99	0.995 111

x	erf x	x	erf x	x	erf x	x	erf x
2.00	0.995 322	2.50	0.999 593	3.00	0.999 977 91	3.50	0.999 999 257
2.01	0.995 525	2.51	0.999 614	3.01	0.999 979 26	3.51	0.999 999 309
2.02	0.995 719	2.52	0.999 635	3.02	0.999 980 53	3.52	0.999 999 358
2.03	0.995 906	2.53	0.999 654	3.03	0.999 981 73	3.53	0.999 999 403
2.04	0.996 086	2.54	0.999 672	3.04	0.999 982 86	3.54	0.999 999 445
2.05	0.996 258	2.55	0.999 689	3.05	0.999 983 92	3.55	0.999 999 485
2.06	0.996 423	2.56	0.999 706	3.06	0.999 984 92	3.56	0.999 999 521
2.07	0.996 582	2.57	0.999 722	3.07	0.999 985 86	3.57	0.999 999 555
2.08	0.996 734	2.58	0.999 736	3.08	0.999 986 74	3.58	0.999 999 587
2.09	0.996 880	2.59	0.999 751	3.09	0.999 987 57	3.59	0.999 999 617
2.10	0.997 021	2.60	0.999 764	3.10	0.999 988 35	3.60	0.999 999 644
2.11	0.997 155	2.61	0.999 777	3.11	0.999 989 08	3.61	0.999 999 670
2.12	0.997 284	2.62	0.999 789	3.12	0.999 989 77	3.62	0.999 999 694
2.13	0.997 407	2.63	0.999 800	3.13	0.999 990 42	3.63	0.999 999 716
2.14	0.997 525	2.64	0.999 811	3.14	0.999 991 03	3.64	0.999 999 736
2.15	0.997 639	2.65	0.999 822	3.15	0.999 991 60	3.65	0.999 999 756
2.16	0.997 747	2.66	0.999 831	3.16	0.999 992 14	3.66	0.999 999 773
2.17	0.997 851	2.67	0.999 841	3.17	0.999 992 64	3.67	0.999 999 790
2.18	0.997 951	2.68	0.999 849	3.18	0.999 993 11	3.68	0.999 999 805
2.19	0.998 046	2.69	0.999 858	3.19	0.999 993 56	3.69	0.999 999 820
2.20	0.998 137	2.70	0.999 866	3.20	0.999 993 97	3.70	0.999 999 833
2.21	0.998 224	2.71	0.999 873	3.21	0.999 994 36	3.71	0.999 999 845
2.22	0.998 308	2.72	0.999 880	3.22	0.999 994 73	3.72	0.999 999 857
2.23	0.998 388	2.73	0.999 887	3.23	0.999 995 07	3.73	0.999 999 867
2.24	0.998 464	2.74	0.999 893	3.24	0.999 995 40	3.74	0.999 999 877
2.25	0.998 537	2.75	0.999 899	3.25	0.999 995 70	3.75	0.999 999 886
2.26	0.998 607	2.76	0.999 905	3.26	0.999 995 98	3.76	0.999 999 895
2.27	0.998 674	2.77	0.999 910	3.27	0.999 996 24	3.77	0.999 999 903
2.28	0.998 738	2.78	0.999 916	3.28	0.999 996 49	3.78	0.999 999 910
2.29	0.998 799	2.79	0.999 920	3.29	0.999 996 72	3.79	0.999 999 917
2.30	0.998 857	2.80	0.999 925	3.30	0.999 996 94	3.80	0.999 999 923
2.31	0.998 912	2.81	0.999 929	3.31	0.999 997 15	3.81	0.999 999 929
2.32	0.998 966	2.82	0.999 933	3.32	0.999 997 34	3.82	0.999 999 934
2.33	0.999 016	2.83	0.999 937	3.33	0.999 997 51	3.83	0.999 999 939
2.34	0.999 065	2.84	0.999 941	3.34	0.999 997 68	3.84	0.999 999 944
2.35	0.999 111	2.85	0.999 944	3.35	0.999 997 838	3.85	0.999 999 948
2.36	0.999 155	2.86	0.999 948	3.36	0.999 997 983	3.86	0.999 999 952
2.37	0.999 197	2.87	0.999 951	3.37	0.999 998 120	3.87	0.999 999 956
2.38	0.999 237	2.88	0.999 954	3.38	0.999 998 247	3.88	0.999 999 959
2.39	0.999 275	2.89	0.999 956	3.39	0.999 998 367	3.89	0.999 999 962
2.40	0.999 311	2.90	0.999 959	3.40	0.999 998 478	3.90	0.999 999 965
2.41	0.999 346	2.91	0.999 961	3.41	0.999 998 582	3.91	0.999 999 968
2.42	0.999 379	2.92	0.999 964	3.42	0.999 998 679	3.92	0.999 999 970
2.43	0.999 411	2.93	0.999 966	3.43	0.999 998 770	3.93	0.999 999 973
2.44	0.999 441	2.94	0.999 968	3.44	0.999 998 855	3.94	0.999 999 975
2.45	0.999 469	2.95	0.999 970	3.45	0.999 998 934	3.95	0.999 999 977
2.46	0.999 497	2.96	0.999 972	3.46	0.999 999 008	3.96	0.999 999 979
2.47	0.999 523	2.97	0.999 973	3.47	0.999 999 077	3.97	0.999 999 980
2.48	0.999 547	2.98	0.999 975	3.48	0.999 999 141	3.98	0.999 999 982
2.49	0.999 571	2.99	0.999 977	3.49	0.999 999 201	3.99	0.999 999 983

For more detailed information, see *Chambers Six Figure Mathematical Tables*, L. J. Comrie, Vol. 2, p. 518 (Chambers, 1949).

Example Figure A1.7

A binary baseband transmission system operates at 50 kbit/s. Logic 1 is represented by +1 volt, logic 0 by −1 volt, the transmission of ones and zeros are equiprobable and there is noise of 0.2 volts RMS present.

Probability of error P_e = area of tail $P_1(x)$ + area of tail $P_0(x)$

$$P_e = 2 \times \text{area one tail}$$

$$= \tfrac{1}{2} \, \text{erfc}[V/(\sigma\sqrt{2})] = \tfrac{1}{2} \, \text{erfc}(5/\sqrt{2})$$

$$= \tfrac{1}{2} \, \text{erfc} \; 3.536$$

$$P_e = \tfrac{1}{2}[1 - (\text{erf} \; 3.536)]$$

$$= \tfrac{1}{2}[1 - 0.999999425]$$

$$= 2.875 \times 10^{-7} \text{ errors per second per bit}$$

At 50 kbit/s, BER $= 2.875 \times 10^{-7} \times 50 \times 10^3$

$$= 0.014375 \text{ errors per second, or approximately} $$
$$1 \text{ error per 70 seconds}$$

If the noise level is doubled to 0.4 volts RMS, the probability of errors increases.

$$P_e = \tfrac{1}{2} \, \text{erfc}(2.5/\sqrt{2}) = \tfrac{1}{2} \, \text{erfc} \; 1.770$$

$$P_e = \tfrac{1}{2}[1 - 0.987691]$$

$$= 6.155 \times 10^{-3} \text{ errors/sec/per bit}$$

At 50 kbit/s, BER $= 6.155 \times 10^{-3} \times 50 \times 10^3$

$$= 308 \text{ errors per second}$$

This shows the disastrous effect that noise can have, even on a digital signalling system.

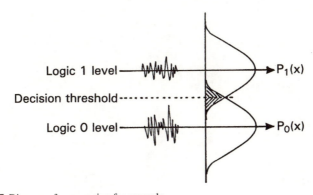

Figure A1.7 Diagram of error region for example.

A1.7   TABLES OF ERROR FUNCTIONS

See Table A1.2 on pages 493–494.

REFERENCES

(1)   Mosteller, F. *et al.* (1970) *Probability with Statistical Applications*. 2nd edn. World Student Series. London: Addison-Wesley Publishing Company.
(2)   Schwartz, M. (1970) *Information Transmission, Modulation and Noise*. 2nd edn. International Student Series. London: McGraw-Hill Kogakusha Ltd.
(3)   Betts, J.A. (1978) *Signal Processing, Modulation and Noise*. London: Hodder and Stoughton Ltd.

Appendix 2

A2.1 NOISE PERFORMANCE OF CASCADED STAGES

For the purposes of noise analysis, the noise generated within a system can be replaced by an equivalent auxiliary input of noise so that the system can be treated as ideal (non-noise-producing).

In Figure A2.1, system and source are correctly matched so that the noise input is kTB watts. The system has a noise factor F and power gain G, so that the total

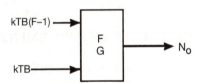

Figure A2.1 Noise performance of single stage.

noise output power is $N_0 = FGkTB$ watts. If the system had been ideal, this would have been $N_0 = GkTB$ watts. Therefore the noise power generated within the system is:

$$FGkTB - GkTB = GkTB(F - 1)$$

This is equivalent to providing the system with an auxiliary noise input of $kTB(F - 1)$ watts.

This concept can be extended for two or more systems in cascade as depicted in Figure A2.2, where the total noise output is:

$$N_0 = kTBG_1G_2 + kTB(F_1 - 1)G_1G_2 + kTB(F_2 - 1)G_2$$

$$= kTBG_1G_2 + kTBF_1G_1G_2 - kTBG_1G_2 + kTB(F_2 - 1)G_2$$

$$= kTBG_1G_2F_1 + kTB(F_2 - 1)G_2$$

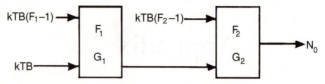

Figure A2.2 Noise performance of cascaded stages.

Noise output due to input alone $= kTBG_1G_2$

$$F_0 = \frac{\text{Total noise power at output}}{\text{Noise power at output due to input alone}}$$

$$= \frac{kTBG_1G_2F_1 + kTB(F_2 - 1)G_2}{kTBG_1G_2}$$

$$= F_1 + (F_2 - 1)/G_1$$

Similarly for three stages in cascade:

$$F_0 = F_1 + (F_2 - 1)/G_1 + (F_3 - 1)/G_1G_2 \qquad (A2.1)$$

A2.2   CCIR FIVE-POINT SCALE OF IMPAIRMENTS

Originally developed under the auspices of the CCIR (now designated as the Radiocommunications Sector of the International Telecommunications Union and referred to as the ITU-RS five-point scale), this provides a subjective grading for both the audio and picture quality of broadcast radio and television signals. The gradings were derived by averaging the resulting assessments made by a panel of experts. When it is necessary to achieve a finer assessment then half-points may be used.

Table A2.1

Quality	Grade	Impairment
Excellent	5	Imperceptible
Good	4	Perceptible but not annoying
Fair	3	Slightly annoying
Poor	2	Annoying
Bad	1	Very annoying

Appendix 3

A3.1   THE UNIVERSAL ANTENNA CONSTANT

Consider two antennas R metres apart and directed towards each other as shown in Figure A3.1, the gains and areas of each being G_1, A_1 and G_2, A_2 respectively. A power of P watts is transmitted from antenna 1 towards antenna 2 so that the power flux density (PFD) at 2 is $PG_1/4\pi R^2$ W/m². The total power received at antenna 2 is therefore $PG_1A_2/4\pi R^2$ W.

Now exchange transmitter and receiver without changing any other parameter. The total power received at 1 is $PG_2A_1/4\pi R^2$ W. Applying the reciprocity theorem:

$$PG_1A_2/4\pi R^2 = PG_2A_1/4\pi R^2$$

$$G_1A_2 = G_2A_1, \quad \text{and}$$

$$G_1/A_1 = G_2/A_2, \quad \text{which is a constant}$$

If this constant can be determined for just one antenna, then it can be applied to all antennas. It is shown in reference (1) that a small Hertzian dipole of length 1, which is much less than half a wavelength, has a gain $G = 1.5$ and radiation resistance $R = 80(\pi l/\lambda)^2$ ohms. If such an antenna is placed in an electric field of E volts/m, it will collect an emf of $E.e^{j\omega t}.1$ V. The maximum power that this will generate under matched conditions will be $(\frac{1}{2}(emf)^2)/4R$ W.

$$\text{Maximum power} = (\frac{1}{2})(El)^2/(4(80(\pi l/\lambda)^2))$$

$$= E^2\lambda^2/640\pi^2 \text{ W}$$

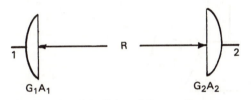

Figure A3.1 Diagram for derivation of the Universal Antenna Constant.

The power flow in the wave is $(\frac{1}{2})E^2/Z_0$, where Z_0 is the impedance of free space $= \sqrt{(\mu_0/\varepsilon_0)} - 120\pi$ ohms. If the effective area of the receiving antenna is A_e square metres, the received power is:

$E^2 A_e/240\pi$ W

Therefore, $E^2 A_e/240\pi = E^2\lambda^2/640\pi^2$ or

$\quad A_e = 3\lambda^2/8\pi$

For the Hertzian dipole:

$\quad G/A_e = 3/2 \times 8\pi/3\lambda^2$

$\qquad = 4\pi/\lambda^2$, the universal constant

The gain G is thus $4\pi A_e/\lambda^2$.

A3.2   APPROXIMATE BEAMWIDTH FOR PARABOLIC REFLECTOR ANTENNAS

Referring to Figure A3.2, where each small elemental area dA is matched to a corresponding area dA' spaced by a radius of half the diameter D, assume uniform illumination of the dish at wavelength λ and uniform phase. For the half power, direction $\theta/2$ has to be such that the contributions to the transmitted power by dA and dA' are in quadrature, i.e. $x = x'$ and $x + x' = \lambda/4$.

Sin $\theta/2 = (\lambda/8)/(D/4) = \lambda/2D$. For high-gain antennas $\theta/2$ is small, so that:

$\quad \sin \theta/2 = \theta/2 = \lambda/(2D)$ or

$\qquad \theta = \lambda/D$ radians

Or for θ in degrees, the half-power beamwidth $= 57.3\lambda/D$.

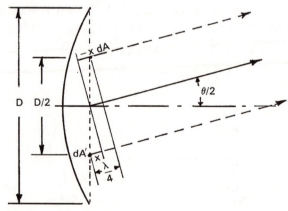

Figure A3.2 The half-power beamwidth.

A3.3 AZIMUTH/ELEVATION ANGLES BY CALCULATOR

A calculator with trigonometrical functions and this algorithm can quickly produce the azimuth/elevation angles. For the northern hemisphere, the convention is to use positive angles for satellites and ground stations west of the Greenwich meridian. (Easterly locations use corresponding negative values.)

(1) Find the angle WEST (the longitude difference). Satellite °W – station °W.
(2) Find X = (cos WEST° × cos(station latitude°))
(3) AZIMUTH = arc tan (tan WEST/sin station latitude). Add 180° if satellite is west of Greenwich meridian.
(4) Calculate $Y = \sqrt{(1 + K^2 - 2KX)}$, where K = 6.608, the distance between the satellite and the earth centre in terms of earth radii.
(5) ELEVATION = arc cos((1 – KX)/Y) – 90°.
(6) Calculate range Z = 6378 × Y km.

Note: for latitudes greater than about 81°, X < 0.15; this indicates that the satellite is below the horizon.

A3.4 CALCULATION OF ANGLE OF ELEVATION α FOR SIMPLE POLAR MOUNTS

With reference to Figure A3.3, and using the cosine rule:

$$\cos \beta = \frac{(r + h)^2 + r^2 - d^2}{2r(r + h)} \tag{A3.1}$$

so that

$$d = \sqrt{((r + h)^2 + r^2 - 2r(r + h) \cos \beta)}. \tag{A3.2}$$

Using the sine rule:

$$\frac{r + h}{\sin(90 + \alpha)} = \frac{d}{\sin \beta} = \frac{\sqrt{(r + h)^2 + r^2 - 2r(r + h) \cos \beta}}{\sin \beta}$$

$$\frac{(r + h) \sin \beta}{\sqrt{((r + h)^2 + r^2 - 2r(r + h) \cos \beta)}} = \sin(90 + \alpha) = \cos \alpha$$

$$\alpha = \frac{(r + h) \sin \beta}{\text{arc } \cos\sqrt{((r + h)^2 + r^2 - 2r(r + h) \cos \beta)}} \tag{A3.3}$$

Substituting for the constants $r = 6378 \times 10^3$ and $h = 35{,}765 \times 10^3$, this simplifies to:

$$\alpha = \text{arc } \cos(1.82 \sin \beta)/\sqrt{(3.38 - \cos \beta)} \tag{A3.4}$$

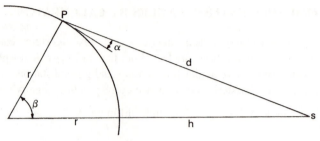

Figure A3.3 The simple polar mount calculations.

This function has been calculated (Table A3.1) and plotted. For values up to latitude (β) of 55°, the relationship is linear to within 1 percent. The angle of elevation can thus be derived from:

$$\alpha = 90° - 1.15385\beta \qquad\qquad (A3.5)$$

A3.5 MODIFIED POLAR MOUNT

In Chapter 3, reference is made to the need to apply a declination correction to the elevation angle of the simple polar mount. This arises chiefly because of the earth-bound observer's view of the Clarke Orbit. From an equatorial viewpoint, the orbit appears as a straight line, running due east to west and passing overhead. If the orbit could be viewed from either of the polar regions, it would be seen to be circular. At all latitudes between these two extremes, the orbit appears elliptical. The simple polar mount provides a tracking arc that is circular, so that it will only coincide with this apparent ellipse tangentially in a southerly direction. At best, it will track only two points if the elevation angle is slightly offset. This may be acceptable if the services of only two satellites are to be used.

Figure A3.4(a) shows a plan view (not to scale) of the earth and the Clarke Orbit, through the equatorial plane, as seen from above the north pole. Point S represents a satellite positioned due south of an earth station, located at Q (T in Figure A3.4(c)). The antenna can be swung through 90° in both an easterly and a westerly direction, to point to two further satellites S_1 and S_2. (S_2 is in a mirror-image position relative to S_1, about the line OS.) Although these points are below the horizon, they are used in this simplified analysis (2) to provide for three-point accurate tracking.

Table A3.1

Latitude°	0	10	20	30	40	50	60	70	80
Elevation°	90	78.22	66.52	54.48	43.65	32.57	22.56	11.12	0

With reference to Figure A3.4(b), the antenna is aimed at satellite S_1, with a declination angle of α. Swinging the antenna through an angle of 90° to point to satellite S causes the required angle α to increase by a small value. The new declination angle $\gamma = \alpha + \beta$, where β is the additional offset angle required to accurately track the three satellites. The angle β is never greater than 1°.

For the three triangles shown in Figure A3.4, the angle ϕ is the earth station latitude and θ is the difference in longitude between S and S_1, and S and S_2.

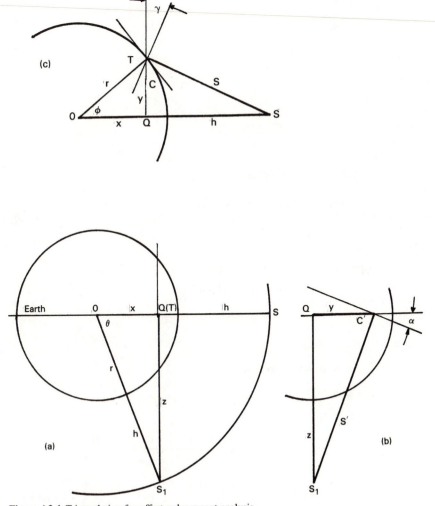

Figure A3.4 Triangulation for offset polar mount analysis.

From Figure A3.4(c):

$$x = r \cos \phi$$

$$y = r \sin \phi$$

$$SQ = (r + h) - x$$

In triangle SQT:

$$C = \text{arc tan } ((r + h) - x)/y$$

$$= \text{arc tan } ((r + h) - r \cos \phi)/(r \sin \phi) \qquad (A3.6)$$

From Figure A3.4(b):

In triangle S_1QT_1

$$C' = 90° - \alpha$$

$$= \text{arc tan } z/y \qquad (A3.7)$$

From Figure A3.4(a)

In triangle S_1QO_1

$$z^2 + x^2 = (r + h)^2$$

$$z = \sqrt{((r + h)^2 - (r^2 \cos^2 \phi))}$$

Therefore equation A3.7 becomes:

$$C' = \frac{\text{arc tan } \sqrt{((r + h)^2 - (r^2 \cos^2 \phi))}}{r \sin \phi} \qquad (A3.8)$$

and

$$\alpha = 90° - C'$$

$$= 90° - \text{arc tan } \frac{\sqrt{((r + h)^2 - (r^2 \cos^2 \phi))}}{r \sin \phi} \qquad (A3.9)$$

From Figure A3.4(c)

$$\gamma = \alpha + \beta, \quad \text{so that}$$

$$\alpha + \beta + c = 90° \quad \text{or}$$

$$\beta = 90° - \alpha - \gamma$$

$$= 90° - 90° + \text{arc tan } \frac{\sqrt{((r + h)^2 - (r^2 \cos^2 \phi))}}{r \sin \phi}$$

$$- \text{arc tan } \frac{(r + h) - r \cos \phi}{r \sin \phi} \qquad (A3.10)$$

Therefore

$$\beta = \arctan \frac{\sqrt{((r + h)^2 - (r^2 \cos^2 \phi))}}{r \sin \phi}$$

$$- \text{arc tan} \frac{((r + h) - (r \cos \phi))}{r \sin \phi} \tag{A3.11}$$

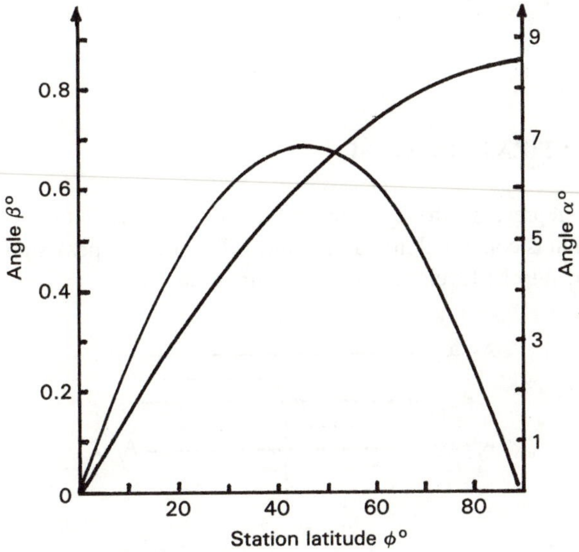

Figure A3.5 Plot of equations A3.9 and A3.11.

If the values for the constants r and h are inserted into equations A3.9 and A3.11, the graphs shown in Figure A3.5 can be plotted. The due south elevation angle for the modified polar mount can then be obtained for any latitude from:

$$90° - (\alpha + \beta + \phi) \tag{A3.12}$$

This value provides tracking to an accuracy within 0.05°.

Author's note: the above analysis is due to an idea presented by Steve Birkill, for which I am particularly gateful.

REFERENCES

(1) Connor, F.R. (1984) *Introductory Topics in Electronics and Telecommunications: Antennas*. London: Edward Arnold.
(2) Birkill, S.J., Technical Director, Satellite TV Antenna Systems Ltd, Staines, UK. Private communication to author.
(3) Stephenson, D.J., Arrowe Technical Services, Merseyside, UK.

Appendix 4

A4.1   QUANTIZATION NOISE

Figure A4.1 represents the quantization errors that are introduced when an analogue signal is converted into digital form. The peak-to-peak signal amplitude (P) is divided into M levels, each of step amplitude 'a'.

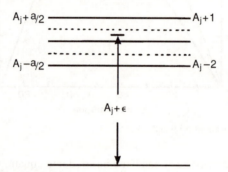

Figure A4.1 Quantization errors.

Statistically, any value to be quantized will fall in the band $A_j \pm a/2$, so that the mean square error $\bar{\varepsilon}^2$ is given by:

$$\bar{\varepsilon}^2 = \frac{1}{a} \int_{-a/2}^{+a/2} \varepsilon^2 . d\varepsilon$$

$$= \frac{1}{a} \left[\frac{\varepsilon^3}{3} \right]_{-a/2}^{+a/2} = 1/a \left\{ \left[\frac{(a/2)^3}{3} \right] - \left[\frac{(-a/2)^3}{3} \right] \right\}$$

$$= \frac{1}{3a} \left[\frac{a^3}{4} \right] = a^2/12$$

The RMS error is therefore $= a/\sqrt{12}$.

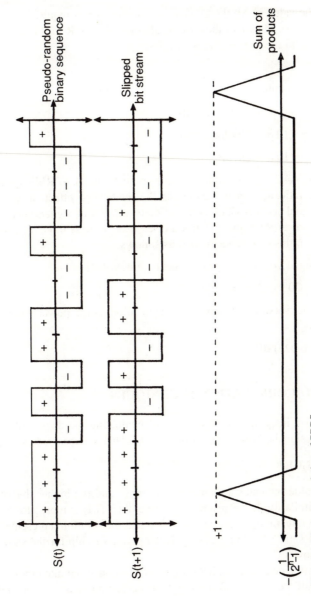

Figure A4.2 Auto-correlation of PRBS.

Now the signal-to-quantization noise power ratio SQNR = $P^2/(a^2/12)$; and since $P = aM$, SQNR = $12a^2M^2/a^2 = 12M^2$, or:

$$\text{SQNR (dB)} = 10.8 + 20 \log M \qquad (A4.1)$$

The larger the value of M, the greater the number of bits required to code each sample, and hence the wider the base bandwidth. The SNR for binary signalling can be related to the bandwidth as follows:

$$M = 2^n$$

where n is the number of bits per sample, so that the

$$
\begin{aligned}
\text{SQNR} &= (10.8 + 20 \log 2^n) \text{ dB} \\
&= (10.8 + 20n \log 2) \text{ dB} \\
&= (10.8 + 6n) \text{ dB} \qquad (A4.2)
\end{aligned}
$$

The equation A4.2 representing the peak-to-peak signal to RMS quantization noise power ratio adequately expresses the annoyance effect of quantization noise on a signal such as video (varying dc level). For ac signals such as audio, the RMS signal to RMS quantization noise power ratio is more appropriate.

These two ratios can be reconciled as follows:

$$\text{RMS signal voltage} = (\text{peak-to-peak value})/(2\sqrt{2})$$

$$20 \log 2\sqrt{2} = -9.03 \text{ dB}$$

so that the ac version of signal to quantization noise power ratio is often expressed as:

$$(1.76 + 6.02n) \text{ dB} \qquad (A4.3)$$

A4.2   AUTO-CORRELATION TECHNIQUES

The correlation integral provides a way of evaluating the degree of similarity between two signals during the period t_1 to t_2. This is expressed as:

$$\int_{t_1}^{t_2} f_1(t)f_2(t) \, dt$$

A positive value indicates a degree of similarity and the higher the value, the greater the similarity. If the result is negative, then $f_1(t)$ is more closely related to $-f_2(t)$. The integral operates on $\{f_1(t)\}^2$ so that the solution represents the total energy in the signal. Dividing this by T, the period or chip for the signal yields its average power.

For correlation detection, an NRZ signal is first converted into bipolar form by subtracting half the signal peak amplitude from each bit value. This signal is then multiplied by the PRBS bit by bit and the product integrated (summed) over the chip period. As shown by Figure A4.2, the output signal is only a maximum when the incoming signal is completely synchronized with the PRBS, otherwise the result is near zero.

Index

Index